THE NORTH AMERICAN CITY

THE AMERICAN

MAURICE H. YEATES

QUEEN'S UNIVERSITY, CANADA

HARPER & ROW, PUBLISHERS

NORTH CITY

BARRY J. GARNER

AARHUS UNIVERSITY, DENMARK

NEW YORK, EVANSTON, SAN FRANCISCO, LONDON

THE NORTH AMERICAN CITY

 For information address Harper & Row, Publishers, Inc., 49 East 33rd Street, New York, N.Y. 10016.

Standard Book Number: 06-047326-6

LIBRARY OF CONGRESS CATALOG CARD NUMBER: 72-148449

Cover: Color photograph—Charles E. Rotkin;
Arcology by Paolo Soleri—The Corcoran Gallery of Art, Washngton. D.C.

To Ned
with deep appreciation
for his stimulating guidance

PREFACE

Settlements form an essential element of the landscape. As such they have traditionally held a dominant place in the curriculum of human geography. Ranging in size, form, and function from the highly complex and increasingly problematic "world cities" down to the most ubiquitous hamlets—now a declining feature of the rural landscape—they are perhaps the most significant expression of human occupancy of the earth's surface. In this book the emphasis is on the upper end of this so-called rural-urban continuum, on places that are largely divorced from the rural scene and that we refer to, rather vaguely, as urban areas. During the past fifty years these have been expanding in size and relative importance the world over. In North America, particularly since the widespread use of the automobile, the movement of population into urban areas, and especially the larger ones, has been gathering increased momentum each decade. This accelerating urbanization has brought with it a significant number of new and extremely complex problems for society, while the traditional ones appear to get worse rather than better.

Concurrent with this rapid growth in urban population and its complex spatial ramifications, it is natural that geographers should become more involved in urban studies. It is not surprising, therefore, that urban geography has emerged in the recent past as a particularly important area of inquiry, and there can be little doubt concerning its continued growth and importance in the future. Urban geography, however, is not merely an academic discipline with interests confined to the curriculum of colleges and universities—although we sincerely hope that this introduction to the subject will find a useful place in this context. To an increasing extent it is a practical area of inquiry with wide application in the affairs of government and business. City and metropolitan planning agencies, industrial and commercial firms, and many other organizations both public and private are increasingly aware of the contribution urban geographers can make toward the solution of their problems.

The emergence of urban geography as an academic subject, rich in its potential application to the solution of contemporary urban problems, is a relatively recent phenomenon. It has been made possible to a large extent by fundamental changes in the methodology of geography, which have had an important effect on the way study is undertaken—and on the things that are studied. Early studies in urban geography tended to focus on the description of specific details of individual towns and cities, and they were essentially characterized by a strong dependence on the relationships between the location of places, their character, and the physical environment. The closest associations of geography in the first quarter of this century were with geology and history, and it was perhaps natural that the major emphasis was given to the *morphology,* or form, of settlements and their historical development. At the time, this emphasis was particularly strong in Europe, where the results of a much more varied cultural history persisted in the landscape; and it had a strong influence on the emerging urban geography and the kinds of studies undertaken by geographers in North America during the first quarter of this century.

In this book we are not very much concerned with the morphological aspects of urban settlements in the traditional sense, nor with the historical details surrounding the evolution of particular settlements. Rather, we have attempted to adopt a more general functional-organizational approach in which the focus is on structure and pattern in the urban fabric and on the processes at work in the contemporary urban milieu. This emphasis reflects the more recent developments in urban geography, developments that have stemmed directly from what has come to be known as the "quantitative revolution" in human geography. The principal effects of this have been to place greater stress on generalizations concerning the spatial structure of urban areas and the interactions between them and to reduce the relative importance of detailed descriptions of individual places. At the same time, the search for order and generalization has been accompanied by a growing concern for developing models and theories of urban structure and by the increased use of a wide range of mathematical methods of analysis. In short, urban geography has come to be viewed by many as a science.

The importance of these recent changes, as they have affected the philosophy and methodology of urban geography, are dealt with in the introductory chapter. The implications of these changes underlie much of the content and the approach adopted in the rest of the book, which is divided into three parts. In the first of these attention is focused on what may be loosely called the "city system." These six chapters are devoted to concepts and generalizations relating to the distribution of settlements, their functional specialization, and the spatial interrelations that bind them together into a complex, functional whole. Urban places are considered as discrete phenomena in the landscape, and they are discussed generally in terms of their aggregate characteristics.

Part II is concerned with urban areas as regions for study in their own right. The emphasis is firmly on the internal structure of urban areas. Patterns in the residential, social, commercial, and manufacturing structure of cities are discussed, and the importance of the theories of urban land use are stressed.  Urban areas, however, are not static but dynamic, functional systems characterized by complex patterns of interrelationships in which the role of transportation is critical. The way in which transportation has affected the growth of the urban area and influenced its structural pattern is explicitly dealt with as a prefatory chapter to this section; and it is implicit in much of the ensuing discussion, particularly in the last chapter, which deals specifically with intraurban movements. Examples have been taken from a wide variety of sources and cover many different cities. The specific chapter contents reflect the fundamental overlap between the work of urban geographers and contemporary urban research in the cognate disciplines of economics, sociology, and political science.

The final part of the book is devoted to what many social philosophers have termed "the urban dilemma." Here the emphasis is on the multiplicity and complexity of problems resulting from the continuing and accelerating trend of urbanization. The relationship between urban geography and planning is implicit in the discussion, and the necessity for planning control over the urban environment is stressed. Although specific attention is given to some of the problems of North American cities, the implications in the main are just as important for urban areas in other economically advanced countries of the world. In many of these other countries a strong conscience for urban planning has already developed, and mention is made of the potential applications of similar arguments and practices in connection with the current situation in North America. It is in this last section, then, that stress is given to the application of the geographer's craft in helping to make a better urban environment for ourselves and future generations.

The contents of this book represent urban geography as we see it today. We are the first to acknowledge its many biases, prejudices, and shortcomings. Most of the literature cited is of recent origin. We have neglected many important earlier contributions, but only because they are difficult to fit into the framework we have adopted. The book is intended as an introductory text in urban geography, mainly for students at colleges and universities in North America. As such, much of the specific factual content may be relevant only indirectly in other parts of the world. The concepts and general ideas presented, however, have direct relevance for the study of cities by geographers the world over; and we hope that in this sense it will be a useful addition to the growing literature on urban geography. Some of the factual content relates to data provided by the 1960 Census of the United States and 1961 Census of Canada. Naturally, these will need to be updated when the 1970 and 1971 census returns are published. Space has been left in two or three of the tables for this purpose, and the reader may wish to provide these data for himself.

It is impossible to thank all the people who have contributed to the formulation of the ideas and opinions in the book. We would, however, like to take this opportunity of acknowledging the assistance and opportunities given to us by the geography department at Northwestern University. We are particularly indebted to E. Taaffe, W. Garrison, and E. Espenshade for the inspiration and attention they gave us. Our special thanks are also extended to Brian Berry for all the intellectual stimulation he has given us over the past years. Among others from whom we have profited greatly in discussion are George Carey, Larry Bourne, Art Getis, Howard Nelson, Brian Osborne, George Nicholson, Rowland Tinline, Alan Frey, Jay Vance, David Harvey, Peter Haggett, and Robert Dickinson. To these and the many others too numerous to mention we extend our warm thanks. We also appreciate the help of the many secretaries who have typed and retyped the manuscript, and especially thank Ulla Redder and Audrey Douglas. Finally, we thank our wives—Marilynn and Vanessa—for their advice, encouragement, and patience in enduring the many disruptions to the normal routine that the writing of this book has involved. Maurine and Harry were especially helpful, for they refrained from drawing on the many drafts, and they slept at vital moments.

Maurice H. Yeates　　　　Barry J. Garner

ACKNOWLEDGMENTS

Since the material cited below is listed alphabetically by author in the References section, the reader will find it easier to consult that section for further information about particular source material used in the text.

The Authors and Publisher wish to express their thanks to the following for permission to reprint or modify material from copyright works:

The American Academy of Political and Social Science for Figs. 1–5, pp. 8–9, 11, from *The Annals,* Vol. 242, 1945 (Paper by C. D. Harris and E. L. Ullman).

The American Geographical Society of New York for the following from the *Geographical Review:* Figs. 2–9, p. 92, and Table I, p. 88, Vol. 33, 1943 (Paper by C. D. Harris); Fig. 7,

p. 396, and Tables II and III, pp. 393 and 398, Vol. 43, 1953 (Paper by J. Brush); Fig. 7, p. 232, Vol. 46, 1956 (Paper by E. J. Taaffe); Fig. 1, p. 185, Vol. 46, 1956 (Paper by R. T. Novak); Fig. 1, p. 165, Vol. 55, 1965 (Paper by A. Pred); Fig. 2, p. 361, Vol. 56, 1966 (Paper by G. Carey); Table II, p. 219, Vol. 56, 1966 (Paper by B. E. Newling); Figs. 6–10, pp. 313, 316–318, and 322, Tables II and III, pp. 315 and 329, and to quote from p. 329, Vol. 57, 1967 (Paper by J. Borchert); Fig. 4, p. 630, Vol. 58, 1968 (Paper by J. Simmons); and for the map on p. 3, from *Focus,* Vol. 20(6), 1970.

Edward Arnold (Publishers) Ltd., London, for Fig. 5.4, p. 119, from *Locational Analysis in Human Geography* by Peter Haggett, 1965; and to quote from p. 298, *Explanation in Geography* by D. Harvey, 1969.

The Association of American Geographers for the following from *Annals of the Association of American Geographers*: Fig. 6, p. 324, Vol. 44, 1954 (Paper by C. D. Harris); Table 1, p. 147, Vol. 49, 1959 (Paper by B. J. L. Berry); Fig. 1, p. 113, Vol. 50, 1960 (Paper by B. J. L. Berry); Fig. 3, p. 8, Vol. 54, 1964 (Paper by B. J. L. Berry); and Table 5, p. 393, Vol. 58, 1968 (Paper by W. A. V. Clark); and for information from pp. 9 and 11, *Air Pollution,* Resource Paper No. 3, by R. A. Bryson and J. E. Kutzbach, 1968.

The Brookings Institution, Washington, D.C. for Table 16, p. 243, from *The Metropolitan Transportation Problem,* revised edition, by W. Owen, 1966.

The Bureau of Business and Economic Research, State University of Iowa, to quote from p. 15, *Iowa Business Digest,* 1960 (Winter) (Paper by E. N. Thomas).

The Canadian Association of Geographers and the authors for the following from *The Canadian Geographer:* Fig. 2, p. 4, Vol. 2, 1958. (Paper by R. Mackay); Tables 3 and 4, pp. 216 and 220, Vol. 10, 1966 (Paper by L. J. King).

The Editor of the *Canadian Review of Sociology and Anthropology* for Table 1, pp. 166–167, Vol. 6, 1969 (Paper by T. G. Nicholson and M. H. Yeates).

The Carnegie Institution of Washington, D.C., for Plates 138A, B, and C, from *Atlas of the Historical Geography of the United States* by C. O. Paullin, 1932.

The Center for Urban Studies, University of Chicago, for Fig. 3.7, p. 91, from *The Impact of Urban Renewal on Small Business* by B. J. L. Berry, S. J. Parsons, and R. H. Platt, 1968.

The Chicago Area Transportation Study for Map 12, p. 21; Figs. 15 and 24, pp. 35 and 48; and Tables 4 and 6, pp. 37 and 47, from *Final Report,* Vol. I, Survey Findings, 1959.

The Detroit Metropolitan Area Traffic Study for Map 4, p. 33, from *Report,* Part I, Data Summary and Interpretation, 1955.

The Editor and Authors for the following from *Economic Geography:* Figs. 12 and 25, pp. 216 and 333, Tables 2 and 1, pp. 204, and 302, and to quote from p. 219, Vol. 30, 1954 (Papers by R. Murphy and J. E. Vance, Jr.); Figs. 3, 10, 12, 13, 14, 15, 16, pp. 27, 31, 33, 35–37, 43 and Table 1, pp. 22, Vol. 31, 1955 (Paper by R. Murphy, J. E. Vance, Jr., and B. Epstein); Figs. 1, 2, 10, pp. 192, 197, 204, Tables 1, 2, 3, 4, pp. 190, 191, 195, and Appendix, pp. 205–210, Vol. 31, 1955 (Paper by H. J. Nelson); Figs. 3, 4, 5, 7, 8, 9, pp. 287, 290, 292, 296, 298–299, Vol. 31, 1955 (Paper by H. L. Green); Table 2, p. 97, Vol. 33, 1957 (Paper by H. J. Nelson); Table 2, p. 150, Figs. 1 and 3, pp. 308 and 310, and Table 2, p. 307, Vol. 34, 1958 (Papers by B. J. L. Berry and W. L. Garrison); Fig. 5, p. 216, Vol. 36, 1960 (Paper by J. E. Vance, Jr.); Fig. 5, p. 9, Vol. 38, 1962 (Paper by E. J. Taaffe); Figs. 6, 7, 8, pp. 325–326, 328, Vol. 38, 1962 (Paper by P. J. Smith); Fig. 3, p. 170, Vol. 39, 1963 (Paper by H. A. Stafford, Jr.); Figs. 1, 6, 7, 14, 15, 30, 31, pp. 216, 219, 221, 231, Vol. 41, 1965 (Paper by R. A. Murdie), and Figs. 1 and 2, pp. 60–61, Vol. 41, 1965 (Paper by M. H. Yeates).

The Federal Reserve Bank of Kansas City, for Table 1, p. 4, from the *Monthly Review,* Vol. 37, 1952.

Gustav Fischer Verlag, Stuttgart, W. Germany, for Figs. 27 and 86, pp. 118 and 448 from *The Economics of Location* by A. Lösch, 1954.

C. W. K. Gleerup Publishers, Lund, Sweden, for Fig. 2, p. 129, from *Proceedings of the I.G.U. Symposium on Urban Geography, Lund, 1960,* edited by K. Norborg, 1962 (Paper by E. L. Ullman and M. F. Dacey).

C. D. Harris for the full list of cities classified by functional specialization.

Harvard University Press, Cambridge, for Fig. 9, p. 63, from *Streetcar Suburbs: The Process of Growth in Boston* by S. B. Warner, Jr., 1962.

Hutchinson Publishing Group Ltd., London, to quote from p. 84, *The Geography of Towns* by A. E. Smailes, 1953.

R. F. Latham for information from *Urban Population Densities and Growth: with Special Reference to Toronto,* unpublished M.A. thesis, Department of Geography, Queen's University, Canada, 1967.

McGraw-Hill Book Co., New York, for Figs. 5A and 6, pp. 102 and 107, from *The Metropolitan Community* edited by R. D. McKenzie, 1933 (Paper by R. E. Park and C. Newcomb); data from p. 167, *Fundamentals of Forestry Economics* by W. A. Duerr, 1960; and to quote from pp. 1–2, *The American City* by R. Murphy, 1966.

The Maryland-National Capital Park and Planning Commission, Washington, D.C., for the diagram on p. 20 of *On Wedges and Corridors,* 1964.

The Massachusetts Institute of Techonology Press, Cambridge, for Table A-5.3, p. 23, from *Principles and Techniques of Predicting Future Demand for Urban Transportation* by B. V. Martin, F. W. Memmott, and A. J. Bone, 1961.

Methuen and Co., Ltd., London, for Fig. 10.1, p. 365, from *Models in Geography,* edited by R. J. Chorley and P. Haggett, 1967 (Paper by F. E. I. Hamilton).

The Author and the Editor, *Netherlands Journal of Economic and Social Geography* (T.E.S.G.) for Figs. 2 and 3, pp. 232–233, Vol. 56, 1965 (Paper by K. R. Cox).

The New Zealand Geographical Society for Table V, p. 157, from *Proceedings, Third N.Z. Geography Conference,* 1962 (Paper by L. J. King).

Northwestern University Press, Evanston, for Figs. 1.1, III.3A, B, C, D, E, F, pp. 6, 22–23, and Tables II.1, and Vol. 6, pp. 9 and 88, from *The Peripheral Journey to Work* by E. J. Taaffe, B. J. Garner, and M. H. Yeates, 1963.

The Authors and Northwestern University, Department of Geography, for the following from *Studies in Geography:* Figs. 2, 16, 19, pp. 14, 55, 61, No. 10, 1965 (Paper by J. L. Davis); Table 1, p. 62, No. 16, 1968 (Paper by D. F. Marble and S. R. Bowlby).

The Ohio State University Research Foundation for Table 20, p. 40, from *The Shopping Center versus Downtown,* by C. T. Jonassen, 1955.

The Pergamon Press, Oxford, to quote from p. 80, *Urban Geography: An Introductory Analysis* by J. H. Johnson, 1967.

Prentice-Hall Inc., Englewood Cliffs, N.J., for Figs. 1.3, 1.4, 2.1, 2.8, 2.9, 2.11, 2.13, 2.15, 2.16, 2.21, 2.23, pp. 6, 27, 32, 33, 36, 38, 39, 43, 49, 52, and to quote from pp. 34–35 from *Geography of Market Centers and Retail Distribution* by B. J. L. Berry, 1967.

The Public Administration Service, Chicago, for Fig. 49 from *Urban Renewal and the Future of the American City* by C. A. Doxiadis, 1966.

The Queen's Printer, Toronto, for Figs. 31, 40, 41, 42, pp. 47, 52, 53, from *Report No. 1,* Metropolitan Toronto Area Regional Transportation Study, 1966.

The RAND Corporation, Santa Monica, for Fig. 2, p. 15, and Table 10, p. 46, from *A Multiple Equation Model of Household Locational and Trip Making Behavior,* Memorandum RM-3086-FF by J. F. Kain, 1962.

P. H. Rees for Fig. 4, p. 47, from *The Factorial Ecology of Metropolitan Chicago,* unpublished M.A. thesis, University of Chicago, 1968.

The Regional Plan Association, New York, for Chart 3, p. 10, from *Anatomy of a Metropolis* by E. M. Hoover and R. Vernon, 1959; Table 22, p. 131, from *Freight and the Metropolis* by B. Chinitz, 1960; and to quote from pp. 19, 106, 113, *1400 Governments* by R. C. Wood, 1961.

The Regional Science Association and the Authors, for the following from *Papers and Proceedings of the Regional Science Association:* Fig. 5, p. 194, Vol. 3, 1957 (Paper by J. D. Carroll and H. W. Bevis); Table I, p. 113, Vol. 4, 1958 (Paper by B. J. L. Berry and W. L. Garrison); Tables 1 and 3, pp. 242 and 247, Vol. 4, 1958 (Paper by I. Morrisset); Fig. 6, p. 165, Vol. 6, 1960 (Paper by D. Huff); Fig. 2, p. 39, Vol. 7, 1961 (Paper by J. D. Nystuen and M. F. Dacey); Figs. 1, 2, 3, 4, 7, 10, 11, 14, 15, 17, pp. 66, 69, 71, 79, 81, 83, 89, 91, 95, and Tables 1, 4, 5, 6, pp. 70, 77, 78, Vol. 9, 1962 (Paper by B. J. L. Berry, H. G. Barnum, and R. Tennant).

The Commission on Geography, Pan American Institute of Geography and History, for Fig. 4 from *Revista Geografica,* Vol. 15, No. 42, 1954 (Paper by R. A. Kennelly).

The Planning Division, Rhode Island Development Council for data on p. 51, *Metropolitanization and Population Change in Rhode Island,* Planning Division Publication No. 3 by S. Goldstein and K. B. Mayer, 1961.

The Royal Statistical Society and the Author for Diagrams on p. 492, *Journal of the Royal Statistical Society,* Series A, No. 114, 1951 (Paper by C. Clark).

Scientific American Inc., for Diagrams on pp. 28 and 30, *Scientific American,* Vol. 210(1), 1964 (Paper by A. J. Haagen-Smit).

The Scripps Foundation, Miami, Ohio, for material on pp. 121–124, *Suburbanization of Manufacturing Activity within Standard Metropolitan Areas,* Studies in Population Distribution, No. 9, by E. M. Kittagawa and D. J. Bogue, 1955.

The Editor of the *Southeastern Geographer* for Fig. 1, p. 33, Vol. 8, 1964 (Paper by C. E. Browning); and the Table on p. 31, Vol. 12, 1968 (Paper by A. W. Stuart).

Stanford University Press, Menlo Park, and the Board of Trustees of the Leland Stanford Junior University, for Fig. V.14, pp. 42–43, and Table II.1, p. 4, from *Social Area Analysis:*

Theory, Illustrative Applications and Computational Procedures by E. Shevky and W. Bell, 1955.

Syracuse University Press, Syracuse, to quote from p. 143, *American Geography-Inventory and Prospect,* edited by P. E. James and C. F. Jones, 1954 (Paper by H. Mayer).

The Editor of the *Town Planning Review* and the Author for Fig. 17, p. 175, Vol. 22, 1961 (Paper by J. P. Reynolds).

The Editor of *Trains,* to quote from p. 40, Vol. 26, 1966 (Paper by J. A. Pinkepank).

The Twentieth Century Fund, New York, for Fig. 3, p. 26, from *Megalopolis* by J. Gottmann, 1961.

E. L. Ullman for Fig. 7, from *Mobile: Industrial Seaport and Trade Center,* 1943.

The University of Chicago Press for Charts I and II, pp. 51 and 52, from *The City* by R. E. Park, E. W. Burgess, and R. D. McKenzie, 1967 edition.

The Editors and the University of Chicago Press for the following from the *American Journal of Sociology:* Chart 10, p. 78, Vol. 35, 1929 (Paper by R. E. Park); Table 1, p. 153, Vol. 60, 1954 (Paper by W. Isard and P. Kavesh); and to quote from p. 156, Vol. 56, 1950 (Paper by R. G. Ford); and for the following from *Economic Development and Cultural Change:* to quote from pp. 167–169, Vol. 3, 1955 (Paper by R. Vining); and Fig. 1, p. 239, Vol. 4, 1956 (Paper by C. H. Madden).

The Editor and the Authors for the following from *University of Chicago, Department of Geography, Research Papers:* Figs. 3, 10, 11, 12, 14, 17, 18, pp. 14, 32, 64, 68, 72, 84, 86, and Tables 1, 2, 6, 19, 49, 50, 51, BI, pp. 17, 20, 42–43, 65, 133, 135, 228, No. 85, 1963 (Paper by B. J. L. Berry); Diagram on p. 2, and Table on p. 3, No. 86, 1963 (Paper by B. J. L. Berry and R. J. Tennant); Fig. 18, p. 78, No. 90, 1964 (Paper by M. Helvig); Fig. 29, p. 169, Table 34, p. 164, and to quote from p. 76, No. 116, 1969 (Paper by R. A. Murdie).

The University of Nebraska Press for Table 5.2 and data from pp. 40, 47, 53, 98, 106, *The Industrial Structure of American Cities,* by G. Alexandersson, 1956.

The University of North Carolina Press for Fig. 2 from *The Urban South* edited by R. B. Vance and N. J. Demerath, 1954 (Paper by R. B. Vance and S. Smith).

The University of Pittsburgh Press for Tables 21, 22, 23, pp. 65, 67, 69, from *Portrait of a Region* by I. S. Lowry, 1963.

The Editors and the University of Reading Press for Figs. 70, 74, 75, 76, pp. 325, 329, 330, from *Essays in Geography for Austin Miller,* edited by J. B. Whittow and P. D. Wood, 1965 (Paper by M. H. Yeates).

The University of Washington Press and the Authors for Figs. 11.5 and 11.6, pp. 213–214, and Table 11.8, p. 221 from *Studies of Highway Development and Geographic Change* by W. L. Garrison, B. J. L. Berry, D. F. Marble, J. D. Nystuen, and R. L. Morrill, 1959; and for Fig. 2.6, p. 21, and Tables 2.1 and 2.2, pp. 16 and 20 from *Studies of the Central Business District and Urban Freeway Development,* by E. M. Horwood and R. R. Boyce, 1959.

The Editor and the University of Wisconsin Press for the following from *Land Economics:* To quote from pp. 223–227, Vol. 24, 1948 (Paper by R. E. Dickinson); and Tables 1, 2, 3,

p. 106, and footnote 3, p. 105, Vol. 52, 1964 (Paper by J. H. Niedercorn and E. F. R. Hearle).

The Upper Midwest Economic Study and J. R. Borchert and R. B. Adams for Fig. 2, Urban Report 3, from *Trade Centers and Trade Areas of the Upper Midwest,* 1963.

The Urban Land Institute, Washington D.C. for the Table on p. 43, from *Metropolitanization of the United States* by J. P. Pickard, 1959.

John Wiley and Sons Inc., New York, for Figs. 8 and 12, pp. 67 and 73, from *Location and Space-Economy* by W. Isard, 1956.

The Authors and Publisher also acknowledge the use of material from United States Government noncopyright publications, and especially for Figs. 28 and 40, pp. 77 and 115, and to quote from p. 76, *The Structure and Growth of Residential Neighborhoods in American Cities* by Homer Hoyt, Federal Housing Administration, 1939.

THE NORTH AMERICAN CITY

“INTRODUCTION TO URBAN GEOGRAPHY”

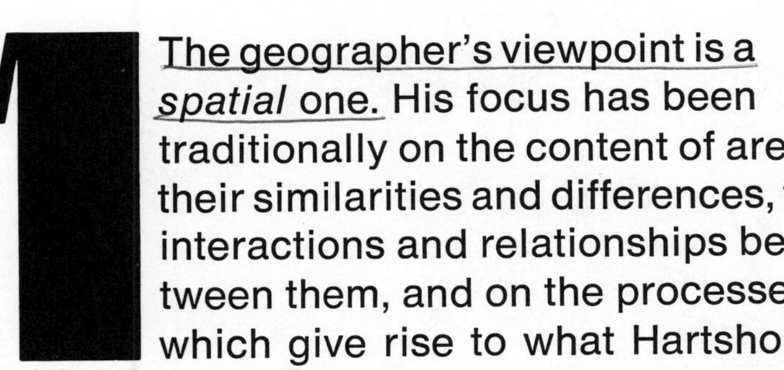

The geographer’s viewpoint is a *spatial* one. His focus has been traditionally on the content of areas, their similarities and differences, the interactions and relationships between them, and on the processes which give rise to what Hartshorne

(1939) termed "areal differentiation." A very general description of the objective of geographical study might be, then, that it *seeks to describe and explain* the areal differentiation of the earth's surface. This statement can be divided into two parts: (1) the first part which is italicized, and (2) the remaining part about areal differentiation. Breaking the statement up in this way is helpful because it distinguishes between two fundamentally distinct, but necessarily related, parts of a discipline. Thus the second part (2) is concerned with what geographers do—with the definition of the subject; while the first part (1) concerns how they do it. This is the basic difference between the philosophy of geography and its methodology.

In this chapter we shall look at both of these aspects as they relate to the growing field of urban geography. On the one hand, the chapter is a brief introduction to urban geography; on the other, it is an introduction to the rest of this book, since the emphasis in much of what follows has its roots in the viewpoints presented in this chapter.

THE NATURE OF URBAN GEOGRAPHY

Urban areas are not only studied by geographers but can be thought of as a laboratory in which studies are undertaken by researchers from many different subjects. Consequently urban geography overlaps with the urban-oriented parts of many other disciplines. Figure 1.1 shows this overlap for some of the more important cognate sciences, the core of which can be thought of as

FIG. 1.1. THE OVERLAP OF URBAN-ORIENTED SCIENCES.

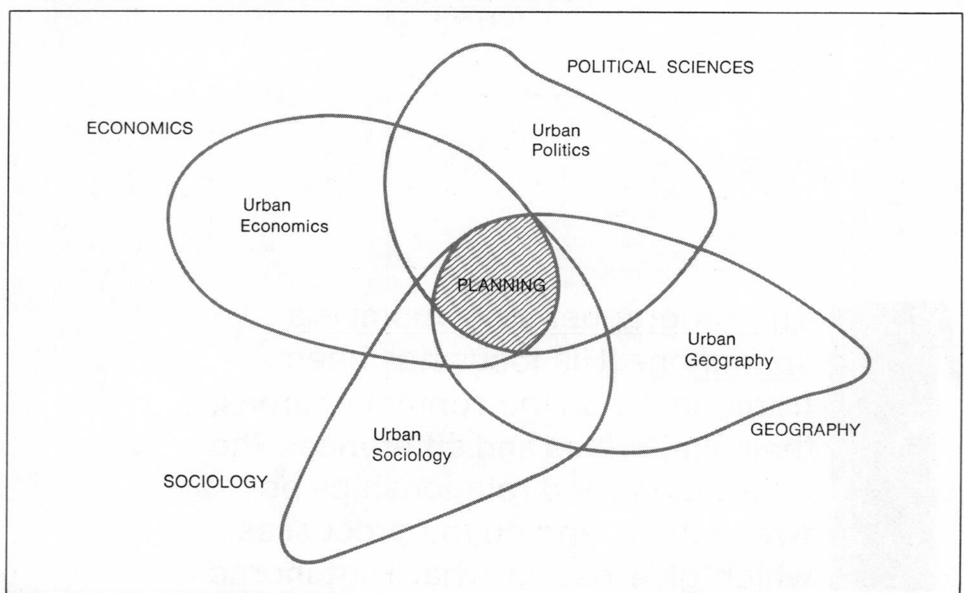

comprising the interdisciplinary science of planning. This overlap between subjects points to a fundamental premise concerning the definition of subjects, namely that sciences are identified "not so much by the phenomena they study as by the integrating concepts and processes that they stress" (Berry, 1964, p. 2). Thus although there may often be a close resemblance between the work of an urban geographer and, for example, that of an urban sociologist, the fundamental difference between the kinds of studies each undertakes results from the fact that the integrating concepts and processes of the geographer are spatially oriented and "relate to spatial arrangements and distributions, to spatial integration, to spatial interactions and organization, and to spatial processes" (Berry, 1964, p. 3). The geographer is essentially concerned with the behavior and processes that form spatial patterns (Taaffe, 1970, pp. 5–8).

In a similar way, the different systematic branches of human geography overlap, each of which may in part focus on the study of urban areas. This is shown in Figure 1.2 for the principal branches of human geography. Thus the economic geographer may be concerned with the location of industry. He can

FIG. 1.2. THE CONVERGENCE ON URBAN GEOGRAPHY.

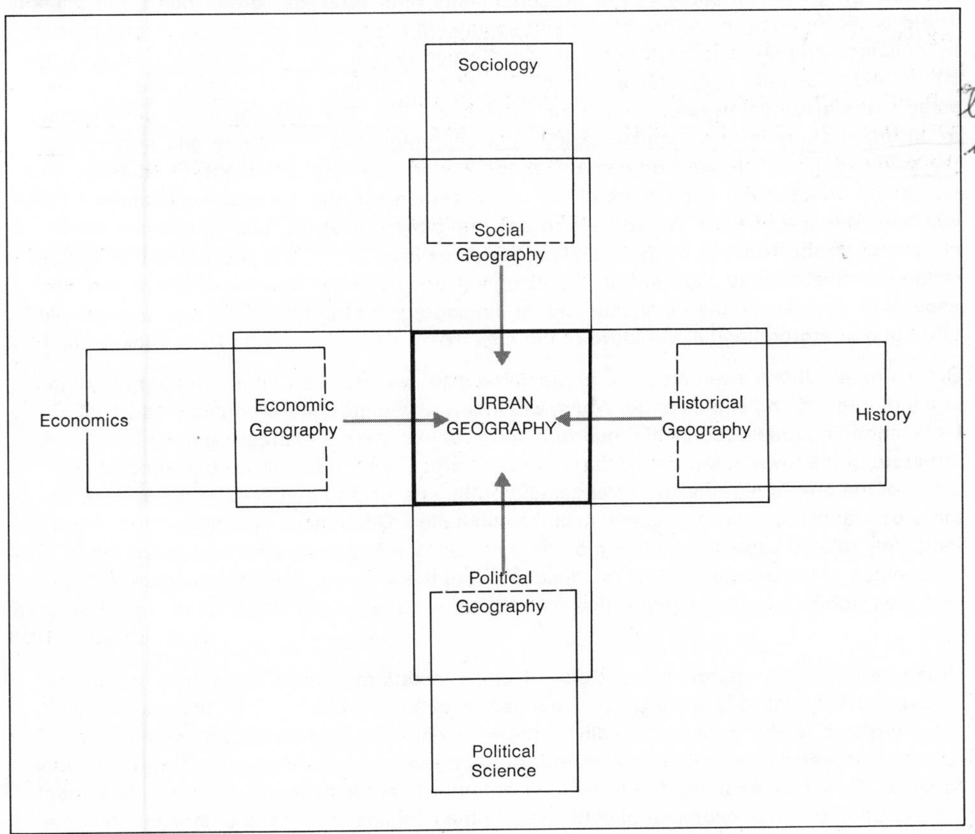

study this general problem with special reference to the industrial structure of urban areas, either looking for patterns in the distribution of industry between them or looking for patterns and processes at work in the location of industry within them. Similar urban bias may be characteristic of the work of political and social geographers, and so on. Hence just as planning may be thought of as being at the core of the overlap between different sciences, so urban  geography can be thought of as an area of convergence of the various systematic branches of human geography. It is largely because of this that urban geography is not so much a well-defined subject on the basis of the facts it deals with as it is an area of inquiry in which the inquiry is spatial and the area urban.

APPROACHES TO URBAN GEOGRAPHY

The easiest way of defining urban geography is to describe what urban geographers do. Four such definitions are presented as follows, and this book can be thought of as constituting a fifth.

> . . . the geographical study of human settlements both rural and urban has three aspects. There is the *physical structure* of the settlement—the character and mode of grouping of its buildings and streets; there is the *process* which determines this structure—that is, the social and economic character and traditions of the community; and third, there is the *stage* in the historical development of the settlement. . . . The first task of the geographer in an urban study is to determine exactly the characteristics of the site and situation of the settlement. . . . Having determined precisely the physical conditions of situation and site which affected the beginnings of the urban settlement, the geographer examines how, with the passage of time, the settlement utilizes, adapts itself to, and transforms these conditions in the process of its formation and expansion. . . . The present urban pattern is the culminating and the central object of the geographical approach. There are two aspects of such study, the functional and the demographic structure of the city; and the plan and build or morphological structure of the city.
>
> R. E. Dickinson, 1948

> But towns are themselves areas of appreciable size, and have an internal geography that is full of interest and significance. When, within any urban area, we recognize industrial belts, shopping areas, residential quarters and suchlike, we are expressing the internal structure of the town in terms of different uses of urban land. It can also be described in terms of the physical forms and arrangement of the spaces and buildings that compose the urban landscape, or townscape, as it may be called. Differences in either or both these intimately related aspects of urban morphology, function and form, give a basis for the recognition of urban regions. It is the description of their nature, their relative disposition, and their social interdependence that constitutes a geographical analysis of an urban area.
>
> A. E. Smailes, 1953

> Urban geographers approach the study of cities in different ways. They may be chiefly concerned with the city as a part of the fabric of settlement. . . . In this case they are interested in the forms of buildings, the arrangements of streets and railroads, or the relations between these things that men build and the functions they are or were intended to serve. They may examine the forms and patterns of settlements as of today, trace back the evolution of the phenomena of settlement to their origins, forecast the changes to come.

Or they may approach the city as an economic phenomenon with associated social and political attributes, by seeking to identify the function or functions underlying city growth or decline, or the role of the city in the economy of the larger area it serves. Actually most urban geographers combine these approaches. Furthermore, they may study cities for the purpose of formulating basic concepts of city growth, city location, or city character; or, they may study cities in order to contribute to the solution of practical problems of urban planning. H. Mayer, 1954

Urban geography deals with the spatial aspects of urban development. Primarily its focus is upon cities, but this focus is broadened to include all areas that are sufficiently city-like in housing density and land-use characteristics to be referred to as urban, and even to include non-urban areas as they relate to cities. The concern is with determining in the field or through plotting of data in the office the areal patterns associated with urban centers and in explaining these arrangements. . . . But the interest is not confined to the contemporary scene. The urban geographer reaches into the past to find explanations of the present areal arrangements and to investigate patterns of the past. He is interested, too, in using his methods to predict the futures of urban areas. R. Murphy, 1966

These definitions suggest that an important distinction can be made between (1) the study of various aspects of the distribution of urban settlements, and (2) the study of the internal structure of urban areas. A useful way of generalizing about the different kinds of study within each of these two major approaches is to use the notion of a "geographical matrix" (Berry, 1964). Such a matrix is outlined in Figure 1.3. It comprises a number of rows and columns. Although in reality there is an infinite number of both, it is normally possible to define a fixed number of them, which is meaningful in the context of a given problem. The columns in the matrix refer to places; we can refer to them generally as urban areas. The rows refer to characteristics—the variables or attributes to be used in study. These have been grouped in the diagram into the main systematic branches of human geography. The intersection of a given column and row defines a *cell* (as shown for the intersection of column i and row j) which contains a *geographic fact.* This is an observation of a single characteristic recorded by its location at a single place.

Approaches to the city system In studies of the distribution of urban places, they are treated in the aggregate, for example, in terms of population size, or total employment in a certain type of economic activity, and so on. Thus in Figure 1.3A, such aggregate indexes constitute the geographic facts in the cells of the matrix. Study of the cells in the whole or in a part of a single row amounts to studying the same characteristic as it occurs at a number of different cities. Here the emphasis is on the spatial variation of a particular characteristic. It can give rise to distributional maps, as for example the distribution of cities according to their population size or their functional structure. Study of the whole or part of a single column amounts to looking at many different characteristics in the same place. In this way we get a partial or complete inventory of general facts about a place, which is characteristic, for example, of much information available about cities in the census and other statistical source books.

An alternative approach is that of comparative study, either of the rows or of the columns. Comparison between rows amounts to the study of spatial associations—the way in which different characteristics are related to each other. An example of this might be the study of the relations between the economic and social characteristics of urban areas (see Nelson, 1957). Comparison of two or more columns amounts to the comparative study of urban areas in terms of selected criteria (see Weber, 1958).

One further possibility is to take a number of adjacent rows and columns that comprise a box of the matrix (Figure 1.3A) and look at its contents. In essence this involves both of the approaches discussed above, and perhaps the best example of this is the classification of urban areas on the basis of their functional specialization as discussed in Chapter 3.

The five basic approaches to the study of the city system discussed so far are, however, deficient in one important respect. The definition of a geographical fact has been based on the observation of a given characteristic at only a single point in time. At any other point in time it could be different, for variation occurs in time as well as space. Changes through time can easily be incorporated if we think of slices cut through different time periods as shown in Figure 1.3A. Each slice represents a matrix containing the same characteristics about the same places—but as they occurred in the past. The addition of the time dimension obviously increases the possibilities for study. Each of the five basic approaches discussed above could be undertaken at any one of the slices through time. This would result in what is generally referred to as *historical urban geography*. Alternatively any one of the five basic approaches could be adopted and comparisons made across a number of different time slices. In this way the emphasis would clearly be on the evolution of patterns and the processes operating to give rise to them. All of these alternative approaches to the study of the system of cities are explicit or implicit in Part I of this book.

Approaches to internal structure Only a slight modification of our geographic matrix is needed to illustrate the approaches to the study of the internal structure of urban areas. For this we can think of each urban area as having a number of columns associated with it as shown in Figure 1.3B. These columns could represent, for example, census tracts within the city or any other small areas we choose to delimit. In this way the characteristics can be recorded at different locations within the urban area. By adding the slices through different time periods, the same basic approaches are again possible, although the emphasis in each will differ. For example, study of all the cells in a given row corresponding to a single urban area would amount to the study of the variation within the city of the selected characteristic, perhaps population density or income. Extension to include the cells in an entire row amounts to a comparative study of the spatial variation of the selected characteristic in a number of different cities, and so on. With other permutations and combinations, the result is a rich diversity of possible approaches and themes in studying the internal geography of urban areas. These are the kinds of approaches discussed in Part II.

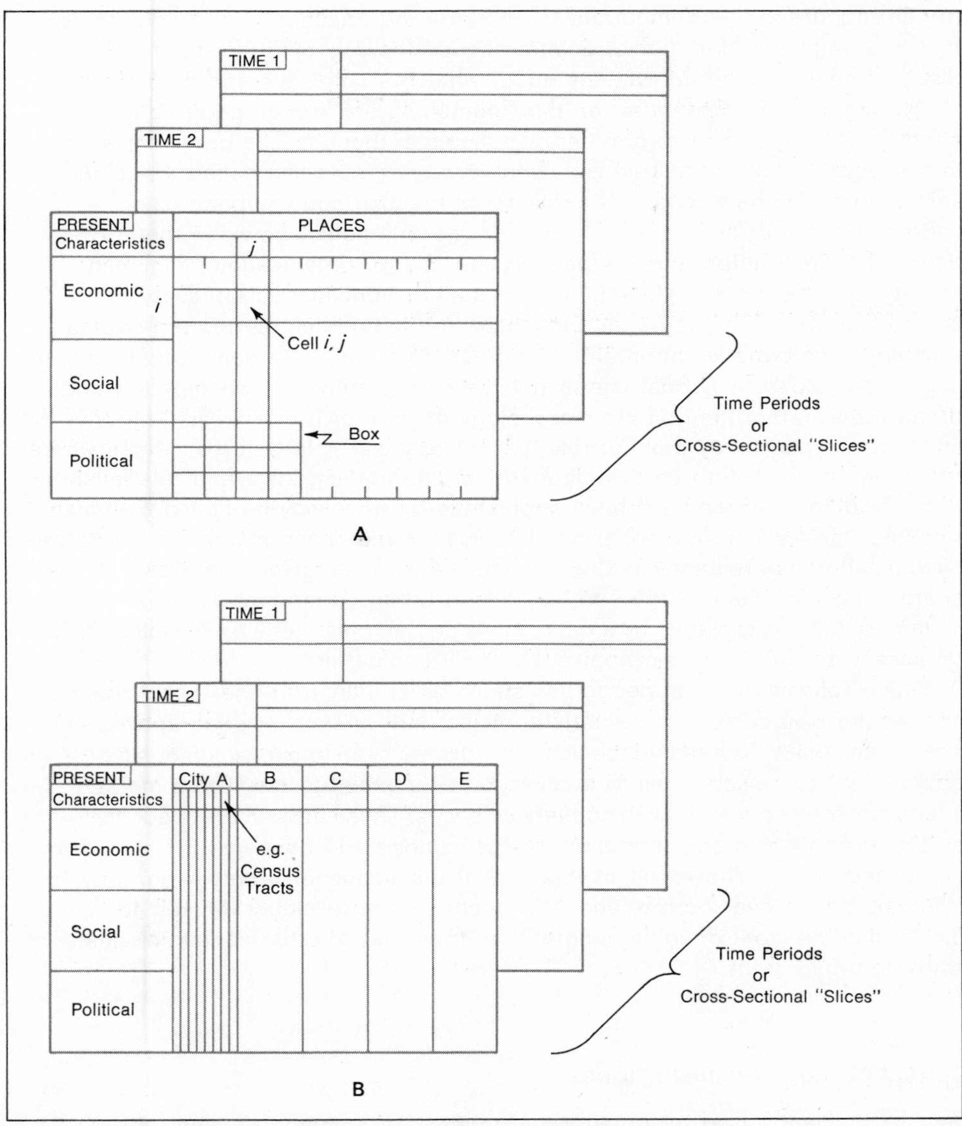

FIG. 1.3. THE "GEOGRAPHIC MATRIX" IN URBAN GEOGRAPHY AS APPLIED TO STUDY OF THE "CITY SYSTEM" (A), AND THE INTERNAL STRUCTURE OF CITIES (B). (*Source:* After Berry, 1963, Fig. 3.)

EMPHASES IN URBAN GEOGRAPHY

Just as there is diversity in the approach to urban geography, so there is considerable variation among urban geographers in their study emphasis. The particular emphasis of an individual is largely a reflection of his philosophy of (urban) geography. The important thing about the philosophy of a science is that it is ultimately a matter of opinion; hence there is plenty of room for disagreement between individuals about what the emphasis and objectives of study ought to be. Because of this, contemporary urban geography is characterized by a number of different schools of thought. The particular emphasis in this book is that associated with what Haggett (1965) has called the locational school, in which the emphasis is explicitly on the distributional patterns of various aspects of human activity and on the interaction between them. Areal differentiation is interpreted largely as the spatial organization of human activity, and the stress is placed firmly on the functional aspects of study.

The kind of urban geography presented in this book is, therefore, just one of a number of alternative approaches that could be adopted—some of which were suggested above. It is characterized by a strong emphasis on function and organization rather than on the morphology or form of urban areas. The physical environment plays only a minor role, particularly within large urban areas where it can be considered to be of only marginal importance. Man-land relationships in the traditional sense have been supplanted by what may be called man-man relationships—a shift in emphasis resulting from the concern with the functional-spatial patterns of relations among people. The detail of history that was characteristic of many of the early studies in urban geography (for example in James, 1931) is replaced by the emphasis on the role of time as it relates to processes at work in the development of the urban pattern.

This emphasis in urban geography stems essentially from the recent reaction against the isolationism characteristic of the early growth of geography (see Ackerman, 1963). As a result, the past decade has been one in which human geography has looked outward to an increasing extent to result in a marked intensification of contacts with cognate sciences. These have in turn become an increasingly rich and fruitful source of analogy and concepts for studies in urban geography. The result of this is that the scope of urban geography is wider now than ever before, and it is becoming increasingly difficult to distinguish the work of some geographers from that of other social scientists studying urban areas.

CONCEPTS AND CONSIDERATIONS

Just as the facts used by urban geographers are common to many other sciences, so are many of its concepts. There are in fact very few concepts that might be considered as truly geographic. Nystuen (1963) identifies the few as those of distance, relative location, site, and accessibility. These are all specifically related to location and ultimately can be viewed as geometrical concepts. For the rest we are more or less completely dependent on other sciences. The cognate fields of economics and sociology have traditionally been a very fruitful source of concepts for spatial analysis. To an increasing extent, social psychology is becoming an important source of concepts, particularly those relating to perception and learning, which are now quite basic postulates for study in the emerging behavioral approach in human geography (see Cox and Golledge, 1969). Many concepts from these cognate disciplines that have been found useful in urban geography are introduced at appropriate places in the text. At this point it is sufficient to stress some basic concepts and considerations that underlie the emphasis given to urban geography in this book.

THE CONCEPT OF REGION

With its spatial viewpoint and focus on area, regions are fundamental to geography. The region is an intellectual construction used to facilitate study. In practice it is a question of placing a boundary around a part of the earth's surface to identify one's study area. Obviously there is an infinite number of ways of dividing up the earth's surface into smaller regions, and this problem has received much attention in the history of geography (Whittlesey, 1954). How and where the boundary of a specific region is drawn is essentially a matter of classification (Grigg, 1965). It is important to keep in mind that, although boundaries are usually shown on maps as lines, in reality changes in the distribution of phenomena over space are marked by zones of transition between regions with well-marked characteristics. Three different kinds of regions are particularly useful in the context of urban geography.

Uniform regions When a characteristic observed at locations is essentially the same over a wide area, it is possible to delimit a region possessing a high level of internal homogeneity. Such a region will never be 100 percent homogeneous since the real world is not that perfect. It is possible, however, to delimit regions that are fairly uniform in their content. Such regions will always be characterized by a certain range of variability in the selected criteria, and there will always be irrelevant differences that must be disregarded in the context of a given problem. Two types of uniform regions can be identified depending on whether a single feature or a combination of different features is used in drawing the boundary. Examples of these are presented in Figure 1.4, and many others appear throughout the book.

An example of a single-feature uniform region in urban geography could be the nonwhite areas of a city (Fig. 1.4A). Although a number of white persons may be living in such a region, and nonwhites living outside it for that matter, the region identified on the basis of this single characteristic will be typified by a very high degree of nonwhite occupancy and hence will be uniform in terms of this stated characteristic. Multiple-feature uniform regions are based on the spatial association of a number of different characteristics. A good example is the "zone in transition" within cities (see Chapter 9), a distinctive area because of the particular combination of features found there, including things such as a high proportion of dilapidated structures, high residential densities, a mixture of land uses, and so on.

Nodal regions A characteristic feature of the *nodal region* is that it has a central point or focus to which surrounding locations are united on the basis of a given kind of interaction. Regions of this type are delimited on the basis of interaction between places. They are functional, and their homogeneity is in terms of internal organization. As with uniform regions, single- and multiple-feature nodal regions may be identified depending on the number of criteria used in drawing the boundary. An example of a single-feature nodal region is the catchment area of a local high school, or the circulation area of a town's newspaper (Fig. 1.4B). An important multiple-feature nodal region is the trade area of a town as discussed in Chapter 4.

Administrative regions Administrative regions are not peculiarly geographic but are nevertheless basic to a great deal of research in urban geography. Their importance lies in the fact that they are the basic spatial units used for the collection of official statistics. Two kinds of administrative regions may be identified. First, there are the political kind such as states, corporate municipalities, and so on. In terms of their political organization they may be thought of as a special type of nodal region. Secondly, there are the ad hoc regions established by government and private agencies for specific purposes. Included in these would be planning regions, such as the TVA, Standard Metropolitan Statistical Areas, and the various small areas, such as census tracts used in the census. The latter are often the basic building blocks used in the construction of uniform regions for particular geographic study. An important

FIG. 1.4. UNIFORM AND NODAL REGIONS IN URBAN GEOGRAPHY: (A) NONWHITE AREAS IN THE CITY OF CHICAGO, (B) NEWSPAPER CIRCULATION AREAS IN THE CHICAGO METROPOLITAN AREA. (*Source:* After Berry, Parsons, and Platt, 1968, Fig. 3.7, and Park and Newcomb, 1933, Fig. 5.)

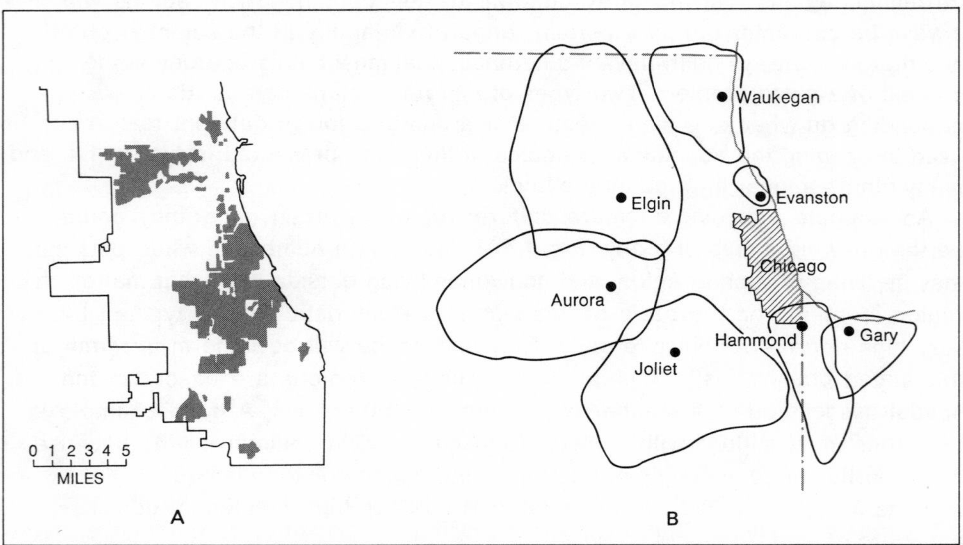

feature of this kind of region is that its boundaries are in the main fixed rather arbitrarily, and often they represent conditions that existed in the past. Hence they form an underlying mosaic over which uniform and nodal regions delimited for specific geographic purposes are superimposed.

THE CONCEPTS OF DISTANCE

Distance is basic to geography. One geographer has even suggested that geography itself is a "discipline in distance" (Watson, 1955). It is certainly true that the concept of the "frictional effect" of distance is one of the important cornerstones on which a considerable part of contemporary urban geography is constructed. As such it is a consideration that runs right through the contents of this text. Distance is a fundamental consideration, because it separates locations from each other, thereby necessitating movement between them to give rise to spatial interaction. So important has this factor been that a considerable part of man's technological effort has been directed at inventing ways of reducing the influence of distance (see Chapters 2 and 8). The history of transportation and communication is thus essentially one of successively reducing the inconvenience of distance. Although this has certainly been achieved for many kinds of spatial interaction, the inconvenience of distance can never be completely removed; and it still constitutes an important factor for understanding spatial relations, particularly for the flows of goods and people between cities which is discussed in Chapter 4.

Distance is a fundamental factor because of the costs involved in overcoming it. These costs are an important consideration in the collective and individual decision-making processes underlying spatial patterns. Decisions are thus often made with the express purpose of minimizing these costs to give rise to what can be thought of as "centripetal forces" acting in space. These forces tend to bring things together to result in various types of agglomeration (see Chapter 6). The urban area itself can be thought to have resulted from centripetal forces; the emergence of "downtown" as the major retail-service area of the city is another example. At the same time distance affords the opportunity for the spatial separation of things from each other. Hence we can also detect "centrifugal forces" operating in opposition to the centripetal ones, resulting in the dispersion of things in space. Spatial organization therefore owes much to the interaction of these opposing sets of forces, which are one of the frameworks for understanding the distribution of activities in space.

LOCATIONAL CONCEPTS

In discussing why things are located where they are, we are explicitly concerned with location. In a most simple way we can think of location as points in two-dimensional space. The location of these can be fixed rather precisely using the grid coordinates of the world's system of latitude and longitude. This determines the absolute location of the point. In discussing the site of a settlement, we are in a general way talking in part about its absolute location. When the absolute locations of a number of points are determined, we create a pattern, the particular features of which are basic to much geographical study. The location of an individual point in a pattern can be discussed from another point of view. Using the notions of distance and direction, we can refer to the location of one point in relation to the locations of the others. This is the concept of *relative location.*

Relative location is a more useful concept than absolute location for most studies in urban geography. In a very general way it approximates the traditional concepts of situation in the work of urban geographers, and for all intents and purposes we might think of the two as synonymous. Thus in talking about the location of a particular industry, we can refer to its position relative to important considerations, such as the source of its raw materials and the market in which its products are sold (see Chapter 6). Hence, relative location becomes an important consideration in the geographical study of cities, particularly since many decisions are made to maximize the advantages of relative location and accessibility. One important result of this is that distinctive associations between phenomena are found in cities.

SCALE

We seldom consider locations as mere points in space but more frequently refer to collections of points or areas. Once we begin to talk about areas, we introduce a further consideration—that of scale, the effects of which are shown diagrammatically in Figure 1.5. Clearly areas can vary considerably in size,

FIG. 1.5. SOME EFFECTS OF SCALE CHANGES IN URBAN STUDY.

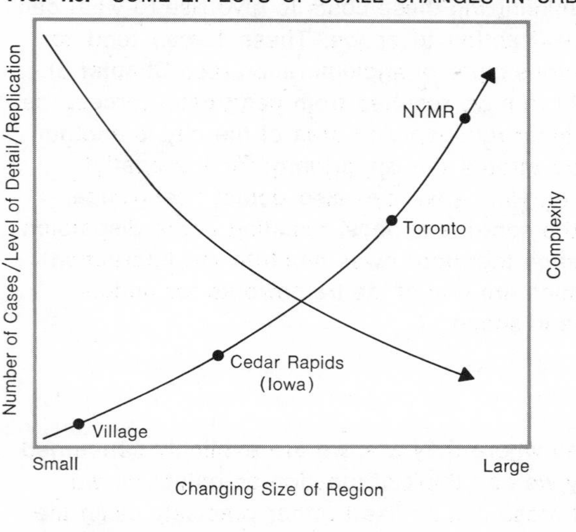

ranging from the smallest imaginable (a point) to the entire world. The size or scale of regions is an important consideration because it relates to the level of complexity of study. As regions get smaller, their complexity decreases—they become in a sense more uniform. A second important effect of scale is that it affects the selection of the significant variables for study. What we may consider to be significant, and hence appropriate, for study in a small region may not be the same as that selected for a larger region. An important effect of this is that much greater detail may be relevant for studying small regions than for large ones.

A good illustration of this is the study of the commercial structure of urban areas (Chapter 12). If this is studied at the city-wide scale, then a particular shopping center may be thought of simply in terms of the number of different functions and establishments it contains. If, however, a single shopping center is used as the region for study, then many other features become important in giving rise to patterns within the center. Another important scale consideration should be borne in mind, namely, that scale affects the kinds of processes operating in space. The processes operating in a large region may not have the same meaning in a smaller one, for which a different set of more local processes must be considered.

A final scale consideration relates to the number of cases (the population in a statistical sense) available for study. As regions get smaller, their number gets larger. For example the New York Metropolitan Region, which in 1960 had a population of about 16 million inhabitants, is the only urban region of this size in North America. In the entire world the number of similar-sized urban regions is restricted to perhaps 10. At the other extreme a considerably larger number of nodal regions centered on small villages is available for comparative study. This number is certainly in excess of 100,000 in North America and several millions in the whole world. The important implication of this is that when a large number of cases is available, there is more opportunity for comparison and repetition in study; and an inductive approach to hypothesis formulation and theory building is possible. Conversely a smaller number of large regions restricts the possibility for this approach and consequently greater stress must be placed on a deductive approach and external reasoning (Haggett, 1965, p. 4).

METHOD IN URBAN GEOGRAPHY

Method should not be confused with technique. In talking about method in urban geography, we are referring to the conceptual framework within which study is undertaken—the methodology of study. During the past twenty years a marked change has occurred in the methodology of urban geography. This has resulted from the growing realization that geography can be considered as a science and that the scientific method can be adopted as the framework for research. This is essentially what the quantitative revolution in geography was about (Burton, 1963). The effect of this has been to change the character of much recent work in urban geography by making it more mathematical. As a result, urban geography is becoming considerably more abstract in its approach.

THE SEARCH FOR ORDER

The methodological changes associated with the quantitative revolution have resulted in great stress on the search for order (Haggett, 1965, p. 2). In this the focus is on the regularities in spatial arrangement, on the association between things in space, and on the processes operating to create them. The nature of the regularities that may be identified depends, however, on what we are prepared to look for and what we see, for "If we ask of a given region whether its settlements are arranged in some predictable sequence, or its land-use zones are concentric, or its growth cyclical, the answer largely depends on what we are prepared to look for and what we accept as order" (Haggett, 1965, p. 2). Order and chaos are not parts of nature but are concepts of the mind. In urban geography the search for order is reflected in the increasing concern with generalization, higher degrees of abstraction, and greater problem orientation.

The concern with generalization Early studies in urban geography were for the most part concerned with places as individuals and comprised detailed descriptions of them. Stress was on the case study approach, but without much regard for what the particular case studied represented in the broader context of areal differentiation. There were exceptions to this, and the early attempt of Griffith Taylor (1942) to see order in the way settlements evolved through time is still today worthy of close inspection despite the marked environmentalist framework he used.

These early studies recognized that the particular combination of detail making up the urban area differed from city to city. The explicit underlying assumption was that each place was unique. This concept of uniqueness has played a key role in the traditional methodology of geography. In a scientific geography, however, it is illogical because it does not permit explanation or the prediction of phenomena; and for science the essential concern is that of explanation. Hence "Science is diametrically opposed to the doctrine of uniqueness. It is willing to sacrifice the extreme accuracy obtainable under the uniqueness point of view in order to gain the efficiencies of generalization" (Bunge, 1962, pp. 8–9). Consequently in most contemporary studies in urban geography much of the fascinating detail about places is purposely sacrificed so that general similarities in spatial structure may be recognized.

More abstract study Generalizations can only meaningfully result if study is undertaken at fairly high levels of abstraction, for it is only in this way that order can be perceived among all the confusing detail. One way of sacrificing detail and thereby making study more abstract is to select more carefully the variables and characteristics thought to be significant in a given context. By restricting the choice of what is included in a study, it is possible to introduce greater clarity, thereby making the identification of order and chaos easier. In this book much interesting detail has been sacrificed in this way, and greater attention is given to regularities that have been identified at fairly high levels of generalization.

Abstract study is brought about in another important way—through the use of mathematics. The symbols of the mathematical languages have much greater precision than words alone. Hence the use of mathematics makes possible a more precise definition of things and a clearer and more objective identification of the underlying relationships. Abstraction is achieved then on two fronts—through greater simplification and more frequent use of symbols. The fundamental objective of both is to make possible the formulation of theory, in which connection very abstract models are often proposed.

The concern with problems To the layman a problem is something that requires a solution. In urban geography such a problem might be where to locate a new shopping center. The solution to this requires the application of the geographer's skills in a specific context outside of the academic world. There is no doubt that geographers are becoming increasingly involved in solving these kinds of applied problems, particularly in the context of urban and regional planning, and will continue to do so in the future.

The solution to these practical location problems can be obtained in fundamentally different ways, however. On the one hand, solutions can be arrived at intuitively, on the basis of the skill and subject-matter knowledge of the individual. Alternatively the problem can be solved by recourse to a theory. For much current research in urban geography, it is this concern with theory that constitutes the fundamental problem. This involves, first, establishing the significant relationships that exist, a problem which can be thought of as the formulation and testing of hypotheses. Increasingly the methods of statistical inference are used for this. Once significant relationships have been identified, the problem becomes that of explaining why they are there. The basic problem is consequently that of answering the questions how? and why?

STAGES IN STUDY

The scientific approach to study involves three distinct but complementary stages. These are (1) description, (2) explanation, and (3) prediction. These stand in relation to each other in that order. Explanation occupies the central position. It is necessarily preceded by description; and it leads logically to prediction.

Description This has occupied a dominant position in geographical studies in the past and must continue to do so in the future. As Klimm (1959, p. ii) said, "It tends to keep us honest in our theorizing." A number of different aspects are included under the general heading of description, all of which have to do with the arrangement of facts so that they can be used meaningfully in later study.

First there is the question of selecting those facts that are relevant for a given problem. This involves observation in its broadest sense. In many cases where data is not readily available, observation directly involves field study. The important thing about this is that it necessitates selection of facts. As Harvey has recently stated,

> Reality presents the observer with a vast inflow of information. It is the function of observation techniques to select and order this information in a way that makes it manipulable and comprehensible. This process is a kind of search procedure, . . . Clearly, the way in which reality is searched, the particular set of filters (some might call them blinkers) which we use, has an enormous influence upon the kinds of questions we ask and the kinds of answers we are able to give (Harvey, 1969, p. 298).

Quite clearly this notion of searching reality implies that we have some kind of hypothesis in mind at the outset and in connection with which we are collecting (observing) information. Hence in this case we are structuring reality in order to test hypotheses about it. An alternative approach, however, is to search reality in order that hypotheses may be identified. The approach is characteristic of much urban geographical research. Vast amounts of information are collected, which are then sifted through in the hope of identifying significant hypotheses. Clearly this is not a very efficient way of undertaking study.

Description also involves the problem of defining the observed facts. It is in this way that specific meaning is attached to them and that they can later be measured. Lastly there is the organization or classification of the facts into some meaningful system. Classification has held a dominant place in the literature of urban geography since it underlies virtually everything we do. Several attempts to classify cities, for example, are discussed in Chapter 3.

Observation, definition, measurement, and the classification of facts enable us to manipulate them in a meaningful way. In geography it is common to express the facts in graphic form, particularly on maps. When we do this, the emphasis is explicitly on the spatial dimension, and the focus is directly on patterns and distributions. Increasingly, however, we use graphs and other more abstract ways of presenting data. In these the spatial parameter is often only implicitly recognized, since the facts have been abstracted from their specific locational context. Throughout this book there are examples of many aspects of the descriptive stage in study and the various ways of representing data in graphic forms.

Prediction In its scientific usage, prediction means a conditional statement, usually expressed as follows: "If *X*, then *Y*." This simply states that if *X* occurs, then it should result in, or be associated with, the occurrence of *Y*. An example can make this clear. Imagine a proposal has been made to build a by-pass highway around a small town in an attempt to reduce traffic congestion in its center. If this is done, it would probably bring about a marked change in the flow of traffic through the town, which may very well have an impact on the town's businesses. Clearly the planner wants to know whether constructing the by-pass will have an adverse effect on the local business community; and if so, how serious this would be.

Obviously the planner cannot experiment by constructing the highway so as to observe what happens. The planner could, however, shed some light on the problem if there was a theory about the impact of by-passes on local business communities. For then the theory could be used to predict the likely effects of the new highway construction. The theory might tell him, for example, that, if the by-pass (X) is constructed, there will in all probability be an increase in business turnover (Y) in the town's center. The planner would like to predict the possible outcome of his decisions in order that he can avoid making mistakes. It is quite clear from this example that prediction is only possible in a scientific sense when we have an adequate theory for the given situation. It is because of this that prediction follows explanation to form the logical third stage in study.

Explanation The critical stage in study is quite clearly that of explanation. Generally explanation can be viewed as any satisfactory answer to a why or how question. Most of the questions asked in urban geography have no single answer, hence there may be a number of alternative explanations, each of which may be satisfactory to different people. The important point is that explanations should be plausible.

The quest for explanation is the quest for theory. Theories are thus at the heart of explanation in science. They are devised in the attempt to answer questions like: why the distribution of shopping centers in a city is the way it is; why there is a consistent decline in interaction between places with increasing distance; how does an area change its social structure over time, and so on. There is, however, considerable confusion over the specific meaning of theory. Since theories are free creations of the human mind, any speculative fantasy may be regarded as a theory of some sort. Scientific theory is, however, much more rigorously defined. Urban geography has very little rigorous theory. In urban geography most of the theories have been borrowed from other sciences and modified slightly or radically to fit the spatial context. To bridge the gap between description and theory, much use is currently made of models; and many examples are found in the chapters of this book.

ON MODELS

As with theories, it is not easy to explain exactly what models are. In fact there is a good deal of variation among geographers, just as there is among philosophers of science, regarding the exact meaning and definition of a model. In everyday language the word model has at least three different meanings. As a noun it signifies a representation as, for example, in the case of a model railroad. For many of us this is perhaps its most familiar meaning. As an adjective the word model implies an ideal as, for example, in the case of a model home or model husband. As a verb, to model means to demonstrate as, for example, is done by some young girls, modeling new fashions in a fashion show.

In its scientific usage, the concept of a model implies all three meanings.

Hence a model is an idealized representation of a part of reality, which is constructed so as to demonstrate certain of its properties. This is the way in which the concept of a model is used in this book. A more catholic view would be, however, that models are primitive theories, laws, hypotheses, hunches, structured ideas, a relation between things, an equation, or a synthesis of data (see Skilling, 1964), and sometimes this much broader interpretation is implicit in geographical study (see Chorley and Haggett, 1967) and at times in this book.

The characteristics of models Models are used as an aid for explanation; as such they can be thought of as a kind of conceptual prop to our understanding. We cannot, however, explain very much about the complex patterns and interrelationships between phenomena in the real world simply by duplicating them camera fashion. This would add very little to our understanding. To explain we must abstract. Thus the first, perhaps the most important, characteristic of a model is that it is an abstraction from reality, a gross simplification of what a situation in the real world is really like. Models do not convey the whole truth, but only part of it; and this is presented in a highly compressed form. This simplification is achieved by selecting what is significant in a given situation. We are forced to distinguish between what we think are the important factors operating and the trivial. In this way we hope to eliminate from consideration much of the incidental detail, thereby clarifying the picture. Hence, a second characteristic of all models is that they are highly subjective approximations to reality, representing the particular researcher's bias, whims, and fancies.

In developing a model we do not expect to explain everything by it, but only that part of reality for which it was specifically devised. For example, the model developed for the journey to work in Chapter 15 will not explain shopping patterns, for which a completely different set of considerations must be taken into account. A third characteristic of models is then that they have a specific range of conditions for which they are relevant. In scientific language, this is referred to as the model's (or theory's) domain.

In presenting a part of the real world in the form of a model, we have to translate the real things under study into something else. This may be some physical structure, like a wave tank used to simulate coastal erosion; or it may be a set of mathematical equations. A fourth characteristic of models is therefore that they are analogies to the real world, the particular form of analogy depending on the type of model used. Lastly models are structured. The significant variables they comprise are viewed in terms of their connections and relationships with each other. Because of this, a good model, like a good theory, should be capable of making predictions about the real world in the sense we have discussed it above. Commonly, these predictions are stated as hypotheses which are then tested against reality.

Types of models The main types of models used in geography are shown in Table 1.1. The experimental models, in which the properties being investigated are translated into some tangible structure, and the natural models, in which

TABLE 1.1. A GENERAL TYPOLOGY OF MODELS USED IN GEOGRAPHY

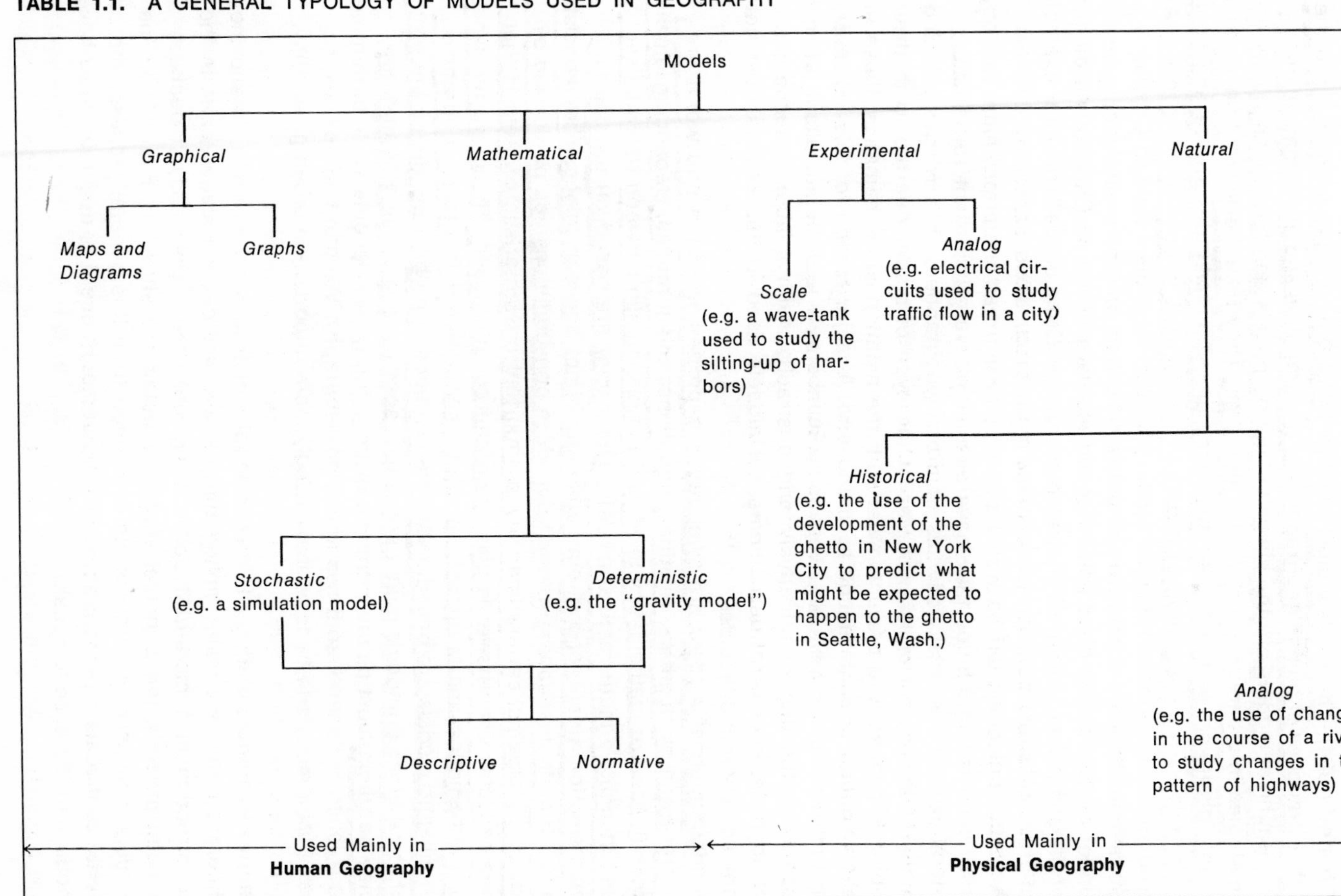

some other circumstance is used as an analogue, are seldom used in urban geography and therefore will not be discussed at any greater length here (see Chorley, 1964). The models most commonly used in urban geography, and the other branches of human geography, are the graphical and mathematical ones.

Graphical models are the simplest kind of models and have been widely used in studies in urban geography for a long time. They take the form of generalized maps, diagrams, or graphs. As such they are essentially descriptive and consist of a stylized representation of a part of reality as it is or is thought to be. An example is the concentric zonal model of urban form discussed in Chapter 9. Sometimes they are normative and portray in graphical form what ought to be under certain stated conditions. A good example of this is Christaller's diagram of the settlement pattern of an area discussed in Chapter 7. Many other examples of graphical models will be encountered in the discussions that follow.

Mathematical models have found their place in urban geography more recently, and since the mid-fifties they have assumed a very important role in the literature and research activities of urban geographers. The reader will find many of the more simple examples of this type of model referred to in this book. For those who are unfamiliar with the notation of mathematics, these may at first glance appear difficult to understand. A major reason for this, however, is that most of us have an aversion to numbers, a real mental block when it comes to thinking quantitatively and abstractly. With a little patience and willingness, however, the mathematical models used in this book should not present any real difficulties.

Mathematical models are symbolic; the properties of the real world are represented by numbers, relations, equations, and formulas. Depending on the specific kind of mathematics used, we can distinguish between *deterministic* and *stochastic* mathematical models. The former are based on the classic mathematical notion of a direct cause and effect between things. They consist of a set of mathematical assertions from which consequences can be derived by the logic of mathematical argument. One important characteristic of them is that one and only one answer is given from the equation used. These are the types of mathematical models most frequently encountered in urban geography. Stochastic models are based on the mathematics of probability. Hence the product of these types of models is in a sense less specific, and a range of answers may be given. Just as the principle of uncertainty has become an important one in science in general, so it has in human geography. We can therefore expect stochastic models to become increasingly more important in urban geography.

Stages in model building In discussing the characteristics of models and their different forms, we have implied that certain well-defined stages exist in the construction of a model. Model building and use is essentially a decision-making process, the principal stages of which are shown in Figure 1.6. The models discussed in this book have resulted from this general process, and can be thought of as representing its final outcome. Hence it is useful to know how models are born, so to speak.

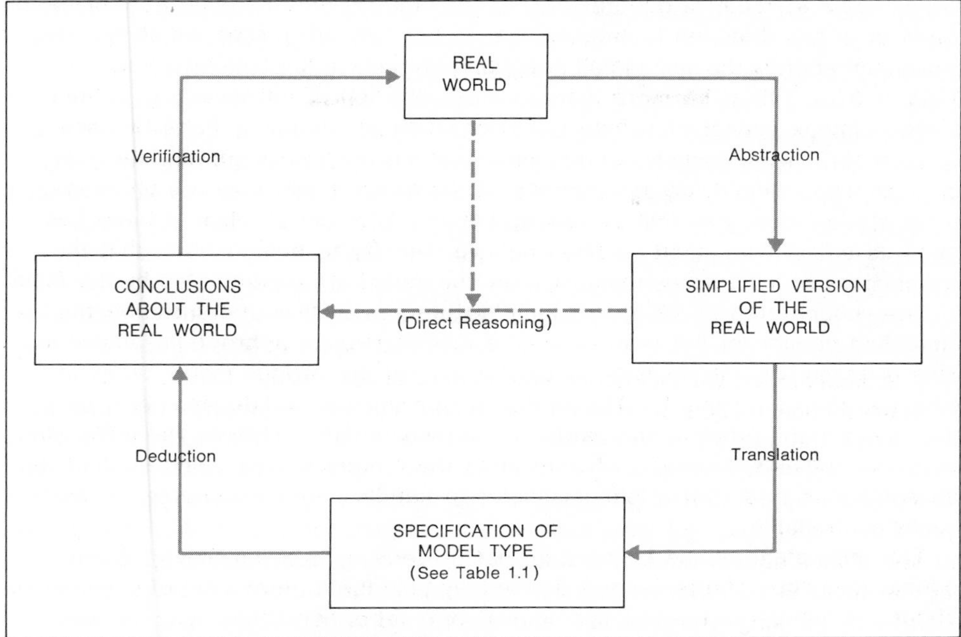

FIG. 1.6. AN OUTLINE OF THE STAGES IN MODEL BUILDING AND USE.

The model-building process consists of a series of stages (the boxes in Figure 1.6) which are linked together in sequence by a series of transformations (connecting lines in Figure 1.6). Together, these form a circuit starting and ending with the part of the real world under study. The first step is to derive a simplified version of the real world. This is obtained by the process of abstraction. This is where huge amounts of information are discarded, where the deadwood is pruned away to reveal what are believed to be the significant variables and relationships operating in a given situation. It is also at this stage that the subjective element in model building comes to the fore. What is selected as being significant for the problem at hand will depend largely on the beliefs of the researcher, on how he consciously or unconsciously thinks the world works. Important things consequently may unknowingly be excluded—throwing away the baby with the bath water is perhaps an appropriate description of this kind of error. Alternatively, "red herrings" may be introduced, which tend to cloud the issue.

The simplified version of the real world, which results from the abstraction process, contains what are thought to be the significant variables and relationships—the bare bones of the problem. These are often accompanied by a set of assumptions stating the circumstances under which the model is meant to hold. This is a way of saying that certain factors are not directly relevant for the model. For example, a common assumption in geographical models is the *isotropic surface,* "a geographical space that has no difference from place to place or in one direction to another; that is, not only are places the same, but movement effort is the same in all directions from place to place" (Nystuen, 1963, p. 375). This is no more than a convenient fiction, introduced to simplify some complex aspect of human behavior, such as shopping behavior (see Chapter 15). The student should remember that it is not always appropriate to criticize these simplifying assumptions on the grounds that they are unrealistic. If the student does feel that something important for the problem at hand has been assumed away, then he must believe, and try to demonstrate, that the conclusions or hypotheses resulting from the model are contradicted by the facts.

The second step in the model-building process is that of translating the simplified version of the real world (the model) into an appropriate analogue. This is essentially the decision to choose one of the various model types or subtypes shown in Table 1.1. The particular type selected will depend partly on the nature of the problem and partly on the researcher's interests. The underlying objective remains, however, of translating the circumstances being studied into an analogous form that is either simpler to handle, more accessible, or more easily controllable.

The third stage in the process is that of deriving from the model some conclusions about the real world. These may take the form of a set of implications about it, a number of testable hypotheses, or a set of actual findings. The way in which these are derived depends directly on the type of formal model used. Thus if an experimental model (i.e. a wave tank) was selected for the purpose at hand, observations would be derived by actual experimentation. When mathematical models are used, the conclusions are obtained as a result of the logic of mathematical deduction.

Finally, the last step is that of comparing the conclusions derived from the model with what is known to exist in the real world. This is the verification stage. Often the findings are verified simply by visual comparison. It is becoming increasingly common, however, to use statistical inference in verifying models. This essentially amounts to a set of rules enabling us to say with a specified level of probability how closely the conclusions from the model match the real world. The great thing about the use of these statistical techniques is that different researchers using the same sets of information should come to the same conclusions.

It is on the basis of using the methods of statistical inference that scientists are able to agree on whether the postulates of the model can be considered a significant explanation of the situation in the real world. If the results of the model can be satisfactorily verified, then the model might be proposed as a theory to be applied in similar situations elsewhere. Hence it is that models are not exactly the same as theories, but can be a useful stage in the formulation of them. As Chorley (1964, p. 128) states,

> A model becomes a theory about the real world only when a segment of the real world has been successfully mapped into it, both by avoiding the discarding of too much infor-

mation in the stage of abstraction . . . and carrying out rigorous interpretation of the model results into real world terms.

An important point to keep in mind about verifying models or theories is that they can never be proved to be true. To say that "I have proved that my model is correct" is a meaningless and impossible statement. Models and theories can be shown to be either consistent with the facts or to be refuted by them, but they can never be proved correct.

To conclude this brief discussion of models and the way they are developed, it is important to stress the point that the stages in the model-building process are connected to form a circuit starting and ending with the real-world situation. The importance of this is that good models, those which may eventually stand as theories, may represent the culmination of a number of cycles through the circuit, each one of which brings the model closer and closer to reality without sacrificing its generality. For example the first pass at the model may result in conclusions at variance with the real world. The researcher must then ask a number of questions concerning why this is so. Have the significant relationships really been specified? Has the baby been thrown out with the bath water? Has the most appropriate form of model been used? Is there an error in the calculations? and so on. The answers to questions like these may result in modifications of the initial model to result in a second, third, and subsequent passes at the problem. The models used in this book often represent the outcome of this kind of reiterative development of an argument.

TECHNIQUES IN URBAN GEOGRAPHY

The way urban geographers undertake their study, their method, is clearly very closely connected with the techniques used. Like any other subject, the techniques in urban geography are many and varied. There is no such thing, however, as a peculiarly geographic technique, despite claims to this effect from time to time. Geographers have, however, often developed better skills with certain techniques than workers from other sciences may have done. For convenience the techniques used in urban geography may be discussed under three headings: techniques of observation, description, and analysis.

Observational techniques Geography has traditionally been regarded as an observational science, in which the role of field work has held a dominant place. Although a large part of the data used by urban geographers can be obtained from already published sources, such as the census or various planning reports and other publications on cities, the nature of many problems necessitates new data which has to be collected from field surveys. Often it is not possible, either through shortage of time or lack of sufficient funds, to collect all the data one might like to; and so resort has to be made to sampling techniques. The techniques of sampling, particularly as they relate to spatial phenomena, are consequently becoming increasingly important in contemporary urban geography at the expense of the complete inventory characteristic of earlier studies. Many of the findings summarized in this book are in fact based on sample surveys rather than complete inventories.

Techniques of description Perhaps the outstanding thing under descriptive techniques is the map, traditionally regarded as synonymous with geography. A very efficient way of describing the characteristics of an area is to present them in map form. Maps constitute a very important descriptive technique in this book: however, there are other ways of presenting material graphically. Diagrams and increasingly graphs are becoming more commonplace in the literature of urban geography. More recently the traditional descriptive techniques have been supplemented with those of statistics and mathematics. These enable much greater objectivity in description than the word language traditionally used. There are many examples of the use of simple descriptive statistics, such as means, standard deviations, correlation coefficients, and so on, in the book.

Analytical techniques If there has been any major change recently in the techniques of urban geography, it has been through the addition of a wide range of powerful techniques of analysis. These are essentially of a mathematical nature; and one group of these is especially important, namely the techniques of statistical inference used for hypothesis testing. It is the application of these techniques that tends to give the impression that much of the work currently undertaken in urban geography is of a fundamentally different nature from that of past studies. However, this is not generally the case and to date these new tools have for the most part been used to tackle traditional problems in a more effective way. The result has been often that new insights have been gained that have enabled researchers to strike out in fresh directions and to explore new *terra incognita.*

“THE CITY SYSTEM”

All of the industrial nations are highly urbanized.

"THE EVOLUTION OF THE URBAN PATTERN"

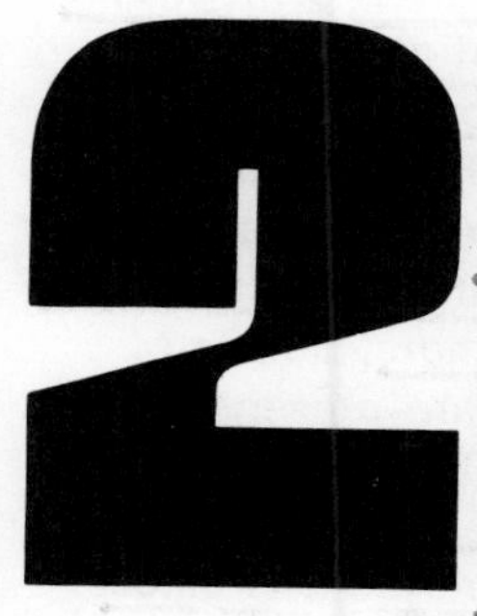

Despite considerable differences in their physical environments and cultural histories, the technically advanced nations of the world today share one thing in common: they are, with some variation, all highly urbanized. Moreover, they

have become so in the recent past. Urbanization is a relatively recent phenomenon, dating essentially from the beginning of the nineteenth century. Even before 1850 no society could be described as predominantly urbanized; and by 1900 only one—Great Britain—could be so regarded. Yet today, scarcely 70 years later, all the industrial nations are highly urbanized; and throughout the entire world the urbanization process is accelerating rapidly.

Quite clearly something dramatic occurred to bring about so radical a transformation of the distribution of population in such a short span of time. The purpose of this chapter is to look more closely at the forces that lay behind the process of urbanization and to trace in general terms the evolution and spread of large cities in the United States from the eighteenth century until the present. The discussion concentrates on the United States as urban growth in Canada has been a more recent phenomenon and developed in a number of different ways. Although the discourse inevitably involves consideration of city function, the main emphasis is on the population size of cities.

THE URBAN TRANSFORMATION

Urbanization is often mistakenly thought of simply as the growth of cities. This confusion arises because, in the past, urbanization and the growth of cities occurred simultaneously (see Table 2.1). Although the two are obviously related, it is important to note a basic difference between them. The process of urbanization, whereby a society is transformed from an essentially rural to a predominantly urban one, has a beginning and an end. In contrast, the growth of cities has no inherent limits. The fundamental distinction stems from the definition of *urbanization* as the proportion of the total population of an area concentrated in urban settlements (Kingsley Davis, 1965). Since the total population can be divided into an urban and a rural part, the proportion urban is a function of both of them. Cities therefore could conceivably grow without any urbanization, provided that the rural population grew at an equal or greater rate. Similarly the growth of cities could continue after everyone was living in urban areas and the process of urbanization was complete, simply by excess births over deaths of the urban population.

Quite clearly, then, the level of urbanization in an area at a given point in time depends on the particular way in which settlements are defined as urban. There is no universal definition of urban settlement, and any definition used must be considered arbitrary and a matter of practical compromise. For example in Denmark, places with 250 inhabitants are considered as urban; in Korea, a place with less than 40,000 is not. In the United States, settlements are defined as urban by the Bureau of the Census if they have 2,500 inhabitants or more. Details of this definition and others used by the Bureau of the Census are presented in Appendix A. On the basis of this definition, the increasing level of urbanization in the United States is shown in Table 2.1 (col. 2). Except for the decade 1810–20, when events were interrupted by the war of 1812, every federal census since

TABLE 2.1. TOTAL NUMBER OF URBAN PLACES AND LEVELS OF URBANIZATION BY SIZE GROUPS IN THE UNITED STATES, 1790–1960

Date	All Cities ≥ 2,500 (1)	U/P[a] (2)	Cities 2,500–24,999 (3)	U/P (4)	Cities 25,000–249,999 (5)	U/P (6)	Cities 250,000–1 Million (7)	U/P (8)	Cities Larger Than 1 Million (9)	U/P (10)
1790	24	5.1	22	3.5	2	1.6	–	–	–	–
1800	33	6.1	30	3.7	3	2.4	–	–	–	–
1810	46	7.3	42	4.1	4	3.2	–	–	–	–
1820	61	7.2	56	3.9	5	3.3	–	–	–	–
1830	90	8.8	83	4.7	7	4.1	–	–	–	–
1840	131	10.8	119	5.3	11	3.7	–	–	–	–
1850	236	15.3	210	6.4	25	6.7	1	1.8	–	–
1860	392	19.8	357	7.9	32	6.7	1	2.2	–	–
1870	663	25.7	611	10.5	45	7.0	3	5.2	–	–
1880	939	28.2	862	11.0	69	8.4	7	8.2	–	–
1890	1,348	35.1	1,224	12.9	113	11.2	7	6.4	1	2.4
1900	1,737	39.7	1,577	13.6	145	11.6	8	5.2	3	5.8
1910	2,262	45.7	2,034	14.7	209	14.2	12	6.0	3	8.5
1920	2,722	51.2	2,435	15.5	262	16.0	16	7.6	3	9.2
1930	3,165	56.2	2,789	16.1	339	16.6	22	10.1	3	9.6
1940	3,464	56.5	3,052	16.5	375	17.1	32	11.2	5	12.3
1950	4,054	59.6	3,534	17.3	479	19.2	32	10.8	5	12.1
1960	4,996	63.1	4,239	18.7	707	22.5	36	11.6	5	11.5
1970	6,435	73.5	5,519	20.9	860	24.0	45	12.1	5	9.8
							50	11.5	6	9.2
New definition[b]										
1950	4,284	64.0	3,800	17.6	443	18.0	36	11.6	5	11.5
1960	5,419	69.9	4,658	19.5	711	22.6	45	12.1	5	9.8
1970	—	—	—	—	—	—	—	—	–	—

[a] Percent of total population living in urban places.

[b] See Appendix A. The figure in column 2 under the new definition includes urban territory outside of places of 2,500 inhabitants.

Source: U.S. Bureau of the Census. *U.S. Census of Population: 1970. Number of Inhabitants, United States Summary,* Table 7. (U.S. Government Printing Office, Washington, D.C., 1971.)

1790 has reported a growing number of people living in cities. The process of urbanization was a very gradual one throughout most of the nineteenth century, mainly because the growth of the urban population in the eastern states was continually being offset partly by the opening up of new rural territory to the west. Despite this by 1870 the United States was 25 percent urbanized; only fifty years later in 1920 over half the total population was urban. Today the proportion is over 70 percent. This increasing degree of urbanization has also been associated with a rapid growth in both the number and size of cities. Particularly significant for the latter was the emergence of urban areas with more than a quarter of a million inhabitants by 1840 and the growth of the million cities by the nineteenth century.

Equal in significance to the growth in numbers and in sizes of urban places since 1790 has been their spread throughout the entire land area of the United States and Canada. This spatial dimension to urbanization is shown for the four major census regions comprising the conterminous United States in Table 2.2 (also see Fig. 2.1). The pattern is clearly one of differential urban concentration and growth in time and space. The Northeast region, which is today the most

TABLE 2.2. URBANIZATION OF POPULATION BY MAJOR CENSUS REGIONS, UNITED STATES, 1790–1960

Date	U.S. (1)	North-east[a] (2)	South (3)	North Central (4)	West (5)
1790	5.1	8.1	2.1	–	–
1800	6.1	9.3	3.0	–	–
1810	7.3	10.9	4.1	0.9	–
1820	7.2	11.0	4.6	1.1	–
1830	8.8	14.2	5.3	2.6	–
1840	10.8	18.5	6.7	3.9	–
1850	15.3	26.5	8.3	9.2	6.4
1860	19.8	35.7	9.6	13.9	16.0
1870	25.7	44.3	12.2	20.8	25.8
1880	28.2	50.8	12.2	24.2	30.2
1890	35.1	59.0	16.3	33.1	37.0
1900	39.7	61.1	18.0	38.6	39.9
1910	45.7	71.8	22.5	45.1	47.9
1920	51.2	75.5	28.1	52.3	51.8
1930	56.2	77.6	34.1	57.9	58.4
1940	56.5	76.6	36.7	58.4	58.5
1950	59.6	75.4	44.6	61.1	59.9
1960	63.1	72.8	52.7	63.9	66.1
1970	—	—	—	—	—
New definition[b]					
1950	64.0	79.5	48.6	64.1	69.5
1960	69.9	80.2	58.5	68.7	77.7
1970	**73.5**	**80.4**	**64.6**	**71.6**	82.9

[a] States included in each major census region are shown in Figure 2.1.
[b] See Appendix A.
Source: U.S. Bureau of the Census. *U.S. Census of Population: 1970. Number of Inhabitants, United States Summary,* Table 18 . (U.S. Government Printing Office, Washington, D.C., 1971.)

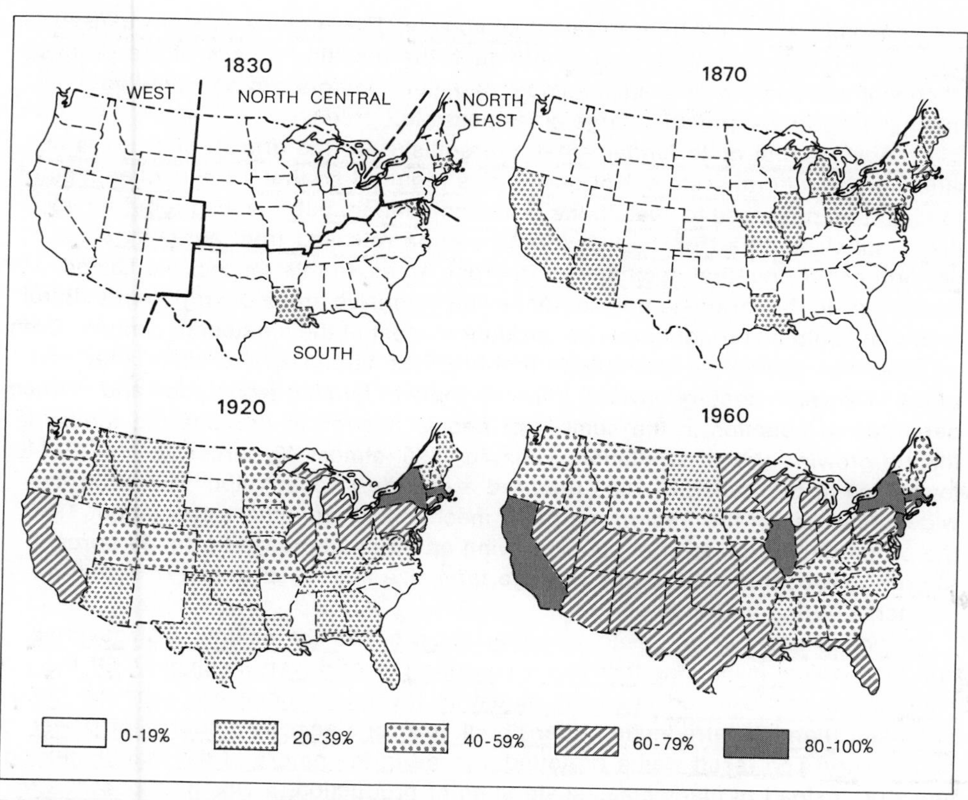

FIG. 2.1 LEVELS OF URBANIZATION IN THE UNITED STATES BY STATES AT SELECTED TIME PERIODS. (*Source:* U. S. Bureau of the Census. *Census of Population 1960. Number of Inhabitants, United States Summary*, Table 10.)

highly urbanized in the United States, was more than 50 percent urbanized by 1880; the North Central and Western regions, together with the nation, by 1920; while the South failed to reach this level before the mid-fifties. Within each major census region, marked differences also occurred in the level of urbanization of individual states at each census period. These differences are shown for four selected dates in Figure 2.1. For example, whereas Rhode Island and Massachusetts were both more than half urbanized by 1870, Mississippi is still today predominantly rural and the least urbanized of all the states (37.7 percent urban in 1960). In terms of levels of urbanization, therefore, many states lag behind those in southern New England by 50 to 60 years, while some states in the deep South lag by more than a century (Lampard, 1968).

GENERAL FACTORS IN URBAN GROWTH

The increase in level of urbanization and the accompanying growth of cities in the United States since 1800 is a reflection of profound changes that occurred in the economic and social organization of society. These changes were caused initially by the industrial revolution. Although the resulting details of the process of change are complex indeed, a number of general factors can be identified that have made the growth of large cities possible.

An obvious, but quite fundamental, prerequisite for the growth of cities is an efficient agricultural system. Not only is this required so that surplus quantities of food can be produced to sustain the urban population, but it is also required so that a substantial part of the labor force can be released from agriculture to perform nonagricultural occupations in urban areas. In this respect the United States was in the fortunate position of having extensive areas of virgin agricultural land that could be brought into use throughout most of the nineteenth century. Even an extensive agriculture was able to produce vast surpluses. From the latter part of the nineteenth century onward, improvements in farming technology and method permitted a reduction in the number of people needed to produce the foodstuff for the growing urban population. Thus, in 1890, almost 40 percent of the 25,746 townships of the nation in 1880 reported a decline in population. Following the widespread use of the tractor and other mechanized equipment after about 1920, the proportion of the total population living on farms decreased from 30 percent to only 5 percent in 1968, while average farm size increased from 147 acres to 377 acres during the same period.

A second basic prerequisite for urban growth was the scientific discoveries and mechanical inventions that made possible power-driven machinery. Of the many inventions ushered in by the industrial revolution, none was perhaps more important than the introduction after about 1830 of steam as a source of power for industry. The result was a profound change in the nature of the manufacturing industry. Instead of many small-scale units of production, it was now possible to concentrate production into bigger factories requiring large numbers of workers. With the introduction of steam power, coal replaced wood and water as the primary source of industrial energy; and thereafter urbanization rapidly became synonymous with industrialization on a large scale. As the scale and complexity of industry increased, a division of labor became a necessity; and strong agglomerative forces based on external economies favored concentration of production and distribution in cities (see Chapter 6). As new innovations appeared, these centripetal forces were reinforced, and the growth of increasingly larger cities was possible.

Although urban growth has largely resulted from economic forces, this does not mean that the growth of all cities was based on the development of manufacturing, nor that the employment in secondary activities dominated the urban labor force. Many smaller cities grew up solely as points of collection and distribution for the areas surrounding them, and this service function is a characteristic function of even the largest cities. Consequently employment in the service, or tertiary, sector of the labor force has been an important factor in the growth of cities, particularly since 1920. Until then employment in the primary (agriculture, forestry, and mining) and secondary (manufacturing) sectors had dominated the structure of national employment and contributed most, either directly or indirectly, to the growth of cities. Although their share of the total employment had been falling steadily since the last decades of the last century, they nevertheless still accounted for 56 percent of the total force in 1920. Since then, however, their share has been less than half and falling rapidly. The most significant increase in employment has been associated with the growth of white-collar occupations. It is the growth of this sector of the labor force that Hall (1966, pp. 25–28) has argued has been without doubt the most important single explanation for the growth of cities, especially the large metropolitan areas, in the twentieth century.

A third important factor was the development that occurred in transportation. An efficient transportation system was essential to bring into the cities not only food in larger and cheaper amounts, but also the raw materials for the growing industries and to distribute the finished products. Moreover, cities could only grow in size if there was a proper intraurban transportation system enabling mass movement of people between home and work places. The growth of cities during the last 150 years has therefore been dependent on a series of technological changes in transportation. Especially important was the introduction and spread of the railroads, which displaced waterways as the dominant mode of moving goods and people after about 1850 and which brought about radical changes in the pattern of urbanization. Although the impact of the railroads on urban growth was dramatic, the introduction of the automobile in the twentieth century has been phenomenal. The widespread use of the automobile and truck in the twentieth century has made possible the decentralization of people and functions within urban areas; it has enabled people to live farther away from their places of work; and it has given rise to the urban sprawl so typical of present-day cities (see Chapter 8).

Fourthly, demographic and social factors have played an important part in city growth. Until relatively late in the nineteenth century, cities—and again especially the larger ones—experienced a natural decrease in population: the number of deaths exceeded the number of births in them. Growth in urban population depended largely on migration of people from rural areas to the growing cities. In the United States this was supplemented by immigration from abroad, which reached a peak in the decade between 1900 and 1910 when some 9 million aliens were admitted. Between 1870 and 1910, immigrants contributed 16.5, 23.5, 14.6, and 23.7 percent, respectively, to decennial increase in the urban population (Lampard, 1968). With greater legal restrictions on immigration, this fell off sharply to 5.1 percent in the decade 1920–30; and this decline has continued since that date.

Since about the turn of the century, however, improvements in medicine and sanitary conditions in urban areas have resulted in a natural increase in city population, so that today urban areas are generally generating their own growth. Rural-urban migration is still important, but as the rural population has experienced an absolute decline, migration from small cities to larger ones has become a more significant mechanism in urban population growth in recent decades (Gibbs, 1963).

Although doubtlessly it is the economic opportunities of the city that exert the greatest pull on migrants, this is reinforced by the social advantages of life in the city. The influence of social factors in urban growth are difficult to isolate; but it is certain that the prospective excitement of city life—despite the superficiality, anonymity, and the transitory character of urban-social relations—has exerted a persuasive influence on migration patterns throughout the period of rapid urban growth. Today the wide range of cultural facilities found in the larger metropolitan centers is important because it encourages a highly educated cadre to live in them. It is from the ranks of these people that key personnel are recruited, which in turn means that the larger cities have become increasingly attractive as the locations for certain types of manufacturing and administrative activities.

THE SPREAD OF CITIES

The present-day distribution of cities in the United States represents the most recent stage in a process of urban growth and spread that essentially began at the end of the seventeenth century. Although slow to start, the process of urban growth gained momentum after about 1850—a momentum that has been accelerating right up to the present day. Throughout this relatively short time span, two general factors have been especially important in influencing the relative locations of growth and decline of cities (Borchert, 1967). The first of these was a series of major changes in the technology of transportation and industrial processes. These brought about a continual reappraisal and definition of natural resources on which large-scale urban growth was based. The second factor was a series of great migrations, which sought to exploit the newly appreciated and changing resource base of the nation. These two factors were, of course, very closely interrelated. The appreciation of new resources was usually brought about by technological change that made them usable and accessible. Together these two factors provide a general framework for understanding the spread of cities and the spatial differentiation of the pattern that has emerged.

From an analysis of major technological innovations, Borchert (1967) identified four epochs in the evolution of the metropolitan pattern in the United States. These are shown in Table 2.3, which summarizes the major innovations, stimuli to urban growth, and new territories settled during each epoch. It should be remembered that this division is only one of many that could be made and that change from one epoch to another was transitional. In addition, the settled area of the United States was expanding westward throughout virtually all of the first three epochs. Hence the new land pioneered during each of these periods "constitutes a region within which all city sites were chosen, and subsequent investments made, under a particular sequence of technological considerations" (Borchert, 1967, p. 308).

The basis for the discussion is a series of maps that show the spread of large cities during each epoch. On the maps, cities are classified by population

TABLE 2.3. CRITICAL STAGES IN THE EVOLUTION OF THE CITY SYSTEM, UNITED STATES, 1790–1960

Epoch	Major Innovation	Stimulus	New Territories
Sail and wagon 1790–1830	—	Agricultural settlement	Eastern Midwest
Age of steam 1830–1870	Steam engine in land and water transportation	Agricultural settlement, small-scale manufacturing, mining, canals	Midwest, Lakes states, Gulf coast
Steel 1870–1920	Steel and electricity	Large-scale manufacturing, mining, tertiary activity	High Plains, West coast, South
Automobile era 1920–1960	Automobile, airplane	Tertiary activity, amenity resources	Gulf coast, South, Southwest

Source: Based on Borchert (1967).

size into five orders (size classes), the lower limits of which increase at each epoch to take account of the fact that the scale of urban growth increases through time. For example, to be considered as a fourth-order city in 1790, a settlement only had to have 15,000 inhabitants. At that time this would have made it a sizable city. In 1960, however, the threshold population size for fourth-order cities was 250,000. The fact that cities were able to increase in population size is largely related to changes that took place in their internal structure. Although these are not discussed here, it should be kept in mind that changes in transportation technology had a profound impact on urban form at each of the different time periods (see Chapter 8).

THE URBAN SYSTEM IN 1790

Figure 2.2 shows that at this date urban settlement in the United States was essentially confined to the Atlantic slope from Maine to Georgia. The economic orientation of the larger cities was primarily commercial, and they functioned as centers of trade and finance for relatively small-sized agricultural hinterlands. They were, in fact, the mercantilistic outposts of England. As such, they were oriented seaward and could in fact be regarded as a peripheral part of the western European city system at this time (Lukermann, 1966).

The major centers were ports either on the Atlantic coast itself or on the navigable rivers, such as the Connecticut, Hudson, Delaware, and Savannah. Of the third or higher order centers, only Worcester, Mass., and Pittsburgh, Pa., were not on the Atlantic waterways. New York and Philadelphia were the largest cities with 33,181 and 28,522 inhabitants respectively. These, together with Boston, Baltimore, and Charleston, S.C., contained just over half of the nation's urbanized population. Although even at this time New York and Philadelphia had spawned a series of suburbs, the most prominent cluster of smaller urban centers based on agricultural trade and small-scale local industry was that dominated by Boston in eastern Massachusetts. The beginnings of a new urban pattern were emerging along the Hudson River to the north of New York. Albany and

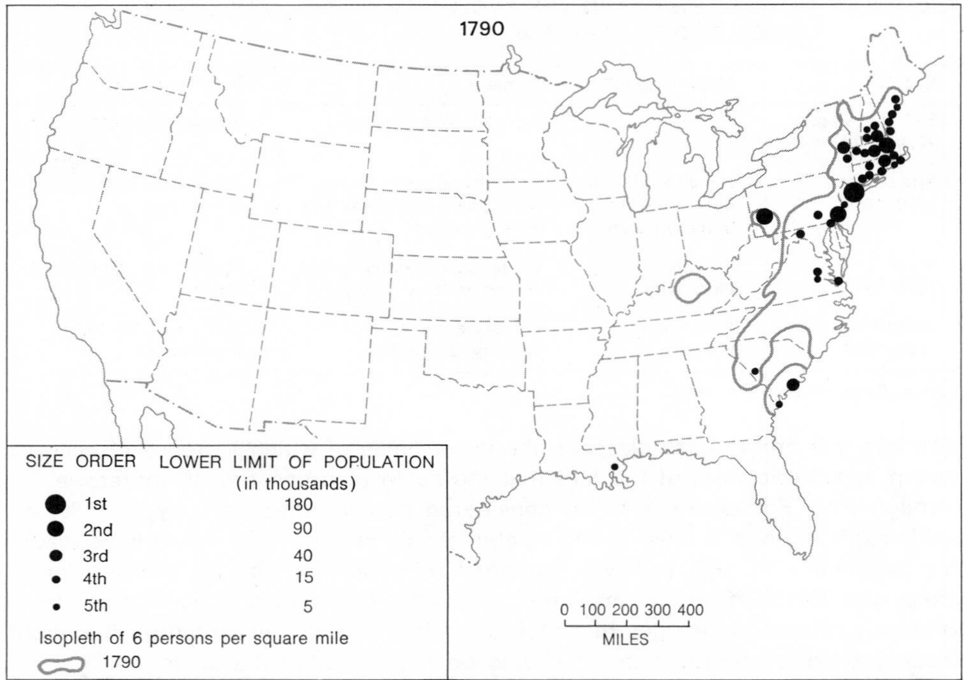

FIG. 2.2. DISTRIBUTION OF MAJOR TOWNS IN THE UNITED STATES, 1790. (*Source:* After Borchert, 1967, Fig. 6.)

Hudson were at this time the first of the transport cities that were to develop later in the Hudson-Mohawk corridor.

THE SAIL-WAGON EPOCH, 1790–1830

The first decades of the nineteenth century witnessed the beginnings of independent urban growth albeit at a modest scale. Towns, and particularly the higher order ones, were becoming the outlets for capital accumulated through commercial agriculture as well as the centers from which the development of the continental interior proceeded. Arable land was the resource that counted, and the infant regional economies were developing a certain archetype: "a good deepwater port was the nucleus of an agricultural hinterland well adapted to the production of a staple commodity in demand on the world market" (Berry and Horton, 1970, p. 22). Figure 2.3 shows that the urban centers that grew most rapidly were associated with the spread of nucleated-clustered agricultural regions westward into western New York State, the Great Valley (of Appalachia), the Bluegrass region, and the Nashville basin. Accompanying this expansion westward, there was a relative decline in growth at a number of small ports and agricultural service centers in eastern New York and New England.

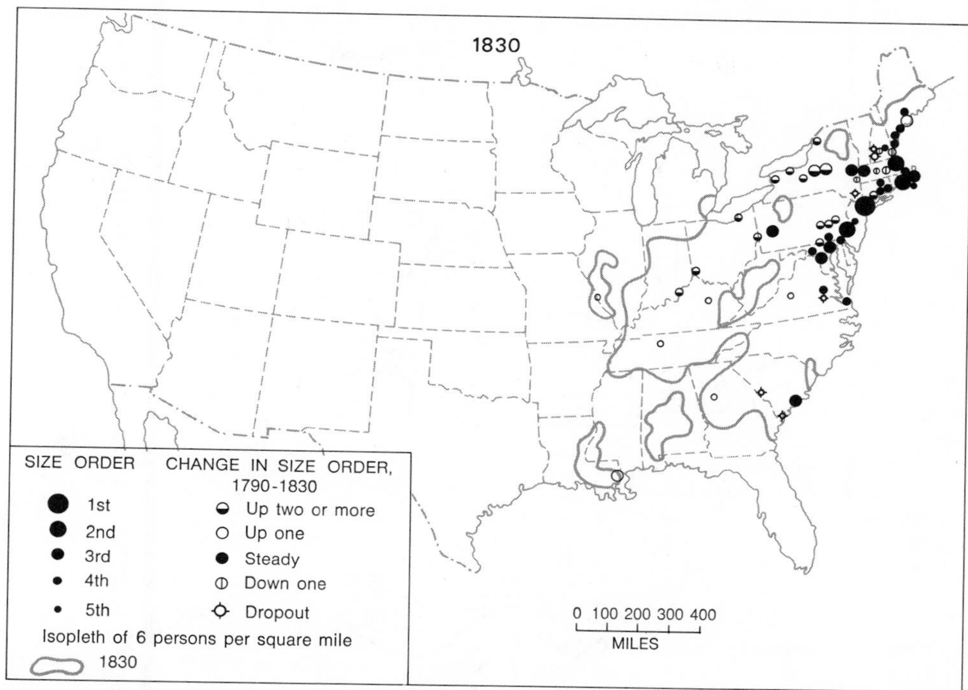

FIG. 2.3. DISTRIBUTION OF METROPOLITAN CITIES IN THE UNITED STATES, 1830. (*Source:* After Borchert, 1967, Fig. 7.)

Despite the spread and consolidation of the network of post roads and turnpikes within the settled area, distance overland was still an effective barrier to movement and especially for goods. Pittsburgh was, for example, still four days distant from New York City in 1830. (Fig. 2.4). Consequently water transportation was still the dominant means, and apart from the new cities in the Great Valley near the anthracite fields, the boom cities were closely tied to inland waterways. Pittsburgh, Cincinnati, and Louisville were developing as small regional centers on the Ohio River system, and St. Louis had emerged as a fourth-order place on the Mississippi. Largely because of the difficulties of overland transportation, the higher order cities on the Atlantic coast retained their dominant positions despite the setbacks of the War of 1812, which brought about the decline of many smaller east-coast ports. Table 2.4 indicates the changes that occurred during the epoch in the number of cities and their population size.

The canal boom The difficulties of inland transportation away from the navigable rivers at this time gave rise to considerable speculation on the construction of canals. These were thought to be the most effective solution to the problem of long distance movement of freight and passengers. As it turned out, however, they proved at best to be only a temporary and inadequate answer; and the boom

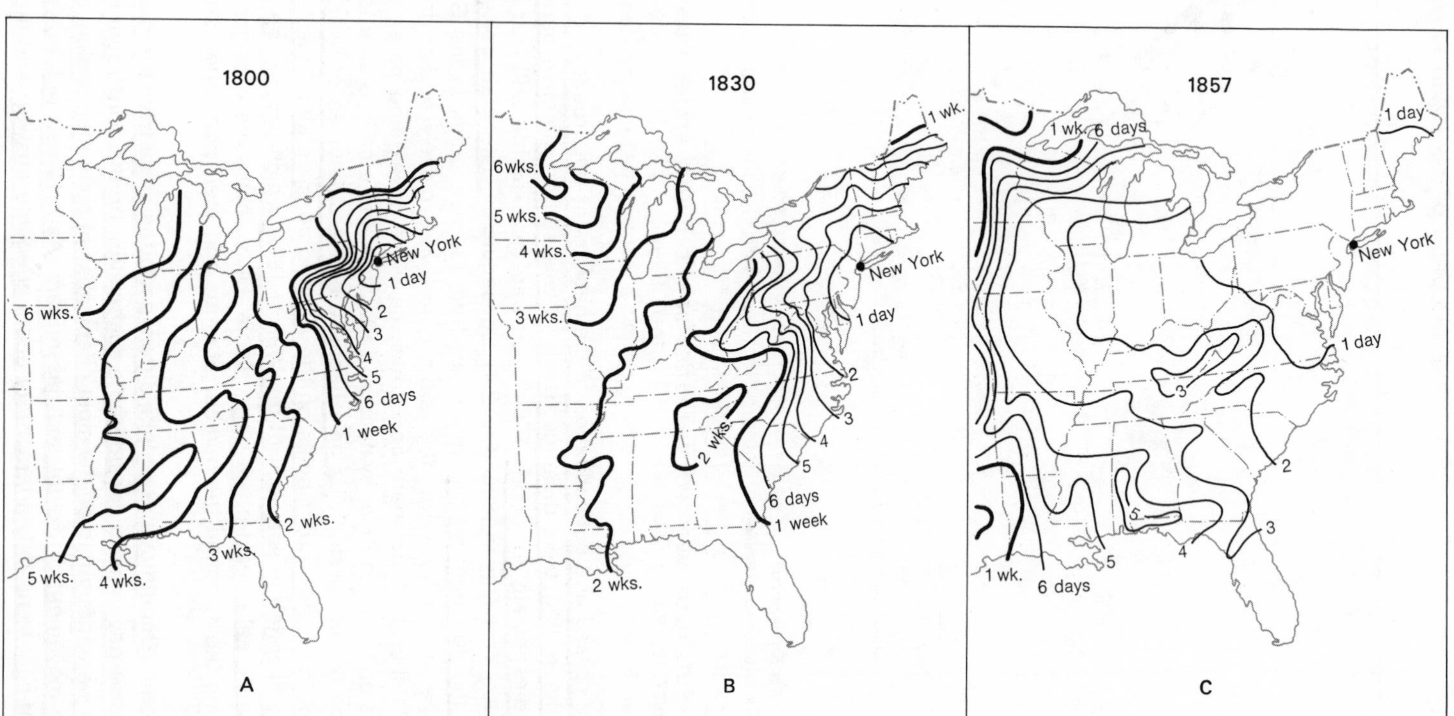

FIG. 2.4. TRAVEL TIMES OVERLAND IN THE EASTERN UNITED STATES AT SELECTED TIME PERIODS. (*Source:* Paullin, 1932, Plate 138A, B, and C).

TABLE 2.4. NUMBER OF CITIES AND TOTAL POPULATION BY SIZE ORDER, UNITED STATES, 1790–1960

Size Order	1790	1830	1870	1920	1960
			Number of Centers		
First	0	0	1	1	1
Second	3	3	6	4	6
Third	8	8	14	16	19
Fourth	20	29	33	51	70
Fifth	8	12	37	75	82
Total	39	52	91	147	178
			Total Population (thousands)		
First	–	–	2,171	8,490	14,760
Second	514	1,120	3,301	10,364	28,826
Third	499	784	3,627	13,918	26,493
Fourth	530	1,812	2,533	12,829	30,473
Fifth	95	300	1,826	6,972	12,647
"SMSA" total	1,638	4,016	13,458	52,573	113,199
U.S. total	3,929	12,866	39,818	105,711	179,323

Source: Borchert (1967), p. 315, Table 2.

in canal building was short lived. Nevertheless, between 1810 and the 1840s, canals spurred urban growth, particularly in New York, Pennsyvlania, and Ohio and to a lesser extent in New Jersey, Indiana, and Connecticut.

The Erie Canal was without doubt the most successful of all canals constructed during the period. Started in 1817, the 350-mile "big ditch" between Albany and Buffalo was opened in 1825 to create a through waterway between the Atlantic Ocean and the Great Lakes. Syracuse, Rochester, Utica, Rome, and other smaller settlements had their origin and periods of great growth following its opening. These towns became the collection and distribution centers for the newly expanding agricultural areas in western New York, and later most of them became commercial-industrial centers. While Buffalo, the western terminal of the canal, increased its population from 2,000 in 1820 to 8,600 in 1830, the canal traffic secured permanently for New York City the commercial leadership of the nation, enlarged her financial resources, and "helped make 'Wall Street' synonymous throughout the United States with monetary power" (Green, 1965, p. 64). The canal was also a prime factor in the city's population increase of 200,000 between 1820 and 1830.

THE AGE OF STEAM, 1830–1870

Although at the beginning of the Age of Steam, intensive agricultural settlement had pushed westward virtually as far as the Mississippi River, all of the larger urban centers except Pittsburgh were still to the east of the Appalachians or in western New York. Figure 2.5 shows that by the end of the period there had been extensive urban growth in the Midwest and that New York City had emerged as

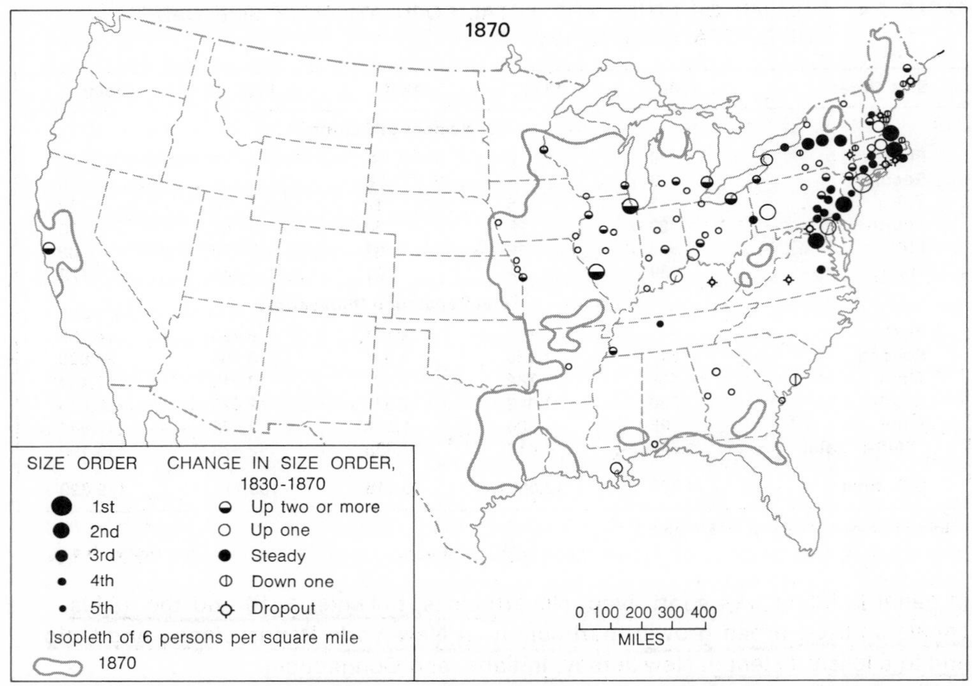

FIG. 2.5. DISTRIBUTION OF METROPOLITAN CITIES IN THE UNITED SATES, 1870. (*Source:* After Borchert, 1967, Fig. 8.)

the nation's only first-order center. By 1870 one-quarter of the country's population was urbanized (Table 2.1), and there had been a rapid growth in both number and population size of cities of all orders (Table 2.4).

This minor urban revolution could only have resulted from one thing: the development of an integrated inland transportation system, which permitted the commercial exploitation of the agricultural, mineral, fuel, and power resources of the newly settled territory. Hence the key to urban growth during this epoch was the development that occurred in transportation technology, based on the application of the steam engine to water and land transportation. This was the era of the steamboat and of the emergence of the railroad.

Although steamboats had been successfully used as early as 1810, it was not until they were constructed in Cincinnati after 1818 that they became the mainstay of river commerce. Even then, the hazardous navigation on the midcontinental rivers delayed their widespread adoption; and it was not until after 1830 that the real build-up of tonnage began on the Ohio-Mississippi-Missouri system and steamboats were widely used in Great Lakes commerce (Borchert, 1967, p. 303). The first decades of the epoch were the heyday of the river towns, particularly New Orleans, St. Louis, and Cincinnati, although all towns and cities located on navigable rivers and lakes benefited from the intensification of the port functions brought about by the steamboat. St. Louis doubled its trade with New Orleans, which even by 1835 had a larger volume of exports than New York City. By 1850 New Orleans had become the third largest city of the nation—a rank it was to lose shortly afterward as a result of the shifting alignment of trade and economic growth brought about by the railroad.

The waterways were not only the main inland transportation routes at this time, they were still the main source of power for the developing manufacturing industries of the period. Although the steam engine had also been applied to industry, its impact was localized owing to the difficulties of transporting coal over long distances. It is in this respect that the canals played an important role, for they enabled the transportation of bulky goods and materials at relatively low costs. But for towns located away from the canals and for the infant railroads, coal was an expensive commodity. Consequently waterpower sites continued to exert a strong influence on the location of small-scale manufacturing industries. Even as late as 1870, water wheels were still providing approximately half of the inanimate energy for manufacturing.

The impact of the railroads The coming of the railroads brought about drastic changes in the pattern of urban centers emerging by 1850. After this date, the railroads, which hitherto were largely concentrated in the eastern states, rapidly spread into the continental interior. In 1850 there were 9,000 miles of track; by 1860 this had grown to 31,000; and by 1870, to 53,000 miles; the continent had been spanned, and the basic framework of America's future railroad network had been established. Regional rail nets focused on the larger coastal and inland ports; smaller nets, often comprising only single lines, centered on the minor ports. In their initial period of extensive growth, the limitations of technology—the iron rails and light equipment—essentially made the railroads complementary to the waterways for long-haul traffic. Lines were built linking the ports with surrounding areas of agricultural, mineral, and timber resources.

As a result most of the boom cities of the epoch were great ports in the Midwest. The importance of places like St. Louis, Cincinnati, Detroit, and Cleveland was reinforced, while by 1860 Chicago had emerged as the nation's most important railroad center, the terminal of eleven trunk and twenty branch and feeder lines. In the older northeastern region, the railroads acted as a new stimulus to urban growth as the settled area of the interior, and hence its products, was brought closer to the east (Fig. 2.4). Boom cities appeared in the anthracite region of Pennsylvania, and Pittsburgh attained second-order rank for the first time, as the railroads and the continuing growth of small-scale manufacturing industry (increasingly based on steam power) brought about an accelerated demand for coal and iron. The "heartland" of North America was beginning to emerge. Outside this area there was relatively little growth of large cities. Fourth- and fifth-order cities had grown up along the Missouri River, while on the West Coast San Francisco had attained second-order status. In the South, New Orleans was still the only large city, and Charleston had experienced relative decline in population size (Fig. 2.5).

THE STEEL EPOCH, 1870–1920

First the steamboat and then the railroad set the nation on a course of industrialization, the main impact of which came with the appearance of abundant quantities of low-priced steel and a rapid development of manufacturing technology. The key to urban growth in the fifty-year period from 1870 to 1920 was the development in manufacturing and its ancillary activities. Initially based on the growth of the iron and steel industry, the development of manufacturing was stimulated by a series of further inventions, which passed into general use by the turn of the century. These included things such as the electric power station (1882) and the gasoline motor (1883). These new inventions ushered in a new era—the neotechnic era—in the growth of cities.

At the same time, significant changes occurred in the organization of industrial and commercial enterprises with the formation after 1870 of limited liability joint stock companies. Backed mainly by the large financial houses, these new companies permitted the development of market-oriented manufacturing industry on a scale never before experienced.

Urban growth based on manufacturing was impossible without good transportation systems—in which the main components during this epoch were the railroad. These continued to push westward opening up new territory for settlement, while the network filled out in the eastern part of the nation. By 1910 there were some 240,000 miles of track in operation. The growing importance of the railroad for the movement of materials, products, and people was associated with the introduction of steel rails, which replaced iron on both the new and existing lines. Steel also made possible the construction of larger locomotives and heavier equipment, which in turn meant longer and cheaper hauls of raw materials, and particularly coal. Thus the average freight charge per ton-mile was reduced from 3.31 cents in 1865 to 0.70 cents in 1892; and the average length of haul increased from 110 miles per ton in 1822 to 250 miles per ton in 1910 (Pred, 1965, p. 174). Rail gauges were standardized (there had been eleven different gauges on the northern systems in 1860), and the introduction of refrigerated boxcars ushered in a new era of specialized agriculture (Borchert, 1967, p. 304).

Changes in the pattern of cities during the steel epoch are shown in Figure 2.6. The expansion of the railroads westward brought about the second major spatial jump in the history of settlement. New cities grew up along the West Coast. By 1920 Seattle, Portland, and Los Angeles had emerged as sizable urban concentrations, while San Francisco maintained second-order status. In the Central Valley of California, the growth of specialized agriculture had resulted in the emergence of a number of fifth-order processing and service cities. Inland, numerous small urban centers had grown up in association with the railroad, but only Salt Lake City and Denver had grown to metropolitan status by the end of the epoch.

The opening up and commercialization of the agricultural resources of the Texas and Oklahoma prairies was associated with the growth of large cities in

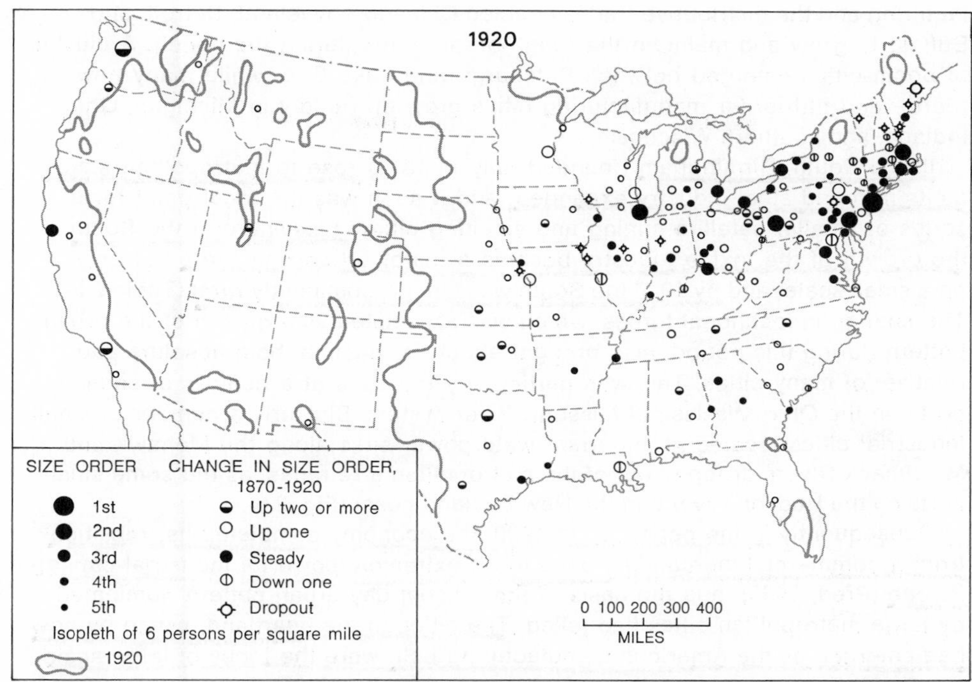

FIG. 2.6. DISTRIBUTION OF METROPOLITAN CITIES IN THE UNITED STATES, 1920. (*Source:* After Borchert, 1967, Fig. 9.)

these regions. Similarly new cities grew up in conjunction with the exploitation of newly accessible and usable mineral resources, such as Butte copper, the Lake Superior iron ores, and the lead and zinc deposits of northeastern Missouri. Also in this period a new major feature in the settlement pattern appeared. As agriculture boomed, service centers and agriculturally oriented manufacturing followed; and the hierarchy of smaller-sized central places emerged to become a distinctive feature in the urban pattern throughout the nation, especially in the Midwestern states (see Chapter 7).

Spectacular as the expansion of settlement and the growth of cities in the new territories of the West was, the most significant changes in the urban pattern occurred in the older settled areas of the East, particularly in the heartland. Here the close juxtaposition of coal, iron ore, and growing urban and rural markets provided the impetus for the large-scale growth of manufacturing cities. Clusters of boom cities appeared in conjunction with the exploitation of high-grade bituminous coal deposits, which accompanied the growth of the iron and steel industry. These were particularly prominent on the coal fields of western Pennsylvania and to a lesser extent on the bituminous coal fields of West Virginia and eastern Kentucky (Fig. 2.6).

Outside the coal field areas of the northern states, the expansion of manufacturing and the distributive trades enabled Chicago, Cleveland, Detroit, and Buffalo to grow and maintain their high-order status during the epoch. A cluster of boom cities emerged between Pittsburgh and Lake Erie, while many new fourth- and fifth-order manufacturing cities grew up rapidly in Michigan, Ohio, Indiana, and southern Wisconsin.

In the South, Birmingham (founded only in 1871) rose to metropolitan status as its iron and steel industry expanded; and it soon was the focal point for a series of smaller satellite mining and smelting cities. Elsewhere in the South, the growth of the textile industry became a major urbanizing force but only on a small scale; and by 1920 the South was still predominantly rural (Table 2.2). The change in locational forces, which was associated with growth of the urban pattern during this period, also brought about the decline, both absolute and relative, of many cities. This was particularly the case at a number of smaller ports on the Ohio-Mississippi-Missouri River system. Similarly a number of small industrial cities located at important waterpower sites along the Mohawk and Merrimack Rivers dropped out of the metropolitan size ranks, as did some small ports on the Hudson River and the New England coast (Fig. 2.6).

Subsequently in the period up to 1920, the economy completed its transition from a commercial-mercantilist base to an extremely powerful industrial-capitalist one (Pred, 1965); and the basis of the present-day urban pattern dominated by large metropolitan cities had jelled. The cities of the heartland, which by now had emerged as the American manufacturing belt, were the focus of large-scale manufacturing and processing industries serving the national market. Outside the heartland, regional economies had developed centered on major regional cities based on specialization in the production of "resource and intermediate outputs for which the heartland reaches out to satisfy (the needs) of its great manufacturing plants" (Perloff and Wingo, 1961, p. 211). As shown in Table 2.4, the five largest cities increased their share of the national population faster than in any other period. Similar rapid increases occurred in the population size of third-order cities although their number remained much as before, while the total number of fourth- and fifth-order cities registered their greatest growth in the epoch.

THE AUTOMOBILE ERA, 1920–1960

The new technology, which came into general use at the turn of the century, created a different type of industry: "Instead of heavy crude products, light and increasingly complex ones; instead of coal, electricity; instead of the universal railway, increasing dependence on the motor vehicle; instead of concentration in congested centers, freedom of location through improved communications" (Hall, 1966, p. 24). Industry, it could now be argued, was free to locate almost anywhere; the logical pattern of neotechnic urban development was almost complete deconcentration. Instead of this, however, economic activity and people continued to concentrate in metropolitan cities, and especially in the larger ones. This process of concentration has continued at an accelerating pace since World War II. The latest phase in the evolution of the urban pattern has been characterized not so much by the development of new cities as by the continued growth of already existing ones into large metropolitan agglomerations.

Figure 2.7 shows the changes that occurred in the urban pattern during this period. Some mining centers declined, as did certain of the coal and railroad cities in the Appalachians and across the Midwest. New or higher-order cities appeared in the oil-field areas from central Kansas to western Texas and the Gulf Coast; and there was a notable concentration of growth in southern Michigan, particularly at Detroit. The influence of amenities on the location of industry and people was reflected in the growth of new metropolitan centers in Florida, the Southwest desert, and in Southern California; while all the cities on the West Coast except Seattle moved up one or two ranks in size order. From 1920 to 1960, there was a net migration from other parts of the country of 11.4 million people to California, Arizona, and Florida.

Thus the influence of amenities and particularly of the automobile have been the major factors affecting recent urban growth. The significant effect of the automobile was that it enabled the decentralization of people and functions out of the increasingly congested central cities into the surrounding suburbs (see Chapter 8). In the decade from 1950 to 1960, for example, the population of the central cities of the 212 areas designated by the Bureau of the Census as Standard Metropolitan Statistical Areas (SMSA's see Appendix A) increased by

FIG. 2.7. DISTRIBUTION OF METROPOLITAN CITIES IN THE UNITED STATES, 1960. (*Source:* After Borchert, 1967, Fig. 10.)

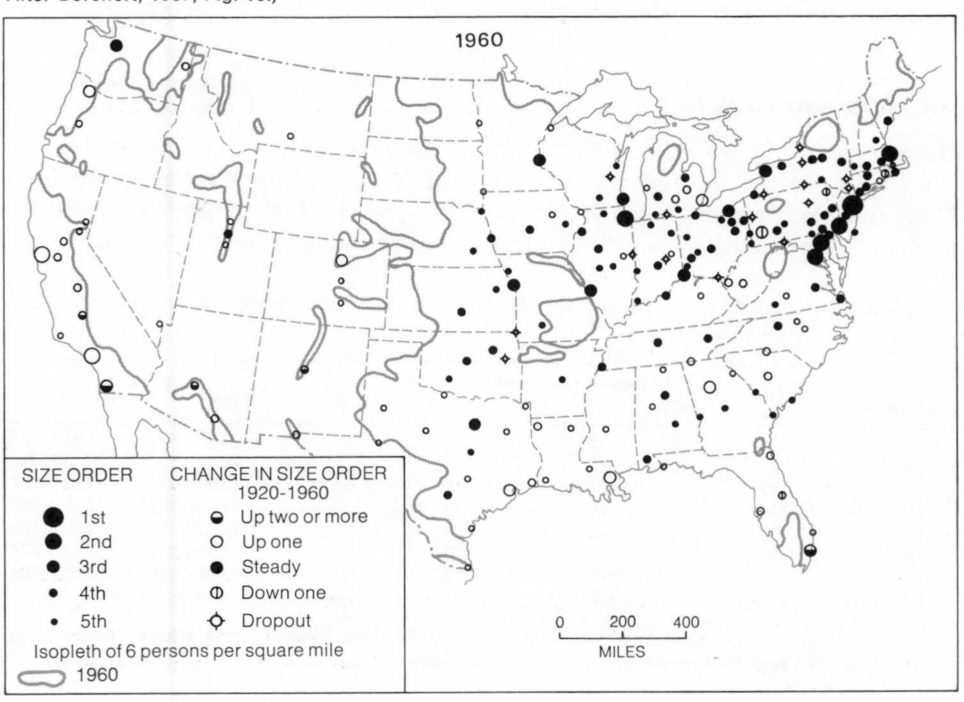

only 10.7 percent compared with an increase of 48.6 percent in their outlying, suburban parts. This suburbanization of the urban population is also reflected in the data presented in Table 2.5. Since 1940 the population of the 212 SMSA's has increased by 55 percent. Moreover, there is a direct relationship between size of metropolitan area and rate of population growth. Thus in the period from 1940 to 1960 those metropolitan areas with 3 million or more inhabitants experienced a 92.8 percent increase in population size. Conversely, there has been an absolute decline in both the numbers of, and growth in, the SMSA's with less than 100,000 inhabitants.

With 63 percent of the total population living in the 212 SMSA's in 1960, the United States had become completely metropolitanized. If people were not actually living within the limits of these areas, modern communications have resulted in their being within their spheres of influence; and the traditional distinction between rural and urban has become meaningless for most purposes. It has moreover become apparent that these metropolitan areas are beginning to grow together to form even larger, more complex super-metropolitan regions. Thus, today, the entire eastern seaboard from Boston to Washington is virtually continuously urbanized—a sprawling 600-mile long super-metropolitan region, which Gottmann (1961) termed "megalopolis." A less spectacular but equally significant coalescence of metropolitan centers to form super-metropolitan regions is also occurring between Pittsburgh and Cleveland, between Chicago and Detroit, along the east coast of Florida, and in the Far West between Los Angeles and San Diego. And as metropolitan growth and sprawl continues, so the problems of living in them become increasingly more complex.

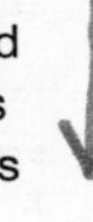

LOCATION AND GROWTH

Our survey of the growth and spread of the larger cities in the United States since the eighteenth century raises many questions for geographical analysis. Three questions are particularly important. First, why did cities grow up where they did? Second, how and why did many cities increase in population size

TABLE 2.5. POPULATION CHANGE IN STANDARD METROPOLITAN STATISTICAL AREAS, 1940–1960

	Number of Areas				Population		
SMSA size[a]	**1970**	**1960**	**1950**	**1940**	**1970**	**1960**	**1950**
3,000,000 or more		5	5	3		31,763,499	25,788,967
1,000,000–3,000,000		19	10	9		29,818,571	16,627,603
500,000–1,000,000		29	21	16		19,214,817	14,439,987
250,000– 500,000		48	44	36		15,829,067	15,209,376
100,000– 250,000		89	89	76		14,497,817	14,045,736
under 100,000		22	43	72		1,761,407	3,205,234
Total		212	212	212		112,885,178	89,316,903

[a] Data relate to areas as defined for 1960.
Source: U.S. Bureau of the Census. *U.S. Census of Population, 1960. Number of Inhabitants, United States Summary.* Table 31. (U.S. Government Printing Office, Washington, D.C., 1961.)

relatively quickly, particularly during the period of rapid industrialization? Third, why were some cities able to grow at a faster rate than, and at the expense of, other cities?

THE LOCATION OF CITIES

In discussing the location of cities, geographers have traditionally differentiated between the *site* and the *situation.* Dickinson (1948, p. 223) sums up the difference as follows: The *site* is "the precise features of the terrain on which the settlement began and over which it has spread," whereas the *situation* "is usually taken to mean the physical conditions (as for the site) over a much wider area around the settlement. But of equal importance are the human characteristics of the surrounding country, since these affect the character and fortunes of the urban settlement." Although valid, this distinction is not quite as rigid as Dickinson and others have suggested, and in practice it is often difficult to separate discussion of the one from the other.

The built-up areas of today's cities usually bear very little relationship to their original sites, which were for the most part selected without any idea of, or consideration for, the scale of urban growth that was often to take place at them. Site selection was often strongly influenced by factors in the physical environment. Things such as the need for shelter and good supply of drinking water, freedom from floods, and perhaps good defensive positions were prime considerations. Often great care was taken in the selection of the initial sites for settlement. This was the case, for example, in the founding of Charleston and Philadelphia, and later in the location of Washington, D.C. More often, however, settlements grew up at particular locations more by chance than anything else, and their subsequent growth had very little to do with their initial site or situation.

Madison, the state capital of Wisconsin, is a good case in point. At first sight the location of this city seems a good example of the role of physical factors; however, the history of the choice of site reveals that the human rather than the physical factor was the most important. For,

	Percentage Change			
1940	**1940–50**	**1950–60**	**1960–70**	**1940–60**
16,476,197	56.5	23.2		92.8
16,210,026	2.6	79.3		84.0
11,056,897	30.6	33.1		73.8
12,007,871	26.7	4.1		31.8
12,077,950	16.3	3.2		20.0
5,005,527	–35.9	–45.0		–64.8
72,834,468	22.6	26.4		55.0

In 1836 the Wisconsin Territorial Legislature was obliged to choose a site for a permanent capital. A total of sixteen localities were considered, all of them owned by speculators, who energetically advanced the claims of their own land. The decision to locate the capital on its present site was taken by 15 votes to 11, and this decision owed more to intrigue than to any careful assessment of site and situation (Johnson, 1967, p. 80).

Although the sites of initial settlements were significant, their situation was usually the more important locational consideration since this had a more direct bearing on the functions they performed and on their subsequent growth. Physical factors were also important in the situational context, particularly as these related to movement. Thus we have seen from the discussion of the spread of cities that many of today's urban giants originated as small settlements on navigable rivers, on good harbors, or at the entrance to passes through difficult terrain. Junction points in the transportation networks of the time were especially important, and locations were frequently selected at river confluences, bridging points, and crossroads. Particularly important were the junctions where different types of transportation came together—the so-called "break of bulk" points at which goods and materials had to be transferred, commonly after processing, from one means of transportation to another. It is not difficult to appreciate how the initial site and situation could affect subsequent development of city function, particularly of these transport-oriented cities.

As technology advanced, so new locational forces became important; and location became more directly related from the start with the functions settlements were to perform. Thus with the early growth of manufacturing, new settlements grew up at waterpower sites. The planned mill towns of the Boston Associates in the 1840s at Lowell, Lawrence, Chicopee, and Holyoke in Massachusetts, and at Manchester and Nashua in New Hampshire are good examples. Later with the spread of the railroads, junctions of different lines became important growth points. In the West the operating needs of the railroads themselves dictated the locations where many new settlements grew up as watering stops or in conjunction with car and locomotive repair shops. As coal became increasingly important, new mining settlements grew up on the coal fields; and older settlements assumed new significance. Similarly settlements were founded in conjunction with the opening up of new mineral ore deposits. Most recently, in the age of leisure, a different natural resource—climate—has influenced location and subsequent development of settlements to result, for example, in the growth of resort cities in Florida and the "retirement cities" in Arizona and California.

A MODEL OF CITY GROWTH

As a general rule the basis for cities is economic, and their population size is largely a reflection of the functions they perform. To answer the question of how cities increase in population size, often in relatively short time periods, we must consider the way in which growth in function brings about a corresponding increase in population. The processes involved are quite complex and vary in their detail at different time periods. Regardless of time and the type of functions involved, one of the important factors in the growth process is what Myrdal (1957) called the "principle of circular and cumulative causation." As it applies to urban growth, this simply states that a given change in functional structure brings about supporting, rather than contradictory, changes. As a result growth is cumulative and often gathers speed at an accelerating rate; in short, growth breeds growth.

Of the many different kinds of functions that may bring about increases in the population size of cities, the most important is the growth of manufacturing and industry. As we have seen, most of today's large metropolitan areas owe their present status to the early development of industry there, particularly during the period of rapid industrialization (1870–1920) when the basic features of the urban system were established. Consequently growth in association with industrialization is particularly important. Under these conditions, Pred (1965) has used the idea of "growth breeding growth" to explain increases in city size in the following way. First imagine an isolated city, whose economy is based on commerce and trade, which imports goods not locally produced from other places. Then imagine that a new large-scale factory is constructed in the city. Sooner or later this event evokes two simultaneous, circular chains of reaction as outlined in Figure 2.8.

The first of these reactions is based on what is called the "multiplier effect," which is discussed in more detail in Chapter 5. Simply put, this works in the following way. The new factory and the increased purchasing power of its work-

FIG. 2.8. THE CIRCULAR AND CUMULATIVE PROCESS OF INDUSTRIALIZATION AND CITY-SIZE GROWTH. (*Source:* After Pred, 1965, Fig. 1.)

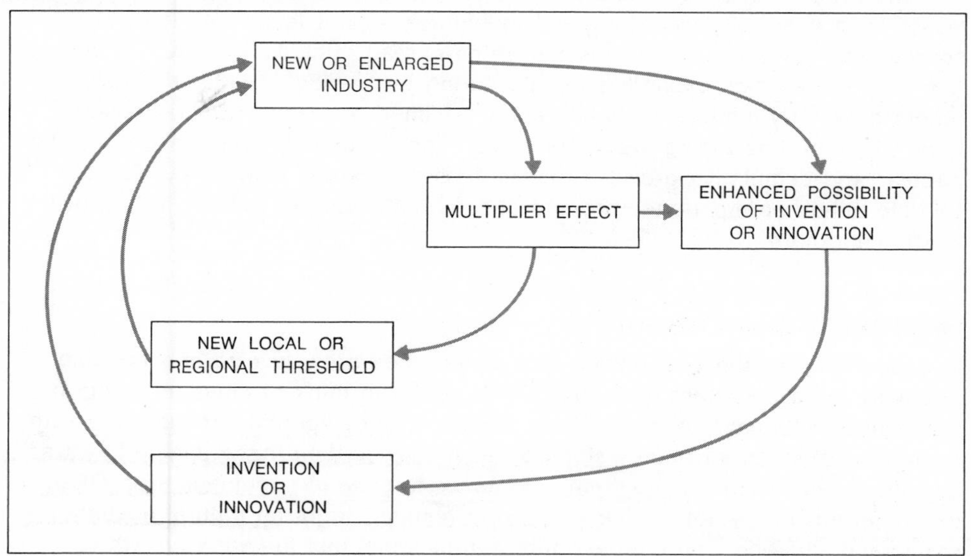

ers create new local demands. This results in the development of a host of new business, service, trade, construction, transportation, professional, and other white-collar jobs. The net result is that the population size of the city increases, which in turn means that the city becomes large enough to support a more specialized manufacturing activity—it attains one or more new local or regional thresholds. These new thresholds will support new manufacturing functions, as well as making possible the enlargement of the existing ones. Once these new factories are constructed, a second round of growth is started and eventually still higher local and regional thresholds are achieved. And so the process continues in a circular and cumulative manner until it is stopped or impeded.

The second reaction, which occurs simultaneously, tends to reinforce the first. It is based on the increased amount of interpersonal interaction derived from the expanding city population. This "enhances the possibilities of technological improvements and inventions, enlarges the likelihood of the adoption of more efficient managerial and financial institutions, increases the speed with which locally originating ideas are disseminated, and eases the diffusion of skills and knowledge brought in by migrants from other areas" (Pred, 1965, p. 166). Once these new inventions or innovations are adopted, new or enlarged industry results, which brings about further population growth and so the process continues in a circular and cumulative fashion until it is diverted or hindered. It is through the multiplier effect implicit in these two reactions that growth in the population sizes of cities is brought about. Although the model is based specifically on the expansion of manufacturing activity and is consequently most applicable in the context of industrialization, the general features of the model offer a plausible basis for understanding urban growth under other conditions (see Chapter 5).

If the process of circular and cumulative growth of cities functioned flawlessly, then every city would expand indefinitely—or at least until natural resources ran out. From our discussion of the spread of cities we noted, however, that only some cities expanded rapidly during the period of industrialization; others grew only moderately, while many declined or stagnated. Quite clearly, then, within an interacting system of cities in an expanding spatial economy, the circular and cumulative growth process does not persist indefinitely. Factors operate to halt or impede the process at some cities and to prevent it from ever starting at others.

DIFFERENTIAL URBAN GROWTH

In accounting for the observation that some cities grow in size and become relatively more important than others, it is useful to think of cities as being in competition with each other to attract functions. In competition, those cities with some kind of initial advantage stand a better chance than those unable to attract specific types of activities to them, and hence to grow in population size. Often the initial advantage for settlement growth resulted from the natural advantages of site and situation. There is no doubt, for example, that the early growth of

New York was aided by the fact that it had good access to the interior via the Hudson-Mohawk corridor, and hence it was able to build up an important import and export trade with the expanding settlements to the west. Conversely other cities on the East Coast, such as Boston and Philadelphia, found it much more difficult to exploit the interior because of physical barriers; and they consequently suffered in the competition for trade and in the accompanying growth of ancillary activities.

Yet despite their initial disadvantages, these cities have emerged as major metropolitan areas. The differential growth of cities therefore cannot be explained solely on the basis of the physical aspects of location. Local enterprise is often a more significant factor bringing about growth. This is well illustrated by events at Baltimore. In 1827 bankers in the city concluded that a railroad over the mountains and into the Ohio valley would be the best means of capturing a share of the western trade that the Erie Canal was diverting in increasing amounts to New York. Within five months a group of local businessmen had prepared a plan, obtained a company charter, raised $3.5 million of capital, and engaged a competent engineer to start construction of the Baltimore and Ohio Railroad. Before this enterprise was five years old, freight was rolling into Baltimore in a volume that gave her undisputed commercial control of most of Maryland; and by 1850 when the iron tracks reached the Ohio valley, the Chesapeake Bay port had attained a position as an outlet for western produce that only New York and New Orleans could challenge (Green, 1965, p. 66).

Regardless of whether initial advantage stemmed from location or from local enterprise, one thing is clear: initial advantage and differential city growth are very closely related to changes in accessibility. In turn, this is brought about by changes in the transportation system. Thus we have noted that, in the period from 1790 to 1860, accessibility to hinterlands was related to navigable waterways; and it was at favorable locations along these that large cities emerged. The coming of the railroads drastically altered the pattern of accessibility to result in the decline of those river towns that did not receive a railroad connection and to change the locational advantages of those that did. A similar, but perhaps less profound, effect on locational advantage has been associated more recently with the automobile and even the airplane (see Goodwin, 1965).

The impact of the railroad was widespread. Figure 2.9 shows the effect the coming of the railroad had on the growth of small service settlements in southwestern Iowa. In 1868, on the eve of the opening of the railroad through the area, a rudimentary pattern of small hamlets had developed (Fig. 2.9A). These were located in association with the distribution of woodlands, which had influenced the settlement pattern of the pioneer farmers. Figure 2.9B shows the pattern eleven years later. The railroad stations became the locations with initial advantage for further growth. Places in the vicinity of stations were abandoned as business moved into the station towns. Size differences emerged among these as some successfully captured small processing activities to tie in with their collection and distribution functions. Others were designated county seats, which gave them initial advantage for further growth. However, despite the

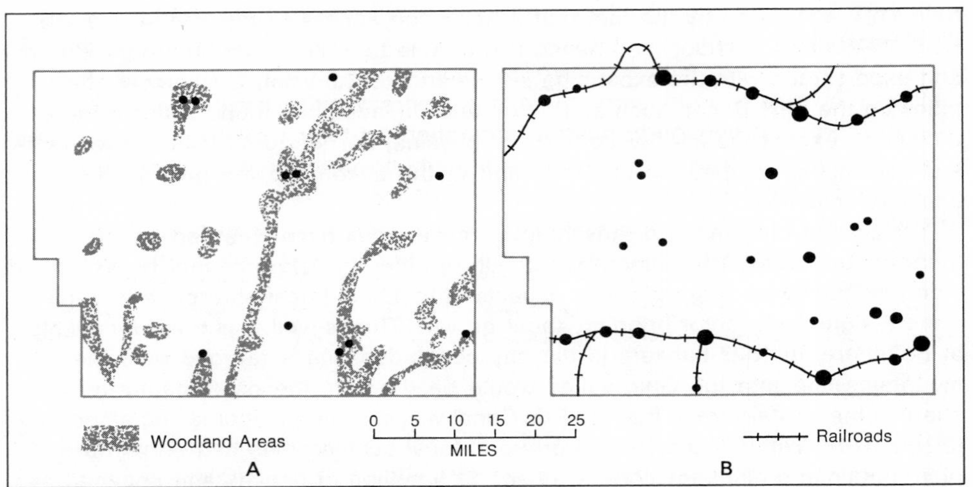

FIG. 2.9. THE DISTRIBUTION OF SERVICE CENTERS IN SOUTHWESTERN IOWA IN 1868 (A) AND IN 1879 AFTER THE COMING OF THE RAILROAD (B). (*Source:* Berry, 1967A, Figs. 1.3 and 1.4.)

changes in accessibility brought by the railroads, none of these rural service centers ever developed into very large cities.

As suggested by the model, large-scale urban growth was dependent essentially on the growth of manufacturing; and it is in connection with the location of this activity that the railroads had their most pronounced impact, resulting in the more rapid growth of some cities at the expense of others. The railroads, by lowering delivery prices of finished goods, enabled industries to increase the size of their markets and to obtain raw materials from greater distances. In turn large-scale production became more feasible and tended to favor the agglomeration at, and growth of, the already efficiently producing centers where small-scale industry may have originally grown up simply by chance. As a result, the lucky cities gained in population as the circular-cumulative process of growth got under way, while growth at the inefficient and nonproducing centers was impeded or delayed until a later time.

The railroads were not the only factor bringing about initial advantages for population growth. Often a change in the production process or a local invention had the same effect. Commonly changes in accessibility and in production occurred together at some cities, which subsequently very quickly generated their own conditions for growth. Similarly other factors such as availability of capital or local entrepreneurial initiative had the effect of creating initial advantages for growth, resulting in differential expansion of some cities at the expense of others.

The changes in initial advantage associated with the coming of the railroads have been stressed because, as we have seen, it was in the period 1870 to 1920 that the basic features of the present-day pattern of cities was established.

Since then, differential urban growth has largely resulted from changes in the national pattern of employment. Berry and Horton (1970) suggest that the most recent differences in relative growth of cities can be attributed to two principal causes. The first is an industry mix effect, whereby cities grow most rapidly that are fortunate enough to have a large share of their workers in the nation's rapid-growth industries. The second is a competitive shift effect, whereby the rapid-growth industries grow most rapidly in cities located in areas having the resources they need. It is the latter effect that underlies the rapid growth of cities in Florida, Arizona, Texas, California, besides Denver, Las Vegas, and Reno in recent decades.

RANK SIZE

An interesting feature of the population-size distribution of cities is shown in Figure 2.10. On the graph, the 212 SMSA's are plotted by their 1960 population size on the Y-axis, and in descending order by their rank in population on the X-axis. When both axes on the graph are scaled in logarithms as they are in Figure 2.10, the result is a smooth progression approximating a straight line.

This intriguing empirical regularity, which is typical of the city-size distribution in many countries (Berry, 1961), is known as the *rank-size rule*. This states that if all cities are ranked in descending order of population size, the population of

FIG. 2.10. THE RANK-SIZE RELATIONSHIP FOR THE 212 SMSA'S IN THE UNITED STATES, 1960.

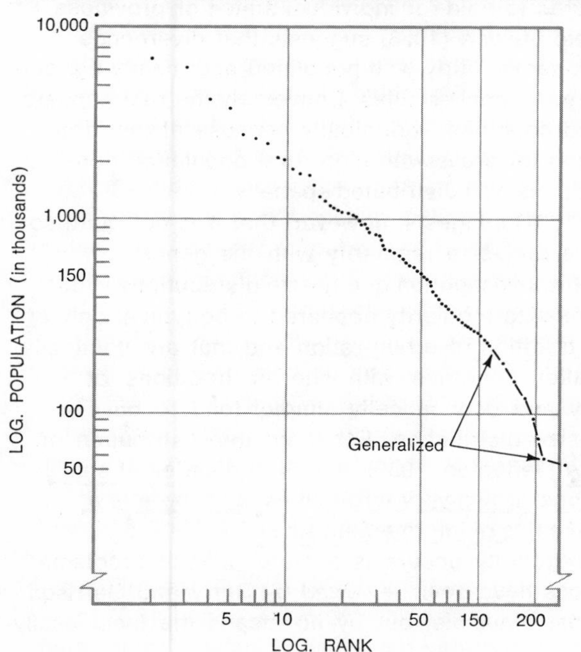

the rth ranking city will be $1/r^{th}$ the size of the largest city. Zipf (1949) stated this mathematically as follows:

$$r \times P_r{}^q = K$$

where r is the rank of a particular city (on the basis of its population size); P_r is the population size of that city; and q and K are constants. When q has a value of 1.0, the value of K is equal to the population size of the largest city (P_1) in the system, and the formula can be restated simply as:

$$r \times P_r = P_1$$

Thus in 1960 the largest SMSA's (P_1) was New York, which had a population of 10,694,633. According to the rank-size rule, the fifth largest SMSA (P_5) should have a population of 2,138,927. In 1960, Detroit was the fifth ranking S.M.S.A., and its actual population was 3,762,360. The difference between the actual and expected population size results from the fact that the value of q in the formula (the slope of the line in Figure 2.10) does not equal 1.0. Thus although the rank-size distribution of cities may accord to a straight line for many countries, and sometimes for even smaller areas, there is normally some variation from the rigid relationship postulated by the rank-size rule.

The deviation of actual from expected rank-size city distributions has prompted a number of researchers to investigate the conditions under which the rank-size rule holds good. Zipf (1949) suggests that the regularity is only characteristic of complete regions; that is, areas that are self-contained and not part of a larger region. Thus it could not be expected to hold for individual states or provinces, but it might for the entire countries. Stewart (1958) suggests that divergence from the rule is greater for homogeneous, fairly well populated and mainly agricultural countries in which there are many smaller cities. Conversely the rule appears to hold fairly well for industrialized countries—principally because of the large size of some industrial centers—and for areas with high rural population densities, and for areas where population is well distributed spatially.

A more recent study by Berry (1961) suggests, however, that it is not quite so easy to relate the occurrence of a rank-size regularity with the general characteristics of a country. From his investigation of city-size distributions in 38 countries, Berry noted that the rank-size regularity appeared to be typical only of larger countries that have a long tradition of urbanization and that are politically and economically complex. Smaller countries with shorter traditions of urbanization, which are politically and economically simple, tend to have a completely different form of city-size distribution. For them the distribution of cities by population size is *primate* (Jefferson, 1939), that is, the series of small towns and cities is dominated by one or two very large cities, and there is a notable deficiency in the number of cities of intermediate sizes.

Explaining why the rank-size regularity occurs is a more difficult problem. Some of the alternative explanations have been reviewed by Berry and Garrison (1958D) and among these the most plausible, but by no means the most easily grasped, is that offered by Simon (1955). Noticing that rank-size distribution approximates many probability distributions, among them the Yule and Pareto, Simon argues that the linear regularity of city sizes is generated by a stochastic process. In this, many forces affect the size of cities, often in a random fashion within the context of growth proportionate to size of city.

Implicit in this explanation is often the notion that cities are integrated through linkages and interchanges between them into a system, the "steady state" of which is the log-linear rank-size regularity noted in Figure 2.10. The plausibility of this explanation is further enhanced by the stability of the rank-size relationship through time. Thus for the United States, Figure 2.11 shows that the general growth of cities since 1790 has not occurred independently of the total population system of which they are a part. Consequently the distribution of the city sizes at each census period has generally approximated the linear form of the rank-

FIG. 2.11. CHANGES IN THE RANK-SIZE REGULARITY IN THE UNITED STATES, 1790–1950. (*Source:* After Madden, 1956B, Fig. 1.)

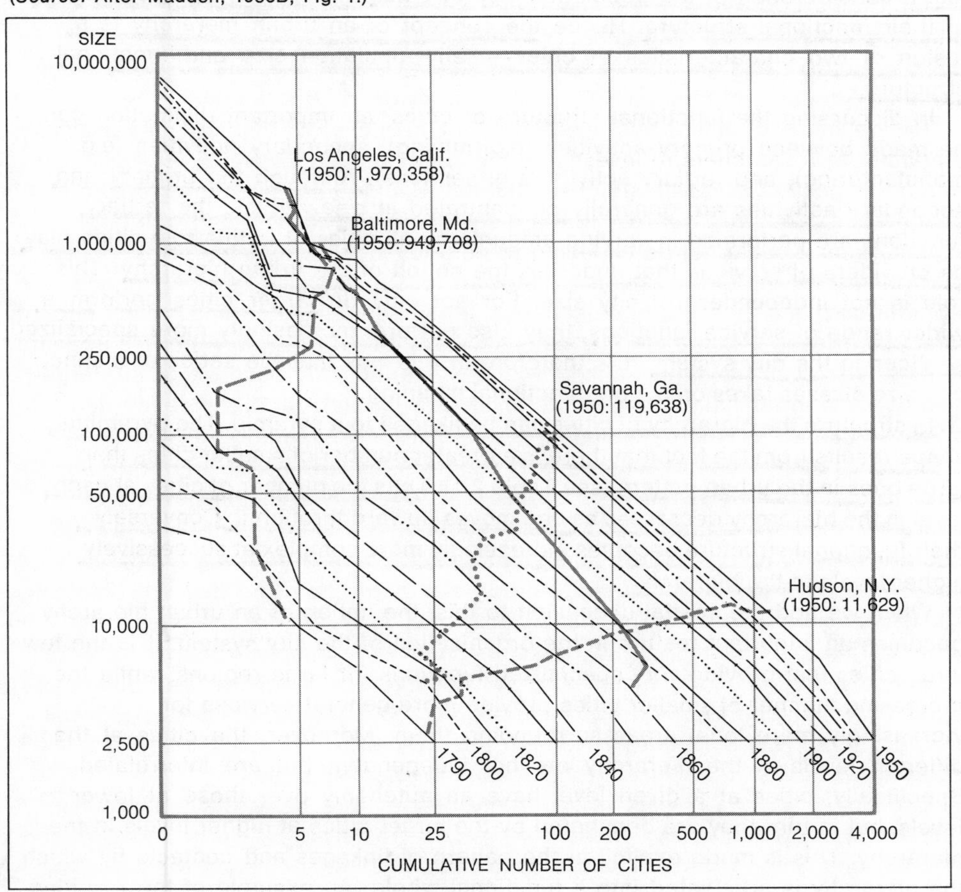

size distribution. However, as indicated for Los Angeles, Baltimore, Savannah, Ga., and Hudson, N.Y., within the fairly stable overall distribution of cities there is often marked divergence in the growth rates of individual places. This is expected because of the factors operating to bring about the differential growth of cities in time.

THE URBAN HIERARCHY

Although the rank-size regularity correctly indicates a continuous distribution of cities on the basis of their population size, for many aspects of urban analysis it is more useful to consider them to be arranged in a series of distinct size classes. Thus instead of a smooth progression from small to large, the hierarchical concept postulates a "stair-like" distribution of cities on the basis of their population size. But the notion of an urban hierarchy involves more than just a consideration of the population size of cities. It explicitly involves aspects of their functional structure. Hence the concept of an urban hierarchy is a fusion of two characteristics of cities—their population size and functional structure.

In discussing the functional structure of cities, an important distinction can be made between primary activities (e.g. mining), secondary activities (e.g. manufacturing), and tertiary activity (e.g. services). Although the primary and secondary activities are generally concentrated in a few cities, the tertiary functions are performed in varying amounts by all cities. It is this role cities play as providers of services that underlies the notion of the urban hierarchy. This role is not independent of city size. For not only do larger cities perform a wider range of service functions, they also perform increasingly more specialized services in the city system. It is therefore in this way that the series of distinct city-size classes takes on a more functional meaning.

In structure the hierarchy of cities can be likened to a pyramid. The pyramidal shape results from the fact that there is a greater number of smaller cities than large ones in the urban pattern (see Table 2.1). Thus the number of cities at each level in the hierarchy decreases as one moves upward through it. Conversely their functional structure becomes increasingly more complex at successively higher levels in the hierarchy.

When we add the spatial dimension to this, the notion of an urban hierarchy becomes an important feature in the organization of the city system. It is the few large cities that provide very specialized functions for large regions, while the increasing number of smaller cities provide more general services for increasingly more local areas surrounding them. Moreover, the cities at the different levels in the hierarchy are not independent but are interrelated. Specifically, cities at a given level have an autonomy over those at lower levels, but in turn they are dominated by the larger cities at higher levels in the hierarchy. This is made explicit in the pattern of linkages and contacts by which the hierarchy is articulated into a functional whole. An example of the resulting

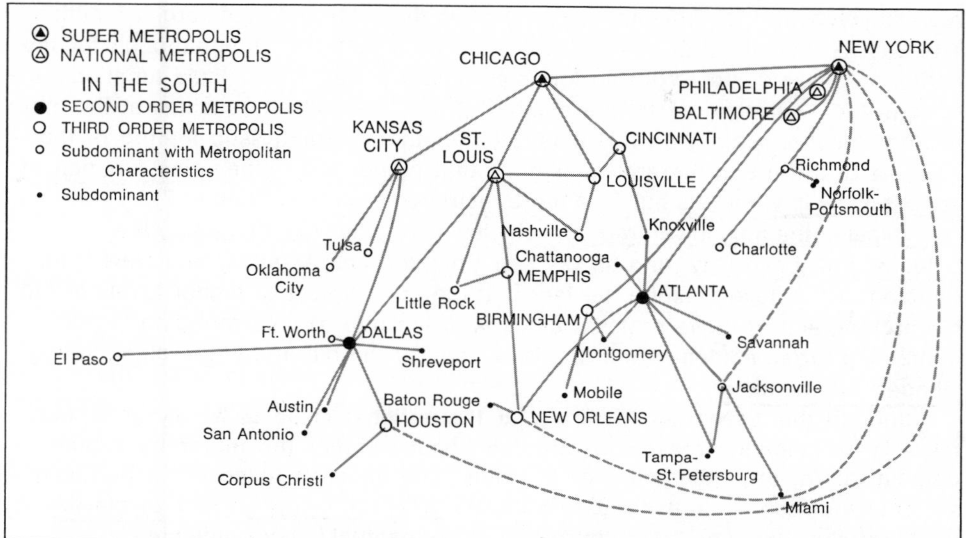

FIG. 2.12. HIERARCHICAL METROPOLITAN ORGANIZATION OF THE SOUTH. (*Source:* After Vance and Smith, 1954, Fig. 2.)

distinctive spatial-functional organization is presented in Figure 2.12 for the larger settlements of the South.

Identification of the number of levels in the hierarchy is a problem in classification, the object of which is to divide the continuous distribution of city sizes into meaningful city-size classes. Consequently the number of different levels proposed depends on considerations such as the scale of analysis—that is, the size of region in which study is undertaken—the method of classification used, the particular interests of the researcher, and, importantly, the purpose for which the hierarchy is being identified. Because of this it is important to keep in mind that there is no single, best specification of the urban hierarchy. Thus the particular scheme shown in Figure 2.12 is, for example, one of a number of alternatives that could be suggested for the cities of the South.

For the United States as a whole, however, Philbrick (1957) has suggested that urban settlements comprise a hierarchy with seven distinct levels. At the pinnacle of the hierarchy is the national metropolis—the nation's "primate city." New York is the sole example of a city at this high level in the United States city system, and it can be thought of as corresponding to cities like London and Paris at the world scale. The influence of New York is nationwide, through such things as the financial activities on Wall Street, the advertising activities of Madison Avenue, and the decisions made in the headquarters offices of many of the country's largest business organizations.

Immediately below this level are the regional metropolises. Los Angeles and Chicago are perhaps the two cities typical of this level in the hierarchy in the United States. They dominate the western and middle parts of the country respectively with their smaller, regional-scale financial and commercial functions. The East is dominated at this regional level by New York. Thus although for the nation as a whole, New York performs a number of very specialized functions, it does at the same time perform a number of less specialized activities at the more limited regional scale. And this illustrates another characteristic feature of the concept of the urban hierarchy—namely that higher level cities also function at successively lower levels but for a more restricted area (see Chapter 7).

Typical of the next lower, regional city level are cities like St. Louis, New Orleans, Salt Lake City, and so on. But Chicago, Los Angeles, and New York function at this level despite the fact that they are typical of higher levels in the hierarchy. Each of these regional cities is at the hub of a surrounding region containing urban settlements at the lower end of the hierarchy: the cities, towns, villages, and hamlets.

Although this seven-tier hierarchy at the national scale is widely accepted, there is no scientific reason for arguing about whether the hierarchy should contain this or any other number of levels. The decision to accept a particular set of size-classes is in itself quite arbitrary. In short, levels, orders, or classes in the hierarchy should be "regarded either as conceptual fictions suitable for manipulation in abstract discourse or as categories of convenience for handling empirical data" (Duncan, *et al.,* 1960, p. 51). In both contexts, the notion of the urban hierarchy is another one of the cornerstones on which much contemporary thinking about the city system has been built.

CITY TYPES AND FUNCTIONS

3

Implicit in the discussion of settlement evolution was the notion that different types of cities may be recognized within the overall urban pattern. For example, from the discussion of location, a simple distinction might be made

between railroad, river, and coastal cities. Similarly different city types might be identified on the basis of their population size or the functions they perform. The recognition of different types of cities in this way necessitates their classification, and it is to this that we turn in this chapter. We shall look at some of the ways in which cities have been classified in urban geography, paying particular attention to the ways in which they have been classified on the basis of their functional structure and economic specialization.

THE PURPOSE OF CLASSIFICATION

In the introductory chapter we noted that, as part of the descriptive stage in study, classification is the basic procedure we use to organize facts. Without classification of some sort it would be impossible to give names to things or to transmit information about them. But there is very little to be gained from organizing facts for its own sake; there must be a purpose. Hence classification is merely a means to an end—a means of organizing facts within the context of a specific problem.

The purpose of classifying cities is twofold. On the one hand classification is undertaken in order to search reality for hypotheses. In this context the recognition of different types of cities on the basis of, for example, their functional specialization may enable us to identify spatial regularities in the distribution and structure of urban functions and to formulate hypotheses about the resulting patterns. On the other hand classification is undertaken to structure reality to test specific hypotheses that have already been formulated. For example, to test the hypothesis that cities with a diversified economy grow at a faster rate than those with a specialized economy, cities must first be classified on the basis of their economic structure so that diversified and specialized types can be identified.

After a thorough review of a large number of attempts at classifying cities, Smith (1965) has rightly concluded, however, the "specific objectives—or, for that matter, objectives in general—are difficult to discern in the statements of purpose . . . . Too often it appears that a major purpose of these studies (if not *the* major purpose) has been the development and presentation of a different classificatory methodology as an end in itself" (Smith, 1965, pp. 539–540). Although this criticism was directed specifically at the voluminous literature on the functional classification of cities, Smith's comments are, for the most part, applicable to the many attempts at classifying cities on the basis of other criteria. The classifications have, more often than not, "proved to be ends in themselves rather than points of departure for further research into the character of urban settlements" (Wilson, 1962, p. 125).

FUNCTIONAL SPECIALIZATION

When Pittsburgh is recognized as a "steel town" or Detroit as the "automobile capital of the world," explicit recognition is given to the existence of city types based on their economic specialization. Of all the various ways in which cities have been classified, those based on the identification of dominant economic function or functional specialization have been by far the most numerous and important in the literature. As the population size of cities increases, so their functional structure becomes increasingly more complex; and the urban economy is based on a broad mixture of activities. Consequently they become more difficult to differentiate one from another on the basis of the functions they perform. This multi-functional character of cities notwithstanding, it is common, however, to find the urban economy dominated by one, perhaps two, major activities. Classification based on functional specialization attempts to identify these dominant activities and to group together those cities that are most similar to each other with respect to their functional specialization.

As the recent review by Smith (1965) indicates, the many approaches that have been adopted in this context may be initially differentiated into those which are quantitative and those which are qualitative in nature. In the former, city types are identified from an analysis of precise numerical data about the functions cities perform. The latter group contains more intuitive schemes that are based on logical deduction and general observation.

QUALITATIVE SCHEMES

Of the classifications made, that undertaken by Aurousseau (1921) is perhaps the most representative of the qualitative schemes. From general observation he identified six urban functions: administration, defense, culture, production, communications, and recreation. Although it was noted that cities may perform a combination of these functions, it was common to find that one type of function dominated to result in specialization.

A similar type of general scheme was that proposed more recently by Harris and Ullman (1945), who recognized three functional types of cities. These were *central places* performing a comprehensive range of services for a more local surrounding area; *transportation cities* performing break-of-bulk and allied activities for a larger region; and *specialized-function cities* dominated by one activity, such as mining, manufacturing, or recreation, and serving wider national, even international markets. They, too, point out that most cities represent a combination of all three factors, although the relative importance of each one often varies from city to city.

The significance of this very general threefold division is the way it relates to the location of cities. This is shown in idealized form in Figure 3.1. The overall pattern created by the distribution of cities can be thought of as being made up of three different layers superimposed on top of each other (Fig. 3.1A). The hierarchy of central places forms the basic layer. Ideally these tend to be evenly spaced throughout productive territory as shown in Figure 3.1B, although the regularity of the pattern is often seriously distorted by the unevenness of the resource distribution. Since cities are dependent on transportation, the symmetry of the central-place arrangement is further modified by the pattern of routes. In turn, these give rise to the second layer of cities in the overall pattern. The development of cities at focal points or breaks of transportation create a linear element along rail lines or at coasts (Fig. 3.1C). Lastly, the specialized-function cities form the third layer. These occur singly or in clusters in conjunction with localized resources, such as coal fields, mineral deposits, at waterpower sites, and so on and result in a clustered element in the pattern as shown in Figure 3.1D. We have seen from the discussion of the evolution of the pattern of cities in the United States how this model of the urban pattern has developed in reality.

QUANTITATIVE SCHEMES

Studies in which functional specialization is identified from analysis of precise numerical data are far more numerous. The common assumption in these studies

FIG. 3.1. LAYERS IN THE SETTLEMENT PATTERN OF A REGION. IDEALLY THE OVERALL PATTERN (A) CAN BE THOUGHT OF AS COMPRISING EVENLY SPACED CENTRAL PLACES (B), TRANSPORT CENTERS (C), AND SPECIALIZED-FUNCTION SETTLEMENTS SUCH AS MINING TOWNS AND RESORTS (D). (*Source:* Harris and Ullman, 1949, Figs. 1–4.)

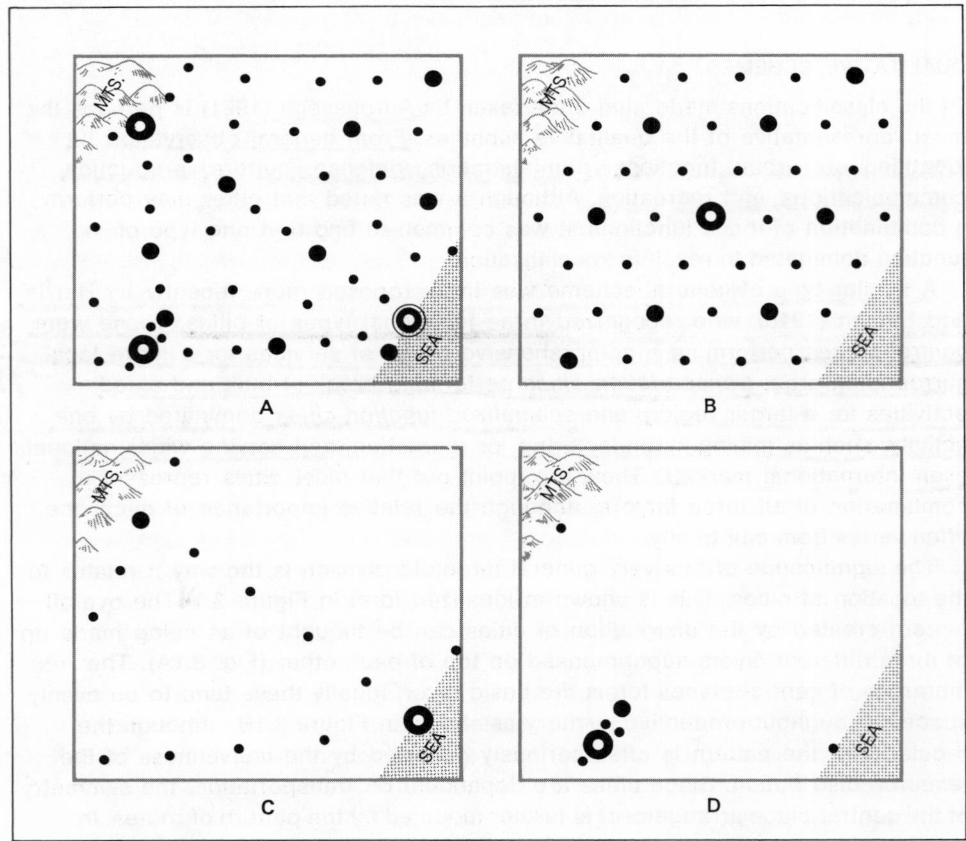

is that the city's labor force is the best indicator of the nature of the urban economy. Groups of cities with similar functional specialization have therefore been most frequently identified from the analysis of employment data. Specialization is said to exist when employment in a given type of activity exceeds some critical level specified by the researcher. For it is only when an abnormally large proportion of the city's labor force is employed in a particular activity that it becomes a distinguishing feature in functionally differentiating that place from all others.

The major difficulty in this approach is immediately apparent. It is, namely, that of deciding at what point an economic activity becomes important enough in the city's economic structure to be of such special significance as to warrant separate classification. In short, the fundamental problem is to meaningfully define the critical level of employment necessary for specialization to exist. There is no single or even best solution to this problem, and in the literature on the functional classification of cities there is little agreement on either the magnitudes of these threshold values or on the ways by which they should be selected. In the last resort, definitions of specialization depend very much on the methods used in classification and the purpose for which it is undertaken. To illustrate this, we will look at two functional classifications in more detail.

THE HARRIS CLASSIFICATION

The classification of the cities of the United States proposed by Harris (1943) can now be regarded almost as a classic in the literature dealing with urban functional types. In this classification cities were defined as functional rather than political units. At the time the classification was proposed, the best approximation to a functional definition of cities was the metropolitan district used by the Bureau of the Census. There were, however, only 140 of these since many cities had less than the minimum 50,000 population required to qualify for metropolitan-district status. To enable a more complete coverage of the cities of the United States, nine city-clusters and 456 smaller cities were defined by Harris as functional units for the purpose of the classification. In this way, a total of 988 cities were combined into 605 functional units.

These were classified on the basis of the activity of greatest importance in each city into one of nine classes. In alphabetical order, these were as follows: diversified (D), university (E), manufacturing (M), political (P), retail (R), mining (S), transportation (T), wholesale (W), and resort-retirement cities (X). Because of the large number of cities found to specialize in manufacturing, it was later thought desirable to subdivide this important category into two: into manufacturing (M′) and manufacturing (M), to result in a total of ten functional types of cities. In the M′-type of manufacturing city, employment in manufacturing overwhelmingly dominated; while in the M-type, although manufacturing could be considered the dominant economic activity, other important but definitely secondary activities were also present.

10 classes of functional units by Harris

10 functional types of cities

The allocation of cities to one of these ten functional classes was based primarily on an analysis of employment data. This could be used to provide a critical index of the relative importance in each city of the various branches of manufacturing and trade. Since employment data was collected, however, on an industrial and trading establishment basis, the returns gave little real indication of the variety of different jobs performed by the labor force employed in each of the major categories. For example, the total work force of an industrial plant would all be recorded as employed in manufacturing. Quite obviously not all the workers in the plant would actually be employed in making things. Many workers would be engaged in secretarial jobs, or employed as maintenance men, or cleaners, and so on. To overcome this shortcoming, Harris supplemented the employment data with data on specific occupations. Both sets of figures were expressed as percentages; the employment figures as percentages of the total workers in manufacturing, wholesaling, and retailing combined, and the occupation figures as percentages of the total gainful workers. For three of the classes—educational, resort-retirement, and political cities—Harris was obliged to use noncensus data, and more intuitive criteria were developed to identify these types of cities.

THE ASSIGNMENT

In assigning cities to one of the ten classes, Harris set up the critical levels of employment needed for specialization in an arbitrary fashion from an intuitive analysis of the employment structure of cities of what he thought were well-defined functional types. A complete list of the criteria established to define specialization for each of the ten functional types is given in Table 3.1. The identification of the cities specialized in manufacturing (M′) is illustrated graphically in Figure 3.2. On the graph the employment figures are plotted on the Y-axis, and the occupational figures on the X-axis. The critical levels established by Harris are shown on the graph by straight lines: the horizontal line is drawn at 74 percent of the total employment in manufacturing, wholesaling, and retailing; and the vertical line, to indicate that 45 percent of the gainful workers are employed in the manufacturing and mechanical industries. Each city can then be plotted on the graph according to its percentages on the two scales.

Cities for which employment and occupation percentages are greater than the specified critical levels will fall in the upper right-hand shaded portion of the graph. These cities are then considered to be specialized in manufacturing and are identified as M′-type places. Cities that fall outside the upper right quadrant of the graph do not satisfy the criteria for specialization in manufacturing. These cities must then be examined with reference to the critical levels established for specialization in each of the other activities and assigned to their oppropriate category. In this way each of the 605 cities is eventually classified according to its specialization in one of the ten functional categories.

The results of the classification are summarized in Table 3.2. As might be expected, the most important types are manufacturing, diversified, and retailing

TABLE 3.1. CRITERIA USED BY HARRIS TO IDENTIFY ECONOMIC SPECIALIZATION

Manufacturing Cities, M′ Subtype.

Employment data: manufacturing employment equals at least 74% of total employment in manufacturing, retailing, and wholesaling.

Occupation data: manufacturing and mechanical industries contain at least 45% of gainful workers.

Note: A few cities with industries in suburbs were placed in this class if the percentage for the occupation data reached 50%

Manufacturing Cities, M Subtype.

Employment data: manufacturing employment equals at least 60% of total employment in manufacturing, retailing, and wholesaling.

Occupation data: manufacturing and mechanical industries usually contain between 30% and 45% of gainful workers.

Wholesale Cites (W).

Employment data: employment in wholesaling is at least 20% of the total employment in manufacturing, wholesaling, and retailing and at least 45% as much as in retailing alone.

Transportation Cities (T).

Occupation data: transportation and communication contain at least 11% of the gainful workers, and workers in transportation and communication equal at least one-third the number in the manufacturing and mechanical industries, and at least two-thirds the number in trade.

Note: This definition applies only to cities of more than 25,000 for which such figures are available.

Resort-Retirement Cities (X).

No satisfactory statistical criterion was found. Cities with a low percentage of the population employed were checked in the literature for this function.

Retail Cities (R).

Employment data: employment in retailing equals at least 50% of the total employment in manufacturing, wholesaling, and retailing and at least 2.2 times that in wholesaling alone.

Diversified Cities (D).

Employment data: employment in manufacturing, wholesaling, and retailing is less than 60%, 20%, and 50% respectively of the total employment in these activities; and no other criteria apply.

Occupation data: with few exceptions, manufacturing and mechanical industries contain between 25% and 35% of the gainful workers.

Mining Cities (S).

Occupation data: extraction of minerals accounts for more than 15% of the gainful workers.

Note: This definition applies only to cities of more than 25,000 for which such figures are available. For cities between 10,000 and 25,000 a comparison was made of mining employment available by counties only, with employment in cities within such mining counties. Published sources were consulted to differentiate actual mining towns from commercial and industrial centers in mining areas.

University Cities (E).

Enrollment in schools of collegiate rank (universities, technical schools, liberal-arts colleges, and teachers colleges) equals at least 25% of the population of the city in 1940.

Note: Enrollment figures were obtained from *School and Society,* 52 (1940), pp. 601–619.

Political Cities (P).

Cities that were state capitals, plus Washington, D.C.

Note: The political function is clearly dominant in only 16 of these; in the rest it is overshadowed by trade and industry.

Source: Harris (1943), Table 1.

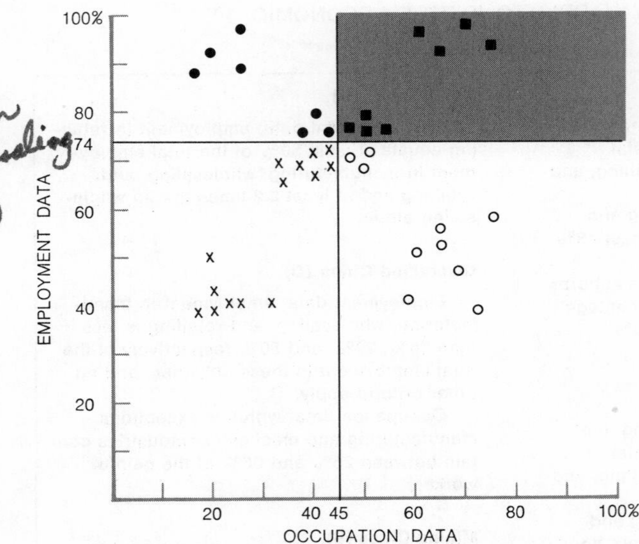

FIG. 3.2. DIAGRAMMATIC REPRESENTATION OF HARRIS' METHOD FOR DEFINING M′-TYPE CITIES.

cities in that order. Together these account for just over 80 percent of the cities classified. Cities specializing in manufacturing turned out to be the most important single type and accounted for 43.5 percent of the total number of cities. This is the case for both the larger metropolitan districts (50,000 or more population) and the other smaller cities (10,000–50,000 population). Also significant is the fact that a larger proportion of the smaller cities are classified as retailing, educational, and mining centers, while the larger metropolitan districts appeared more frequently to specialize in manufacturing, transportation, and wholesaling.

TABLE 3.2. SUMMARY OF THE RESULTS OF THE HARRIS CLASSIFICATION

		Metropolitan Districts		Other Cities	
Activity Type	**Totals**	**No.**	**%**	**No.**	**%**
(M′) Manufacturing	118	25	17.8	93	20.0
(M) Manufacturing	140	38	27.1	102	22.0
(D) Diversified	130	33	23.6	97	21.0
(R) Retail	104	12	8.6	92	20.0
(T) Transportation	32	14	10.0	18	4.0
(W) Wholesale	27	11	7.9	16	3.0
(X) Resort-Retirement	22	5	3.6	17	3.7
(E) Educational	17	–	–	17	3.6
(S) Mining	14	1	0.7	13	2.8
(P) Political	1	1	0.7	–	–
Totals	605	140	100.0	465	100.0

Source: Harris (1943), full mimeographed list of cities.

THE DISTRIBUTION OF FUNCTIONAL TYPES

The distribution of the various functional types of cities is shown in Figure 3.3, and a complete listing of the 605 cities by type is presented in Appendix B. The pattern of the manufacturing cities approximates very closely that expected from our discussion of the spread of cities in the previous chapter. Cities of this type are notably concentrated in the manufacturing belt of the United States, with two narrow extensions southward in the Great Valley and along the Piedmont Plateau. Outside of these areas, cities specializing in manufacturing are notably absent. The few are mainly associated with the processing of raw materials such as lumber, ores, and oil, or the processing of perishable products such as fruit, vegetables, and fish.

The distribution of the cities specializing in retailing is quite different. Cities of this type are generally located outside of the manufacturing belt and its border zones and are notably concentrated in a band running north-south through the central, agricultural part of the country. These cities are mostly smaller ones, which for the most part act as service centers for fairly small surrounding rural regions (see Chapter 7).

Diversified cities, in which both trade and manufacturing are well developed, are well distributed throughout the eastern part of the United States. They are noticeably concentrated in a transitional area between the concentration of manufacturing cities in the heartland and the band of retail cities to the west of it. Within the manufacturing belt, diversified cities are those at which trade is well developed, while within the band of retail cities they are associated with local industries, particularly processing raw materials such as grains and oil.

Cities classified as specialized in wholesaling are found mainly in the South and in western parts of the country. Two types of wholesale cities can be recognized. First, there are the smaller cities associated with the assembly, packaging, and marketing of agricultural produce. Examples are Redlands, California (oranges), Sanford, Florida (celery), Hopkinsville, Kentucky (tobacco), and Suffolk, Virginia (peanuts). Secondly, there are larger cities, such as San Francisco, Seattle, Sioux Falls, and Dallas, which are predominantly engaged in the distribution of goods over wider areas.

Transportation cities include both coastal and inland ports and railroad centers. A number of the latter are associated with passes through mountains (e.g. Altoona, Pennsylvania), while others are the focal points of movement within the manufacturing belt. The distribution of mining centers requires little comment. For the most part they are associated with the pattern of the coal fields; 10 of the 14 cities in this category are coal-mining towns. The others are located in conjunction with other mineral deposits, such as copper (Butte, Montana) and iron ore (for example, Ironwood, Michigan). The educational cities are mostly small places dominated by the large state universities; and they are notably concentrated in the Midwestern states. Lastly, the distribution of resort and retirement cities reflects the influence of amenity factors on location. These types are notably concentrated in Florida, Southern California, and the desert Southwest.

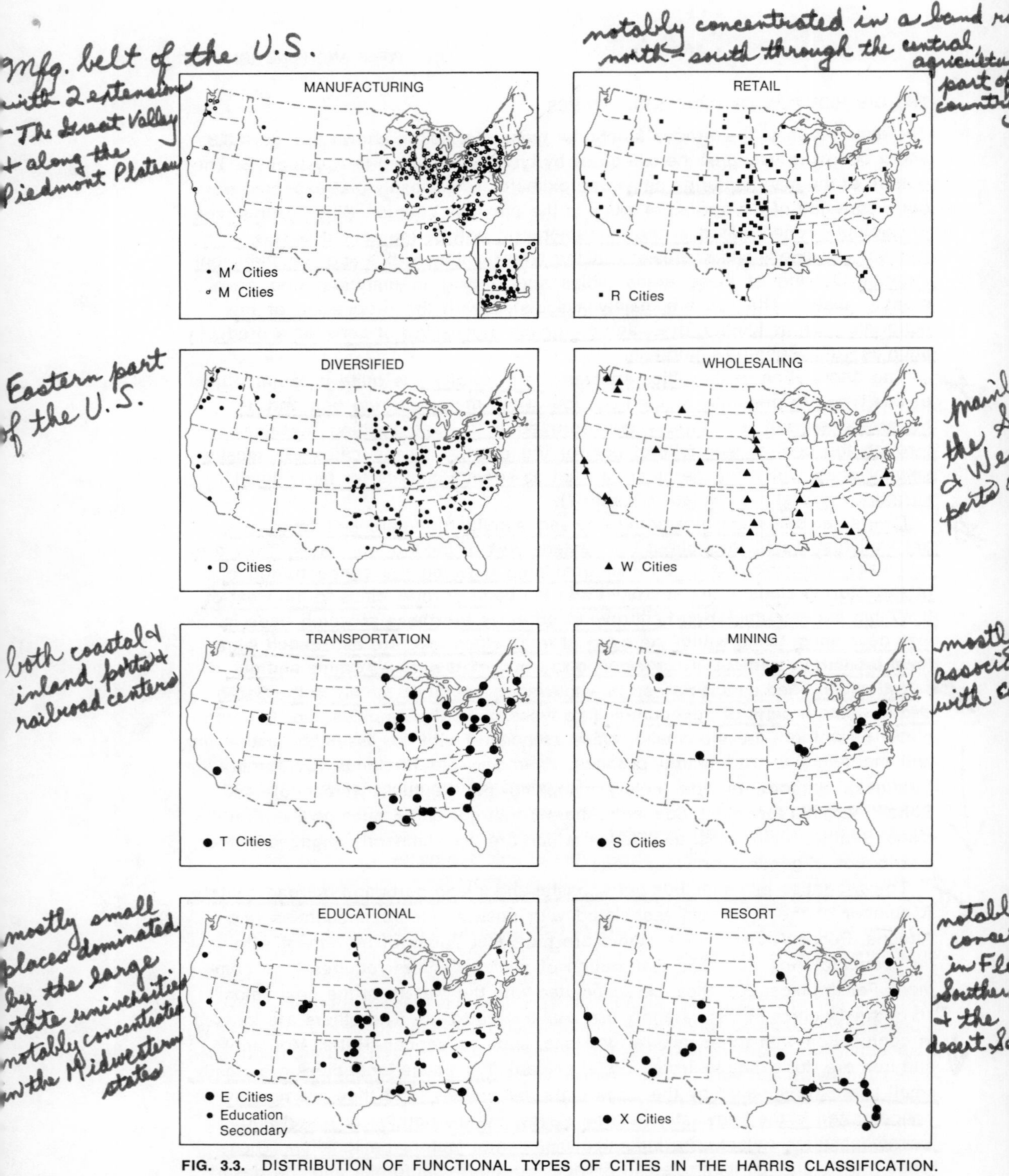

FIG. 3.3. DISTRIBUTION OF FUNCTIONAL TYPES OF CITIES IN THE HARRIS CLASSIFICATION. (*Source:* Harris, 1943, Figs. 2–9 inclusive.)

COMMENT

The Harris classification, which has been widely used as the basis for further studies in urban geography, is not without its shortcomings. Two weaknesses in particular should be stressed. The first of these is the essentially intuitive way in which Harris defined specialization. The validity of the criteria listed in Table 3.1 is open to question, and it has been said that Harris failed to identify the well-recognized types on which these were built up (Mayer, 1956). Secondly, cities were permitted to specialize in only one type of activity. As a result, "The labels attached to many urban settlements often hid more about their occupational structure than they revealed" (Johnson, 1965, p. 68). For example, although New York City and Chicago are the nation's two principal wholesale centers and are both important manufacturing, transportation, and educational centers, the importance of these functions at these cities is not revealed in the classification. Both are considered simply as diversified cities. For these and many other large urban centers, the idea of attaching a simple descriptive label is highly dubious.

NELSON'S SERVICE CLASSIFICATION

An attempt was made to overcome these shortcomings in a more recent classification of cities in the United States proposed by Nelson (1955). In this, a more objective, statistical definition of specialization was employed. As a result cities could be more realistically classified according to their multiple functional specialization; and, moreover, it was possible to specify the degree to which cities were specialized in the various activities.

In the classification, cities were defined as functional units although differently from the definition used in Harris's work. After 1940, metropolitan districts were superseded by two new census units—Standard Metropolitan Areas and Urbanized Areas (see Appendix A). Nelson decided that urbanized areas best suited his purpose, and so these were used wherever possible. To ensure as complete a coverage of cities as possible, these were supplemented by all urban places outside the urbanized areas that had populations between 10,000 and 50,000. As a result a total of 897 cities were included.

These were classified on the basis of ten major functional types, details of which are presented in Table 3.3. The first nine functions were obtained by condensing the twenty-four industry groups given in the *Census of Population, 1950.* The final category was added to ensure that the classification was exhaustive; cities were assigned to this class when they failed to satisfy the criteria of specialization in any of the other functions. In addition, each of the categories except for diversified was further subdivided into three classes to indicate the degree of specialization at a particular city.

The classification was based on employment figures expressed as percentages of the total labor force. An example is given for four sample cities in Table 3.4. Clearly there is considerable variation between the cities in the percentages of

TABLE 3.3. THE PRINCIPAL ACTIVITY TYPES IN NELSON'S CLASSIFICATION

Letter Code	Type	Corresponding Major Industry Groups from State Volumes, Table 35 of *U.S. Census of Population: 1950, Vol. 2, Characteristics of the Population*
Mi	Mining	Mining
Mf	Manufacturing	Manufacturing
T	Transportation and Communication	Railroads and railway express services Trucking services and warehousing Other transportation Telecommunications
W	Wholesale trade	Wholesale trade
R	Retail trade	Food and dairy produce stores and milk retail Eating and drinking places Other retail services
F	Finance, insurance, and real estate	Finance, insurance, and real estate
Ps	Personal services	Hotels and lodging places Other personal services Entertainment and recreational services
Pf	Professional service	Medical and other health services Educational services, government and private Other professional and related services
Pb	Public administration	Public administration
D	Diversified	.... ("Cities with insufficient proportion of their labor force in any single service to warrant special classification.")

Source: Nelson (1955), Table 1.

the labor force employed in each of the nine activities. This variation is more readily appreciated when the data for all cities are tabulated in the form of frequency distributions as shown in Figure 3.4. On each of the graphs, the percentage of the labor force engaged in the given activity is measured on the X-axis; and the number of cities, or frequency, is plotted on the Y-axis. The shapes of the resulting graphs indicate that the percentages employed vary between the different activities and also between different cities.

At one extreme the graph for manufacturing reflects the widespread occurrence of this activity in all cities. No city is without some employment in manufacturing; a few manage to get by with less than 5 percent, and a few can even boast of more than 60 percent. No less than 91 of the 897 cities have over 50 percent of their workers in manufacturing. At the other extreme, the concentrated nature of mining is indicated on the graph by the very high proportion of cities with hardly any employment recorded in this activity. In all, 673 cities have less than 1 percent of their labor force employed in mining, and most of these are

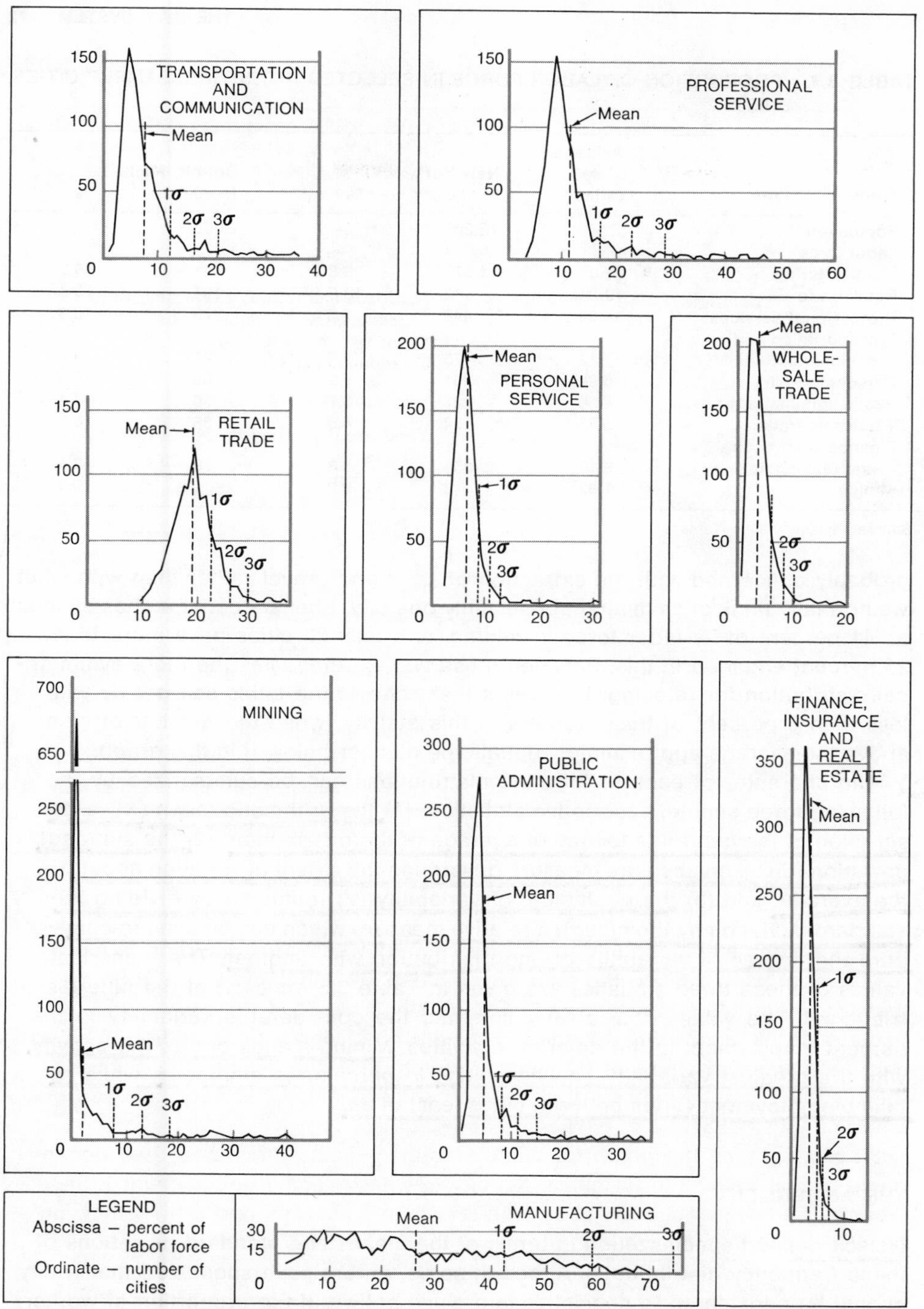

FIG. 3.4. FREQUENCY DISTRIBUTIONS FOR NINE KINDS OF EMPLOYMENT IN AMERICAN CITIES. (*Source:* Nelson, 1955, Fig. 1.)

TABLE 3.4. PROPORTION OF LABOR FORCE IN SELECTED ACTIVITIES, SAMPLE CITIES, 1950

	Average of 897 Cities	New York, N.Y. In 000's	%	Detroit, Mich. In 000's	%
Population	–	12,296	–	2,659	–
Labor force	–	6,099	–	1,068	–
Manufacturing	27.07	1,573	25.8	501	46.9
Retail trade	19.23	822	13.5	164	15.3
Professional services	11.09	448	7.3	73	6.9
Transportation and communications	7.12	475	7.8	71	6.7
Personal services	6.20	361	5.9	59	5.5
Public administration	4.58	227	3.7	36	3.4
Wholesale trade	3.85	274	4.5	33	3.1
Finance, insurance, and real estate	3.19	353	5.8	36	3.4
Mining	1.62	3	0.05	0.3	0.01

Source: Nelson (1955), Table 2.

probably concerned with the extraction of sand and gravel rather than with what we normally think of as mining per se. Only one city, Shenandoah, Pa., has as much as 41 percent of its labor force in mining, and only 25 cities have more than 25 percent engaged in this. Between these two extremes lies the more symmetrical distribution for retailing. It appears that none of the cities can get by with less than 6 percent of their workers in this activity, while the number of cities above the average approximately equals the number below it in this graph.

The character of each of the nine distributions can be summarized by the following three simple, descriptive statistics: (1) the arithmetic mean ($\bar{X}$), a description of the central tendency or average of the distribution; (2) the standard deviation (*S.D.*), an absolute measure describing the extent of variation about the average; and (3) the coefficient of variability (*V*) (obtained by dividing the standard deviation by the mean), a relative measure which can be used to compare the degree of variability of one distribution with another. The numerical values of these three statistics are given in Table 3.5 for each of the nine distributions. The values of *V* clearly illustrate the considerable variability in the percent employment in the different activities. Mining stands out as the activity with the greatest variability between cities in percentage employed, while retailing employment varies between cities least of all.

THE ASSIGNMENT

Nelson defined specialization in terms of the means and standard deviations of these frequency distributions. Although some writers have suggested that a city should be considered to specialize in a given activity if the proportion of workers employed in it exceeds the average amount for all cities, Nelson decided that this was insufficient as a definition of specialization. Instead he argued—

Kearney, Neb. In 000's	%	Rochester, Minn. In 000's	%
12.11	–	29.88	–
3.28	–	13.0	–
0.27	8.3	0.81	6.1
1.18	36.2	2.72	20.7
0.84	25.6	4.39	33.3
0.32	9.7	0.73	6.3
0.36	11.0	1.40	10.6
0.20	6.1	0.41	3.1
0.22	6.6	0.42	3.1
0.13	3.9	0.39	2.9
0.005	0.15	0.01	0.09

although not very clearly—that the proportion of a city's labor force in a given activity should exceed the mean by at least one standard deviation before it could be considered to be specialized in that activity. These critical values are shown on the graphs in Figure 3.4 by the Greek letter σ, and their numerical values are given in row 4 of Table 3.5. For a city to be classified as specializing in manufacturing it therefore must have at least 43.11 percent of its labor force employed in this activity. Similarly specialization in personal services requires at least 8.27 percent of the labor force to be employed in this activity, and so on for each of the other types.

The standard deviations were also used as the basis for indicating the degree of specialization in each of the activities. An example will make this clear. For a city to be considered specialized in mining, it must have at least 6.63 percent of its labor force engaged in this activity (Table 3.5). Many cities, however, have considerably more than this; and this excess can be measured in terms of one, two, or three standard deviations from the mean. Hence if the proportion engaged in mining was between 6.63 and 11.64, the city was classified as a Mi1 type; if it was between 11.64 and 16.65 percent it was classified as a Mi2 type; and if the proportion was greater than 16.65 percent, it was classified as a Mi3 city. Shenandoah, Pa., with 41 percent of its total workers engaged in mining, qualifies as a Mi3 city—indicating its extreme degree of specialization in this activity. Exactly the same procedure was adopted for every other activity type, and hence three levels of specialization could be identified for each functional type.

In the final classification, letter and number codes are given to each city. The letters indicate the activities in which the city specializes; and the numbers, the degree to which specialization occurs. For example, Kearney, Neb., specializes in four different activities and is classified as WPs2Pf2R3, indicating that its employment is more than 3 S.D.'s above the mean in retailing, over 2 S.D.'s in both professional and personal services, but only 1 S.D. in wholesaling. On the

TABLE 3.5. AVERAGES AND STANDARD DEVIATIONS IN PERCENTAGES FOR ACTIVITY TYPES IN NELSON'S CLASSIFICATION (1950)

	Manufacturing	Retail Trade	Professional Services	Transportation and Communication	Personal Services
Average	27.07	19.23	11.09	7.12	6.20
Standard deviation	16.04	3.63	5.89	4.58	2.07
V-coefficient	59.25	18.87	53.10	64.30	33.38
Average plus 1 SD	43.11	22.86	16.98	11.70	8.27
Average plus 2 SD	59.15	26.49	22.87	16.28	10.34
Average plus 3 SD	75.19	30.12	28.76	20.86	12.41

Source: Nelson (1955), Table 4.

other hand, Pekin, Ill., does not satisfy the requirements for specialization in any of the nine activities; and so it is recorded as a diversified (D) city. The complete list of cities classified is presented in Appendix C.

The aggregate results of the classification presented in Table 3.6A show that although three-quarters of the cities specialized in only one activity, specialization in two or even three activities is not uncommon. El Centro, Calif., is really multifunctional, specializing in five activities—R3W3PsPbF. Table 3.6B shows the total number of cities recorded by activity type and degree of specialization.

TABLE 3.6. SUMMARY OF THE RESULTS OF NELSON'S CLASSIFICATION

(A) Number of Functions in Which Cities Specialized

	Number of Activity Groups					
	1	2	3	4	5	Totals
No. of cities	679	149	62	6	1	897
Percentage of total (897)	75.7	16.6	6.9	0.7	0.1	100.0

(B) Number of Cities by Activity Type and Degree of Specialization

	Totals		1 S.D.		2 S.D.		3 S.D.	
Activity	No.	%[a]	No.	%	No.	%	No.	%
Manufacturing	183	20.4	153	83.6	29	15.8	1	0.6
Retail trade	137	15.3	110	80.3	21	15.3	6	4.4
Finance, etc.	123	13.7	93	75.7	13	10.6	17	13.7
Wholesale trade	107	11.9	73	68.2	21	19.6	13	12.2
Transportation	96	10.7	51	53.1	22	22.9	23	24.0
Personal services	92	10.3	57	61.9	24	26.1	11	12.0
Public administration	85	9.5	45	52.9	19	22.3	21	24.8
Professional services	81	9.0	42	51.8	16	19.7	23	28.5
Mining	46	5.1	12	26.1	12	26.1	22	47.8
Diversified	246	27.4	n.a.	n.a.	n.a.	n.a.	n.a.	n.a.

[a] These do not add to 100 percent because of multiple classification.
Source: Nelson (1955), Appendix.

Public Administration	Wholesale Trade	Finance, Insurance, and Real Estate	Mining
4.58	3.85	3.19	1.62
3.48	2.14	1.25	5.01
75.98	55.59	39.19	309.26
8.06	5.99	4.44	6.63
11.54	8.13	5.69	11.64
15.02	10.27	6.94	16.65

Nearly a third of the 897 cities do not specialize in anything in particular and are best represented as diversified cities. Manufacturing appears most often as the activity in which cities specialize, followed by retailing, finance, and wholesaling.

There are also marked variations in the degree of specialization in the given activities. Apart from mining, most cities have only a low degree of specialization in a given activity. The textile area of Brandon-Johnson, N.C., is the only city with a large enough proportion in manufacturing to warrant classification as an Mf3 city. Conversely, the extreme specialization typical of mining communities is well brought out by the fact that just under one-half of cities specializing in this activity are in the Mi3 class. Levels of such extreme specialization as this are not noted for the other types, although it is significant that about a quarter of the cities specializing in professional services, transportation, and public administration are characterized by this high degree of specialization.

POPULATION CHARACTERISTICS

Like Harris, Nelson presented the results of the classification on a series of maps and commented on the resulting distributions. The maps for mining and manufacturing cities are presented in Figures 6.1 and 6.4 respectively. Of greater interest, however, was a further study based on the results of the classification (Nelson, 1957). In this Nelson investigated whether the different types of cities showed any variation in their population characteristics. Although the results of this later study were not very conclusive, a number of interesting findings emerged. These are summarized in Table 3.7 for the S.D.2 and S.D.3 cities in each of the nine functional categories. Nelson used only these more specialized cities in his analysis, because he felt that differences in population characteristics would be most marked in them.

The manufacturing and professional service cities appeared to be the most extreme in population characteristics. Cities of the former type grew on the average considerably more slowly than other types in the decade 1942 to 1950. They had the highest participation in the labor force and the highest median incomes, but their populations were associated with the lowest average number of school

TABLE 3.7. AVERAGES OF SELECTED POPULATION CHARACTERISTICS FOR ALL CITIES AND S.D.3 AND S.D.2 CITIES IN NELSON'S CLASSIFICATION

	All Cities	Mf3 & Mf2	R3 & R2	Pf3 & Pf2	T3 & T2	Mi3 & Mi2
% increase in population, 1940–1950	27.9	2.2	39.4	65.0	17.5	31.1
% 65 years old or older	8.6	7.6	9.0	7.6	9.7	7.4
Average years of school completed	10.0	8.9	10.5	12.3	10.4	9.7
Participation in labor force (% of males over 14 years of age)	77.8	82.8	77.1	55.8	78.0	79.2
Participation in labor force (% of females over 14 years of age)	32.8	35.9	30.3	34.1	29.2	27.1
% unemployed	5.1	5.4	6.7	3.6	4.7	5.5
Median income	$2,643	$3,134	$2,560	$1,674	$2,733	$2,882
Number of cities	897	30	27	39	50	34

Source: Nelson (1957), Table 2.

years completed. In contrast, professional service cities grew much more rapidly than any other type of city in the period from 1942 to 1950. They were also associated, understandably, with the highest number of school years completed, but they had low rates of participation in the labor force and the lowest median incomes of all types of cities. This is in part associated with their large student populations. Other significant associations were the high growth rate at personal service cities, the high unemployment figures at retail and wholesale cities, and, as was to be expected, the low rate of female participation in the labor force at mining centers.

COMMENT

Despite what appears to be a more objective method in city classification, we cannot say that the results presented by Nelson are better or worse than those of Harris. Both schemes must be evaluated independently on the basis of whether they adequately do the job for which they were intended. Since the concept of specialization is a relative one, any definition of it must be considered arbitrary. In this context Nelson's attempt to reduce the subjective element is worthy of praise, even if the subjective element in classification cannot be altogether removed. Notwithstanding, the use of the standard deviation to identify specialization can be criticized on the grounds that the frequency distributions shown in Figure 3.4 are not normal and in the absence of such a distribution the $\overline{X}$ and S.D. mean very little. This would, however, not appear to be a condemning criticism because Nelson's use of this statistic was purely descriptive. The technical problems of normality only become a problem in the context of statistical inference.

Pb3 & Pb2	Ps3 & Ps2	W3 & W2	F3 & F2
40.0	61.0	30.4	35.6
7.3	9.2	7.7	10.0
10.8	11.0	9.9	11.1
77.8	73.2	80.0	75.6
33.0	33.3	33.0	34.6
4.7	5.8	6.9	4.1
$2,658	$2,227	$2,566	$2,780
41	36	36	35

Preferences for one classification over another are often made on the basis of whether cities are assigned to a single class or to many. The argument for classification by a single dominant function largely rests on the fact that the results are easier to use, and especially to map. Simplicity, however, would seem to be an attribute of declining importance in current geographic studies; and preferences based on this kind of argument are not particularly meaningful in the context of classification. It is undoubtedly more realistic to recognize that some cities specialize in several activities just as it is to recognize that the economy of others may be dominated by a single activity. Because of this, it would appear that classifications like Nelson's, which recognize multiple specialization, are potentially more useful and rewarding than those which do not, despite the fact that the results may be more difficult to handle using simple methods in subsequent analyses.

There are of course many other reasons for preferring one classification over another. The final choice, however, among alternative methods should be based primarily on the "demonstrated greater relevance or predictive power of one classification in comparison to its alternatives, in the context of a well defined problem" (Duncan, et al., 1960, p. 35). Despite the potential usefulness of the findings, it is unfortunate that both Harris's and Nelson's classifications were apparently undertaken more to illustrate method than to search or structure reality in a problem framework.

The effect of city size One question that has not been asked so far pertains to the effect of city size on economic specialization: "Does it make sense to speak of cities as specializing in wholesaling, retailing, manufacturing, etc., if, in fact, the amount of each of these activities is directly proportional to the size of the city?" (Hadden and Borgatta, 1965, p. 39). There appears to be little if any agreement among geographers on the answer to this question. Some have stated categorically that ". . . only the average or total of the whole urban society . . . can be used as a measure of comparison" (Steigenga, 1955, p. 108); others argue that in defining specialization it makes more sense to "construct national means for towns of approximately the same size rather than to group urban centers of 1,000 people with, say, metropolitan populations 200 to 300 times larger" (Pownall, 1953, p. 333).

The problem of giving one definition for specialization for all cities is that one presupposes that approximately the same proportion of the population is engaged in identical activities in cities regardless of their size. That this is clearly not so is shown in Table 3.8. Considerable variation in proportions employed in the different activities occurs between cities of different sizes. There does not, however, appear to be any consistent change with size of city; and largely because of this, Nelson decided against including the size variable in his classification. The answer to the question of the modifying effects of city size can presumably only be found in the context of the specific problem for which the classification of cities is devised. Obviously when hypotheses based on city size are to be tested, it is essential that city-size differences are incorporated into the method used.

Basic employment In both Harris' and Nelson's classifications, figures for total employment were used in differentiating between cities on the basis of their functional specialization. As we shall see in Chapter 5, the total labor force of a city can be separated into two parts, (1) the basic component that is concerned with the production of goods and services for export outside the community, and (2) the nonbasic component that exists to service the workers in the basic sector. It is generally recognized that the fortunes of cities depend to a large

TABLE 3.8. PERCENTAGES EMPLOYED IN ACTIVITY GROUPS BY CITY SIZE

	Manufacturing	**Retail**	**Professional Services**	**Wholesale**	**Personal Services**
In cities of from					
10 000 to 24,999	26.65	19.66	11.34	3.72	5.79
25,000 to 49,999	26.07	19.07	11.98	3.87	7.09
50,000 to 99,999	29.31	18.56	9.76	4.24	6.47
100,000 to 249,999	29.77	18.07	9.50	4.21	6.61
250,000 to 499,999	28.10	17.81	9.22	4.40	6.86
500,000 to 999,999	27.21	18.16	9.17	5.10	6.72
1,000,000 and over	30.86	16.32	8.97	4.15	6.42
Average	27.07	19.23	11.09	3.85	6.20

Source: Nelson (1955), Table 3.

extent on the amount of their basic employment, for it is this which ultimately makes possible the growth of the city as a result of trade with other cities and regions.

Because of this, some writers have suggested that it makes better sense to identify urban functional specialization from an analysis of basic rather than total employment. This problem was implicitly recognized by Harris who assigned higher percentages to some functions than to others in defining specialization (see Table 3.1). In this way he attempted to "rule out local service employment in activities that exist merely to serve workers employed in the primary (Basic) activities" (Harris, 1943, p. 87). Explicit recognition of this problem is found in the classifications of American cities by Alexandersson (1956), of Canadian cities by Maxwell (1965), and in the index of functional specialization proposed by Ullman and Dacey (1962).

MULTIVARIATE CLASSIFICATION

If the object of classifying cities is to group together those that have the greatest similarity in functional structure rather than simply to indicate a dominant function, then different methods must be used than those employed by Harris and Nelson. For when deviations from an average are used as the basis for identifying specialization, important groupings are frequently hidden.

This problem can be illustrated with reference to the way in which Harris identified cities specializing in manufacturing shown graphically in Figure 3.2. It will be remembered that, on the graph, all cities falling in the upper right-hand quadrant were considered to specialize in manufacturing. However, close inspection of the graph suggests that five distinct clusters can be identified as shown in Figure 3.5. Each of these clusters contains cities that are most similar to each

Public Administration	Transportation and Commerce	Finance, Insurance, Real Estate	Mining	Total No. of Cities
4.39	7.03	2.96	2.11	550
4.80	6.98	3.22	1.03	166
4.79	7.75	3.39	0.48	59
5.22	7.14	3.74	0.71	71
6.40	7.58	4.38	1.24	25
4.96	8.83	5.06	0.41	14
6.92	7.35	4.75	0.16	12
4.58	7.12	3.19	1.62	897 Total

other in terms of the two stated criteria. Although groups of cities with similar functional structure can be readily identified when only two differentiating characteristics are used as in Figure 3.5, the problem becomes quite complex when

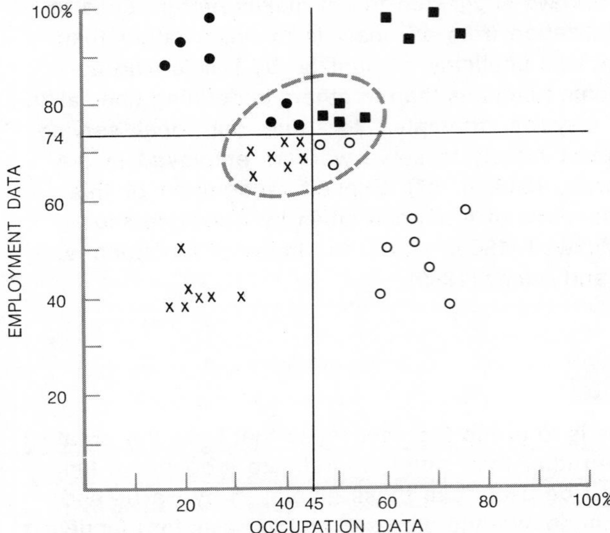

FIG. 3.5. CLUSTERS OF CITIES WITH SIMILAR KINDS OF FUNCTIONAL SPECIALIZATION.

similarities in functional structure are to be identified on the basis of many urban characteristics considered together. When this is the case, more sophisticated multivariate methods of taxonomy have to be used.

BASIC PROCEDURES

The procedures most commonly followed in the more complex kinds of classifications are outlined in Figure 3.6. To start with the data is arranged in the form of an $n \times m$ data matrix. In this, there are m columns each one of which corresponds to a different characteristic of the cities, and there are n rows each one of which corresponds to a different city. The cells of the matrix contain the information to be used in the classification.

It was, of course, a data matrix similar to this which Nelson used as a starting point for his classification. That one had nine columns—one for each of the different activities, and 987 rows corresponding to the cities. The cells in the matrix contained the percentages of each city's labor force employed in the nine activities. Thus the percentage breakdown of a city's labor force was recorded along a row, as shown for Detroit in row 2 and for New York City in row 3 in Figure 3.6. Variations among the cities in the proportions employed in the various activities is indicated by the column figures. It was this column information that Nelson was primarily interested in, first for the construction of the frequency distributions and second for calculating the arithmetic means and standard deviations.

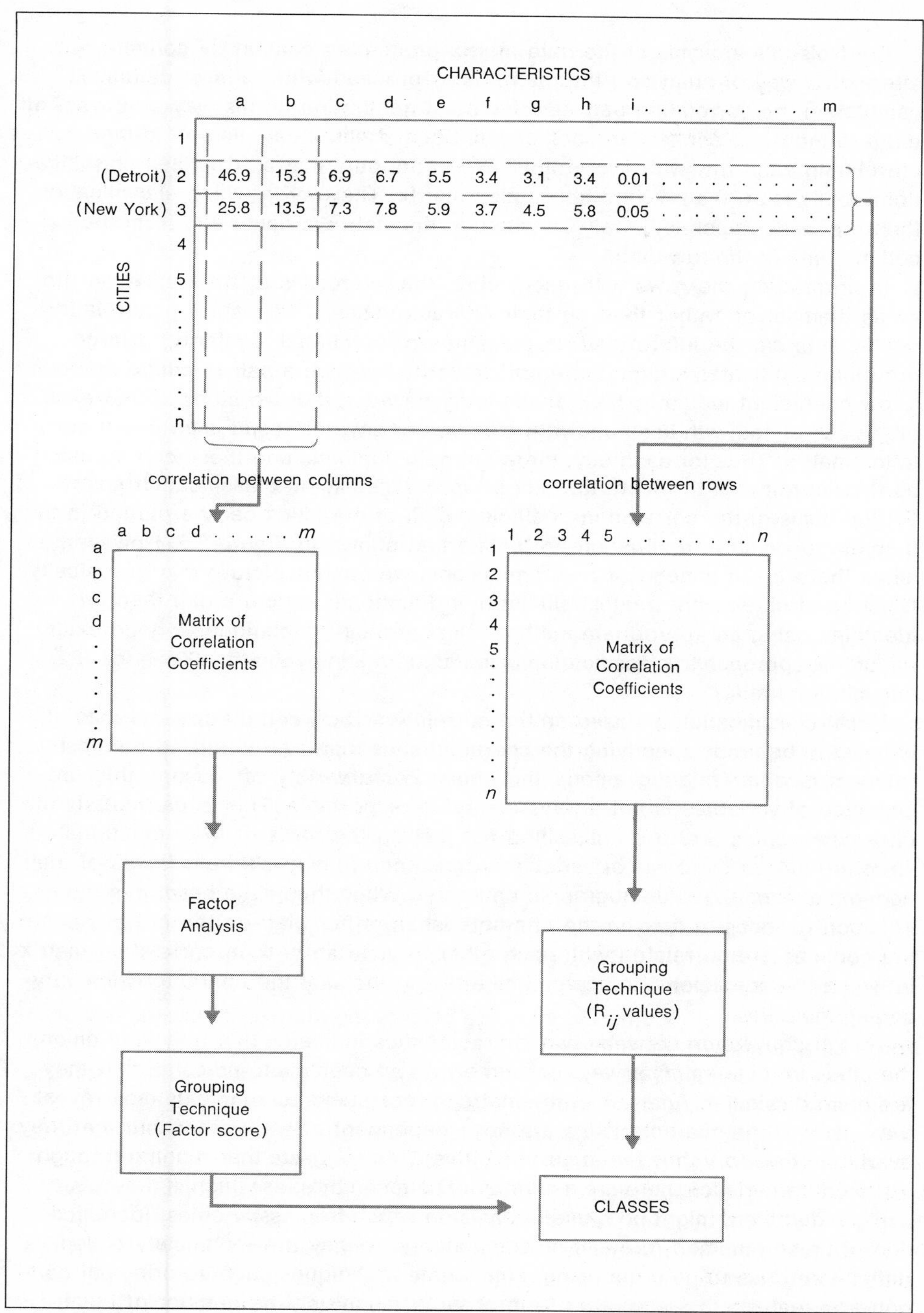

FIG. 3.6. FLOW CHART OF PROCEDURES USED IN THE MULTIVARIATE CLASSIFICATION OF CITIES.

But Nelson's analysis of the data matrix proceeded column by column. An alternative way of analyzing the matrix is to proceed with pairs of columns, calculating the correlation between them and generating in this way a new set of data—a matrix of correlation coefficients. Such a matrix can also be formed by correlating each row with every other row in the data matrix. Complex classifications really start, then, with a correlation matrix. The way in which classification then proceeds depends largely on whether this matrix is generated from the column data or the row data.

In correlating the rows with each other, the interest is at the outset on the cities themselves rather than on their characteristics. The resulting correlation coefficients can be interpreted as measures of functional similarity; a large correlation indicates a high degree of similarity between a pair of cities, whereas a low coefficient indicates lack of similarity between the two cities. Since each city is correlated with itself and with every other city, the result is an $n \times n$ correlation matrix. Thus for each city, there are n coefficients, and these can be used as the coordinates to locate the city in an n-dimensional classification space. On the basis of the correlation coefficients, all of the cities can be plotted in the n-space to result in a situation not unlike that shown in Figure 3.5. However, since there are n instead of two dimensions, we cannot picture this graphically. Clusters of cities with greatest similarity in functional structure can then be identified using an appropriate mathematical grouping technique. A good example of this approach to classification is that undertaken by Smith (1965B) for 422 cities in Australia.

When classification is based on the correlations between the rows of data, it is usual to begin by specifying the characteristics that are thought to be most relevant in differentiating among the cities. For a variety of reasons this preselection of variables is not always desirable or possible. This is particularly the case when cities are to be classified not just on the basis of their functional structure but on the basis of variables representing many different facets of their economic, social, and demographic character. When this is the case, it is more common to focus at first on the characteristics rather than on the cities. Hence the columns are correlated with each other to yield an $m \times m$ correlation matrix in which the coefficients indicate similarities in the way the characteristics vary among the cities.

A high correlation between two characteristics indicates that they vary among the cities in a very similar way; conversely a low coefficient indicates that they are quite dissimilar. Analysis of the matrix of correlation coefficients may reveal that many of the characteristics are not independent of each other, but that they overlap in the story they tell about the cities. This suggests that running through the m characteristics there are a number of common threads which, if they can be identified, might be a useful basis on which to classify cities. Identification of these common threads, or components as they are technically called, is difficult and has to be done using multivariate techniques such as principal components analysis or some other form of factor analysis. The number of identified components will determine the dimensions of the classification space, in which each city can be located by its factor scores. Application of a suitable grouping technique will then identify clusters of cities that are similar to each other with respect to these scores, and hence their characteristics. Examples of the uses of this procedure are the classifications of British towns by Moser and Scott (1961), of American cities by Hadden and Borgatta (1965), and of Canadian cities by King (1966).

A MULTIVARIATE ANALYSIS OF CANADIAN CITIES

King's (1966) multivariate analysis and classification of Canadian cities is of interest not only as an illustration of the basic procedures just described, but also because it sheds a little light on the way the Canadian city system has changed through time. In this study the principal components method was used to analyze more than 50 characteristics of Canadian cities in both 1951 and 1961. The basic dimensions of the city system resulting from the use of this method were then used as a framework for classifying the 106 cities. In summarizing King's study, we will focus on the analysis of the 1961 data.

URBAN DIMENSIONS IN 1961

To capture some of the many ways in which the 106 cities varied, measurements on 54 economic, social, demographic, and locational characteristics were included in the analysis for 1961. A sample of the kinds of measurements used in the analysis is given in Table 3.9. When put together, the observations on each city formed a 106×54 data matrix, each column of which was correlated with every other to result in a 54×54 matrix of correlation coefficients. This matrix was then subjected to a principal components analysis, the results of which suggested that variation in the structure of Canadian cities could be expressed in terms of eleven basic dimensions. These eleven dimensions together accounted for 83 percent of the total variance in the data matrix.

The first six components could be readily interpreted from the way in which the original variables loaded onto them. In order of importance these dimensions were as follows:

(1) An urban manufacturing, and especially textile manufacturing, dimension.
(2) The second component was clearly identified with the population structure of cities located in Quebec province and indicated that the demographic character of these is distinctly different from cities in English-speaking Canada.
(3) The third dimension was identified with the socioeconomic structure of the Toronto and Montreal metropolitan areas.
(4) This dimension indexed aspects of the residential role of many cities, and particularly their high socioeconomic status. The Ontario cities generally rank high on this component.
(5) The fifth dimension principally indexed the service function of many older and comparatively isolated communities, such as Quebec City, Halifax, N.S., and

TABLE 3.9. SELECTED CHARACTERISTICS USED IN THE MULTIVARIATE ANALYSIS OF CANADIAN CITIES, 1961

Demographic Variables
Percent women aged 15–39
Percent total population aged 14 and under
Percent total population French ethnic origin
Number of males per 100 females
Population immigrating from overseas in previous decade

Social Variables
City population density
Percent occupied dwellings single detached
Percent occupied dwellings occupied over 10 years
Percent occupied dwellings needing major repairs
Median value of dwellings
Percent wage-earners earning over $4,000 annually

Economic Variables
Percent total population in active labor force
Percent total labor force in primary industry
Percent manufacturing labor force in textiles, clothing, etc.
Percent total labor force in manufacturing
Percent labor force in proprietary, managerial, and professional occupations

Locational Variables
Distance to nearest central city of a metropolitan area
Having port facilities
Located on Canadian National Railways network
Number of cities in 100 mile radius
Number of through highways

Source: King (1966), Table 3.

St. Johns, Newfoundland. It is interesting to note that the cities of Ontario generally rank low on this dimension.
(6) This component stressed the importance of what may be generally referred to as urban depression as one of the basic ways in which cities vary one from another.

The remaining five dimensions were much more difficult to interpret and can perhaps best be considered as being mainly of a statistical interest.

CITY GROUPINGS IN 1961

In 1961, then, the 106 Canadian cities could be differentiated on the basis of their scores on each of these eleven underlying dimensions. Using these scores as coordinates, each city could be plotted in an abstract, eleven-dimensional classification space. Cities having roughly similar scores on the different dimensions would cluster together in this. The application of a mathematical grouping technique then enabled these clusters of generally similar cities to be identified. In this way King suggested that the 106 cities could be classified into eleven distinct groups as shown in Table 3.10. Perhaps the most interesting aspect of the resulting grouping is its fairly close correspondence to accepted broad regional divisions of Canada.

The first two groups contain what may be thought of as the eastern frontier industrial cities. The eight cities comprising Group 1 generally have high scores on the first and second dimensions but rank low on the third component. The low rank on the third dimension is also characteristic of the important metal producing cities contained in Group 2. Since the cities in this group, with the

TABLE 3.10. CITY GROUPINGS, CANADA, 1961

Frontier Industrial Cities	
Group 1.	**Group 2.**
Chicoutimi, Que.	Arvida, Que.
Rouyn, Que.	Glace Bay, N.S.
Jonquiere, Que.	New Waterford, N.S.
Thetford, Que.	Sault Ste. Marie, Ont.
Edmunston, N.B.	Trail, B.C.
Rimouski, Que.	Sydney, N.S.
Hull, Que.	Sudbury, Ont.
Timmins, Ont.	
Southern Ontario Residential	
Group 3.	
Barrie, Ont.	Brantford, Ont.
Orillia, Ont.	Guelph, Ont.
Trenton, Ont.	Brockville, Ont.
Belleville, Ont.	Peterborough, Ont.
Chatham, Ont.	Woodstock, Ont.
St. Thomas, Ont.	Waterloo, Ont.
Owen Sound, Ont.	Galt, Ont.
Stratford, Ont.	Kitchener, Ont.
Niagara Falls, Ont.	
Quebec Cities	
Group 4.	
Cap de la Madeleine, Que.	Joliette, Que.
Grand'Mere, Que.	St. Hyacinthe, Que.
Magog, Que.	St. Jean, Que.
Victoriaville, Que.	Trois Rivieres, Que.
Sorel, Que.	Jacques Cartier, Que.
Drummondville, Que.	Montreal North, Que.
Granby, Que.	St. Michel, Que.
St. Jerome, Que.	Cornwall, Ont.
Valleyfield, Que.	
Service Centers	
Group 5.	
Brandon, Man.	Pembroke, Ont.
Regina, Sas.	Calgary, Alb.
Saskatoon, Sas.	Edmonton, Alb.
Lethbridge, Alb.	St. Boniface, Man.
Medicine Hat, Alb.	Winnipeg, Man.
Moose Jaw, Sas.	Vancouver, B.C.
Prince Albert, Sas.	North Bay, Ont.
Penticton, B.C.	Ottawa, Ont.
Charlottetown, P.E.I.	London, Ont.
Fredericton, N.B.	Kingston, Ont.
Truro, N.S.	Moncton, N.B.

TABLE 3.10. (Continued)

Metropolitan Complexes	
Group 6.	**Group 7.**
Montreal, Que.	Forest Hill, Ont.
Toronto, Ont.	Leaside, Ont.
	Mount Royal, Que.
	Outremont, Que.
	Westmount, Que.
Heterogeneous Groups	
Group 8.	**Group 9.**
Dartmouth, N.S.	Fort William, Ont.
Levis, Que.	Port Arthur, Ont.
Halifax, N.S.	New Westminster, B.C.
St. Johns, Nfld.	North Vancouver, B.C.
Saint John, N.B.	Victoria, B.C.
Eastview, Ont.	Oshawa, Ont.
Quebec City, Que.	St. Catherines, Ont.
Verdun, Que.	Windsor, Ont.
Hamilton, Ont.	
New Toronto, Ont.	**Group 10.**
Mimico, Ont.	Sherbrooke, Que.
Lachine, Que.	
Longueuil, Que.	**Group 11.**
La Salle, Ont.	Sillery, Que.
St. Laurent, Que.	
Sarnia, Ont.	
Shawinigan, Que.	

Source: King (1966), Table 4.

exception of Arvida, are all outside Quebec, they also rank low on dimension two. This cluster of frontier industrial cities was also a notable feature in the grouping of cities in 1951. The fact that they have remained distinct over the decade 1951 to 1961 perhaps suggests that the urban system in Canada is not a highly connected one, but rather that it is relatively immature. These cities are therefore strongly dependent on the processing of natural resources or on a particular basic industrial function. This dependence is reflected in their demographic, social, and economic character, which is distinctly different from that of the more diverse and mature cities found elsewhere in Canada.

The distinctive feature about cities in Group 3 is their regional concentration in southern Ontario. The most outstanding feature is their high scores on the fourth dimension, that of high socioeconomic residential status. King suggests that these cities form a well developed subsystem which is relatively homogeneous in terms of the urban characteristics included in the study. A similar regional concentration and homogeneity in structure is also typical of the cities in Group 4, which for the most part contains the smaller cities in Quebec. Without exception, the cities in this group rank relatively high on the first two urban dimensions.

In contrast, the cities comprising Groups 5, 6, and 7 are distinguished not as much by their regional concentration as by their type. Thus Group 5 contains cities that function predominantly as service centers of one kind or another. As such they rank high on the fifth urban dimension—the service function of older and comparatively isolated communities. Groups 6 and 7 reflect the growing dominance of the two largest Canadian metropolitan areas, Toronto and Montreal. The two central cities themselves combine to form Group 6, while their higher socioeconomic status suburbs cluster together to form Group 7. Interpretation of the remaining groups is not so easy in terms of either locational association or functional type. They can best be described as being of heterogeneous character.

CONCLUSION

In this section we have noted that urban functional specialization is a distinctive feature of the city system. The identification of different types of cities is based on their classification, which consequently is an important and necessary feature in urban study. The examples have illustrated the variety of approaches to the problem of identifying city types and the variation in the results which they generate. Because of this it is important to stress again that there is no such thing as a best classification and to reiterate that any classification can only be evaluated in the context of the problem for which it was devised. The unfortunate thing is, as the examples have shown, that all too often the identification of city types and functions has been undertaken without any specific problem in mind.

SETTLEMENTS AND INTERACTION

4

Settlements do not, and cannot, exist in isolation. The people and activities they contain interact with those at other places to result in an extremely complex pattern of linkages and contacts. The need for interaction has been hinted at in the previous chapters, and it is through these contacts that urban areas are integrated into a functional system. It is, moreover, the various kinds of interaction that ultimately makes possible the spatial division of labor essential for urban functional specialization discussed in the last chapter. In this chapter we extend the discussion of the settlement pattern by focusing attention on the contacts between a city and the area surrounding it and on the pattern of linkages and contacts between cities themselves. Some of the basic principles and concepts are discussed and the more general models of interaction are introduced.

SOME BASIC CONSIDERATIONS

The basic principles and concepts concerning interaction include: the friction of distance, transferability, the principle of least effort, intervening opportunities and complementarity. Although they interact with each other, they can be discussed separately.

THE FRICTION OF DISTANCE

In separating locations from each other, distance exerts an attenuating effect on interaction. This effect is widely known as the *friction of distance*, and it gives rise to an inverse relationship between interaction and distance. Two examples of this are shown in Figure 4.1. In the first the fall-off of the volume of Class I railroad freight movements with distances up to 1,500 miles is shown for the continental United States (Fig. 4.1A). On a smaller scale the second shows a comparable kind of decay for the number of truck trips within a 350-mile radius of Chicago (Fig. 4.1B). Although some form of distance decay is a general characteristic of all spatial behavior, the degree of friction exerted by distance varies depending on the type of interaction. Some movements are more sensitive to the effects of distance than others. On graphs like those shown in Figure 4.1, this is reflected by the slope of the line that best fits the scatter of dots—the steeper the slope, the greater the frictional effect of distance and hence the rate of distance–decay.

TRANSFERABILITY

Differences in the sensitivity of movement to the effect of distance are most clearly revealed when actual physical flows are involved. For people the degree of sensitivity largely depends on the frequency and purpose of trips; for goods it depends on the type of product being moved. For all types of interaction, sensitivity is also directly or indirectly related to the mode of transportation or communication used. The fact that different products move with unequal ease is a particularly noticeable feature in the pattern of commodity flows and is related to the transferability of a product. In introducing this concept, Ullman (1956) did not give it any precise definition but simply said that it was related to distance,

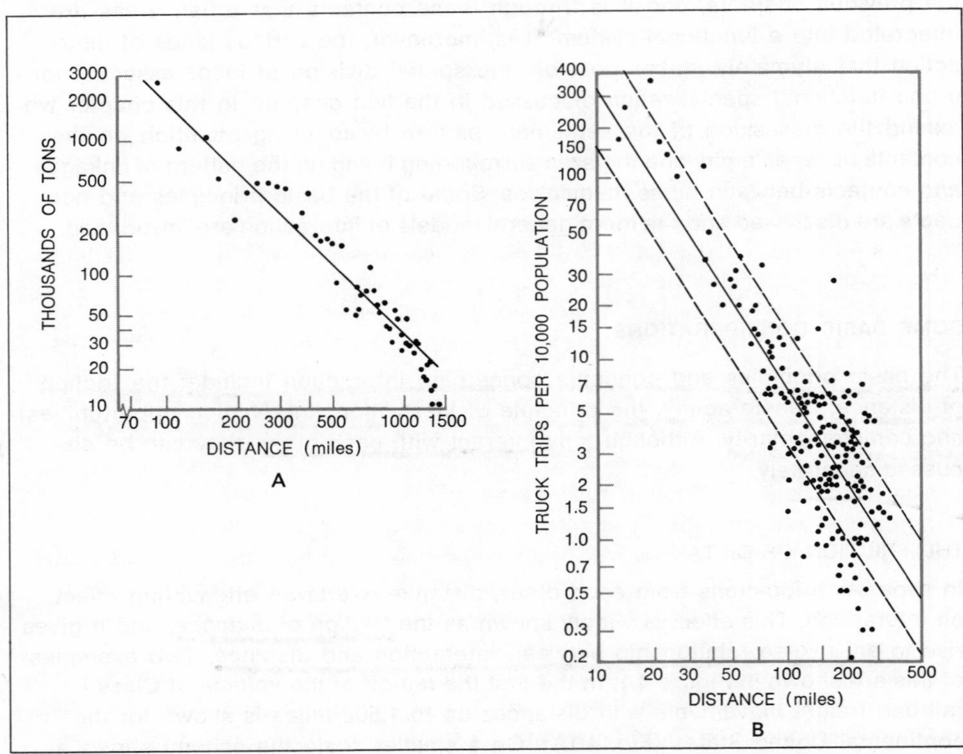

FIG. 4.1. DISTANCE-DECAY REGULARITIES FOR CLASS I RAILROAD SHIPMENTS IN THE UNITED STATES (A), AND THE NUMBER OF TRUCK TRIPS IN THE CHICAGO REGION (B). (*Source:* After Isard, 1956, Fig. 12, and Helvig, 1964, Fig. 18.)

measured in real terms of transfer time and costs. It is, however, clear that the transferability of a product is largely a function of its specific value; that is, its value per unit weight. Table 4.1 shows a very good example of the effect of specific value on transferability. The generalization stemming from this and other research is that low-value products generally move short distances, whereas high-value products move relatively longer distances. Although the concept of transferability is most applicable to flows of goods, it can be thought of as a general notion for the study of spatial interaction. For example, a similar transferability effect is typical of shopping trips. People are normally only prepared to

TABLE 4.1. RELATIVE TRANSFERABILITY OF THREE TIMBER PRODUCTS

	Timber Products		
	Veneer Logs	Pulpwood	Mine Props
Specific value*	150	20	5
Maximum railroad haul in miles	400	100	25

* Dollars per ton.
Source: Haggett (1965), p. 41.

travel short distances to purchase low-value goods but much farther to purchase more expensive items (see Chapter 7).

THE PRINCIPLE OF LEAST EFFORT

The friction of distance and transferability are expressions of the fact that movement involves costs. These can be measured in a variety of ways. Obvious examples are the time it takes to travel a given distance, or the physical effort this requires. Ultimately, however, it is the economics of distance that really matters. Distance may be thought of as an inconvenience with a dollar sign attached. The details of the relationship between dollars and distance are extremely complex and vary with type of interaction, and modes used, and the characteristics of the transportation and communications networks involved (see Chapter 6). In some circumstances costs of movement may be more or less independent of distance because transportation companies have the ability to manipulate the prices charged. In this way the friction of distance may be increased or decreased and transferability radically altered.

Since the inconveniencing effects of distance cannot be avoided altogether, attempts can at least be made to reduce them as much as possible. This notion of least movement has occurred in various forms in many disciplines, ranging from classical physics to operations research. In the social sciences, it was introduced by Zipf (1949) as the "principle of least effort." Although he defined effort in a rather special way, it is considered more widely by urban geographers to include any inconvenience of distance. In this way, the principle can be more generally interpreted as that of distance-minimization.

Distance-minimization forms a basic building block for many location and interaction models in urban geography (Yeates, 1963). In its strictest interpretation, the concept assumes that human beings are rational and that economic factors govern their behavior. In a spatial context, decisions are made so as to minimize costs since "the minimization of cost is the controlling force" in space relationships. Although this is a convenient argument for conceptual purposes, empirical observations suggest that interaction patterns rarely correspond to this ideal. This is illustrated in Figure 4.2 for patterns of interstate flows of aluminum bar. The actual flow is shown in Figure 4.2A. The pattern that would occur if the total distances involved were minimized is presented in Figure 4.2B. Comparison of the two maps clearly indicates that actual flows are far from optimal, implying that interaction is considerably more complex than envisaged by the principle of least effort.

Men are not entirely rational beings who act wholly within an optimizing framework. But neither are men fools who completely disregard the effect distance has on their spatial behavior. Hence although distance may not be minimized in interaction, it is fair to assume that attempts are made to reduce its inconvenience as much as possible and that this distance-reduction behavior is an important element underlying patterns of spatial interaction. For example, distance-reduction behavior is one of the factors involved in distance-decay regularities.

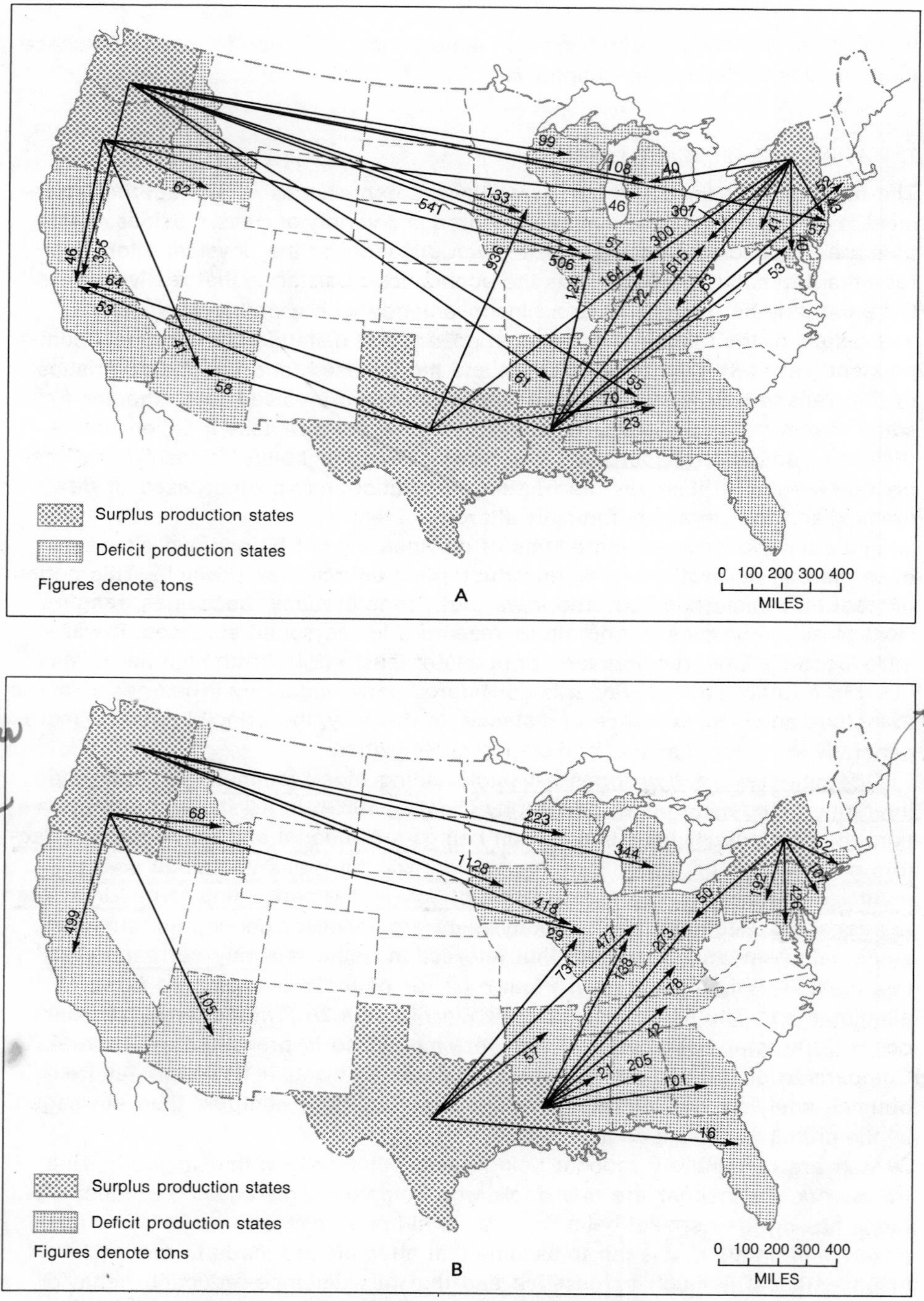

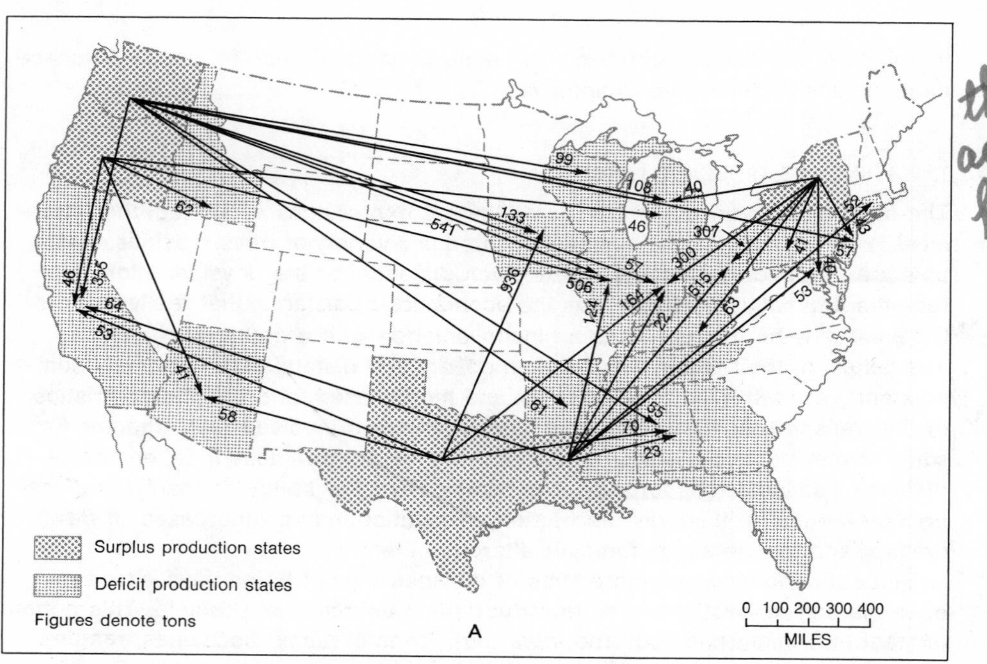

Surplus production states

Deficit production states

Figures denote tons

0 100 200 300 400

MILES

B

FIG. 4.2. INTERSTATE FLOWS OF ALUMINUM BAR, UNITED STATES. THE ACTUAL PATTERN OF FLOWS (A) BEARS LITTLE RESEMBLANCE TO THAT WHICH SHOULD OCCUR IF ALL DISTANCES WERE MINIMIZED (B). (*Source:* Cox, 1965. Figs. 2 and 3.)

INTERVENING OPPORTUNITIES

A concept allied to distance-minimization is that of *intervening opportunities*. These can be thought of as acting in two ways to result in a kind of place substitution. First, as a direct way of reducing the costs associated with distance, nearby places are substituted for those farther away. This effect of intervening opportunities is a particularly noticeable feature of the pattern of commodity flows. For example, at the end of the last century, few forest products moved from the Pacific Northwest to the Eastern Seaboard, despite the existence of cheap water transportation between the two regions. This can be explained by the fact that the then extensive forest resources of the Great Lakes region were better placed to serve the demands for timber in the urban East. The Great Lakes region acted as an intervening opportunity for the supply of forest products which made possible a considerable reduction in the delivered price of timber at eastern cities.

Secondly, intervening opportunities can be thought of as a kind of filter affecting movements, particularly the movements of people, and one which indirectly brings about place substitution. For example, there would most probably be a much higher degree of interaction between Boston and Philadelphia were it not for the fact that New York is located between them to siphon off what might otherwise be through traffic. The filter effect of intervening opportunities is a particularly important factor in understanding migration patterns and is generally important as an underlying factor in distance-decay regularities.

COMPLEMENTARITY

A final consideration concerns the conditions required for interaction to occur between places. Although the need for interaction arises from the fact that people and activities are concentrated to varying degree at specific locations, which are separated by distance, this in itself is not necessarily sufficient to actually bring about interaction. Something else is needed. Ullman (1956) has suggested that this something else is *complementarity*. This concept states quite simply that interaction only occurs between specific places when there is a supply at one and a demand at the other. Specific complementarity between places in supply and demand terms therefore forms the underlying basis of interaction.

Admittedly complementarity is most applicable to the flow of goods and materials between cities, but like transferability it can be considered a general notion relevant for flows of people and messages, especially when these are in conjunction with economic activities.

NODAL REGIONS

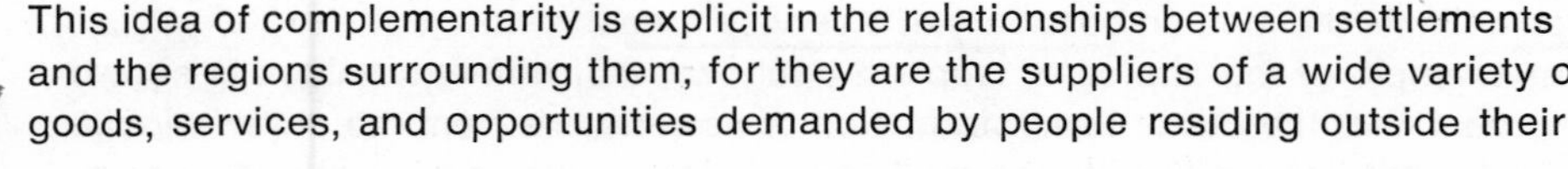

This idea of complementarity is explicit in the relationships between settlements and the regions surrounding them, for they are the suppliers of a wide variety of goods, services, and opportunities demanded by people residing outside their built-up areas. On the basis of the interaction that results, each city can be considered the core of a wider nodal region over which it exerts a dominating influence. As distance increases away from the city, its influence weakens as a result of the combined effects of the friction of distance, transferability, and least effort; and eventually the influence of another city becomes dominant over the closer area surrounding it. The nodal regions centered on cities may be delimited on the basis of either a single criterion or many criteria considered together. We shall refer to the former, single-feature nodal regions as *service areas*, and the latter, multiple-feature nodal regions as *tributary areas.*

SERVICE AREAS

The service areas of a city may be delimited using a wide variety of criteria. Examples might be the city's wholesale area, the distribution area of its newspapers, its milk delivery area, the area served by its radio or television stations, the catchment areas of its retail stores and other service functions, its commuting area, and so on. The choice among the various alternatives will depend on the size of the city and on the purpose of study. That city size should be an important consideration follows from our discussion of the urban hierarchy in Chapter 2. Cities at higher levels in the hierarchy supply more specialized services for larger surrounding areas. For these, wholesale and newspaper distribution areas may best represent the city's sphere of influence. Conversely, the more restricted influence of smaller, lower level cities may be indicated by such indexes as their retail service or high school catchment areas.

Boundary problems Regardless of the specific criteria used, a city's service areas all share one thing in common: they are theoretically continuous in extent. Unlike, for example, administrative areas that have discrete limits, they are unbounded. This feature is demonstrated diagrammatically in Figure 4.3, which shows a cross section through an idealized service area. The diagram also indicates a second important aspect of service areas; they have a very rapid fall-off close to the city and a very slow, almost asymptotic fall-off toward the periphery.

Since nodal regions are theoretically continuous, it is not possible to describe them on the basis of their absolute outer limits. Instead, subjectively determined boundaries must be drawn to delimit them for analytical purposes. Because of the gradational nature of field intensity, a series of boundaries can be selected. These can be thought of as comprising a series of isopleths of descending value outward from the center. The value of the particular isopleth selected will depend on many things, but since it is generally the innermost, intensive part of the service area that is most representative of the city's influence, higher rather than lower values are normally used. Frequently, the 50 percent isopleth is selected which delimits the median boundary of a service area.

An example of the choice of isopleth boundaries of different values is shown in Figure 4.4 for the out-of-town circulation of newspapers from the city of Mobile, Ala. The inner line represents the median boundary enclosing the intensive part

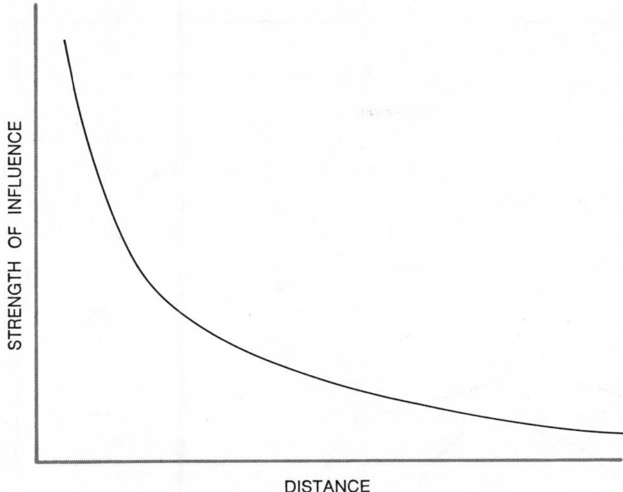

FIG. 4.3. CROSS SECTION OF AN IDEALIZED SERVICE AREA.

of the field. Within this area Mobile newspapers account for at least 50 percent of the out-of-town circulation. The declining influence of Mobile with distance is indicated by the location of the second, outer boundary. This encloses the area within which Mobile's newspapers have at least 20 percent of the total out-of-town circulation. This example also illustrates the difficult problems of generalizing about the extent of a city's influence over the area surrounding it. Quite clearly, the size of a service area varies depending on the particular boundary selected.

A second example of the use of isopleth boundaries is shown in Figure 4.5 to illustrate the limiting effect that competition from another center has on the extent of a city's sphere of influence. The isopleths on this map pertain to the number of telephone calls generated in southern New England to New York City and Boston. The line of equal influence of the two centers is indicated by the location of the median boundary. This is generally closer to Boston than it is to New York, indicating that the influence of larger cities normally extends over a wider area than that of smaller cities. The location of the isopleths also demonstrates the way in which the intensity of service areas declines with distance away from the focus and shows that, in competition, the influence of different centers overlaps.

The transferability effect Although the distance-decay characteristic of nodal regions in Figure 4.3 is typical of all kinds of interaction, the specific form of the curve varies depending on the particular criterion under consideration. Thus for some activities the curve may be steeper; for others it may be shallower. This might be thought of as resulting from a general transferability effect on interaction.

As a result of this, the size of service areas measured by their median boundaries

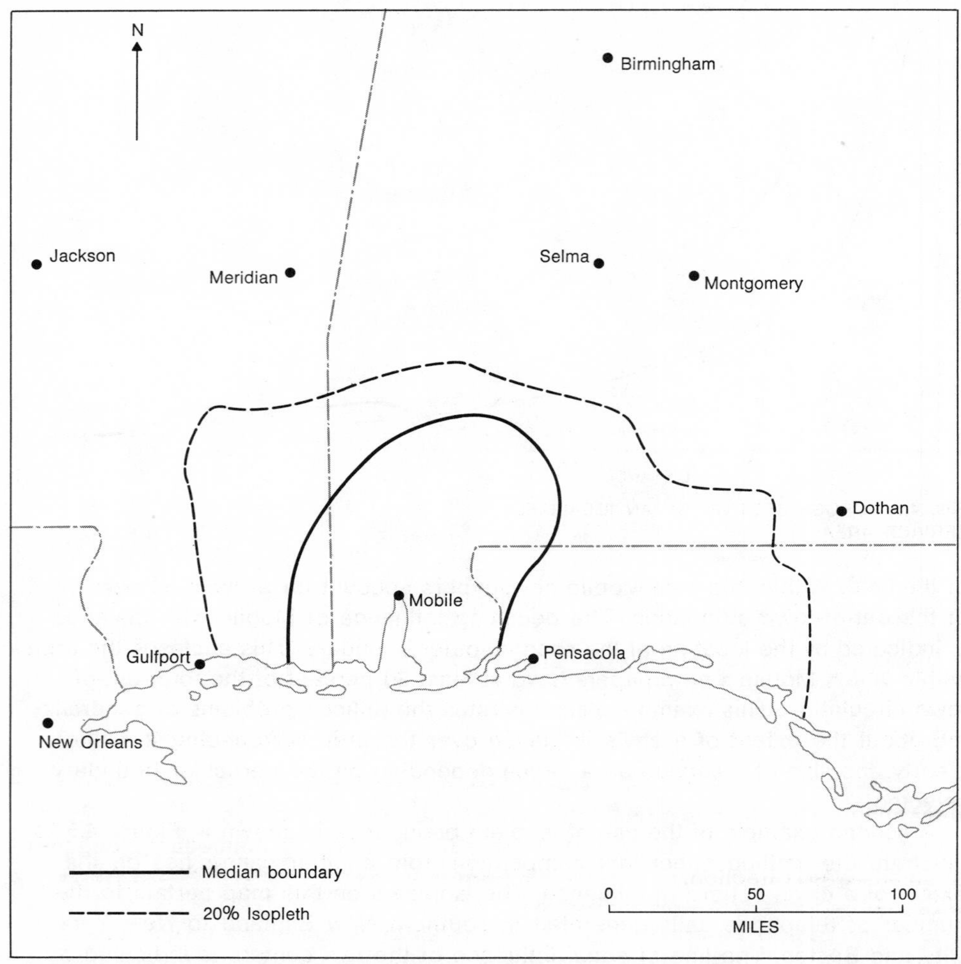

FIG. 4.4. THE MEDIAN AND 20.0 PERCENT BOUNDARIES FOR THE NEWSPAPER NEWSPAPER SERVICE AREAS OF MOBILE, ALA. (*Source:* After Ullman, 1943, Fig. 7.)

varies for different activities. This is shown for a number of different functions in Figure 4.6. The median boundary for Mobile's retail service area encloses a rather compact area immediately adjacent to the city, a fact that reflects the high friction of distance associated with shopping journeys. In contrast the median boundary for the wholesale distribution of drugs, a higher-level function, lies considerably farther away from the city. Between these two extremes, the areas for newspaper circulation, wholesale grocery, wholesale meat, and wholesale produce are arranged in order of generally increasing size. The map also indicates that the intensity of a particular service area declines at different rates depending on direction from the city. The result of this is that fields vary in

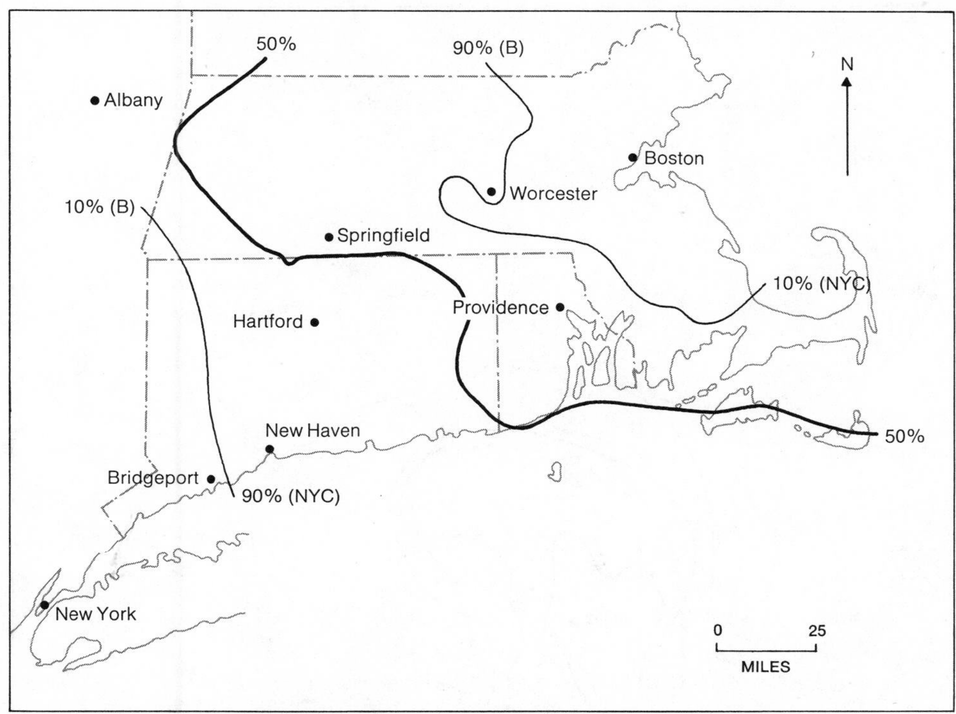

FIG. 4.5. TELEPHONE HINTERLAND BOUNDARIES IN SOUTHERN NEW ENGLAND. (*Source:* After Green, 1955, Fig. 5.)

their shape. Thus Mobile's retailing service area extends more to the west of the city than to the east. In contrast the wholesale drug area is noticeably elongated in an eastward direction.

The shape of service areas On a perfectly uniform plane and if distance-minimization were the controlling force in interaction, then the ideal shape of service areas would be a perfect circle. Given all the imperfections of the real world, it is perhaps not surprising to find that this ideal is only rarely found. In reality, service areas generally tend to be more amoeba–like with lobes and indentations. Nevertheless, despite these distortions, there is abundant evidence suggesting that they often approximate something like a circular form. This is generally the case, for example, for those shown in Figure 4.6. Under certain conditions, however, the shapes of service areas have been noted to depart quite markedly from anything like a circular form. Haggett (1965) has drawn attention to two commonly found types: truncated and distorted service areas.

Truncation occurs when the influence of a center is constrained by a barrier. Perhaps the classic example of this was that given by Lösch (1954) for the financial sphere of influence of El Paso, Texas, reproduced here in Figure 4.7.

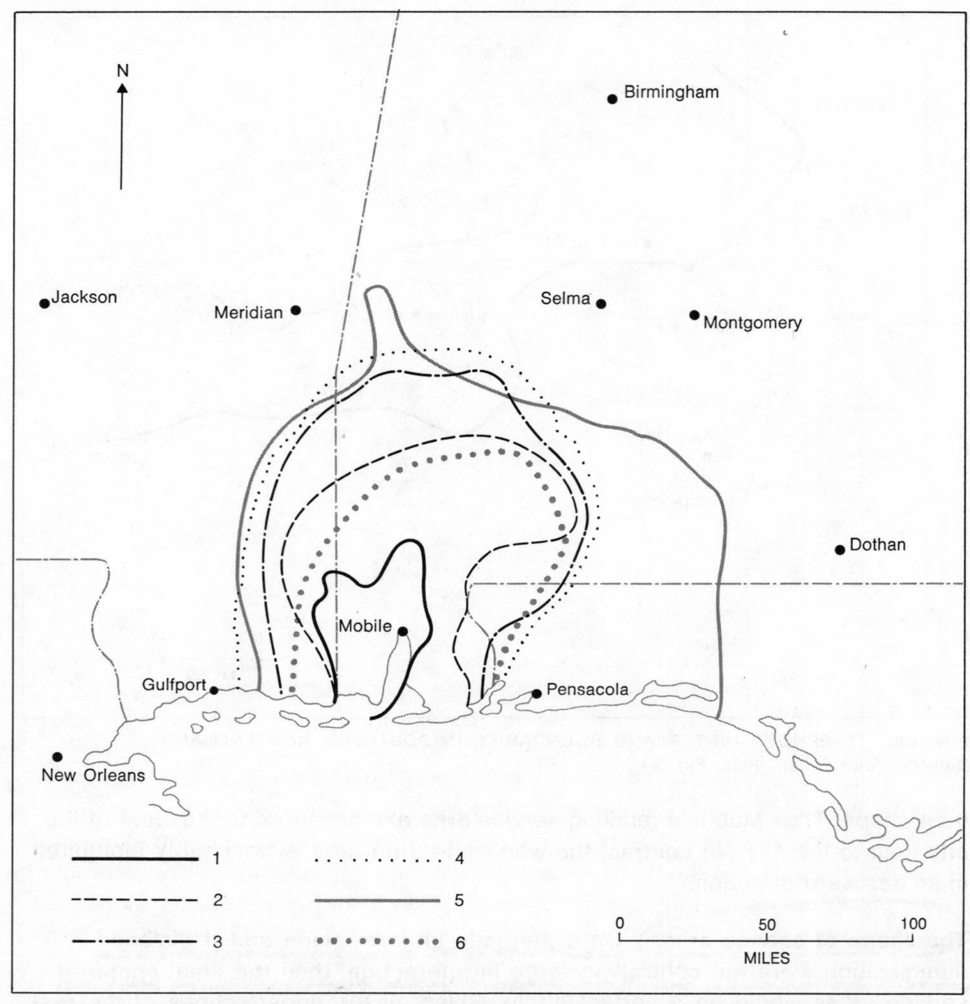

FIG. 4.6. SELECTED SERVICE AREAS OF MOBILE, ALABAMA. MEDIAN BOUNDARIES ARE SHOWN FOR (1) RETAIL TRADE, (2) WHOLESALE GROCERY, (3) WHOLESALE MEAT, (4) WHOLESALE PRODUCE, (5) WHOLESALE DRUG BUSINESS, AND (6) NEWSPAPER CIRCULATION. (*Source:* After Ullman, 1943, Fig. 7.)

On the map each dot represents a bank keeping an account at a central bank in El Paso. The presence of the international boundary restricts this city's influence to the south, so that the extent of the field on the Mexican side is only about half that of the corresponding part in Texas. In effect the cities south of the border are much farther away from El Paso than is indicated by their physical distances. The barrier effect is not only confined to political boundaries but can result from natural barriers, such as unbridged rivers, extensive swamps, mountain ranges, besides artificially induced economic barriers like tolls. The

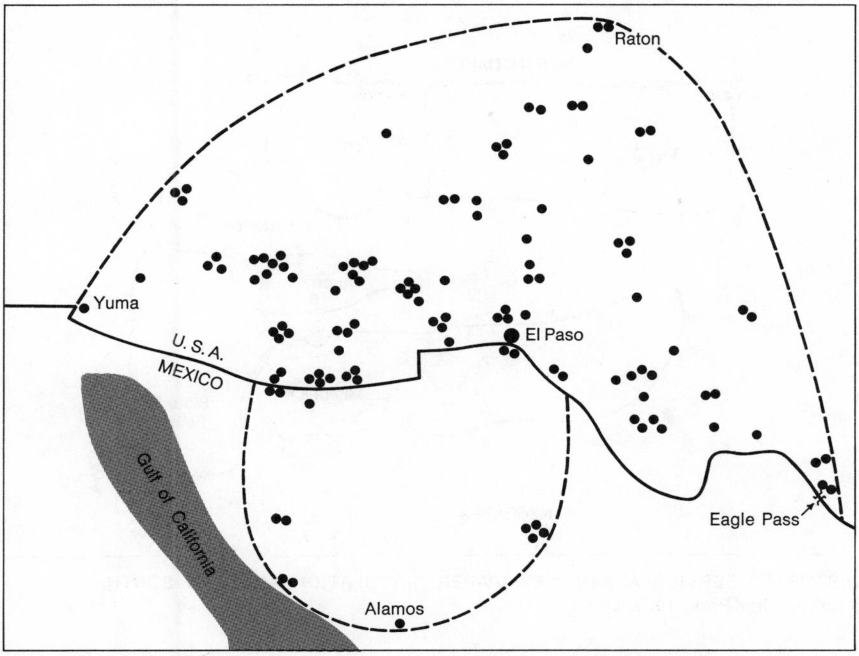

FIG. 4.7. A TRUNCATED SERVICE AREA: THE FINANCIAL SPHERE OF INFLUENCE OF EL PASO, TEXAS. (*Source:* Lösch, 1954, Fig. 86.)

effect of the latter has been noted by Vance (1962) to be an important feature affecting the shape of trade areas in the Bay Region of San Francisco.

Distortion occurs for a variety of reasons. A common example is the elongation of service areas in the direction away from a competing center. This is particularly evident in the pattern of newspaper circulation areas in South Dakota. Figure 4.8 shows how the fields for Aberdeen, Huron, and Mitchell are considerably more extensive in a westerly direction away from the competing influence of Sioux Falls and Watertown, and the larger centers off the map to the east.

Changes in the size of service areas The size and shape of service areas are not static, but are subject to variation through time. One of the principal reasons for this is that cities themselves change in size. As they grow larger, their influence normally extends over a wider area. Another reason is that many activities have become increasingly more concentrated at fewer cities to result in their larger spheres of influence. The ultimate factor, however, underlying changes in size of service areas is the revolution that has taken place in transportation and communication. The reduced friction of distance brought about by newer forms of transportation and communications media has generally resulted in the extension of the influence of cities, and particularly the larger ones, over increasingly wider areas.

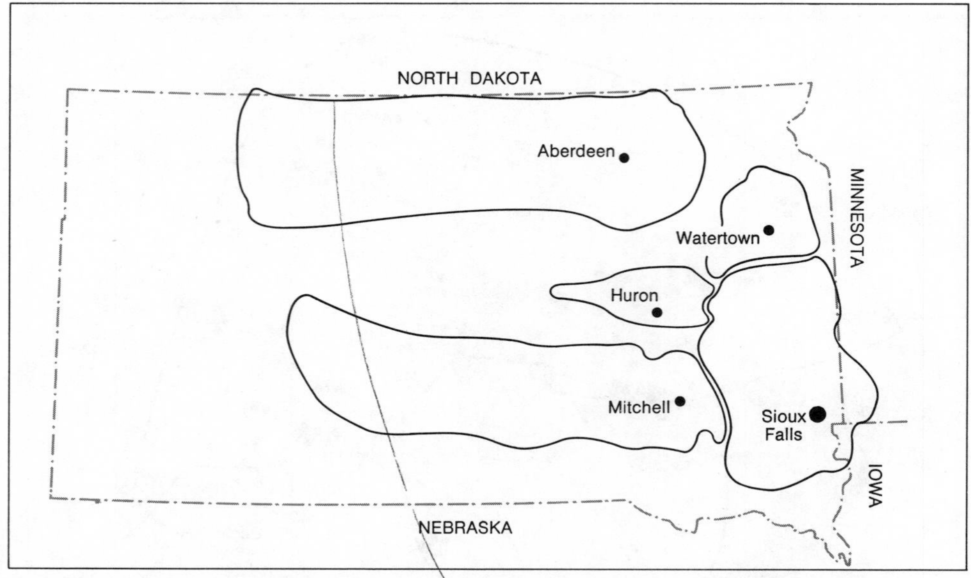

FIG. 4.8. DISTORTED SERVICE AREAS: NEWSPAPER CIRCULATION AREAS IN SOUTH DAKOTA. (*Source:* After Park, 1929, Chart X.)

This effect of changing mobility has particularly affected the size of retail trade and commuting areas of cities. Vance (1960) has documented the changing extent of the commuting field for Natick, Mass. The results of his investigation are presented in Figure 4.9 for Natick's *employment field,* defined as the area in which residents of Natick travel to work. At the end of the last century, Natick's employment field was restricted to the neighboring municipalities along the railroad. With the coming of the street railroad in 1885, the pattern began to change; and by 1915 residents of Natick were traveling to work to towns in a much wider, but still essentially linear, zone around Natick. By 1931 the improved mobility brought about by the automobile was clearly visible. The effect of this was to fill in the gaps unserved by the street railroad (which by this time had nearly all been abandoned) and to push the outer boundary of the field farther away from the city. Finally, by 1951, Natick's employment field, which was at this time more or less completely automobile-oriented, extended over an amorphous area of about 1,200 square miles.

TRIBUTARY AREAS

If several representative single-feature nodal regions focusing on a particular city are delimited and superimposed over each other on a map, it is possible to outline in a general way the boundary of the area over which the city exerts a more or less total dominance. This multiple-feature nodal region is variously referred to as the city's tributary area, trade area, hinterland, or urban field.

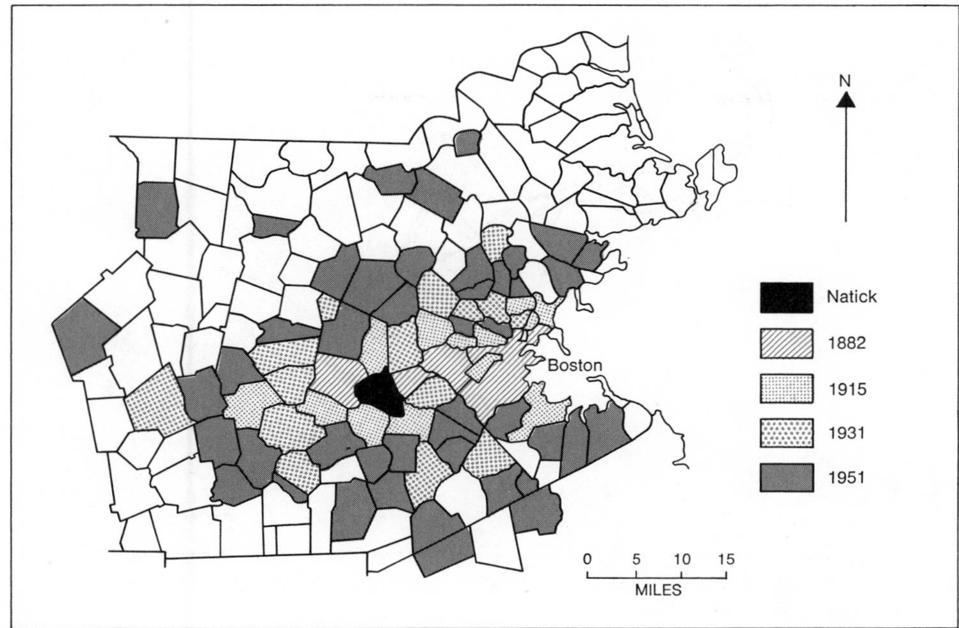

FIG. 4.9. CHANGES IN THE EXTENT OF THE EMPLOYMENT FIELD FOR NATICK, MASS., 1882–1951. (*Source:* Vance, 1960, Fig. 5.)

Tributary areas may be delimited using a variety of different methods, each of which has its difficulties and shortcomings. A commonly adopted method is that of locating what may be called the *modal boundary*. In this method the boundaries of several individual service areas are established first, and then the modal boundary is located so as to pass through the zone where the individual boundaries roughly coincide.

This was the approach adopted by Green (1955) to locate the hinterland boundary between New York City and Boston. In this study, Green mapped seven functional indicators: the purchase of railroad coach tickets; an estimate of truck freight movements to New York and Boston; metropolitan newspaper circulation; long distance telephone calls; the origin of vacationers; the business addresses of directors of major firms; and the metropolitan correspondents for banks in southern New England. The median boundaries that Green located for five of these functional indicators together with the modal boundary that generalizes them are shown in Figure 4.10A; and the hinterlands that were finally established using this method are illustrated in Figure 4.10B.

It is quite clear from this example, as it is from others, that it is difficult to generalize the gradational nature of a city's spheres of influence with a single-line boundary of this kind. Since the many service-area boundaries rarely follow each other closely, the use of the modal-boundary method can at best only be considered as a highly subjective approximation to the overall tributary area

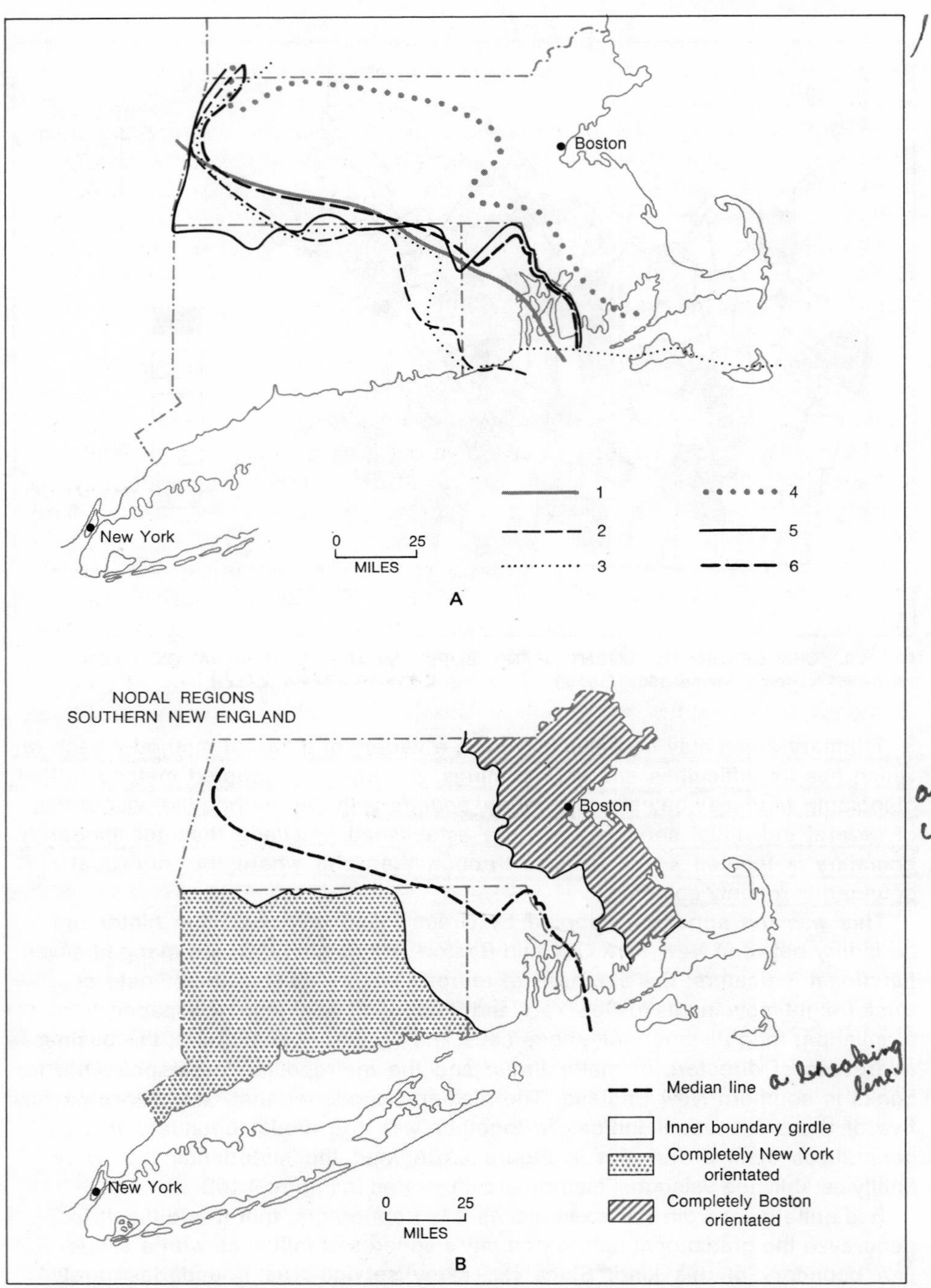

FIG. 4.10. HINTERLAND DELIMITATION. (A) THE MODAL BOUNDARY (6) BETWEEN NEW YORK CITY AND BOSTON IS BASED ON THE MEDIAN BOUNDARIES FOR (1) RAILROAD COACH PASSENGER FLOWS, (2) NEWSPAPER CIRCULATION, (3) TELEPHONE CALLS, (4) BUSINESS ADDRESSES OF DIRECTORS OF MANUFACTURING FIRMS, AND (5) CORRESPONDENT BANKS. (B) THE RESULTING HINTERLANDS FOR NEW YORK CITY AND BOSTON. (*Source:* After Green, 1955, Figs. 3, 4, 5, 7, 8, and 9.)

of the city. It is perhaps most applicable for delimiting the trade areas of small central places (see Chapter 7), for which it is possible to undertake intensive and detailed field work.

When tributary areas are to be delimited for a number of cities, and particularly those at higher levels in the hierarchy, it is, however, impossible to undertake such detailed investigations of the relationships between cities and their tributary regions. Consequently a number of shortcuts have been proposed to outline the limits of urban trade areas. A usual method is to select only one index thought to be particularly representative of the relationships between city and region, such as local bus flows, wholesale trade areas, and newspaper circulation areas.

Although it is obvious that no one single index will ever be entirely satisfactory for delimiting tributary areas, data on newspaper circulation has a number of distinct advantages. First, this information is often readily available for the whole country, as for example from the data compiled by the Audit Bureau of Circulation for the United States. Secondly and more importantly, the contents of newspapers are a very good indication of the social, political, and economic ties between a city and the people living in its area of circulation. Its opinion columns represent the city's political outlook; advertisements inform people about the goods, services, entertainments, and other activities offered by the city; while news and features of a local appeal help keep readers informed about the happenings in the city. Hence the newspaper is an important factor in developing a community of interest within a city's tributary area. An early attempt at delimiting the hinterlands of metropolitan centers in the United States, using newspaper circulation data, is shown in Figure 4.11.

The law of retail gravitation A different kind of shortcut method that has been widely used in the delimitation of tributary areas is the more abstract approach proposed by Reilly (1931). This method, which was originally devised to outline the retail-trade area of a city, is based on the use of a simple mathematical formula instead of on the choice of a particular single service or functional indicator. Using the theory of gravitation from Newtonian physics as an analogy, Reilly argued that, all things being equal, two cities attract retail trade from any intermediate city or town approximately in direct proportion to the populations of the two cities and in inverse proportion to the square of the distances from these two cities to the intermediate town. The breaking point between two cities that are in competition for trade in their intermediate area can be determined quite simply from the following formula:

$$\text{Breaking point from City A} = \frac{\text{Distance between A and B}}{1 + \sqrt{\dfrac{\text{Population of City B}}{\text{Population of City A}}}}$$

The breaking point established by the use of this formula is the boundary where the attraction of the two competing cities is exactly equal.

An example will make clear the application of this restatement of Reilly's Law.

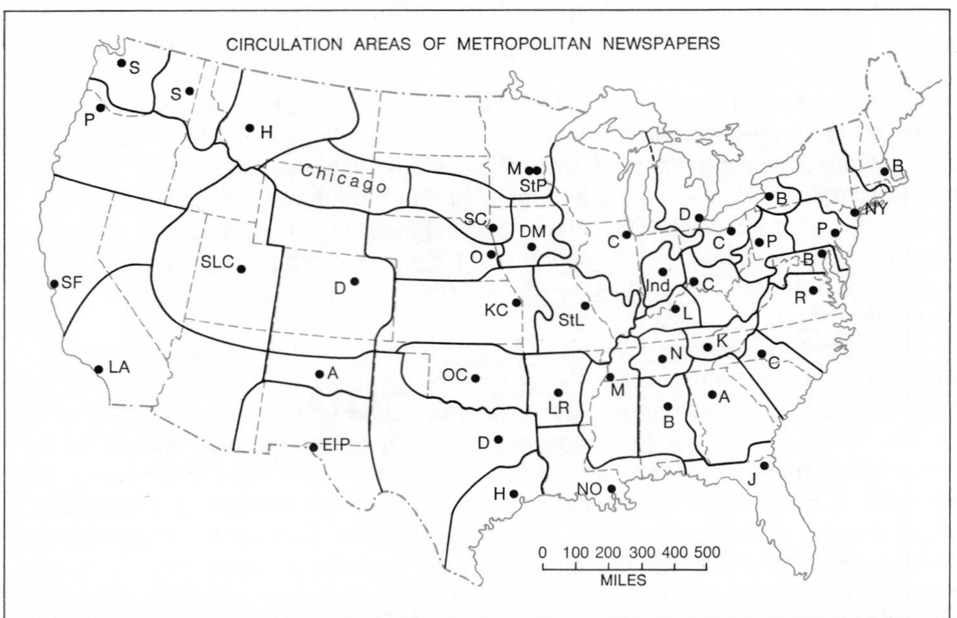

FIG. 4.11. METROPOLITAN TRIBUTARY AREAS IN THE UNITED STATES BASED ON NEWSPAPER CIRCULATION, 1933. (*Source:* After Park and Newcomb, 1933, Fig. 6.)

In 1960 the urbanized areas of St. Louis (City A) and Kansas City (City B) had populations of 1,667,693 and 921,121 respectively. These two cities are located 252 miles apart. Using the Reilly formula, the breaking point between them is:

$$\frac{252 \text{ miles}}{1 + \sqrt{\dfrac{921{,}121}{1{,}667{,}693}}}$$

which equals 144.6 miles. St. Louis would therefore be expected to capture retail trade in the area up to 144.6 miles in the direction of Kansas City. The fact that Kansas City dominates over a smaller distance is consistent with our generalization that smaller cities have more restricted tributary areas than larger ones.

The use of this formula as a shortcut method for determining the boundaries of tributary areas is of course restricted to the breaking point between only two cities. Thus to determine the complete trade area of a given city, the formula must be used to establish the breaking points between the city and all of its competitors. The breaking points calculated in this way can then be joined to indicate the extent of the city's trade area. An hypothetical example of the kind of tributary area resulting from this method is presented in Figure 4.12. It is quite clear from the geometrical shape of this example that the delimitation of tributary areas using this method must be considered as essentially diagrammatic

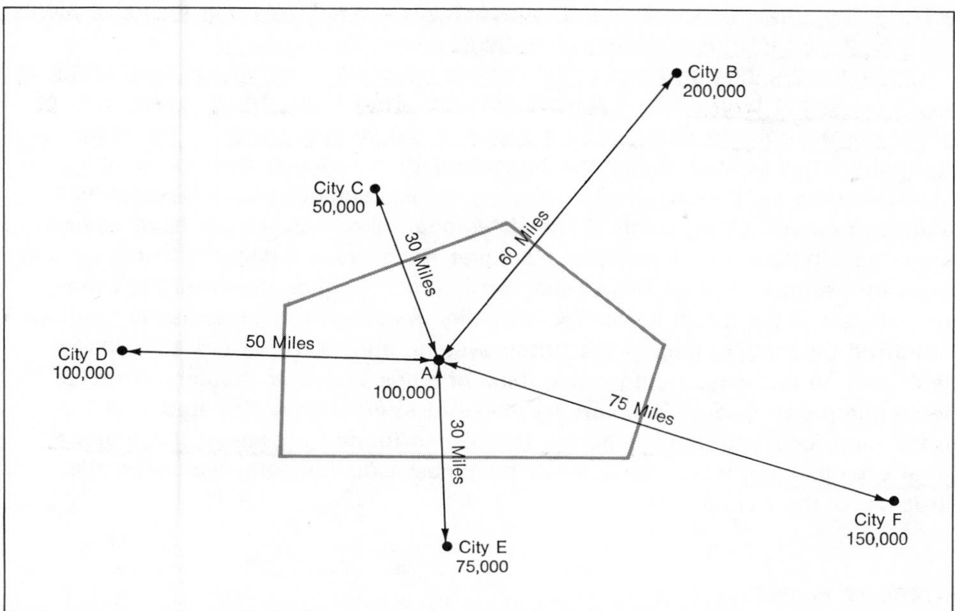

FIG. 4.12. HYPOTHETICAL TRIBUTARY AREA BASED ON REILLY'S LAW OF RETAIL GRAVITATION.

and only as a highly generalized representation of reality. This notwithstanding, the Reilly approach has proved a useful one in the study of spatial interaction.

THE MOSAIC OF TRADE AREAS

The influence that each city exerts over the surrounding countryside is reflected in the size of its tributary area. Normally this varies, as we have seen, with the size of the city. Thus the tributary areas of smaller cities are generally local in extent compared to the hinterland of a metropolis, which may often extend over many hundreds of square miles (see Fig. 4.11). If the tributary areas were to be delimited for all cities in a region and then superimposed on a map, the result would resemble something like a mosaic of overlapping nodal regions of varying size. The question then remains of how these varying-sized tributary areas fit together.

The answer is found in the notion of the urban hierarchy discussed in Chapter 2. There we noted that cities at the various levels in the hierarchy differed in both their population size and in the kinds of functions and activities they perform. The lower-level cities with their more general service provision consequently exert an influence over a more local area, which is reflected in their smaller tributary areas. By contrast, centers at higher levels in the hierarchy provide increasingly more specialized activities for much larger tributary areas. Moreover it was also pointed out that cities at higher levels in the hierarchy perform the functions of centers at successively lower levels, but for increasingly more restricted territories surrounding them.

Consequently the mosaic of nodal regions covering a region can be thought of ideally as being built up of layers of different-sized trade areas, each layer of which corresponds to cities and functions at the various levels in the urban hierarchy. Thus nested within the hinterland of a regional metropolis like Chicago, there are several smaller tributary areas, each of which is associated with the regional cities. Each of these regional cities will in turn have nested within its tributary area a number of smaller trade areas belonging to the smaller cities in the area. And so this nesting structure continues down through the lower levels in the urban hierarchy. In reality, however, this ideal nesting pattern is blurred by irregularities in the urban system, although it is not completely destroyed. In this way, then, we can think of cities and their tributary areas as being integrated through the various levels of interaction associated with the urban hierarchy into what Philbrick (1955) has termed a system of functional areal organization, which as a result becomes a fundamental feature in the structure of the city system.

INTERCITY FLOWS

Interaction within the city system is not confined to the relations between cities and their surrounding tributary areas. Equally important are the linkages and contacts, often over greater distances, between cities themselves. These intercity flows are of course implied in the idea of the nested hierarchy of the trade areas referred to above, and it is to a consideration of selected aspects of these that we now turn.

In highly urbanized societies such as the United States and Canada, the total volume of intercity interaction can only be described as phenomenal. Consider what is involved: the movements of goods and materials to industries and markets; the movements of people for business and pleasure; the flow of messages and information necessary for the various aspects of social, economic, and political life; and so on. Moreover, the volume of all kinds of interaction has increased in the comparatively recent past at a staggering rate. Some of the more obvious reasons for this are the continued concentration of people and activities into larger urban areas; the increasing complexity and scale of contemporary economic and social organization; and the increased level of mobility and spatial awareness resulting from improved living standards and technological developments in transportation and communication. In fact it is difficult to conceive of any change, whether it be technical, economic, political, or social, that does not ultimately have some direct effect on the volume and pattern of interaction between cities.

TOTAL VOLUMES

A general impression of the total magnitude of intercity freight and passenger traffic for the United States is given in Tables 4.2 and 4.3. Since 1940 the volume of intercity freight traffic has increased by about 170 percent to an all time high of 1.8 billion ton-miles. The increase in passenger traffic is just as staggering. In 1950 it amounted to 0.5 billion passenger-miles, whereas only seventeen years later in 1967 it totaled 1.02 billion passenger-miles. Exact details of intercity flows of messages and information are more difficult to obtain, but a general idea of the magnitudes involved can be obtained from the following national statistics. In 1969 the U.S. Post Office estimated it handled 81.2 billion pieces of domestic mail, compared to 44.6 billion in 1950. In 1968 a total of 109.1 million telephones were installed within the United States compared to only 43.1 million in 1950. Finally in 1968 there were 5,236 commercial broadcasting stations in the United States compared to 2,336 in 1950.

Tables 4.2 and 4.3 also show the relative importance of the different networks

TABLE 4.2. VOLUME OF DOMESTIC INTERCITY FREIGHT TRAFFIC BY TYPE OF TRANSPORTATION, U.S.A.

		Percent of Total Volume by				
Year	**Total Volume**[a]	**Railroads**[b]	**Motor Vehicles**	**Inland Waterways**[c]	**Oil Pipelines**	**Airways**[d]
1940	0.65	63.2	9.5	18.1	9.1	0.002
1950	1.09	57.4	15.8	14.9	11.8	0.029
1960	1.33	44.7	21.4	16.6	17.2	0.058
1967	1.77	41.9	22.0	15.5	20.4	0.146
Percentage point change						
1940–1967		−21.3	+12.5	−2.6	+11.3	+0.144

[a] In billions of ton-miles. A ton-mile is the movement of a ton (2,000 lbs) of freight for one mile.
[b] Includes electric railways, express, and mail.
[c] Includes Great Lakes and Alaska for all years and Hawaii beginning 1959.
[d] Includes express, mail, and excess baggage for domestic services.
Source: *Statistical Abstract of the United States, 1969,* Washington, D.C., U.S. Bureau of the Census (1969), Table 801, p. 539.

TABLE 4.3. VOLUME OF DOMESTIC INTERCITY PASSENGER TRAFFIC BY TYPE OF TRANSPORTATION, U.S.A.

		Percent of Total Volume by				
Year	**Total Volume**[a]	**Private Automobiles**	**Airways**[b]	**Commercial Motor Carriers**	**Railroads**[c]	**Inland Water-ways**[d]
1950	508	86.2	1.9	5.2	6.4	0.2
1960	783	90.1	4.3	2.5	2.7	0.3
1967	1,020	87.2	8.5	2.4	1.5	0.3
Percentage point change						
1950–1967		+1.0	+6.6	−2.8	−4.9	+0.1

[a] In billions of passenger-miles. A passenger-mile is the movement of one passenger for the distance of one mile.
[b] Includes domestic commercial services, private and business flying.
[c] Includes electric railways.
[d] Includes Great Lakes.
Source: *Statistical Abstract of the United States, 1969,* Washington, D.C., U.S. Bureau of the Census (1969), Table 802, p. 539.

in the pattern of intercity traffic. For freight traffic, the railroads dominate. This is expected since the railroad network is flexible and particularly suitable for the transportation of heavy and bulky goods. Next in order of relative importance come the highway network, oil pipelines, and inland waterways. The use of airways for freight traffic is still insignificant despite the fact that it has become relatively more important since 1940. Changes in the relative importance of the different networks are much as expected and largely reflect the increased competition of newer forms of transportation. Thus the traditional importance of waterways and railroads have declined. This is particularly noticeable in the case of railroads, which in 1940 accounted for nearly two-thirds of intercity freight traffic. Conversely the highway and oil-pipeline networks have become relatively more important since 1940.

Comparison of these figures with those shown in Table 4.3 for intercity passenger traffic clearly points up the basic differences between the networks and means used for the flow of people. For these, the highway network is supreme; and in this the use of the automobile is dominant. The only other important mode for passenger traffic are the airlines, which are becoming increasingly more important. The railroad and inland waterways are relatively insignificant for passenger traffic, and much of the flow by railroad is accounted for by intercity commuting.

THE GENERATION OF FLOWS

The amount of interaction of a given type that an individual city generates is determined by many factors. Two general factors, however, stand out as being particularly important at all cities in accounting for variation in the volume of interaction generated. These factors are the population size of the city and its functional specialization.

We have noted before the importance of city size in connection with interaction. Size of cities is a generally good indicator of their economic and social diversity. Thus Chicago generates a considerably greater volume of interaction of all kinds than does, for example, Des Moines, Iowa, simply because of its higher position in the hierarchy and hence greater importance in the city system. An example of the relationship between city size and interaction generated is given in Figure 4.13, in which wholesale sales are used as an implicit measure of interaction with other places. A sample of fifty SMSA's is plotted on the graph according to their rank importance on the two variables; rank 1 is given to the largest numbers in both cases. The line on the graph indicates what the relationship would look like if it were perfect. Although the scatter of points on the graph corresponds fairly well to this line, the relationship clearly becomes considerably more blurred at the smaller places. This is indicated by the greater scatter of points at the upper end of the graph. The cities falling below the line are of particular interest, since these generate a greater volume of wholesale sales than expected from their population totals.

These cities indicate the influence of functional specialization, the effect of

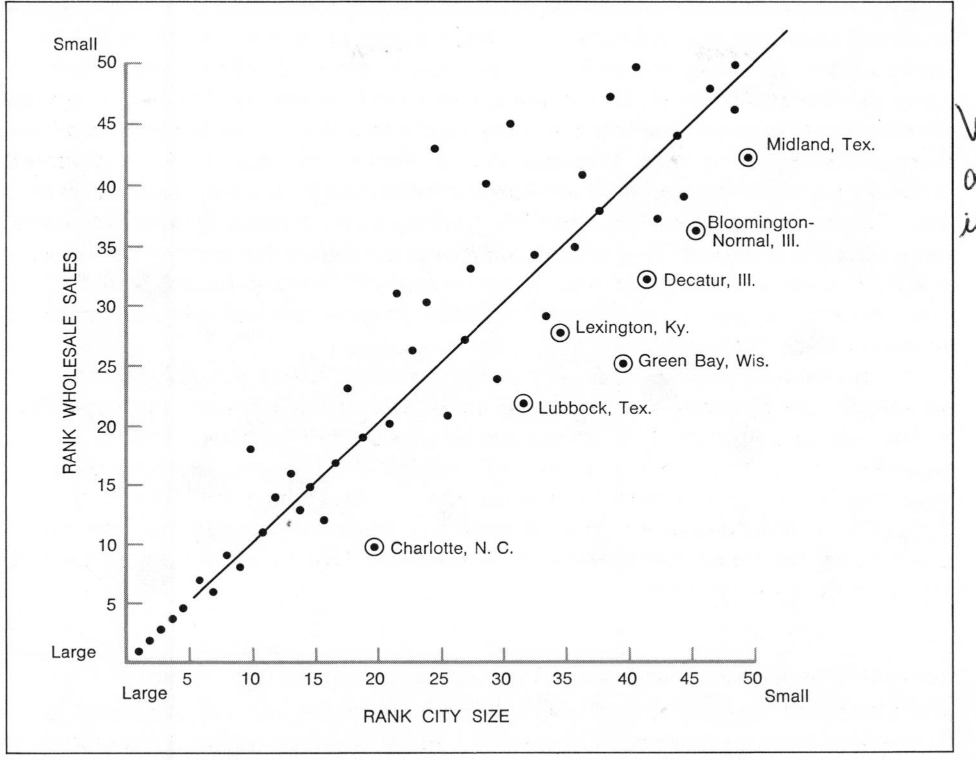

FIG. 4.13. THE RELATIONSHIP BETWEEN CITY SIZE AND VOLUME OF WHOLESALE SALES. (*Source:* U. S. Bureau of the Census. *Statistical Abstract of the United States,* 1969, pp. 864–915.)

which is clearly revealed from a study by Taaffe (1956) of air transportation and the urban pattern in the United States. The results of this study are summarized in Figure 4.14. On the map, cities are plotted as circles proportional to the number of air passengers generated per 1,000 inhabitants (the air-passenger index), and they are shaded according to their dominant function in the Harris classification of cities discussed in Chapter 3. If all cities generated the same volume of air-passenger traffic per 1,000 inhabitants, each circle on the map would be the same size. Clearly this is not the case. Close inspection of the map reveals that variation in the air-passenger index between cities is highly correlated with city function. Thus the resort and special function cities have an extremely high average index of 679. Wholesale cities have an average index of 442—a reflection of the high per-capita air traffic generated by their commercial function. In contrast the nine manufacturing cities have an average index of only 234. Diversified cities, which can be thought of as representing a division of the wholesale and manufacturing functions, fall between these two types with an average index of 345.

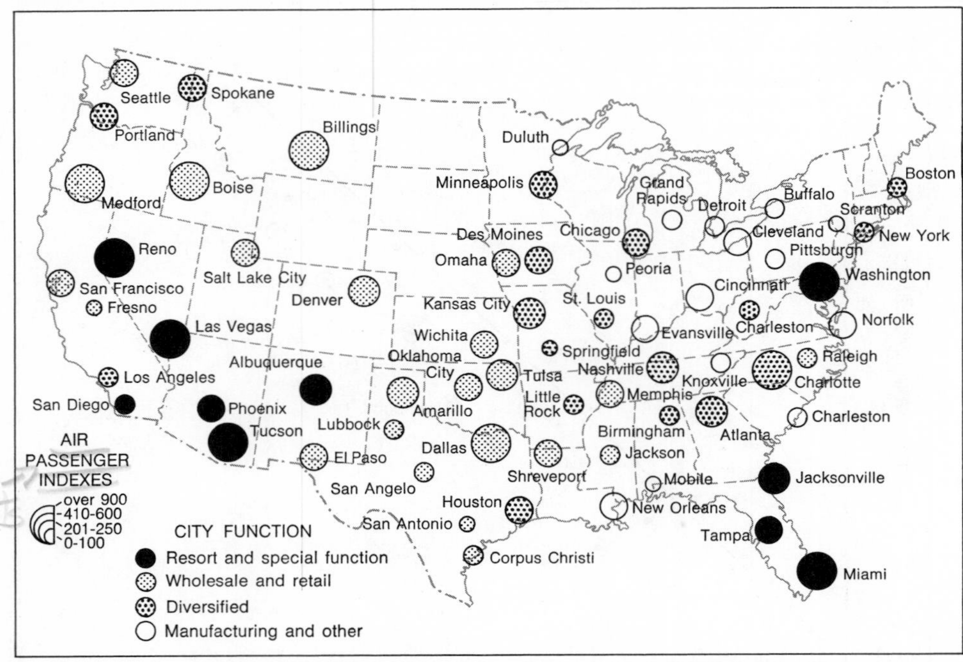

FIG. 4.14. THE RELATIONSHIP BETWEEN CITY FUNCTION AND VOLUME OF AIR PASSENGER TRAFFIC GENERATED AT SELECTED U.S. CITIES. (*Source:* Taaffe, 1956, Fig. 7.)

FLOWS BETWEEN CITY PAIRS

The total volume of a given kind of intercity interaction is the aggregate of a gigantic number of specific flows between individual pairs of cities. Again, variation in the volume of contacts between a given pair of cities depends on the interplay of many factors. In the research on intercity flows, however, it has been demonstrated that such variations can largely be accounted for by two general factors: (1) the size of the two cities, and (2) the distance separating them. Specifically, the total volume of interaction between a given pair of cities appears in general to be proportional to their sizes and, because of the friction of distance, inversely proportional to the distance between them. This formulation is the basis of the gravity model, which is discussed later in the chapter.

The general correspondence between the actual volume of flows between cities and that expected on the basis of their size and separation appears as a widespread feature of intercity interaction. An example is presented in Figure 4.15. This is taken from a study by Mackay (1958) of telephone calls between Montreal and samples of cities in (1) Quebec Province, (2) the rest of Canada, and (3) the United States. For each of the three sets of cities studied, the close correspondence between actual volume of calls and that expected on the basis of city size and distance is clearly visible. What is more interesting on this graph, however, is that each of the three sets of cities form a distinct pattern.

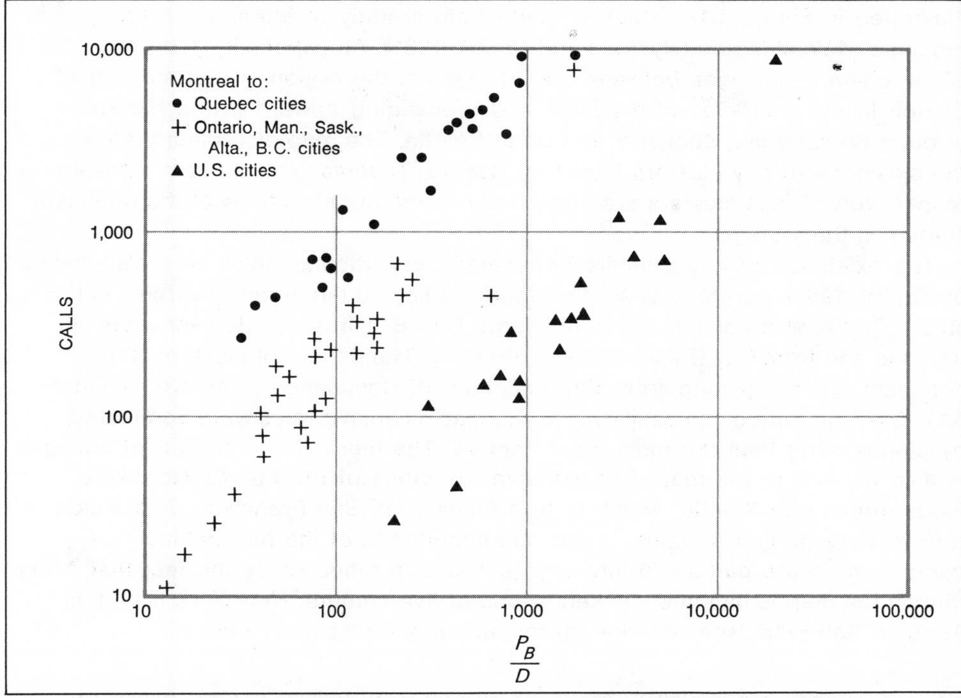

FIG. 4.15. THE RELATIONSHIP BETWEEN ACTUAL AND EXPECTED NUMBER OF TELEPHONE CALLS FROM MONTREAL TO SAMPLE CITIES IN QUEBEC, ENGLISH-SPEAKING CANADA, AND THE UNITED STATES. (*Source:* Mackay, 1958, Fig. 2.)

This reflects the influence that political boundaries have on intercity interaction. Thus the volume of telephone calls between Montreal and other cities in Quebec was 5 to 10 times higher than that between Montreal and cities with corresponding P/D values in English-speaking Canada. The effect of the international boundary is even more striking. Comparison of the actual volume of telephone calls and that expected on the basis of city size and distance indicates that the cities in the United States are in effect 50 times farther away from Montreal than is indicated by their physical distance.

THE HIERARCHY OF FLOWS

A distinctive feature of the pattern of intercity flows is that it mirrors the hierarchical arrangement of cities and tributary areas. Thus small cities tend to be dominated by medium-sized ones, which in turn are dominated by larger, higher-level centers in the hierarchy. One result of this is that within the overall pattern of interaction distinct clusters, or subsystems of cities may be identified within the city system, each of which is dominated by a particular city. The hierarchy of cities contained within the hinterland of a metropolis is a good example.

This hierarchical structure in the pattern of intercity flows is clearly illustrated in Figure 4.16, which is taken from a study of telephone messages in the state of Washington (Nystuen and Dacey, 1961). An especially good example of the chain of linkages between the 40 cities in the region is that starting at Dayton in the southeast of the state and proceeding upward in the hierarchy through Walla Walla, Spokane, and on to Seattle. The map also clearly shows the existence of city clusters based on Seattle, Tacoma, Yakima, and Spokane respectively. These clusters are interpreted as the nodal regions of the dominant centers in the system.

The existence of city clusters dominated by particular cities was also found by Taaffe (1962) in a study of air-passenger traffic and the urban hierarchy. In this study, City A was considered to dominate City B if it accounted for more air traffic to and from City B than did any other city. The pattern of clusters and dominant cities resulting from this definition of dominance is shown in Figure 4.17. Only the thirteen cities shown on the map as open circles were dominated by places other than the nine major centers. The hierarchical pattern of linkages is also implicit in the map. For example the cities of the Pacific Northwest focus directly on Seattle, which in turn focuses on San Francisco, and which in turn focuses on Los Angeles. In fact the importance of the hierarchical component in the pattern of intercity air traffic is reflected by the fact that every city on the map is ultimately linked to one of five centers: New York City, Los Angeles, San Francisco, and the Texan centers of Dallas and Houston.

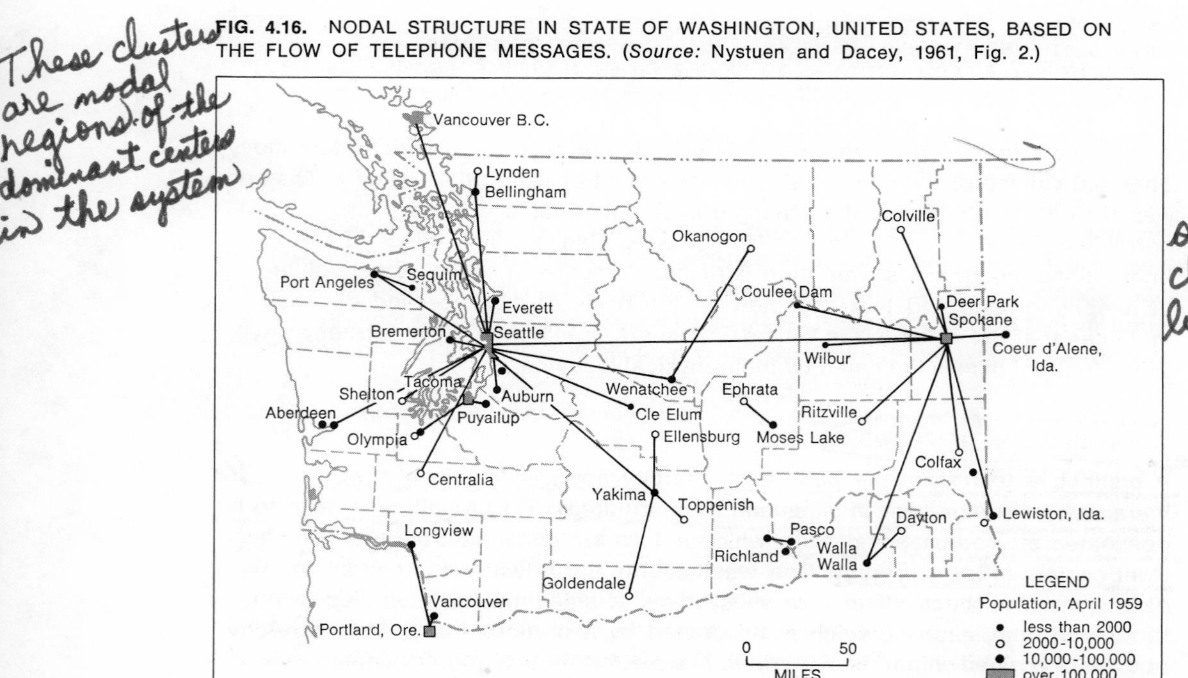

FIG. 4.16. NODAL STRUCTURE IN STATE OF WASHINGTON, UNITED STATES, BASED ON THE FLOW OF TELEPHONE MESSAGES. (*Source:* Nystuen and Dacey, 1961, Fig. 2.)

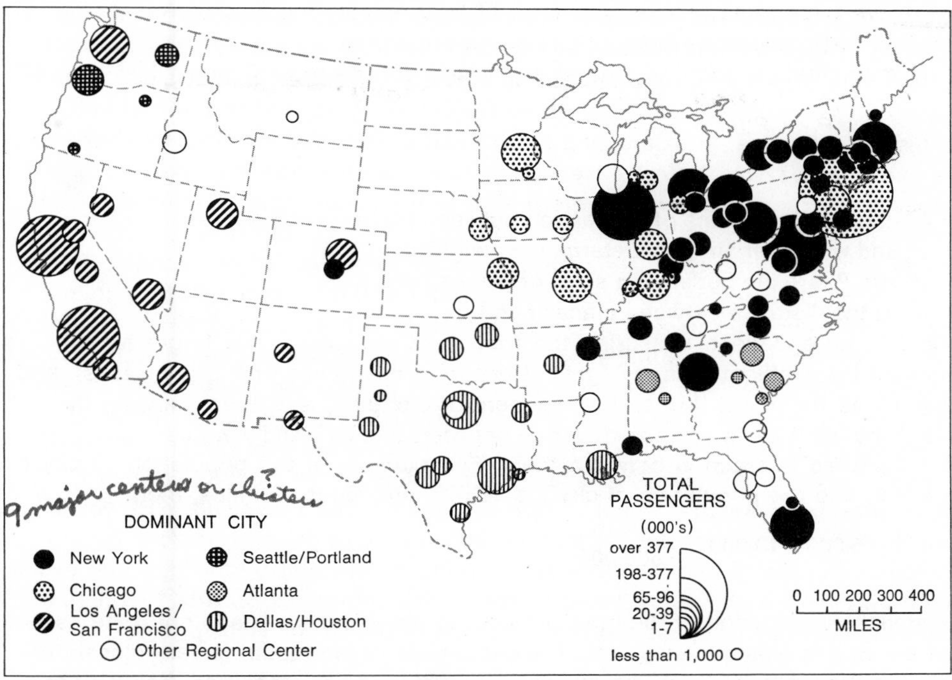

FIG. 4.17. DOMINANT CITIES IN THE URBAN HIERARCHY DEFINED IN TERMS OF NUMBERS OF AIR-PASSENGERS GENERATED. (*Source:* Taaffe, 1962, Fig. 5.)

INTERACTION MODELS

The importance of the various kinds of interaction for spatial organization and the many regularities found to exist in flow patterns have led to the development of a wide range of interaction models. Excellent reviews of many of these are found in Isard (1960), Olsson (1964), and Haggett (1965). In this section we will concentrate on the more elementary gravity models, a derivation of them known as potential models, and the intervening opportunity model.

THE GRAVITY MODEL

The gravity model is the oldest, simplest, and most widely used of all interaction models. Although variations of it have been used since the first half of the nineteenth century (Carrothers, 1956), it was not until the 1940s that it was given the more general form by which it is recognized today. Based on ideas from Newtonian physics, the gravity model postulates that interaction between two centers of population varies directly with some function of the population size of the two centers, and inversely with some function of the distance between them. We have already seen one form of this, namely the Law of Retail Gravitation proposed by Reilly (1931) discussed above.

In mathematical form, a general expression for the gravity model is:

$$I_{ij} = \frac{(w_i P_i)(w_j P_j)}{(D_{ij}^b)} \tag{4.1}$$

in which I_{ij} is the volume of interaction between places i and j,
w_i and w_j are empirically determined weights,
P_i and P_j are the population sizes of places i and j,
D_{ij} is the distance between places i and j,
and b is an exponent measuring the friction of distance. If we forget for the moment the problem of the weights attached to the values of P (the masses), and assume as Reilly did that b, the exponent of distance, is 2, then knowing the two population sizes and the distance between places i and j we can compute the expected interaction between them. For example, if the population of city i is 5,000, and the population of city j is 10,000, and D_{ij} is 10 miles, then:

$$I_{ij} = \frac{(5{,}000)\ (10{,}000)}{10^2} = 500{,}000$$

Obviously, application of the gravity model in empirical studies is not quite as simple as this example suggests. The usefulness of the model is very closely related to the ways in which the masses and distance are measured, and also to the values which are given to the exponent of distance and the weights in Equation (4.1).

Mass and distance Although the population size of cities has most commonly been used as the measure of mass in the gravity model, other measures have been used in empirical studies. Clearly the particular measure used depends on the problem under consideration. For example, Isard (1960, p. 505) suggests that in studies of intermetropolitan migration, urban employment opportunities or income may be a better measure than population size. Similarly in the context of a marketing problem, total dollar volume of sales of a city may be a more appropriate measure of mass than population. Other possibilities include such things as value added in manufacturing, car registration at a place, number of families, economic opportunities, newspaper circulation, total number of retail outlets, and so on.

Similarly different ways of measuring distance than in miles are justified on the basis that different things are more or less relevant in different types of studies. Thus although miles have been most commonly used to measure distance, other possibilities are driving time, the cost of travel, effort or energy required to overcome the frictional effect of distance, number of traffic lights, and so on. Although some of these other ways of measuring distance may appear to be more logical in a given situation, many studies have shown, however, that they only marginally improve the performance of the model in empirical study. Thus one of the conclusions that Ray (1965) arrived at in a study of freight movements by railroad between cities in Canada was that "distance measured in cost does not perform significantly better than distance measured in terms of miles" (Ray, 1965, p. 66).

The weights The problem of weighting the masses in the gravity model is a very difficult one. In many applications, the weights attached to the population are set equal to 1.0, but many studies have shown that the model's performance can be greatly improved if other values are selected. The basic reason for attaching weights to the masses is to bring out the differences in the populations used. Thus Dodd (1950) sharply pointed out that the average Chinese farmer does not make the same contribution to sociological intensity as someone living in the Los Angeles metropolitan area. Following this line of argument, it has been suggested that when population is used as the mass, it should be weighted by indexes measuring such differences as sex, age, income, occupation, years of schooling, and so on. However, the essence of the gravity model is its simplicity; and although some kind of weighting may be necessary, this very quickly makes the model cumbersome and difficult to work with.

The distance exponent Perhaps the most difficult problem in applying the gravity model is the selection of the value for *b*, the distance exponent. From a theoretical standpoint, it has been argued that the value of the exponent should be either 1.0 or 2.0. The latter value was that preferred by Reilly. From empirical studies it has been shown, however, that in actual situations the value of the distance exponent often departs quite radically from either of these figures and may lie anywhere in the range 0.5 to 3.0. For example, Iklé (1954) found values of 0.69 for trips by car between the Central Business District (CBD) of Dallas and the rest of the city, 2.57 for automobile trips between Fort Wayne, Ind., and selected counties in that state, and 1.07 for airline trips between cities in the United States.

Variation in the value of the distance exponent is to be expected because distance exerts a different frictional effect depending on the type of interaction considered. As we have seen, different products move with unequal ease and hence differences in transferability are reflected in the value of the exponent. It is not surprising to find, therefore, that several studies have demonstrated that marked differences occur in the value of *b* by type of trip. Thus Carroll and Bevis (1957) have found lower values for the distance exponent for trips to work than for shopping trips or trips to school (see Fig. 15.8). It is also quite clear from other studies that the value of the exponent varies through time, a fact which may reflect the decrease in the frictional effect of distance associated with improvements in transportation.

THE POTENTIAL MODEL

The gravity model enables us to calculate the expected interaction between a pair of cities. However, if we are interested in the interaction between place *i* and all other places including itself, then a number of calculations must be made and the results summed. Thus the expected interaction between place *i* and place

1, or I_{i1}, must be added to that between place i and place 2 (i.e. I_{i2}), and so on. This can be represented in equation form as follows:

$$\sum_{j=1}^{n} I_{ij} = \sum_{j=1}^{n} \frac{(P_i)(P_j)}{D_{ij}^b} + \frac{(P_i)(P_i)}{D_{ii}^b} \qquad (4.2)$$

in which the symbols have the same meaning as in Equation (4.1) and D_{ii} is some average radius of the area occupied by the place. Since P_i may be factored from the right-hand side of Equation (4.2), by dividing both sides by P_i we get:

$$\sum_{j=1}^{n} \frac{I_{ij}}{P_i} = \sum_{j=1}^{n} \frac{P_j}{D_{ij}^b} + \frac{P_i}{D_{ii}^b} \qquad (4.3)$$

Now the numerator on the left-hand side of Equation (4.3) is the total interaction of place i with all other places including itself. Hence by dividing this by the value of P_i, the total interaction associated with place i is expressed on a per-capita or a per-unit mass basis. Expressed in this form, the total interaction at place i is known as the *potential at i,* and is usually designated as $_iV$. By definition, then, the potential at place i is given by:

$$_iV = \sum_{j=1}^{n} \frac{P_j}{D_{ij}^b} + \frac{P_i}{D_{ii}^b} \qquad (4.4)$$

The interpretation to be given to the population potential at a place calculated in this way is not yet entirely clear. It may well indicate the total proximity of people to the place, a kind of measure of aggregate accessibility of the place to all others in the system. In this sense the potential at a place may be regarded as an index of likely interaction. Because of this, the concept of potential has mainly been used as a descriptive device. Since potentials may be calculated for many different points in space, it is possible to plot them on a map. Interpolation between the mapped points then enables contours of equal potential to be drawn. An example of the kind of surface that results from this mapping is shown in Figure 4.18 for the United States.

It is interesting to compare this map with Figure 2.7 showing the distribution of metropolitan areas in 1960. The dominance of New York City is clearly brought out. East of the Sierras, every contour line closes round New York. In this part of the country, all other major cities are local peaks on the downward slope away from the national metropolis. West of the Sierras, three local peaks occur. One centers on Seattle, and the other two on San Francisco and Los Angeles respectively. An example of the use of such a potential surface for more analytical purposes is presented in Chapter 6.

THE INTERVENING-OPPORTUNITY MODEL

This approach to modelling interaction was proposed by Stouffer (1940) as an alternative to the gravity formulation. Stouffer argued that no necessary rela-

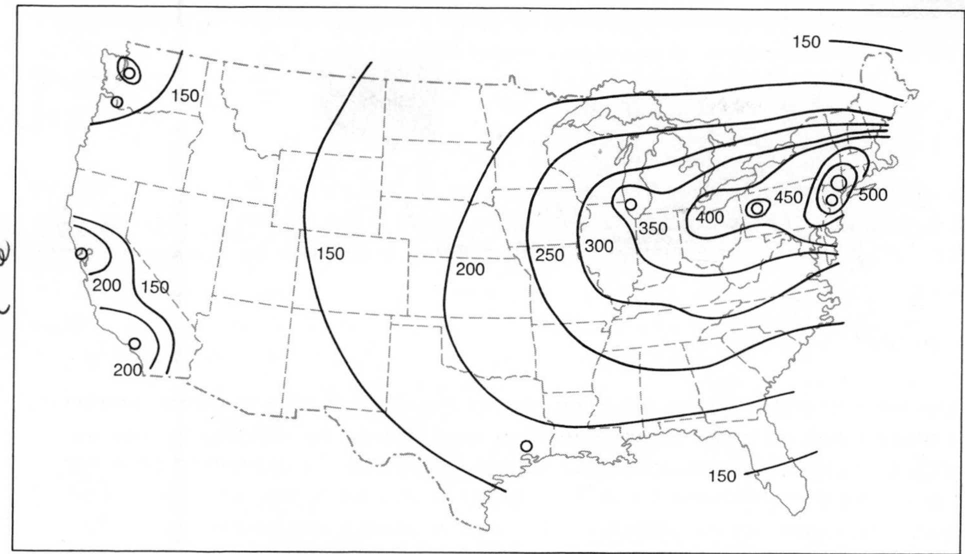

FIG. 4.18. CONTOURS OF EQUAL POPULATION POTENTIAL IN THE UNITED STATES, 1940. (*Source:* Isard, 1956, Fig. 8. Adapted from *Theory in Marketing* by Reaves Cox and Wroe Alderson, eds., published by Richard D. Irwin, Inc., 1950, under the sponsorship of the American Marketing Association.)

tionship existed between interaction and distance as it had been used in the gravity and other interaction models. Rather, he suggested that in the context of migration, the number of people moving a given distance is directly proportional to the number of opportunities at that distance and inversely proportional to the number of intervening opportunities. This relation can be expressed as follows:

$$M_{ij} = (N_j / N_{ij})K \tag{4.5}$$

in which

M_{ij} is the expected interaction between places *i* and *j*,
N_j is the number of opportunities at place *j*,
N_{ij} is the number of opportunities intervening between places *i* and *j*,
and *K* is a constant.

The main problem in applying the intervening-opportunities model is that of defining opportunities in a suitable way. In his original presentation, Stouffer used the number of migrants that had earlier moved into the area. However, this definition and that used by others involves a certain circularity in reasoning. Despite this, application of the model has shown it to give better predictions of interaction in some cases than the more straightforward gravity type of model.

"THE ECONOMIC BASE OF SETTLEMENTS"

We have observed that one of the major reasons for the collection of groups of people into settlements has been specialization of activities. This division of labor automatically implies trade, and settlements are therefore centers of trade. There is a movement of goods into and out of all settlements, for in order to specialize, people have to sell the product of their labor. In a nonbarter society this means that people sell the product of their labor for money in order to purchase the other necessities of their everyday life. In terms of the collection of people into settlements, this means that settlements must sell part of the product of the gross labor of the inhabitants of the settlement elsewhere in order to import not only necessary foodstuffs but also raw materials for further production. It is this necessary trade between settlements and other areas that has provided the background philosophy for the concept of the economic base of cities (Andrews, 1953) and is, in turn, one of the cornerstones of the urban economic multiplier.

THE BASIC-NONBASIC CONCEPT

A settlement can therefore only exist if it can sell its goods and services beyond its borders. Part of all production, however, is sold within the settlement and does not, therefore, earn outside income for the settlement as a whole. This distinction lies at the core of the basic-nonbasic concept.

THE MEANING OF ECONOMIC BASE

The economic-base concept implies that the reason for the growth of a settlement region lies in the goods and services it produces locally but sells beyond its borders. The more goods and services a settlement can produce and sell beyond the immediate environs of the city, the more income it will earn, and the more settlement growth will be generated. Thus the economy of the settlement region can be divided into two parts. The basic part refers to the goods and services produced within the settlement but sold beyond the settlement region; the nonbasic sector refers to the goods and services produced within the settlement but sold within the settlement region (Blumenfeld, 1955).

In terms of the basic-nonbasic concept, economic activity within a settlement can therefore be expressed as a simple equality:

Total activity in the settlement = Total activity in basic industries + Total activity in nonbasic industries

or, symbolically as:

$$(TA) = (BA) + (NBA)$$

This equality can be expressed in income terms as:

Total income in the settlement = Total income derived from basic industries + Total income from nonbasic industries

Therefore, if half the income of an urban area originates in nonbasic activities, the other half must come from basic activities.

These two proportions can be expressed as a ratio which is termed the *basic-*

nonbasic ratio. In the example cited if half the income comes from nonbasic activities and the other half comes from basic activity, the ratio can be written 1:1. Alternatively if a quarter of the settlement income comes from basic activities, then three-quarters of the income will come from nonbasic activities; and the ratio is written 1:3. The convention is for the basic side of the ratio to come first and to be represented as unity.

The multiplier If the basic-nonbasic ratio is constant, a unit increase (U) in basic activities will yield an increase in total settlement activity equal to the product of U and the sum of the basic-nonbasic ratio. Thus if the basic-nonbasic ratio is 1:3, an increase of 10 in basic activities will yield an increase of 40 in total settlement activity ($40 = 10 + 30$). Thus the ratio is a simple form of the economic multiplier (Tiebout, 1956), and in an urban context is described as the *urban economic multiplier*.

The concept of the multiplier depends on the assumption that

$$(\mathrm{NBA}) = v(\mathrm{TA}) \text{ which can be rewritten as } (\mathrm{TA}) = \frac{1}{v}(\mathrm{NBA})$$

where v is a parameter indicating a constant relationship between nonbasic and total activity. Therefore,

$$(\mathrm{TA}) = \frac{1}{1-v}(\mathrm{BA}) = m(\mathrm{BA})$$

where m is the multiplier (Berry, 1967B). In the basic-nonbasic example above, m is defined as 4, and v as 0.75. Thus m may be written variously as

$$m = \frac{1}{1-v} = \frac{1}{1-\dfrac{(\mathrm{NBA})}{(\mathrm{TA})}} = \frac{\mathrm{TA}}{\mathrm{BA}} = 1 + \frac{\mathrm{NBA}}{\mathrm{BA}}$$

As a consequence the multiplier m links the basic component to total activity, and the constant v links the nonbasic component to total activity. But the implication of the term multiplier is that changes in the quantity of basic activity cause changes in the amount of total activity.

Some research analysts have made extensive use of the multiplier concept for projection purposes (Hoyt, 1961; Andrews, 1953). By evaluating future prospects of expansion in basic activities of settlements and then applying multipliers obtained from basic-nonbasic ratios estimated from the existing industrial composition, they have forecast the impact of expansions in basic activities on total activity within the settlement.

EMPIRICAL ESTIMATES OF THE BASIC-NONBASIC RATIO

Most estimates of the basic-nonbasic ratio have been from employment data because this is the kind of data that is most easily obtained for settlements. Using an employment definition the equality can be written:

Total employment in a settlement = Total employment in basic industries + Total employment in nonbasic industries

The ratio can be calculated in two ways. One way is to estimate the total employment in a settlement's basic and nonbasic activities and to express these as a ratio. Thus it is estimated for 1961 that basic employment in Gainesville, Florida, totaled 12,171, whereas the nonbasic employment totaled 17,097. This implies a basic-nonbasic ratio of 1:1.4, which implies that for every five basic workers in Gainesville, Florida, in 1961 there were seven nonbasic workers.

A second method using employment data is to calculate the ratio between an increase in employment in a settlement's basic activities and the increase in employment in its nonbasic activities between two time periods. Both the first and the second method are illustrated in Table 5.1 for Wichita, Kansas, for 1940 and 1950. From this table it can be calculated that the basic-nonbasic ratio in 1940 was 1:2.5, and for 1950 the ratio was 1:2.0; however, the basic-nonbasic ratio based on the change in employment between 1940 and 1950 was 1:1.6.

It could be hypothesized that there should be some regularity in the trend of the basic-nonbasic ratio with settlement size. As settlements get larger, more and more of the employed population is concerned with producing things that are sold within the settlement area. Thus it could be suggested that the basic proportion of settlement employment should get smaller with an increase in size of population of a settlement. Conversely the ratio should get larger and larger with increasing settlement population. The fact that such trends are difficult to discern have led to a critical evaluation of the basic-nonbasic concept (Lane, 1966).

DISCUSSION OF THE BASIC-NONBASIC CONCEPT

One of the most persuasive favorable evaluations of the basic-nonbasic concept has been put forward by Alexander (1954). He asserts that the division of a city's economic activities into export and local categories illustrates a space-relationship and is thus of more interest to geographers than simple analysis of the urban area as a whole. He points out several ways in which the basic-nonbasic concept can aid in an understanding of cities.

TABLE 5.1. BASIC AND NONBASIC EMPLOYMENT IN WICHITA, KANSAS, 1940 AND 1950

Component	1940 Employment	1950 Employment	1940–1950 Employment Change
Nonbasic	37,148	59,325	22,177
Basic	14,943	29.250	14,307
Total	52,091	88,575	36,484

Source: Federal Reserve Bank of Kansas City (1952), p. 4.

1. The concept brings into sharper focus the economic ties of a city or region to other areas. Further, the composition of a city's or region's basic activities may be quite different from that of its total economic structure. Since it is the basic activity which is important to economic existence and growth of a city or region, the explicit identification of such activity is significant for analysis for distinguishing between types of regions.

2. The concept makes possible a more satisfactory classification of cities in terms of regional functions. Certain basic activities express a city's service to a surrounding region; by reference to these activities a city can be better classified in terms of their economic specialization.

3. The concept provides a new and important method of classifying individual business. For example, two firms might be engaged in manufacturing but because of the location of their markets, one could be basic and the other a service.

The limitations of the basic-nonbasic concept are both technical and conceptual (Isard, et al., 1960, pp. 194–205). A primary difficulty involves the unit of measurement with which the ratio is calculated. Employment figures have usually been used, but these do not equal income because of different wage levels. In fact what the ratio is really seeking to determine is the amount of income brought into an urban area. Furthermore if one can use employment and payrolls, a difficulty arises due to the fact that unearned income is ignored. Unearned income in some urban areas may be very large, for example in some of the retirement holiday resorts.

Another set of problems arises due to the difficulty of determining which firms are basic and which are not. Most firms sell some of their produce within an urban area and some beyond. It is therefore necessary to determine which part of a firm's employment or which part of a firm's payroll is spent on basic activities and which part is derived from nonbasic activities. In this context another difficulty arises due to linked activities. Many firms are established as subsidiaries feeding other firms; for example, coal can be mined locally and sold for fuel to a local steel producer who exports finished steel. The question arises whether the coal mine is a basic or nonbasic activity. In most studies this would be classified as a nonbasic activity because its output is consumed locally.

An overwhelming technical difficulty arises due to the problem of defining the limits of a settlement. Thus far we have used vaguely the terms settlement, urban area, and urban region; but if numbers are to be used and if ratios are to be calculated, these numbers have to pertain to a defined area. Roterus and Calef (1955) suggest that the ratio can be affected by the size of the area. For example a firm that is basic to Chicago may be nonbasic in the context of Illinois as a unit. Ultimately if the world is taken as a unit, then all activities are nonbasic. One answer to this problem in terms of the context of the problem may well be to define a settlement or urban area as a *functional economic area* as suggested by Fox and Kumer (1965) and Berry (1967C).

The conceptual limitations are rather more subtle than the technical limitations but equally as important. The ratio is, in fact, an average over the whole range of economic activities in a settlement. Increases in activity in some industries may, however, generate greater growth than a similar increase in activity in other industries. Consequently the ratio fails to distinguish between the higher and lesser growth generating activities. Furthermore the ratio fails to take into account the feedback effect of growth in industrial activity. For example it can be argued that settlement size itself creates growth. Large settlements demand services that are established to satisfy these wants. These firms might export part of their product even though they were established as city-serving activities. The fact that a firm is partially a basic activity may therefore be quite incidental to its primary function, which is to provide goods and services for the settlement itself.

MINIMUM REQUIREMENTS AND THE ECONOMIC STRUCTURE OF U.S. CITIES

A number of attempts have been made to determine in abstract terms the expected proportion of a city's economic activity that serves the settlement itself and that amount that is basic to the city's growth. One method has been developed by Alexandersson (1956) and another has been adapted by Ullman and Dacey (1962) to U.S. cities. In this section we will discuss both these methods and indicate how Alexandersson's technique can be applied to a broader understanding of the basic variation in economic structure of U.S. cities. Both techniques attempt to estimate the minimum proportion of a settlement's economic activities that can be regarded as being city serving; and of the two, Alexandersson's is by far the most simple.

THE USE OF THE FIFTH PERCENTILE IN AN EMPLOYMENT ARRAY

Alexandersson used the 1950 census of population to obtain the occupations of employed persons by industry groupings for each city or urbanized area with a population of 10,000 or more. Thus 864 cities were used in the analysis. For each city he calculated the percent of employed persons in that city working in each one of 36 employment groups. Then, for each employment group, the cities were arrayed by these percentages from the lowest to the highest; and the percentage at the fifth percentile was designated as the *k* value for that industry.

As an example consider the employment array for the wholesale trade—one of the four employment groupings in the trade category (Table 5.2). It can be seen that the city with the largest proportion of its total employment concerned with wholesale trade is the city of Sanford in Florida. This city can therefore be ranked number 864 and can be referred to as the 100th percentile town in the ranked array. The city with the smallest proportion of its employment occupied in wholesale trade is Richland, Washington, with 0.01 percent of its employed persons working in wholesale trade. Out of a total of 864 towns the fifth-percentile town will be the 43rd town in the array, which in 1950 had 1.4 percent of

TABLE 5.2. EMPLOYMENT ARRAY: WHOLESALE TRADE, 1950

Per-centile	Rank	Settlement	Percent of Employed Persons in Wholesale Trade
100	864	Sanford, Fla.	18.7
	863	Suffolk, Va.	16.9
	862	Mercedes, Tex.	16.7
	.	.	.
	.	.	.
	.	.	.
5	43		1.4
	.	.	.
	.	.	.
	.	.	.
	4	Kannapolis, N.C.	0.4
	3	Kings Park, N.Y.	0.2
	2	Oak Ridge, Tenn.	0.2
	1	Richland, Wash.	0.01

Source: Alexandersson (1956), p. 98; and Morrisset (1958), pp. 240–241.

its employment working in wholesale trade. Thus only 5 percent of the cities have 1.4 percent or less of their employed persons working in wholesale trade and 95 percent of the cities have more than 1.4 percent of their employed persons working in wholesale trade. Accumulated frequency distributions (ogive curves) for wholesale trade and for four other categories are presented in Figure 5.1. The more concentrated an industry in a small number of settlements the closer the curve will be to the vertical axis, and the sharper it will change direction.

Alexandersson considered that these *k* values indicate the minimum percentage of economic activity one would expect in a particular industry in any city. The fifth percentile was chosen after some experimentation. Alexandersson tried using the first percentile settlement but found that the lower end of the distribution showed highly abnormal employment patterns. The fifth-percentile towns, however, seemed in fact to exhibit more the characteristics that were expected of most settlements. It is interesting to observe that the *k* values add up to 37.7 percent (Table 5.3), indicating that this percentage of almost every city's workers must be employed to meet the minimum requirements of a city's economy. This percentage implies a basic-nonbasic ratio of 1:0.6.

Of course, the sum of the *k* values does not represent the minimum requirements of all cities in the United States, because the towns at the bottom of the array would represent the minimum amount. The fifth-percentile town, however, can be interpreted as being the minimum town above the tail end of the abnormal towns in the ranked array. Consequently, this figure can be interpreted as indicating the minimum percentage of employment that is to be expected on the average to serve the requirements of a city's economy in the United States.

Variations in *k* It has previously been suggested that the large cities should have more city-serving or nonbasic activities in them than the smaller cities. Morrisset

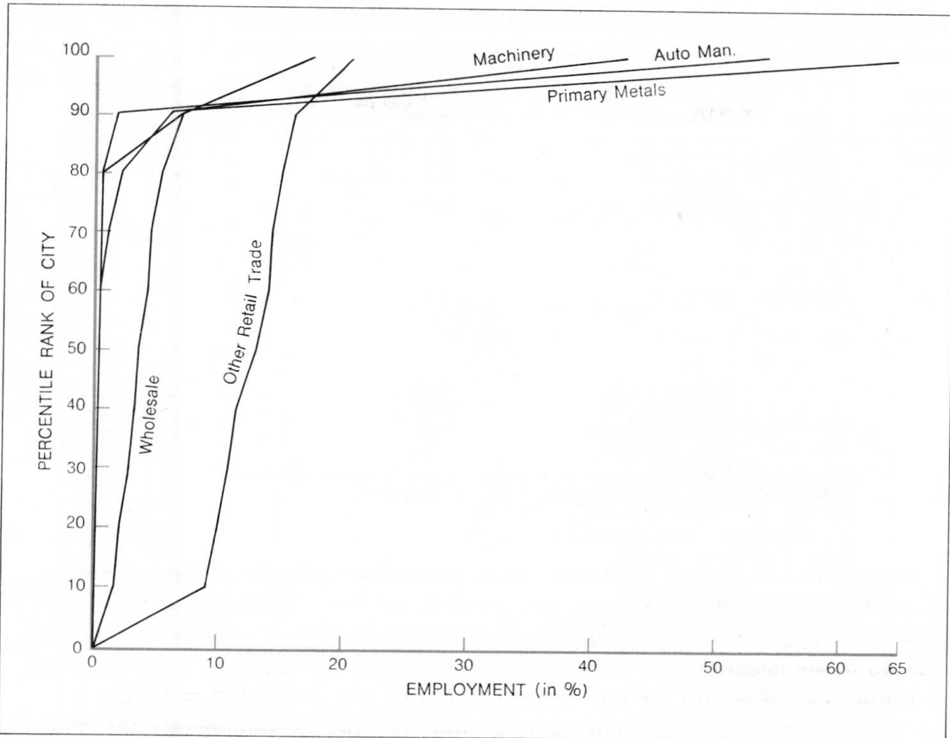

FIG. 5.1. ACCUMULATED FREQUENCY DISTRIBUTIONS FOR EMPLOYMENT IN FIVE INDUSTRIAL CATEGORIES AT UNITED STATES CITIES. (*Source:* Based on information from Alexandersson, 1956, Table 5.2.)

(1958) examined this proposition and another concerning regional variations in the extent of nonbasic activities in settlements by making use of Alexandersson's concept of the minimum percentile. Morrisset used Alexandersson's data less 123 of the settlements in the array. These were college towns and special administrative centers, such as Washington, D.C. The remaining 741 were divided into 7 size categories in three regions, the Northeast, the South, and the West of the United States. These size categories and regional divisions are indicated in Table 5.4

From this table it can be observed that the sums of the *k* values increase with city size in both the Northeast of the United States and in the South and West. In other words, large cities do tend to have more of their total economic structure devoted to service activities than small cities (the basic-nonbasic ratio for cities with more than one million inhabitants category in the South and West is 1:2.4). Furthermore the service (or nonbasic) component seems to be higher in the cities of the South and West than in those of the Northeast of the United States. This is because cities in the Northeast of the United States seem to be devoted far more to manufacturing than those in the South and West. Manufac-

TABLE 5.3. *K* VALUES AND NATIONAL PERCENTAGES U.S.A., 1950

	k	National Percentage
Mining	0	.9
Construction	3.5	6.2
Durable manufacturing	.3	15.9
Furniture, and lumber and wood products	0	1.3
Primary metal industries	0	2.6
Fabricated metal industries	0	1.8
Machinery, except electrical	.1	2.9
Electrical machinery, equipment and supplies	0	1.8
Motor vehicles, and motor vehicle equipment	0	2.0
Transportation equip., excl. motor vehicles	0	1.1
Other durables	.2	2.4
Nondurable manufacturing	1.6	14.2
Food and kindred products	.7	3.0
Textile mills products	0	2.2
Apparel and other fabricated textile products	0	2.4
Printing, publishing, and allied industries	.7	2.1
Chemicals and allied products	.1	1.3
Other nondurable goods	.1	3.2
Transportation and utilities	2.9	9.2
Railroads and railway express service	.4	2.9
Trucking service and warehousing	.5	1.3
Other transportation	.5	2.0
Telecommunications	.6	1.4
Utilities and sanitary	.9	1.6
Trade	14.2	22.6
Wholesale trade	1.4	4.4
Food and dairy products and milk retailing	2.7	3.5
Eating and drinking places	2.1	3.6
Other retail	8.0	11.1
Services	15.2	30.8
Finance, insurance, and real estate	1.8	4.5
Business services	.2	1.1
Repair services	1.1	1.6
Private households	1.3	3.3
Hotels and lodging places	.3	1.1
Other personal service	2.1	3.0
Entertainment and recreation services	.7	1.2
Medical and other health services	1.8	3.6
Education service	2.6	3.9
Other professional and related services	1.2	2.2
Public administration	2.1	5.3
Total	37.7	100.0

Source: Morrisset (1958), Table 1.

turing towns are more concerned with basic activities, exporting their finished products to the rest of North America and the rest of the world.

Furthermore, reading across Table 5.4, it can be observed that the *k* values for individual employment categories increase with the size of the cities. In other words all industries tend to become more city serving in the larger settlements.

TABLE 5.4. *K*-VALUES ($P_{.05}$) BY REGION AND CITY SIZE U.S.A., 1950

	Alex-ander-son's k	Northeast Population[a]							South and West Population[a]						
		10	25	50	100	250	500	1000	10	25	50	100	250	500	1000
Mining	0	0	0	0	0	0	0	0	0	0	0	0	0	0	0
Construction	3.5	*2.4*	*2.7*	*3.0*	*3.4*	*3.8*	*4.0*	4.2	*4.2*	*4.4*	*4.6*	*5.0*	*5.7*	*6.1*	*6.4*
Durable Mfg.															
Furniture	0	0	.1	.1	.2	.3	*.4*	*.4*	.1	.1	.1	.2	*.4*	*.5*	*.5*
Prim. Metals	0	0	0	.1	.1	.3	*.5*	*.4*	0	0	0	0	.1	.2	.3
Fab. Metals	0	.1	.1	.1	.2	*.5*	*1.1*	*1.4*	0	0	.1	.2	.3	.4	.7
Machinery	.1	.1	.2	.3	.5	*.9*	*1.0*	*1.0*	.1	.1	.1	.1	.2	.4	.8
Elec. Mach.	0	0	.1	.1	.1	.2	*.7*	*.7*	0	0	0	0	0	.1	.2
Mot. Vehic.	0	0	0	0	0	.1	.3	.3	0	0	0	0	0	.1	.1
Transport. Eq.	0	0	0	0	0	.1	.1	.2	0	0	0	0	0	0	.1
Other dur.	.2	.2	.3	.4	*.6*	*1.0*	*1.3*	*1.3*	.1	.1	.2	.3	*.6*	*.8*	*.8*
Nondurable Mfg.															
Food Mfg.	.7	.5	.6	*.8*	*1.0*	*1.4*	*1.8*	*1.8*	.7	*.8*	*.8*	*1.0*	*1.3*	*2.0*	*2.7*
Textile Mfg.	0	0	0	0	0	0	0	.1	0	0	0	0	0	0	.1
Apparel	0	0	0	0	.1	.2	.2	.2	0	0	0	0	.2	.5	.6
Printing	.7	*.5*	*.6*	*.7*	*.8*	*1.1*	*1.4*	*1.4*	*.6*	*.7*	*.7*	*.9*	*1.1*	*1.3*	*1.3*
Chemicals	.1	.1	.1	.1	.1	*.3*	*.6*	*.7*	0	.1	.1	.1	.2	*.4*	*.6*
Other Nondur.	.1	.1	.1	.2	.3	*.6*	*1.2*	*1.5*	0	0	.1	.1	.2	*.5*	*.8*
Mfg. not spec.	–	0	0	0	.1	.1	.1	.1	0	0	0	0	.1	.1	.1
Transp. & Util.															
Railroads	.4	.4	.4	.4	.4	*.5*	*.7*	*.9*	.3	.4	*.5*	*.7*	*1.1*	*1.2*	*1.5*
Trucking	.5	*.4*	*.4*	*.5*	*.6*	*.8*	*.9*	*1.0*	*.5*	*.5*	*.6*	*.7*	*.9*	*1.0*	*1.2*
Other Transp.	.5	.4	*.5*	*.5*	*.5*	*.6*	*.8*	*1.1*	*.5*	*.6*	*.7*	*.8*	*1.0*	*1.4*	*2.1*
Telecom.	.6	*.5*	*.6*	*.7*	*.7*	*.8*	*.9*	*1.1*	*.8*	*.8*	*.8*	*.9*	*1.0*	*1.1*	*1.4*
Utilities	.9	*.7*	*.8*	*.8*	*.9*	*1.1*	*1.3*	*1.3*	*.8*	*.9*	*.9*	*1.0*	*1.1*	*1.2*	*1.4*
Trade															
Wholesale	1.4	.9	*1.1*	*1.3*	*1.6*	*2.2*	*2.8*	*3.0*	*1.4*	*1.6*	*2.1*	*2.7*	*3.8*	*4.7*	*5.1*
Food Stores	2.7	*2.7*	*2.7*	*2.7*	*2.7*	*2.8*	*2.8*	*2.9*	*2.7*	*2.7*	*2.7*	*2.7*	*2.7*	*2.8*	*2.8*
Eating	2.1	*1.9*	*2.9*	*2.0*	*2.1*	*2.5*	*2.8*	*2.9*	*2.1*	*2.2*	*2.3*	*2.4*	*2.7*	*2.9*	*3.0*
Oth. Retail	8.0	*7.2*	*1.5*	*7.9*	*8.3*	*8.9*	*9.2*	*9.2*	*9.0*	*9.2*	*9.4*	*9.9*	*10.6*	*10.8*	*10.8*
Services															
Fin. and Ins.	1.8	*1.5*	*1.6*	*1.7*	*1.9*	*2.3*	*2.6*	*3.0*	*1.7*	*1.9*	*2.1*	*2.4*	*3.2*	*4.1*	*4.7*
Bus. Serv.	.2	*.2*	*.3*	*.3*	*.4*	*.6*	*.7*	*.7*	*.2*	*.3*	*.3*	*.4*	*.6*	*.7*	*1.0*
Repair Serv.	1.1	*1.0*	*1.0*	*1.0*	*1.0*	*1.1*	*1.2*	*1.2*	*1.1*	*1.2*	*1.2*	*1.3*	*1.5*	*1.5*	*1.6*
Private HH.	1.3	*.8*	*.9*	*.9*	*1.0*	*1.3*	*1.4*	*1.4*	*.8*	*.9*	*1.1*	*1.2*	*1.9*	*1.9*	*1.9*
Hotels	.3	*.2*	*.2*	*.2*	*.3*	*.4*	*.5*	*.5*	*.3*	*.4*	*.4*	*.5*	*.8*	*1.0*	*1.0*
Oth. Pers. Ser.	2.1	*1.7*	*1.9*	*2.0*	*2.0*	*2.0*	*2.0*	*2.0*	*2.2*	*2.2*	*2.3*	*2.4*	*2.5*	*2.5*	*2.5*
Entertain.	.7	*0.5*	*.5*	*.6*	*.8*	*.8*	*.8*	*.8*	*.8*	*.8*	*.8*	*.9*	*.9*	*.9*	*1.0*
Med. Ser.	1.8	*1.6*	*1.7*	*1.9*	*2.1*	*2.5*	*2.7*	*2.7*	*1.5*	*1.8*	*2.0*	*2.2*	*2.6*	*2.8*	*2.8*
Education	2.6	*2.2*	*2.2*	*2.3*	*2.4*	*2.6*	*2.6*	*2.6*	*2.9*	*2.9*	*2.9*	*2.9*	*2.8*	*2.8*	*2.7*
Oth. Prof.	1.2	*1.0*	*1.1*	*1.2*	*1.3*	*1.5*	*1.6*	*1.6*	*1.2*	*1.2*	*1.3*	*1.4*	*1.6*	*1.9*	*1.9*
Pub. Admin.	2.1	*1.7*	*1.9*	*2.0*	*2.2*	*2.4*	*2.6*	*3.0*	*2.3*	*2.4*	*2.5*	*2.6*	*3.0*	*3.2*	*3.7*
Total	37.7	31.5	34.1	36.8	40.7	48.6	55.6	58.7	38.9	41.2	43.7	47.9	56.8	64.3	71.0

[a] in thousands.

Note: The values in italics are those for which $k \geqq \frac{\text{national percentage}}{4}$. The *k* values were read from smoothed curves.

Source: Morrisset (1958), Table 3.

It can therefore be concluded that the economic structure of the city becomes more city serving as the size of the settlement increases. Regionally there is more specialization in cities in the Northeast than in cities of the South and West. The increase in size of the urban economic multiplier implied by this relationship is therefore due to the fact that there are greater possibilities for interindustry linkages in larger cities. Large urban areas have a diversity of economic activities which both produce for, and purchase from, other industries in the area. Thus the size of the multiplier is related to the possibilities for a diversity of interindustry linkages, possibilities that are much greater in large urban areas due to the diversity of the industrial base.

Morrisset also used the fifth-percentile values to obtain some idea of the degree to which industries are distributed ubiquitously—that is, found in all settlements—and the degree to which they are found sporadically—that is, those that are found only in a few settlements. Morrisset quantitatively defined the term sporadic as a situation where the *k* value of an industry is less than one-quarter of the national percentage. Alternatively, if the *k* value is one-quarter or greater than the national percentage, it will be termed ubiquitous. The ubiquitous industries are indicated in italics in Table 5.4; and the general distribution of italicized figures indicates that, as city size increases, more and more industries are classified as ubiquitous in both the Northeast of the United States and in the South and West. It can therefore be concluded that the economic structure of large cities is much more diversified than the economic structure of small cities.

THE ULLMAN-DACEY MINIMUM-REQUIREMENTS APPROACH

Another method of analyzing the basic-nonbasic structure of urban areas was used by Ullman and Dacey (1962, 1969) in the United States. All cities in an area are divided into groups according to their population size. Each group will contain cities of about the same range in population. Then, for any industrial activity, the city in each group that has the lowest proportion of its employment in that particular industry is judged to represent the minimum requirement for an industry in a city of that particular size range.

These minimum requirements for each industry are plotted on a graph against city population size (Fig. 5.2). A straight line fitted to these points represents the average increase in minimum requirements with city size. Ullman and Dacey found, for fourteen industry categories using six size groupings of American cities, that in all cases the minimum requirements increased with city size. From Figure 5.2 it can be observed that retail trade has the highest minimum requirement. Using this graph, the minimum requirements for any city of a particular size can be calculated. For example, Sioux City has a population of 100,000 and is therefore expected to have 0.6 percent of the total labor force in agriculture serving the city itself, 1.8 percent in wholesale trade, 1.8 percent in durable manufacturing, 3 percent in nondurable manufacturing, 3.4 percent in construction, and 3.8 percent in transportation. Reading farther along the graph to the highest proportion, 14 percent of the total labor force will be in retail trade serving the city itself. Thus if the total labor force of an urban area is known, it will be possible to calculate the amount of labor that one would expect to find in nonbasic activities in a city of any size. Once the nonbasic total is calculated, then a basic-nonbasic ratio can be estimated.

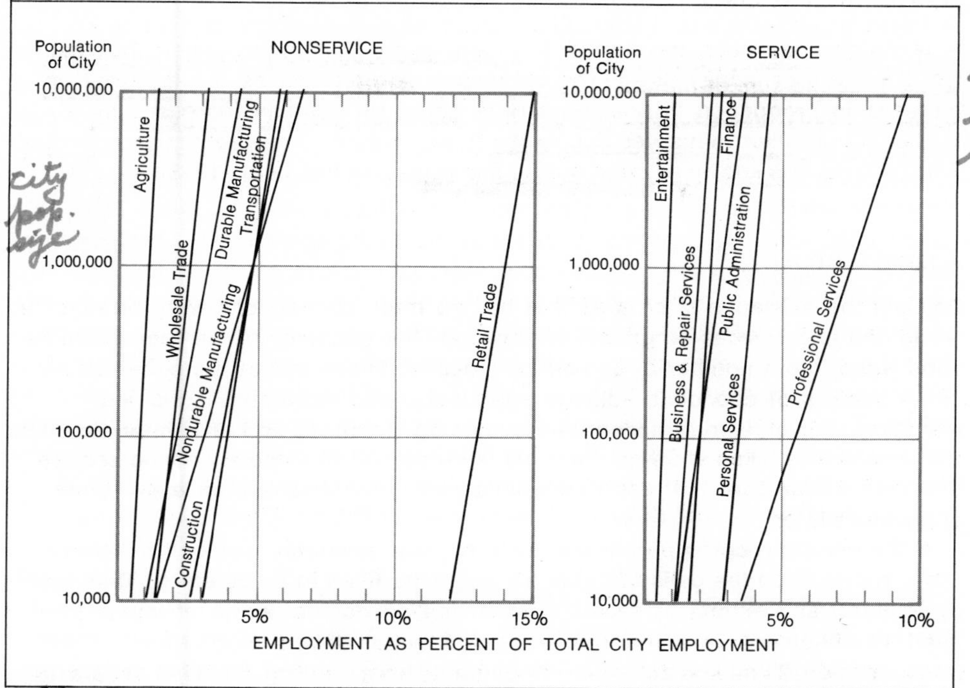

FIG. 5.2. THE RELATIONSHIP BETWEEN CITY SIZE AND MINIMUM REQUIREMENTS FOR 13 INDUSTRY TYPES FOR UNITED STATES CITIES. (*Source:* Ullman and Dacey, 1962, Fig. 2.)

The minimum-requirements approach is very useful in that like Morrisset's use of Alexandersson's *k* values, it emphasizes the changing structure of cities with city size. However, by taking the minimum value in an industry grouping, there is a very strong danger that an abnormal urban area may be chosen as giving the minimum requirements for that particular grouping. For example in the group of fourteen cities with over one million people in them, Washington, D.C., with 2.3 percent of its employment in durable manufacturing, formed the low for this box in the table. Obviously Washington, D.C., by its very nature as the capital of the United States, is bound to have a quite abnormal employment structure. However, the technique of fitting regression lines to the data attempts to average out these abnormalities.

All these approaches to evaluating the economic base of settlements disregard the fact that it is the flow of money into the settlement that generates economic activity. The employment definition of the urban economic multiplier is at best a poor substitute for detail concerning the actual money flow within the urban economy. Furthermore the use of money flows emphasizes that a settlement is, in fact, an economic system (like an individual family household) that has to be financially solvent if it is to be viable.

INPUT-OUTPUT MODELS

A technique has been developed in recent years that incorporates the real world pattern of money flows. The technique also recognizes the fact that an increase in production in one industry is going to result in increases in production in other industries due to the linked nature of all productive activities. This technique is known as *input-output analysis* (Leontief, et al., 1953).

A SIMPLE MODEL

Assume the existence of an area that has no trade connections with the outside world and experiences no growth of any kind. The economy of the region can be subdivided into a number of sectors of industry. These will be simplified to six major sectors of economic activity: agricultural and extractive industries, manufacturing industry, transportation, housing, financial, and all others. Presume that a census is taken showing the value of output for all these economic sectors and also the amount that each economic sector purchases from every other economic sector.

If the census records purchases made by each economic sector from every other sector, then the cells of Table 5.5 would be filled in by columns. Thus the agricultural and extractive sector buys 20 million dollars' worth of inputs from itself, 10 million dollars' worth from industry, 5 million dollars' worth from transportation, 30 million dollars worth of inputs from housing, 5 million dollars worth from the financial sector, and 10 million dollars' worth from all others, making a total of 80 million dollars' worth of purchases by the agricultural and extractive sector. Likewise, the purchases by the transportation sector are 5 million from the agricultural extractive sector, 5 million dollars from industry, 15 million dollars from transportation, 10 million dollars from housing, 15 million dollars from the financial sector, and 10 million dollars from all others, the total being 60 million dollars' worth of purchases.

On the other hand, if sales are recorded, the table can be filled by rows. Thus

TABLE 5.5. INPUT-OUTPUT FLOW (IN MILLIONS OF DOLLARS) IN A HYPOTHETICAL URBAN REGION

Industry Producing / Industry Purchasing	Agriculture and Extractive	Industry	Transportation	Housing	Finance	All Others	Total Gross Outputs
Agriculture and extractive	$20	$ 25	$ 5	$ 20	$ 5	$ 5	$ 80
Industry	10	40	5	40	10	15	120
Transportation	5	10	15	15	10	5	60
Housing	30	25	10	5	10	30	110
Financial	5	10	15	10	5	5	50
All others	10	10	10	20	10	10	70
Total Gross Inputs	$80	$120	$60	$110	$50	$70	$490

the agricultural and extractive sector retained 20 million dollars for its own use, sold goods to the industrial sector worth 25 million dollars; to the transportation sector worth 5 million dollars; to the housing sector worth 20 million dollars; to the financial sector worth 5 million dollars; and a further 5 million dollars' worth to all others. Thus, with perfect data in a closed system, total sales should equal total purchases. In this particular case the total purchases ($80 million) by the agricultural and extractive sector equals the total sales ($80 million) of the agricultural and extractive sector. It will be seen from Table 5.5 that all inputs equal all outputs in this very simple system. A table of this kind is known as an *input-output* table.

Advantages of input-output tables Input-output tables of this type obviously have many advantages. In the first place they record concisely a large amount of information about the economy and the intersectoral relationships between various major groupings of economic activities. Furthermore the table provides a framework for data collection, it reveals gaps, and it shows how they can be filled. For example if it is not known how much the housing sector purchases from the financial sector, it is a simple operation to add up all the other purchases; and, knowing that inputs equal outputs, subtract inputs from the output of 110 million dollars' worth of goods, to find that housing purchases 10 million dollars from the financial sector.

These tables also facilitate a comparison of the magnitudes of sectors and show where further subdivisions might be illuminating. For example the totals for the financial sector and the transportation sector are reasonably small; but for the manufacturing industry and housing sectors the totals are very large. These sectors might be further subdivided. The manufacturing industry sector, for example, might be subdivided into durable and nondurable industries. The housing sector might well be subdivided into high-cost housing and low-cost housing. The most important use of input-output tables, however, is that they offer a technique for projecting the impact of an increase in economic activity in any one or more sectors.

THE USE OF INPUT-OUTPUT TABLES FOR DETERMINING PROJECTIONS

Consider the financial column of Table 5.5. The column lists the inputs of each sector of the economy of the region into the financial industry. At the bottom of the column is the total value of inputs, which equals the total value of outputs of the financial sector. If this figure is divided into each figure in the column, then the cents worth of inputs per dollars of output in the financial industry is obtained. For example in the financial sector each dollar of output requires 10 cents worth of inputs from the agricultural sector, 20 cents' worth of inputs from the industrial sector, 20 cents' worth of inputs from the transportation sector, 20 cents' worth of inputs from the housing sector, 10 cents' worth of inputs from the financial sector, and 20 cents' worth of inputs from the all-others sector.

Similar values can be calculated for each one of the columns where the cents' worth of input per dollar of output are expressed with respect to the total value of inputs in each sector (Table 5.6). These cents' worth of input per dollar of output can be used for projection purposes if it is assumed that they remain constant through time. In this sense they can be regarded as constant production coefficients.

Presume that consumption in the housing sector is to increase by $10 million over a period of years (*X* years). What impact will this increase in consumption have on the economy of the entire region? To begin with, it is assumed that these housing expenditures are allocated in accordance with their proportions in Table 5.6 Thus, a further $1.8 million will be spent in the agricultural and extractive sector, $3.7 million in the industrial sector, $1.4 million in the transportation sector, $0.4 million in the housing sector itself, $0.9 million in the financial sector, and $1.8 million in all other sectors.

These can all be considered final demands, and as a consequence the housing row can be eliminated from the projection. This is because the magnitude of disposable income over *X* years has already been implied, and accordingly the total of inputs required to earn this income. Thus, not to remove the housing row would lead to double counting (Isard, et al., 1960, p. 332). Similarly the housing column is eliminated, for the total of housing expenditures by time *X* has also been implied.

The projection In order for the housing sector to consume the various quantities listed above, these themselves have to be produced. Thus the $1.8 million (see Table 5.7) from the agricultural and extractive sector has to be produced, and the first column of Table 5.6 indicates the dollar value of inputs that is required from every industry to produce this. Therefore, if we multiply down the first column of Table 5.6 by $1.8 million, we obtain the inputs from every industry that are required to produce this total output. Similarly, the $3.7 million production necessary in the industrial sector has to be produced, and the dollar value of inputs required to produce this output can be calculated by multiplying down column 2 of Table 5.6 by $3.7 million. Likewise the $1.4 million from the transpor-

TABLE 5.6. CENTS WORTH OF INPUTS PER DOLLAR OF OUTPUT

Industry Producing / Industry Purchasing	Agriculture and Extractive	Industry	Transportation	Housing	Finance	All Others
Agriculture & extractive	$ .25	$ .21	$ .08	$ .18	$ .10	$ .07
Industry	.12	.34	.08	.37	.20	.22
Transportation	.06	.08	.25	.14	.20	.07
Housing	.39	.21	.17	.04	.20	.43
Financial	.06	.08	.25	.09	.10	.07
All others	.12	.08	.17	.18	.20	.14
Total Inputs	$1.00	$1.00	$1.00	$1.00	$1.00	$1.00

TABLE 5.7. FIRST-ROUND INPUT REQUIREMENTS

	AE	I	T	H	F	AO	Total Outputs
AE	$ 450,000	$ 777,000	$ 112,000		$ 90,000	$ 126,000	$1,555,000
I	216,000	1,258,000	112,000		180,000	396,000	2,162,000
T	108,000	296,000	350,000		180,000	126,000	1,060,000
H							
F	108,000	296,000	350,000		90,000	126,000	970,000
AO	216,000	296,000	238,000		180,000	252,000	1,182,000
Total Inputs	$1,800,000	$3,700,000	$1,400,000		$900,000	$1,800,000	$6,929,000

TABLE 5.8. SECOND-ROUND INPUT REQUIREMENTS

	AE	I	T	H	F	AO	Total Outputs
AE	$ 388,750	$ 454,020	$ 84,800		$ 97,000	$ 82,740	$1,107,310
I	186,600	735,080	84,000		194,000	260,040	1,460,520
T	93,700	172,960	263,000		194,000	82,740	808,000
H							
F	93,300	172,960	265,000		97,000	82,740	711,000
AO	186,600	172,960	180,200		194,000	165,480	899,240
Total Inputs	$1,555,000	$2,162,00	$1,060,000		$970,000	$1,182,000	$4,986,070

TABLE 5.9. THIRD-ROUND INPUT REQUIREMENTS

	AE	I	T	H	F	AO	Total Outputs
AE	$ 276,828	$ 306,709	$ 64,640		$ 71,100	$ 62,947	$ 782,224
I	132,877	496,577	64,640		142,200	197,833	1,034,127
T	66,439	116,842	202,000		142,200	62,947	590,428
H							
F	66,439	116,842	202,000		71,100	62,947	519,328
AO	132,877	116,842	137,360		142,200	125,894	655,173
Total Inputs	$1,107,310	$1,460,520	$808,000		$711,000	$899,240	$3,581,280

TABLE 5.10. INPUT REQUIREMENTS BY ROUND FOR $10 MILLION OUTPUT IN THE HOUSING SECTOR IN A HYPOTHETICAL URBAN REGION

	First	Second	Third	Fourth	Fifth	Sixth	Total
AE	$1,555,000	$1,107,310	$ 782,224	$ 557,752	$ 399,731	$ 260,034	$ 4,662,051
I	2,162,000	1,460,520	1,034,127	740,698	531,903	382,219	6,311,467
T	1,060,000	808,000	590,428	426,998	307,563	221,234	3,414,223
H							
F	970,000	711,000	519,328	375,065	270,057	194,229	3,039,678
AO	1,182,000	899,240	655,173	472,560	339,947	244,410	3,793,330
Total	$6,929,000	$4,986,070	$3,581,280	$2,573,073	$1,849,201	$1,302,115	$21,220,749

TABLE 5.11. HYPOTHETICAL INTERMETROPOLITAN TRANSACTIONS TABLE, 19—
CENTS WORTH OF INPUTS PER DOLLAR OF OUTPUT

	Metropolitan Region I:								
Industry Producing	**Heavy Manufacturing** (1)	**Power and Communication** (2)	**Transportation** (3)	**Trade** (4)	**Insurance and Rental** (5)	**Business and Pers. Serv.** (6)	**Educational and Other Serv.** (7)	**Construction** (8)	**Households** (9)
Metropolitan Region I:									
1. Heavy manufacturing	33	1	3	1		9	1	18	3
2. Power and communication	1	11	3	2	8	4	2		1
3. Transportation	2	2	5	1	1	1	2	4	3
4. Trade	1		2		2	3	5	9	12
5. Insurance and rental activities	1	1	3	5	7	5	4	2	12
6. Business and personal services	1	1	2	7	1	4	2	3	3
7. Educational and other basic services							1		10
8. Construction		4	6		10		1		
9. Households	34	58	58	63	53	46	50	40	1
Metropolitan Region II:									
10. Light manufacturing	4	1	2	2	1	14	15	4	20
11. Power and communication									
12. Transportation									
13. Trade									
14. Insurance and rental activities									
15. Business and personal services									
16. Educational and other basic services									
17. Construction									
18. Households									
Region III:									
19. Agriculture and extraction	6	5	4	1	2		4	18	6
20. Power and communication									
21. Transportation									
22. Trade									
23. Insurance and rental activities									
24. Business and personal services									
25. Educational and other basic services									
26. Construction									
27. Households									

Note: The columns do not add up to 100 due to rounding and the fact that all values less than 0.01 have been deleted.
Source: Isard and Kavesh (1954), p. 153.

Industry Purchasing																	
Metropolitan Region II:									Region III:								
Light Manufacturing (10)	Power and Communication (11)	Transportation (12)	Trade (13)	Insurance and Rental (14)	Business and Pers. Serv. (15)	Educational and Other Serv. (16)	Construction (17)	Households (18)	Agriculture and Extraction (19)	Power and Communication (20)	Transportation (21)	Trade (22)	Insurance and Rental (23)	Business and Pers. Serv. (24)	Educational and Other Serv. (25)	Construction (26)	Households (27)
2	1	3	1		9	1	18	3	1	1	3	1		9	1	18	3
28	1	2	2	1	14	15	4	20	6	1	2	2	1	14	15	4	20
1	11	3	2	8	4	2		1									
2	2	5	1	1	1	2	4	3									
2		2		2	3	5	9	12									
1	1	3	5	7	5	4	2	12									
2	1	2	7	1	4	2	3	3									
						1		10									
	4	6		10		1											
25	58	58	63	53	46	50	40	1									
21	5	4	1	2		4	18	6	28	5	4	1	2		4	18	6
									1	11	3	2	8	4	2		1
									3	2	5	1	1	1	2	4	3
									2		2		2	3	5	9	12
									4	1	3	5	7	5	4	2	12
									1	1	2	7	1	4	2	3	3
															1		10
										4	6		10		1		
									40	58	58	63	53	46	50	40	1

tation sector, and the $0.9 million from the financial sector, and the $1.8 million from the all-others sector have to be produced; and the inputs required for this output can be calculated by cross-multiplying down the respective columns. If these inputs are now added up by type of input, we obtain the first round of input requirements (Table 5.7).

These first-round input requirements are directly required to produce the final demand items that housing is calculated to consume at time period *X*. However, these first-round input requirements also have to be produced; and the input required to produce these outputs can be obtained by a multiplication procedure similar to that used to obtain the first-round input requirements. The inputs required to produce $1.555 million of output in the agricultural and extractive sector can be obtained by multiplying this figure down the first column of Table 5.6 to obtain the figures in the first column of Table 5.8. In a similar fashion, each of the output requirements in Table 5.7 have to be produced; and these can be calculated as explained previously and added to produce the second round of input requirements. Thus the second round of input requirements are necessary to produce the first round. As these second round of input requirements have to be produced a third round must also be calculated (Table 5.9).

The round-by-round requirements have been calculated and added to produce the figures in Table 5.10. It is to be noticed that after the fourth round these figures converge, a situation that is bound to occur inasmuch as the housing row and columns have been deleted. This convergence of the data means that the projection does not have to continue indefinitely, and in this particular example the round-by-round projections have been discontinued at the sixth stage. By this time it is estimated that $10 million of consumption in the housing sector by time period *X* will have resulted in a further increase of $21.1 million of economic activity. Thus over this time period the multiplier has been 3.12.

INTERREGIONAL INPUT-OUTPUT MODELS

The simple one-region input-output model discussed in the previous section can be expanded into a more complex interregional input-output model to incorporate regional differences in concentration of economic activity. For example in the hypothetical model presented by Isard and Kavesh (1954) a model with respect to three regions has been developed; and this is presented in Table 5.11.

In this model there are two metropolitan regions and one broad agricultural region, which in spatial terms links the area around the two metropolitan regions into one unit. Each region has nine major sectors of economic activity. These are listed in Table 5.11. There is, however, one basic variation in economic activity between each region; and it is this activity that provides the export base of the economy of each area. For example in Metropolitan Region 1, heavy manufacturing is the basic activity, sending exports to Metropolitan Region 2 and Region 3. In Metropolitan Region 2, light manufacturing is the basic activity and all other activities are nonbasic; and it is this activity which provides the basic employment for that area. In the third region, agriculture is the basic economic activity, and it is this region that supplies the necessary foodstuffs for the two metropolitan areas. Concomitantly, this region imports heavy manufactured goods and light manufactured goods from the two metropolitan regions. Each region is self-sufficient in the other eight sectors of economic activity.

The assumption that each region is self-sufficient in eight sectors of economic activity and has only one sector of activity as a basic activity is, of course, unrealistic. The model is, however, simplified by this assumption; and in Table 5.11 the cents worth of input per dollar of output are entered to illustrated that an input-output model of this kind can be developed into a table that can be used for projection purposes.

Thus the basic-nonbasic concept and the concept of the urban economic multiplier can be developed into a sophisticated procedure for projecting the impact of future expansion or development of one sector, or group of sectors, of industry in one or more regions. One of the chief problems of this kind of model is that it is difficult to construct. The amount of data needed is immense; and if many sectors of industry are being considered, the storage-space requirement in computers is also very great. The interregional input-output model does, however, emphasize in a very real way that all regions are economically interlinked and that changes in the level of economic activity in one region may also result in changes in the level of economic activity in other regions. The model takes into account the fact that an increase in demand in one sector of economic activity has repercussions on all other sectors of economic activity in all regions. Furthermore, it is important to note that the model provides a mechanism for estimating the multiplier effect of any increase or decrease in economic activity in any sector in any region.

SETTLEMENTS AS CENTERS OF MANUFACTURING

The evolution of the North American city is closely related to the development of manufacturing, for it is invariably the underlying cause of growth or stagnation, depending on the nature of the industry mix and the extent of local interlinkages

between plants. If an urban area is favored with a number of rapid growth firms, and if these firms are closely linked to the rest of the industrial base of the community, then the multiplier effect of an increase in economic activity in any one will be great, for the cummulative effect of such an increase in economic activity will be transmitted throughout the region. Thus it is important in an overview of settlements as centers of manufacturing (Stevens and Brackett, 1967) to examine the factors that help to explain why the employment in, and types of, manufacturing vary in amount between urban areas.

This varying spatial distribution of secondary and primary employment is based on decisions concerning the location of manufacturing that involve both economic and behavioristic considerations. Usually economic considerations are interpreted as involving locational decisions designed to maximize profits, an incentive function that assumes rationality (McGuire, 1964, p. 19). In a situation of perfect competition where a firm's actions do not significantly affect its competitors or its market, an entrepreneur is aware of the situation that exists and can act rationally to seek to maximize a profit. Likewise at the other end of the competitive spectrum in a monopolistic situation, where a firm is so powerful that it is not affected by the actions of others, an entrepreneur can also act rationally to seek to maximize a profit. In an oligopolistic situation, however, where a few sellers produce either almost identical products (steel, nylon, and so forth) or differentiated products (automobiles, cigarettes, and so forth), it may well be that sales maximization rather than profit maximization is the chief economic consideration (Baumol, 1958). If this is so, competition for markets and therefore market locations would be more important than in situations where it is assumed that the chief economic consideration is profit maximization.

Behavioristic considerations are much more complex for they involve decisions based on (1) the assumption that it is a group of actors within the firm rather than an individual who is the firm that acts; (2) a recognition that the behavior of the actor is conditioned by personal as well as economic factors; and (3) the fact that the rewards or goals sought by the actors are usually so complex that any decision (such as location decision) is a compromise of rewards or goals. Consequently the behavioristic considerations with respect to the allocation of industry between settlements are very difficult to place in a theoretical framework (Pred, 1967 and 1969).

GENERAL FACTORS AFFECTING THE LOCATION OF MANUFACTURING

In general the myriad economic and noneconomic factors that are thought to affect the location of manufacturing can be listed as raw materials, fuel, labor, wage levels, unionization, consumer demand, capital, space (land), climate, water, taxes, transportation, government, and foreign trade. There are others that can be important with respect to the location of manufacturing within urban areas, but these will be discussed in Chapter 14; in this chapter we are specifically concerned with factors influencing the location of manufacturing at settlements.

RAW MATERIALS

Traditionally industrial location analysis has placed great emphasis on the role of raw materials in attracting manufacturing. This factor proved particularly important with respect to the development of manufacturing in the late eighteenth and early nineteenth century in North America. For example, the early location of the wool and textile industry in New England is commonly attributed to the abundant local supply of raw wool in that area. More recently the location of the pulp and paper industry within the general vicinity of forested areas such as New Brunswick, Canada; the fruit packing and canning industry near truck farms and orchards in California; and the cheese and butter processing industries within dairying areas such as in Wisconsin reemphasize the importance of raw material locations.

FUEL

Fuel, whether it be from coal, natural gas, petroleum, nuclear power, or hydroelectricity, is a common input to all industry. Fuel is used to create energy, and as a consequence one type frequently can be substituted for another. In early industrial North America steam provided energy, and this steam was created by boiling water using coal or wood as the fuel. Today the great proportion of manufacturing activity uses electricity for energy, and so one type of fuel is easily substituted for another. Thus the selection of one type of fuel as against another frequently depends on its energy-producing efficiency as measured by its Btu (British thermal unit) content. The recent revival of the coal industry in the United States is thus related to the fact that by 1967 coal was the cheapest fuel available for power production in the nation as a whole. The cost per million Btus in 1967 for coal was $.248 compared with $.258 in 1961; whereas the cost of producing 1 million Btus in 1967 from crude oil was $.324 ($.355 in 1961) and natural gas was $.250 ($.251 in 1961). The regional variations in these costs are also extremely important, for the use of coal is less expensive in the North and East but more expensive in the South and West, whereas oil is less expensive in the South and West but more expensive in the North and East.

LABOR

The availability of labor and its productivity are vital factors in every industrial activity, though labor requirements are by no means uniform for all industries. Some manufacturing industries require large volumes of cheap unskilled labor, whereas others require skilled labor and are not so concerned with the price. Thus those industries with a high labor to capital ratio are likely to be strongly influenced by labor costs and productivity in their location, whereas those industries with a low labor to capital ratio are more likely to be influenced by nonlabor factors. It is generally considered that much of the recent growth of manufacturing in the Southeast of the United States can be explained partially by the availability of large quantities of low-cost labor in that area. On the other hand, although wages in Southern California are extremely high, the rapid growth of modern electronics industries in that area can be explained in part by the availability of a large labor pool of highly skilled technical workers.

In fact rarely does the availability of labor alone influence the location of manufacturing. Admittedly there are cases where an abundant supply of labor, such as female labor, does attract a firm that can use large quantities of this type of resource. But most firms, considering present-day mobility, feel that, if a labor surplus does exist in an area, it is as much a result of its poor quality as anything else. Consequently firms may well seek to avoid locating in such areas. The whole question of labor availability is therefore extremely complex, and in North America the trade-off between productivity and wage rates is a less important consideration than some of the other factors being discussed in this section.

CONSUMER DEMAND

Demand, or markets, is becoming an increasingly important factor affecting the location of manufacturing. This is because an increasingly large proportion of modern industrial activity is devoted more to the production of consumer needs than producer goods. Furthermore, these consumers are becoming increasingly concentrated in the largest urban areas, which are also becoming on a per capita basis increasingly more wealthy. In fact a large proportion of the growth of modern economic activity is devoted to the production of consumer goods and the fulfillment of desires for these goods created by the "North American way of life." This demand is kept buoyant by large-scale advertising and continuous and ever-increasing changes in fashions and styles. As urban societies are much more likely to accept and in fact encourage changes of this type, it is likely that consumer demand will show little sign of abatement in the future. Market considerations consequently are likely to increase in importance.

CAPITAL

Although capital is rarely considered as an important factor affecting the location of manufacturing, there is evidence to suggest that in some capital-scarce parts of North America this has been a very real factor inhibiting industrial growth. Firms are much more likely to construct, expand, and modernize in those areas where they can easily obtain short-term credits and capital advances. These areas usually have many financial institutions where incomes and profits are large enough to permit the accumulation of surplus capital. Thus it is not surprising that industrialists find it easier to locate and expand within large metropolitan regions than within relatively poor peripheral rural areas.

LAND

Although space, or land, is very important with respect to the location of manufacturing within urban areas, there is sufficient evidence to indicate that it is also quite an important consideration on a regional basis. For example Fuchs (1962, p. 98) suggests that there is a high correlation between the availability of land and manufacturing employment and value added at the state level of aggregation in the United States. This is probably due to two main factors. First, the great increase in the use of the automobile for commuting has meant that many manufacturing plants have to provide vast areas of land for parking and that the cost of this land has become an important variable in their decision-making matrix. Secondly, most manufacturing plants use assembly-line methods requiring considerable areas of horizontal space, and this along with potential expansion plans requires even greater areas of flat level land assignable to the plant itself. Thus, those states that have quantities of cheap, serviced industrial land available are more likely to attract manufacturing than those that do not.

CLIMATE

Although a vast proportion of the total manufacturing activity of North America is in the North and East of the United States and along the northern shores of Lake Erie and Lake Ontario, this does not imply that these areas are ideally suited for industrial development in terms of climate. As far as managers and workers are concerned, there is little doubt that most people prefer to live in a mild and equable climate; and much of the expansion of modern manufacturing has in fact taken place in those parts of North America where such climates exist. This is, of course, partly due to the fact that a considerable proportion of modern industrial growth is associated with the aircraft industry, which prefers to locate in areas where testing can take place the year round. Furthermore, the U.S. Armed Forces, which are an important source of income in some areas, have also chosen to locate their bases in warmer climates, so that outdoor training need not be curtailed during certain times of the year. Thus it is not surprising that Fuchs indicates at the state level of aggregation that those states with warmer climates have experienced a relatively greater rate of growth in manufacturing during the last thirty years (Fuchs, 1962, p. 98). This factor is likely to be of increasing importance in the future as more and more people seek locations where year-round outdoor recreation is possible.

GOVERNMENT Policy

Of increasing importance in recent years is the degree to which governmental activities affect the location of manufacturing. This can occur in a number of directions, two of which have proven to be extremely important. The first concerns the expenditures of government for defense purposes, which have risen to almost half of the national budget of the United States during the past decade. These expenditures have not been spread evenly across the country, and the impact of the expenditures have been both positive and negative.

Thus a recent study by Bolton (1965) indicates that defense purchases have encouraged a rapid growth of the defense industry in the West and South of the United States but have had a very small effect on industrial expansion and location in the North and East except for Connecticut. This is because much of modern defense expenditures are concerned with the development of sophisticated armaments and missile systems requiring technologically advanced industries that are less likely to be located in the older industrial areas.

A second way in which government has affected the location of manufacturing is through regional development policies that are either concerned with alleviating areas of unemployment or areas of slow growth and economic stress through programs of tax holidays and capital grants (Yeates and Lloyd, 1970). Thus in Canada the federal government attempts to attract industry to locate in the Maritime Provinces and in the slow-growth areas of Quebec and Northern Ontario and the Prairie Provinces. Similarly in the United States federal programs are in effect to promote industrial growth in Appalachia. At a more local level, states and local governments attempt to attract manufacturing also with tax inducements, free land, or cheap buildings. As a result of these different programs of inducement at all levels of government, it is becoming increasingly apparent that government policy is an important factor in determining the location of manufacturing.

FOREIGN TRADE

Fuchs (1962, pp. 89–90) suggests that two kinds of changes in foreign trade patterns could affect the location of manufacturing. One would occur if the direction of trade altered, for example from being primarily directed to Europe to being associated with Asia. Such a change could result in a significant relocation of industries, particularly those that are involved with exports. Another possibility is that there could be significant change in the raw materials being used, which could be exported from an entirely different area. This too could affect the location of industrial activity. The indication is that such changes have not really been all that dramatic during the last forty years, and this has not been a significant factor in industrial location in the United States. There has, however, been a significant increase in trade between Canada and the United States. This has reinforced the concentration of industrial location in Southern Ontario and in Montreal in Canada, and there has undoubtedly been a concomitant but less pronounced effect in adjacent areas in the United States. This effect has been particularly well demonstrated for Southern Ontario by Ray (1965) who suggests that the U.S. parent companies do in fact tend to regionally differentiate in the location of their branch plants.

TRANSPORTATION

The influence of transportation on the location of industry is evident throughout North America. This is particularly well illustrated by the ribbons of manufacturing plants found along railroad routes and by the growth of industry along or within the vicinity of major interstate highways. In particular those areas that are favored with many different types of transportation facilities such as water, rail, highways, and airports are particularly well suited to the location of manufacturing. Chicago is a particularly good example of a manufacturing area that is well served with railroads, water transportation through canals and the Great Lakes, interstate highways and good air links to the rest of North America and the world.

THE INFLUENCE OF TRANSPORTATION COSTS ON LOCATION

Transportation is so important in urban geography that it can be used as a basic theme for tying together into some general theoretical statements many factors considered to be affecting the location of manufacturing plants. Our discussion will proceed with an analysis of the locational framework, variations in transport costs by type of commodity, and the influence of labor costs.

THE LOCATIONAL FRAMEWORK

Certain locations of industry, such as mining, are easily explained, for the extraction of raw materials has to take place where the raw materials are located. Although many cities with 10,000 or more inhabitants in 1930 had part of their work force employed in mining, Harris (1943) classified only fourteen of them as "mining" towns. Of these, the great majority are coal mining towns, located in Colorado, Southern Illinois, and the Appalachian areas of West Virginia and Pennsylvania (Fig. 6.1A). The remaining minority are iron mining towns in Michigan and Montana, and the copper mining city of Butte, Montana. Nelson's (1955) multifunctional classification designates many more towns as having a concentration of employment in mining (Fig. 6.1B). Of the 897 cities with 10,000 or more people in 1950 included in the Nelson analysis, 46 are defined as mining towns. A notable addition to the coal mining and iron mining towns delimited by Harris in 1930 are the petroleum cities of Texas, Oklahoma, and Kansas in 1950. The raw materials produced in mining towns are then refined (partially

FIG. 6.1. THE DISTRIBUTION OF MINING TOWNS AS CLASSIFIED BY HARRIS (A) AND BY NELSON (B). (*Source:* After Harris, 1943, Fig. 7 and Nelson, 1955, Fig. 10.)

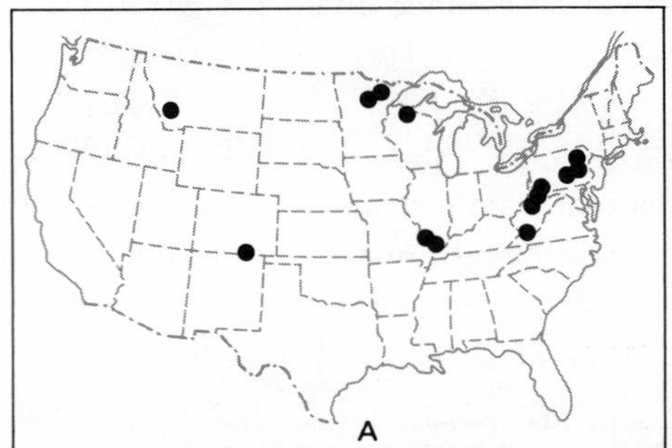

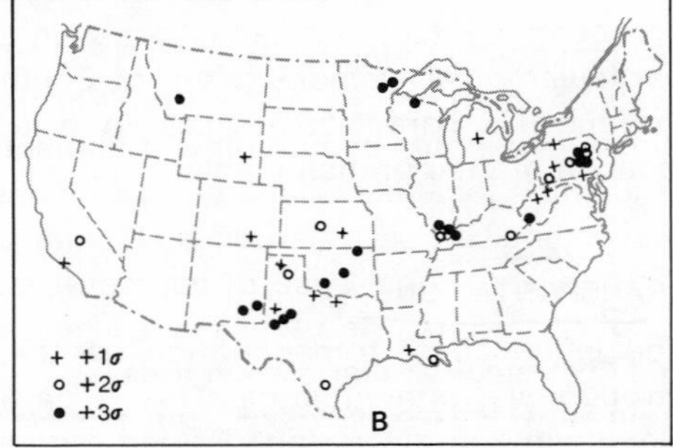

manufactured) or used directly as inputs into other industries. The manufacturing of these raw materials into finished products is often a complex process involving many different kinds of manufacturing activity and often many different individual firms.

It is therefore much more simple to regard all industries as manufacturing concerns that receive inputs of one kind or another (either in the form of raw materials or partially processed raw materials) and perform some manufacturing process. Upon completion of this process, the goods then have to be sold either to other industries (to which they become inputs) or to consumers (final demand). This sequence of events involves the movement of goods and materials, which consequently incur transportation costs.

Source of inputs The classical work in the theoretical analysis of the location of manufacturing industries was undertaken by Alfred Weber (1929), who recognized two major classes of location of inputs to the manufacturing process. One class is the *ubiquities,* which are materials available everywhere at the same price. On the macro-scale the best example of this type of input would be air. At the regional or local level examples of this type of input could be electricity, if the rates are uniform over a large area, and water, if it can be piped to any particular locality.

The second type of inputs recognized by Weber are *localized materials.* These are material inputs that can be obtained only in a geographically well-defined locality. In order to simplify an understanding of the locational effect of these, Weber classified them into two different types. The simplest are the pure materials, which enter to the extent of their full weight into the finished product. Examples of this type of material input are yarns in the textile weaving industry and prefabricated products, such as tires, steering wheels, and electrical wiring, in the automobile manufacturing industry.

The second and more complex type of localized material recognized by Weber are the gross materials, which impart only a proportion, or none, of their weight into the finished product. An extreme type of gross material, at the opposite end of the scale from the pure materials, is fuel, which adds no weight to the finished product. There are, however, many types of gross materials between fuel and the pure materials. The mineral ores, such as iron ore and zinc ore in the metalliferous industries and wood in the furniture industries, are clear examples of this group.

The destination of outputs The destination of the output of a firm can be referred to as the *market area* of the firm. For those industries that produce outputs used directly as inputs by one other manufacturing concern, the market area of the firm is a single location. Similarly those industries that produce goods for a single settlement can be regarded as having one single market area. Thus in the simplest locational case of all, where only ubiquities are used as the material input of the firm, and there is a single market area, the manufacturing process will take place at that market area.

In most cases, however, the market area is distributed quite widely over

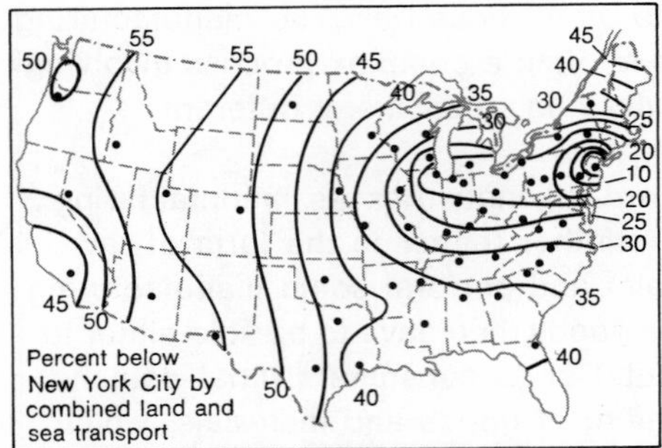

FIG. 6.2. MARKET POTENTIAL SURFACE FOR THE UNITED STATES BASED ON COMBINED LAND AND SEA TRANSPORTATION. (*Source:* Harris, 1954, Fig. 6.)

space and involves not only one settlement but many settlements. Harris's market potential map (Fig. 6.2) indicates that, although New York City has the highest market potential in 1950, there is a broad area covering the eastern seaboard from Boston to Washington, D.C., and extending westward to Chicago in which each settlement has 80 percent or more of the market potential of New York City (Harris, 1954). Maps of population potential produced by Warntz (1965) would tend to suggest this pattern has hardly changed in recent years. Thus, even if ubiquities only are used, the location of the manufacturing plant is not immediately obvious.

The *principle of the median location* suggests that, if a firm using ubiquitous materials as inputs wishes to minimize the cost of distributing its output to its market area, it will locate in the median position with respect to the distribution of consumers (Alonso, 1964). The operation of this principle can be demonstrated with respect to the location of a firm and the distribution of its purchasers along a line (Fig. 6.3). If the firm locates at D (in the middle), the transportation costs to supply the consumers at A, B, C, D, E, F, G, H, and I will be 45; if it locates at F, they will be 43; but if the firm locates at E (the median location), the total costs of transportation will be 42 units. The principle of the median location is, of course, one very persuasive reason for consumer-oriented industries locating in the largest urban areas of all.

The spatial distribution of manufacturing towns Both Harris and Nelson present maps of manufacturing towns that are roughly similar (Fig. 6.4). There is a marked

FIG. 6.3. DIAGRAMMATIC REPRESENTATION OF THE PRINCIPLE OF THE MEDIAN LOCATION (EACH INTERVAL REPRESENTS ONE UNIT OF TRANSPORT COSTS).

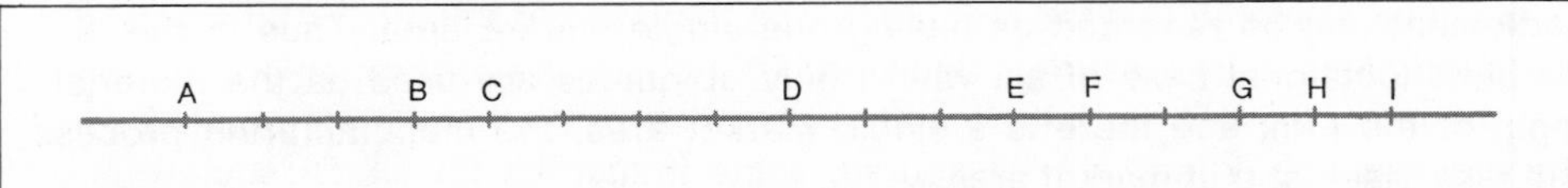

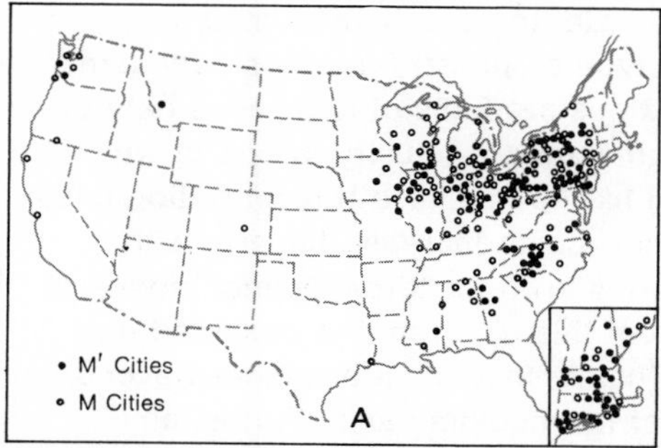

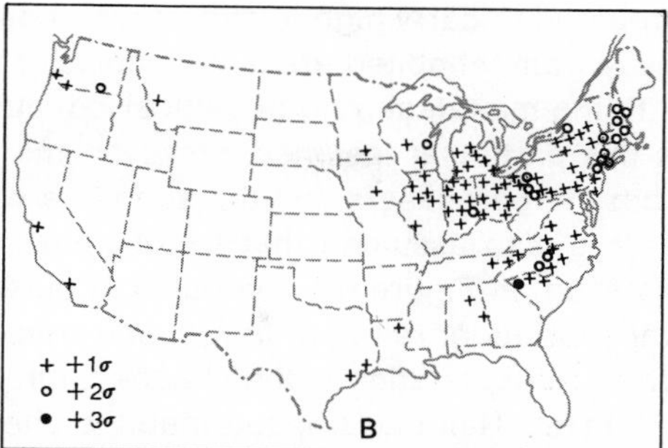

FIG. 6.4. THE DISTRIBUTION OF MANUFACTURING TOWNS AS CLASSIFIED BY HARRIS (A) AND BY NELSON (B). (*Source:* After Harris, 1943, Fig. 2 and Nelson, 1955, Fig. 2.)

concentration on both maps of manufacturing towns within the area of highest market potential (Fig. 6.2), and in the southeastern part of the United States, particularly along the Appalachian Piedmont ("fall-line" towns). There is a noticeable absence on both maps of towns with a concentration of employment in manufacturing west of the Mississippi River.

TRANSPORTATION COSTS AND LOCATION

The previous discussion has emphasized the fact that the spatial considerations involving the source of inputs and the destination of outputs in the manufacturing process involve considerations of transportation cost. It is also clear that these considerations operate within a very complex framework of types of material input and output, each of which also has vital spatial connotations. In order to see how these considerations intertwine to affect the intersettlement location of industry, we shall develop a set of simple models, the first group being concerned with transportation costs, and the second, with weight loss.

Variations in transportation costs We shall assume that there is one source of a particular raw material for a manufacturing company and that this concern also has one area to which it sells. The source of inputs and the destination of outputs are spatially differentiated. The manufacturing firm therefore has to decide whether it is going to establish itself either at the location of its raw materials or at the marketplace, or at some location between these two sites. Each of these decisions involves some transportation costs. Either the raw materials have to be shipped to the marketplace or the finished products have to be shipped from the raw material location to the marketplace, or the raw materials have to be shipped part way, processed, and the manufactured product then shipped to the marketplace.

It will be assumed that the manufacturing firm seeks to minimize these transportation costs in its locational decision. This is not an unreasonable assumption, because these costs simply add to the price of the finished product at the marketplace. There are, of course, some industries for which society is prepared to carry high transportation costs in order to have them located far away from inhabited areas. Examples of this type of industry are those concerned with the manufacturing of explosives and noxious products of a gaseous nature. In this particular instance, however, the manufacturing industry is one in which both the purchasers and the suppliers would like to minimize transportation costs.

It is also assumed that these transportation costs increase linearly with distance. In Figure 6.5 general cost curves are shown for three distinct modes of transportation: railroad, barge, and truck. From this diagram it is observed that water transportation is the cheapest for long hauls; that is, all distances beyond 360 miles. Railroad transportation is cheapest for medium hauls; that is, any distance between 100 and 360 miles. Truck transportation is the cheapest for short hauls; that is, any distance within 100 miles of any particular location. In this particular model we shall assume that there is only one means of transportation connecting the two places and that this is the railroad.

It is also assumed that a given quantity of raw material yields the same quantity of finished product. In other words, these materials are pure materials, for they do not incur any weight loss in manufacturing. In the first set of models to be discussed, this assumption is kept rigid and various assumptions concerning transportation costs are relaxed; in the second series of models to be discussed, gross materials are used; that is, weight loss is allowed to occur.

Transportation Costs Increase Linearly with Distance

In the simplest model of all we assume that transportation costs increase linearly with distance, a situation which has been exemplified in Figure 6.5. Furthermore, the cost of shipping the raw material (R) from the raw material location (SR) to the marketplace (MP) is exactly the same as shipping the finished product (P) from SR to MP. As transportation costs increase linearly with distance at the same rate for both R and P, the same total transportation cost is incurred at any location between the raw material site and the marketplace.

This situation is indicated in Figure 6.6 by the line T.T.C. (total transport costs). This line is calculated by constructing two transportation cost lines, one

FIG. 6.5. TRANSPORT COSTS INCREASE LINEARLY WITH DISTANCE.

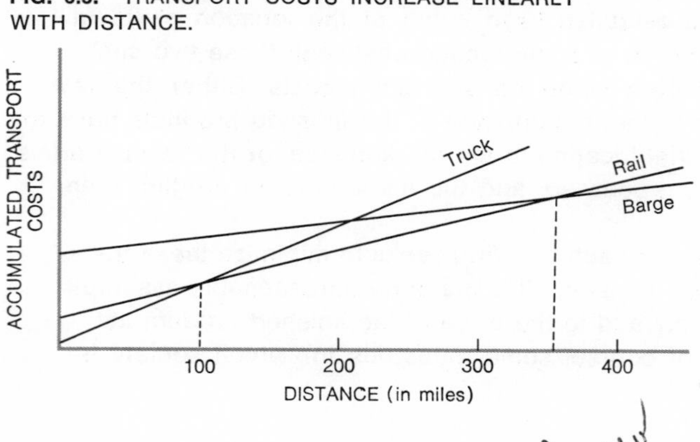

know

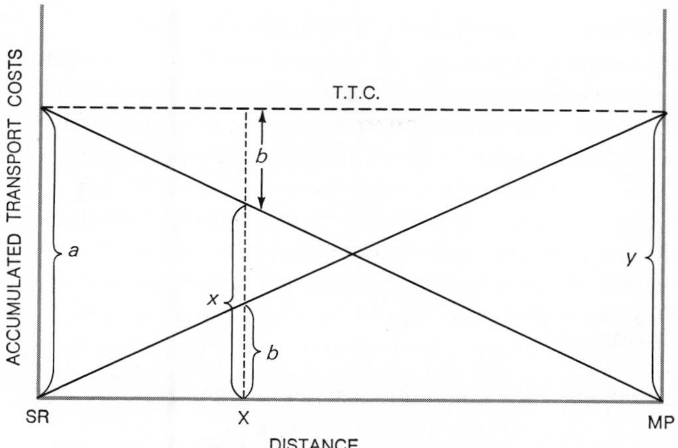

FIG. 6.6. THE EFFECT OF EQUAL COSTS OF TRANSPORT FOR RAW MATERIALS AND FINISHED PRODUCTS ASSUMING TRANSPORT COSTS ARE LINEARLY RELATED TO DISTANCE.

for raw materials, with its orgin at SR, and one for finished products, with its origin at MP. The line from SR indicates the costs of transporting R, and that from MP indicates the cost of transporting P. Thus if the manufacturing firm locates at SR, the transportation charge will be $a =$ TTC. If the firm locates at MP, the transportation charge will be $y =$ TTC. If the firm locates at X, the transportation costs will be b for transporting the raw material to X and x for transporting the finished product to MP. It is obvious that $x + b =$ TTC. In this particular situation, therefore, the manufacturing concern can locate anywhere.

Transportation Costs Increase at a Decreasing Rate with Distance

In reality, however, transportation costs increase at a decreasing rate with distance (Fig. 6.7). This is because the freight rate structure increases by zones (Fig. 6.8). Thus a certain amount is paid for the first few miles, an additional amount for the next few miles, and so on. The width of each zone increases with

FIG. 6.7. TRANSPORT COSTS INCREASE AT A DECREASING RATE WITH DISTANCE.

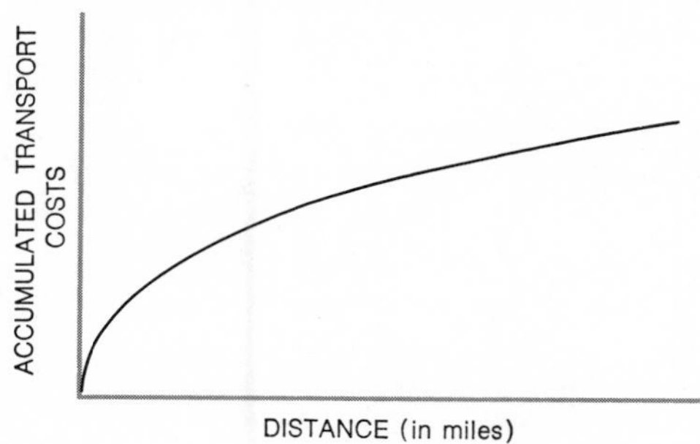

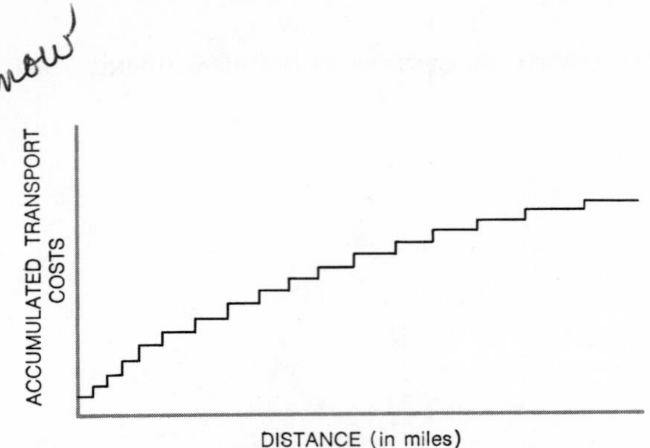

FIG. 6.8. FREIGHT RATE ZONES RESULT IN A STEPPED TRANSPORT COST FUNCTION.

distance from the point of shipment. As a consequence the average freight rate structure is curvilinear and not linear (as suggested in Figure 6.5).

In this situation, if the same quantity of raw materials yields the same quantity of finished products and the freight rate curves for both the raw material and the finished product are the same, the manufacturer can locate either at the raw material location (SR) or at the marketplace (MP). However, the industry cannot locate at any point in between, because at intervening locations the total costs of transportation will be higher than incurred at either SR or MP (Fig. 6.9).

Transportation Costs for Finished Products Are Different from Those for Raw Materials

Transportation costs are usually higher per ton for the finished product than they are per ton of raw material. Figure 6.10 illustrates this quite clearly for

FIG. 6.9. THE EFFECT OF EQUAL TRANSPORT COSTS FOR RAW MATERIALS AND FINISHED PRODUCTS ASSUMING A CURVILINEAR RELATIONSHIP BETWEEN TRANSPORT COSTS AND DISTANCE. COMPARE THIS DIAGRAM WITH FIG. 6.6.

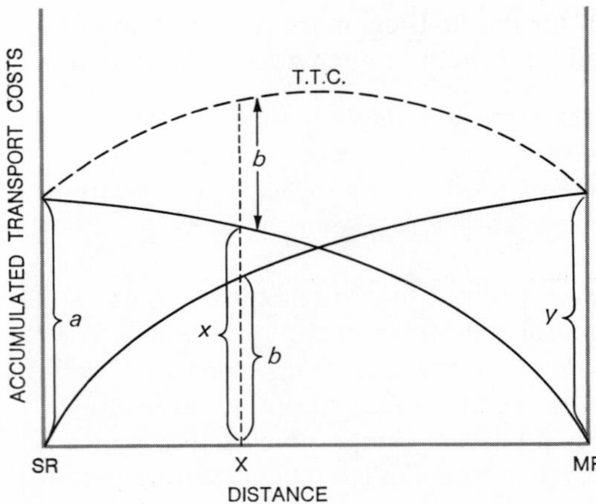

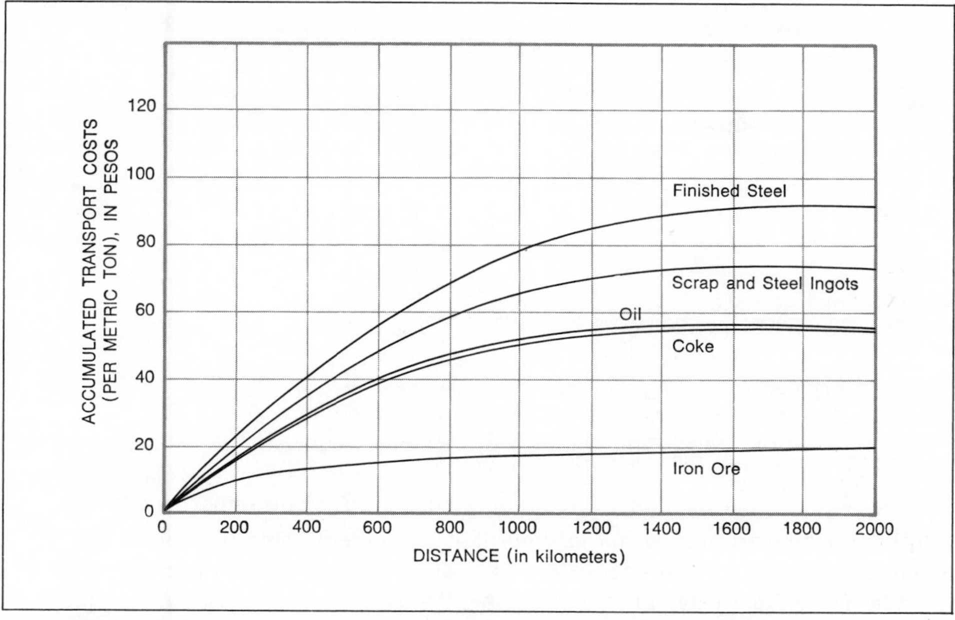

FIG. 6.10. TRANSPORT COSTS FOR FINISHED PRODUCTS ARE NORMALLY HIGHER THAN THOSE FOR RAW MATERIALS AND PARTIALLY FINISHED PRODUCTS. (*Source:* Kennelly, 1954, Fig. 4.)

Mexico. In this case finished steel has much higher transportation costs per ton than scrap and steel ingots, which in turn are much higher than those for oil, coke, and iron ore. One major reason for these differences is that as manufactured goods have increased in value due to the process of manufacturing, transportation costs constitute a lower proportion of the total product than if they were transported in an unprocessed form. Manufactured goods are therefore said to be capable of bearing a higher transportation charge (Hoover, 1963, p. 25). Consequently transportation companies charge higher freight rates for these goods.

In Figure 6.11 the freight rate curve for the finished product is therefore steeper than that for the raw material. Consequently the transportation charges per ton will be lower if the industry locates at the marketplace than if it locates at the raw material location. Thus, in a situation where a given quantity of raw material yields the same quantity of finished product, the industry will locate at the marketplace for the total cost of transportation will be minimal at that location.

Variation in weight loss Thus far we have assumed that the material inputs used are pure materials that incur no weight loss in the manufacturing process. We have previously indicated that the concept of weight loss as developed by Weber refers to the weight by which a given unit of input is reduced during the manufacturing process. Thus, a weight loss of 40 percent would indicate that a given quantity of input was reduced in weight by 40 percent in the manufacturing process.

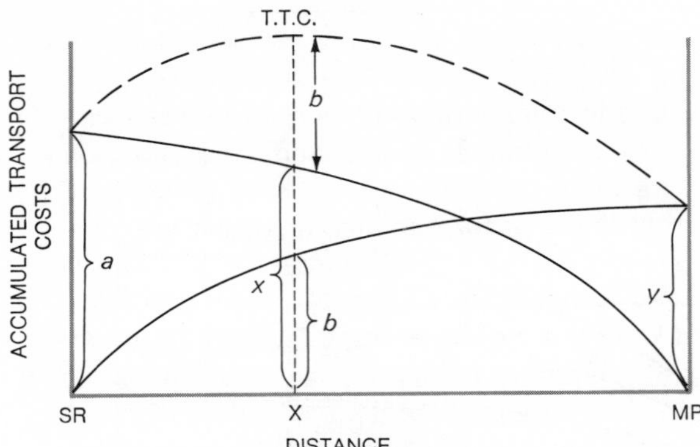

FIG. 6.11. THE EFFECT OF HIGHER TRANSPORT COSTS FOR FINISHED PRODUCTS THAN FOR RAW MATERIALS ASSUMING A CURVILINEAR RELATIONSHIP BETWEEN TRANSPORT COSTS AND DISTANCE. COMPARE THIS DIAGRAM WITH FIG. 6.9.

In this particular case let us assume that the freight rates per ton of a manufactured product average for the total distance between SR and MP, $20 per mile. The freight rates for raw materials (R) average for the same distance $15 per mile. Let us assume that 1,000 tons of raw material are to be processed into finished product (P), the amount of which will vary according to the weight loss in the production process.

If the manufacturing firm establishes itself at the marketplace, it will always have to transport 1,000 tons of ore to MP. As a consequence, the total transportation cost will be $15,000 per mile. If the weight loss is 20 percent, and the firm locates at SR, 1,000 tons of raw material will yield 800 tons of finished product and the total cost of shipping this amount will be $16,000 per mile. Thus with a weight loss of 20 percent, the firm will gain an advantage of $1,000 per mile by locating at the marketplace. However, with a weight loss of 40 percent, 1,000 tons of R yields 600 tons of P. As the cost of transporting this amount at the manufactured product rate is $12,000 per mile, the firm will gain an advantage of $3,000 per mile, if it locates at the raw material site. Consequently, given the transportation cost structure for finished products and raw materials, the higher the weight loss, the more likely it is that a firm will locate at the source of inputs, taking only transportation costs and weight loss into consideration.

Special cases Within this framework of transportation costs and weight loss, there are a number of irregular or unusual situations. In this section we shall discuss three of these: transshipment points, intransit freight rate privileges, and the basing-point system.

Transshipment Points

In the transference of products from one location to another, often more than one means of transport has to be used. An obvious example of such a situation is where a given destination is separated from a source of input by a land surface and a water surface, resulting in the use of some form of water transportation, such as ship or barge, and land transportation, such as railroad or trucks. At the junction of two transportation surfaces of this kind, or at any point where two different means of transportation meet, the goods have to be transshipped. There are many different kinds of transshipment points, an obvious example being seaports.

In the case of seaports, as with many other kinds of transshipment points, not only do goods have to be moved from one means of transportation to another, but they also must be broken down into different units because an ocean-going vessel can carry goods in larger units than the land transportation media, such as a railroad car. It is therefore not uncommon to find a great deal of industry located around port areas for, although it may be feasible to ship bulky goods over great distances by water, due to the fact that shipping costs per mile for this media are relatively low, transportation of the material by a land media would be very expensive. As a consequence, it may well pay an industrial firm to locate at the port and gain the advantages of cheap water transportation, then break down the bulk of the raw material by a manufacturing process and send the product to the marketplace, even though the freight rate would be higher. This, of course, would be particularly true for those raw materials that have a high weight loss. Also, ports and break-of-bulk points are often sites for industry because they can collect raw materials from many locations. In fact, in the days before the development of the railroad, inland cities could not grow very large, for transportation costs were at a maximum at these locations. "It is no accident that the large cities of antiquity grew where they had access to sea-going ships and usually they developed at the mouth of rivers where they also had access to downriver transportation" (Gilmore, 1953, p. 23).

Intransit Freight Rate Privileges

There are many cases, however, where industries locate between their raw material sources and their market areas, even on the same surface of transportation and even along the same means of transportation. One reason for this is that some industries receive intransit freight rate privileges from transportation companies. This system permits industries to transport their raw materials from a particular location, to manufacture the product at some intermediate point, and then transport the finished product to the marketplace: They pay the same rate as if they had transported the raw material directly to the marketplace, and there undergone the process of manufacturing.

The reason for a situation of this kind can often be traced back to some historical sequence. An industry may have located at a particular point because raw materials were there, but then these raw materials became exhausted. When the railway system expanded farther into the hinterland, the owners of the industry and the owners of the railway system might well have come to some agreement concerning intransit freight rate privileges, which was a mutual advantage at that time to both parties concerned. The railway would not want to lose the business and would not want to waste the facilities that might well have been built at the manufacturing plant. In turn the manufacturing company might not want to uproot itself and incur costs of relocation. It is however quite obvious that, if this situation continues for many years, the added costs of these freight rate privileges has to be paid by somebody; and if it is not by the manufacturing company, then it is by the railroad company, and whoever pays will pass these costs on to other users.

The Basing-Point System

The basing-point system developed particularly in the United States in the late nineteenth and early twentieth centuries in the steel industry. The operation of steel firms entails great expenses in plant construction at particular locations. The transportation costs involved for finished products are therefore fairly low in proportion to the total cost involved in the production process. At the turn of the century the greatest concentration of steel production in the United States was at Pittsburgh. Consequently steel producers in Pittsburgh were able to exert persuasive powers over all others regardless of where they were located. These persuasive powers involved the establishment of delivered prices from Pittsburgh as the selling price for all steel producers regardless of where they were located (Pittsburgh "plus").

Thus a simple basing-point system indicates that the price that a purchaser pays per ton of steel is equal to the price per ton of steel at place X plus the cost of transporting that product from X to the location of the buyer. Thus with Pittsburgh "plus," even if the steel were produced in Chicago and purchased in Chicago, the buyer would pay the cost of transportation as if it were produced in Pittsburgh and transported from Pittsburgh to Chicago. In order to conceal this situation, the only prices quoted for steel were the delivered prices; and the customer was not allowed to pick up the steel for himself. This system later evolved into a multiple basing-point system. The basing-point procedure is primarily a price-fixing system and consequently is now illegal.

The geographical implications of this system were easily exaggerated, for it still pays the producer to locate near his market if the transportation cost situation indicates (Hoover, 1963, pp. 56–57). For example, a steel producer in Los Angeles sells to the Los Angeles market at a price that includes transportation costs of the finished product from Pittsburgh. This charge is profit to the company and can be used in an attempt to offset any other locational disadvantage of the Los Angeles site.

OTHER LOCATIONAL CONSIDERATIONS

In the previous section we have considered the effect of transportation costs on the location of manufacturing. In this section two other groups of locational factors that tend to influence the location of industry are discussed. These can be defined as labor differentials and agglomerative principles.

Labor differentials Spatial variations in the cost of labor are particularly important for those industries that are labor intensive. Manufacturing will be influenced by factors concerning labor, particularly when there are a number of equally advantageous locations. There are two aspects of labor that can influence the location of manufacturing. The first is where wage rates for similar quality workers are much lower in one area than in another. The second is where the quality and productivity of workers in one area is much higher for the same wage rate than in others. Both these factors, of course, influence the cost of labor as an input to the firm.

Labor cost differentials are maintained as an important spatial factor influencing the location of manufacturing as long as they remain for a relatively lengthy period of time. Of course, if workers in one area realize that for the same quality and quantity of work they can receive a greater wage rate in another location, they will tend to move. Thus, in a perfectly mobile society labor cost differentials will not influence the location of industry to any great extent.

There are, however, various reasons why people do not move. One of these, of course, is that sometimes people prefer to stay with the friends and in the environment that they have known for a long period of time, even though working in that environment results in their receiving a lower wage rate than they might earn elsewhere. Labor cost differentials in theory, however, have a short-run effect; for in the long term, labor migration will tend to even out differentials of this kind.

Agglomerative principles Agglomerative economies arise from a number of factors that either interact or act singly as a cause of lower costs at particular locations. In this section we will discuss three of these factors. The first of these can be attained by the individual firm by increasing the size of the plant to permit either horizontal integration or vertical integration of its production process. Horizontal integration involves the firm's buying out or amalgamating with a number of competitors who produce a similar product. The result is that with a larger gross output the expanded firm can now achieve economies of scale. Economies of scale can also be achieved by vertical integration when a firm combines in a single productive process the plants that produce the input to the factory and also the marketing companies that sell the finished products.

Another agglomerative factor arises from external economies. External economies are difficult to define, but they refer to situations where an industry has a locational advantage because of some situation that exists beyond the influence of the firm. Such a situation can occur when an individual receives the advantages of large-scale production by locating next door to another firm that produces a similar or sequential product. An example of this kind of situation is the clothing industry in New York, where many small firms group together and thereby receive the advantages of horizontal integration without actual amalgamation.

A third agglomerative factor arises from the urbanization economies created by large urban areas through sheer size. It has been tentatively suggested that the forces of agglomeration are particularly strong in cities of 350,000 or more persons (Thompson, 1965, p. 35). Large cities reduce training costs for labor for particular industries, because there will be a large labor pool containing a variety of skilled workers in such areas. Also large cities tend to have larger banks, which will enable the firm to obtain loans more easily to cover short-term fluctuations in demands for cash. There are also the accumulated fixed investments of an urban mass, such as electricity, sewerage, transportation lines, rapid transit, and so forth, which provide advantages for a particular firm in that it will not have to create these fixed investments for itself.

It may be suggested, however, that these urbanization economies become diseconomies in very large urban masses. Current disagglomerative factors such as congestion, overcrowding, pollution, crime, and so forth, will be discussed as urban problems in the last part of the book.

AN EVOLUTIONARY MODEL OF SETTLEMENT GROWTH

The fact that settlements are both service centers and centers of industry has been combined by Martin (1969), along with the economic-base concept, into an impressionistic generalization concerning the growth of urban areas with respect to their industrial base. Martin's model is a long-run theory of internal growth and casts some light on the reason why economic base ratios discussed in the previous chapter tend to change. The model also incorporates growth in response to industrial development. For definitional purposes the theory distinguishes four categories of implantation of industry. These are:

TYPE A. Basic industries that are the original implantations.

TYPE B. Non-basic industries that enter the settlement through some kind of linkage with the original implantations, and basic industries that enter the urban area because of the availability of external economies created by the Type A group. Thus the Type B group depends to one extent or another on the industrial environment created by the Type A basic group.

TYPE C. This group consists of firms and government ventures and institutions that serve the special needs created by growing urban areas. Examples of this type of firm and government activity are water plants and associated services, electricity generating plants, public transport facilities, and the construction industry.

TYPE D. This group consists of services and institutions that serve the essential urban needs of the population. The range of activities in this group are basically the service functions related to settlements as central places.

A dynamic view of the growth of the urban area distinguishes three stages:

1. The stage of original implantations.
2. The stage of linked implantations and external economies.
3. The metropolis stage.

Since activities of Type D come in automatically with population growth, the stage theory does not have to account for these. Furthermore, the evolutionary model is not chronologically mutually exclusive. Even if the city had attained Stage 2, it can still attract firms belonging to Stage 1, although the order of appearance of the stages cannot be inverted.

The first stage is characterized by the implantation of private firms and public institutions that choose a particular urban area for reasons other than the size of the existing population within the city or the presence of other firms. If firms of this type continue to enter and if those already existent continue to grow, then these firms establish the settlement as a growth pole; for these firms are basic industries that provide the essential employment foundations for urban growth.

The settlement has entered Stage 2 when it attracts firms that come in mainly because other firms have come before them. The second stage is an outcome of Stage 1 and is brought about by the appearance of internal markets for intermediate products and external economies. Internal markets are created by linked industries. These linkages can be forward, lateral, or backward. It must be remembered, however, that in many cases these are not external economies because the entering firms have internalized the economies by a rational locational decision. External economies appear because the original implantations of Stage 1 have created the facilities for services that have become part of the infrastructure of the urban area. Thus Stage 2 is categorized by the implantation of firms of Type B and a few of Type A. Along with this urban growth there has, of course, been the concomitant development of central place activities of Type D.

The third stage is a direct consequence of the two preceding stages. It is recognized by the appearance of external diseconomies and the great appearance of nonbasic service industries designed to satisfy the needs of the urban population. These, of course, are particularly those of Type C and Type D. The external diseconomies of water and air pollution, traffic congestion, slums, high crime rates, and so on, are not internalized by the firms or institutions within the urban area; but they do appear in the rising costs of providing utilities and administering the urban mass. In a sense these urban diseconomies create further growth because the population of the urban area is forced to spend part of its income on goods and services to reduce these ill effects of urban growth. Furthermore, there may be capital transfers into the urban area to counteract these ill effects. Also, the growing population has certain needs which must be fulfilled by the implantation of other industries of a nonbasic variety to serve them. The evolutionary model also suggests that the diseconomies of large urban areas may not, in fact, impinge upon growth of metropolitan areas.

The economic facets of a model of this type have been investigated and substantiated by Pred (1966) for the United States in the nineteenth century. In addition, Pred suggests that growing urban areas contain an additional advantage in that the "possibilities of invention and innovation with industries" is "enhanced by an intensifying network of interpersonal communications and confrontations" (Pred, 1966, p. 84). This innovation aspect of urban industrial growth is placed in a probabilistic context by Thompson (1965), who points out that if a town of 50,000 people is likely to produce an industrial innovator once every ten years, then a town of half a million may produce one per year.

Thus it is not just the introduction of basic industries into a settlement that encourages growth. Large urban areas create growth for themselves by being large and having a predominant nonbasic component which shields them against short-run fluctuations in basic industry employment (Thompson, 1965). Furthermore, economies of scale and the oligopolist nature of much of modern industry work in favor of a small number of large urban areas and against the development and growth of industries in smaller settlements.

"SETTLEMENTS AS SERVICE CENTERS"

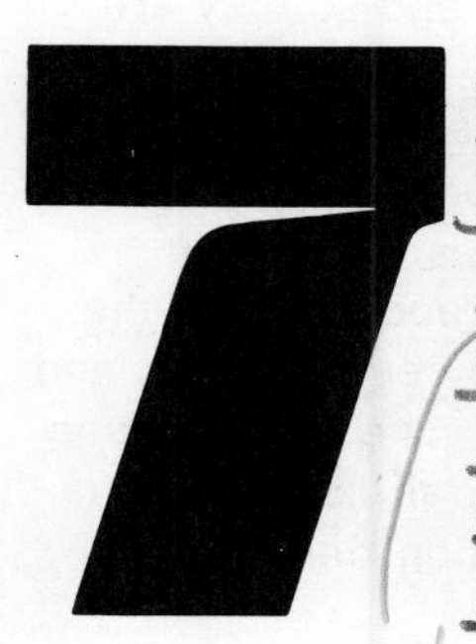

Whereas primary and secondary activities tend to be specialized, the tertiary activities are more generally distributed and are performed in varying amounts by all settlements. The most ubiquitous of all tertiary activities are those connected with the distribution and exchange of goods and services. Without exception, cities are market centers concerned with either the collection of goods from, or the distribution of goods and services to, the people living in the surrounding areas and beyond. For some settlements this marketing function may be overshadowed by other more specialized roles they play in the economic organization of society. But for innumerable others, and especially the smaller settlements in agricultural regions this is often their dominant and only reason for being in the landscape. These are called *central places.* In this chapter we shall discuss the role of settlements as central places, examine some of the spatial regularities that are apparent in the provision of goods and services from them, and review the models generally known as central place theory.

CENTRAL PLACES

Strictly speaking, central places are settlements that are exclusively supported by their role as market centers. As such, "they are neither more nor less than a cluster of retail and service establishments located in a place that provides a convenient point of focus for consumers who visit them to purchase the goods and services they need" (Berry, 1967A, p. 3). The retail and service businesses they provide are known as *central functions,* and these are supplied by establishments (retail stores and service offices). When more than one central function is provided by a single establishment, each is counted separately and called a *functional unit.* For example a drugstore is a central function; it is provided by an establishment that may comprise a number of functional units (drugs, lunch counter, hardware, and so on). The importance of a central place is assessed by the number of different kinds of functions it provides, rather than by its population size.

Quite obviously, central functions are provided by larger cities as well as by smaller ones. But many of them are provided mainly for the inhabitants of the city itself, rather than for people living around about it. In this sense then, larger cities also act in part as market centers for people living in their immediate hinterlands. But the importance of their role as market centers is usually overshadowed by other more specialized functions they perform for much wider areas. Thus although larger places are recognized as performing the central place function, this is not crucial for their continued existence, and so they are not normally thought of as being central places per se.

The tendency for smaller places in agricultural regions to act predominantly as service centers was hinted at in Nelson's (1955) classification of cities. A more complete picture of the nature and distribution of central places is given in Figure 7.1, for South Dakota. Settlements have been classified according to the number of different central functions they provide rather than by employment, and all settlements regardless of their population size are included. The most striking feature about the pattern is the way that the distribution of central places mirrors the distribution of rural population in the state. Rural population densities

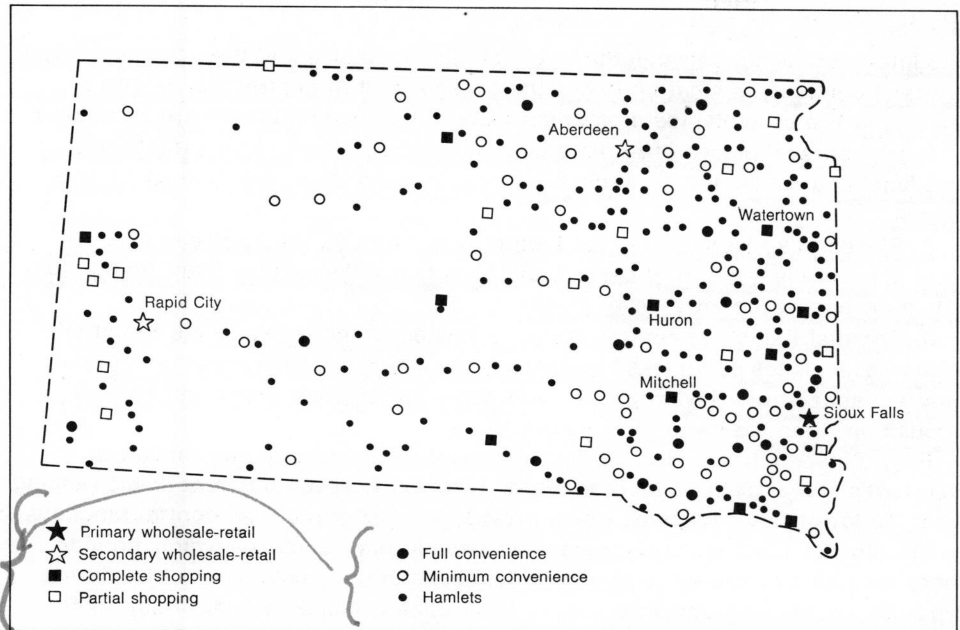

FIG. 7.1. A HIERARCHY OF SERVICE CENTERS IN SOUTH DAKOTA. (*Source:* Borchert and Adams, 1963, Fig. 2.)

decrease from east to west as farming changes from intensive corn livestock fattening to the more extensive cattle ranching on the semiarid rangelands in the western part of the state. Correspondingly the number of central places decreases from east to west, and they become spaced more widely apart.

In visiting marketplaces on a regular basis, consumers want locations that permit them to conduct their business with a minimum amount of effort. Hence central places must be highly accessible to, and be located at points central to, their tributary areas. This quality of location is referred to as *centrality*. The centrality of a place is thought to be reflected by its size measured in terms of the number of different central functions it provides. Thus the larger the functional size of a place, the greater its centrality. Conceptually, centrality, like functional size, is a continuous variable; but in practice it is thought of as having meanings at different scales or levels corresponding to groups of central places of roughly similar functional size. The "full convenience" centers indicated in Figure 7.1, for example, do not all provide exactly the same number nor the same kinds of central functions. They are, however, similar enough to be identified as a class of central places distinct from the functionally more complex "complete shopping" centers or the simpler "hamlets." Hence they are said to be characterized by a higher level of centrality than the hamlets but a lower level of centrality than the complete shopping centers.

THE HIERARCHY OF CENTRAL PLACES

The interrelationship between the levels of functional size and their corresponding levels of centrality is what underlies the organization of central places into a hierarchy. The essential features of the hierarchy of central places are as follows:

1. Higher level places offer more central functions, have more establishments and functional units, and normally are larger in population size than lower level places.

2. Places at a given level in the hierarchy perform all the functions of lower level places plus a group of central functions that differentiates them from, and sets them above, the lower level places.

3. The distribution of central places is related to the levels in the hierarchy. Higher level places occur less frequently in the landscape than lower level places; they are spaced more widely apart and serve larger trade areas and tributary populations than the lower level places.

From Figure 7.1, the size characteristics of the hierarchy are implicit in Borchert's (1963) classification of central places into seven different levels ranging from the lowest level hamlets, which provide at most one or two central functions, to the highest level places—primary wholesale-retail centers—which provide more than 32 different kinds of central functions in conjunction with 14 different types of wholesaling activities. Lower level central places are distinctly more numerous in the state than higher level places; the sequence runs 263 hamlets, 91 convenience centers, 29 shopping centers, and 3 primary wholesale-retail centers. And the differences in population density notwithstanding, lower level places are clearly spaced closer together than the higher level places.

The hierarchy of central places emerges as the fundamental feature in the spatial organization of marketing on account of differences in both the supply of, and the demand for, different goods and services. On the demand side, goods and services are purchased with different frequencies, and consumers differ in the proportions of their incomes they spend on the various goods and services available. On the supply side, some central functions can be supported in greater numbers than others, because of their lower thresholds, or entry requirements.

The threshold concept The establishments providing central functions are small firms, and like all firms they must operate at a profit if they want to stay in business permanently. To do this, they must realize enough sales to at least cover their operating costs, including as part of these a reasonable wage for the entrepreneur. The minimum sales that an establishment must secure in order to survive is called its *threshold*. This varies in size, largely depending on the operating scale of the central function.

Because of the practical difficulties of measuring thresholds, population has been used as a substitute for sales in empirical studies. Moreover, since it is difficult to talk about the minimum population required to support an individual establishment, it is usual to refer to the average establishment for a particular type of central function. Operationally then, the threshold is defined as the minimum population needed to support a given type of central function. It is only by satisfying this threshold that the central function can appear in the landscape. In this way, the different central functions can be thought of as being arrayed along a continuum of threshold size.

Variation in the size of thresholds is perhaps the most important clue in understanding why some central functions are found more often than others in a region. For threshold size is directly related to ubiquity. Hence lower threshold functions can enter the system more easily and occur more frequently than higher threshold functions. Moreover, since the threshold of a given central function is partly a response to how frequently it is demanded, thresholds are directly related to the notion of centrality. It follows that the higher the threshold for a central function, the greater the level of centrality it needs in space. It is for this reason that the higher threshold functions are located at higher level central places in the hierarchy.

Thresholds in Snohomish County

The agreement between threshold size, frequency of occurrence, and the location of central functions is nicely illustrated from a study of 33 central places in Snohomish County, Washington (Berry and Garrison, 1958A). Actual threshold sizes for central functions were estimated from a statistical analysis of the relationship between the population size of central places and the number of establishments of a given function at them. The graph showing the relationship between number of filling stations and population size of places is presented in Figure 7.2 as an example. Each point on the graph corresponds to one of the 33 central places; for example, Lynwood had 9 filling stations and a population of 500 at the time of the study. This graph, like those constructed for each of the other 51 central functions, indicates an *exponential* relationship between the two variables; that is, as places become larger they add fewer establishments of a given central function for each new increment in population. The average relationship of the scatter of points on the graph can be expressed by the best-fitting curve of the exponential growth series, $P = ab^N$, in which P is the population size of a place, N is the number of establishments of the given central function, and a and b are parameters that are estimated empirically from the data. The line representing the average relationship of this sort for filling stations and population size has been drawn in the graph in Figure 7.2.

The equations for the best-fitting curves were then used to estimate the threshold populations needed to support the first complete establishment of each of the 52 different central functions. This was done by calculating the value of P in the equation when $N = 1$. The ranking of the 52 central functions by their threshold population size obtained in this way is given in Table 7.1. From the table, thresholds are shown to range between 196 for filling stations, the lowest order central function in the study area, to 1,424 for health practitioners, which emerges as the highest order function included in the study. Thus, for example, the critical level of demand needed by a drugstore is 458 people and, on average, it can only

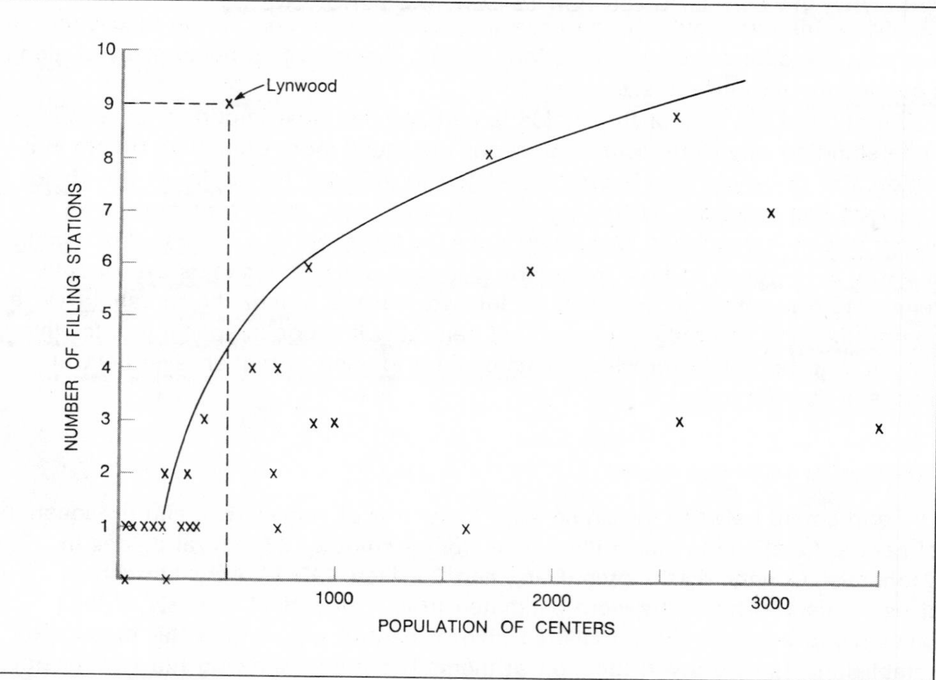

FIG. 7.2. RELATIONSHIP BETWEEN NUMBER OF FILLING STATIONS AND POPULATION SIZE OF CENTRAL PLACES IN SNOHOMISH COUNTY, WASHINGTON. (*Source:* After Berry and Garrison, 1958A, Table 2.)

be supplied from a central place with at least this number of inhabitants. Drugstores would therefore not be found at a place with only 200 inhabitants, which would be only large enough to support one filling station. At this small size of central place the level of centrality is too low, and the diseconomies of scale too great for it to support higher threshold central functions.

The exponential relationship indicated that the population needed to support a second establishment of a given type is not simply twice the size of the threshold for that function, but is in fact more than this. This is illustrated by the curves for four of the central functions shown in Figure 7.3. The shapes of the curves differ according to the threshold size of the functions; high threshold functions (e.g. drugstores) have shallower curves than low threshold functions (e.g. filling stations). This indicates that high order functions need a larger increment in population to support the second establishment than lower order functions do. Another interesting point is revealed from the way the curves tail off to the right. This indicates that the increment in population needed to support each additional establishment gets larger; thus the increment in population needed to support, say, the fifth filling station at a place is greater than that which was needed to support the fourth filling station, and so on. Hence the duplication

TABLE 7.1. THRESHOLD SIZES FOR 52 CENTRAL FUNCTIONS IN SNOHOMISH COUNTY, WASHINGTON, 1958

Central Functions	Threshold Sizes	Number of Establishments for P = 938	P = 2800
Filling stations	196	6.3	9.9
Food stores	254	3.3	5.5
Churches	265	6.0	10.2
Restaurants and snack bars	276	5.3	9.2
Taverns	282	3.4	5.6
Elementary schools	322	3.1	5.2
Physicians	380	3.6	6.8
Real estate agencies	384	3.7	6.9
Appliance stores	385	3.4	6.3
Barber shops	386	2.1	3.3
Auto dealers	398	3.9	7.6
Insurance agencies	409	4.0	7.8
Fuel oil dealers	419	2.8	5.3
Dentists	426	2.7	5.1
Motels	430	2.7	5.2
Hardware stores	431	2.2	3.9
Auto repair shops	435	2.4	4.4
Fuel dealers (coal, etc.)	453	2.2	4.2
Drugstores	458	1.9	3.3
Beauticians	480	2.1	3.8
Auto parts dealers	488	2.0	3.7
Meeting halls	525	1.8	3.3
Feed stores	526	2.0	3.9
Lawyers	528	1.7	3.2
Furniture stores	546	1.9	3.7
Variety stores, 5 & 10	549	1.7	2.9
Freight lines and storage	567	1.8	3.2
Veterinarians	579	1.7	3.3
Apparel stores	590	1.5	2.6
Lumberyards	598	1.5	2.7
Banks	610	1.4	2.3
Farm implements	650	1.4	3.2
Electric repair shops	693	1.3	2.2
Florists	729	1.3	2.3
High schools	732	1.2	2.1
Dry cleaners	754	1.2	2.1
Local taxi services	762	1.2	2.3
Billiard halls and bowling	789	1.2	2.3
Jewelry stores	827	1.1	2.0
Hotels	846	1.1	2.3
Shoe repair shops	896	1.1	2.3
Sporting goods stores	928	1.0	1.8
Frozen food lockers	*938*	*1.0*	*2.0*
Sheet metal works	1076	0.9	1.6
Department stores	1083	0.8	1.5
Optometrists	1140	0.8	1.5
Hospitals and clinics	1159	0.8	1.5
Undertakers	1214	0.8	1.3
Photographers	1243	0.8	1.2
Public accountants	1300	0.7	1.4
Laundries and laundromats	1307	0.7	1.3
Health practitioners	1424	0.7	1.3

Source: Berry and Garrison (1958A), Table 2.

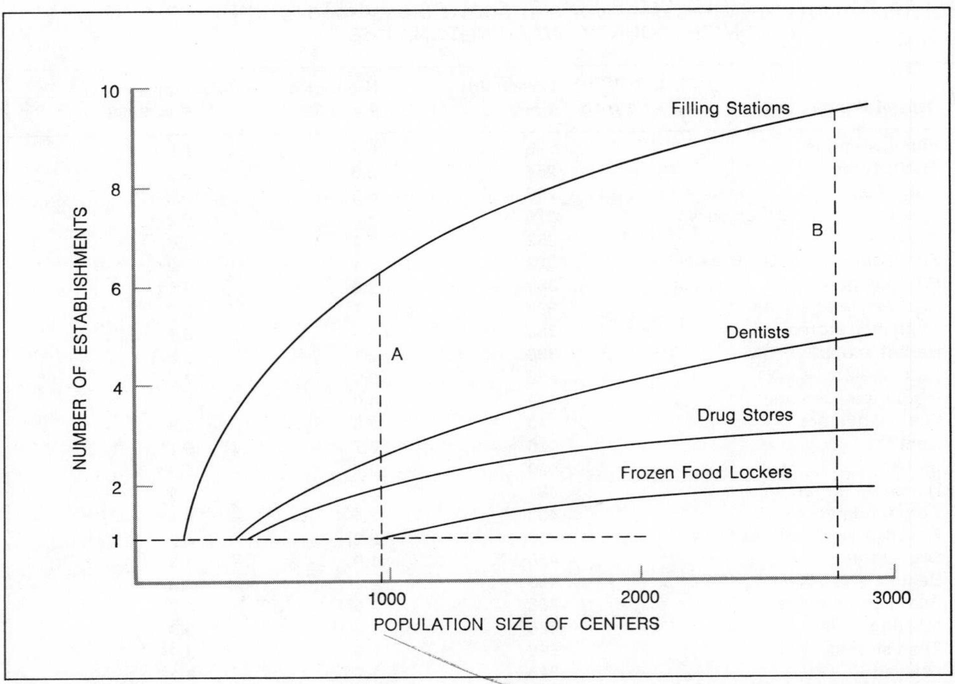

FIG. 7.3. RATES OF DUPLICATION FOR SELECTED CENTRAL FUNCTIONS IN SNOHOMISH COUNTY, WASHINGTON. ON THE GRAPH, LINE A INDICATES THAT A THRESHOLD OF 938 PEOPLE IS NEEDED TO SUPPORT ONE FROZEN FOOD LOCKER, AND LINE B, THAT 2800 PEOPLE ARE NEEDED TO SUPPORT TWO FROZEN FOOD LOCKERS. BY READING ACROSS FROM THESE LINES, THE NUMBER OF ESTABLISHMENTS FOR EACH OF THE OTHER FUNCTIONS CAN BE MEASURED. THE EXACT VALUES ARE PRESENTED IN TABLE 7-1. (*Source:* After Berry and Garrison, 1958B, Fig. 1.)

rate of establishments differs between functions in line with their threshold size and, for any given function, it slows down as the population size of central places gets larger. One of the implications from this is that economies of scale are possible and establishments get bigger in the larger central places.

To illustrate these features of the relationship between the population size of places and numbers of establishments of central functions imagine that the population of a central place was 938. At this size it is large enough to provide all functions along the threshold continuum up to and including frozen food lockers (Table 7.1). Since the threshold for this function is by coincidence also 938, exactly one establishment of this type would be supported there. The numbers of establishments of each of the lower order functions that could be supported are given in the second column of Table 7.1. Thus, for example, there would be enough demand to support 1.9 drugstores, 2.7 dentists, 3.6 physicians, and 6.3 filling stations. But it is not possible to have half of a dentist! So we would in effect find only 1 drugstore (2 would be submarginal), 2 dentists, 3 physicians, and 6 filling stations; and presumably an opportunity exists for some of the establishments to earn sales over and above those needed to exactly satisfy thresholds.

The population needed to support two frozen food lockers at a place is not simply twice 938 (i.e. 1876) but is in fact 2,800. A place of this size is large enough to provide the highest threshold function in the study area, a health practitioner, and hence all the other functions can also be provided on account of their lower thresholds. The number of establishments of each function that could be supported are indicated in the third column of Table 7.1. Thus, despite the considerable increment in population size at this place, we would expect to find, for example, only 3 drugstores, 5 dentists, 6 physicians, and 9 filling stations.

This example shows that the kind of central functions provided at a place is related to the highest threshold function that it can support. This in turn is related to its population size. As population size increases, the number of establishments of the lower order functions that can be supported also increases. It is in this way, then, that the lower order central functions occur more frequently in the landscape than higher order functions. This is shown for Snohomish County in Figure 7.4. Filling stations, the lowest threshold function in the area, occur most frequently, with just under 100 establishments in the 33 central places. As is expected from their higher threshold, only four health practitioners are supported by the 33

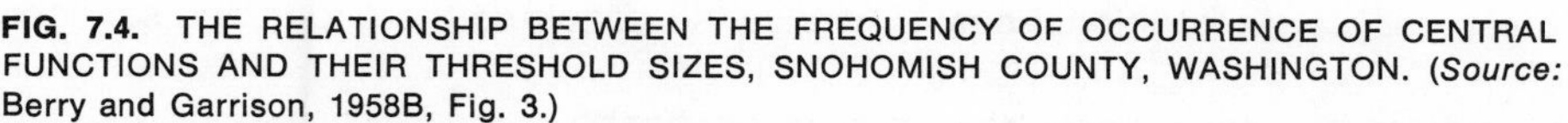

FIG. 7.4. THE RELATIONSHIP BETWEEN THE FREQUENCY OF OCCURRENCE OF CENTRAL FUNCTIONS AND THEIR THRESHOLD SIZES, SNOHOMISH COUNTY, WASHINGTON. (*Source:* Berry and Garrison, 1958B, Fig. 3.)

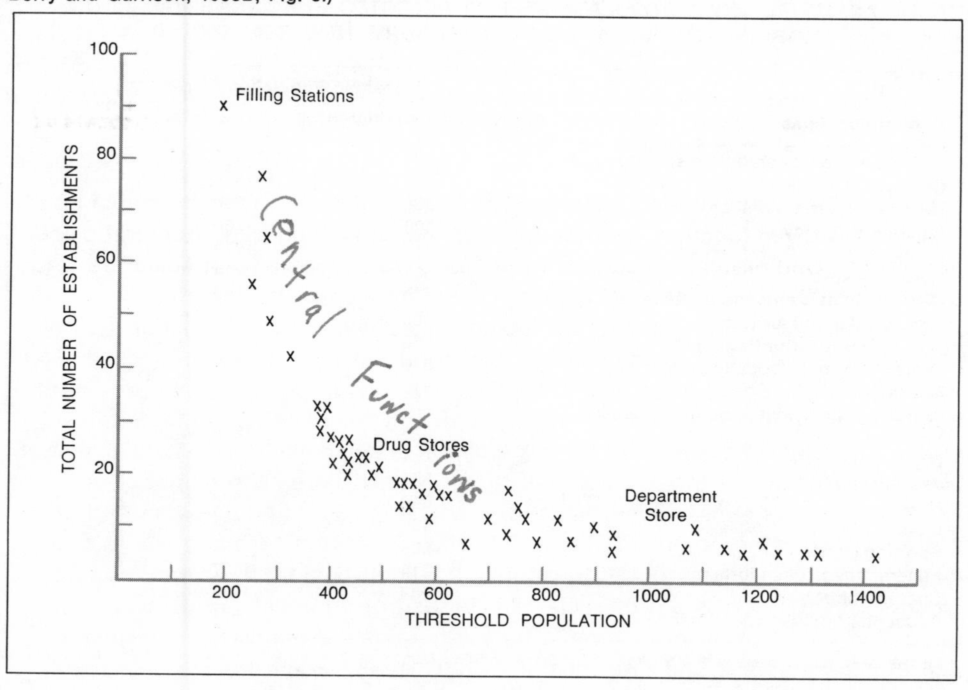

central places. The frequency of occurrence of the other functions ranges between these limits in general accordance with threshold size.

It should be remembered, however, that the absolute values of these presented in Table 7.1 are true only for the 33 places in Snohomish County. Thus when King (1961) repeated Berry and Garrison's study design in a study of central places on the Canterbury Plains, New Zealand, a different set of numerical values was obtained. Of course we might expect this on account of the different cultural environment in that part of the world. However, the interesting thing is that despite such differences Table 7.2 shows that there is still considerable agreement on the rank order of comparable central functions, albeit that one or two of them (i.e. dentists, beauticians, florists, and motels) are notably more specialized in Canterbury. So the ranking proposed by Berry and Garrison should be interpreted with caution and viewed only as a general indication of the comparative ease with which the different central functions can enter the landscape in the United States.

The range of a good The threshold concept has been discussed in terms of the people actually residing in central places. But part of the minimum population needed to support a given function at a central place will be scattered in the area around it—and after all, it is to serve these consumers that central places exist. For these people, an additional cost is involved in acquiring the goods and services

TABLE 7.2. THRESHOLD POPULATIONS FOR SELECTED FUNCTIONS IN WASHINGTON, U.S.A. AND CANTERBURY, NEW ZEALAND

Central Functions	Threshold Population Size in Washington	Threshold Population Size in Canterbury
Motor service station (filling station)[a]	196	261
Doctors (physicians)	380	491
Hairdressers (barber shop)	386	668
Insurance agency	409	250
Dentists	426	1019
Hardware store	431	414
Garage & motor engineer (auto repair)	435	293
Beauty salon (beautician)	480	1126
Barrister & solicitor (lawyers)	528	830
Draper & mercer (apparel stores)	590	388
Bank	610	759
Agricultural machinery (farm implements)	650	431
Florist	729	1280
Dry cleaner	754	781
Jewelry stores	827	926
Hotel	846	356
Motel	430	954
Sporting goods	928	797
Funeral director (undertaker)	1214	1137
Photographer	1243	1156
Accountant (public accountant)	1300	671

[a] The name in parentheses is the term used by Berry and Garrison.
Source: King (1961), Table V.

they need arising from the journey they must undertake to the central place. This travel cost, measured as a combination of money, time, and effort, must be added to the cost of the good at the market. The actual price paid for good, the delivered price, will vary depending on how far away from the central place the consumer resides. The delivered price will therefore increase directly with the length of the shopping trip as shown in Figure 7.5A.

Because of this, consumers are normally not willing to travel very far to obtain items they need frequently. Less frequent purchases can often be postponed, "so that a single longer trip can accomplish several things—not only shopping, but socializing, entertainment, politics, and so on" (Berry, 1967A, p. 3). The maximum distance the dispersed population is prepared to travel to purchase a good from a central place is called the *outer range of the good.* Conceptually the outer range will have an ideal limit, which marks the locations where the price of the good is so high that demand for it is zero (see Fig. 7.5B). In practice, however, it is more useful to refer to the real limit of the outer range of a good, which coincides with locations at which "the net reward to the consumer of a purchase is equalled by the cost of obtaining it" (Golledge, 1968, p. 240). In addition, each good will also have an inner range, which incorporates its threshold requirement.

The outer range (real limit) delimits the service area of a central place for the good, or central function in question. The service area will be different for each of the central functions and may also be different for the same central function at each central place, because of the competition in the supply of the good from other centers. Christaller (1966) suggests that some of the other factors influencing the outer range for a particular business type are the price of the good at the central place, the number of inhabitants of the central place itself, the density and distribution of the population surrounding central places, and the income and social conditions of the consuming population.

THE EMERGENCE OF HIERARCHIES

Together the concepts of the threshold and the range of a good may be used to demonstrate how hierarchies of central places emerge in the landscape. Imagine that *n* different central functions are to be provided in a region and that these are ranked from 1 to *n* in order of their threshold requirements—as for example in Table 7.1. The *n*th central function, with its largest threshold, will require the largest market area to support it. Translated into spatial terms its inner range will have the greatest diameter (see Fig. 7.5B). In the Snohomish County example, a health practitioner with its threshold of 1424 people would represent the *n*th central function while filling stations with thresholds of only 196 would represent central function 1.

Following the argument presented by Berry and Garrison (1958C), we can imagine that central function *n* will be provided from the A-level central places. As many A centers can be supported in the region as there are threshold sales to support establishments supplying this central function. Since these are competing with each other spatially, they will be distributed so as to minimize consumer

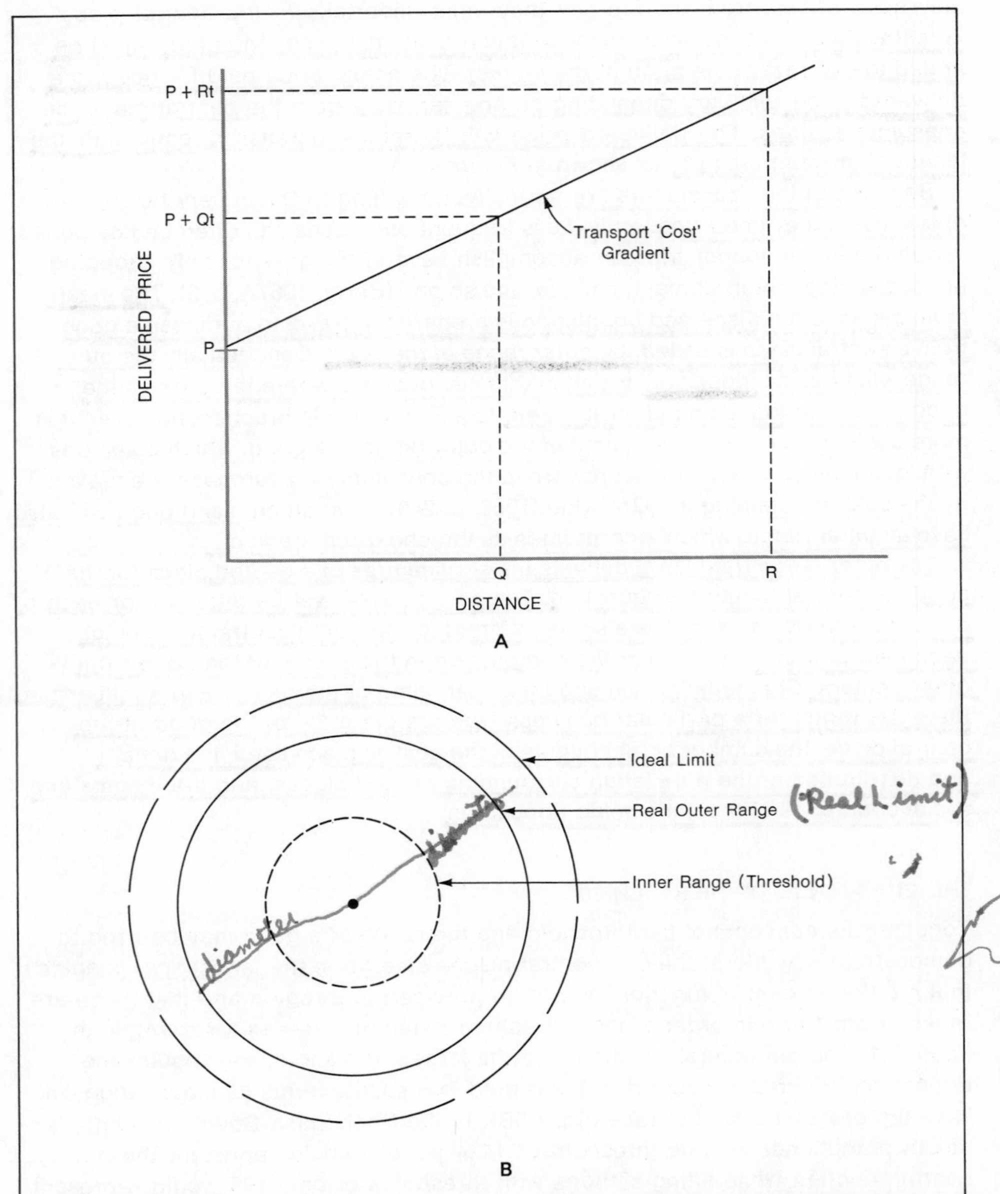

FIG. 7.5. THE RANGE OF A GOOD. (A) THE DELIVERED PRICE OF A GOOD INCREASES WITH DISTANCE TRAVELED TO PURCHASE IT. (B) SPATIAL EXPRESSIONS OF THE RANGE OF A GOOD.

movement in order to satisfy their threshold most efficiently. The question then arises as to how the $n - 1$th central function will be provided (in Table 7.1, central function $n - 1$ corresponds to laundries with a threshold of 1307). Presumably these will also be supplied from the A centers, since they have sought out locations of greatest centrality in the region. In addition advantages will be gained from clustering together with the higher threshold functions at the A centers because of consumers' multiple purpose shopping trips. In the same way, central functions $n - 2$ through 1 will also be provided from A centers.

Some of the n central functions may, however, be supplied from smaller central places than the A centers. These smaller places will arise whenever there is a large enough demand to satisfy thresholds of lower order functions outside the threshold market areas of the A centers. Imagine, for example, that such a situation exists for central function $n - i$. Because there are enough sales in the region outside the threshold market areas for $n - i$ provided at the A centers, greater efficiency will be reached if this function is provided from a second level of central place which we can call B centers. Berry and Garrison (1958C) refer to function $n - i$ as a *hierarchical marginal good* because it is just possible for it to be provided from the next lower level of centers in the hierarchy. These B centers will also provide all lower threshold functions below the hierarchical marginal good; that is, they will provide functions $n - (i + 1)$ through 1.

A new set of centers can come into existence for every hierarchical marginal good in the system. For example, if function $n - j$ (with lower threshold requirements than business type $n - i$) is another hierarchical marginal good, it can be supplied from a third set of centers which we can call C centers. By the same arguments as above, these C centers will be able to provide all lower threshold functions as well.

The cumulative hierarchical structure that builds up in this way is indicated diagrammatically in Table 7.3. In the table the set of functions supplied from each level of central place is indicated by the X's. Thus, in the ideal case, the A centers will provide all central functions; the B centers will provide all functions with thresholds equal to, or lower than, $n - i$; the C centers those functions with thresholds equal to or less than that of $n - j$; and the M centers will only be able to supply the lowest threshold functions below $n - k$. Hence the C places and people in the trade areas of the C centers rely upon either B or A centers for goods $n - i$ through $n - (j - 1)$ and upon the A centers for goods n through $n - (i - 1)$. Similarly, the B centers will rely upon the larger A centers for the provision of goods n through $n - (i - 1)$. According to the premise that each center locates central to

TABLE 7.3. THE SUPPLY OF *N* GOODS FROM *M* CENTRAL PLACES

	Goods													
Centers	n^{+*},	$n-1$,	$n-2$,	.....	$n-i^{+}$,	$n-(i+1)$,	.....	$n-j^{+}$,	$n-(j+1)$,	.....	$n-k^{+}$,	$n-(k+1)$,	.....	1
A	X	X	X	X	X	X	X	X	X	X ..	X	X	X	X
B					X	X	X	X	X	X ..	X	X	X	X
C								X	X	X ..	X	X	X	X
.										..	.	.	.	.
.										..	.	.	.	.
.										..	.	.	.	.
.										..	.	.	.	.
M										..	X	X	X	X

* The symbol + denotes the hierarchical marginal good.

the maximum trade area it can command, all levels of central places will be located at places from which they can serve most efficiently the tributary areas with the goods and services they provide. Because of this, we would expect the higher level centers with their greater needs for centrality to be spaced more widely apart than the more closely spaced smallest level centers in the hierarchy.

HIERARCHIES: EMPIRICAL EXAMPLES

Hierarchies have been recognized in innumerable studies of the central places in small regions. The results of two such studies are presented here; a full listing of others is available in Berry and Pred (1964).

Southwestern Wisconsin The part of southwestern Wisconsin studied by Brush (1953) is shown in Figure 7.6. This area contained 235 agglomerated settlements ranging in size between 20 and 7,217 inhabitants. Brush classified these in an

FIG. 7.6. A HIERARCHY OF CENTRAL PLACES IN SOUTHWESTERN WISCONSIN. (*Source:* Brush, 1953, Fig. 7.)

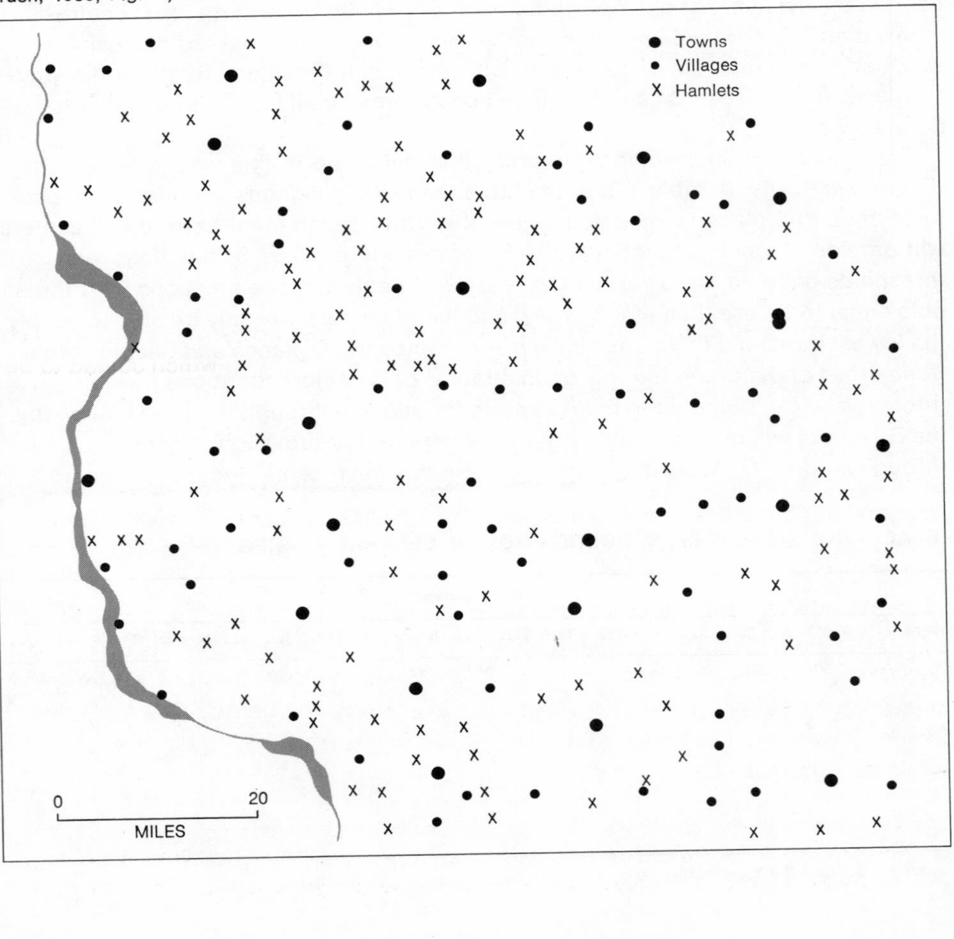

ad hoc way into 142 hamlets, 73 villages, and 20 towns from empirical observation of the kinds of retail and service activities provided from them. No cities, the next highest level in the hierarchy, were located in the study area although Madison, the Wisconsin state capital, lies just outside its eastern boundary.

Hamlets are merely rudimentary service centers offering one or two convenience, low threshold functions. Settlements were classified as hamlets if they had (1) at least five residential structures or other buildings used for commercial or cultural purposes clustered within one-quarter of a mile, and (2) they provided at least one but not more than nine central functions. Typical hamlets in this area provided only a grocery (or general store) and an elementary school, although taverns, filling stations, and churches were frequently provided by them.

Villages provided a minimum of ten central functions and services. In addition to those typically found at the hamlet level, a village had to include (1) at least four of the following: automobile sales, farm implement dealers, appliance and hardware stores, lumberyards, and livestock feed agents; and (2) three other essential services, such as a telephone exchange or postal delivery, automobile repair shop, or a bank. Brush noted that a public high school was provided in more than half of the settlements classified as villages which, as a rule, were incorporated for local government purposes. Although the villages can be considered as incomplete service centers lacking the personal and professional services typical of higher level centers, they nevertheless constitute significant centers for the supply of goods and services most frequently demanded by the farm community surrounding them.

Towns display many of the features of economic specialization that are generally considered to be typically urban in the United States. For not only do they provide the goods and services available from lower level centers but also several more specialized central functions and services. Settlements had to have (1) at least 50 retail establishments to be classified as a town, of which 30 had to be types other than grocery stores, taverns, and filling stations; (2) banks and weekly newspapers; (3) high schools, and (4) four professional services—physicians, dentists, veterinarians, and lawyers. Brush noted that the towns were usually organized as fourth-class cities in Wisconsin (a legal status to which settlements become eligible upon reaching a population of 1,000). In addition, many of them were county seats although this was not a necessary nor a dominant feature of the towns studied.

In classifying settlements into levels in the hierarchy, there is no doubt that Brush established rather arbitrary divisions and then proved what he had in fact assumed. This criticism applies to many of the earlier central place studies, which were usually based on a priori methods of classification. This objection to Brush's study and the many others like it was made clear by Vining (1955, p. 167) when he said that:

> Clearly it is arbitrary to divide the array [of settlements] into three partitions rather than into a greater or lesser number; and similarly arbitrary is the determination of where to put the dividing points in separating the different classes or types. Having drawn the lines,

one may list certain kinds of activities which are typically found within each of the designated classes of center, . . . not all members of a class will contain all the activities listed and most of the communities within a class will contain activities not listed. [This] . . . is not an independently derived basis for a classification of communities by type.

This criticism notwithstanding, the general findings from Brush's study were significant; and it occupies an important place in the history of central place studies. It marked the turning point between the earlier, highly subjective research and the more objective analyses based on quantitative methods typical of recent work. Indeed, it was Vining's (1955) reaction to Brush's classification of centers that prompted Berry and Garrison (1958A) to undertake their now classic study of central places in Snohomish County, Washington. Using mathematical grouping methods and statistical tests of significance, they were able to establish discrete levels in the hierarchy of service centers and so to seriously challenge the frequent claim that, "Like pool, pond, and lake, the terms hamlet, village, and town are convenient modes of expression, but they do not refer to structurally distinct natural entities" (Vining, 1955, p. 169).

Southwestern Iowa One of the most comprehensive studies of service centers was that undertaken by Berry in 1960. Of interest here are the studies undertaken in three contrasted areas of the American Midwest and particularly that in southwestern Iowa (Berry, Barnum, and Tennant, 1962). This nine-county study area, shown in Figure 7.7, is a homogeneous and highly productive farming region typical of the mixed crop-livestock economy of the corn belt. Rural population densities average 15.5 persons per square mile increasing close to Omaha–Council Bluffs to 20.4 persons per square mile and decreasing to 12.7 persons per square mile in Adams County—the poorest part of the region investigated.

The level of settlements in the hierarchy was established using a method called *direct factor analysis*, which was applied to data matrices recording the presence and absence of central functions at each place. This method not only ensured greater objectivity than had been possible in earlier analyses but also avoided the need in the classification process for preselecting central functions characteristic of the different levels in the hierarchy as Brush (1953) had done. The resulting hierarchical structure in the study area is illustrated in Figure 7.7. It has the numerical sequence: 35 hamlets, 36 villages, 20 towns, 8 cities, and 1 regional capital. Actually, as Berry (1967A) points out, Council Bluffs is probably a regional city and Omaha a regional metropolis in the context of Philbrick's (1957) terminology discussed in Chapter 2, for in other parts of the country these levels have distinct locations in the spatial system. With the exception of the hamlets, the sequence is consistent with the notion that lower order centers occur more ubiquitously than higher level centers in the landscape. The fact that hamlets, once the basic feature of the settlement pattern in agricultural regions, occur less frequently than expected partly reflects the decline in rural population in this area during the past decades. For as the number of rural dwellers has decreased, so it has become more difficult for functions in these smallest centers to satisfy

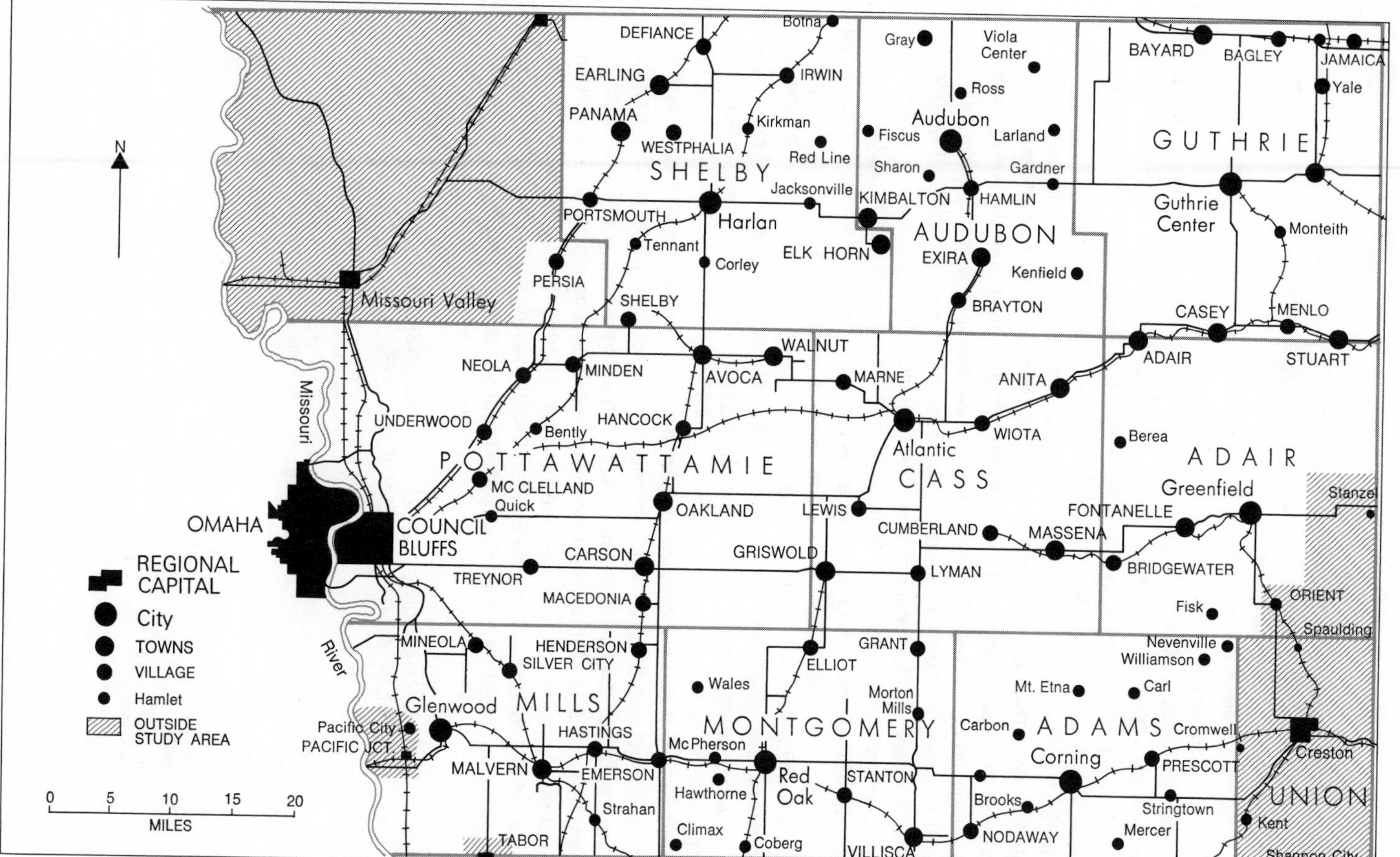

FIG. 7.7. A HIERARCHY OF CENTRAL PLACES IN SOUTHWESTERN IOWA. (*Source:* Berry, Barnum, and Tennant, 1962, Fig. 1.)

their thresholds. Together with the increased mobility of the rural farm population today and the associated shift in patronizing villages, many of the hamlets have disappeared from the landscape as service centers.

The size characteristics of typical centers at the various levels of the hierarchy are presented in Table 7.4. The hamlets, which are omitted from the table, had populations up to 100, seldom more than 4–6 retail businesses, and usually they provided only a filling station and a general store. From the factor analysis, a group of centers was identified which had between 10 and 26 central functions. These were the villages. The functions typical of the village level are indicated in Table 7.5; they are essentially low threshold, basic convenience types for which there is frequent demand. The second grouping indicated was of towns having from 28 to 50 central functions. In addition to the functions performed at the village level, towns provided a selection of higher threshold activities of the sort indicated in Table 7.5. Although functionally more complex than the lower level villages, which cannot profitably provide the higher order functions, the towns are characterized by a simpler set of functions than the cities. In southwestern Iowa these had in every case more than 55 central functions, which include those listed in Table 7.5. All the cities are county seats, providing specialized high threshold activities as well as the functions typical of lower level centers, and have well-developed central shopping districts whose major attractions include functions such as clothing stores, shoe stores, florists, and jewelers.

An indication of the importance of service provision at the city level is the total taxable sales at them. In 1960 Atlantic and Red Oak, for example, had sales of $16 million and $14 million respectively. This compares with total sales of between $2 to $2.5 million at the town-level centers. The dominance of Council Bluffs–Omaha in the region is indicated by the high level of sales there which approached $70 million in Council Bluffs alone! The larger size that this reflects is illustrated by the fact that in Council Bluffs there were over 1100 retail and

TABLE 7.4. SIZE CHARACTERISTICS IN THE HIERARCHY OF CENTRAL PLACES IN SOUTHWESTERN IOWA, 1960

	Level of Center	Population	Number of Central Functions	Functional Units
City	Red Oak	6421	90	312
	Atlantic	6890	92	411
Town	Griswold	1207	50	102
	Anita	1273	50	84
	Villisca	1690	43	90
	Oakland	1340	49	97
Village	Lewis	501	24	43
	Elliott	459	26	42
	Stanton	514	21	28

Source: Berry, Barnum, and Tennant (1962), p. 81.

TABLE 7.5. CENTRAL FUNCTIONS TYPICAL OF LEVELS IN THE HIERARCHY OF CENTRAL PLACES, SOUTHWESTERN IOWA, 1960

(A) The Village-level functions	
Gas and service station	Meeting hall
Automobile repair	Hardware
Bars	Farm materials
Restaurants	Farm sales
Grocery	Farm implements
Post Office	Oil fuel bulk station
Local government facility	Barber
Church	Beauty shops
(B) The Town-level functions	
Furniture	Doctors
Appliances	Dentists
Variety	Building services
General clothing	Building materials
Drugstores	Radio-TV sales and service
Banks	Movers and haulers
Insurance agents	Funeral home
Real estate	Veterinarian
Telephone exchange	Automobile accessories
Cleaners	Farmers' cooperatives
(C) The City-level functions	
Women's clothing	Newspaper publisher
Men's clothing	Office of labor union
Shoes	Sales of new automobiles
Jewelry	Sales of used automobiles
Florist	Specialized automobile repairs
Supermarket	Automobile wrecking
Bakery	Cleaners and laundry (operator)
Liquor store	Self-service laundry
Other medical practice (e.g. optometrists, etc.)	Shoe repairs
Lawyer	Plumbing
Hotel	Fixit
Motel	Movies
County government	Indoor amusements (billiards, etc.)
	Drive-in eating places

Source: Berry, Barnum, and Tennant (1962), Tables IV–VI.

service establishments in 1960, including an array of department stores, specialty shops, professional services, and cultural facilities—high threshold functions that require very high degrees of centrality in the landscape.

STRUCTURAL RELATIONSHIPS IN THE HIERARCHY OF SERVICE CENTERS

One of the fundamental features of the hierarchy is that higher level centers have more central functions, larger populations, a greater number of establishments and functional units, and as we shall see below, larger trade areas encompassing more people. The existence of such structural regularities in the hierarchy in southwestern Iowa is clearly illustrated in Table 7.6. The high

TABLE 7.6. STRUCTURAL RELATIONSHIPS IN THE HIERARCHY, SOUTHWESTERN IOWA, 1960

Correlation Coefficients*

		P	*LP*	*F*	*LF*	*CF*
P	Population of Center	X	–	.98	–	.89
LP	Log. of Population		X	–	.96	.95
F	No. of Functional Units			X	–	.93
LF	Log. of Functional Units				X	.98
CF	No. of Central Functions					X

Regression Equations

1. $P = 17.64F - 162.7$
2. $LP = 1.24LF + 0.731$
3. $LP = 0.02CF + 2.095$
4. $LF = 0.018CF + 1.045$

* Pearson product moment correlation coefficients. The maximum value that these can attain is 1.0; the closer the value to this, the higher the degree of correlation between the two variables.
Source: Berry, Barnum, and Tennant (1962), Table 1.

correlation coefficients indicate the strong positive relationships between the relevant variables, while the regression equations show these relationships to be linear and log-linear in form.

THE POPULATION: FUNCTIONAL UNITS RELATIONSHIP

The marked linear relationship between the population size of places and their corresponding number of functional units, shown graphically in Figure 7.8, points up the importance of the service function at settlements in the region. Where in addition to the service function other activities form an important part of the economic base of settlements, marked deviation from the general trend can be expected. This is clearly shown on the graph for the two cities of Glenwood and Red Oak. In this region, these are the only places supporting part of their population with other noncentral functions. As a result, both places have significantly larger populations than is expected from the number of functional units they contain. Glenwood is the site of the Iowa State Institution for the Feeble Minded, which had 1,800 inmates in 1960, while Red Oak has three small manufacturing plants employing at that time a total of 776 workers. If it is assumed that the 332 male workers at the Red Oak plants are heads of households with 4 persons per household, then an excess population of 1,300 is indicated for Red Oak. Subtracting 1,800 and 1,300 from the total populations of Glenwood and Red Oak, respectively, has the effect of bringing these places into line with the places that are exclusively central places.

THE POPULATION: CENTRAL FUNCTION RELATIONSHIP

A number of studies have examined the relationship between the population size and number of central functions of places. The results of these studies have established this to be curvilinear (or linear when population is transformed into

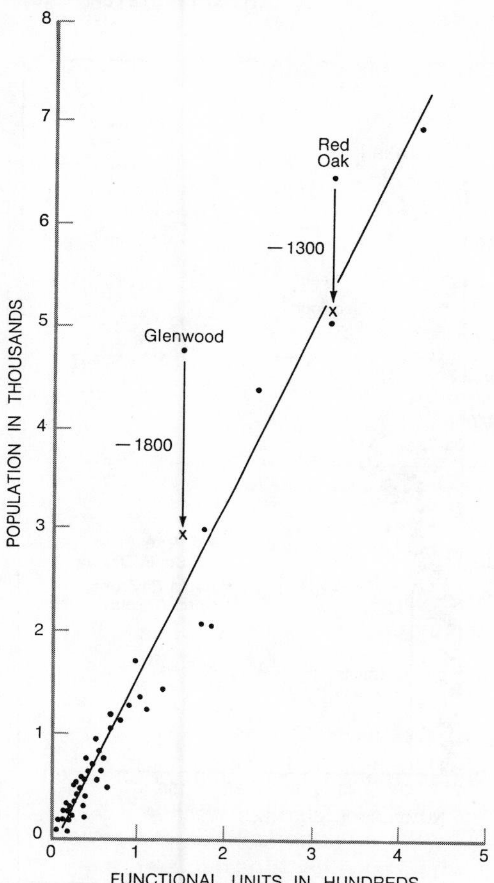

FIG. 7.8. THE RELATIONSHIP BETWEEN THE NUMBER OF FUNCTIONAL UNITS AND THE POPULATION SIZE OF CENTRAL PLACES IN SOUTHWESTERN IOWA. (*Source:* Berry, Barnum, and Tennant, 1962, Fig. 2.)

logarithms), indicating that as settlements become larger they add fewer new functions for each new increment in population. Thomas (1960, p. 15) has suggested one explanation for the curvilinear nature of this relationship, namely that,

> there may be definite limits to the functional complexity of urban places. As cities become larger, greater numbers of establishments and [central] functions are formed within them. Once a certain level is reached, however, establishments are added much more rapidly than functions. This suggests that to a considerable extent greater numbers of people found in larger places do not desire different kinds of functions, but merely convenient access to the same ones.

Figure 7.9 illustrates the nature of the relationship in two studies. For small towns in southern Illinois, Stafford (1963) found that the variation in number of central functions at places was very highly correlated ($r = 0.89$) with variation in

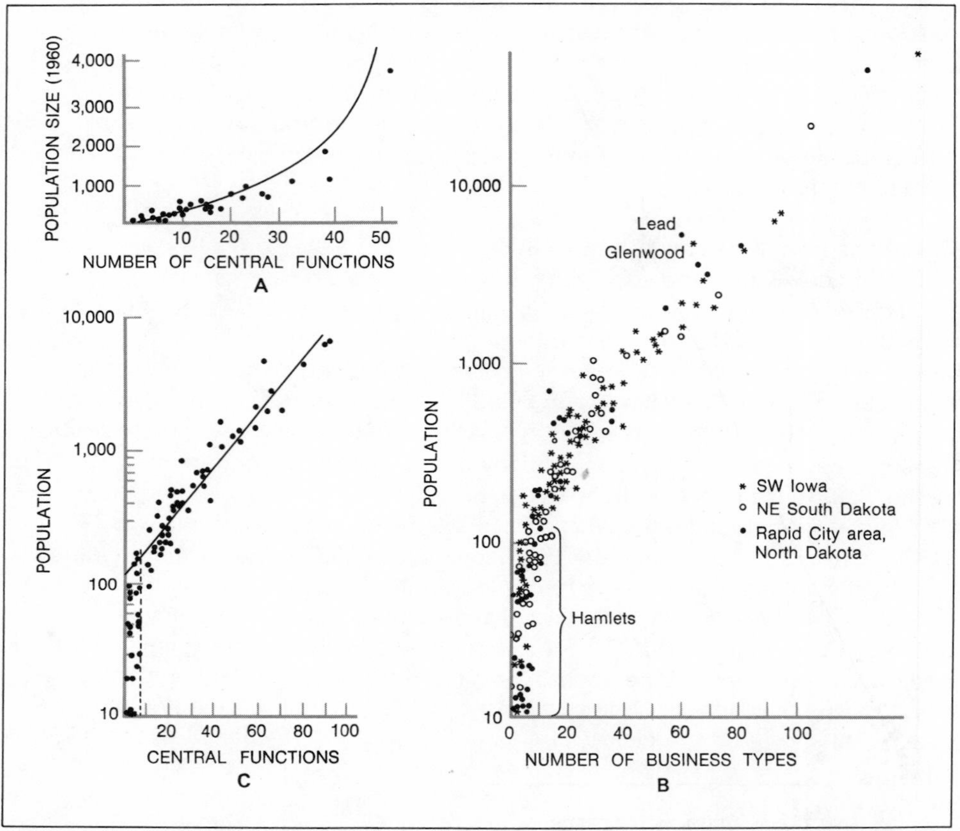

FIG. 7.9. THE RELATIONSHIP BETWEEN THE NUMBER OF CENTRAL FUNCTIONS AND THE POPULATION SIZE OF CENTRAL PLACES IN (A) SOUTHERN ILLINOIS, (B) SELECTED MIDWESTERN AREAS, AND (C) SOUTHWESTERN IOWA. (*Source:* Stafford, 1963, Fig. 3; Berry, 1967A, Fig. 2–11; and Berry, Barnum, and Tennant, 1962, Fig. 3.)

their population size (Fig. 7.9A). Similar high positive correlations have been established in Canterbury, New Zealand, by King (1961) in Snohomish County, Washington, by Berry and Garrison (1958A), and in the three areas in the American Midwest studied by Berry, Barnum, and Tennant (1962). The consistency of the relationship in these latter areas is shown in Figure 7.9B. When the hamlets are excluded from the calculations, correlations of 0.95, 0.93, and 0.91 are typical of the southwestern Iowa, northeastern South Dakota, and the Rapid City, N.D., areas respectively.

The reason for omitting the hamlets from the relationship is made clear from a closer look at the graph for southwestern Iowa (Fig. 7.9C). Clearly two distinct trends are evident in the graph. First, there is the marked log-linear trend of the relationship between population size of places and the numbers of central functions they perform at the village-level places and above (i.e. at places with more than 10 central functions). Second, there is a different kind of relationship between the variables for the smaller hamlets—with between 1 to 8 central functions and populations less than 100. For these places the relationship is weak indeed and apparently does not conform with that typical of the larger level centers. Rather, the hamlets are contained within an equipossible area on the graph reflecting their position of decline in the settlement pattern.

Deviations from the general trend In southwestern Iowa no place appears to deviate markedly from the general trend of the population size–central function relationship. The scatter of points about the line of average relationship is much as we would expect, given the imperfections of the order in the real world. In other situations, however, places may stand out on account of their significant deviation from the line of best fit. We have already seen examples of this in the case of Glenwood and Red Oak in Figure 7.8, and such deviant cases might be expected whenever the rigidity of the central place system is disturbed by the occurrence of noncentral place functions.

The two typical kinds of deviant cases are shown diagrammatically in Figure 7.10A. First, under certain conditions places may have far more central functions than might be expected from their population size. On the graph these will fall below the line of best fit, and examples of this kind are shown by the open circles in Figure 7.10A. Second, some places may well have far greater populations than would be expected from the number of central functions they provide. On the graph deviants of this kind will fall well above the line of best fit, as shown by the closed circles in Figure 7.10A. Evidence of the first type of deviant case has been presented by Thomas (1961) for certain places in northwestern Iowa. In this area several centers had more central functions than could be supported by their resident and tributary area populations, due to their role as tourist centers serving a much frequented recreational region. Hence these places had a range of additional functions that were not found to be characteristic of the other central places in Iowa and that distorted the regularity in the hierarchy there.

Examples of the second type of deviant places are given for Snohomish County, Washington, by Berry and Garrison (1958A). As shown in Figure 7.10B, a number of centers deviate from the average relationship here, which in any case is not as well developed as it is in other areas. The six centers with excessive populations perform some other functions in addition to their role as a central place. For example, Snohomish is the county seat and supports extra population with jobs in local government; Lake Stevens is a recreational area.

The other deviant places are associated with causes of a more universal nature. They reflect the distortion brought about by the impact of an expanding metropolitan community upon an independent central place hierarchy: for "as the commuting range of the metropolis shifts outwards, previously independent central places are drawn within the web of intrametropolitan relations"

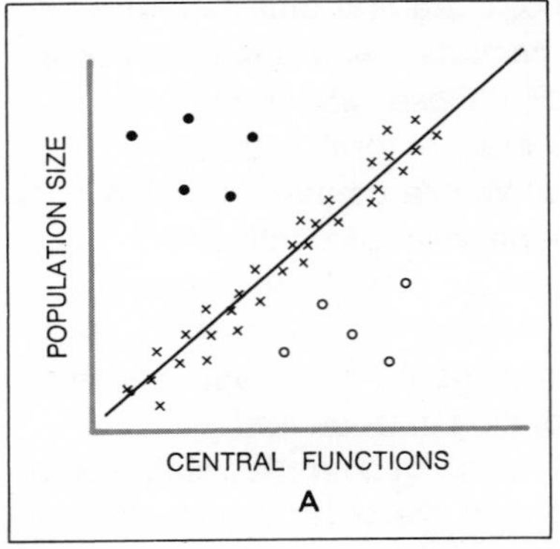

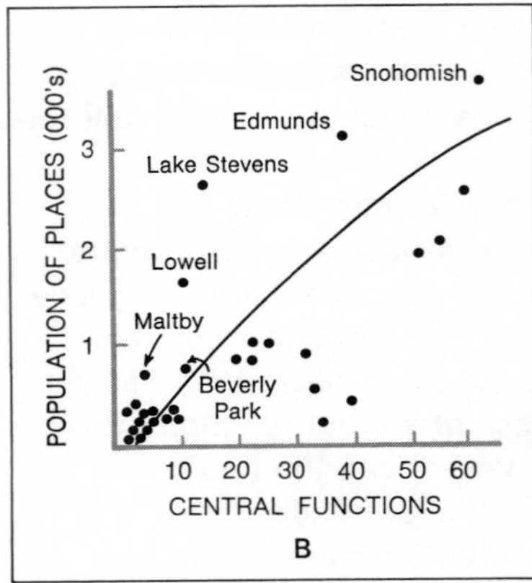

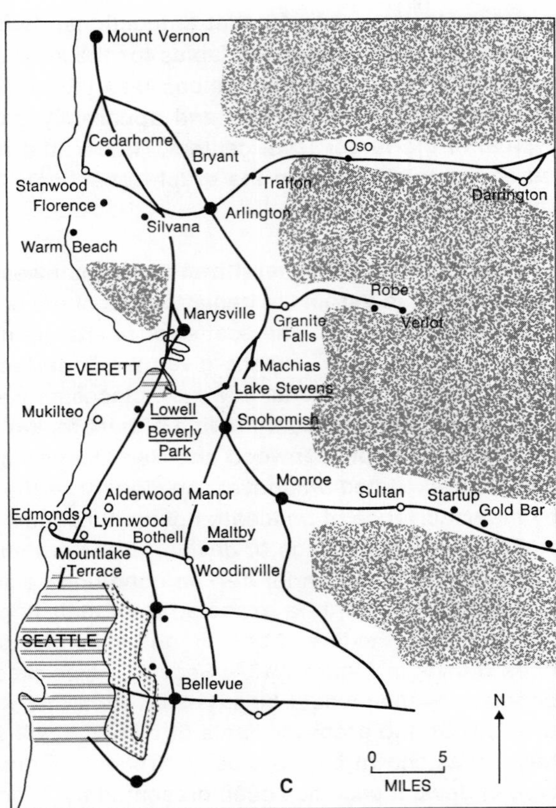

FIG. 7.10. DEVIANT CASES IN THE CENTRAL FUNCTIONS–POPULATION SIZE RELATIONSHIP: (A) DIAGRAMMATIC REPRESENTATION; (B) DEVIANT CASES IN SNOHOMISH COUNTY, WASHINGTON; AND (C) THE LOCATION OF PLACES IN THE SNOHOMISH COUNTY STUDY AREA. (*Source:* Berry and Garrison, 1958A, after Table 2, and Berry, 1960, Fig. 1.)

(Berry, 1960, p. 112). The result of this process is a population–function imbalance at nearby places, which become residential suburbs for the larger centers. Thus in the Snohomish study area, Edmunds and Maltby lie within the commuting range of Seattle, and in addition to being central places act as residential suburbs. Similarly, but perhaps to a lesser extent, Lowell and Beverly Park perform the same role with respect to the regional city of Everett (Fig. 7.10C).

THE ESTABLISHMENT: POPULATION SIZE RELATIONSHIP

The notion implicit in the relationship between population and number of central functions discussed above is that the population of places is dependent on the total number of different kinds of retail and service activities provided by them. It is this number that in part determines and in part depends on the centrality of a place. The relationship between the number of different establishments and population size of centers that logically follows from this is illustrated in Figure 7.11. This relationship is double logarithmic. Straight lines drawn on the graph thus indicate constant rates of change between the two variables. Hence the rate of growth of total number of establishments is proportional to the rate of population growth at centers. Berry (1967A) points out that in the growth process, there will be varied responses by the establishments. In some cases new establishments will be added, in others existing stores will simply grow in size, and in yet other cases preexisting establishments may begin to specialize.

THE CENTRAL FUNCTION: FUNCTIONAL UNITS RELATIONSHIP

Figure 7.12 shows the log-linear relationship between numbers of functional units and central functions. The graph is similar to that shown in Figure 7.9C for population and number of central functions in that two distinct areas can be recognized: (1) the equipossible area containing the hamlets, and (2) the log-linear relationship for the higher level centers (villages and above). However, unlike the relationship shown in that graph, the trend of the relation-

FIG. 7.11. THE RELATIONSHIP BETWEEN THE NUMBER OF ESTABLISHMENTS AND THE POPULATION SIZE OF CENTRAL PLACES IN SELECTED AREAS OF THE MIDWEST, UNITED STATES. (*Source:* Berry, 1967A, Fig. 2–13.)

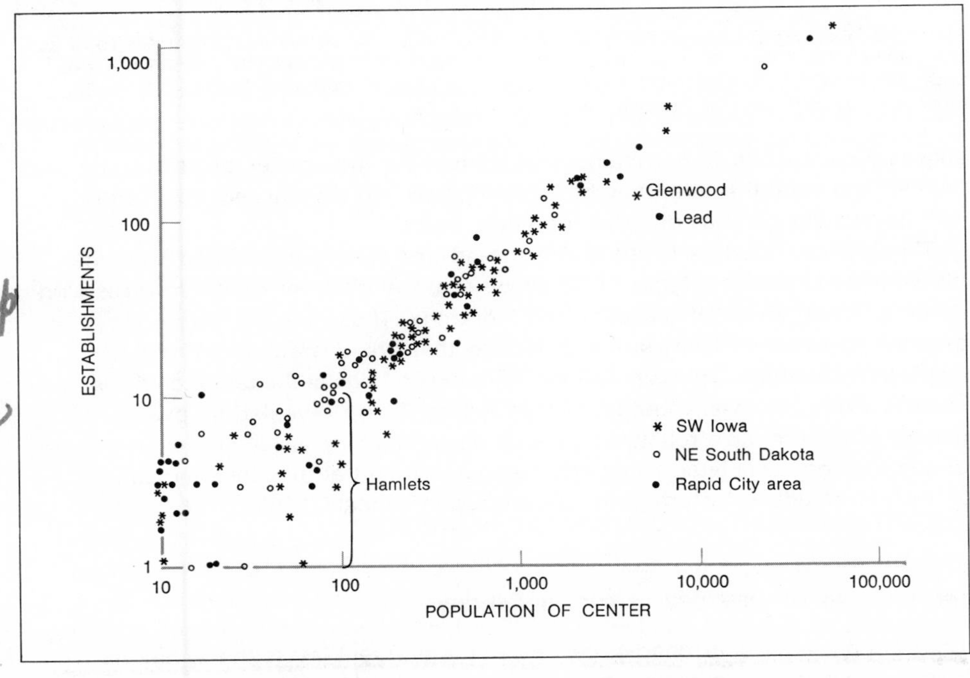

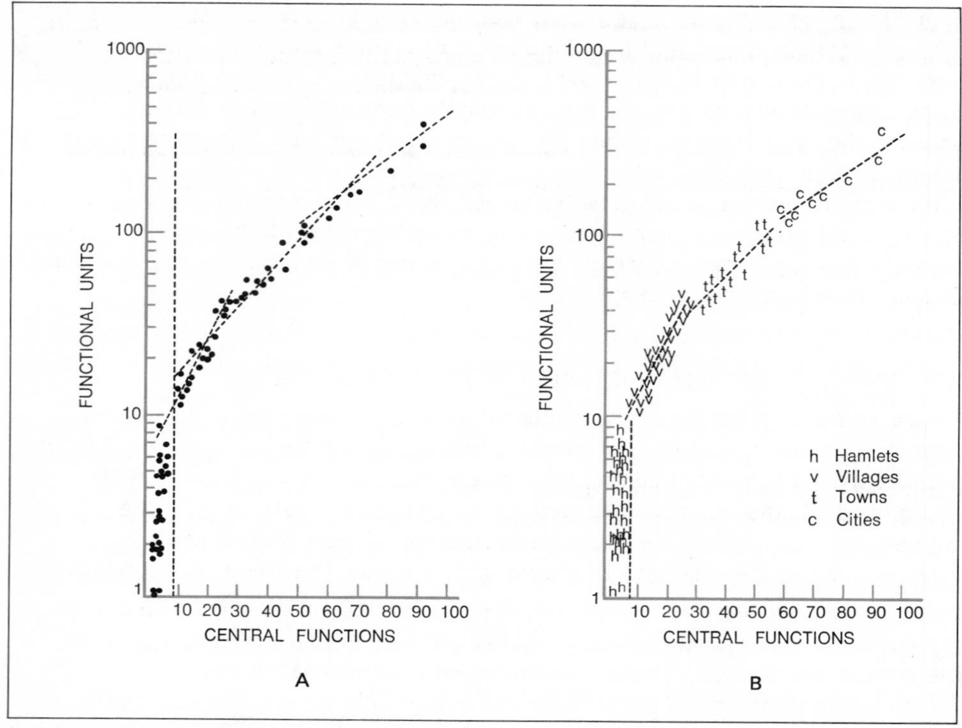

FIG. 7.12. THE RELATIONSHIP BETWEEN CENTRAL FUNCTIONS AND FUNCTIONAL UNITS IN SOUTHWESTERN IOWA. SEVERAL REGIMES APPEAR TO BE PRESENT ON THE GRAPH (A), EACH OF WHICH CORRESPONDS TO A DISTINCT CLASS OF CENTRAL PLACES (B). (*Source:* Berry, Barnum, and Tennant, 1962, Figs. 4 and 7.)

ship in Figure 7.12A is not maintained throughout the scatter of points. Instead, the overall scatter may be broken down into several regimes, each with its own significantly different log-linear trend.

These discontinuities in the overall trend are clearly associated with the hierarchical structure. Figure 7.12B shows that the different regimes correspond to the different levels of places in the hierarchy. These are set within the broader framework of city-size regularities that are characteristic of aggregative analysis. This is consistent with the findings of the factor analysis used by Berry to classify centers in this region. These revealed an overall pattern of general size relationships with discontinuities associated with groups of centers and associated kinds and numbers of central functions indicative of the hierarchical structure (Berry, Barnum, and Tennant, 1962).

THE SPACING OF CENTERS IN THE HIERARCHY

The frequency of occurrence of centers at the different levels in the hierarchy is reflected in their spatial distribution: higher level centers should, on the average

at least, be spaced more widely apart than lower level centers. Data in support of this hypothesis has been presented in many studies of central place patterns, and two sets of findings are given in Table 7.7. In southwestern Wisconsin, Brush (1953) found that despite some considerable range in distances between centers at the same level, the mean intercenter distances varied directly with level in the hierarchy. In a study of the distribution of service centers in southern England, Bracey (Brush and Bracey, 1955) found that higher order centers were spaced over twice as far apart as lower level centers. The interesting point emerging from these findings is that despite considerable difference in the physical structure and economic and social history of the two areas, there is close agreement in the spacing of higher (towns) and lower (villages) level places—at about 21 miles and 10 miles respectively.

The distribution of central places in southwestern Wisconsin (see Fig. 7.6) is best described as a random pattern, even though the tendency for centers to group themselves in rows or clusters is quite pronounced (Dacey, 1962). Hence the mean distance between those villages grouped in rows is only 6.8 miles, while towns grouped in rows are on average only 12.2 miles apart. Another notable feature of the pattern is the discontinuous belts of hamlets around the higher level towns, from which they are separated by an average distance of of 6.9 miles. In contrast the villages are nearly twice as far away from the towns, from which they are separated by an average distance of 11.3 miles.

The spatial pattern of central places in this area is largely the result of site influences and transport innovations during the nineteenth century. The linear element in the pattern can be attributed largely to the influence of the railroads. Distribution and collection points on the long-distance lines were original sites of agglomeration for numerous trade centers, and rail connection was essential to ensure growth. Earlier locations had been at river landings,

TABLE 7.7. THE SPACING OF CENTERS AT DIFFERENT LEVELS IN THE HIERARCHY

(A) Southwestern Wisconsin

	Spacing of Central Places in Miles		
	Hamlets (142)	**Villages (73)**	**Towns (20)**
Mean distance apart (straight line)	5.5	9.9	21.2
Range in distance	1.0–12.0	3.5–18.5	7.0–38.0

Source: Brush, 1953, Table II.

(B) Southern England

	Spacing of Central Places in Miles	
	Lower Level Centers (44)	**Higher Level Centers (26)**
Mean intercenter distance	8.0	21.0

Source: Brush and Bracey, 1955, Table 1.

lead deposits, county seats, and mill-dam sites. Although in the period 1830–1880 some of these early places attained the status of villages or towns in the absence of the railroad, most of them were unable to survive for long. The more or less scattered distribution of hamlets in the voids between the higher level places is accounted for by the dispersion of the farm population throughout the area before 1880. Then the wagon roads were the sole means of access to areas away from the rivers and the few railroads that had already been constructed at that time. Although hamlets emerged at the same kinds of sites as the early villages and towns, they remained relatively isolated from the main currents of movement through the region and consequently experienced stunted growth.

The influence of the railroads was equally important in the evolution of the central place pattern in the area studied by Berry in southwestern Iowa (see Fig. 2.9). The railroads, coupled with the rectangular land use survey of the Midwest, were largely responsible for the evolution of the rectangular or rhomboidal pattern characteristic of this area. The essential features of this are shown diagrammatically in Figure 7.13. The sequence of centers along the main north-south and east-west routes is: city, village, town, village, city. Thus each city is surrounded by four towns, and each town and city by four villages. On average there are two towns for every city, and for every town and city there are two villages. The ratio of lower level centers to the next highest level is therefore two.

CONSUMER TRAVEL AND THE HIERARCHY

The levels of the central place hierarchy are the results of the common behavior of consumers in acquiring goods and services of a given order. It is the movements of both dispersed rural populations and the inhabitants of the central places themselves that provide the means whereby the structural components of the hierarchy are welded together into a central place system.

FIG. 7.13. THE RHOMBOIDAL PATTERN OF CENTRAL PLACES IN IOWA. (*Source:* Berry, 1967A, Fig. 2–15.)

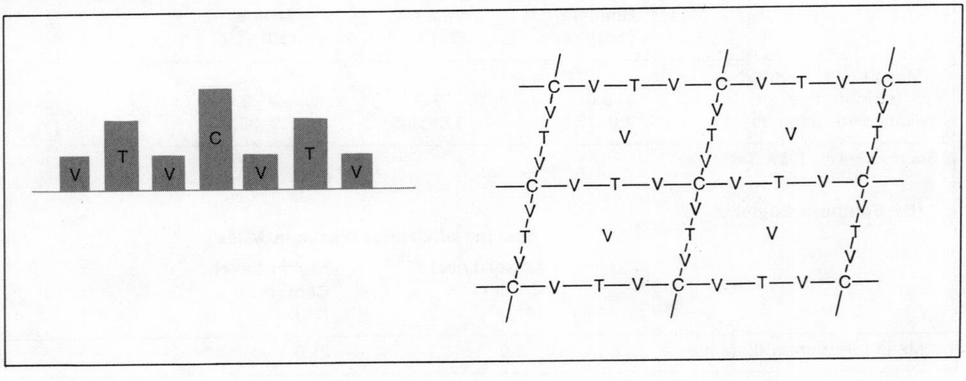

Figures 7.14–7.17 illustrate typical patterns of consumer travel for different order goods and services. These maps were constructed from the results of a questionnaire survey of 150 rural families and 170 families residing at central places within a small part of the southwestern Iowa study area shown in Figure 7.7 (Berry, 1967A). On these maps, desire lines (straight lines from farm residence to marketplace) are used to indicate the shopping trips of rural farm dwellers. The shopping trips for the urban residents (those living at the central places themselves) are shown by wheels; if a good or service is obtained within the center itself, a spoke is added to the wheel, and if it is obtained from another center an arrow is drawn linking the two centers.

The pattern of clothing purchases—a city-level good—shown in Figure 7.14 indicates the way in which Red Oak and Atlantic (the two county seats) and the regional capital dominate the surrounding farms and smaller centers in the provision of this good. This is particularly true for the journeys of the urban dwellers who show a marked preference for one of the three larger central places. The pattern of trips by farm families is almost identical and shows a clear division in patronizing the county seats, consistent with the notion of distance minimization in spatial interaction. The tendency for larger places to attract customers over longer distances is reflected in the way the regional capital extends its influence into the western part of the study area. Clothing is not provided normally from centers below the city level in the hierarchy because the maximum trade areas of these smaller places do not include enough population or sales to satisfy the threshold for this higher order good. The few trips made to low-level centers shown on the maps are accounted for by older farmers buying work clothes from the general stores in the smaller places (Berry, 1967A, p. 16).

Figure 7.15 shows the pattern of travel for lower order, town-level goods. The main difference between the maps for clothing purchases and those for furniture purchases is the emergence of the town of Griswold as a focus in the pattern of consumer movements. This is particularly well marked on the map of rural preferences (Fig. 7.15B). Griswold, located on the watershed between the market areas of the higher level centers for clothing, is able to secure enough sales to make the supply of furniture profitable. Capturing furniture sales

FIG. 7.14. SHOPPING PREFERENCES FOR CLOTHING, SOUTHWESTERN IOWA: (A) URBAN DWELLERS, (B) RURAL DWELLERS. (*Source:* Berry, Barnum, and Tennant, 1962, Fig. 17.)

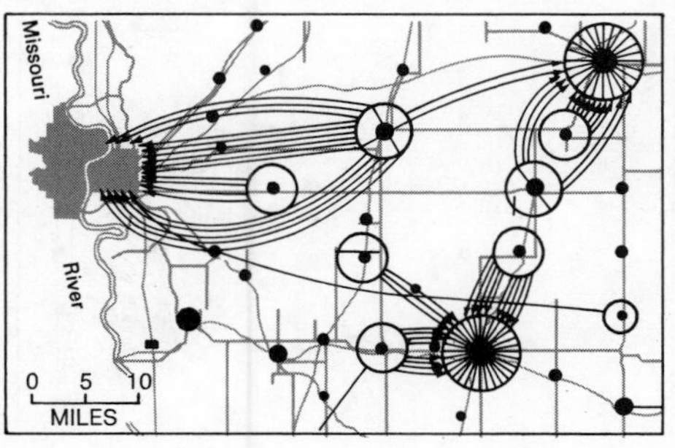

A

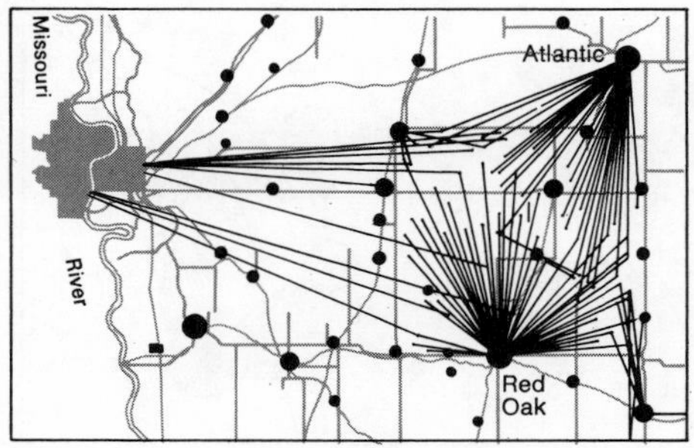

B

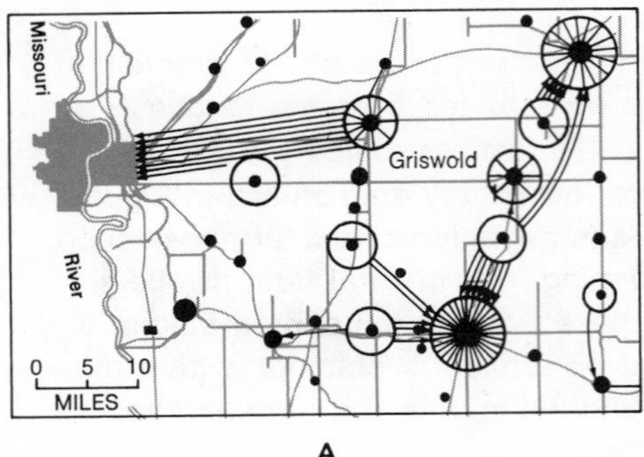

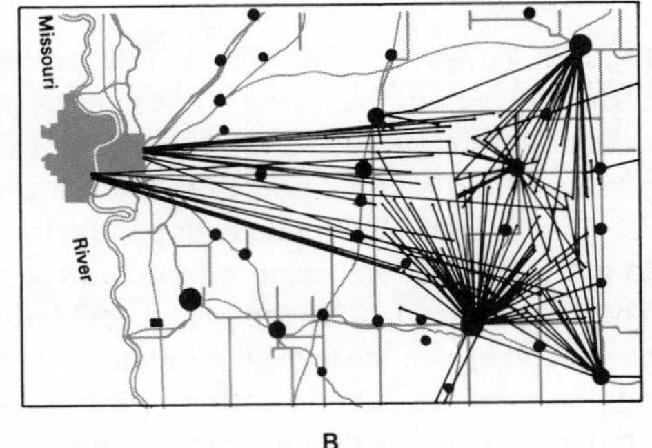

FIG. 7.15. SHOPPING PREFERENCES FOR FURNITURE, SOUTHWESTERN IOWA: (A) URBAN DWELLERS, (B) RURAL DWELLERS. (*Source:* Berry, Barnum, and Tennant, 1962, Fig. 15.)

from both Red Oak and Atlantic in this way results in the smaller market areas for these places for furniture than was the case for clothing. The pull of the regional capital over longer distances is still apparent and is strong enough to detract from the importance of the town of Oakland in the provision of furniture for surrounding farm families. As a result Oakland is unable to secure as much of the demand for furniture as Griswold. The hierarchical structure is clearly expressed in these patterns; drawing power is noticeably related to level of center. The regional capital attracts over longer distances, followed by the two cities of Atlantic and Red Oak, which draw from intermediate surrounding areas, while the small towns (Griswold, Oakland, and Villisca) only attract sales from local areas.

In contrast to these consumer travel patterns for high-order shopping goods, Figure 7.16 shows the different picture for a high-order convenience good—dry cleaning. Although the trade areas of Atlantic, Red Oak, and Griswold are unchanged for this good, the influence of the regional capital in the area has disappeared. Rural and urban consumers seem to travel to the nearest supply point for this commodity. Thus the town of Oakland is shown to attract consumers from the local area for dry cleaning in a way that was not possible for furniture sales. Dry cleaning is a relatively frequently demanded good, and hence

FIG. 7.16. SHOPPING PREFERENCES FOR DRY CLEANING SERVICES, SOUTHWESTERN IOWA: (A) URBAN DWELLERS, (B) RURAL DWELLERS. (*Source:* Berry, Barnum, and Tennant, 1962, Fig. 14.)

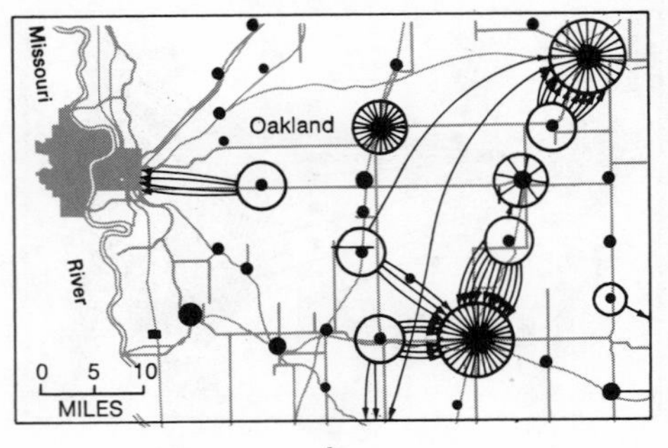

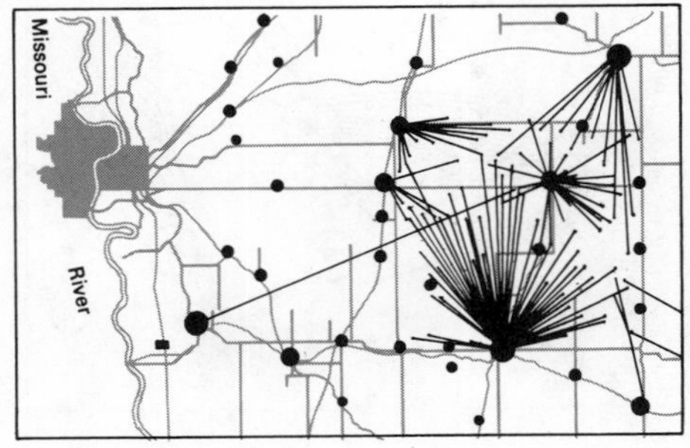

consumers are not prepared to travel long distances for it. This stands in contrast to the buying of furniture which, although an infrequently demanded good, is associated with larger expenditures. As a result, consumers want to be able to shop around before purchasing and so are prepared to undertake longer journeys to the regional capital where there are more opportunities for doing this.

What happens to the pattern when the economic reach of the villages is large enough to support a function is shown for the purchase of groceries in Figure 7.17. Groceries are an example of a true convenience good for which there is a high frequency of demand. Hence consumers are only prepared to travel short distances for their purchases. That this is so in the study area is clearly evident on both maps. Urban dwellers prefer to shop for groceries where they live, while farm families travel to the nearest centers providing this order good. The small trade areas of the villages have been created at the expense of the county seats rather than the towns; the trade areas for foodstuffs from these larger centers consequently show a considerable diminution in size. For this order good, the reach of centers is very clearly related to their size; villages attract fewer farmers but over shorter distances than towns. These in turn have smaller trade areas than the cities.

In summary the maps indicate the close agreement between the patterns of consumer movement and the structure of the hierarchy in the area. Higher level places attract consumers over longer distances than lower level places consistent with their higher degrees of centrality. Moreover the trade areas of the higher level centers are more extensive than those of lower level places for goods of similar order. The trade areas for centers at any level for goods of a given order seldom overlap, and where they do, it is usually at the margins between centers where consumers have a distinct choice of patronage (Golledge, 1967). In general consumers do seem to be systematically selecting the closest central place for the purchase of goods of different orders. This is made possible by the fact that, as thresholds drop, establishments providing goods can squeeze into the interstitial areas between the larger centers. Finally centers do appear to be located central to the areas they dominate in the

FIG. 7.17. SHOPPING PREFERENCES FOR GROCERIES, SOUTHWESTERN IOWA: (A) URBAN DWELLERS, (B) RURAL DWELLERS. (*Source:* Berry, Barnum, and Tennant, 1962, Fig. 11.)

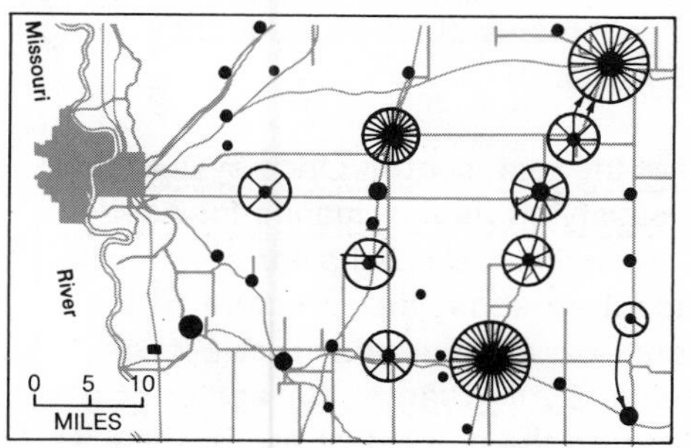

A

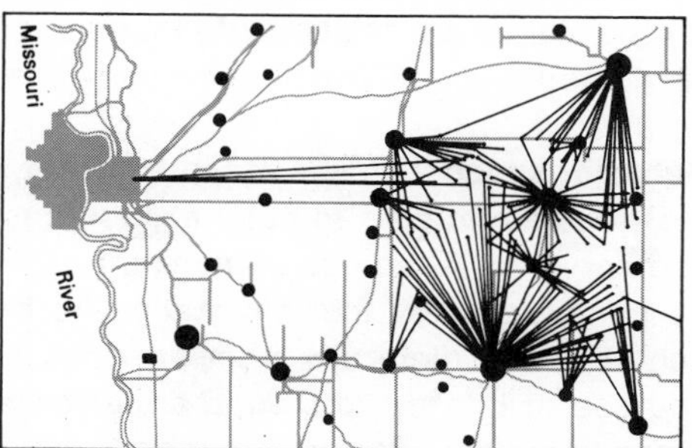

B

provision of goods and services, although the maps do show exceptions to this because of the definite boundaries of the area chosen for the intensive investigation. As Berry states, "If a system is defined as an entity comprising interacting interdependent elements, then we certainly seem to be dealing with a central place system of markets, consumers, and the multiple interactions and interdependencies among them" (Berry, 1967A, p. 13).

FACTORS AFFECTING CONSUMER TRAVEL

Consumer travel patterns naturally raise the question of the factors influencing the distances traveled by rural dwellers to central places for the purchase of goods and services. These can be summarized under three headings: (1) the characteristics of the individual and his spatial preferences, which are a function of his (2) movement imagery, and (3) behavior-space (Huff, 1960).

Individual characteristics Included under individual characteristics are the usual factors such as age, sex, income, and education, which are generally implicit in the notion of socio-economic status. By and large, the higher the status of individuals the greater their price willingness and the more prepared they are to travel to purchase goods. Thus, for example, Berry has noted from his studies in the Midwest that low-income groups tend to patronize closer centers than higher income groups in the purchase of central goods (Berry, Barnum, and Tennant, 1962). Within the central place system, the low-income consumers tend to visit the small, lower level centers and only occasionally visit centers at higher levels. Conversely higher income groups frequently travel longer distances to purchase both convenience and shopping goods from the higher level centers.

Movement imagery Huff defines movement imagery as "the perceived movement of the consumer from one region to another in his quest for a desired goal object" (Huff, 1960, p. 163). The consumer's movement imagery is affected by factors such as means of travel, travel time, and the general opportunity costs involved in overcoming the frictional effects of distance. This is implicit, of course, in the above noted difference between the space behavior of upper and lower income groups, since they most probably perceive the frictional effects of distance in different ways. And it is this notion that accounts, in part, for the significant relationship found in empirical studies between frequency of trip and distance traveled for convenience goods.

Behavior space This is essentially that part of the total central place system that individuals perceive as potential sources for satisfying their demands for goods and services. At any given moment of time, the individual's behavior space will be conditioned by the information he has acquired about the structure of the central place hierarchy from previous personal experience and from outside sources of information, such as advertisements. By and large, the ability of a place to satisfy consumer demands will depend on the number of establishments and central functions it provides—its centrality. This is borne out in empirical studies that have found size of center to be the most significant factor influencing the distance traveled in the purchase of goods and services (Murdie, 1965).

An Example

A vivid example of the way these three general factors affect travel patterns was provided recently by Murdie (1965) in a study of the central place system in parts of Waterloo and Wellington counties, southwestern Ontario, shown in Figure 7.18. Alongside the modern Canadian settlement in this area, there exists a considerable Mennonite population, many of whom still cling to the Old Order. In dress, consumption, and travel they have essentially retained the habits of two centuries ago. Their dress is plain; most of the families' clothes are made at home from yard goods. The simplicity of their home life is reflected in the low demand for goods, and the traditional horse and buggy remains as the sole means of transportation for the normal routine of day-to-day affairs. Moreover their information level is low because they do not use the telephone, radio, or television, and contact with the modern order is mainly via local newspapers. Hence, arising from their particular culture, we might expect to find that the Old Order Mennonites have markedly different behavior-spaces and movement imagery than their modern Canadian counterparts.

That this is so is very clearly illustrated by the patterns of travel for two contrasted goods shown in Figures 7.19 and 7.20. These maps suggest that the central place hierarchy is being used in different ways and that, in fact, there are two different systems corresponding to the two groups of consumers. Figure 7.19 shows the travel pattern for the two groups for a modern good and indicates that both groups assume the same general level of spatial interaction. Banks are typical of less ubiquitous services that have developed in the central place structure more recently and long after the establishment of the first Mennonite settlements in the region. Old Order Mennonite demand for this and similar services is affected very little by the cultural traditions and church doctrine of the group.

When these traditions do affect the demand for goods and services, markedly different travel patterns result. An example is given in Figure 7.20 which shows the movements of modern Canadians for clothing and of the Mennonites for yard goods. The pattern for modern Canadians fits the now-established notions of consumer behavior in the central place system. Kitchener dominates the area in the supply of this city-level good. In contrast to this, the Mennonite pattern is much more localized in nature. For them style, choice, and comparative shopping are unimportant; and their demand for yard goods is easily satisfied by the relatively unspecialized stores in the nearest hamlets, villages, and towns.

This difference in spatial behavior is even more clearly portrayed on graphs showing the distances traveled by modern Canadians and the Old Order Mennonites for clothing and yard goods respectively. In Figure 7.21 the graph for the former group shows that the maximum distance traveled is directly related to the size of center measured in terms of number of central func-

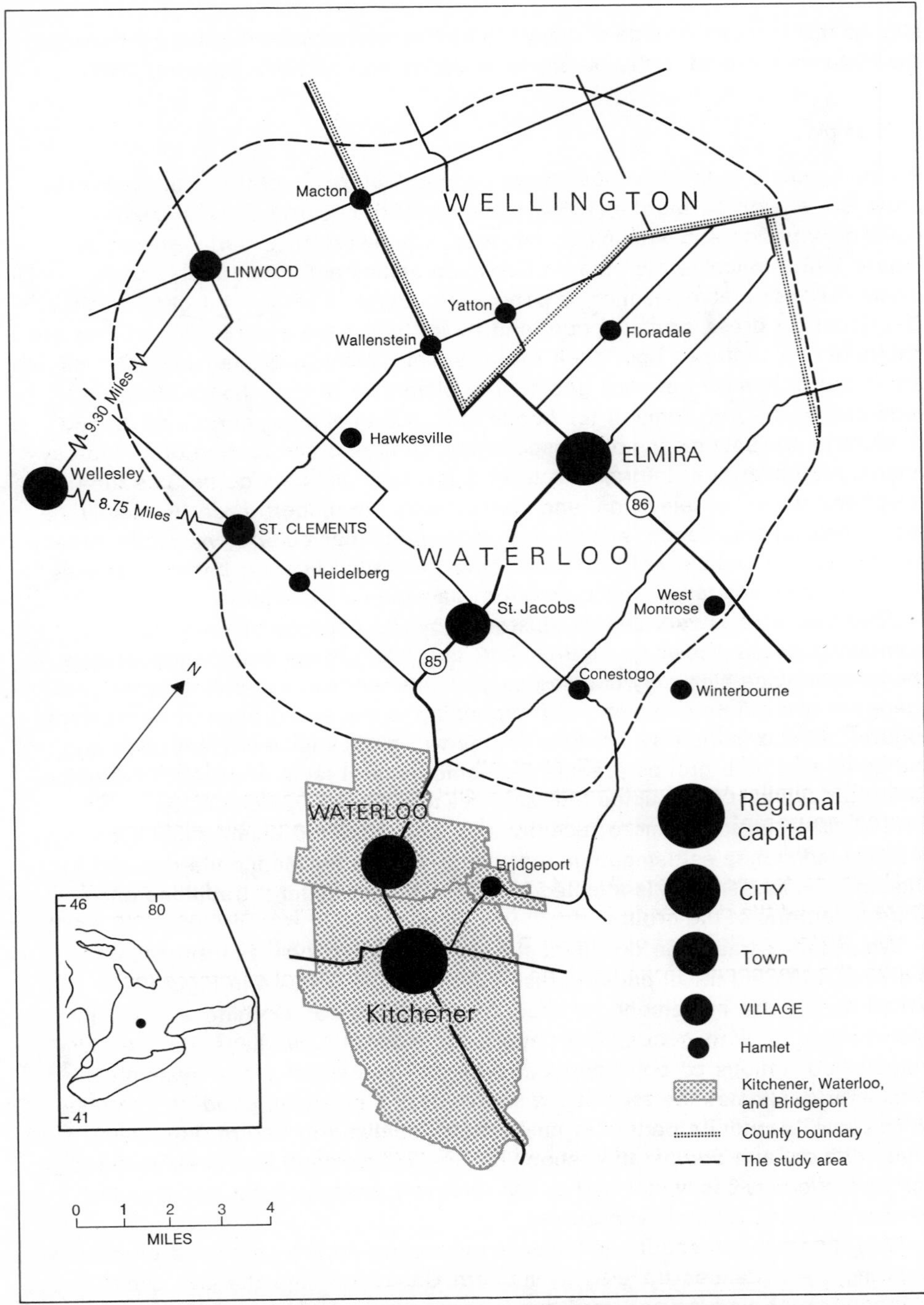

FIG. 7.18. A HIERARCHY OF CENTRAL PLACES IN SOUTHWESTERN ONTARIO, CANADA. (*Source:* Murdie, 1965, Fig. 1.)

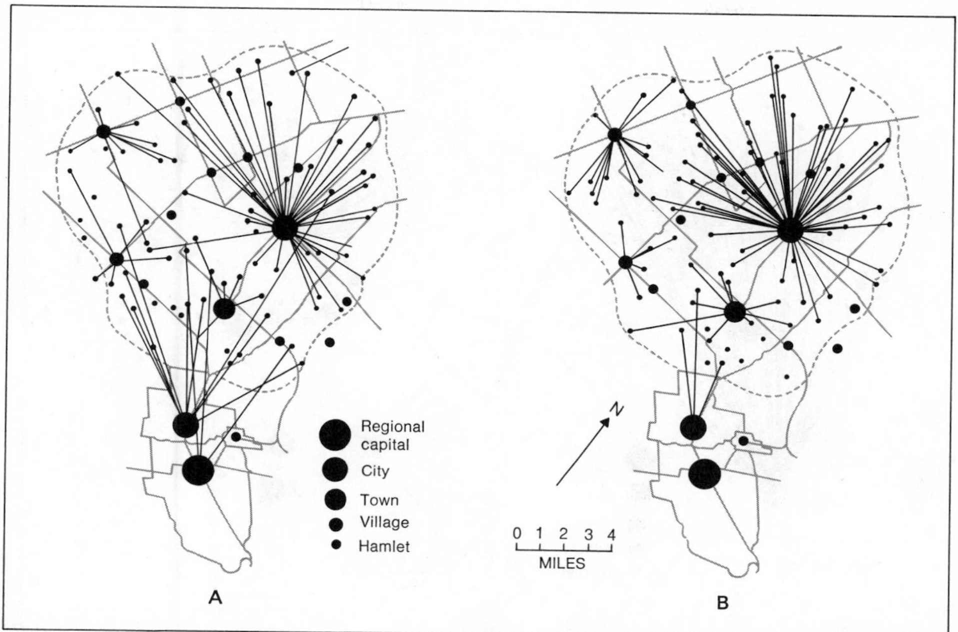

FIG. 7.19. BANKS USED BY (A) "MODERN" CANADIANS AND (B) OLD ORDER MENNONITES, SOUTHWESTERN ONTARIO. (*Source:* Murdie, 1965, Figs. 6 and 7.)

tions. This is not the case for the Mennonite group, indicating that the centrality of a place has no effect at all on the distances traveled for these and other similar traditional goods. The Old Order Mennonites travel to the nearest source of supply regardless of its size; on average this distance is about 6 miles.

However, for modern goods and services—such as banks—we have seen that there is very little difference in travel habits between the two groups. Both travel longer distances to larger centers. But it is worth noting that even for these goods, the Mennonite group uses the system at a lower level of interaction than the modern Canadians, tending to travel shorter distances to get the goods than their modern Canadian counterparts. Hence, for both traditional goods and to a lesser extent for modern goods, the Old Order Mennonites exhibit markedly different space preferences because of their different behavior space resulting both from their cultural doctrine (especially its effect upon demand for goods) and the inability of their Old World transportation to overcome the frictional effects of distance.

TRADE AREAS

The pattern of consumer behavior shown on the maps indicates the extent of the market areas of the different centers. The maximum trade area for a given center will be a function of the highest threshold good provided from it. Since

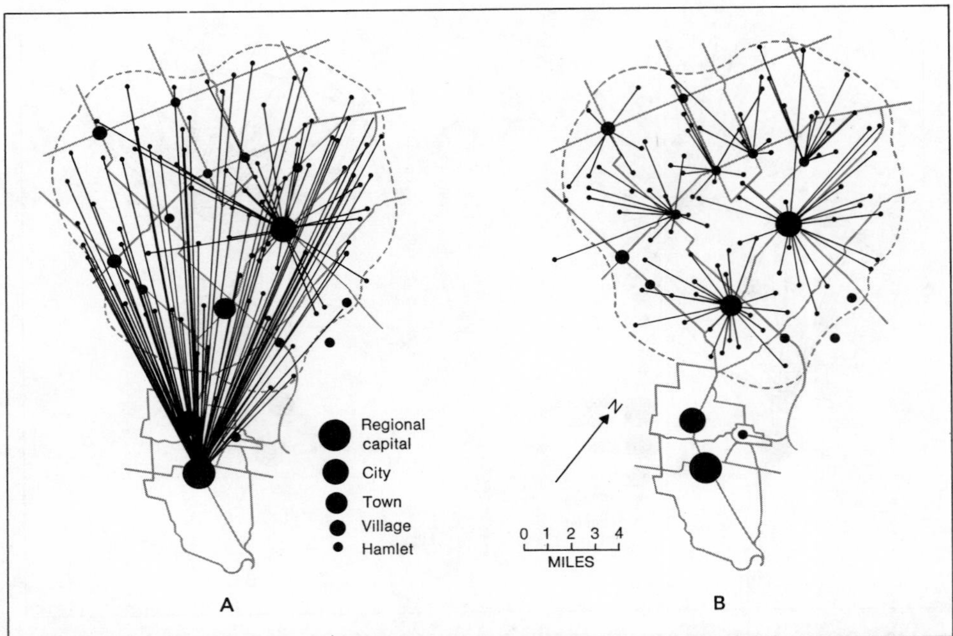

FIG. 7.20. SHOPPING PREFERENCES FOR CLOTHING OF (A) "MODERN" CANADIANS AND (B) OLD ORDER MENNONITES, SOUTHWESTERN ONTARIO. (*Source:* Murdie, 1965, Figs. 14 and 15.)

higher order goods and services are provided from higher level centers, the larger places will have larger trade areas encompassing larger total populations. This is shown for the centers in southwestern Iowa in Figure 7.22.

Several points about the graph should be noted. First, centers at the different levels in the hierarchy occupy distinct regimes within the overall scatter of points similar to the steplike pattern shown in Figure 7.12. These regimes are marked by upper limits corresponding to the maximum economic reach of the different level centers. The villages, serving on average a radius of about 5 miles, have maximum market areas of about 90 square miles. In this area they reach between 500 to 600 consumers, which with their own populations makes a total population served of about 1,100. The towns serve an area with a maximum radius of about 8 miles, have trade areas of up to 200 square miles containing total populations of about 4,200. Cities have maximum trade areas of approximately 1,000 square miles containing 20,000 consumers to give total populations served of about 30,000.

Second, the relationship between size of trade area and total population served is double logarithmic. Hence the line drawn on the graph at an angle of 45° traces out a line of equal population densities. The overall scatter of points lies very close to this line indicating the relationship between the size of trade area and density of population within this area. However, the separate regimes

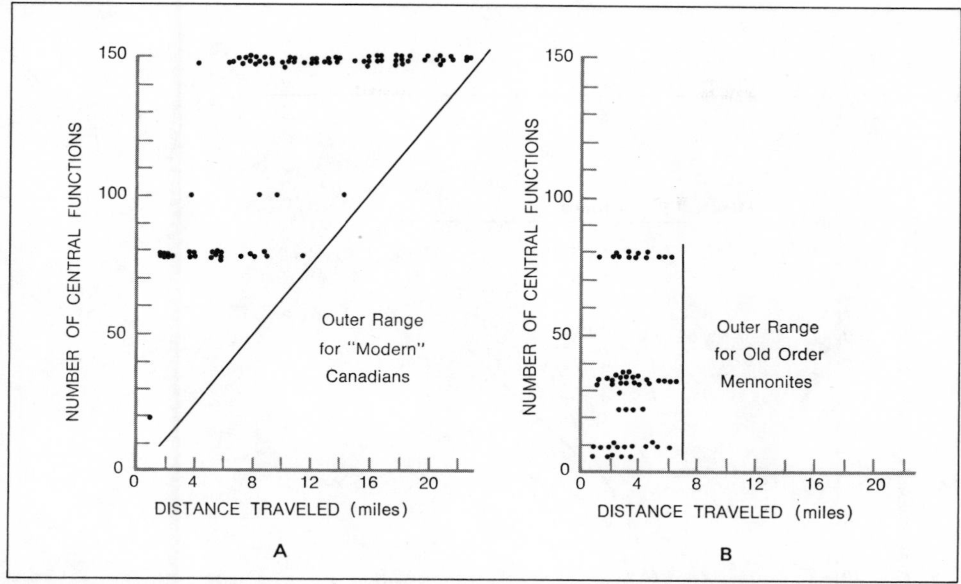

FIG. 7.21. DIFFERENCES IN THE RANGES OF CLOTHING AND YARD GOODS IN SOUTHWESTERN ONTARIO. WHEREAS THE DISTANCES TRAVELED BY "MODERN" CANADIANS (A) ARE RELATED TO THE SIZE OF CENTER VISITED, THE DISTANCES TRAVELED BY OLD ORDER MENNONITES (B) ARE INDEPENDENT OF SIZE OF CENTER. (*Source:* Murdie, 1965, Figs. 30 and 31.)

of the different level centers slope upward at angles greater than 45°—as shown for example by the dashed line for the trend of the villages. These therefore must serve areas with different population density characteristics. The villages at the upper end of the regime have larger trade areas than those at the lower end, but larger areas with lower density of population. This pattern is created because rural population densities decline with distance away from the urban centers, and other things being equal, centers with larger trade areas will therefore have lower density of population (Berry, 1967A, p. 26).

Comparable data to that given in the graph is presented for southwestern Wisconsin in Table 7.8. The trade areas in Brush's study were derived from maps of vehicular traffic flows between centers. Although these probably do not correspond exactly with the boundaries of the market areas, Brush believed that they were reasonable approximations to them (Brush, 1953, p. 395). The mean total population served by the villages and towns in this part of Wisconsin are very similar to that supporting the Iowa centers at the same levels in the hierarchy. The interesting thing to note, however, is that the size of the trade areas is smaller in southwestern Wisconsin that that of centers at the same level in Iowa. This again reflects the differences in density of population between the two areas; in Wisconsin, average densities are nearly twice as high as they are in southwestern Iowa; consequently trade areas are smaller in extent.

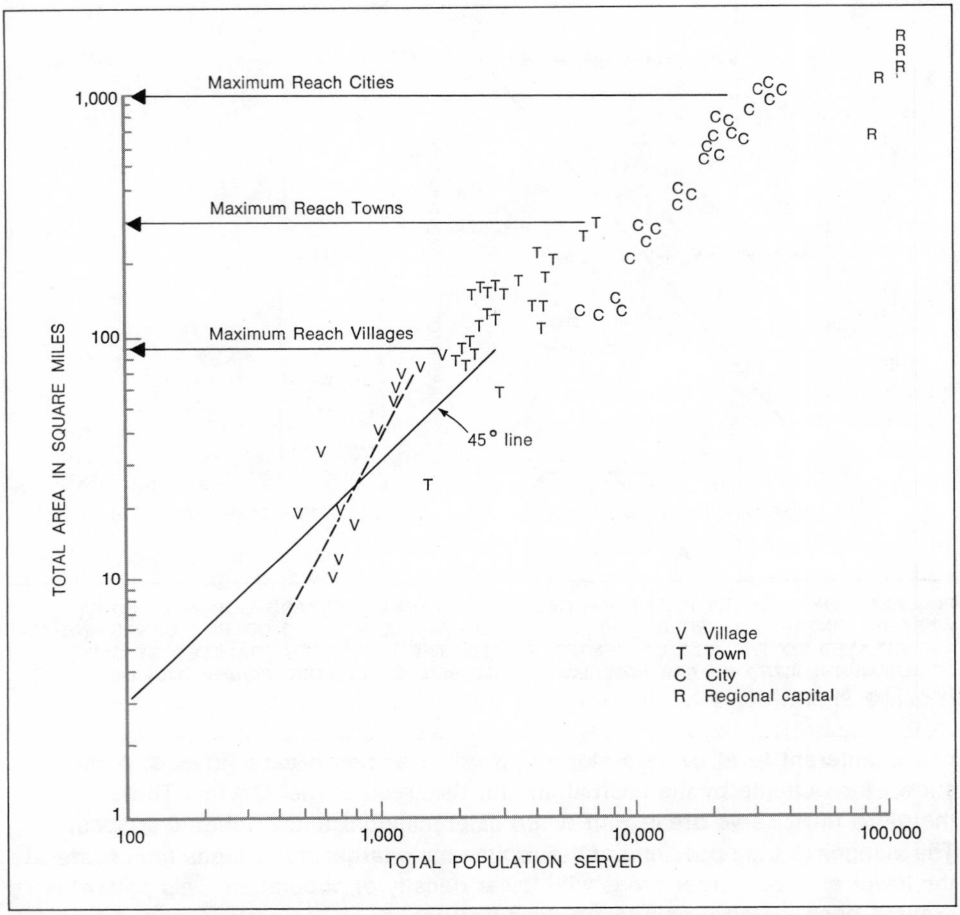

FIG. 7.22. THE RELATIONSHIP BETWEEN THE SIZE OF TRADE AREAS AND TOTAL POPULATION SERVICED BY CENTRAL PLACES. (*Source:* Berry, 1967A, Fig. 2–1.)

We have seen how the discrete structural levels of the hierarchy are associated with discrete sizes of trade areas. How, then, do these fit together in the spatial context? An indication of what happens is given diagrammatically in Figure 7.23. The trade areas of the lower level centers nest within those of the successively higher level centers. In this way the maximum trade area of cities will contain the trade areas of towns, which in turn will contain within them the much smaller trade areas of the villages. The exact ordering of this nesting pattern will depend very much on the particular spatial arrangement of the different levels of centers in the hierarchy of different regions. Hence in some regions, for example in the part of Iowa shown on the maps, the villages may nest within the city trade areas rather than in those of the towns; but the towns nest within the maximum trade areas of the cities.

TABLE 7.8. TRADE AREA CHARACTERISTICS IN SOUTHWESTERN WISCONSIN

Trade Area	62 Villages[a]	13 Towns[a]
Mean size of trade area in square miles	32.2	129.1
Range in size of trade areas in square miles	9.6–76.8	27.2–241.6
Mean trade area population	608	2439
Mean center population	486	3373
Mean total population served	1094	5812

[a] Only those centers with their traffic areas completely within the boundary of the study area are included.
Source: Brush (1953), Table III.

Systematic variation in hierarchies Figure 7.22 indicated that local variation in population density in southwestern Iowa had a direct effect upon the size of trade areas of centers. For any given level of center, larger trade areas were associated with lower population densities. If the hierarchy is sensitive to these local conditions, it is realistic to expect that variations will occur in the central place structure in association with regional variations in population density. That this is so is indicated in Figure 7.24. On this graph, the relationship between trade-area size and total population served by centers is given for the centers in southwestern Iowa (Corn Belt) together with comparable data for centers in four other areas of contrasted density. These range from the low densities of between 2 to 5 persons per square mile in the rangelands of southwestern South Dakota, and the densities between 6 to 9 persons per square mile in the wheatlands of northeastern South Dakota through to the high densities of part of the city of Chicago (Urban on the graph).

The centers in the hierarchies of the different areas show a high degree of systematic variation under the different density conditions. The graph indicates

FIG. 7.23. SCHEMATIC REPRESENTATION OF THE NESTING OF TRADE AREAS.

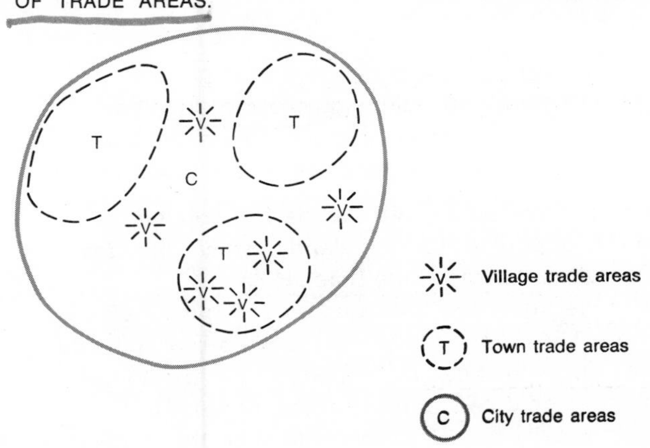

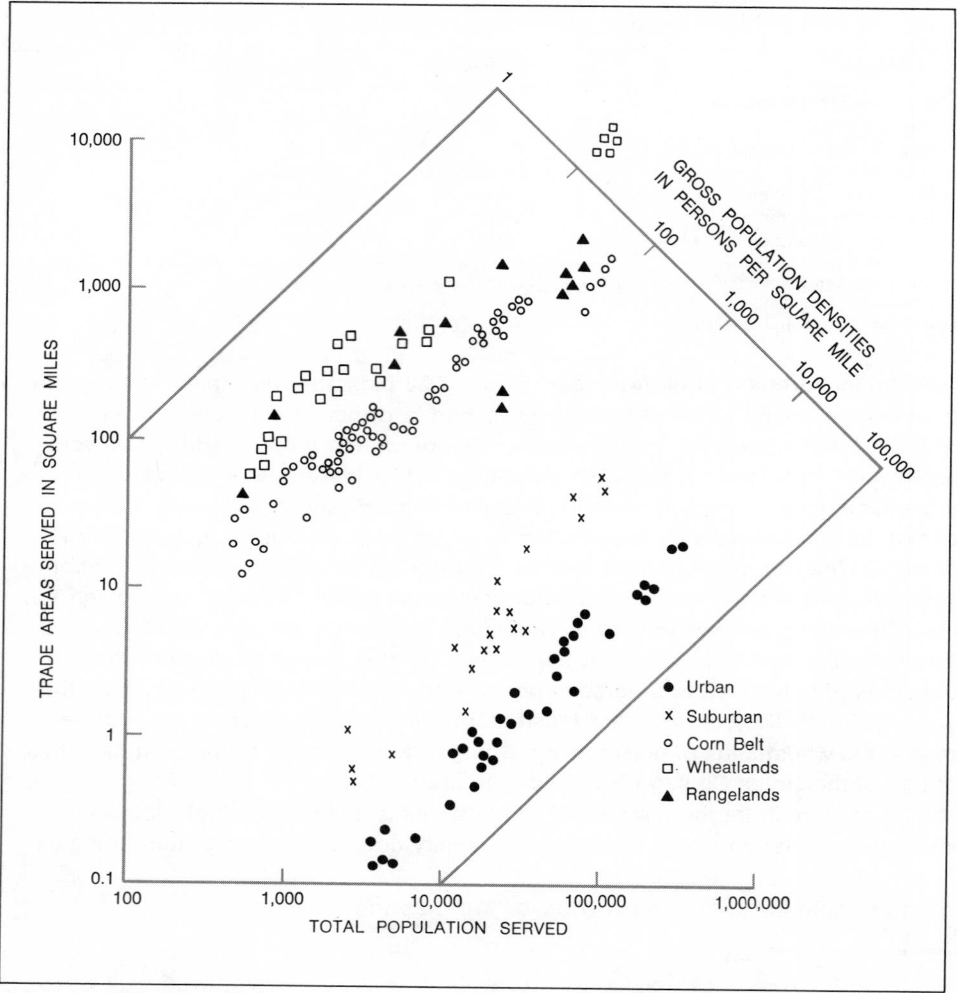

FIG. 7.24. RELATIONSHIPS BETWEEN THE SIZE OF TRADE AREAS AND TOTAL POPULATION SERVICED BY CENTRAL PLACES VARY ACCORDING TO THE DENSITY OF POPULATION. (*Source:* Berry, 1967A, Fig. 2–8).

the significant increase in the size of trade areas with decreasing population densities. The only exception to this occurs in the rangelands, which includes the higher density mining and recreational areas of the Black Hills.

When the different levels in the hierarchy are indicated as in Figure 7.25, another interesting feature emerges. The different levels of the hierarchy in the five regions are so consistent that their upper limit can be indicated by straight lines. These slope backward to the right and indicate that trade areas increase in size with decreases in population density but at slower rate than the decline

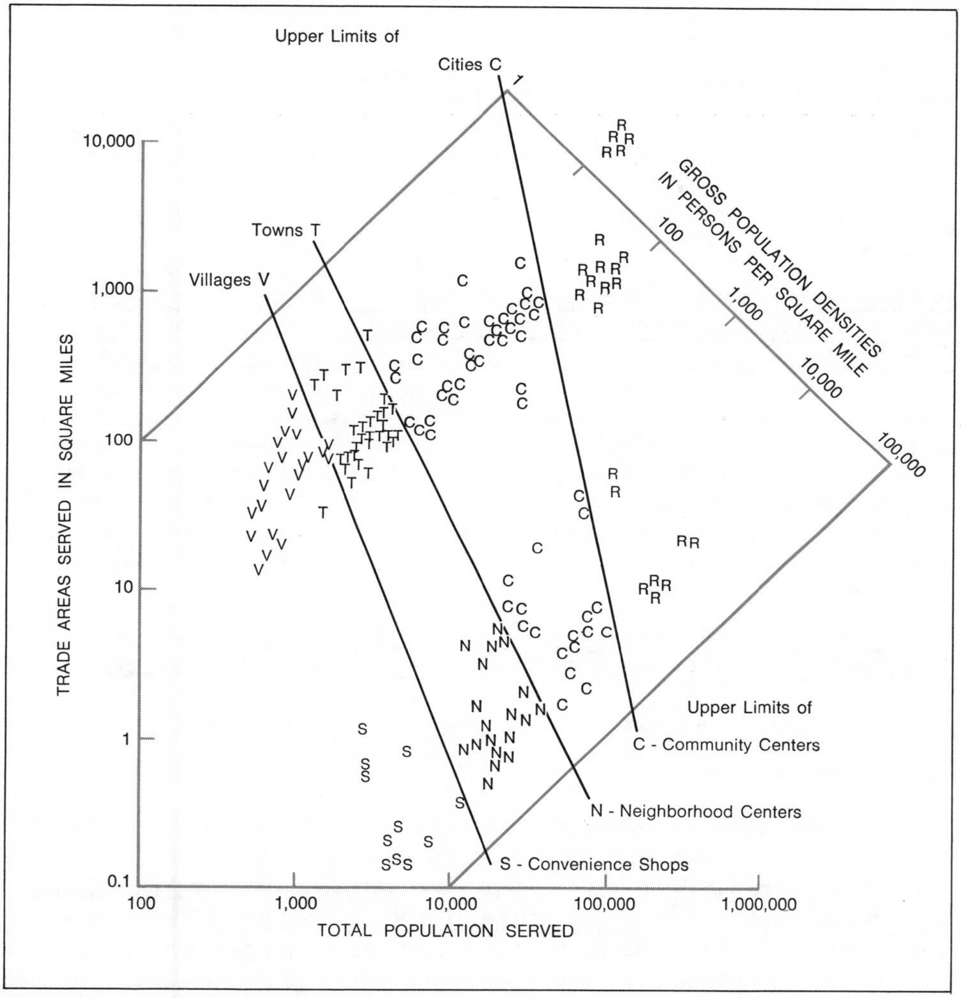

FIG. 7.25. SYSTEMATIC VARIATION IN THE HIERARCHY OF CENTRAL PLACES IS RELATED TO DIFFERENCES IN THE DENSITY OF POPULATION. (*Source:* Berry, 1967A, Fig. 2–9.)

in population density. The result of this is that the total population served by centers at a given level in the hierarchy also decreases.

This has a direct effect on the satisfaction of thresholds at centers. Functions with the highest thresholds at any given level of the hierarchy are forced to move up to the next higher level. Berry argues from this that a reduction is brought about in the population sizes of the centers themselves, because their economic base has declined with the loss of the higher threshold functions (Berry, 1967A, p. 33). Thus the upper limit in population size of towns in southwestern Iowa is about 1700; in the rangelands of South Dakota, towns do not exceed about 500 population. Because of this, the towns in South Dakota are no longer able to support the following central functions: furniture stores, appliance stores, variety stores, insurance and real estate agents, movers and haulers, funeral homes, doctors and dentists. Similarly, the lower threshold functions of farm implement dealers, barber shops, and beauty salons are no longer found at the village level as they are in southwestern Iowa but have moved up to become town-level functions in South Dakota.

Berry (1967A, pp. 34–35) explains this upward shift in the level of functions as follows:

> To maintain a given array of activities, market areas must increase in size in direct proportion to the drop in population densities; the maximum distance consumers are willing to travel to the center must increase in similar proportion to the density decline. Evidently consumers are willing to travel farther where densities are lower, for movement will generally be easier where people are fewer and congestion is less, so that the economic reach of centers does increase. The change is less than proportionate, however, so center's functions must adjust to the declining numbers of consumers that can be reached within the trade areas of increasing radius. Similarly, at very high densities, congestion will not completely localize consumer movements, so that business centers of any given level within cities reach more consumers and are functionally more complex than their rural counterparts.

Thus, systematic variations in the hierarchy can be incorporated into the central place system through the concepts of the threshold and range of the good.

CENTRAL PLACE THEORY

The empirically observed regularities in the provision of goods and services from central places discussed above suggests that they may be formalized in a more abstract way. This was recognized as long ago as 1933 by Walter Christaller, whose name today is synonymous with central place theory. The ideas he presented were subsequently taken up by August Lösch, who before his untimely death in 1945 formulated Christaller's ideas in a more rigorous way and developed them further. Since the publication of these earlier works, the ideas they contained have been added to by many other researchers, notable among whom are Beckmann (1958) and Dacey (1965).

CHRISTALLER'S K=3 SYSTEM

Christaller's model of the size and distribution of central places is based on what he calls the *marketing principle* (Christaller, 1966). This gives rise to a geometrical system in which the number 3 takes on special significance. Hence his model is widely known as the K=3 system (the K is just an arbitrarily selected index letter used as a shorthand notation for the settlement pattern). To get rid of as many of the complicating influences acting on settlement patterns as possible, Christaller developed his model for an abstract area with the following characteristics: (1) the area was a featureless plain devoid of natural or man-made features, (2) movement was possible in any and every direction, a situation described as an *isotropic surface,* (3) population, and by implication purchasing power, was continuously and uniformly distributed, and (4) consumers act rationally in space according to the principles of distance minimization.

If on this abstract surface consumers are to be supplied from central places with a given good, according to assumption (4) the trade areas for the good will be circular in shape. If it is further assumed that the good is to be provided from as many central places as possible, the maximum possible size of the circular trade areas will be equal to the inner range for the good, since an area of this size will contain just enough consumers to satisfy its threshold. The most efficient packing of these trade areas in the plain is shown in Figure 7.26A. In this way, the total area of the plain that is not served by a central place is at a minimum, and the number of central places and trade areas is at a maximum. Two important features of the resulting pattern are that (1) central places are distributed according to a triangular-hexagonal pattern, and (2) each trade area is tangential to six others.

However, with this arrangement, some consumers, namely those living in the shaded interstitial areas of Figure 7.26A, will not be provided with the good in question. If these people are to be supplied, then the circular trade areas must overlap as shown in Figure 7.26B. Consumers living in the areas of overlap must choose which center they will visit. Assuming that the consumer is rational and motivated by least effort principles, he will choose the center closest to him, for in this way he can consume as much as he wants at minimum cost. The result is a bisection of the areas of overlap and the circular trade areas are replaced by hexagons as shown in Figure 7.26C. This geometric pattern forms the basis of Christaller's K=3 system.

FIG. 7.26. THE EMERGENCE OF HEXAGONAL TRADE AREAS: (A) THE MOST EFFICIENT PACKING OF CIRCULAR TRADE AREAS ON THE PLAIN, (B) OVERLAPPING CIRCULAR TRADE AREAS, (C) HEXAGONAL TRADE AREAS COVERING THE PLAIN COMPLETELY AND WITHOUT OVERLAP.

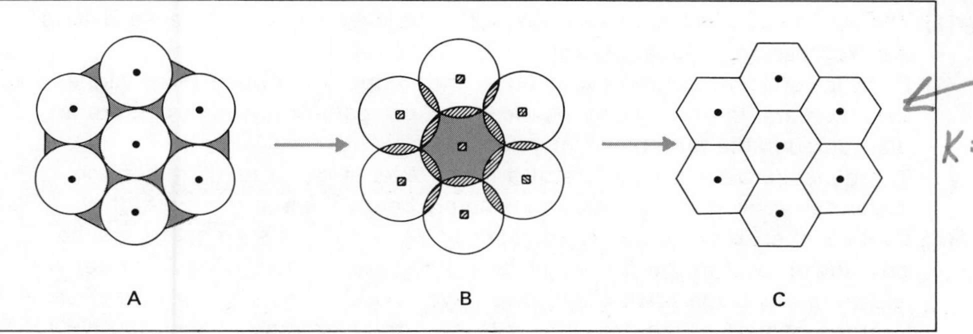

So far the discussion has been in terms of the provision of only one good. In reality a number of different goods and services are provided. The question is how the different order goods will be provided within the framework of the hexagonal pattern. The answer is shown in Figure 7.27. This was developed by Christaller in the following way:

The locations of the highest order good were selected as a starting point. Since this good has the largest threshold requirement, it will also have the largest hexagonal trade area. The places from which this good is provided (primary centers) are shown in the diagram by the large solid dots, and their trade areas by the thick solid lines. Christaller considered these locations to be the sites of central places from which all lower threshold goods are also provided. It follows that the minimum size of trade areas required to support these successively lower order goods will be progressively smaller than that for the highest order good. One of these lower order goods will have a threshold size just large enough for it to be provided from a new location, and an enterprising businessman could establish himself there. The trade area for this good will be a hexagon exactly equal in size to the trade area for the same good provided from the primary centers. In terms of the previous discussion this good is an example of an hierarchical marginal good. Since the existing centers already provide all goods down to this order, the only location possible from which the threshold for this good can be satisfied is the midpoint between three of the original primary centers. The locations of these secondary centers are shown in the diagram by the large open dots and their trade areas by the heavy dashed lines. These secondary centers will provide all goods having thresholds smaller than that of the hierarchical marginal good typical of centers at this level. By repeating the argument a third, fourth, and succeeding times, the pattern fills out to give a system of nested trade areas and a hierarchy of different level centers. By definition, each higher level center in the hierarchy provides all goods supplied from successively lower level centers plus a group of higher order functions that set it above the lower level centers in the system. For reasons of clarity, only the three largest-sized centers in this kind of hierarchy are shown in Figure 7.27.

From the geometrical properties of the hexagonal-triangular pattern the following generalizations about the K=3 system can be made:

(1) The frequency of occurrence of the different levels of central places follows the progression, from large to small, 1, 2, 6, 18, 54, 162, . . . , *n*.

(2) Each lower level center is located at the midpoint between three higher level centers, thereby giving rise to a uniform pattern in which centers are distributed in the form of a triangular lattice.

(3) The distance between centers at a given level is equal to $\sqrt{3}$ times the distance between the centers immediately below them in the hierarchy.

(4) Every higher level center is surrounded by a ring of six centers of the next lower level in the hierarchy, and these are located at each corner of its hexagonal trade area. Each lower level place is therefore served equally by three centers of the next higher level in the hierarchy—hence the K=3 system.

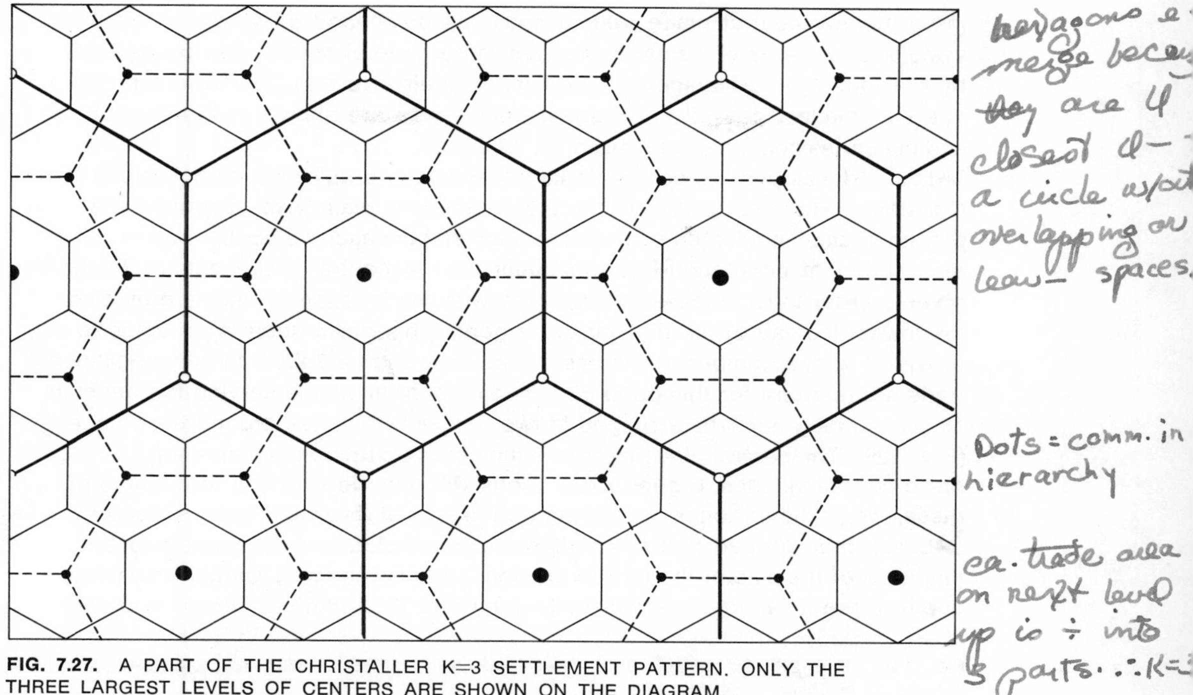

FIG. 7.27. A PART OF THE CHRISTALLER K=3 SETTLEMENT PATTERN. ONLY THE THREE LARGEST LEVELS OF CENTERS ARE SHOWN ON THE DIAGRAM.

(5) The trade area of a higher level center is exactly three times larger than that of the next lower level centers. It comprises its own trade area at this lower level, plus one-third of the trade areas of each of the six surrounding centers (see Fig. 7.27).

(6) In this way, the progression of trade areas from largest to smallest is 1, 3, 9, 27, 81, 243, . . . , *m*.

THE LÖSCHIAN LANDSCAPE

Lösch's (1954) contribution to central place theory was essentially twofold. First, he provided a more explicit and rigorous economic argument of the rationale underlying hexagonal trade areas. The more rigorous analysis of supply and demand was based on the economic theory of the firm, and this made possible a more exact specification of the spatial demand cone for a given good. Lösch was also able to prove mathematically that the hexagon is the most advantageous shape for trade areas, since it requires a smaller amount of land to generate a given level of total demand than any of the possible alternatives (i.e. a triangle or a square). Consequently hexagons enable the best possible packing of trade areas in a region to the mutual advantage of both consumers (through distance minimization) and producers (because the largest number of independent enterprises is possible).

Second, in building on Christaller's initial ideas, Lösch demonstrated that a more general central place system could be developed in which the K=3 system is just a very special case. This more general system can be derived by rearranging the hexagons, by changing their size and their orientation. The six smallest possible hexagonal trade areas are shown in Figure 7.28, and the series continues with sizes 16, 19, 21, 25, ...

Lösch developed his economic landscape from a different starting point than Christaller. He first assumed that the featureless plain was covered by a pattern of small nucleated settlements (hamlets) instead of a continuous distribution of population. He then built up the central place pattern in the reverse order to Christaller by beginning with the location of places providing the lowest instead of the highest order good. This basic good is assumed to be provided from a number of villages as shown in Figure 7.29. The basic hexagonal trade area pattern for this good comprises a central village serving the nearest 18 surrounding hamlets, arranged in two concentric circles around the village (Fig. 7.29). The central place pattern is then built up from the location of these central villages. Higher order goods will only be supplied from some of these, the particular ones depending on the size of threshold to be satisfied.

Lösch then argued that if the different thresholds are considered to be multiples of the size of the basic hexagons, goods requiring market areas from one to three times this size will be located in a K=3 pattern, goods requiring

FIG. 7.28. THE SIX SMALLEST SIZE TRADE AREAS IN THE LÖSCHIAN LANDSCAPE. (*Source:* After Lösch, 1954, Fig. 27.)

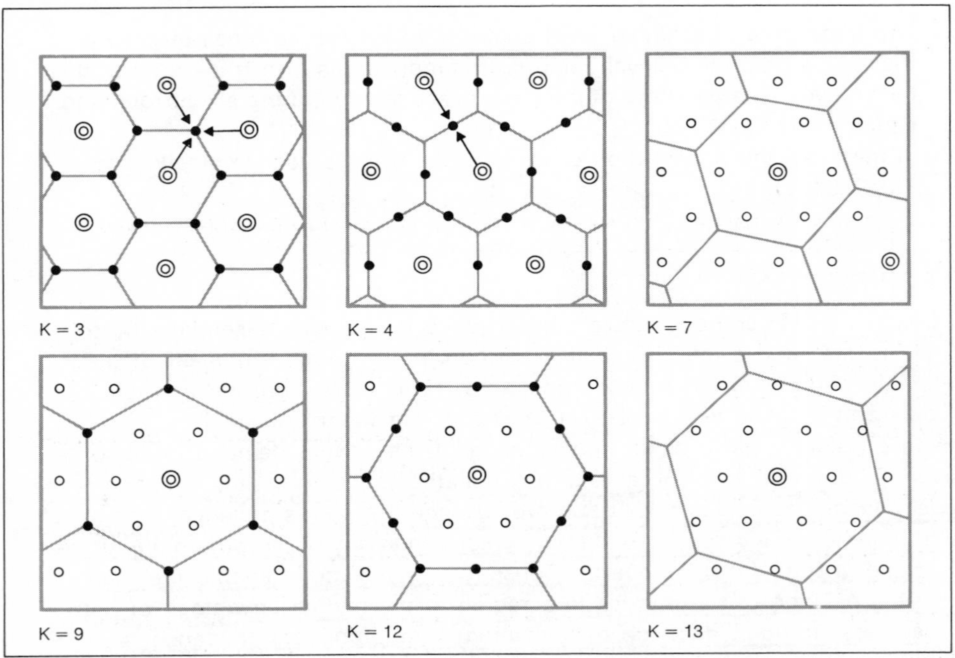

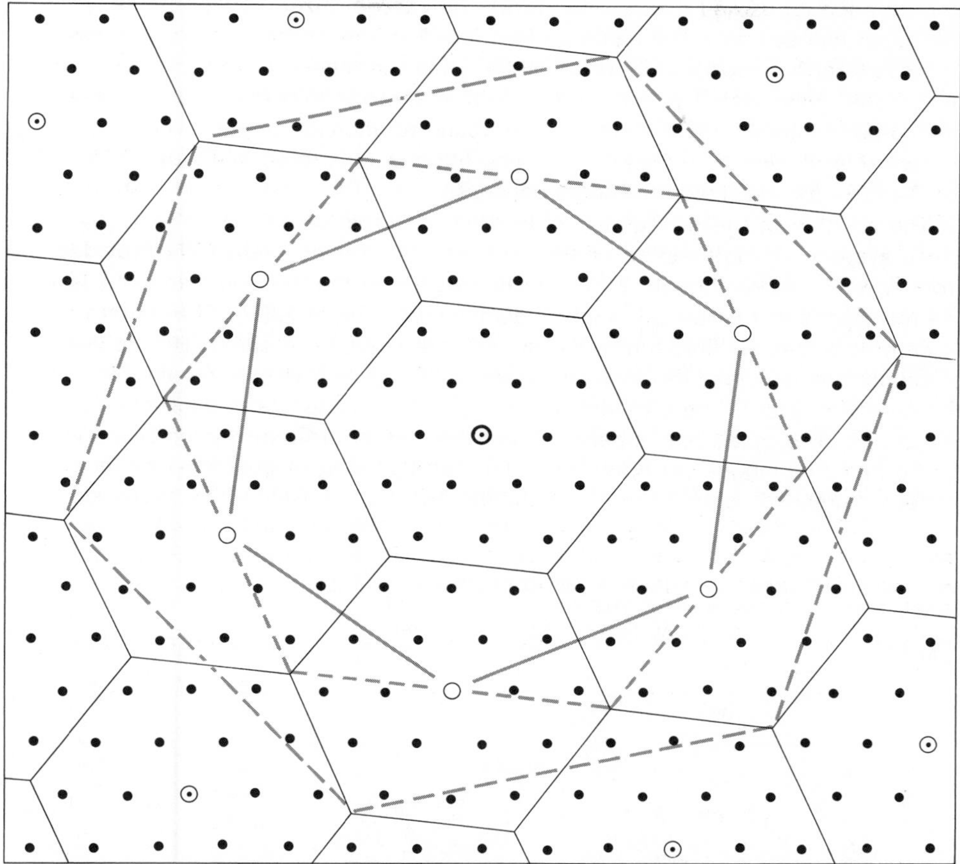

FIG. 7.29. THE OVERLAP OF THE THREE SMALLEST SIZE TRADE AREAS IN THE LÖSCHIAN LANDSCAPE. THE MAP ALSO SHOWS THE BASIC HEXAGONS SERVED BY THE CENTRAL VILLAGES AND THE TRIANGULAR LATTICE OF SMALL NUCLEATED SETTLEMENTS COVERING THE PLAIN.

four times its size will locate in a K=4 pattern, those requiring from five to seven times the basic trade area size locate in a K=7 pattern, and so on up through the different orders of goods. In this way the landscape is covered by networks of hexagons of different sizes. An example of the three smallest market area sizes in the Lösch system is given in Figure 7.29. Since it is only possible to obtain these by changing their orientation (see Fig. 7.28), it should be clear that the different order goods can be supplied from different sets of centers depending on the way the hexagonal network of a given size is laid down.

To overcome this problem, Lösch introduced a further requirement: the amount of agglomeration of activities at central places in the system must be the maximum possible. To satisfy this requirement, one central village in the basic hexagonal network is arbitrarily selected as an initial starting point. For convenience let us call this A. The increasingly larger sized hexagonal networks are superimposed over the basic pattern, so that one of the centers in each of these larger networks coincides with A. Then the different hexagonal networks are rotated (with their centers fixed at A) until there is maximum coincidence of all other centers in the pattern. The particular rotation about place A needed to give this maximum degree of agglomeration is illustrated in Figure 7.30 for the ten smallest sized hexagonal networks.

The rotation of the hexagonal trade area networks gives rise to a central place system with interesting characteristics. Since every activity is provided from A, this can be thought of as the metropolis in the system. Radiating from the metropolis will be six 60° sectors as shown in Figure 7.31A. The pattern of central places within each of the six sectors will be the same. The details of the pattern for one of the sectors are shown in Figure 7.31B. In the diagram, the numbers refer to the different order of goods provided from each place; the lowest order good is numbered 1, and the market area for this corresponds to the basic hexagons used as the initial starting point in building up the pattern. Number 2 refers to the next highest order good, which is associated

FIG. 7.30. THE EXACT ORIENTATION OF HEXAGONAL TRADE AREAS NECESSARY FOR THE MAXIMUM AGGLOMERATION OF CENTRAL FUNCTIONS AT CENTRAL PLACES.

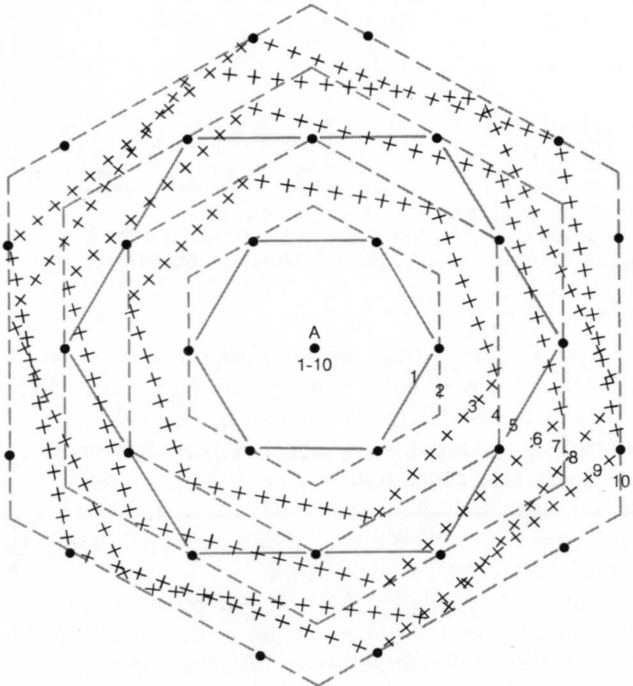

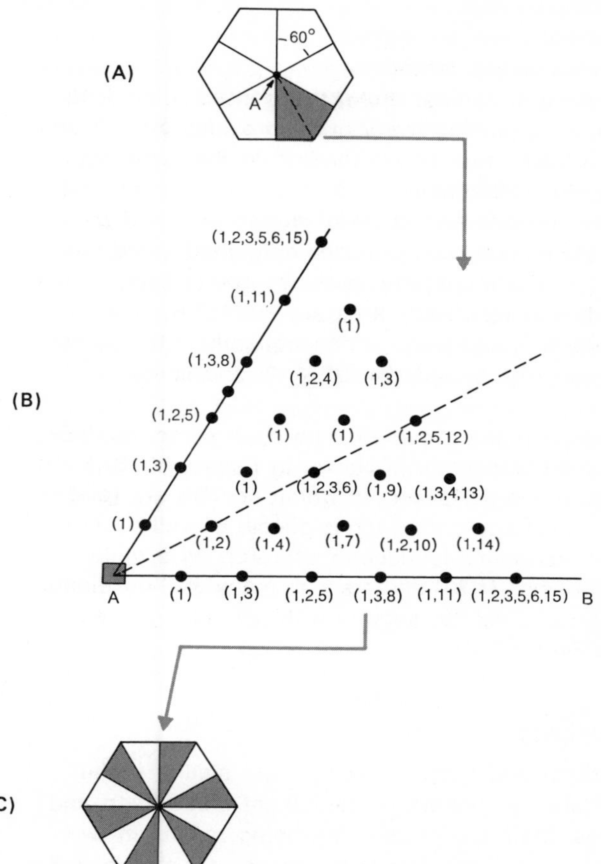

FIG. 7.31. DETAILS OF THE LÖSCHIAN ECONOMIC LANDSCAPE: (A) SIX SECTORS AROUND THE METROPOLIS; (B) DETAILS OF THE LOCATION, SIZE, AND FUNCTIONAL STRUCTURE OF PLACES IN ONE OF THE SECTORS; (C) "CITY RICH" AND "CITY POOR" SECTORS.

with trade areas of the K=3 type, and so on up the scale. The different order goods and their corresponding market area sizes are shown in Table 7.9.

TABLE 7.9. ORDERS OF GOODS AND CORRESPONDING TRADE AREA SIZES IN THE LÖSCHIAN ECONOMIC LANDSCAPE

Order of good	1	2	3	4	5	6	7	8	9	10	. . .*n*
Size of trade area needed K =	basic	3	4	7	9	12	13	16	19	21	. . .*m*

Using the diagram and the table, we have the following information about the different centers:

(1) The total number of goods provided.
(2) The types of goods provided.
(3) The number and size of trade areas served.

This can be illustrated by taking the places along the transect from A to B in Figure 7.31B as an example. By definition every place provides good 1 and is consequently the center of a trade area corresponding to the basic size of a hexagon in the system (see Fig. 7.29). Above this level there is considerable variation between places in the number and kinds of goods provided by them. Thus for example, the closest place to A provides only good 1 and serves only a basic-sized trade area. The place next to it provides goods 1 and 3 and is therefore at the center of a basic-sized trade area and one of K=4; the place next to this provides goods 1, 2, and 5 and is consequently at the center of a basic-sized trade area, one of K=3, and one of K=9; and so on outward from A.

On the basis of the numbers of goods provided from each place, another interesting feature of the Löschian landscape is shown in Figure 7.31B. Each sector can clearly be divided into two parts; one in which centers are relatively specialized in the provision of goods and one which is devoid of well-developed central places. The result is an economic landscape centered on a multi-functional metropolis and comprising six 30° sectors with many well-developed central places (city-rich sectors) and six 30° sectors with few such places (city-poor sectors) as shown in Figure 7.31C.

CHRISTALLER AND LÖSCH COMPARED

It is clear that although Christaller and Lösch start out with similar initial assumptions concerning the triangular pattern of settlement distribution and hexagonal-shaped market areas, their subsequent reasoning results in two completely different central place patterns. The basic reason for this is that Christaller starts with the location of the highest threshold good and proceeds downward from this, whereas Lösch begins with the most ubiquitous, lowest threshold good and subsequently builds upward. On the basis of the resulting different patterns, it has been suggested that Christaller's model is really only relevant for the geography of tertiary activity, whereas the more flexible Löschian model is also relevant for the geography of secondary, market-oriented manufacturing activity.

The most important difference between the two systems is, however, in the type of hierarchy each contains. In the Christallerian system, all places at the same level not only provide the same number of functions but also the same kinds of functions. In graphic form it can be represented as a completely filled-out triangular matrix as shown in Figure 7.32A. Thus it is a very rigid type of hierarchical system. Despite this it has been an extremely useful conceptual framework for empirical investigation. The Löschian type hierarchy is much more variable. Centers that are at the same level in it provide the same number of functions, but do not necessarily provide the same kinds of functions.

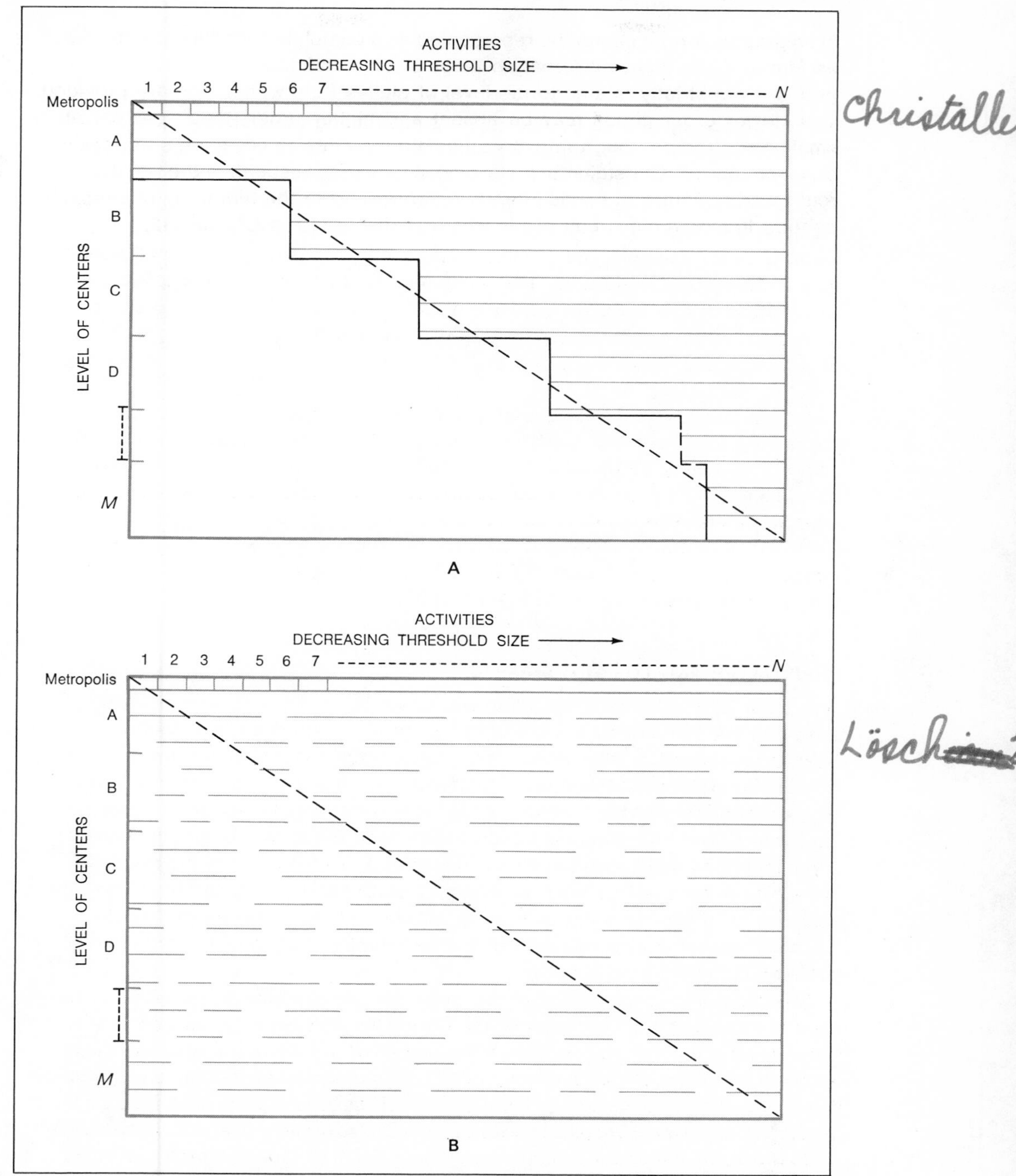

FIG. 7.32. SCHEMATIC REPRESENTATION OF THE (A) CHRISTALLER AND (B) LÖSCH CENTRAL PLACE HIERARCHIES.

In its graphic form it cannot be represented as a complete triangular matrix, but as Figure 7.32B shows it forms an incomplete rectangular one. The order of goods is not strictly related to the level of places from which they are provided. Thus lower order goods may be absent and higher order goods present at smaller centers. Although this more flexible structure is not quite so appealing conceptually as Christaller's hierarchy, it does correspond more to the real world structure of service centers, particularly to the hierarchy of shopping centers found within urban areas which is discussed in Chapter 12.

"THE INTERNAL STRUCTURE OF URBAN AREAS"

"URBAN GROWTH AND URBAN TRANSPORT"

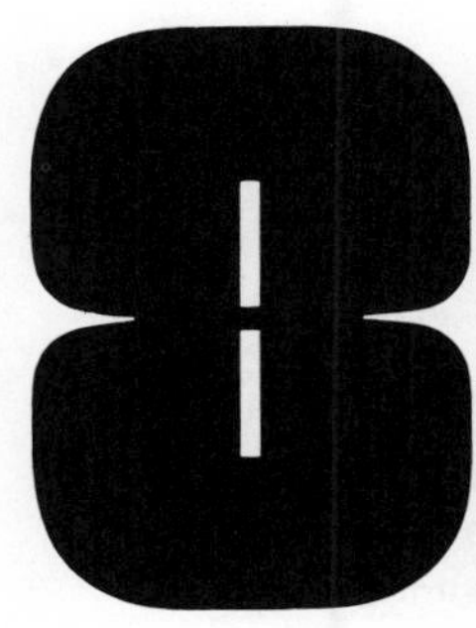

In Part I settlements were observed to perform a variety of activities of both a service and manufacturing nature. These activities are, of course, located within urban areas. It is the purpose of Part II to analyze the internal structure of the North

American city in terms of these uses. At the outset it is important to recognize that the locations of these uses change over time, a high grade residential area may be replaced by lower grade residences or vice versa. Change is, in fact, the essence of the North American city; it is in a continual state of flux. In order to begin the analysis of the internal structure of the North American city we shall therefore first examine the process of change. As much of the ensuing analysis is concerned with the effect of accessibility on land use, our primary concern in this chapter will be to discern the influence of changes in transportation technology on the growth, structure, and form of the urban area.

A basic problem arising in an examination of the effect of changing technology on the urban area is that improvements in urban transportation tend to culminate and overlap each other at the end of the nineteenth and beginning of the twentieth century. Thus it is difficult to follow a strict temporal sequence in terms of discrete time periods. We shall, however, attempt to maintain the central temporal theme by examining some of the more important technical innovations in their historical sequence as they became important to the growth and form of the North American city (Adams, 1970). These changes will be examined in the following conceptual sequence: (1) the pedestrian city, (2) the railroad, (3) the streetcar, (4) rapid transit, and (5) the internal combustion engine.

THE PEDESTRIAN CITY

The central principle derived from our analysis of the economic base concept is that urban areas can grow only by producing and exporting goods, so that they may have the purchasing power to import the necessities and luxuries of their everyday life (Gilmore, 1953, pp. 1–23). The general conditions for rapid urban growth and large urban areas did not exist until the days of the Industrial and Agricultural Revolutions. The Agricultural Revolution made it possible for a few persons to produce a large food surplus, and the Industrial Revolution could take place only with the agglomeration of the surplus rural population into urban places to provide labor for factories. Consequently before the Industrial Revolution, urban areas tended to be rather small in population size, except for those very few involved with particular economic, administrative, and financial activities. These were primarily located along the eastern seaboard of North America.

COMPACTNESS AND TRANSPORT COSTS

Even though the population of some of these cities during the early stages of the Industrial Revolution was quite large, the cities were quite compact. The reason for this compactness was that the costs of transportation for both people and goods were very high due to the primitive means of transportation available. This primitiveness was related to the sources of power available for intraurban transportation at that time. The two basic forms of power available were based on the strength and stamina of humans and horses. Human beings either walked, carried, or pulled goods and each other around, or horses performed this task. The horse-drawn omnibus was first used in North America in New York City by about 1830, and in 1885, 593 omnibuses were licensed to operate over 27 different routes in the city (Hecker, 1951, p. 1). The greater strength and durability of horses of course made them preferable to humans as power sources. But horses were expensive and costly to maintain, and so even companies using horses for pulling omnibuses (where economies of large-scale use might prevail) were beginning to find by 1880 that this form of power was prohibitively expensive.

Horse power At that time "horses cost from $125 to $200 each, and a transit company had to own from five to eight times as many horses as cars" (Holton and Due, 1964, p. 4). But not only were horses expensive to buy, they were also expensive to maintain. In return for four to five hours of service each day, a horse would consume about 30 pounds of hay and grain and had to be provided with ancillary services such as stables, blacksmiths, veterinarians, and other facilities. On top of these costs was the additional fact that horses, like human beings, grow old and at all times were susceptible to diseases and epidemics. For example in 1872 the great epizootic, an equine respiratory disease, killed over 2,250 horses in three weeks in Philadelphia and disabled 18,000 horses in New York City. Disasters of this kind could obviously seriously disrupt an already slow and expensive form of urban transportation.

Home and work in the pedestrian city People therefore did not, on the whole, move around the city as much as they do today. In fact Vance states that ". . . the large-scale movement of people within the city is a rather recent phenomenon" (Vance, 1960, p. 191). Before and during the early stages of the Industrial Revolution, people tended to live either close to or within the same building as their place of work. Only the wealthy could afford to move from one district to another as a daily event. Even then Warner notes that in Boston in 1850 ". . . streets of the well-to-do lay hard by workers' barracks and tenements of the poor; many artisans kept shop and home in the same building or street; and factories, wharves, and offices were but a few blocks from middle-class homes" (Warner, 1962, p. 19). A lack of cheap transportation thus bound the city together into a dense compact unit. As very few people traveled frequently between districts within the larger urban areas, each district was able to form its own identity. Therefore in the days of the pedestrian city, social distance and physical distance amounted to very much the same thing.

The Horsecar

Although the rich and the poor could live side by side, the innovation of the horsecar permitted the city to spread out along restricted lines and began the division of the middle classes from the poorer classes within the city. The first horse-drawn car on street rail lines in North America started regular operation in New York City in 1832 (Hecker, 1951, p. 1). The economic success of this line led to the use of the horsecar in New Orleans, Chicago, Baltimore, St. Louis, Cincinnati, Pittsburgh, and Newark by 1860. Prior to the innovation of the horsecar, only the very wealthy could afford to live beyond the city and work in the city, for only they could afford the maintenance of carriages. Thus the horsecar began the spatial separation of the middle and lower classes, with the wealthier families living at the periphery of the city in suburbs (Ward, 1964, p. 484).

However, the expense and slowness of the horsecar virtually kept the city as a pedestrian city for most people until the 1880s. Up to that time many imaginative alternatives to the horsecar were investigated. One of the best was the steam engine, but it was cumbersome, noisy, and dirty, and above all tended to frighten horses, causing pandemonium and panic when emitting blasts of steam. An attempt at isolating the steam engine on elevated rails was undertaken with a reasonable degree of success in 1872 in New York City along Greenwich Street between the Battery and Cortland Street. One of the chief problems confronting the widespread use of this type of system seems to have been that the center of gravity of the engine and the carriages was rather high, resulting in unfortunate mishaps on curves and sharp turns. For example, at a later date, the elevated railway curve 73 feet above 110th Street in New York City was known as "suicide corner."

Cable cars The most successful replacement for the horsecar was the cable car, which was first operated in San Francisco in 1873. These cars were probably introduced first in San Francisco because of the steep grades in certain sections that precluded the possibility of citywide horsecar operations. Between 1877 and the mid 1890s, 48 cable railways were constructed in various cities in the United States, the most extensive system being in Chicago, which consisted of 82 miles of track. Two outstanding disadvantages of cable cars however led to their gradual decline. The first is their restricted speed of operation, for the car can move only as fast as the cable; and if the cable is moving fast, hooking and disengaging the car is difficult. The second disadvantage was the very high cost of construction, for the cables have to be laid underground. Thus the number of cable lines has declined, so that today only San Francisco operates cable cars, and this it does in order to protect and preserve one aspect of its image of uniqueness.

THE RAILROAD

We have previously mentioned that the steam engine had little impact on the internal movement of people within the North American city. Although the railroad had become the prime mover of goods and people between cities during the latter half of the nineteenth century, the steam engine proved much too cumbersome and dangerous to be applied to the daily ebb and flow of people and goods within urban areas.

Even as far as suburban commuting was concerned, it was also an expensive mode of transportation. Most railroad companies, which by 1880 received as much as 80 percent of their revenues from the transferral of goods, simply could not afford to allocate part of their rolling stock to the restricted daily transportation of people from suburban areas to the central city. There were, however, some companies that operated extensive commuter services that were highly profitable. For example, the Illinois Central Railroad began commuter services in the southern sector of Chicago in 1856, and by 1893 it handled nearly 14,000 commuters a day (a third of what it carries today). During the period of a fair in Chicago that year, the Illinois Central Railroad set a passenger record never since equaled: 500,000 passengers in one day.

Exurbs The greatest impact of the railroad on urban structure and form was experienced with the growth of exurbs, or settlements beyond and spatially distinct from the immediate environs of the urban area. Vance (1964, p. 43) notes that after 1864 in the San Francisco area there was a rapid growth of railroad towns, such as Burlingame, San Mateo, San Carlos, Belmont, and Atherton. All these exurbs had one characteristic in common: they were among other things the location of estates of the wealthy who gained their livelihood in the city. Those of the city wealthy, who chose to live in a rural environment, located in and around the exurbs because they were able to purchase relatively large estates that permitted the creation of ". . . an impression that the owner was of the country rather than of the city" (Vance, 1964, p. 43). These locations were made accessible by a method of transportation (the train) that was accepted as genteel.

Thus the railroad contributed to a further spatial stratification of society in that the wealthiest of all were now permitted (if they so chose) to live at considerable distances from the urban area yet maintain their vital social contacts and daily business interests in the central part of the city. The pattern of growth resulting from the influence of the railroads was quite restrictive, for it could only occur in nucleations along the radial lines of the railroad companies.

THE STREETCAR

Weber, writing in the last decade of the nineteenth century, noted with alarm the appalling congestion of cities in the western world (Weber, 1899). We have observed that this appalling congestion could be attributed in large part to the technology of urban transportation available at that time. For most people it was still impossible to live very far away from their place of work or from alternative employment opportunities; and as a consequence, most people lived in areas of very high population density around the central business district (CBD).

Furthermore, the public means of transportation were slow and space consuming (a horse and carriage takes up more space than an automobile). These factors, along with narrow streets, resulted in terrible overcrowding. Weber's solution to this congestion was to advocate decongestion. This decongestion was not really feasible until the advent of the electric streetcar or trolley (Smerk, 1967). 

THE ADVANTAGES OF THE ELECTRIC STREETCAR

The electric streetcar was first used successfully on the Richmond Union Passenger Railway in Virginia in 1888 and subsequently adapted by Whitney in 1889 in Boston. The immensely superior and efficient operation of the streetcar in Boston resulted in over 200 systems being built or ordered for North American cities in the following three years. By 1902, 97 percent of street railway mileage was electrically operated; whereas, in 1890, 70 percent of street railways had used animal power. In 1901 there were about 15,000 miles of electric railway in the United States (Hilton and Due, 1964, p. 7). The innovation of the streetcar did not come a moment too soon for alleviating congestion in the city, for at the turn of the century the United States population was increasing at a rate of 1.3 million per year as a result of heavy immigration, greater life expectancy, and a relatively high birth rate. Most of this population increase was being experienced by the cities. Thus Vance states that

> It is hard to say whether the trolley produced the metropolis or vice versa. In any event, we may date the transformation of most American cities from the stage of simple urbanism to complex metropolitanism in the first or second decade following the introduction of trolleys (Vance, 1964, p. 50).

The electric streetcar was greatly superior to the other forms of urban transportation available at that time. In the first place a streetcar system, though expensive, was economically feasible to construct within the city. Some horse-drawn cars were already running on rails along the main radials, and the electric streetcar could make use of these facilities. Furthermore, in the construction of new lines there was not the problem of excavating as there was with cable cars. The power source could be provided easily with overhead wires; and though they might look unsightly, few people would complain if it were possible to decrease congestion. Compared with steam engines, the power source was much more efficient and could be applied quietly in creating motion. On top of these attractions, the streetcar could be quite fast, though this advantage was somewhat negated by the necessity for frequent stopping. All these advantages were enhanced by the relatively lower costs of transportation that, for many cities, were developed as a flat rate which allowed transference between lines. Thus it is not surprising that the trolley became the first form of public transportation to be used on a large scale by employees going to and from their place of work.

The electric streetcar consequently made it possible for the population of urban areas to spread out and thereby to decrease residential densities. For the

population to spread out, however, land had to be provided and serviced, and homes had to be built. The innovation of the trolley therefore led to great increases in land sales, land values, and land speculation, particularly along the areas adjacent to the main transportation arteries.

THE EFFECT OF THE ELECTRIC STREETCAR AND SPECULATION

Warner (1962), in his seminal analysis of the effect of the electric streetcar on the suburban development of Roxbury, West Roxbury, and Dorchester—all in the southern sector and immediately adjacent to the central city of Boston—provides a quantitative estimate of the effect of this transportation innovation. Most of the land in these three independent towns, which became suburbs in the latter part of the nineteenth century, was beyond the zone of dense settlement in the "walking city" of Boston prior to 1850. In 1870 after the first fifteen years of the horsecar, which prompted a tentative beginning of suburbanization in these towns, the population of these three towns stood at 60,000. By 1900 the population of these three towns had boomed to 227,000. This increase in population was housed in 22,500 new houses, of which 53.3 percent were single-family houses, 26.6 percent were two-family houses, and the remainder were multi-family dwellings. Developments of this kind could only take place through the integration of the expansion of streetcar lines and land development.

Thus throughout much of North America, the expansion of "streetcar suburbs" involved close cooperation between the developer-speculator and the transit lines, which were often strategically placed and threaded through preplatted subdivisions. It was the developer who, therefore, determined the land use. If the developer thought an area of land was capable of supporting high value housing, then the land was platted accordingly with large lots. Furthermore, the developer built according to his estimate of the tastes and values of the prospective buyers.

THE SUBURBANIZATION OF THE MIDDLE CLASSES

The vast majority of the prospective buyers were not the very wealthy. They were, in fact, that mass of the total population commonly referred to as the middle class, which includes a wide variety of incomes and occupations. As the occupational structure of society in North America was becoming more complex with the progression of the Industrial Revolution, particularly placing a greater emphasis on organizational and managerial skills, the ranks of the middle classes were continually expanding. It was this broad group that was gaining in affluence, through (it was thought) the virtues of unfettered capitalistic enterprise, and which the streetcar "liberated" from the central city. As the land developer built for this middle class, it was not so much the expense of transport on the streetcar that prevented the lower classes from moving to the suburbs, but the cost of housing and living in the suburbs. Although there were undoubtedly certain groups who would not be permitted to buy in the suburbs, it was generally supposed that any person who could afford to pay middle-class surburban house prices could move into these areas. The fact that some groups could not afford to pay these prices because of a whole series of integrated discriminatory laws, mores, and traditions, was rarely recognized (Ward, 1968).

Thus the streetcar not only affected urban form by encouraging residential development in the vicinity of the electric streetcar lines radiating from the central city, it also brought into focus the beginning of a spatial socio-economic pattern considered to be symptomatic of the modern North American metropolis. The socio-economic patterns involve house structures, the spatial separation of families by economic class, new health standards, and a weak community structure.

House structures Prior to this period of the mass suburbanization of the middle classes, urban wealth had attained a visible appearance through housing structures either by estates or by streets of well-designed row houses that achieved their prosperous effect through a repetition of more or less identical imposing fronts. In these new suburbs the gridded streets and (subdivided) lots, all with some small frontage on the street, resulted in a suburban style of individualized houses ". . . arranged in such a way as to produce for the public the gratifying view of a prosperous street" (Warner, 1962, p. 151). These houses almost filled their entire lots and, though individually designed, were basically similar in style along each street. For example, they usually had structural features such as gables or shingles, which were adapted as imitations from the homes of the more wealthy.

These houses gave the appearance of being solid, prosperous, and family oriented. They therefore gave a physical expression of the satisfaction and confidence of the middle-class owner in the economic underpinnings of the North American way of life. Home ownership was, however, not as frequent as this appearance of prosperity implied. The unregulated mortgage market of that time resulted in high down payments and short-term nonamortizing mortgages that restricted home ownership. In the case of Boston, only one-quarter of its families owned their own homes in 1900. Furthermore, the pleasant semirural environment desired by the suburban dweller was rarely attained, for the vast majority of the subdividers and builders were not trained in architectural methods and construction techniques that would achieve and preserve this desired atmosphere.

Spatial economic differentiation Thus the streetcar, by further stimulating and accelerating the rate of suburbanization, also indirectly affected the spatial socio-economic differentiation of society. Because the suburbs, and suburban type housing, specifically catered in large part to the middle class, and as this housing was in turn differentiated by street and area into price and style groupings, the population of the suburbs was spatially stratified according to income.

Warner (1962, p. 157) notes that ". . . in an atmosphere of rapid change, the income-graded neighborhoods rendered two important services to their residents." In the first place, the evenness of wealth found within local areas meant a uniformity and conformity in social and economic values. The middle classes found this acceptable, because it was felt to be highly desirable that these values be passed on to their children. If all people in the same area held the same values, then it would be possible to pass these values on to successive generations. Consequently the local educational system, churches, clubs, and so forth came to reflect these values; and these institutions rarely publicly questioned them because the apparent affluence of the middle class proclaimed them to be right.

This latter aspect interacts with the second important service rendered by income-graded neighborhoods to their residents. The evenness of wealth gave the adults in the community a sense of shared experience, for each family would be affected by the same economic forces and similar uncertainties. Thus bank managers and doctors living on the more wealthy middle-class streets would hold the same views of social change and fervor for philanthropic missions. The less wealthy areas, on the other hand, would perhaps have a grouping of people with slightly different attitudes, particularly as they might be on the way up or trying to get ahead.

Warner indicates that this kind of socio-economic variation was spatially expressed in concentric form (Fig. 8.1) in the southern sector of Boston in 1900. By this date the edge of the old pedestrian city of Boston was between 2 and 2½ miles from Boston City Hall (which was considered to be the center of downtown Boston). The range of lower middle-class to middle-class housing extended a mile to 3½ miles farther from the City Hall, and its outer limit is roughly demarcated by the outer limit of linear, or radial street railway service. Beyond this band, the very wealthy were served by commuter railroads. With time, as the radial streetcar lines extended in length, and the cross-town services continued their interstitial infilling, the socio-economic bands continued to move outward from the central city.

Rising health standards This rapidly accelerating suburbanization of the middle classes had an important side effect on the provision of public services, such as parks, and utilities in the North American city. The frequent plagues and epidemics that were the scourge of nineteenth century urban areas had given rise to a growing demand for better methods of garbage and sewage disposal, lighting, heating, water, and facilities for improving urban life. The rapid growth of the suburbs, following the innovation of the electric streetcar, provided an environment where the technological advances made in the provision of services and utilities could be put into large-scale effect. The middle classes were generally well disposed toward the provision of services and utilities of this kind and often favored their installation by public or municipal authority.

New suburbs were therefore built and planned with these provisions in mind. Thus the land was subdivided in an orderly fashion, and often utilities were laid

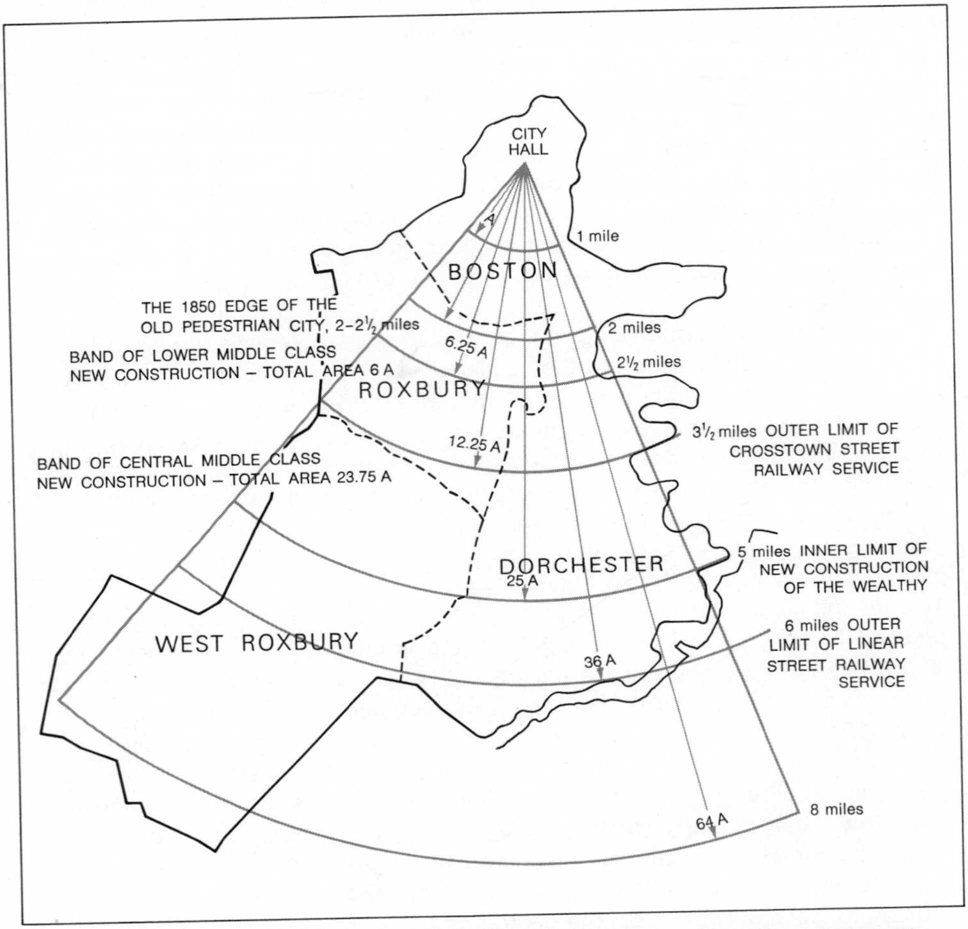

FIG. 8.1. APPROXIMATE CLASS BUILDING ZONES OF THE THREE TOWNS OF ROXBURY, WEST ROXBURY, AND DORCHESTER IN 1900. ON THE MAP, A EQUALS 357.4 ACRES. IT IS THE AREA OF A 64-DEGREE SEGMENT OF A CIRCLE WHOSE RADIUS IS ONE MILE. THE OTHER RADII ARE MARKED IN MILES FROM BOSTON'S CITY HALL AND THE AREAS GIVEN IN TERMS OF A. (*Source:* Warner, 1962, Fig. 9.)

before the home builders began their work. These rising municipal standards were also followed by the home builders who through middle-class demand found it expedient to follow, and sometimes to lead, regulations concerning plumbing, gas fitting, and fire safety. Perhaps more importantly, the demands of the middle-class suburbs had an important feedback on the old central "walking" city itself, in that the provision of utilities and better housing became a matter of general metropolitan concern.

Community structure and government The negative effects of the suburbanization of the middle classes counterbalance to a large degree these important positive benefits. These negative effects are most apparent with respect to metropolitan government. Although it might be thought that the collecting together of a group of people with similar aims, incomes, objectives, and tastes might produce a strong coherent community and political structure, the suburbanization of the middle classes achieved almost exactly the opposite. Warner (1962, p. 160) contends that the philosophical basis of the suburb at the turn of the century was founded on the concept of the freedom of the family as a unit to pursue its own economic and cultural objectives. Of course, these objectives had to be within the acceptable norms of middle-class society. For example, belief in God and family attendance at church were undoubtedly a middle-class social and cultural norm at the end of the nineteenth century; but there was no stipulation as to which religion was generally acceptable, though undoubtedly some religions were less acceptable than others. This, of course, is not meant to imply that the suburban middle classes were the only churchgoers, but it is meant to suggest that the social action as much as the philosophical and ethical basis was extremely important among this group.

The important point is that a view of life, centered on what was best for the individual family, resulted in a lack of perspective in considering problems of other parts of the metropolitan area. Participation in local community politics was generally limited, and those aspects of political life that did achieve importance were generally quite parochial in nature. Thus, although some of the standards of the middle classes concerning health and welfare were percolating down to the lower classes, this was usually by accident rather than by public policy. Furthermore, the separation of the middle classes from the central city led to the isolation of this group from the growing and burgeoning problems of the central city. It could therefore be considered that the streetcar suburb began the self-defeating fragmentation of metropolitan structure and interests that is so evident as one of the major shortcomings of metropolitan government today.

RAPID TRANSIT

Rapid transit is a cross between the streetcar and the railroad. Although earlier systems used steam engines, rapid transit involves the application of the electric motor to a system involving rail lines placed in structures that are isolated from the rest of the city. Thus rapid transit facilities are able to proceed at a faster pace than streetcars and can consist of more than one carriage, as with a train. Consequently rapid transit tends to be quicker and safer, and its carrying capacity can be expanded or restricted simply by the addition or removal of carriage modules. Although the system is quite rigid once constructed, with good planning it can be designed as an integrated part of the overall urban transportation system, for the rail lines may be elevated, on the surface, or subsurface. The great density of activity at the center of the city immediately points to the advantage of the subsurface aspect of rapid transit.

As both the streetcar and rapid transit involved the use of the electric motor, it is not surprising that both methods of transportation were applied simultaneously to urban transportation. However, as rapid transit involved much greater fixed costs in its construction, its application was slower and more deliberate than that of the streetcar. Consequently rapid transit on elevated lines was first introduced into Chicago by the South Side Elevated Railroad using steam engines in 1892, which were converted to electric motor cars in 1897 and 1898. Boston's first rapid transit facility started operation in 1891, and Philadelphia's in 1905. In New York City the first subway was put into operation in 1904. Because of the high capital construction costs fewer lines were built with little attempt at catering for cross-town movements. However, the development of rapid transit had a great impact on the form and structure of the city. This impact can be seen particularly in its emphasis on the radial or sectoral growth of the city, and by the rise of the area around local transit stations as centers of economic activity.

SECTORAL GROWTH

Rapid transit is only efficient when it is moving large numbers of people daily. Consequently rapid transit systems were constructed to connect the central business district (CBD) as the chief place of employment and commercial activity, with the principal areas of urban population. The direction of growth in most cases had already been defined by the horsecar, the cable car, and the streetcar. For example, in Chicago rapid transit routes on elevated lines (the El) followed a predetermined pattern established by the horsecar (Fig. 8.2) and cable cars (Fig. 8.3). The south- and west-side lines (Fig. 8.4) were constructed prior to the north-side lines, which followed the direction of growth marked by the cable and horsecar systems.

Rapid transit in the north sector of Chicago As rapid transit was expensive to establish, few feeder lines were constructed; and the lines emphasized the radial nature of the preceding transportation systems. Thus, in the case of Chicago, a clear south, west, and north pattern of growth emerged as the rapid transit lines pressed their stems to the periphery and began to precede urban development. Davis (1965) indicates three zones of development associated with the growth of the El in northern Chicago. In the first zone, within three miles of the CBD, the El had little effect as the land was already settled when the El began its operation in 1900. Between three and four miles from the CBD is a transition zone that incurred a limited degree of building activity following the opening of the El. Beyond this zone the El provided a great impetus to urban development immediately following the opening of El services in 1900.

This urban development coincided with an increase in construction, an increase in population, and an increase in land values along the rapid transit line. But these changes were greater farther away from the CBD. For example ". . . land value changes were greater with El impact the farther one moved from the CBD, as zone 3 increased its land values by 66.40 percent more than zone 2 from 1892 to 1905" (Davis, 1965, p. 88). However, even though these changes increased with distance from the CBD, the intensity of construction, the density of population,

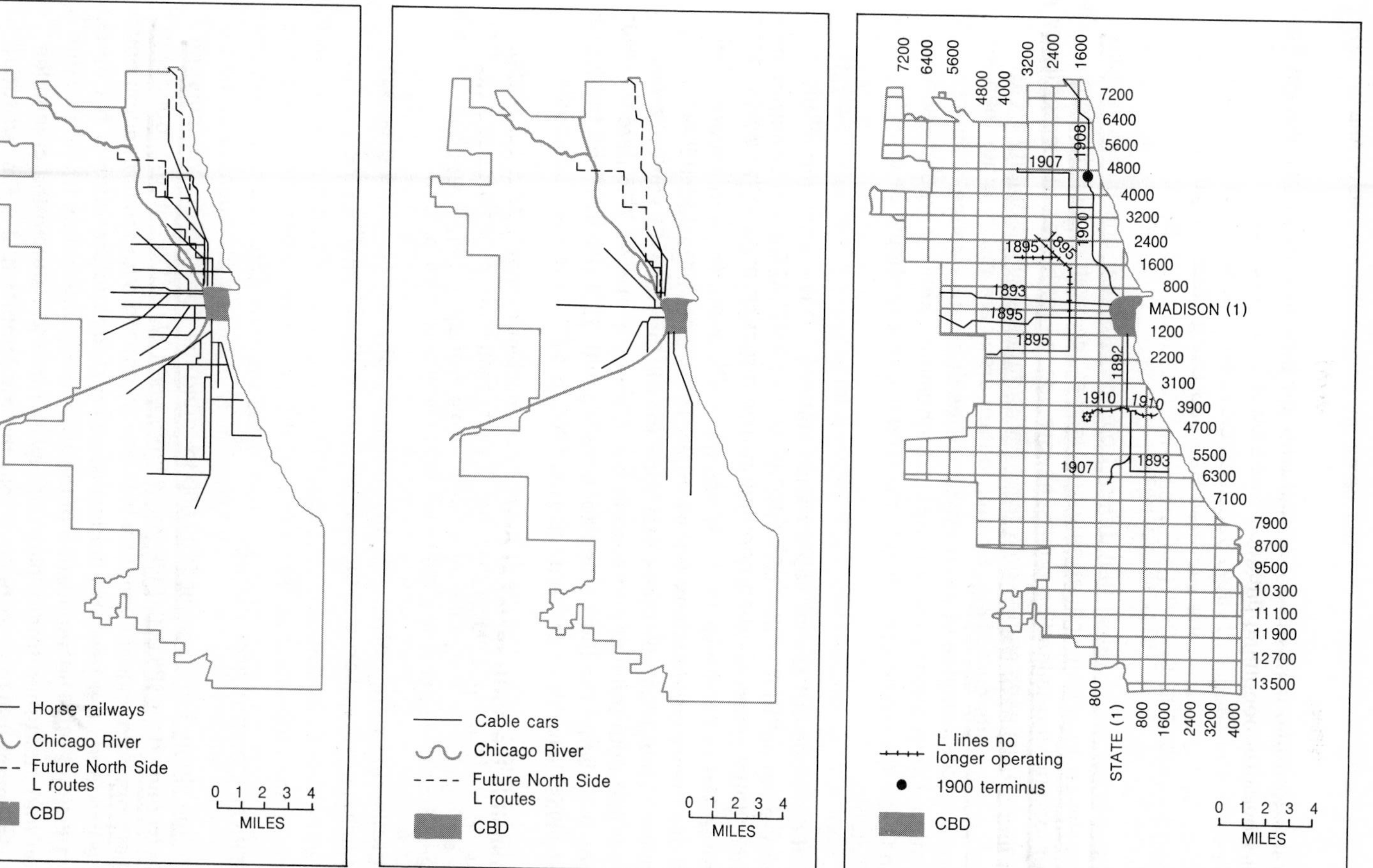

FIG. 8.2. PRINCIPAL HORSE RAILWAYS IN THE CITY OF CHICAGO, 1890. (*Source:* Davis, J. L., 1965, Fig. 16.) **FIG. 8.3.** PRINCIPAL CABLE-CAR ROUTES IN THE CITY OF CHICAGO, 1893. (*Source:* Davis, J. L., 1965, Fig. 19.) **FIG. 8.4.** THE ELEVATED SYSTEM IN THE CITY OF CHICAGO SHOWING DATES OF INITIAL OPERATION AND STREET PATTERN. (*Source:* Davis, J. L., 1965, Fig. 2.)

and the value of urban land still decreased with distance from the CBD, though the curve was obviously becoming flatter.

RAPID TRANSIT AND THE GROWTH OF OUTLYING CENTERS OF ECONOMIC ACTIVITY

A further aspect of rapid transit that differs from the streetcar and therefore adds a new dimension to urban spatial structure is that the system has discrete passenger loading and unloading points that are spaced farther apart than ordinary streetcar stops. Thus each station on a rapid transit facility has a tributary area from which it draws its customers. Some tributary areas are much larger than others, due to a coalescence of rapid transit routes or a convergence of street transportation. Consequently there is apt to be business activity around each rapid transit station, which according to the land use theory should be orderly and predictable.

Patterns of development around rapid transit stations Davis also empirically examined the impact of El stations on the pattern of new residential construction, land values, and population density in the northern sector of Chicago. Although the evidence showed some variation, it was generally found to be in accordance with land use theory expectations. For example, in the case of residential construction "Total block-by-block statistics for all forty-one El station areas . . . reveal that both the first and second block zones averaged 77.5 percent new settlement . . . while the third block zone trailed with 72.4 percent, and the fourth block zone was last with 71 percent" (Davis, 1965, p. 177). In terms of land values

> The average front-foot value of all the El station areas first block zones in 1911 was $68.70. This figure was 11.84 percent higher than that of the second block zone's average of $61.40, 41.94 percent higher than that of the third block zone's average of $48.40, and 95.67 percent higher than that of the fourth zone's $35.11 per front foot (Davis, 1965, p. 122).

Similar gradations were noted with population density patterns, the greatest changes being observed around those El stations farthest from the CBD.

THE INTERNAL COMBUSTION ENGINE

In 1903 when Henry Ford sought $100,000 to found the Ford Motor Company, he was able to raise only $28,000. Five years later when W. C. Durant, the founder of General Motors, told an investment banker that eventually a half million automobiles would be produced per year, the banker showed Durant to the door of his office (Moore, 1954, p. 279). The application of the streetcar to intraurban traffic and its extension into interurban traffic, plus the use of rapid transit and the commuter railroad, led many persons to believe that the automobile had a limited future. However, the forces that these new innovations had set in motion in reshaping and restructuring the city proved to be ideally suited to the internal combustion engine as applied to the automobile. All the facets of urban life that came to the fore with the innovation of the streetcar—the suburbanization of the middle class, the desire for travel and recreation beyond the city, the emphasis on individual and family group activities, the beginning of the outward migration of employment opportunities and cross-town commuting—could be developed a great deal further with the use of the automobile.

The rate of increase in automobile use in North America during the first few decades of the twentieth century has been quite dramatic. Table 8.1 presents data concerning the number of persons per registered automobile and taxi in the United States from 1900 to 1969. The measure is referred to as an *automobile ownership ratio*, and in 1900 there appears to have been approximately one automobile for every 10,000 people. By 1910 the rate of automobile ownership had increased fiftyfold; and from about 1922 onward there has been more than one automobile for every ten persons in the United States. If the rate of automobile ownership continues to increase at the present rate, by 1975 there will be at least 115 million cars in the United States.

This rate of increase in automobile ownership is very strongly related to the ever-increasing wealth in the United States. On a family basis, the wealthier the family, the greater the number of automobiles in that family. For example, in 1963 only 53 percent of the families with less than $3,000 annual income owned an automobile; but 95 percent of the families with incomes of between $7,500 and $10,000 owned one automobile, and 30 percent of them owned two cars or more (Owen, 1966, p. 36). As the proportion of families in the middle-income groups is expected to continue to rise, a much greater proliferation can be expected in the future in the use of the automobile and in increased mobility.

Previous discussion has indicated that the distribution of wealth within the city is not even. Wealthier families tend to live at the periphery of the city, and the less wealthy tend to live toward the center. Thus, the spatial rate of automobile ownership also varies, with a much higher rate of automobile ownership at the periphery. As it was the suburbanized middle class that first began the widespread

TABLE 8.1. AUTOMOBILE OWNERSHIP IN THE UNITED STATES FOR SELECTED YEARS BETWEEN 1900 AND 1967

Year	Auto Registrations (in '000)	Population (in '000)	Auto Ownership Ratio
1900	8	76,094	9,511.3
1910	470	92,407	196.6
1920	8,131	106,466	13.1
1930	23,035	123,077	5.3
1940	27,466	132,594	4.8
1950	40,339	152,271	3.8
1960	61,682	180,684	2.9
1969	86,560	203,213	2.3

Source: U.S. Bureau of the Census, *Statistical Abstracts of the United States: 1969*, Washington, D.C., 1970, pp. 5 and 544.

use of the automobile for both work and social travel, it was at the periphery of the city that the impact of the automobile on urban structure and form began to be felt. This impact was accentuated by the fact that in areas of low population density mass transit facilities could not hope to compete with the automobile. Thus it was at the fringe of the city that the automobile first began to shape the city (Vance, 1964, p. 61).

THE AUTOMOBILE SHAPES THE CITY

The commuter railroad encouraged the growth of the upperclass exurbs, the streetcar stimulated the expansion of the middle class into suburbs, and rapid transit further accentuated the radial growth of the city. The innovation of the automobile made possible an even greater physical expansion of the city, but most importantly it permitted the spread of population into areas between the major radial lines leading into the city. The ensuing continuing decrease in density of the suburban population has resulted in communities that are even more spread out than the streetcar suburbs and even more difficult to provide with a wide range of community services—except those facilities that had become entrenched as the norms of middle-class life. These include piped drinking water, sewage facilities (though many surburban homes have septic tanks), churches, and community schools. In terms of social and economic behavior, there has been an even greater emphasis on the individual family and the use by that family of modern technology in the home (particularly in the kitchen).

This modern suburban development is dependent almost entirely on the automobile for transportation, for public transport is infrequent, if available at all, in the suburbs. In many cases the male home-owner finds it essential to use an automobile to get to work; and if he uses rapid transit or the commuter railroad he either leaves his car at the railroad station, uses a car pool, or is driven there by his wife ("kiss'n'ride"). Thus the automobile, in helping to create the modern interstitial suburb, has also helped to create a further demand for automobiles; for if one car is used in the daily journey to work, the wife must also have an automobile in order to shop, take the children to school, visit the doctor and the dentist, and pursue sundry social or philanthropic activities. It is partially in reaction to this suburban syndrome that the "women's liberation movement" has evolved.

The effect of the automobile on urban structure is not, however, felt only at the urban fringe. In order to speed traffic through the city and into the CBD, most North American cities are criss-crossed with limited access highways and expressways. These make it possible for the suburban dweller to visit the CBD without seeing much of the old central city. Thus the conditions of the central city are hidden behind the concrete canyons of the expressway until dramatic events bring these conditions into the public eye. The insularity of the middle classes, first encouraged by the streetcar and rapid transit, has therefore been greatly accentuated by the automobile.

The automobile has created a new urban form. The outmigration of people, commercial activity, and much of modern industry has changed the North American city from a phenomenon closely organized around a single central core to being a metropolis in which the central core plays a less dominant part. Vance suggests that the North American city of the middle twentieth century has become noncentric, and that this is emphasized by the fact that the 1960 U.S. Census shows that the ". . . greatest single movement of workers was from one outlying area to another, rather than from the periphery to the core" (Vance, 1964, p. 68).

THE EFFECT OF THE INTERNAL COMBUSTION ENGINE ON OTHER MODES OF URBAN TRANSPORTATION

The internal combustion engine has not only had an impact on the shape of the city, it has also affected the other forms of urban transportation that had been developed immediately prior to it. In some cases the internal combustion engine has provided a cheaper and much more flexible replacement. Probably the best example of this is the diesel engine bus, which is a much more efficient machine than the streetcar. The streetcar, being confined to its rails and unable to move in and out of the regular flow of traffic in order to discharge and take on passengers, was rapidly outmoded with the innovation of the bus. However, the necessary fixed-cost capital outlays that had been incurred in the establishment of streetcar systems meant that they remained functioning long after they had, in effect, become obsolete. Thus it was not until 1945 that bus passenger traffic in the United States exceeded that of the streetcar (Table 8.2). Since 1945 there has been a great decline in streetcar traffic, so that by 1963 motor-bus traffic was twenty times greater than that of the streetcar. A minor innovation during this latter period was the trolley coach, which is, in effect, a cross between the motor bus and the streetcar, being dependent on electric wires but not confined to rails.

People are not the only commodities requiring mobility within the urban area. The inputs into, and the outputs from, industries require shipment; also the

TABLE 8.2. PASSENGER TRAFFIC BY STREETCAR, TROLLEY COACH, AND MOTOR BUS IN THE UNITED STATES, FOR SELECTED YEARS BETWEEN 1905 AND 1963 (IN BILLIONS OF TOTAL PASSENGERS)

Year	Streetcar	Trolley Coach	Motor Bus
1905	5.0		
1920	13.7		
1925	12.9		1.5
1930	10.5		2.5
1935	7.3	0.1	2.6
1940	5.9	0.5	4.2
1945	9.4	1.2	9.9
1950	3.9	1.7	9.4
1955	1.2	1.2	7.3
1960	0.5	0.7	6.4
1963	0.3	0.4	5.8

Source: Owen (1966), Table 16.

multitude of goods and services of different kinds have to be transported to all parts of the urban area. Some commodities, such as water, gas, and electricity, can be provided with their own specific transport networks; but many others are not suitable to pipe or wire dispersion. The primary conveyor of material into and from most large cities is the railroad, though the application of the diesel engine to motor vehicles has given rise to a rapidly growing interurban trucking industry in recent decades. The development of the interstate highway system in the United States, and limited access highways in Canada, has further encouraged the growth of this intercity truck traffic.

The truck is, however, preeminent for the movement of goods within the city. Prior to the development of the internal combustion engine, within-city commodity movements were undertaken primarily with horse-drawn vehicles. Very little commodity movement was undertaken by streetcars, cable cars or rapid transit, as all these systems are inflexible for local deliveries. Thus, though horses were quickly superseded for the movement of people, they remained in service much longer for the movement of goods. The development of the internal combustion engine was therefore vital for the efficient transport of goods within the rapidly expanding North American city, and has been an extremely important factor in permitting the decentralization of industry (Moses and Williamson, 1967).

CHANGING TRANSPORTATION TECHNOLOGY AND THE NORTH AMERICAN CITY

From the preceding discussion it is possible to recognize three major periods of technological innovation in urban transportation in North America. These periods conform very closely to those suggested by Borchert as applicable to interurban transportation in North America (Borchert, 1967).

(1) The first period, prior to 1870, involved movement based primarily on the horse, or individual locomotion by foot. As a consequence the urban area was compact and can be described as a "pedestrian" city.

(2) From 1870 to 1920, and particularly around those two decades at the turn of the century, the North American city witnessed dramatic technological innovations. These, in terms of urban transportation, involved the streetcar, cable car, and electric rapid transit. This was a period of great suburban expansion of North America with the strong development of urban radials. Although many forms of urban transportation existed at this time, this period can be characterized as that of the "streetcar," as it was this innovation that led to some of the most dramatic changes in urban structure and form.

(3) The third or present period, starting in 1920, brought the automobile to the fore as being an important means of urban transportation. This last period is therefore designated as the "automobile era."

Urban growth in North America has not been uniform through time. Some cities have grown predominantly in the nineteenth century and others in the twentieth century. It can be suggested that in general the cities of the South and

Southwest are newer and products of the twentieth century, while those of the Northeast and Southeast are more the products of the nineteenth century. In Table 8.3 twelve of the largest Standard Metropolitan Statistical Areas (SMSA's) in the United States are listed and the proportions of the population of each urban area in 1960 that was achieved during each of the three intraurban transportation eras. Thus Boston, by 1870, had achieved a population that was 27 percent of its 1960 population size. Between 1870 and 1920 it achieved a further 48 percent of its 1960 population size, and between 1920 and 1960 the additional 25 percent was added. Since people require space and housing structures in which to live, it might therefore be assumed that quite a large proportion of present-day Boston was built to house the pre-1870 population, and that an even larger area was consumed to house the population growth that occurred in the streetcar era. Further down the table it can be observed that 85 percent of Los Angeles' growth occurred during the automobile era, only 15 percent in the streetcar era, and none at all prior to 1870. The table tends to substantiate the proposition that the larger cities of the Southwest and West are the products of the automobile era, while those of the Northeast and Southeast are much more the products of the nineteenth century.

Borchert (1967) suggests that this variation in epochal growth expressed in Table 8.3 has very important implications for an understanding of urban obsolescence and renewal. Cities that grew primarily in those eras before the automobile will have a transportation system and a set of physical structures that are antiquated and invariably obsolete with respect to the automobile. Those cities that have grown up entirely within the automobile era will be noncentric and have a different structure and appearance from those that did not. "The nation's new construction has been concentrated, in any given epoch, not only in new neighborhoods and new suburbs but also in what have been, for all practical purposes, new cities. The residue of obsolescent physical plant has also become concentrated, not only in certain districts of most cities but in virtually the entire

TABLE 8.3. PERCENTAGES OF POPULATIONS OF SELECTED 1960 SMSA'S ATTAINED IN MAJOR HISTORICAL EPOCHS

SMSA	Pre-1870	1870–1920	1920–1960
Boston	27%	48%	25%
New Orleans	25	23	52
Philadelphia	24	38	38
Pittsburgh	17	56	27
New York	14	44	42
Washington, D.C.	10	19	71
Chicago	8	47	45
San Francisco–Oakland	7	26	66
Detroit	6	29	65
Dallas–Ft. Worth	3	30	67
Seattle-Tacoma	0	42	58
Los Angeles	0	15	85

Source: Borchert (1967), Table 3.

area of some" (Borchert, 1967, pp. 328–329). The impact of those new technological innovations upon all aspects of urban structure and form has therefore varied greatly throughout North America. Although a general pattern of change can be observed in terms of technological innovations, each of which has specific impacts on the structure of the city, no one urban area will have exactly the same structure and form as another.

“THE LAND USE SYSTEM”

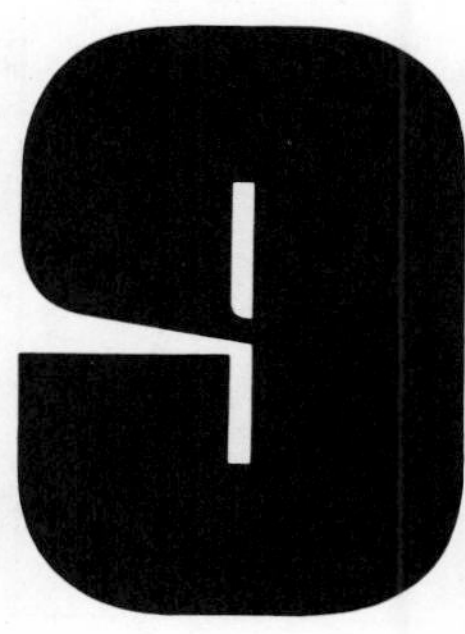

The accelerating growth and areal spread of the North American city through time, which was made possible by technological innovations in transport and communications, has involved the visible physical location, relocation, and expansion of land uses that comprise the fabric of these urban areas. This chapter is concerned with a statement of the major uses of urban land and with a discussion of various theories and descriptive models that can be used to understand the spatial variation in the intensity of urban land use. Central to the discussion is the fact that urban land use is in a continual state of flux, though some parts of urban areas tend to grow and change at a greater rate than others.

MAJOR GROUPS OF URBAN LAND USES

The land use of urban areas can be divided into six major categories. These are residential, industrial, commercial, roads and highways, public and semipublic land, and vacant land. The major studies inventorying the proportion of urban land in each of these uses have been undertaken by Bartholomew (1955) and Niedercorn and Hearle (1964). In this section the source of data that will be used primarily is that presented by Niedercorn and Hearle, which was obtained from a questionnaire sent out under the auspices of the RAND Corporation to 63 large American cities, of which 52 returned replies.

Land use may be presented in either gross or net terms. Gross land use includes in each land use category the area of streets abutting the land in question. Net land use treats streets as a separate land use category. Niedercorn and Hearle found that most of the returned questionnaires gave estimates in net terms, and so Tables 9.1 and 9.2 provide a separate category for roads and highways. Four urban areas (Denver, Houston, Milwaukee, and Philadelphia) responded with gross estimates and consequently were dropped from the study. The 48 remaining cities are listed in Table 9.3.

Residential uses consume more land in American cities than any other type. According to Niedercorn and Hearle, 29.6 percent of all urban land and 39 percent of all developed land is devoted to residential use. This latter figure is very close to that provided by Bartholomew (1955) for central cities in the United States, where, for a sample of cities representing a much wider population range, he

TABLE 9.1. MEAN PROPORTION OF LAND DEVOTED TO VARIOUS USES IN 48 LARGE AMERICAN CITIES

Type of Use	Proportion of Total Land	% of Developed Land
Total developed	77.0	100.0
Residential	29.6	39.0
Industrial	8.6	10.9
Commercial	3.7	4.8
Road and highway	19.9	25.7
Other public	15.2	19.6
Total undeveloped	23.0	—
Vacant	20.7	—
Underwater	2.3	—

Source: Niedercorn and Hearle (1964), pp. 105–110.

TABLE 9.2. CHANGES IN MEAN PROPORTION OF LAND USE

Type of Use	Mean Percent of Land Devoted to Various Uses at Different Times in 22 Cities				Mean Percent of Land Devoted to Various Uses at Different Times in 12 Cities			
	% of Total		% of Devpd.		% of Total		% of Devpd.	
	Early Data	Late Data	Early Data	Late Data	Early Data	Late Data	Early Data	Late Data
Total developed	75.5	78.4	100.0	100.0	80.2	85.7	100.0	100.0
Residential	29.0	31.0	38.5	39.8	30.0	32.5	37.4	37.9
Industrial	8.5	8.5	11.0	10.4	10.0	10.6	12.4	12.4
Commercial	4.1	4.0	5.3	5.0	4.5	4.4	5.5	5.0
Road and highway	20.7	19.8	27.9	25.4	20.3	21.0	25.4	24.5
Other public	13.2	15.1	17.3	19.4	15.4	17.2	19.3	20.2
Total undeveloped	24.5	21.6	—	—	19.8	14.3	—	—
Vacant	23.3	20.4	—	—	18.4	12.9	—	—
Underwater	1.2	1.2	—	—	1.4	1.4	—	—

Source: Niedercorn and Hearle (1964), pp. 105–110.

estimates that 39.6 percent of the developed land is devoted to residential activity. Residential land, in turn, can be divided into a number of subclasses. By far the dominant use of residential land is for single-family dwellings. Bartholomew estimates that 31.8 percent of the total developed area is in this use. Two-family dwellings, represented by the duplex, consume about 4.8 percent of the developed land and multifamily apartments and tenements consume about 7.6 percent of urban land.

The second largest single category of land use is roads and highways. This class of use consumes nearly 20 percent of the total land found in the forty-eight urban areas responding to the RAND survey questionnaire. In terms of the developed land in urban areas, roads and highways comprise over a quarter of the total land use. This figure is higher for the parts of the city closest to the center of the city than it is for the periphery where streets are spaced farther apart.

TABLE 9.3. THE 48 CITIES

Albany	Jersey City	*Pittsburgh
Baltimore	Kansas City (Mo.)	Portland (Oreg.)
Birmingham	**Long Beach	**Portsmouth (Va.)
*Boston	**Los Angeles	*Providence
*Buffalo	Louisville	Rochester
**Chicago	Memphis	*St. Louis
*Cincinnati	*Miami	St. Paul
*Cleveland	Milwaukee	Sacramento
Columbus (Ohio)	*Minneapolis	**San Antonio
**Dallas	New Orleans	San Diego
**Dayton	*New York	**San Francisco
Denver	*Newark	San Jose
*Detroit	Oakland	**Seattle
Ft. Worth	**Oklahoma City	Syracuse
Hartford (Conn.)	Philadelphia	Washington, D.C.
Houston	Phoenix	Youngstown

* Single asterisk indicates 12 sample cities.
** Double asterisk indicates 22 sample cities (including those with single asterisk).

All other uses comprise a remarkably small proportion of the total land in urban areas. Industrial uses, involving heavy and light industry as well as railroad properties and airports, comprise 8.6 percent of the land available in urban areas. Commercial uses—involving wholesale, retail, and service activities—consume only 3.7 percent of urban land. General public uses—such as for schools, public buildings, parks, playgrounds, cemeteries, and so on—comprise a little over 15 percent of urban land. In total it seems that about 20.7 percent of urban land at present is vacant, and 2.3 percent is under water.

LAND USE CHANGES

Thus far the discussion has involved a description of the average land uses in relatively large urban areas in the early 1960s. An interesting aspect of land-use studies is to see the way in which land uses have changed through time. Table 9.2 is divided into a 22-city category and a 12-city category, showing changes in land use between two time periods. The 22-city table contains information from those cities that supplied data for two or more years. The average interval between these time periods is about 10.2 years. As a consequence, the data has been divided into an early group and a late group. From this table a number of points can be observed. First, residential and other public land uses have increased relative both to total area and to total developed land. Second, road and highway uses on the whole have decreased. Third, industrial and commercial uses have remained about the same, although declining slightly as proportions of developed land. These figures may well have been influenced by an increase in area of the cities through annexation of surrounding territory.

As a consequence, the 12-city table contains those cities that had not annexed any land between the early and the late period being discussed. The average interval in this subsample is about 9.8 years. The major point emerging from an analysis of this table is that the ratio of land in urban use to the total increased for all categories except commercial, which decreased slightly. Secondly, the largest increase was in residential land, and the next largest increase was in public land. Thirdly, the proportion of total area remaining vacant has decreased substantially. In other words, the 22-city table is in fact influenced a great deal by annexation. As a consequence, it would appear that unless the city is annexing land, vacant land in central cities is fast disappearing. For those cities that cannot sprawl, a substantial growth of city population and employment will therefore not be possible unless land use densities are increased. Urban growth can only be sustained either by an increase in density or by the consumption of more space at the periphery of the urban area.

THE LOCATION OF LAND USES WITHIN URBAN AREAS: A CASE STUDY OF CHICAGO

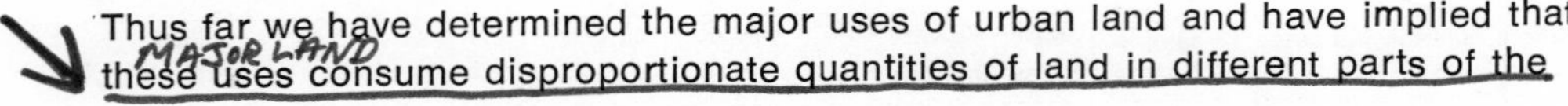

Thus far we have determined the major uses of urban land and have implied that these uses consume disproportionate quantities of land in different parts of the city. In terms of developed urban land itself, the indication has been that much more land is developed within the central city than at the periphery. This situation is clearly evident for Chicago in 1955 where 90 percent or more of the land located within 8½ miles of the CBD was developed, whereas beyond 16 miles less than 50 percent was developed for urban uses (Fig. 9.1). Thus it is evident that a very small proportion of the old, highly built-up part of the city is vacant (Browning, 1964).

The amount of developed land consumed for residential purposes at the center of the city is, however, limited. Residential land in Chicago consumes 41.2 percent of the total developed land, but within two miles of the CBD less than 20 percent of the land is devoted to this use (Fig. 9.2). In this innermost zone the largest single use is the space occupied by streets, commercial activities, and transportation facilities. Streets and transportation facilities are major users of land in all zones, consuming respectively 31 percent and 11.7 percent of all developed land in Chicago. Commercial activities, on the other hand, use only 4.8 percent of all developed land within the city but consume nearly one-quarter of all developed land at the center of the city. Manufacturing activities use over one-tenth of the land between 4 and 12 miles from the center of the city, and residential areas consume over one-third of the land in this area.

ELEMENTARY LAND USE THEORY

The ensuing chapters are concerned with a discussion of the various factors that affect the location of these various land uses. At the outset, however, it is

FIG. 9.1. PERCENTAGE OF THE TOTAL LAND IN USE BY DISTANCE FROM THE CBD, CHICAGO URBAN REGION. (*Source:* Browning, 1964, Fig. 1.)

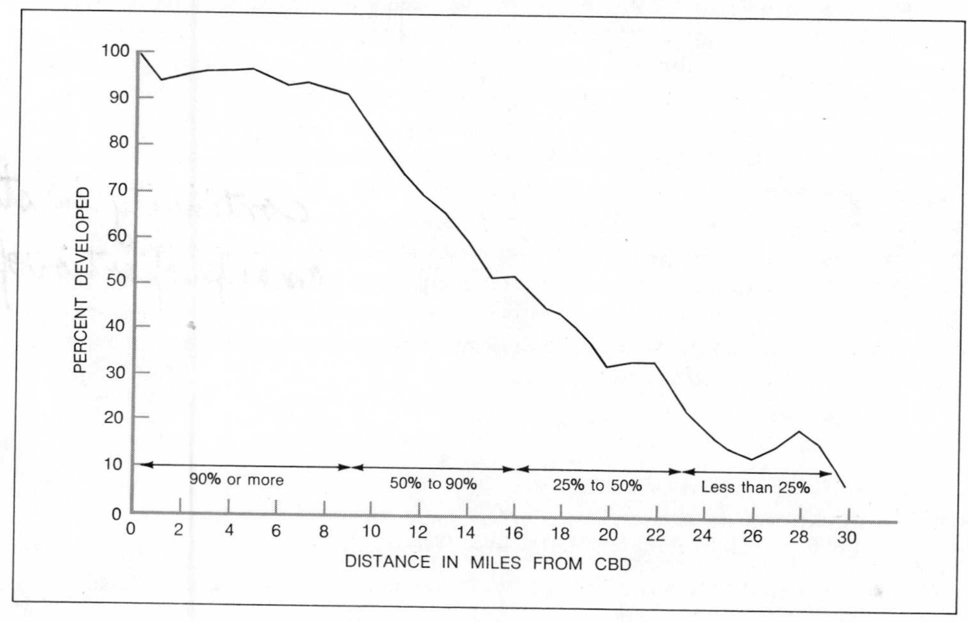

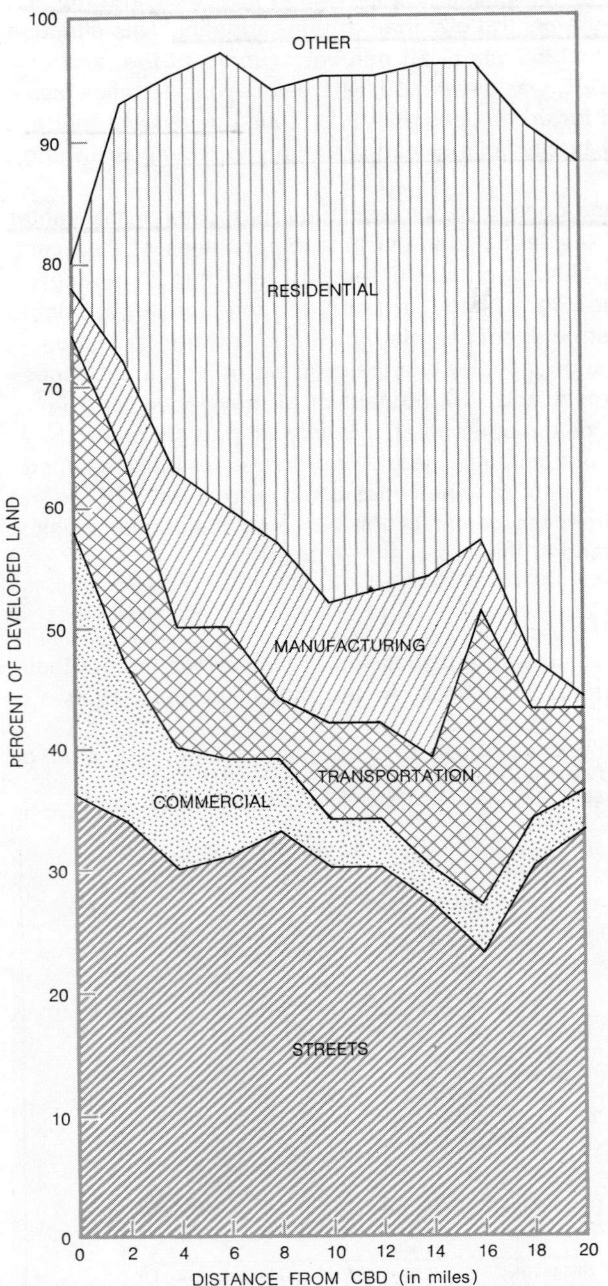

FIG. 9.2. VARIATIONS IN THE PROPORTION OF LAND IN SELECTED USES WITH DISTANCE FROM THE CBD. (*Source:* Based on Browning, 1964, pp. 34–35.)

continuity in streets as a proportion of lan

important to develop a general theoretical base that casts some light on the distribution of the intensity of land use in urban areas. The major starting place for land use theory is the work of Johann Heinrich von Thünen (1783–1850). Thünen's writings represent the first serious effort to systematize patterns in economic space (Hall, 1966; Chisholm, 1962); and though his land use theory was developed with respect to an agricultural environment, it has had great impact on the analysis of urban location problems.

Thünen envisaged the situation of a country with no connections with the outside world. A metropolis is located within an unbounded plain over which uniform soil and climatic characteristics prevail. Furthermore, transport possibilities are equal in any direction over this plain, a characteristic sometimes referred to as an *isotropic surface*. The costs of transportation, however, increase with distance. The metropolis provides manufactured goods for the rural community, and the rural community provides the agricultural products for the workers in the metropolis. Prices for manufactured goods and agricultural products are stable and are set at the marketplace, which is the metropolis.

Economic rent Assume that the price at the marketplace for one acre of wheat is $4. As all the land over the whole plain is equally fertile, one acre of wheat provides the same quantity at any location. Assume that there are three locations, A, B, and C (Fig. 9.3). A is closest to the marketplace, B is the next closest to the marketplace, and C is farthest from the marketplace. If the transportation cost for one acre of production of wheat from A to the marketplace is 40 cents, A will receive $3.60 for one acre of production. B is farther away from the marketplace than A and his transportation cost can be assumed to be about $1 for one acre of production. The price that he actually receives therefore will be $3 for one acre of wheat. C, the farthest away of all, has a transport cost

FIG. 9.3. VON THÜNEN'S CONCEPT OF ECONOMIC RENT. THE ECONOMIC RENT OF A WITH RESPECT TO C IS $1.10, AND OF A WITH RESPECT TO B IS $0.60.

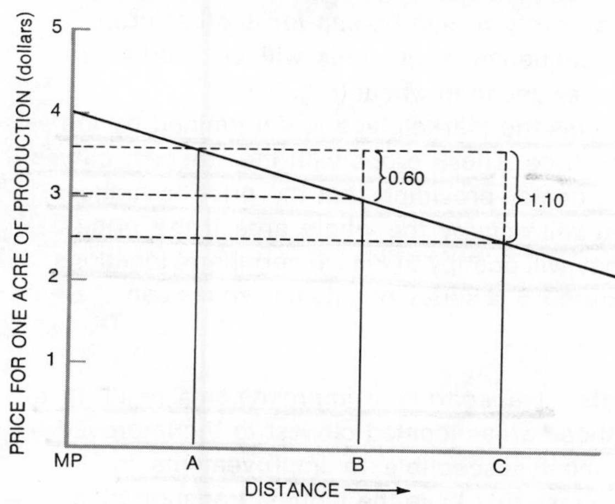

of $1.50 for one acre of production. The price that he receives therefore is, in effect, $2.50 for one acre of production.

If all the farmers have equal standards of living and put in the same effort and have the same costs of production, they will all wish to locate at A or closer than A to the marketplace. C, for example, will perceive that he can make $1.10 more for exactly the same effort at A than at C. This difference, in effect, represents the economic rent of A with respect to C. In general terms, the *economic rent* can be defined as the difference in returns received from the use of a unit of land compared with that received at the margin of production. In this particular case, the difference is due solely to variations in distance.

Zonation of land use and intensity implications In Figure 9.3 economic rent decreases with distance from the marketplace. The slope of the rent line is affected by the cost of transportation, which is in turn determined by the relative bulk, weight, and perishability of the commodity being transported, as well as by the distance that the commodity has to be transported. Assume now the existence of a second commodity, that of vegetables. Vegetables can be produced very intensively, but they are very bulky and perishable. As a consequence, the transportation cost for vegetables is very high. The price for the sale of one acre of production of vegetables is also high. Let us assume that this price is $6 for one acre of vegetable production. Due to the high transportation costs for transporting vegetables to the marketplace, the economic rent curve will be steep as is indicated in Figure 9.4.

Assume the existence of another product, potatoes, for which the price at the marketplace is $5 for one acre of production. The economic rent curve for this commodity is less steep than for vegetables, but steeper than that for wheat. This is because potatoes are not so highly perishable as vegetables, but they are more bulky than wheat. The farmer will always produce that crop which yields the highest price per acre. He will do this either out of choice or because he is forced to do it, because other farmers realize that they can produce that crop at a location and receive a greater return than he can for another crop at that particular location. As a consequence, vegetables will be produced closest to the marketplace, then potatoes and then wheat (Fig. 9.5).

Thus the position of the crop vis-à-vis the marketplace is determined by the slope of the rent line and the market price. Those crops with the steepest curves will always be located closest to the center providing that the price is highest. The crops with a shallow rent curve will occupy the whole area if the price at the market is highest; otherwise they will occupy the more peripheral locations. By rotating the zones indicated in Figure 9.5, a series of land use zones can be generated (Fig. 9.6).

Effect of transportation improvements Transportation improvements result in a decrease in transportation cost for those areas located closest to the improved facility. The commodities that are most susceptible to improvements in transportation media are, of course, those that have the highest transportation cost. In Figure 9.7 the effect of water transportation on the surface configuration

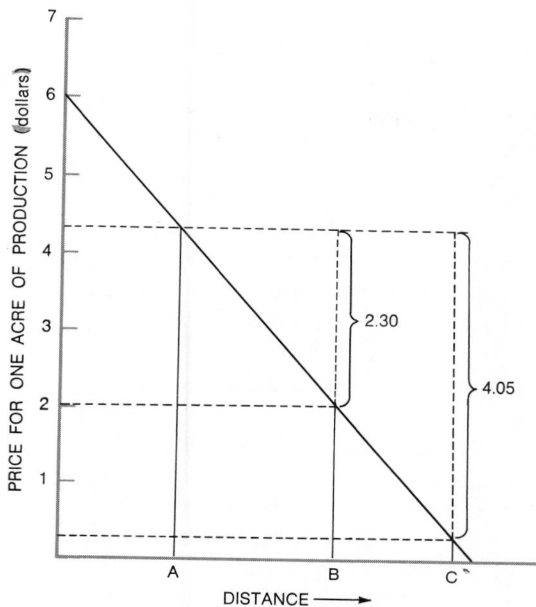

FIG. 9.4. ECONOMIC RENT CURVES FOR VEGETABLES. THE ECONOMIC RENT OF A WITH RESPECT TO C IS $4.05, AND OF A WITH RESPECT TO B IS $2.30.

FIG. 9.5. ECONOMIC RENT CURVES FOR THREE COMPETING LAND USES.

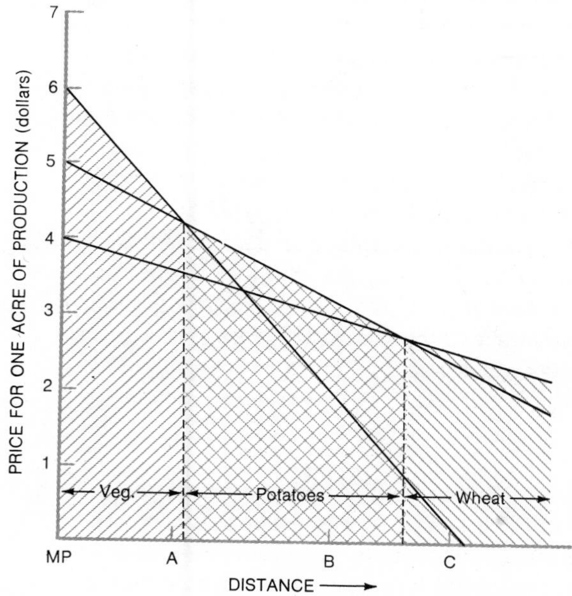

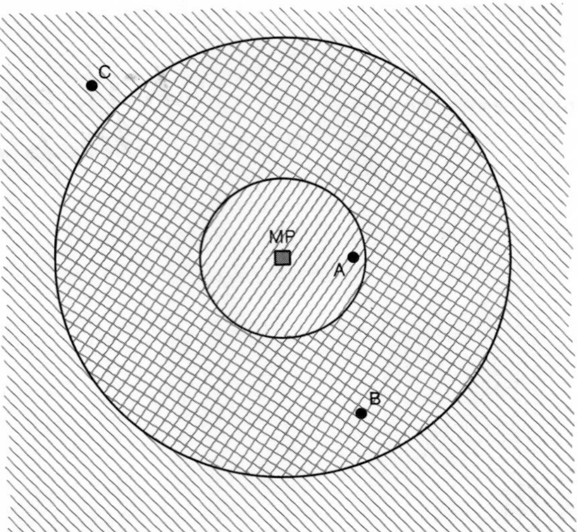

FIG. 9.6. CONCENTRIC LAND USE ZONES DERIVED FROM ROTATING THE ECONOMIC RENT CURVES SHOWN IN FIG. 9.5.

FIG. 9.7. DISTORTION IN THE CONCENTRICITY OF LAND USE ZONES RESULTING FROM AN IMPROVEMENT IN TRANSPORTATION.

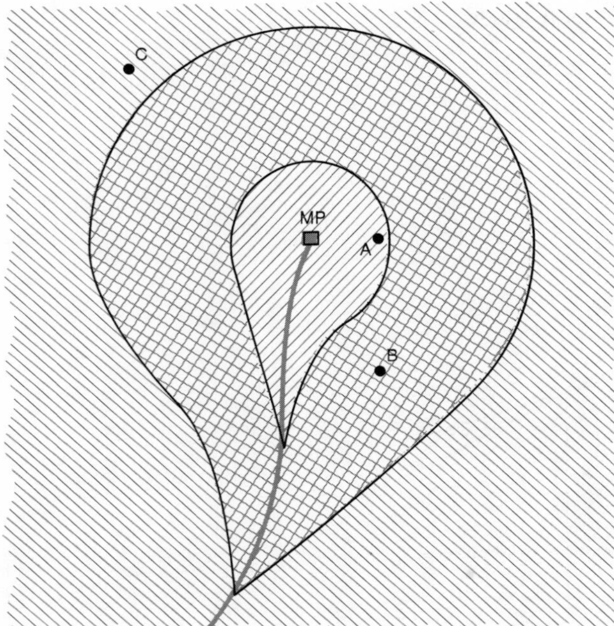

of land uses is shown. Because agricultural commodities can be hauled directly to the river's edge and thence moved to the city by inexpensive barge or boat, each zone of production becomes elongated in a direction roughly parallel to the stream. The innermost zone changes least because water transportation is no faster than wagons; and as growers of perishables are most interested in the time it takes to get to the marketplace, the innovation of water transportation has little effect. However, for those commodities that are bulky, the innovation of water transportation is extremely important as is indicated by the extension of the wood zone and the other crop zones along the water route.

Figure 9.8 presents an intuitive application of the land use theory, at a high

FIG. 9.8. DIFFERENT ACTIVITIES REQUIRE DIFFERENT LEVELS OF ACCESSIBILITY.

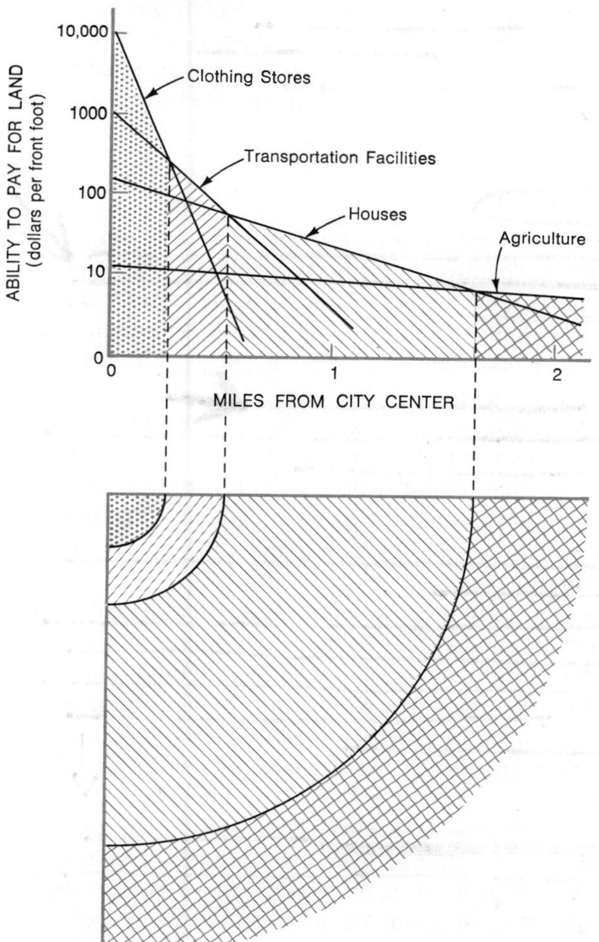

order of generality to the urban area. In this diagram the focus of accessibility is the central business district, and four types of land use are arrayed with respect to this location. Those activities requiring the greatest centrality with respect to the urban market locate in the innermost zones, while those least susceptible to accessibility considerations locate at the periphery (Nourse, 1964, pp. 114–125). It must be remembered, however, that an urban area is not a surface over which transport is homogeneous in any direction; therefore distortions to this highly generalized diagram will be great. These distortions are discussed in detail in the ensuing chapters.

DESCRIPTIVE MODELS OF URBAN LAND USE

In this section we shall deal with three descriptive models of urban land use. The first is Burgess's (Park, et al., 1925) concentric zone model, which was formulated in the early 1920s. The second is Hoyt's sector theory (1939), and the third is the Harris-Ullman (1945) multiple nuclei model. Finally, we shall see how the land use development of one urban area, that of Calgary, fits these models through time.

THE BURGESS CONCENTRIC ZONE MODEL

The concentric zone model suggests that the pattern of growh in the city can best be understood in terms of five concentric zones and a sixth lying beyond the immediate confines of the urban area (Fig. 9.9). This particular model was developed to try to explain the sociological pattern of the North American city and was based primarily on intensive research in the Chicago area during the early part of the present century. The six concentric zones are:

1. The central business district (CBD), which is considered to be the focus of commercial, social, and civic life, and of transportation. This area contains the department stores, smart shops, huge office buildings, clubs, banks, hotels, theaters, museums, and so on, which are of importance to the whole urban area.

2. The fringe of the CBD. This second zone surrounds the CBD and is an area of wholesaling, truck, and railroad depots.

3. The zone in transition. This is a zone of residential deterioration that used to be quite wealthy but, as the city expanded and immigration occurred from rural areas and from overseas, this area became filled with low-income families and individuals. As a consequence, it contains the slums and rooming houses that are so common to the peripheral areas of the CBD. Business and light manufacturing encroach into this area because of the intensive demand for services and supply of cheap labor.

4. The zone of independent workingmen's homes. This zone consists primarily of industrial workers, who have escaped from the zone of transition. It might be regarded, therefore, as an area of second generation immigrants and families who have had enough time to accumulate sufficient wealth to be able to purchase their own homes.

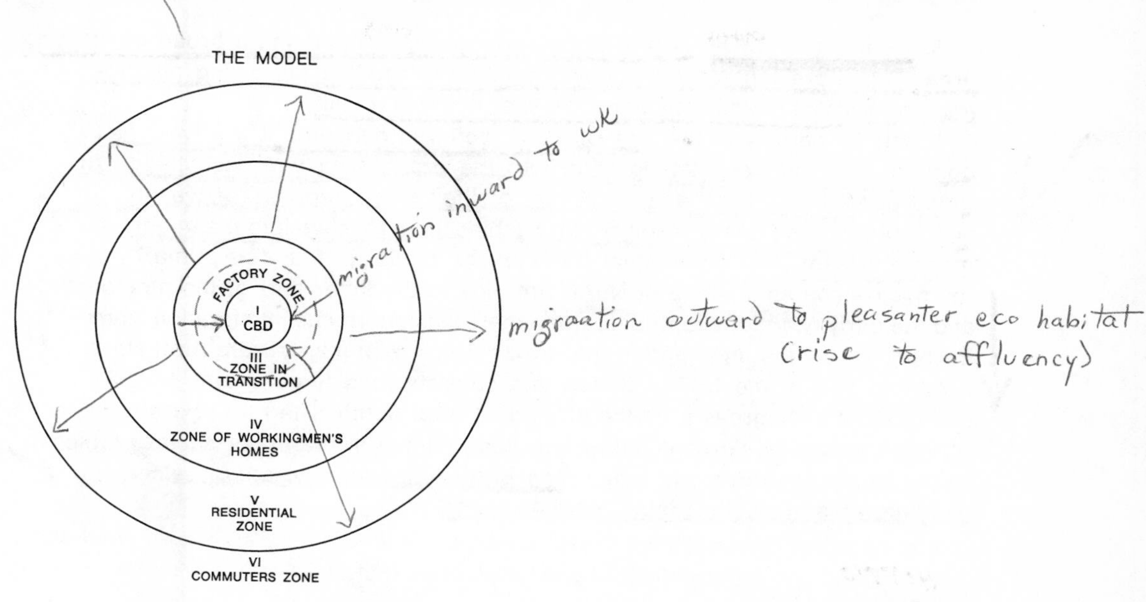

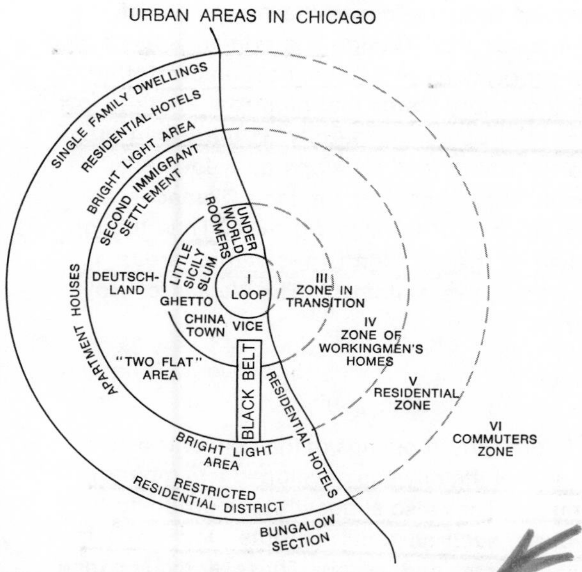

FIG. 9.9. THE BURGESS CONCENTRIC ZONE MODEL OF URBAN STRUCTURE. (*Source:* After Park, et al., 1967, Charts I and II.)

5. High-class residences. This is a zone of better residences containing single-family dwellings and exclusive restricted districts. There are a few high-income apartment buildings.

6. Commuters' zone. This is the outermost zone containing a broad commuting area. These are the suburban areas containing satellite cities and middle- and upper-class residences along rail lines or rapid transit.

It can be perceived that the Burgess model is dynamic. It involves the concept of continuous immigration into the urban area and assimilation of these people into the "American way of life" via a process of wealth accumulation and family stability that enables them to move into the middle-income stream. The conceptual basis of the model is founded primarily on the socio-economic scene of North America in the latter part of the nineteenth and the early twentieth centuries, when there was enormous immigration from Europe. Today the immigration into urban areas is primarily from rural North America; and in the United States this consists to a large extent of the immigration of Negroes from the urban and rural South. The rate of assimilation of these people is extremely slow and has resulted in the major social problems of the North American city today. The Burgess model envisages assimilation of immigrants of all kinds into the urban scene.

THE SECTOR THEORY

The sector theory has been developed with respect to the movement of residential neighborhoods in the American city. Though it is primarily concerned with the movement of high-rent neighborhoods, it has implications for other types of housing as well. Basically the theory states that high-rent areas follow definite sectoral paths outward from the center of the city as the urban area grows. Concomitantly if one sector of a city first develops as a low-rent residential area, it will tend to retain that character for long distances as the sector is extended through the process of the city's growth. Thus though the sector theory is basically applied to the location of residential areas, it is nevertheless a notable general descriptive statement. The details of Hoyt's model will be discussed in Chapter 10.

MULTIPLE-NUCLEI THEORY

Harris and Ullman (1945), recognizing the shortcomings of the concentric zone theory and the sector theory, suggest that the city has developed a number of areas that group around separate nuclei. They also suggest that a grouping of specialized facilities has developed, such as retail districts, port districts, manufacturing districts, university districts, and so on. These activities tend to group together because they profit from cohesion, such as wholesale merchants and financial institutions. On the other hand, certain unlike activities are detrimental to each other, such as heavy industry and light industry, which are usually not found together, for the former is smoky and dirty and the latter is suburban in type, using electrical power. Also, in many cases towns grew by combining together, such as Minneapolis–St. Paul (Dickinson, 1964, pp. 328–329). As a consequence, one would expect to find a division of the city based upon

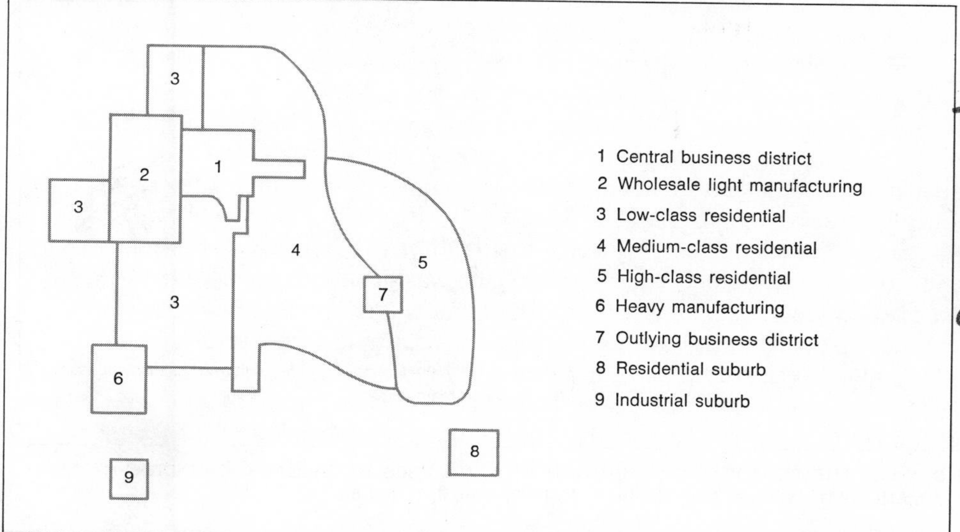

FIG. 9.10. THE HARRIS-ULLMAN MULTIPLE NUCLEI MODEL OF URBAN STRUCTURE. (*Source:* Harris and Ullman, 1945, Fig. 5.)

grouping of certain activities. Such a grouping is indicated in Figure 9.10.

One of the problems of the three descriptive models just discussed is that they are overly simplistic. They try to explain a land use pattern without clearly stating any assumptions. Also, it is very difficult to distinguish the different location decisions behind commercial and industrial development and residential location. A worthwhile descriptive model should include these decisions in the form of theories. Models of this type are developed and discussed later. In fact, Smith (1962), in a study of Calgary, states that these three models are not independent and that they all have some relevance.

THE INTERNAL STRUCTURE OF CALGARY

Hoyt's sector theory, however, seems to be most meaningful with respect to Calgary. The innermost of Burgess's five concentric zones—the CBD and the wholesale light manufacturing core, and the surrounding residential zone in transition—are readily apparent in Calgary, but the remaining zones are by no means clear. Broad general concentric patterns occur, but they are disrupted by radial cross zones of industry. Consequently the sector diagram of Calgary, Figure 9.11, includes most of the major elements of the land-use pattern in a way that would not have been possible in a concentric-zone diagram. Furthermore, the sector model does recognize the essential dynamics of Calgary's growth, which is the outward progression of generalized land-use types along radial lines of transportation. One of the major reasons for this is that residential land use has avoided areas of potential industrial value, such as

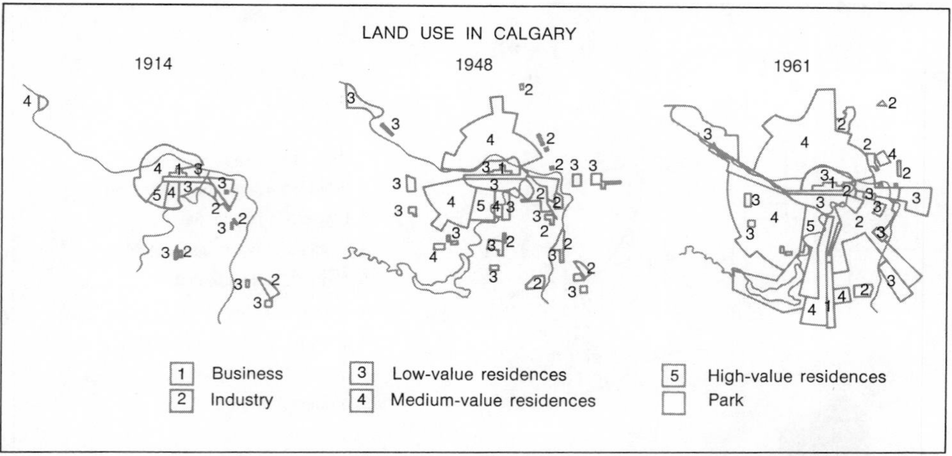

FIG. 9.11. THE SECTORAL DISTRIBUTION OF LAND USES IN CALGARY, CANADA, 1914, 1948, AND 1961. (*Source:* After Smith, P. J., 1962, Figs, 6, 7, and 8.)

the Bow Valley, and sectoral growth between the industrial areas has been encouraged by zoning.

There is evidence in the most recent diagram for 1961 that the Calgary pattern is breaking down into a more flexible multiple-nuclei pattern, with the CBD and wholesaling district and the Bow Valley industrial zone still being dominant. Newer industrial estates and residential areas are developing at the periphery of the city, causing the growth of further commercial business zones in that area. This trend is accelerating today with many areas containing residential sprawl beyond the urban area.

A GENERAL DESCRIPTIVE MODEL

Taking these various changes into consideration, it might be possible to develop a general descriptive model that pertains to the current era. This model is presented in diagrammatic form in Figure 9.12. The first zone is the central business district, which is the area of maximum vertical development of office buildings, the largest department stores, and numerous recreational, financial, and entertainment facilities. The second area can be described as the fringe of the CBD, which contains elements of a sector pattern radiating out from the city center. This area will be most prominent in those urban areas where there is a waterfront running through the downtown area. It contains blighted residences as well as wholesaling districts and industrial sectors.

The third area is the middle zone or the gray area as described by Hoover and Vernon (1959). In this area one finds a mix of activities including high-rent apartment buildings and low-rent areas usually related to industrial sectors. There is also middle-income housing, particularly of the two-family variety, with the highest densities of housing prevailing toward the fringe of the CBD

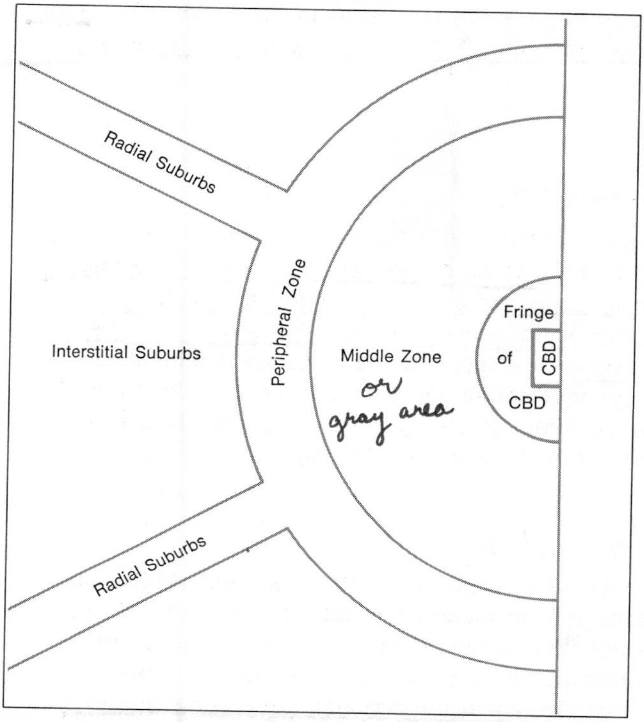

FIG. 9.12. IDEALIZED STRUCTURE OF URBAN AREAS.
(*Source:* After Taaffe, et al., 1963, Fig. 1.1.)

and the lowest densities at the periphery. The fourth zone is a concentric peripheral area consisting primarily of single-family residences of a middle-income variety. It is in this area that there has been great development of light industry, particularly of the kind that uses large quantities of electricity and needs enormous amounts of space for horizontal expansion. This type of industry is often truck oriented and therefore found on urban arteries and close to limited access highways. The peripheral zone also contains large shopping centers, which need vast areas of space for parking and which serve both the gray area and the zones beyond this peripheral belt.

The fifth zone consists of the radial suburbs that string out along older commuter railroads and the newer high-speed limited access expressways and throughways feeding into the heart of the modern city. Upper- and middle-income suburbs are found closer to these transport arteries. Between these radial fingers one finds the interstitial zones. This area consists of a mix of subdivision housing and truck farming and dairying activities. Residential subdivisions are rapidly taking the place of farmland, which is often held vacant by speculators. These subdivisions are developed by real estate promoters as high-income, middle-income, and low-income subdivisions, depending on the

Interstitial Suburb

intensity of development and array of services offered to the subdivision. This is the area of the most rapidly expanding residential development in North America today.

LOCATION AND INTENSITY OF LAND USE

This section is concerned with a discussion of factors influencing the intensity of land use. As it is believed that the value of land at a location is determined to a degree by the intensity of land use, and on the other hand, that high land costs exert very strong pressure to increase densities, this section will be concerned primarily with land values. Factors of a spatial nature that influence land values are discussed in general terms and then applied specifically to the city of Chicago. Furthermore the effect of zoning on land use and land values is discussed, and a specific case examined in north Chicago.

LAND VALUE AND INTENSITY OF LAND USE

A number of writers such as Hoyt (1933, 1960), Muth (1961), and Knos (1962) have indicated that there is a complex interrelationship between intensity of use and the structure of land values. This seems clear from the discussion of Thünen's theory of economic rent and its relationship to the intensity of land use—the more intensive the use, the higher the economic rent pertaining to a piece of land. In Thünen's model, this intensity of use depends on location in relation to the market. In a perfect economy, where every person is able to bid freely for a piece of land, the contract rent for a plot of land would be raised so that it would be equal to its economic rent. Of course in many instances in the real world this true economic rent is never the real contract rent for a given location. Land ownership does not change very quickly, particularly in older established urban areas, and there is very rarely a perfectly competitive situation.

A definition of urban land value The value of a piece of land should however be related to the use to which it is put. Urban land economists seem to be in general agreement about the way in which an individual or firm estimates the value of a given piece of land. It seems that the value of urban land results from a "discounting of future net income attributable to land by virtue of its location" (Wendt, 1957, p. 229). This theoretical definition of land value has been presented by Knos (1962, p. 7) as follows:

$$LV_i = \frac{R_i - C_i}{r}$$

where, LV_i = land value at any i^{th} location.

R_i = expected gross revenue to be received from the property, including the improvements. This expected gross revenue depends on the size of the market, the average income of the spending units within the market, and relative competition to be expected from other uses.

C_i = expected costs, such as local property taxes, operating costs, interest on capital invested in present and future improvements, and depreciation allowances on present and future improvements.

r = the capitalization rate, which is the average interest rate for all investments. This item is a function of current interest rates, allowances for expected risk, and expectations concerning capital gain.

Economic models of this kind occur in Wendt (1957), Hurd (1924), and Ratcliffe (1949, 1957). The point that is geographically relevant in this rather classical economic definition of land value is that the expected revenues and the expected costs change with location (Wendt, 1961). Furthermore the intensity of land use is now measured in monetary terms as the amount to be accrued from a particular location.

It is quite easy to envisage this kind of model applying to industry and commercial activities. The same kind of model can be developed for housing locations, though it may not be possible to measure all aspects of revenue and costs in monetary terms. For housing many intangibles must be taken into account. It is quite clear that transportation costs theoretically must play an important part in residential land value determination. The farther a person is located from his place of work, the greater his expected costs because of increased transportation costs. However this kind of theoretical discussion is offset by many individual preferences. A person may live miles away from his work place because of friends or relatives that the family does not wish to leave or because he simply prefers the district.

Thus it is the location of the site that is the chief factor in determining the value of land in an urban environment. The important question arising at this juncture is: location with respect to what? Hurd (1924) neatly summarized the problem as follows: "Since value depends on economic rent, and rent on location, and location on convenience, and convenience on nearness, we may eliminate the intermediate steps and say that value depends on nearness. The next question is nearness to what?" (Hurd, 1924, p. 13). According to Pendleton (1962), nearness, or accessibility, to something really means distance, measured in some appropriate way. The question therefore can be restated as: distance from what?

Accessibility and land value. If we presume that city growth spreads from a central core on a level plain, then in terms of commercial location, the center of the city should be a major focus of high land values. The reason for this is that as the city develops and expands, the communication network of the urban area expands radially, thereby ensuring that all locations at equal distances from the center are equally accessible to the center of the city. As a consequence, the center of the city is the area of minimum aggregate travel cost for the whole urban area; and commercial activities requiring the largest hinterland possible, either as a labor source or as a market, will desire to locate close to the center. A concentrated grouping of those activities requiring central locations results in the formation of a central business district. Thus the peak value intersection (PVI) or the corner of highest land value in the central business district is theoretically the point of minimum aggregate travel costs for the whole urban area.

As a city grows and expands, outlying business centers will be established; and the major arteries connecting these business centers with each other and with a central business district will become ribbons of commercial and business development. The land value pattern should reflect varying accessibilities to these different centers in the hierarchy. Over the whole city relative accessibility to the central business district should be important for all areas, and individual parts of the city should reflect varying accessibility to outlying business centers. This particular situation is suggested in Figure 9.13, wherein the land-value

FIG. 9.13. DIAGRAMMATIC REPRESENTATION OF URBAN LAND VALUES. (*Source:* Berry, 1963, Fig. 3.)

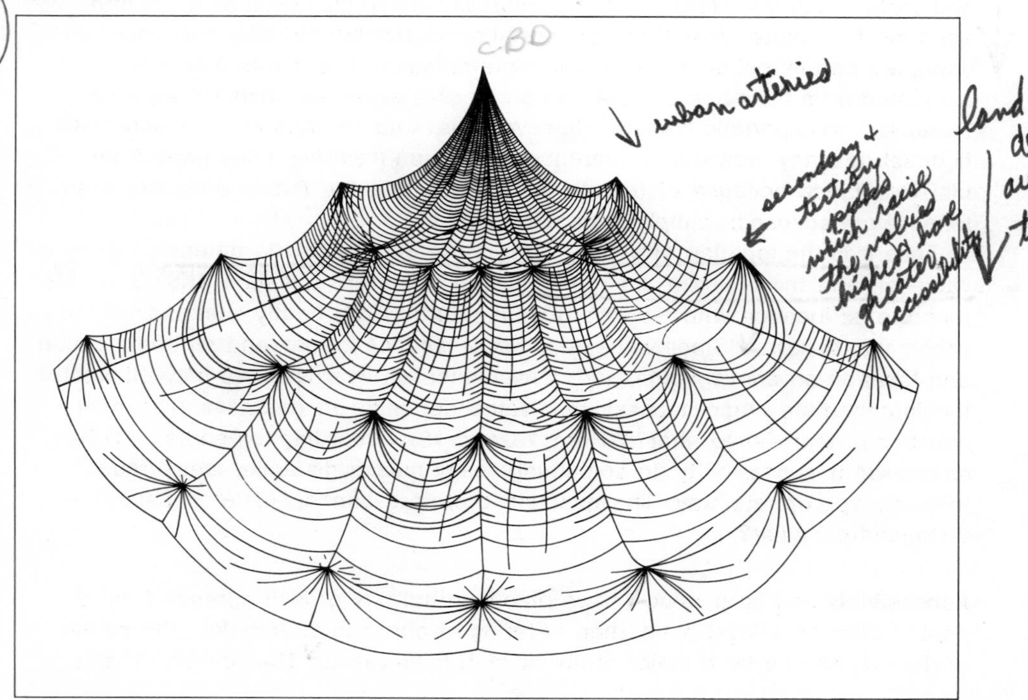

surface is reflected as a circus tent, the highest point being at the CBD, with the ridge lines being the urban arteries of relatively greater land value, and the intersections giving rise to local peaks.

A land value surface The hypothetical structure of a land value surface can be examined with respect to Chicago for the period between 1910 and 1960 (Yeates, 1965A). Land value data can be obtained from Olcott's *Blue Book of Chicago Land Values,* which has been published annually since 1907. These valuations give a front-foot value for every block in the city. Corner valuations, except in a few instances, are not given but have to be estimated by the user from the front-foot estimates using certain rules laid down by Olcott. Thus, though within-block variations are impossible to analyze, between-block variations can be studied. Furthermore, Garner (1966, pp. 185–188) indicates that there is a very close correlation between assessed values and Olcott's estimates of land value.

The land value maps (Fig. 9.14) are constructed from a sample of 484 front-foot land values located within the 1960 city limits of Chicago. In order to facilitate later statistical analysis, the data is normalized by means of a logarithmic transformation; and in order to facilitate comparison of the land value maps between the time periods, the transformed data is converted into standard scores. The isoline interval chosen for each map is one standard deviation, so each map can be compared because the intervals are comparable and related to their respective means.

A visual analysis of the maps yields some interesting observations. Throughout the whole time period, the highest land values are found within and adjacent to the central business district, the center being the peak value intersection at State and Madison, and from this area there is a sharp decline in all directions. This decline is logarithmically fairly uniform in 1910, but by 1960 it does not exhibit the same consistency. The contraction of the mean isoline and the general reduction of land values on the south side of the central business district are quite evident, as is the presence of residual outliers, which indicate the position of regional business and shopping centers. It could be suggested, therefore, that the effect of distance from, and consequently access to, the central business district on land values appears to have diminished in importance during the past fifty years, while the front-foot value of locations in the vicinity of outlying regional service centers has increased.

A further locational factor that appears to influence the general spatial distribution of land values is Lake Michigan, for relatively higher land values are found close to the lake shore. The 1950 and 1960 maps, however, suggest that land values within the vicinity of Lake Michigan on the north side of the city are generally increasing and higher than those on the south side where values are declining. This is possibly a reflection of the nonwhite, low-income nature of the southern area which discourages high-rise apartment speculation.

Land at the periphery of the city appears to be becoming relatively more valuable than land in the middle of the city. On the 1960 map, this tendency is

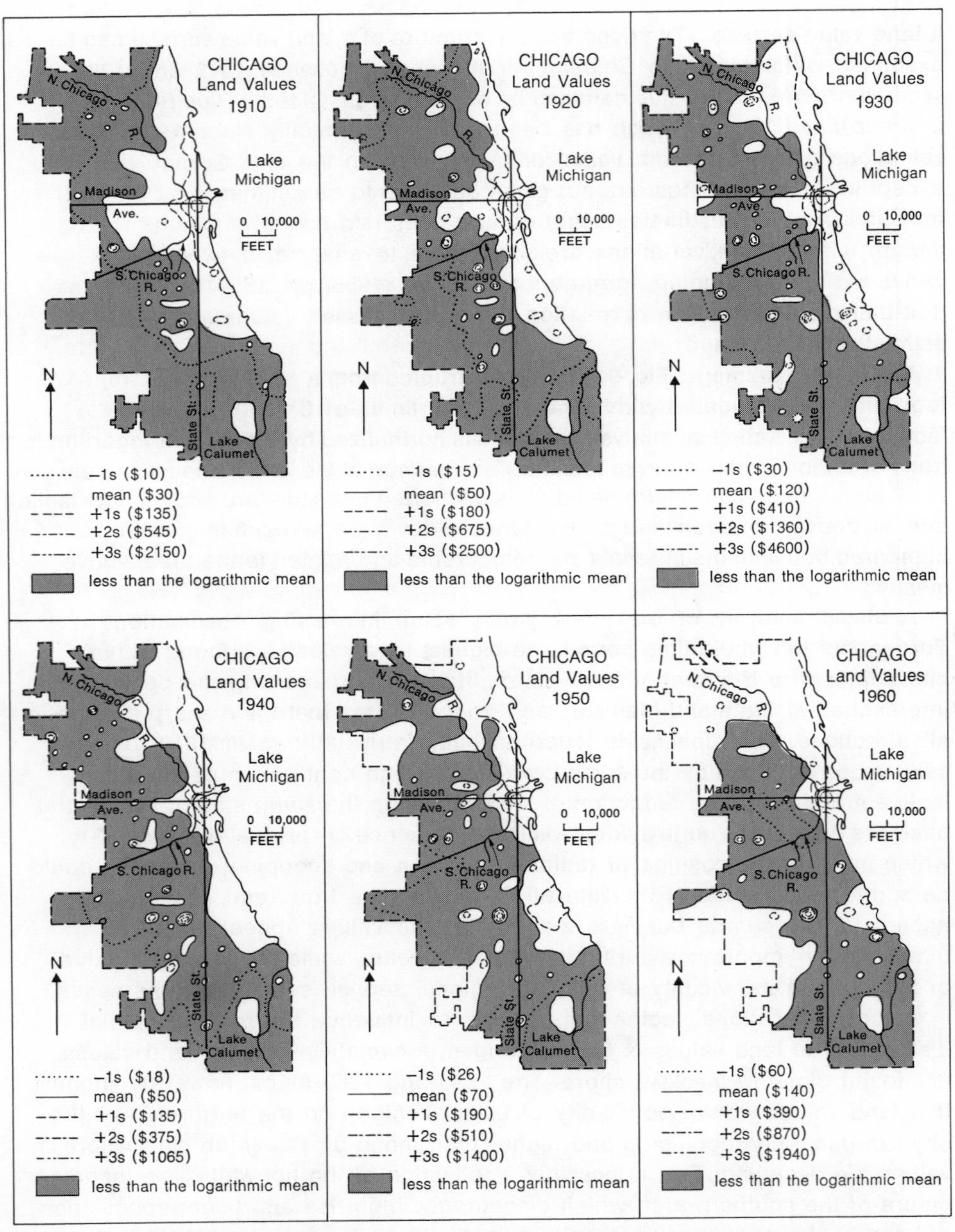

FIG. 9.14. LAND VALUE SURFACES IN THE CITY OF CHICAGO, 1910–1960. (*Source:* Yeates, 1965A, Figs. 1 and 2.)

much more strongly developed in the north than in the southwest and hardly present at all in the west. The great rise in land values at the periphery of the city in the north is probably a reflection of the high-income nature of this area. The absence of any rise to the west is the result of the political boundary on the west being closer to the center of the city than the boundary to the north or south; and thus peripheral developments that are within the city on the north or south are absent in that area.

Thus it would seem that in the case of Chicago the effect of three specific locational factors should be examined. The first is the effect of variation in location with respect to the central business district, the center of which is defined as the intersection of State Street and Madison Avenue, the PVI of Chicago. The second is the effect of variation in the location of sites with respect to Lake Michigan. Lake Michigan appears to have been an area of amenity attractions, which have increased in importance during the past fifty years. The third is variation in location with respect to regional shopping centers. There are, of course, numerous outlying shopping centers in the Chicago urban area. For the purpose of this discussion those outlying shopping centers defined as "major regional center" and "smaller shoppers' goods centers" by Berry (1963) will be combined and classified as regional centers.

A fourth locational factor that might well be important, as defined in the theoretical analysis by Thünen, is location with respect to transportation improvements. In this discussion the effect of the elevated–subway stations on land values is examined. This is the only variable that changes through time, because the rapid-transit system has changed considerably in elevated coverage during the last fifty years, maximum mileage having been attained in the 1930s. It is expected that this variable will prove to be more important in early years than in later years, because in the early part of the century people were more dependent on this form of rapid transit. In today's automobile society, the elevated–subway system is not quite so important.

A descriptive model of urban land values The factors influencing the spatial distribution of land values outlined above can be examined together in a multiple regression model. In general form, a multiple regression model can be represented as follows:

$$Y = a + b_{Y1.234}X_1 + b_{Y2.134}X_2 + b_{Y3.124}X_3 + b_{Y4.123}X_4 + e$$

where, Y = the dependent variable

X_1, X_2, X_3, X_4 = four independent variables
b = regression coefficients pertaining to each independent variable
a = a constant, sometimes referred to as the Y intercept
e = an error term

An important feature of a multiple regression model is that the b–coefficients indicate the change in the dependent variable associated with a unit change in an independent variable, with all the other independent variables in the equation being held constant. Thus, $b_{Y2\cdot134}$ is read as "the change in Y per unit change in X_2 with X_1, X_3, and X_4, held constant." For the sake of convenience, this profusion of subscripts will be reduced in the ensuing discussion to the form b_1, b_2, b_3, and b_4.

The hypothesized model can be expressed with respect to the spatial distribution of Chicago land values as follows:

$$V_i = a - b_1C_i - b_2M_i - b_3E_i - b_4S_i$$

where, V_i = logarithm of the land value at any i^{th} location

C_i = logarithm of distance of the ith location from the CBD
M_i = logarithm of distance of the ith location from Lake Michigan
E_i = logarithm of distance of the ith location from the nearest elevated–subway station
S_i = logarithm of distance of the ith location from the nearest regional shopping center
$i = 1, 2, 3, \ldots, n$; n being the sample size based on a systematic stratified random sample design of 484 points.

The data has been transformed into logarithms in order to satisfy one of the major assumptions of tests of significance using the normal distribution; that is, that the residuals are distributed normally. The signs of the regression coefficients are negative because the discussion has indicated that land values should decrease with distance from the CBD, Lake Michigan, stations of the elevated subway–system, and regional shopping centers.

The above model has been tested with respect to the spatial distribution of land values in Chicago for 1910 and 1960. The multiple correlation coefficients, coefficients of determination, and regression coefficients are represented in Table 9.4. The model describes the 1910 land value distribution extremely well. The four variables taken together explain 76.2 percent of the variation in land values. Furthermore the signs of the regression coefficients are as hypothesized. As all the variables are measured in common distance units, the magnitudes of the regression coefficients indicate the relative importance of each variable in the equation. Clearly, the most important variable is distance from the CBD. Thus it may be concluded that in 1910 relative accessibility of locations to the CBD was the basic determinant of land values. Accessibility to Lake Michigan

TABLE 9.4. CHICAGO LAND VALUES: CORRELATION COEFFICIENTS (R), COEFFICIENTS OF DETERMINATION (R^2), AND REGRESSION COEFFICIENTS, 1910 AND 1960

Year	R	R^2	C	M	E	S
1910	.873	76.2%	−.935	−.469	−.300	−.035*
1960	.335	11.2%	−.250	−.120	+.029*	−.124

* Not significantly different from zero at t (.05).

and stations on the elevated system were the second and third most important determinants of land values. In general, outlying regional shopping centers do not significantly affect the land value surface.

The model for 1960 explains very little of the variation in land values, but the signs of the regression coefficients are as hypothesized, with one exception. The exception is the value of land with respect to distance from stations on the elevated–subway system. The regression coefficient pertaining to this variable is positive though not significantly different from zero. The change in sign and value of the regression coefficient provides some land value evidence for the relative decline in importance of this form of rapid transit in Chicago. Although the signs of the other variables are as hypothesized, the values of the regression coefficients are much less than they were in 1910. Distance from the CBD is still the most important variable, but the relative accessibility of locations to Lake Michigan and regional shopping centers are now equally important.

Thus, as far as the growth of Chicago during the last half century is concerned, it would appear that centrifugal forces (Colby, 1933) have become paramount and are reflected in the changing land value surface. Highway improvements and the almost universal use of the automobile, plus social changes resulting in a shorter work week and generally higher wages and salaries, have meant that families and entrepreneurs are less inclined to locate near the center of the city or close to their work place. Consequently the effect of accessibility on land values is not so important as it has been in the past. Furthermore, whereas in 1910, commercial, business, and industrial activities as well as housing were relatively free to locate in any part of the city, during recent decades this freedom has been limited by zoning.

THE EFFECT OF ZONING

As a city grows it becomes increasingly obvious that land has to be set aside for certain uses and that certain elements in the land use mosaic should be kept apart. Noxious industries should not be allowed to locate close to schools, and zoned commercial areas should be kept apart from housing developments. Areas set apart for housing should be zoned for intensity of development, because people buying property in a low-density, single-family area would not wish to see their district ruined by high-rise apartments that would raise population densities and create social problems with which the district might be unable to cope. For these reasons, and many others, city governments increasingly zone land use to ensure the best development of the urban area.

Thus the growth and development of the city through time would seem to warrant an investigation of the effects of zoning on land-value variations. Of course, the extent to which zoning is rigorously applied varies from city to city in North America. Indeed, it has been said that "Houston, Texas, which has grown up without the exercise of any zoning powers at all, is little diffierent from any other North American city" (Buchanan, 1964, p. 225). However, zoning has been in operation in Chicago since the 1930s, and its regulations have been followed with a degree of rigor since World War II.

Zoning and land values in Rogers Park, Chicago In the Rogers Park district of North Chicago (Fig. 9.15) zoning has resulted in fairly uniform residential development (Yeates, 1965B). The most widespread land use in the area in 1960 is classified as general residence (Fig. 9.15), which means that apartment building is permitted over the whole area; and in fact, three-floor apartments are most common. The occupants of the apartments and single-family houses are generally of middle income and white. Two other considerable land uses consist of areas zoned business and commercial. The business areas demarcate zones of retail and shopping activities, whereas the commercial areas delineate zones occupied by financial activities, small workshops, and hotels. There are two other land uses found in the Rogers Park district, but the variations of land values in these areas are not very great.

The Rogers Park district is far enough away from the central business district in Chicago for that particular distance variable to have very little effect on the land value surface. Comparison of Figures 9.16 and 9.17 indicates that the spatial distribution of land values in the business and commercial zones is

FIG. 9.15. LAND USE ZONING IN ROGERS PARK, CITY OF CHICAGO, 1961. (*Source:* Yeates, 1965B, Fig. 70.)

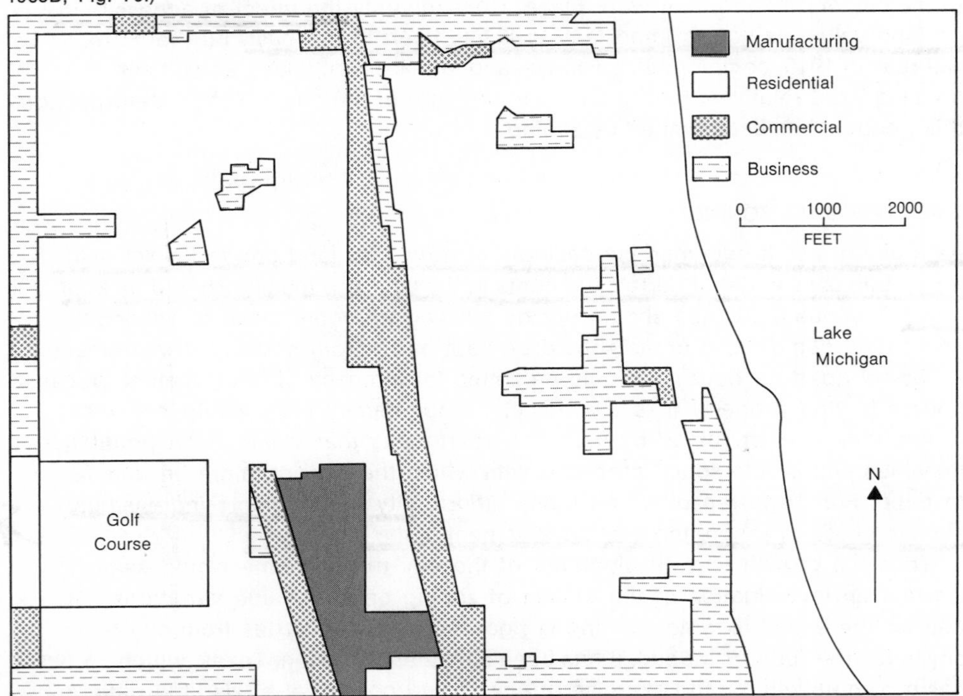

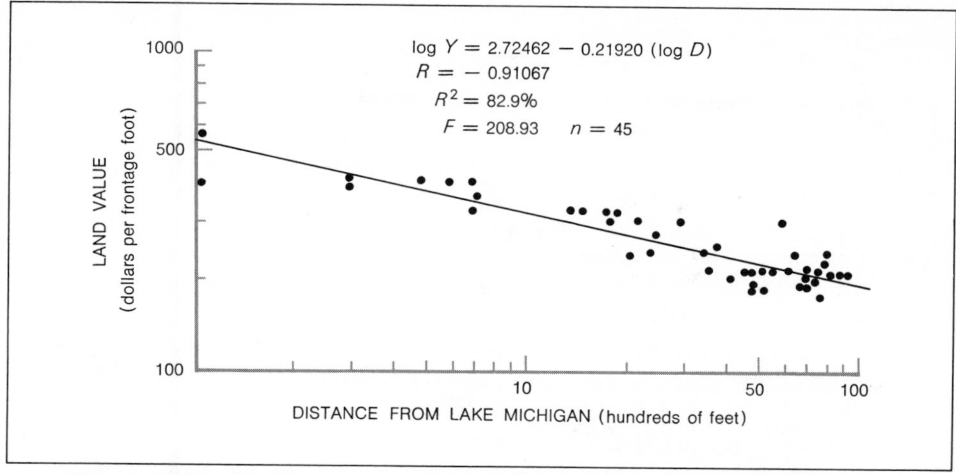

FIG. 9.16. VARIATION IN RESIDENTIAL LAND VALUES WITH DISTANCE FROM LAKE MICHIGAN, ROGERS PARK IN THE CITY OF CHICAGO. (*Source:* Yeates, 1965B, Fig. 74.)

affected by forces different than those in the residential zones. In Figure 9.16 there appears to be a very close relationship between land values in areas zoned residential and distance from Lake Michigan. The area bordering Lake Michigan has, in fact, become an outstanding area of high land values for residential purposes for a number of reasons. In the first place, it has great amenity attractions; the beaches and bathing areas along the lake shore provide excellent facilities for Chicagoans during the hot and often humid summer. For city dwellers the open view and evening lake breezes make urban dwelling a little more pleasurable. Furthermore the Lakeshore Drive and the elevated rapid transit facility running along the lake connect the CBD to suburbs north of the city limits of Chicago. Thus, locations along the lake shore are enhanced in value by the nearby presence of these transportation advantages.

Figure 9.17 indicates that land values in business and commercial areas are not related to distance from Lake Michigan at all. In fact, there is very little reason for business or commercial activities to locate near the lake, as such a location would involve a truncation of their potential market area. It is reasonable to hypothesize that land values in business and commercial areas would, in fact, be most influenced by distance from the center of the outlying shopping areas. Figure 9.18 indicates that such an arrangement does, in fact, occur. The theoretical basis for this arrangement is discussed later in the chapter concerned with the internal structure of commercial areas.

Zoning and planning The evidence discussed with respect to changes in the spatial distribution of Chicago land values between 1910 and 1960 indicates the important effect of zoning on the land value surface as cities grow. As the urban area expands and the population increases, it becomes more and more

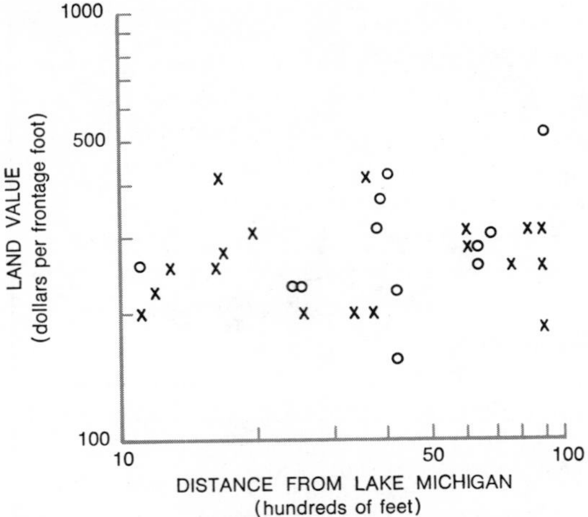

FIG. 9.17. VARIATION IN BUSINESS AND COMMERCIAL LAND VALUES WITH DISTANCE FROM LAKE MICHIGAN, ROGERS PARK IN THE CITY OF CHICAGO. (*Source:* Yeates, 1965B, Fig. 75.)

necessary to plan city services and land uses. Zoning is the method most commonly used to plan and control land uses and separate various uses, one from another, in order to maintain property values and appearance. The individual or firm is then allowed freedom of choice of location within the appropriate zoned area.

FIG. 9.18. VARIATION IN BUSINESS AND COMMERCIAL LAND VALUES WITH DISTANCE FROM OUTLYING SHOPPING AREAS, ROGERS PARK IN THE CITY OF CHICAGO. (*Source:* Yeates, 1965B, Fig. 76.)

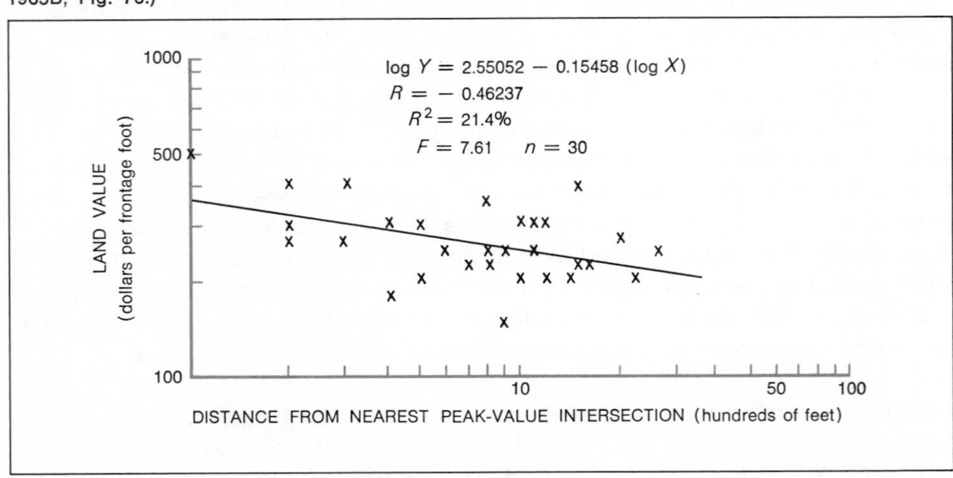

Theoretically the optimum zoning is that which allows the land to be occupied by its highest and best use. The concept of highest and best use refers to the use that envisages the highest discounted future net income at a location. It would seem that the attainment of this goal by zoning would be extremely difficult. The aim, however, is sound as it results in a maximizing of a taxable base. It is therefore necessary that a zoning board should take very good care to satisfy the demand for each kind of land use. If too little commercial land is provided, for example, the land values in areas zoned commercial may be inflated; on the other hand, if too much land is provided, values may fall and submarginal commercial activities may enter.

In a growing urban area the problem of determining the amount of land to be zoned in each category takes on another dimension, that of trying to forecast future demand for a given general land use. It is in this situation that zoning and urban growth are particularly interrelated. Zoning is highly desirable, but as the urban area grows the quantity and location of areas devoted to specific uses has to change. In too many cases, rezoning takes a great deal of time and numerous public hearings. The result is that a decision concerning land in the past is often stamped upon land in the present. Thus zoning may result in a slow adjustment to new conditions arising from urban growth. The urban geographer, by attempting to discern the factors that influence the internal structure of urban areas, is groping toward a theoretical base that will permit planning for the continuous readjustment of urban land use.

“THE LOCATION OF RESIDENCES”

We have observed in the previous chapter that residential land use consumes by far the largest proportion of the total developed land within urban areas. According to the data provided by Niedercorn and Hearle (1965), residential land use in large North American urban areas consumes 39 percent of the total developed land. This figure is supported by the information of Bartholomew (1955) for central cities in North America. In this chapter we will be concerned with three particular aspects of urban residential location. In the first section the general location of people within urban areas is discussed, and some mathematical models concerning the distribution of population densities are presented. In the second section we will discuss some general hypotheses that have been formulated with respect to various patterns of residential location in the North American city. In the third section we will attempt to determine those factors that have the greatest influence in the locational decision.

THE DISTRIBUTION OF PEOPLE WITHIN URBAN AREAS

A brief analysis of population density maps of two North American cities reveals a few general characteristics (Fig. 10.1). Population densities on the

FIG. 10.1. POPULATION DENSITY MAPS OF (A) DETROIT, 1953 AND (B) CHICAGO, 1956. (*Source:* After Detroit Metropolitan Area Traffic Study (D.M.A.T.S.), 1955, Map 4, and Chicago Area Transportation Study (C.A.T.S.), 1959, Map 12.)

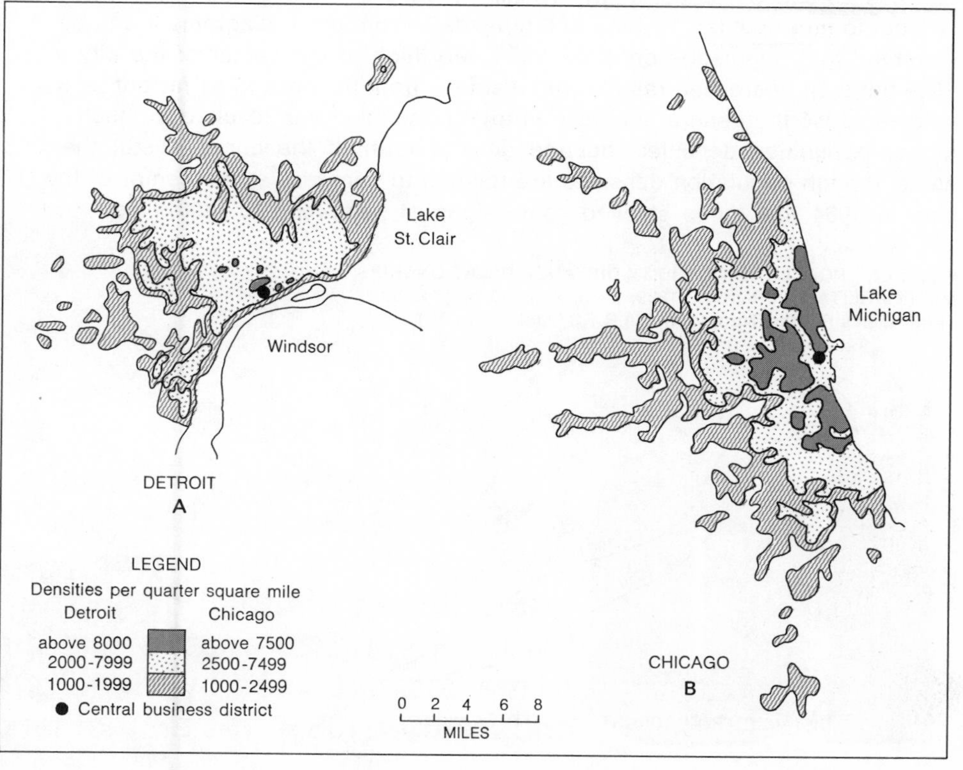

whole seem to be greater at the center of the city than at the periphery, and the decline in the population density surface away from the center of the city is very steep to begin with and then flattens out. There are, of course, some departures from this general pattern. In particular, in both cases the density of population at the center of the city seems to be relatively low, increases to a peak, and then decreases away from the center as previously described. Furthermore there are noticeable instances where population densities tend to be relatively higher along the major radials leading into the central city. Aside from these departures, however, it seems that a very close relationship exists between population density distribution and general accessibility within urban areas.

CHANGES IN POPULATION DENSITY PATTERNS

We have observed in Chapter 8 that as the city has grown and expanded the distribution of people within the urban area has changed accordingly. In the early days of the pedestrian North American city, population densities were very high at the center of the city and decreased rapidly from the central focus of economic activity. With changing technology and the accompanying decentralization of economic activities, the population of the North American city has spread out accordingly. These changes are well illustrated with respect to metropolitan Toronto in Figure 10.2. From these diagrams it can be observed that population densities were very high at the center of the city in 1899 but then decreased rapidly with distance from the core to as far out as 6 miles. In 1956 the general increase in total population has resulted in much higher population densities, but the general form of the curve is still the same, though population densities are tending to decrease at the center of the city. In 1964 this curve showed some signs of beginning to flatten out.

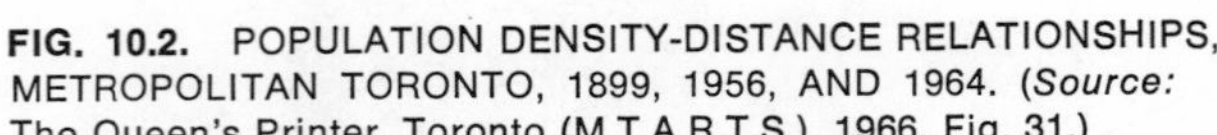

FIG. 10.2. POPULATION DENSITY-DISTANCE RELATIONSHIPS, METROPOLITAN TORONTO, 1899, 1956, AND 1964. (*Source:* The Queen's Printer, Toronto (M.T.A.R.T.S.), 1966, Fig. 31.)

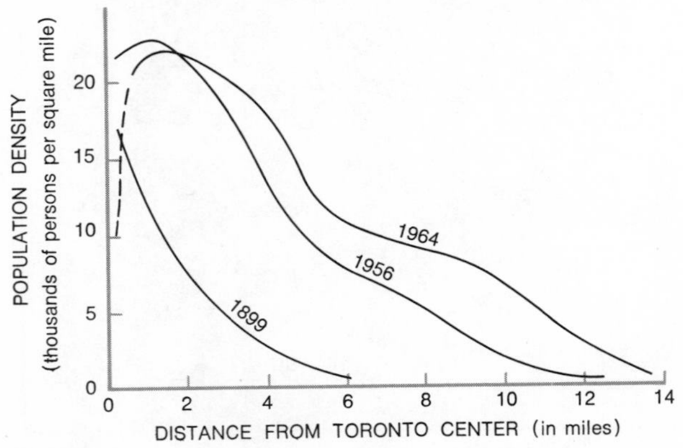

These recent changes in population density are well illustrated by the maps for metropolitan Toronto from 1951 to 1963 (Fig. 10.3). In 1951 it can be observed that population densities are very high in the center of the city, though there is a general decrease right at the center which is the intersection of Queen and Yonge streets, and that there is a general decline to the periphery. However, a very strong radial spread of relatively higher population densities is observed along the major radials, particularly leading to the north, northwest, west, and east. The map for 1956 indicates a contraction of the highest density area, but a general spreading out of densities ranging between 627 and 3,200 persons per square mile and the beginnings of an infilling between the major radials. This trend is continued through to 1961, particularly with an infilling in the northwest between the major radials leading to the west and north. Finally, in 1963, the last map indicates that the area of lower population densities at the center of the city has expanded slightly and that the infilling between the radials has continued apace. Concomitantly densities along the radials have continued to increase, particularly at the periphery of the metropolitan area.

These changes are summarized quite well in the population growth rate map in Figure 10.4. This map illustrates the variation in growth rate of population in metropolitan Toronto for the ten-year interval between 1951 and 1961. During this period those areas closest to the center of the city decreased in population while the greater increases are found at the periphery of the city or in the interstitial areas to the northeast. Thus the pattern of growth rates indicates a decline at the center of the city and high positive growth rates at the periphery.

FIG. 10.3 CHANGES IN POPULATION DENSITY DISTRIBUTION IN METROPOLITAN TORONTO, 1951–1963. POPULATION DENSITIES ARE MEASURED IN PERSONS PER SQUARE MILE. (*Source:* Latham, 1967, from data on pages 53–59.)

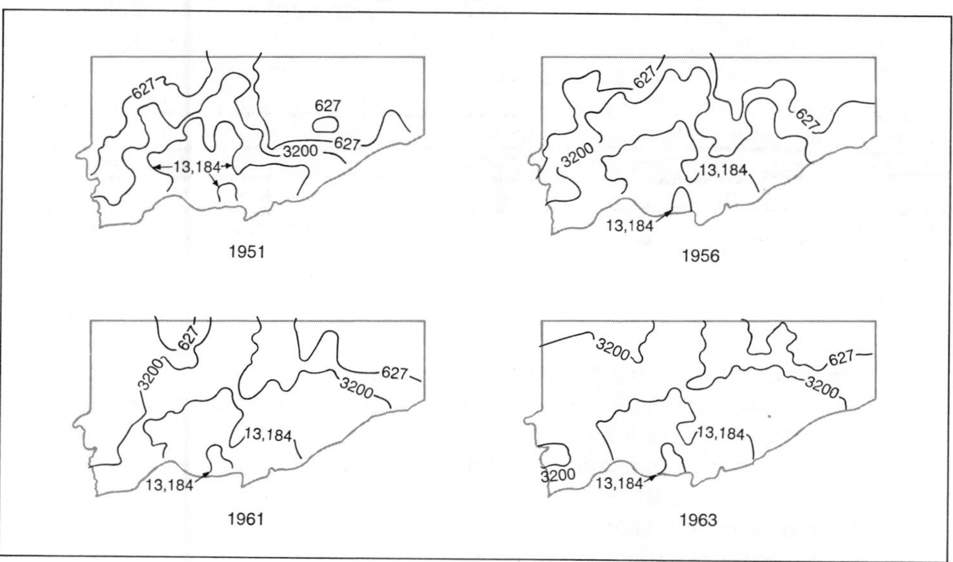

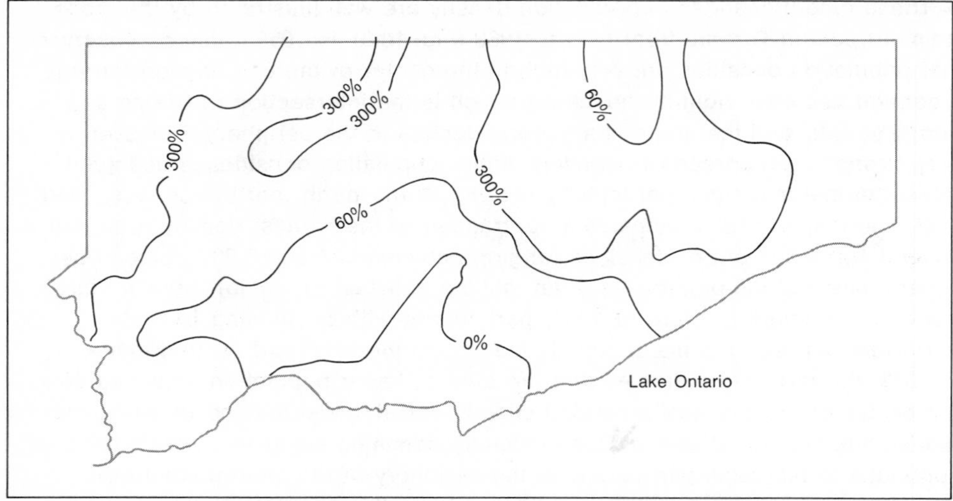

FIG. 10.4. POPULATION GROWTH RATE IN METROPOLITAN TORONTO, 1951–1961. THE ISOLINES SHOW THE PERCENTAGE CHANGE DURING THE PERIOD FROM 1951 TO 1961.

This pattern is typical of most North American cities in which the population growth rate increases with distance from the center of the city rather than decreases with distance from the center of the city as with population densities.

SOME MATHEMATICAL MODELS OF URBAN POPULATION DENSITIES

One of the most stimulating attempts at postulating a general mathematical statement concerning the distribution of population densities within urban areas has been presented by Colin Clark (1951B). Having collected data for many urban areas throughout the world, he concludes that urban population densities are related in some systematic way to distance from, or accessibility to, the center of the city. Specifically he suggests that urban population densities decrease in a negative exponential fashion (that is, decrease at a decreasing rate) with distance from the CBD. The formulation of this model is presented in equation form as follows:

$$D_d = D_o e^{-bd}$$

where D_d = population density at distance d from the CBD

D_o = a constant indicating the population density at distance zero, i.e., at the center of the city

$-b$ = a parameter indicating the rate of decrease of population with distance; i.e., the slope of the curve

d = the variable distance

e = base of the natural logarithms

In general terms all that an equation of this type indicates is that population densities decrease rapidly at first with distance from the CBD and then tend to flatten out. This situation is expressed in Figure 10.5 which, as can be observed, is very close to the situation expressed in three time periods for Toronto in Figure 10.2. The curve presented in Figure 10.5 can be transformed into a straight line by the transformation of the population density variable into natural logarithms:

$$\ln D_d = \ln D_o - bd$$

where $\ln D_d$ = natural logarithm of the population density at distance d from the CBD

$\ln D_o$ = natural logarithm of the constant

The evidence from various North American cities that Clark produces as support for this suggested model is presented in Figure 10.6, where the population densities are averages for annular rings, the locus of which is located at the center of each city. The population density data is transformed into natural logarithms.

The density gradient and time From the data presented by Clark, it can also be observed that the densities not only decrease with distance from the center of the city but that the lines are generally steeper in 1900 than in 1940. The steepness of the line is indicated by the parameter b which represents the rate of decrease of population densities with distance from the center of the city. In all cases the value of this parameter has decreased between 1900 and 1940. For example in St. Louis the b parameter has a value of $-.75$ in 1900 but $-.45$ in 1940. If the value of b were zero, the population density curve would

FIG. 10.5. CLARK'S MODEL OF URBAN POPULATION DENSITY.

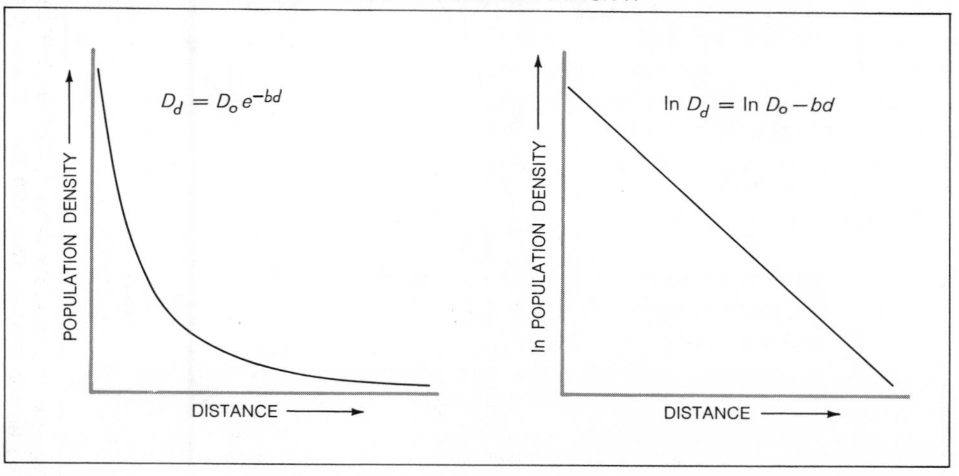

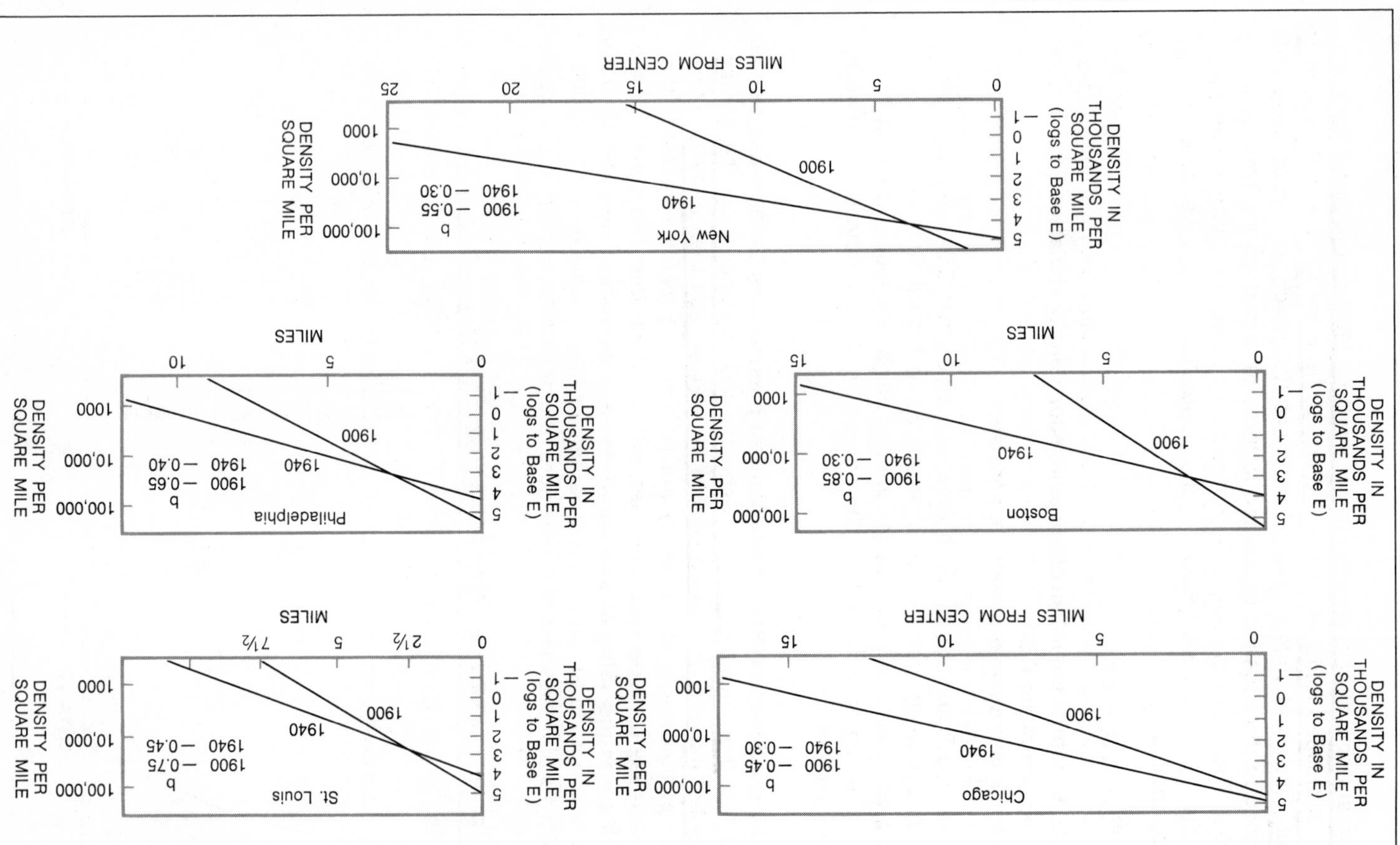

FIG. 10.6. POPULATION DENSITY-DISTANCE RELATIONSHIPS FOR SELECTED CITIES IN THE UNITED STATES, 1900 AND 1940. (*Source:* Clark, 1951B, p. 492.)

be flat, indicating that population densities were evenly distributed throughout the urban area.

Newling regards this as one of the most interesting features of Clark's data, and after examining information from other urban areas, he concludes that the population density gradient decreases through time in a constant, systematic fashion (Newling, 1966). In fact he suggests that the mathematical form of this relationship is the same as that suggested by Clark relating population densities to distance from the center of the city. His hypothesis with respect to density gradient and time is expressed diagrammatically in Figure 10.7A, B, where it is suggested that the density gradient decreases rapidly through time in the earlier time periods, but then tends to decrease less rapidly as the value of the density gradient gets very small. This situation with respect to a particular hypothetical setting is expressed in Figure 10.7C with a very steep density gradient in 1900 but a shallower gradient in 1940 and a gradient that is very close to zero in 1960.

The equation for this relationship is expressed as follows:

$$b_t = b_{t-\alpha}e^{-ct}$$

where b_t = density gradient at time t
$b_{t-\alpha}$ = a constant, indicating the density gradient at an earlier period $t-\alpha$
$-c$ = a parameter indicating the rate of decrease of the density gradient with time
t = the variable time
e = the base of the natural logarithms

This equation does not of course imply that time itself causes these changes, but that processes, taking place over a period of time, cause these changes. Some of these processes have been described in Chapter 8 with respect to innovations in urban transportation. Clark supports this argument by suggesting that the decline in the density gradient is related to changing transportation

FIG. 10.7. CHANGES IN THE POPULATION DENSITY-DISTANCE RELATIONSHIP THROUGH TIME.

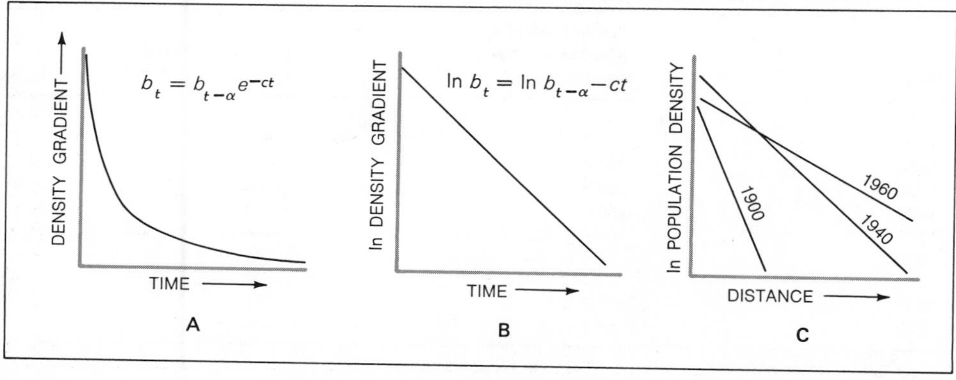

technology and particularly the introduction of the use of the automobile (Clark, 1957).

Concurrent with this decline in density gradient has been the change in the densities at the center of the city. The change in central densities does not, however, appear to be as consistent in North American urban areas as that for the density gradient itself (Berry, et al., 1963; Newling, 1964). In fact, it appears that the density at the center of the city increases for a period of time, and then decreases in recent years. This is well illustrated by the data prepared by Winsborough (1961) for Chicago. In Table 10.1 it can be observed that, whereas the density gradient has declined consistently since 1860, the central density rose and reached a peak somewhere between 1900 and 1910 and then declined thereafter. On the other hand, the data for Toronto suggests that the central densities have remained fairly consistent (Fig. 10.2).

The reason for these differences may well be related to the different epochs in which urban areas show their greatest growth. If an urban area grew rapidly in population when urban transportation technology permitted limited radial expansion of the city, then "piling up" inevitably occurs in the central locations. However with changing technology, decentralization of activities has become possible thereby permitting central densities to decline so that the greatest densities are now found at some distance from the central city and are perhaps moving outward in a tidal wave (Blumenfeld, 1954). It is in this context that Newling (1969) has modified Clark's model by suggesting a second degree polynomial in order to take into account the central density crater (Fig. 10.8).

Population growth rate and distance We have observed with respect to Figure 10.2 that the recent growth of population in Toronto appears to be much greater at the periphery of the city than at the center and that at the center of the city population densities are in fact declining (Fig. 10.3). Newling (1966) suggests that this relationship is also systematic throughout the urban area and that the form

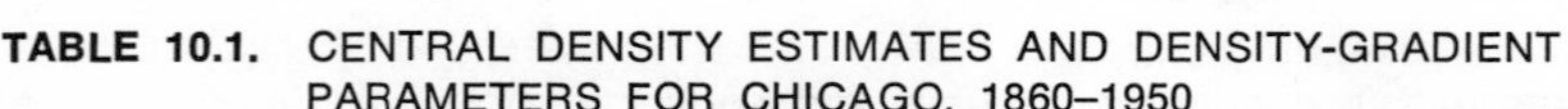

TABLE 10.1. CENTRAL DENSITY ESTIMATES AND DENSITY-GRADIENT PARAMETERS FOR CHICAGO, 1860–1950

Year	Central Density (thousands per square mile)	Density Gradient (natural logarithms)
1860	30.0	—.917
1870	70.8	—.877
1880	96.6	—.781
1890	86.3	—.508
1900	100.0	—.415
1910	100.0	—.369
1920	73.0	—.251
1930	72.8	—.215
1940	71.1	—.210
1950	63.7	—.182

Source: Data quoted by Newling (1966), p. 219, from Winsborough (1961).

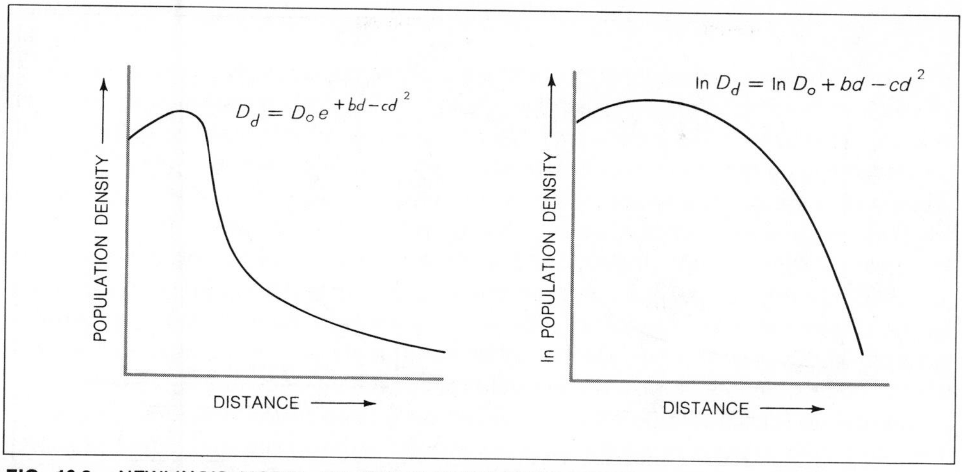

FIG. 10.8. NEWLING'S MODEL OF URBAN POPULATION DENSITY.

of this relationship can also be expressed in terms of an exponential equation. This equation takes the form

$$(l + r)_d = (l + r)_o \, e^{gd}$$

where $(l + r)_d$ = population growth rate at distance d, usually empirically defined as the population at distance d at time period t divided by the population at some earlier time period

$(l + r)_o$ = a constant, indicating the population growth rate at the center of the city

g = a parameter indicating the rate of increase of the population growth rate with distance from the CBD

d = the variable distance

e = base of the natural logarithms

The hypothesized ideal relationship of the growth rate with respect to distance is expressed diagrammatically in Figure 10.9, and here it can be observed that the population growth rate is very low at the center of the city but increases at an increasing rate with distance from the center.

There are two basic reasons for this pattern. The first is that, as population densities tend to be low at the periphery of the city, any increase in population usually exhibits a high rate of increase. On the other hand, an increase of population in an area of large population will not show up high in terms of rate of increase. Secondly, the fertility rate at the periphery of North American urban areas is much greater than at the center of the city. This is because at the periphery of the city in the suburbs the population is younger and the birth

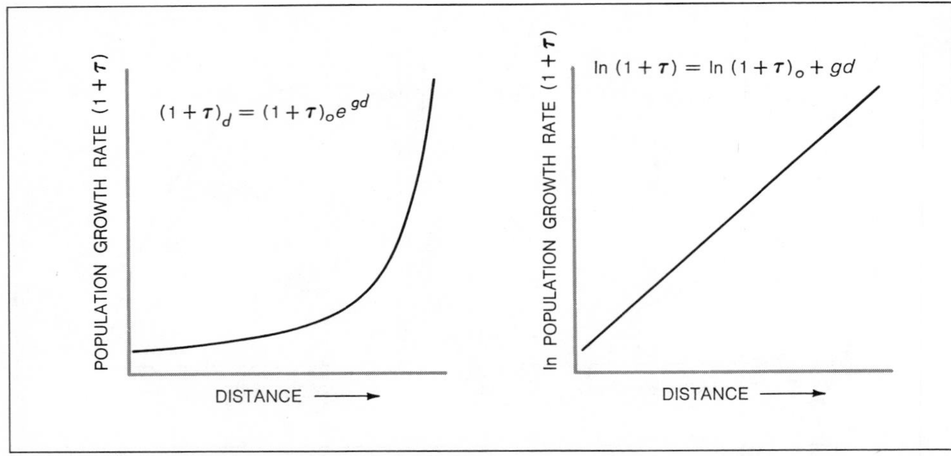

FIG. 10.9. DIAGRAMMATIC REPRESENTATION OF THE RELATIONSHIP BETWEEN POPULATION GROWTH RATE AND DISTANCE FROM THE CBD.

rate is a great deal higher than at the center of the city where the population tends to be a great deal older.

The relationship between the population growth rate and densities If population densities decrease with distance from the center of the city and the growth rate increases with distance from the center of the city, then it is reasonable to assume that the growth rate decreases with population density. Thus the relationship should take the form

$$(I + r)_d = AD_d{}^{-k}$$

where $(I + r)_d$ = population growth rate at distance d
A = a constant, indicating the growth rate when the population density is close to zero
D_d = population density at distance d
$-k$ = a parameter indicating the rate of decrease in population density as the growth rate increases

In natural logarithmic form this equation can be expressed as

$$\ln (I + r)_d = \ln A - k (\ln D)_d$$

This relationship is expressed diagrammatically in Figure 10.10, which suggests that areas of high population density have lower population growth rates than areas of low population densities. Thus at the periphery of the city, where there are low population densities, there are high growth rates; and at the center of the city, where there are high population densities, there are low growth rates.

The situation expressed by the equations relating the population growth rate to

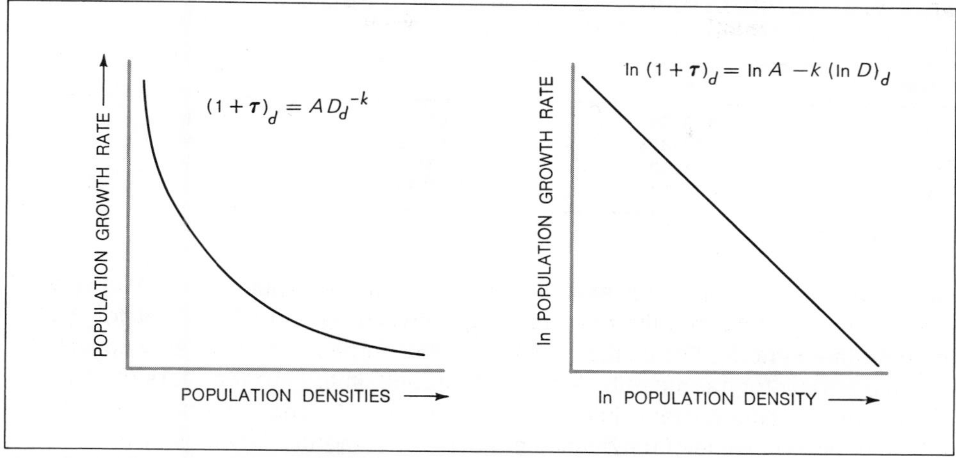

FIG. 10.10. DIAGRAMMATIC REPRESENTATION OF THE RELATIONSHIP BETWEEN POPULATION GROWTH RATE AND URBAN POPULATION DENSITY.

distance and the population growth rate to densities suggests, according to Newling (1966, p. 214), a "rule of intraurban allometric growth." The term *allometric* implies that each part of the urban area is growing in a related pattern to the growth of all other parts. In terms of urban populations, not only is the population growth rate related in a systematic fashion to distance from the center of the city, but also to the density of population itself.

THE URBAN POPULATION OF TORONTO: A CASE STUDY

We have therefore identified four models with respect to urban population densities. These are

$$D_d = D_o e^{-bd} \quad (1)$$
$$b_t = b_{t-\alpha} e^{-ct} \quad (2)$$
$$(l + r)_d = (l + r)_o e^{gd} \quad (3)$$
$$(l + r)_d = AD_d^{-k} \quad (4)$$

These urban population models can be tested with respect to Toronto by using the data that pertains to four time periods between 1951 and 1963. The data refers to the growth in population densities and was enumerated with respect to over 300 equal-area hexagonal cells. Thus, although the data pertains to areas, each one of these is of the same size.

With respect to population densities in metropolitan Toronto, it can be suggested that the relationship postulated by Clark is fairly good for metropolitan Toronto (see Table 10.2). It must be noted, however, that Latham and Yeates (1970) suggest that the second degree polynomial modification postulated by Newling (1969) may be more explicit with respect to the 1963 situation. Continuing with the Clark

TABLE 10.2 METROPOLITAN TORONTO: POPULATION DENSITY-DISTANCE RELATIONSHIPS, 1951–1963

Date	ln D_o	b	R^2
1951	4.73739	−0.21327	64.63
1955	4.86463	−0.19309	67.06
1961	4.81760	−0.15777	64.57
1963	4.80274	−0.14789	63.82

Source: Latham (1967).

model, however, the variances explained by the negative exponential model applied to each time period are quite high, ranging between 63 and 67 percent for the different time periods. The central density parameter has remained fairly constant but the *b* parameter has steadily decreased through time. Thus the Clark model fits the Toronto data for four time periods between 1951 and 1963 fairly well. In fact the decline in value of the density gradient (*b*) conforms very closely to the model suggested by Newling. In Figure 10.11 the density-gradient values have been plotted against time on semilogarithmic paper, and each one of the points fits very closely to the "best-fit" line.

With respect to the population growth rate, models (3) and (4) are also applicable to the situation in metropolitan Toronto between 1951 and 1961. The relationship between the population growth rate and distance from the center of the city is significantly positive, but the variance explained is not very high ($R^2 = 12.4\%$). This is undoubtedly due to the great sectoral variation in growth rates exhibited in Figure 10.4. Interestingly, however, the negative relationship between the 1951-61 decadal growth rate and 1951 population densities is much higher ($R^2 = 45.7\%$). This latter relationship therefore has important implications for urban planners, who are vitally concerned with developing rational models of urban growth.

FIG. 10.11. RELATIONSHIP BETWEEN THE SLOPE OF POPULATION DENSITY GRADIENTS AND TIME IN METROPOLITAN TORONTO.

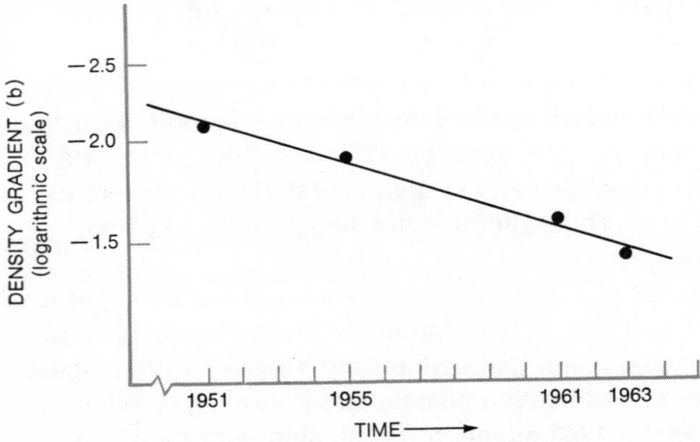

PATTERNS OF RESIDENTIAL LOCATION

Some general descriptive models of urban land use proposed by Burgess (1925), Hoyt (1939), and Harris and Ullman (1945) have been discussed in Chapter 9. These models allocate residential land use within the urban area according to different criteria. The Burgess model suggests that residential patterns will be concentrically spread throughout the city, with the lowest income residential area being found closest to the center of the city and the highest income residential area at the periphery. Thus, in terms of residential types, the implication of the model is that many multifamily dwellings will be found close to the center of the city, with single-family dwellings on larger parcels of land at the periphery. However Burgess's model applies specifically to the problem of assimilation of socio-economic groups within the North American city. The Harris-Ullman model is a general description of the typical location of all types of land use. The model presented by Hoyt, however, relates specifically to the location of residential areas in North American cities.

THE SECTOR THEORY

Hoyt (1939) based his sector theory on an intensive study of the internal residential structure of 142 North American cities in the 1930s. From an analysis of the average block residential rental values of these cities. Hoyt presents a number of specific conclusions. Among these some of the most important are:

1. The highest rental area is located in one or more specific sectors on one side of the city. Generally these high-rent areas are in peripheral locations, though there are instances when a high-rent sector extends continuously out from the center of the city.

2. High-rent areas often take the form of wedges, extending in certain sectors along radial lines leading outward from the center to the periphery of the city.

3. Middle-range rental areas tend to be located on either side of the highest rental areas.

4. There are some cities in which large areas of middle-range rental units tend to be found on the periphery of low-rent residential areas as well as high-rent areas.

5. All cities have low-rent areas, and these are frequently found opposite to the location of the high-rent areas, and usually in the more central locations.

On the basis of these observations, Hoyt rejects the concentric circle theory of city structure and proposes a sectoral pattern as being more persuasive. Accordingly he arranges the rent areas of 30 cities in an ideal pattern of concentric circles in order to show that the greatest variation is not between concentric circles but between sectors (Fig. 10.12). Thus Hoyt states

> From the evidence presented, therefore, it may be concluded that rent areas in American cities tend to conform to a pattern of sectors rather than of concentric circles. The highest rent areas of the city tend to be located in one or more sectors of the city.

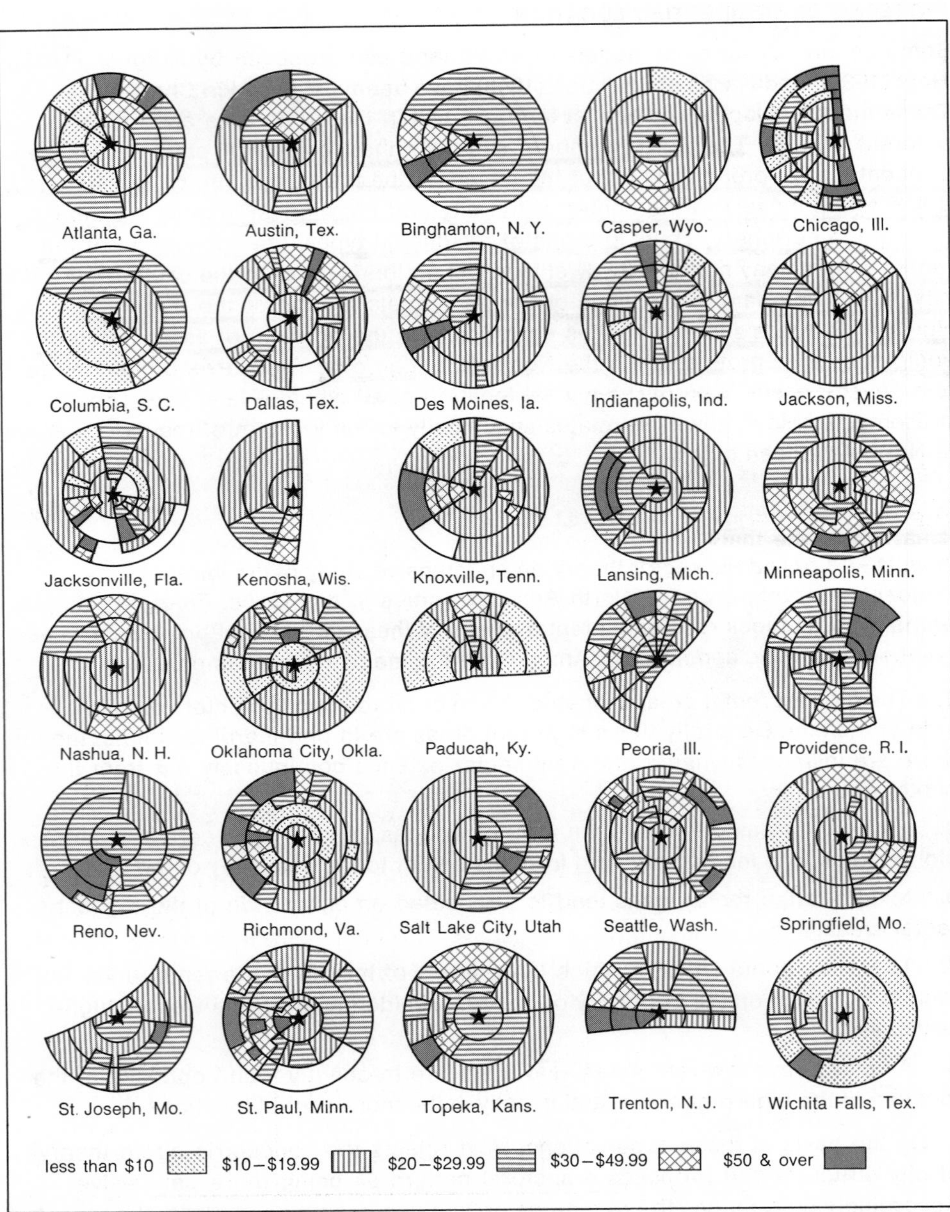

FIG. 10.12. IDEALIZED PATTERN OF RENT AREAS IN 30 AMERICAN CITIES. (*Source:* Hoyt, 1939, Fig. 28.)

There is a gradation of rentals downward from these high-rent areas in all directions. Intermediate-rent areas, or those ranking next to the highest rental areas, adjoin the high-rent area on one or more sides, and tend to be located in the same sectors as the high-rent areas. Low-rent areas occupy other entire sections of the city from the center to the periphery. On the outer edge of some of the high-rent areas are intermediate-rent areas (Hoyt, 1939, p. 76).

In fact, it appears that in no city studied by Hoyt was there a regular upward gradation of residential rental values from the center to the periphery in all directions.

Factors influencing high-grade and low-grade residential development

One of the specific concerns of Hoyt's early analysis of the structure and growth of residential neighborhoods in American cities is the location of high-rent residential areas. Following an analysis of the location of high-rent residential areas in a number of North American cities, he proposed a sector theory of neighborhood change. This theory states: "The high-rent neighborhoods of the city do not skip about at random in the process of movement—they follow a definite path in one or more sectors of the city" (Hoyt, 1939, p. 144). To illustrate this particular point, Hoyt presents cartograms showing the shift in location of high-rent residential areas in six North American cities (Fig. 10.13). The diagrams clearly indicate that the principle has some validity. For example in Boston the high-rent residential area was originally located on the western side of the city and it remained in this sector to 1936 with a new area on the periphery to the southeast. Likewise in Minneapolis the high-grade residential area has always been in the southwestern sector.

Factors influencing the movement of high-rent residential areas

Hoyt (1939, p. 114) indicates the significance of studying the location and movement of high-rent residential areas when he suggests that "the movement of the high-rent area is in a certain sense most important because it tends to pull the growth of the entire city in the same direction." The high-rent residential area in North American cities always has its point of origin at the periphery of the CBD near the retail, financial, and office activities. This point is always farthest removed from the side of the city that has industry or warehouses. The growth of the high-rent residential areas, and concomitantly the city, usually follows one or more principles.

The first of these is that the movement of high-rent residential areas tends to proceed from the given point of origin along established lines of travel or toward another existing nucleus of buildings or trading centers. Thus in many North American cities there are well-known fashionable boulevards along or near which many of the wealthiest and established families are located. Second, high-rent areas tend to be developed on high ground, free from the risk of floods, and to spread along lake, bay, river, and ocean fronts where such waterfronts are not used for industry. Well-known examples of this type of location are the Gold Coast along the waterfront of Lake Michigan in Chicago, Knob Hill in San Francisco, and the "upper-class highlands" in the Bel-Air district of Los Angeles. In a similar context, it is estimated that in Pittsburgh rental values increase by 10 cents for every foot in altitude (Blumenfeld, 1959).

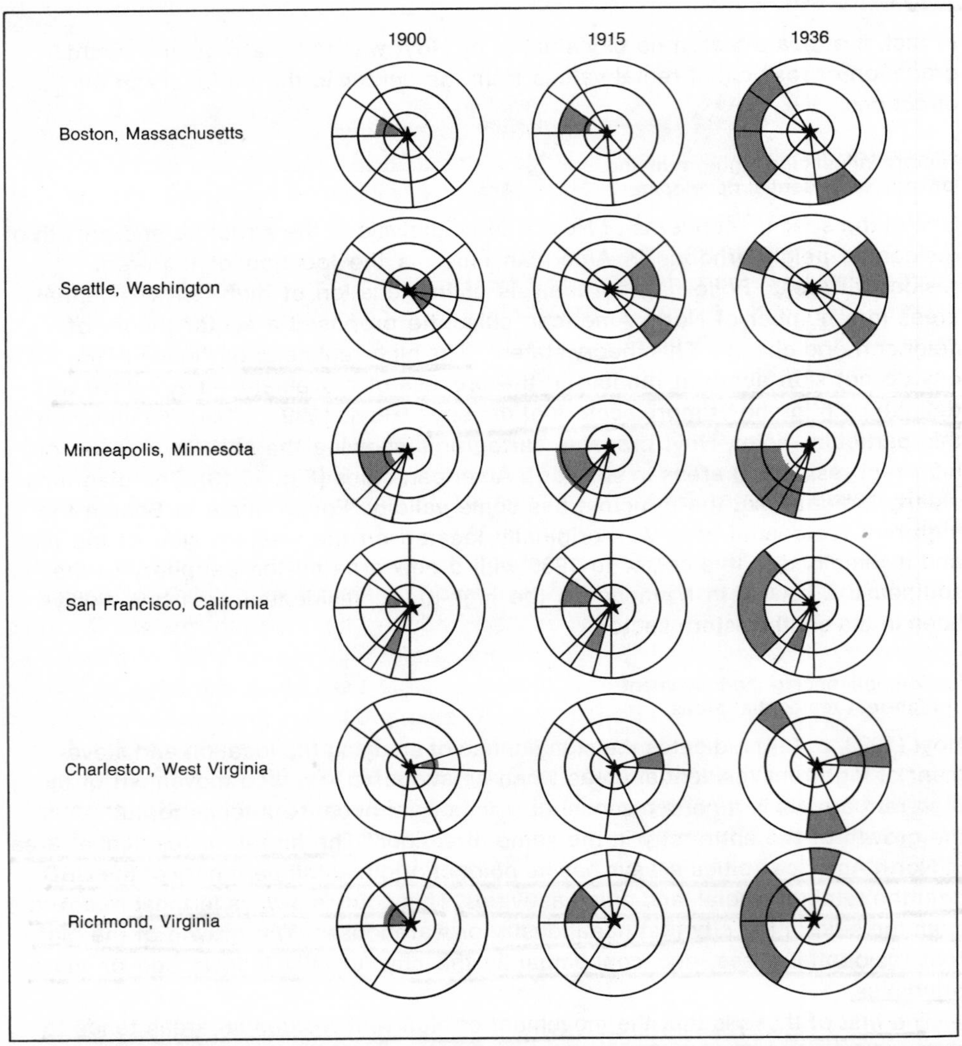

1900 1915 1936

Boston, Massachusetts

Seattle, Washington

Minneapolis, Minnesota

San Francisco, California

Charleston, West Virginia

Richmond, Virginia

FIG. 10.13. THE CHANGING PATTERN OF HIGH-RENT AREAS IN SIX AMERICAN CITIES, 1900–1936. (*Source:* Hoyt, 1939, Fig. 40.)

High-rent residential districts also tend to grow toward the section of the city that has free, open country beyond the edges, and away from dead-end sections that are limited by natural or artificial barriers to expansion. The implication of this particular principle is that there have to be possibilities for further growth and development as well as space for expansion. Thus the development of new golf courses and country clubs today acts as a lure for high-rent residential growth in many North American cities. Another lure is the homes of leaders of the community, for higher priced neighborhoods tend to develop around these. This principle

recognizes the basic snob appeal of most high-rent residential locations, which follows from the quite human desire of most people to wish to locate close to their peers. Thus in the early development of New York the homes of the Astors and the Vanderbilts were the forces that pulled the development of the city in a particular direction.

Trends in the location of office buildings, banks, and stores can also pull higher priced residential neighborhoods in the same general direction. The recent growth of outlying shopping centers in North American cities has resulted in the out migration of a number of retail and service activities. Very often the establishment of a high-class shopping center in which well-known sophisticated department stores, banks, and so forth, are located can result in the growth of adjacent upper income districts by giving an aura of class to the surrounding area. Also the decentralization of office activities can result in the expansion of high-rent residential areas in a particular direction. Frequently these areas are linked by rapid transit lines, which themselves provide good locations for expensive high-rise apartments and condominiums. In Washington, D.C., for example, the best areas are also on the main transportation lines, particularly those leading to the White House, such as Connecticut Avenue, Massachusetts Avenue, and Sixteenth Street.

Finally, real estate promoters may bend the direction of high-grade residential growth. This is of course one of the most important factors influencing residential growth within the city, particularly as the location of the high-rent residential areas appears to have such an important feedback effect on the location of other residential areas and economic activities as well. Ever since the days of the development of the streetcar suburbs, real estate promoters have been increasingly concerned with planning the development and growth of quality residential areas. The profits from such ventures are frequently quite high, particularly today when many promoters form companies that build complete communities, with shopping and business facilities and residential uses all forming part of an overall plan. This is because the highest profits are realized in the construction of the highest-priced residential facilities. The profit margin for the lower-priced residential units is much less, and so contractors are usually less inclined to build lower-income communities.

Factors influencing the location of low-income residential development

In general it is frequently considered that the location of low-income residential areas is strongly influenced by the costs of commuting to work. This particular argument is well expressed by Alonso (1960) in his application of land-value theory to the location of residential areas in cities. His argument suggests that because the costs of transportation form a large part of the total budget of low-income families, but a comparatively smaller part of the total income of wealthier families, low-income families are much more susceptible to the costs of transportation and therefore consider this factor much more in their locational decision. Low-income groups are therefore much more work-place oriented, and low-income residential areas are generally found much closer to the chief areas of employment

within the city. If industrial employment is concentrated close to the CBD, the low-income residential areas will be on that side of the city closest to this area.

It has been noted, however, that there has been a dispersal of employment opportunities to the periphery of many cities (discussed in detail in Chapter 14). This, along with the widespread use of the automobile, has extended the zone of possible location of workingmen's homes to cover, in the case of small cities, almost the entire urban area; and in large cities, a great proportion of it. Under these conditions the individuals who suffer the most are those who cannot afford to purchase and maintain an automobile. In these latter instances their location is very much constrained by the availability of public transportation; and in most cities in the United States, this is a facility that is declining in both quality and availability.

A second factor influencing the location of low-income residential areas is that they are very often occupied by those members of North American society who have suffered or still do suffer to a greater or lesser degree from discrimination, both in terms of employment and in terms of the possibilities of residential site selection. In numerous North American cities Negroes, Puerto Ricans, Indians, and so forth, have suffered from job discrimination, lack of equal opportunity, and a limited availability of housing. This has resulted in the location of these individuals becoming constrained to a certain part or sections of the city. These groups then disperse outward from an original location in a clustered manner (Morrill, 1965). The processes underlying this segregation and dispersion are discussed in the ensuing chapter.

A third factor influencing the location of low-income residential areas refers to the physical attributes of the urban space. The higher incomes seek and can afford the better and most picturesque locations. The middle income takes the next best, leaving the worst and poorest urban sites for the lowest income groups of all. Thus the low-income residential areas are frequently found on the worst drained land and on the side of the city that is the least secluded. Very frequently these areas are also on the side of the city that suffers the most air pollution from surrounding industry, and in many cases the range and scale of the facilities serving the community are badly planned. There is very frequently a shortage of parks, the schools are the oldest and most overcrowded, and the medical facilities are poorly developed. All these conditions ensure that the area will remain in the occupance of the low-income groups.

In terms of change, it has frequently been observed that low-income groups tend to move in and occupy the land and houses or parts of houses previously occupied by the rich. This process is a basic element in Burgess's model and is observed also by Hoyt's sector model. In this latter case as the high- and middle-income groups move outward along a given sectoral path, they are replaced by the low-income groups who occupy the large houses by subdividing them. It is interesting to note that this process has been reversed in a number of urban areas, particularly in those residential areas that contain a number of well-built and well-designed homes that can be modernized. The catalyst for this type of change can be urban renewal, as in the case of Philadelphia, or the introduction of an avant garde "Bohemian" element which gives the neighborhood an artistic appearance and therefore makes it more attractive, such as in Greenwich Village, New York City.

THE LOCATIONAL DECISION

The individual or family's locational decision is the result of a multitude of complex forces. From the individual or family's point of view, two aspects of this decision are paramount. The first involves the location of the house with respect to other features of the urban area, and the second relates to the characteristics of the dwelling unit itself. These two elements are not independent, for frequently the type of dwelling unit is related to its location. For example single-family units are generally found at the periphery of urban areas, whereas multifamily dwelling units are generally found in the central part of the city. Also, new units are found at the periphery and older units are generally found closer to the center. Thus these two elements of the location decision cannot be isolated one from the other. We will therefore examine the location decision in terms of the spatial elements of this decision. These elements are those characteristics that affect the decision-making units. On the demand side these may be described as the location of employment opportunities, the life cycle and social class, and on the supply side we will refer to the supply of housing. As the effect of employment opportunities has been described previously, the discussion at this juncture will concentrate on the life cycle, social class, and the supply of housing.

THE LIFE CYCLE AND THE LOCATIONAL DECISION

North American society is a mobile society. In fact it is estimated that 20 percent of the population of the United States changes residence annually (Simmons, 1968, p. 621). On the average an individual family will move eight or nine times in a lifetime, and five of these moves are considered to be life-cycle moves; that is, moves related to the changing composition of the family of which the individual forms a part (Rossi, 1955, p. 9). The average distribution of these life-cycle moves is indicated in Figure 10.14. Particularly noticeable are the clusters of moves around the period of early adulthood.

FIG. 10.14. CHANGES OF RESIDENCE RELATED TO STAGES IN THE LIFE CYCLE. (*Source:* Simmons, 1968, Fig. 4.)

AGE	STAGE	MOVES
0	Birth	
	Child	1 (Birth–Adolescent)
10	Adolescent	
20	Maturity	1
	Marriage	1
30	Children	1
40		
	Children mature	
50		
60		1 (Children mature–Death)
	Retirement	
70	Death	
80		

This cycle related specifically to middle-class white America.

Typically the situation in Figure 10.14 may be characterized as describing the following situation. During the early years of a person's life, the individual's locational decision is made by his parents, who are the heads of the family. The one move that generally occurs during this period is related to a move made by the parents. Frequently this move is in fact related to the requirements of the children; but generally speaking, the individual with whom we are concerned is not directly brought into the decision making. The next move, which generally occurs during the period of maturity, is frequently associated with the individual's gaining of independence, either as a result of leaving school and getting a job, or frequently in middle-class North America, going on to college or university. The next move comes with marriage. The individual has now once again become part of a family and the decision making is not on the basis of the individual's requirements but of the family's requirements. At this stage in life, the young family may have a large joint income from the two individuals working, and their locational decision may well we determined by a desire for proximity to good and varied recreational facilities. Thus the family may well be located in a downtown area where they can afford a reasonably expensive apartment because of their joint incomes (Bourne, 1968, p. 214).

This conditional wealthy situation and its concomitant desire for a broad range of recreational amenities is usually changed by the arrival of children. Other factors now enter the locational decision. In particular, these are usually the changing housing requirements that the young couple considers to be associated with the raising of children. These housing requirements usually relate to single-family dwelling units with gardens or enclosed play areas and an elementary school within walking distance. Most Americans generally believe that these conditions are available in the suburbs and not available in downtown areas. In particular it must be noted that the desire for locations within the districts of good schools is generally preeminent for the middle class. The last move mentioned in Figure 10.14 may well be a desire for more housing space as the family gets larger, a move as a result of the family decreasing in size due to the children leaving home, or simply retirement.

It is evident that the situation referred to in Figure 10.14 relates specifically to middle-class white America. Many people have more complex life cycles, but the general effect of the life cycle on decision making is quite clear. In fact it may well be suggested that not only the life cycle but the life style is increasingly becoming the major determinant of residential location, for in a sense the cycle greatly affects the style of living (Erikson, 1968). In particular, it is evident that the life style led, or presumed to be followed, by the conditional wealthy has a great effect on the design and services offered by downtown high-rise apartments and on the advertising industry.

SOCIAL CLASS AND RESIDENTIAL LOCATION

One of the fundamental realities of the social structure of North America is that there is a fairly rigid set of social classes. Social class in this environment is greatly determined by occupation, income, race, and in the highest classes of all, family. In the ensuing chapter we will suggest that urban areas in North America can be subdivided into distinct social class communities in which there is very little variation in class type. Thus if a person or family attains a higher social rank through a change in occupation or an increase in income, this change may well be associated with a change in residential location. However, Lipset and Bendix (1959) suggest that only a small proportion of North Americans leave the social class into which they were born, so change in social class only affects a small proportion of residential location decisions.

Thus, most people who change their location of residence do so to a part of the city that is of the same social class as that from which they originated. If there is a move upward, this is usually to an area of the city occupied by the next higher social class; a movement downward is usually to an area of the next lower social class. This situation is admirably expressed with respect to data from Rhode Island in Table 10.3. From this table it can be observed that 63.8 percent of all persons who moved from the highest social-class area moved to another high social-class area, and that 51 percent who moved from the second highest social-class area moved to an area that was also of the second highest social class. Noticeably the values on the diagonal of the matrix are always very large but decrease toward the lower social-class areas. Here 48.1 percent of the people who originated in the lowest social class moved to another area that was also of the lowest social class, and 17.4 percent moved up to the next higher (class 4) and 17.3 percent moved up two classes (to class 3). The general upward mobility of society is indicated by the fact that the largest percentages on the off-diagonals are to the left of the diagonal, whereas the smaller percentages are to the right (indicating downward movement).

Of course, this pattern is severely disrupted in many North American cities by ethnic patterns. In some instances particular ethnic groups are very much restricted in their spatial location. Furthermore some have a range of social ranks within their own particular area which have very definite spatial locations. For example in North America some urban areas have particular Jewish suburbs of various income levels and Catholic areas of particular income levels. Thus the process often works within minority groupings as well as among the majority. As the barriers between the ethnic groups progressively disappear, it is likely that the locational criteria of social class based purely on the criteria of income will increase in strength.

TABLE 10.3. MOVES AMONG SOCIAL AREAS (IN PERCENTAGES)

Social Class (origin tract)	1	2	3	4	5
1 (High)	63.8	12.0	11.3	8.2	4.7
2	8.2	51.0	20.6	13.3	6.9
3	6.1	18.8	50.4	16.7	8.0
4	5.1	13.0	21.0	52.7	8.2
5 (Low)	4.1	13.2	17.3	17.4	48.0

Source: Goldstein and Mayer (1961), p. 51.

THE SUPPLY OF HOUSING

A very important element influencing the locational decision is the varying supply of housing available to the consumer. On the one hand not all types of housing are built everywhere in an urban community. Modern high-rise apartments are frequently located downtown or close to limited access expressways. Single-family dwelling units with large yards usually are found at the periphery of the city, duplexes and row houses with small yards are commonly found in the central city. Thus if a family desires a particular type of dwelling unit, it can locate only where that type of dwelling unit is available. Also the dwelling units themselves vary in age and style, and frequently they group in various parts of the city.

Dwelling units become available for occupancy through being vacated or through new housing stock. Vacated dwelling units can occur at one extreme through the elimination of the family (by death), but more commonly vacancies occur through people changing their residence by moving. Given the rapid rate of increase of the North American population, it is evident that housing space for new families can be provided only by increasing the stock through new construction. This new housing stock is usually located at the periphery of the urban area, for land in sufficient quantities is available only in these fringe zones. This is reinforced by the fact that it is easier to obtain federally insured mortgages on new housing than for renovated older housing. Thus in a sense the federal governments in both the United States and Canada have encouraged the sprawl of the city and have done little to support the possible redevelopment of the central city.

The filtering process The mobility of families from one housing submarket to another involves a filtering process (Smith, 1964). This process can be perceived in both economic and social terms. In an economic sense the process describes

> . . . the changing of occupancy as the housing that is occupied by one income group becomes available to the next lower income group as a result of a decline in market price . . . (Ratcliff, 1949, p. 321).

From the point of view of the house itself, this can be interpreted as the

> . . . change over time in the position of a dwelling unit or group of dwelling units within the distribution of housing prices and rents in the community as a whole (Fisher and Winnick, 1951, p. 49).

The implication of the economic view of filtering is that if the relative price of the housing decreases more rapidly than the quality, then the lower-income groups will be able to afford successively better quality housing.

The latter implication reveals the social interpretation of the filtering concept. A rapid rate of downward filtering in relative house prices will make possible an upward filtering of income groups into better quality housing. Conversely, a low rate of downward filtering in house prices would result in limited possibilities of upward filtering of income groups into better quality housing (Grebler, 1952).

Factors affecting the rate of filtering In general terms there are two factors affecting the rate of filtering—the rate of construction of housing and the demand, or rate of family formation. If the rate of new housing construction, implying a favorable mortgage market, is in excess of the demand, then it would be possible for the relative value of older housing to decrease quite quickly. The depth of the downward filtering of the housing stock varies according to the range in value of the new housing being constructed. If new housing were available primarily for the upper-income groups, then upward filtering would be possible for all income groups, with the low-income group occupying the homes previously owned by the more wealthy. The provision of only low-income housing would limit upward filtering to the low-income groups.

The suggestion therefore arises that better housing for all can be encouraged by a vigorous rate of construction of middle- and high-priced housing. This will encourage a high rate of downward filtering of houses, and therefore a high rate of upward filtering in house quality for all socio-economic groups. The ethical morality of providing new housing for only the wealthy, however, is dubious. Probably a better policy would be to provide new housing in all price ranges—the rate of upward filtering that results may be lower but at least new housing would be available to some people in every income group.

If the demand is in excess of the supply, the value of the housing stock may decrease more slowly than the quality, and in extreme cases the values may well not decrease at all; and all types of homes may show a relative increase. Under these conditions the possibility for the upward filtering of socio-economic groups into better quality housing is severely limited. In fact, there may be a downward filtering of socio-economic groups into lower-quality housing, with the higher-income groups preempting the homes previously occupied by the less wealthy. Under these conditions the lowest incomes suffer the most as they are forced to occupy marginal or substandard dwellings at quite high rents (Lansing, et al., 1969).

Thus the filtering concept has important policy and planning implications. In terms of policy, the intricate interrelationship of mortgage markets and the type of housing being provided has very important social implications. For the urban planner, the variation in the rate of filtering in different parts of the city is a vital indicator of neighborhood change, and therefore possible blight. Also it is evident that filtering is one of the chief processes involved in the resorting of people within the city into groups according to different criteria. The results of this resorting are described in Chapter 11.

"THE SOCIAL GEOGRAPHY OF URBAN AREAS"

11

A quick "windshield" inspection of a cross section of residential streets in any North American city reveals a variety of social, economic, and ethnic characteristics. In some areas the houses are new, large, and obviously occupied by high-income families. Other areas are older, consisting of walk-up apartments, children are playing on the streets, and the small local stores are owned by people with Germanic, Scandinavian, or other ethnic-sounding names. The differences between these two areas are based on a number of criteria, such as housing, density, and ethnicity; though in some instances a single characteristic may convey the image of the area. For example in Novak's (1956) study of Puerto Ricans in Manhattan, a grouping of contiguous census tracts, each with more than 40 percent of the population Puerto Rican, was sufficient to define a community.

COMMUNITIES AND NEIGHBORHOODS

The concept of community and neighborhood is essentially ecological and has its urban roots in the pioneering work of Park, Burgess, and McKenzie at the University of Chicago in the 1920s (Burgess and Bogue, 1964, pp. 2–14). They assumed that the processes recognized by plant and animal ecologists as operating in the natural environment could be applied, with modification, to the social sphere. Thus human ecology developed as a science which is ". . . fundamentally interested in the effect of position, in both time and space, upon human institutions and human behavior" (Park, et al., 1925, p. 64).

The geographic importance of the ecological view is, of course, that it is essentially spatial and behavioristic. Man, though he may be acculturated or conditioned by his cultural heritage, is, nevertheless, an animal with basic animal instincts concerning territory and space. Indeed, Chombart de Lauwe (1965, pp. 94–98) indicates that there is a complex interrelationship between the space habitually occupied by man and the way in which man perceives and understands that space. Furthermore, he contends that there are cultural variations in the way in which space is perceived and in man's reaction to it.

In terms of urban densities, the same writer suggests that there are certain critical space limits above and below which French working-class families develop psychological disturbances. Pathologies are apparently at a minimum with 90–140 square feet of interior household space per person and increase both above and below these limits.

In terms of exterior space, there is some evidence to support the notion that man is happiest in a prescribed safe territory. If an individual regards the environment as threatening and unsafe, then he is more likely to subconsciously desire and protect a safe home (Rainwater, 1966). Young children need prescribed spatial limits and are quite happy in playing within a limited territorial range, as long as the basic facilities for play, such as sand boxes, climbers, and so forth, are available (White, 1963). Even older children have a closely defined territory: "A typical Harlem Negro up to the age of thirteen usually lives in a four-block territorial world" (Bragdon, 1967, p. 32), and youth gangs are basically concerned with territorial protection.

THE COMMUNITY

The term *community* is one of the most widely used but difficult to understand terms in the literature of urban geography. Frequently, the word is used synonymously with *neighborhood,* but in the context of this discussion it will have a specific meaning. We will regard the community as a

> social unit which consists of persons who share a common geographic area interacting in terms of a common culture and which incorporates a range of social structures which function to meet a relatively broad range of needs of all persons who make up the social unit (Popenoe, 1969, p. 70).

In this sense the community is comparable with the *quartier* in French urban areas (Caplow, 1952, p. 547). In both these cases the community is a clearly defined area of subculture of the urban landscape having a distinctive appearance, with its own local industry and commerce, its housing forms, family types, collective attitudes, formal associations, and frequently its own dialect and folklore. Thus in many settlements the community may well be bounded by the municipal limits of the entire urban region, while in large cities it may well be just one part of the metropolis.

Social area analysis One approach at defining communities in urban areas has been through the technique of social area analysis, a method originally proposed by Shevky, Bell, and Williams (1949; 1955). The method involves the application of a set of procedures for classifying census tracts with respect to three indexes: economic status, family status, and ethnic status. These indexes are derived from a set of hypotheses concerning the nature of societal change through time. Society is viewed as having changed from a rural to an urban-industrial state, and this change is represented by an increasing scale of complexity of social organization. The three postulates that provide the foundation for the indexes are presented in Column 1 of Table 11.1.

The first hypothesis suggests that as society changes from a rural to an urban-industrial state, there is a change in the range and intensity of relations between families and individuals. The statistics considered by Shevky and Bell (1955) as interpretive of these trends involve the changing distribution of skills associated with industrialization. These refer, in particular, to the decreasing importance of manual productive occupations and a growing importance of clerical, supervisory, and management occupations. Thus society becomes differentiated by the derived construct *economic status,* or *social rank.* Columns 5 and 6 indicate the census tract data used by the social area analysts to determine the economic status of a particular census tract.

The second postulate suggests that the structure of the family is affected by the differentiation of functions that occur with the changing structure of productive activity. These are directly related to a decrease in the importance of primary production and a growing importance of activities of a secondary and tertiary nature. In the primary-rural state the entire family is involved in a production process that is agrocentric. The urban-industrial family, on the other hand, is less

TABLE 11.1. STEPS IN (SHEVKY) CONSTRUCT FORMATION AND INDEX CONSTRUCTION

Postulates Concerning Industrial Society (Aspects of Increasing Scale) (1)	Statistics of Trends (2)		Changes in the Structure of a Given Social System (3)		Constructs (4)		Sample Statistics (Related to the Constructs) (5)		Derived Measures (From Column 5) (6)	
Change in the range and intensity of relations	Changing distribution of skills; lessening importance of manual productive operations — growing importance of clerical, supervisory, management operations.	→	Changes in the arrangement of occupations based on function.	→	Social rank (economic status)	→	Years of schooling, employment status, class of worker, major occupation group, value of home, rent by dwelling unit, plumbing and repair, persons per room, heating and refrigeration.	→	Occupation, schooling, rent.	Index I
Differentiation of function	Changing structure of productive activity. Lessening importance of primary production — growing importance of relations centered in cities — lessening importance of the household as economic unit.	→	Changes in the ways of living — movement of women into urban occupations — spread of alternative family patterns.	→	Family status (urbanization)	→	Age and sex, owner or tenant, house structure, persons in household.	→	Fertility, women at work, Single-family dwelling units.	Index II
Complexity of organization	Changing composition of population: increasing movement — alterations in age and sex distribution — increasing diversity.	→	Redistribution in space, changes in the proportion of supporting and dependent population, isolation and segregation of groups.	→	Segregation (ethnic status)	→	Race and nativity, country of birth, citizenship.	→	Racial and national groups in relative isolation.	Index III

Source: After Shevky and Bell (1955), p. 4.

unitary and may well be concerned with a number of different kinds of occupations. The family status index therefore consists of derived measures (Column 6 derived from Column 5) concerning female fertility ratios, the proportion of women at work, and the ratio of single-family dwelling units to all others in a census tract.

Ethnic status, the third construct of the social analysts, is based on a hypothesis that the population becomes more complex with the increasing scale of urban industrial activity and that this complexity is a result of mobility and a redistribution of the population in space. Thus there is, in effect, a tendency for the sorting out of population in terms of its age, sex, and ethnic background. In North America this resorting is particularly marked by ethnic composition and color. The statistics used to compile this index of segregation relate particularly to race, country of birth, and citizenship. Those census tracts with a high proportion of their population consisting of a particular race, or coming from a particular country, are considered to be areas of high ethnic status.

The Social Areas of San Francisco, 1950

As an example of the use of social area analysis for defining the spatial location of different types of communities, the constructs are presented as defined by Shevky and Bell for San Fransisco in Figure 11.1. These maps are part of a much larger study that, in fact, pertained to the whole San Francisco Bay area in 1950. Figure 11.1A illustrates the spatial distribution of the social rank construct and indicates that the highest social rank tracts are on the western and northern part of the peninsula, whereas the lower ranked tracts are generally on the east facing the bay. This, of course, reflects the historical development of San Francisco, for industry, commerce, and shipping activities are located on the bay.

The family status map (Fig. 11.1B) shows that the highest family status (or low urbanization) tracts are in the southern part of San Francisco, whereas the lowest family status (or high urbanization) is in the central and northern part of the city. Finally, the tracts of greatest segregation are generally in the eastern part of the city, with the greatest concentration being in the core or downtown part in the northeast. A generalized composite of these three constructs (Fig. 11.1C) indicates the existence of a high social rank–low family status quadrant in the southwest, a high family status–low social rank area with some segregated tracts in the east and south, a high social rank–low family status area with a number of segregated tracts in the central and northern part of the city, and a small area of low family status–low social rank tracts with some segregation in the old wharf area of the city in the central part.

The Social Areas of Winnipeg, 1961

There have been some severe criticisms of social area analysis involving both the theoretical base and the statistics used in the methodology (Hawley and Duncan, 1957; Udrey, 1964). Although the social area analysts cite the works of Clark (1951A), Florence (1952), Ogburn (1933), and Wirth (1938) in support of their thesis,

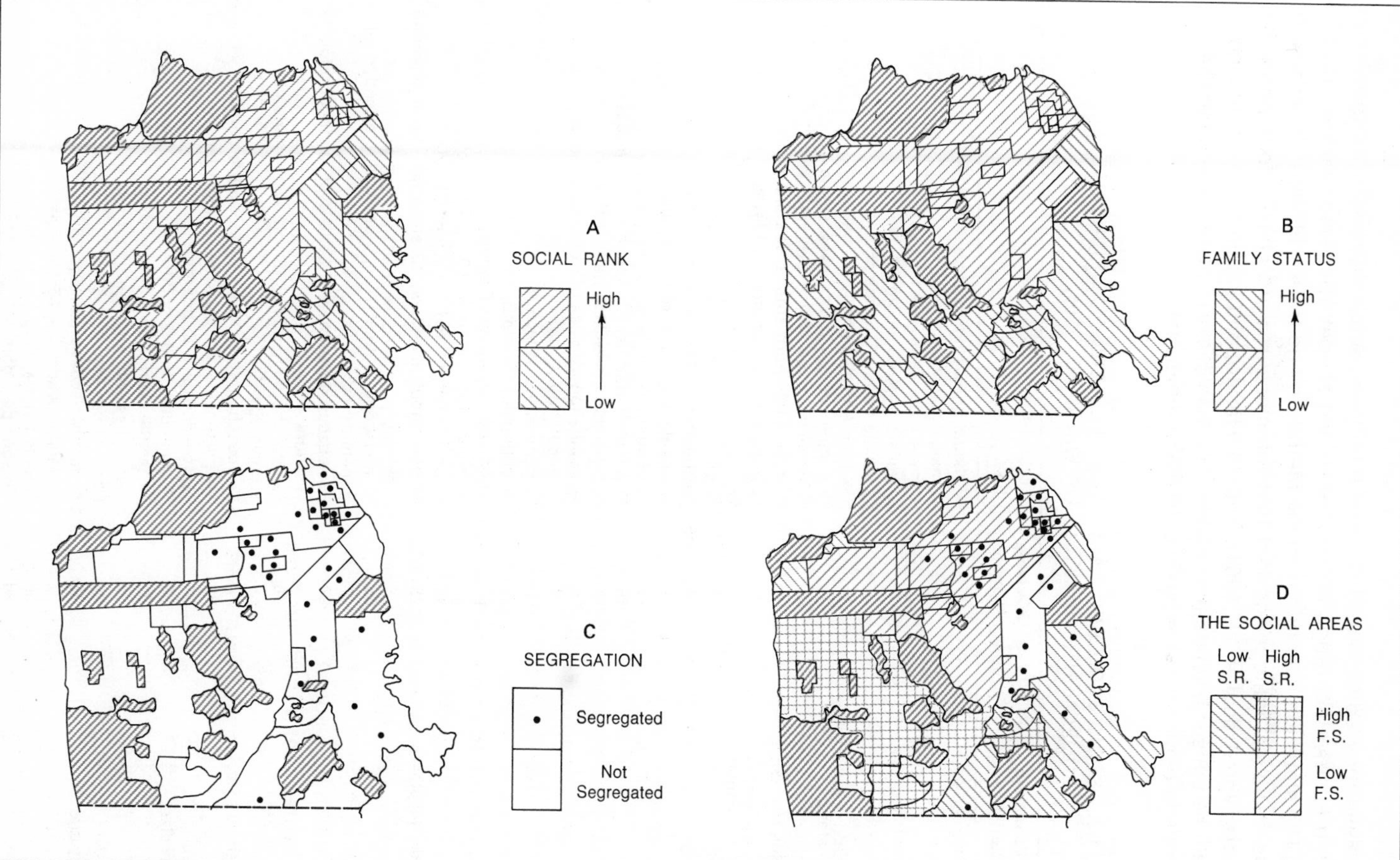

FIG. 11.1. THE SOCIAL AREAS OF SAN FRANCISCO, 1950. (*Source:* After Shevky and Bell, 1955, Fig. V. 14.)

nevertheless they admit that ". . . the theory, as presently stated, is too sketchy. It needs elaboration in both detail and scope" (Bell and Moskos, 1964, p. 416). The statistical objections to the method range from criticisms of census tracts as statistical units to the fact that the measures are chosen to support the constructs (Van Ardsol, et al., 1961). With this latter point in mind, it is interesting to use all the census tract data available for urban areas to observe whether the constructs do conform to the basic underlying dimensions.

TABLE 11.2. SOCIO-ECONOMIC VARIABLES SELECTED FOR PRINCIPAL COMPONENTS ANALYSIS OF WINNIPEG, 1961

Socio-Economic Characteristics	Variable Number	Title
Population change	1	% annual population change, 1956–1961
Age structure	2	% male population, age 0–19
	3	% male population, age 65 and over
	4	% female population, age 0–19
	5	% female population, age 65 and over
Sex ratio	6	Sex ratio (females per 1,000 males)
Marital status	7	% population age 15 and over, single
	8	% population age 15 and over, married
Birthplace	9	% population, born outside of Canada
	10	% population immigrated, 1946–1961
Ethnic allegiance	11	% population, British Isles ethnic group
	12	% population, French ethnic group
	13	% population, German ethnic group
	14	% population, Polish ethnic group
	15	% population, Ukrainian ethnic group
	16	% population, other European ethnic groups[a]
	17	% population, speaking neither English nor French
	18	% population, Anglican Church of Canada
	19	% population, Greek Orthodox
	20	% population, Jewish
	21	% population, Lutheran
	22	% population, Roman Catholic
	23	% population, Ukrainian (Greek) Catholic
	24	% population, United Church of Canada
Educational status	25	% nonschool attenders, 15 and over, never attended school
	26	% nonschool attenders, 15 and over, attended elementary school
	27	% nonschool attenders, 15 and over, attended high school
	28	% nonschool attenders, 15 and over, attended university
Household size	29	% households, occupied by 6 or more persons
	30	% households, occupied by a single family
	31	% households with boarders
Family size	32	% families with 0–2 children
	33	% families with 5 or more children
	34	% families with children under age 6
	35	Persons per family
Family age	36	% family heads, under age 25
	37	% family heads, age 65 and over
	38	Rooms per dwelling
	39	Persons per room

Nicholson and Yeates (1969) use principal components analysis to determine the basic dimensions of socio-economic variation in Winnipeg in 1961. Each one of the 84 census tracts is characterized by 70 different variables, each of which is a percentage measure of a socio-economic characteristic (Table 11.2). In effect, these variables comprise almost all of the measured socio-economic characteristics available in the census data—a few were deleted because of inappropriateness or lack of complete coverage. The analysis indicated that nearly 76 percent of the variation in the original 70 variables could be accounted for by five dimensions.

TABLE 11.2. (Continued)

Socio-Economic Characteristics	Variable Number	Title
Amenities	40	% households, with flush toilet (excl. use)
	41	% households, with refrigerator
	42	% households, with television
	43	% households, with passenger automobile
Working women	44	% females age 15 and over, in labor force (L. F.)
Male labor-force structure	45	% male L. F. wage earners
	46	% employed male L. F., managerial
	47	% employed male L. F., professional and technical
	48	% employed male L. F., clerical
	49	% employed male L. F., sales
	50	% employed male L. F., services & recreation
	51	% employed male L. F., transport and communication
	52	% employed male L. F., craftsmen and related activities
	53	% employed male L. F., laborers
Female labor-force structure	54	% employed female L. F., managerial
	55	% employed female L. F., professional and technical
	56	% employed female L. F., clerical
	57	% employed female L. F., sales
	58	% employed female L. F., service and recreation
	59	% employed female L. F., craftsmen and related activities
	60	% employed female L. F., transportation and communication, primary and laborers
Wage and salary income	61	Average male wage and salary income
	62	Average female wage and salary income
	63	Wage and salary income per family
Family income	64	% families, with incomes under $3,000
	65	% families, with incomes $3,000–$7,000
	66	% families, with incomes $7,000–$10,000
	67	% families. with incomes $10,000 and over
Residential stability	68	% population, age 5 and over, nonmovers 1956–1961[b]
	69	% population, age 5 and over, movers from central city, 1956–1961
	70	% population, age 5 and over, movers from fringe area, 1956–1961

[a] These comprise European ethnic groups other than British, French, German, Italian, Dutch, Polish, Russian, Scandinavian, and Ukrainian.

[b] Variables 68–70 are based on "estimates of population by mobility status (which were derived from a 20 percent sample of persons 15 years old and over residing in private households," Census of Canada, Dominion Bureau of Statistics, *Migration, Fertility and Income by Census Tracts,* Series CX, Bulletin CX–1, Catalogue 95–541 (1961), p. 1. The remainder of the variables are based on complete census returns.

The first of these is a dimension describing census tracts consisting of many high- and middle-income families of British Isles ethnic stock, which belong to the Anglican or United Church. The male labor force described by this component usually has completed high school, in many cases has a university education, and as a consequence is employed in professional, managerial, and technical occupations. Although only a few of the females work, those that do are often clerical or professional employees, and they earn relatively high salaries. The general affluence of the group defined by this component is indicated by the fact that it is well equipped with amenities such as automobiles and television. This dimension therefore defines a group that can be defined as high- and middle-income Anglo-Saxon Protestants, the characteristics of which conform very closely to those of the social rank construct of the social area analysts.

The second dimension describes a group consisting of large, but mostly young families living in single-family houses. Most of the adult population is married; most of them own cars; and although many have only a few years of education, they nevertheless receive middle-range incomes from work in transportation and communication activities or as craftsmen. There is a relative absence of elderly people and females in the labor force within this group. Thus the second component describes a group that can be defined as consisting of young, middle-income families, the characteristics of which comprise those of the family status construct.

The third dimension consists of a group composed primarily of "Other European" and Jewish people, many of whom have attended university and are now employed in a managerial capacity; and generally family incomes are greater than $10,000 per year. This component can therefore be described as representing general non-Anglo-Saxon affluence. The fourth component consists of French-speaking Roman Catholics and large families, characteristics that obviously describe the French-Canadian ethnic group. The last dimension describes census tracts that contain a large proportion of Eastern European Ukrainian (Greek) Catholics, which have received few recent immigrants and which are undergoing a population decline. These tracts have relatively few young people in them and few large families or households and obviously describes a residual Eastern European group. These last three components together define three distinct dimensions conforming very closely to the ethnic status construct of the social area analysts.

NEIGHBORHOODS

Communities subdivide into smaller areas called *neighborhoods.* Burgess illustrates the distinction by adopting a land value definition of a community:

> The centers of local communities are to be found at the point of highest land value in the intersection of two business streets . . . If high land values indicate the center of the community, the lowest land values generally define its periphera. But if the intersection of two business streets determines the trade center, these same streets divide it into neighborhoods (Park, et al., 1925, pp. 148–149).

Each neighborhood has its own public school, its own church, its own social center, and frequently its own local shopping street. These characteristics usually act singly or in harmony as the focus of the neighborhood, the limits of which are usually set by the average length of convenient walking distance. It is interesting to note that Burgess comments favorably on the role of the neighborhood as a moral decision-making force.

The automobile and the associated spreading out of the city have resulted in a change in the concept of the neighborhood beyond the central city. Although many subdivisions are constructed with some rudimentary knowledge of the neighborhood concept, frequently this goes only so far as religious institutions. Planned shopping centers are usually built to cater to a number of neighborhood subdivisions, and the busing of children to large economic high schools reinforces the fluidity of society. Thus the trend beyond the central city seems to be away from the neighborhood as a social unit and toward the community as a unit of organization. The problem that emerges frequently, however, is that people identify more readily with small spatial units than with larger ones. In these cases what is needed is some catalyst to foster neighborhood-community affiliation.

PATTERNS

The urban geographer is usually interested in the manner in which these socio-economic areas are distributed within the city. Maps of social variation can be constructed using a variety of methods. At one extreme can be distinguished the univariable map, and at the other extreme is the multivariable map. The most important aspect of this type of analysis is the search for order in spatial patterns, and the fundamental concern involves the development of some rationale to explain this pattern. This procedure should in fact be reversed, but research in urban social geography usually has not progressed from theory to patterns, but the other way around.

UNI- AND MULTIVARIABLE PATTERNS

Univariable patterns are those that are described on the basis of a single characteristic. Thus in the context of the definition of regions they are synonymous with single-factor regions. Multivariable patterns describe regions based on a number of characteristics which have to be synthesized to define a single dimension. This synthesis results in the definition of multifactor regions, as discussed in Chapter 1.

Puerto Ricans in Manhattan Figure 11.2A is based on the proportion of the total population in each census tract in Manhattan in 1950 that can be classified as Puerto Rican. Novak (1959) states that at that time only 5 of the 284 census tracts in Manhattan were between 40 and 76 percent Puerto Rican, and none exceeded 76 percent. These tracts are to the south of a black ghetto known as Harlem, and

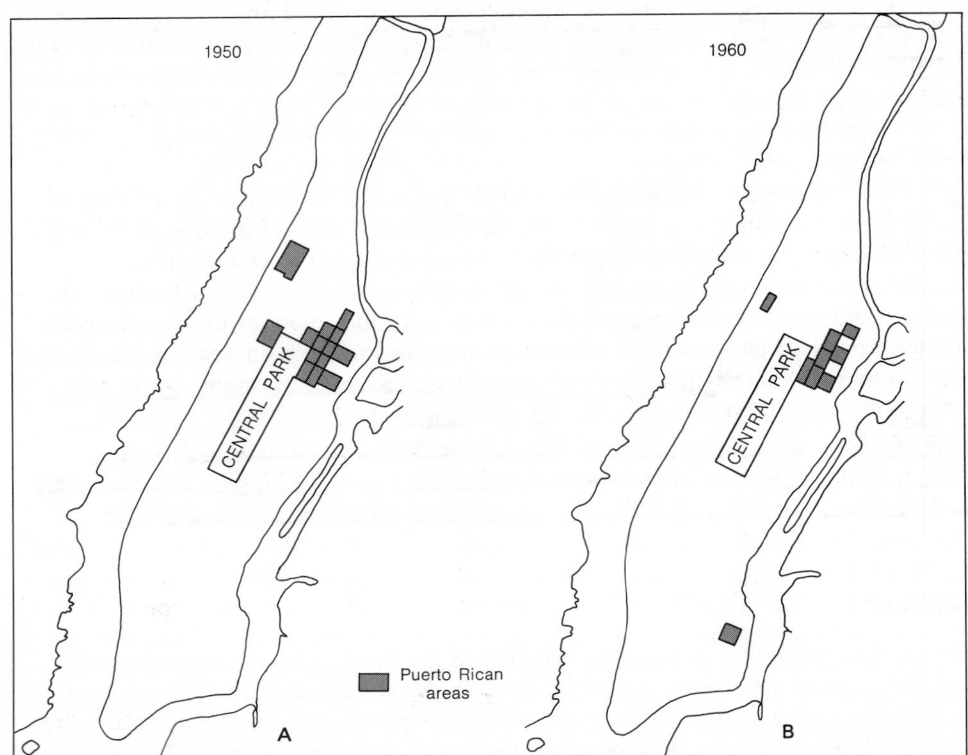

FIG. 11.2. THE DISTRIBUTION OF PUERTO RICANS ON MANHATTAN ISLAND, NEW YORK CITY: (A) THE 1950 PATTERN DELIMITED BY NOVAK; (B) THE 1960 PATTERN DELIMITED BY CAREY. (*Source*: Adapted from Novak, 1956, Fig. 1, and Carey, 1966, Fig. 2.)

for that reason form the core of an area that is referred to as "Spanish Harlem" or "the Barrio." The reasons for this and other minor centers of concentration in Manhattan are considered by Novak to be twofold: (1) low-cost housing where extended families can coexist or friends live with others who speak the same language; (2) the availability of public transportation, which is vital for the majority of Puerto Ricans who are employed in the downtown service trades.

A multivariable analysis of the 1960 census tract data for Manhattan (Fig. 11.2B) provides more detail concerning the socio-economic characteristics of this Puerto Rican subgroup, and a modification of the distributional pattern described by Novak. As a result of a principal components analysis of thirty-three socio-economic variables, Carey (1966) defines a Puerto Rican subpopulation factor as including many children of elementary and high school age, with the labor force employed in the garment trades and eating and drinking places, and generally unsound and overcrowded housing. The map illustrates that the Puerto Rican core area extends eastward to cover seven census tracts rather than five.

The social geography of Metropolitan Toronto, 1951 and 1961 One of the most comprehensive multivariate ecological analyses of an urban area has been undertaken by Murdie (1969) for Metropolitan Toronto using a principal components analysis of 86 socio-economic variables. These variables concerned occupations, income, dwellings, ethnic backgrounds, language, religion, sex, and school characteristics of census tracts. The results of this analysis indicate that there are nine significant dimensions of variation in both time periods and that the variable constituents of the dimensions are comparable between time periods. The dimensions that show the greatest consistency are those summarizing variations in economic status, family status, and recent growth. The remaining dimensions are also similar at both time periods, for

> a factor describing ethnic status in the 1951 analysis separated into two independent factors in the 1961 analysis: Italian ethnic status and Jewish ethnic status. In contrast, two independent factors from the 1951 study which were identified as service-employment and household characteristics consolidated into one component comprising both household and employment characteristics in the 1961 analysis (Murdie, 1969, p. 76).

Thus, factors comparable to the social-area constructs are the dominant underlying dimensions of the original 86 socio-economic variables in both 1951 and 1961.

The spatial relationships of these social areas or communities and ethnic groups of Toronto are expressed diagrammatically in Figure 11.3. It is to be noted that Murdie recognizes concentric zones distorted by the underlying pattern of transportation, with small families close to the center of the city and large families at the periphery. Juxtaposed with this concentric pattern is a zonal arrangement of census tracts of low and high economic status families and individuals. Finally, clustered around the metropolis but conforming to the underlying concentric family status and zonal economic status patterns are certain ethnic groups.

Recurring patterns Evidence for the concentric, zonal, and clustered patterns presented by Murdie for Toronto has been recognized previously by a number of social area analysts. Anderson and Egeland (1961) concluded from social-area analyses of Akron (Ohio), Dayton (Ohio), Indianapolis (Indiana), and Syracuse (New York), that family status was concentric phenomenon and social rank sectoral. De Vise notes a rather more confusing pattern for metropolitan Chicago:

> The rings are shown to contain towns of similar residential employment functions. Sectors, at least within the first two rings, are found to have towns of similar income characteristics. Zones, the composites of rings and sectors, are seen as areas of relatively homogenous functions and characteristics (De Vise, 1960, p. 6).

These empirical studies, and others, have led Berry (1965) to hypothesize that, in general, there are three spatial patterns of socio-economic variation. The first is the axial or sectoral variation of neighborhoods by socio-economic rank. The second is the concentric variation of neighborhoods according to family structure. The third is the localized segregation of particular ethnic groups in pockets, which conforms to some multiple nuclei pattern.

These hypotheses are represented diagrammatically in Figure 11.4. Social rank varies from high to low, and its theoretical spatial distribution conforms closely to the locational mechanisms implicit in Hoyt's sector theory. The family status (or, its inverse, urbanization) construct has its conceptual counter-

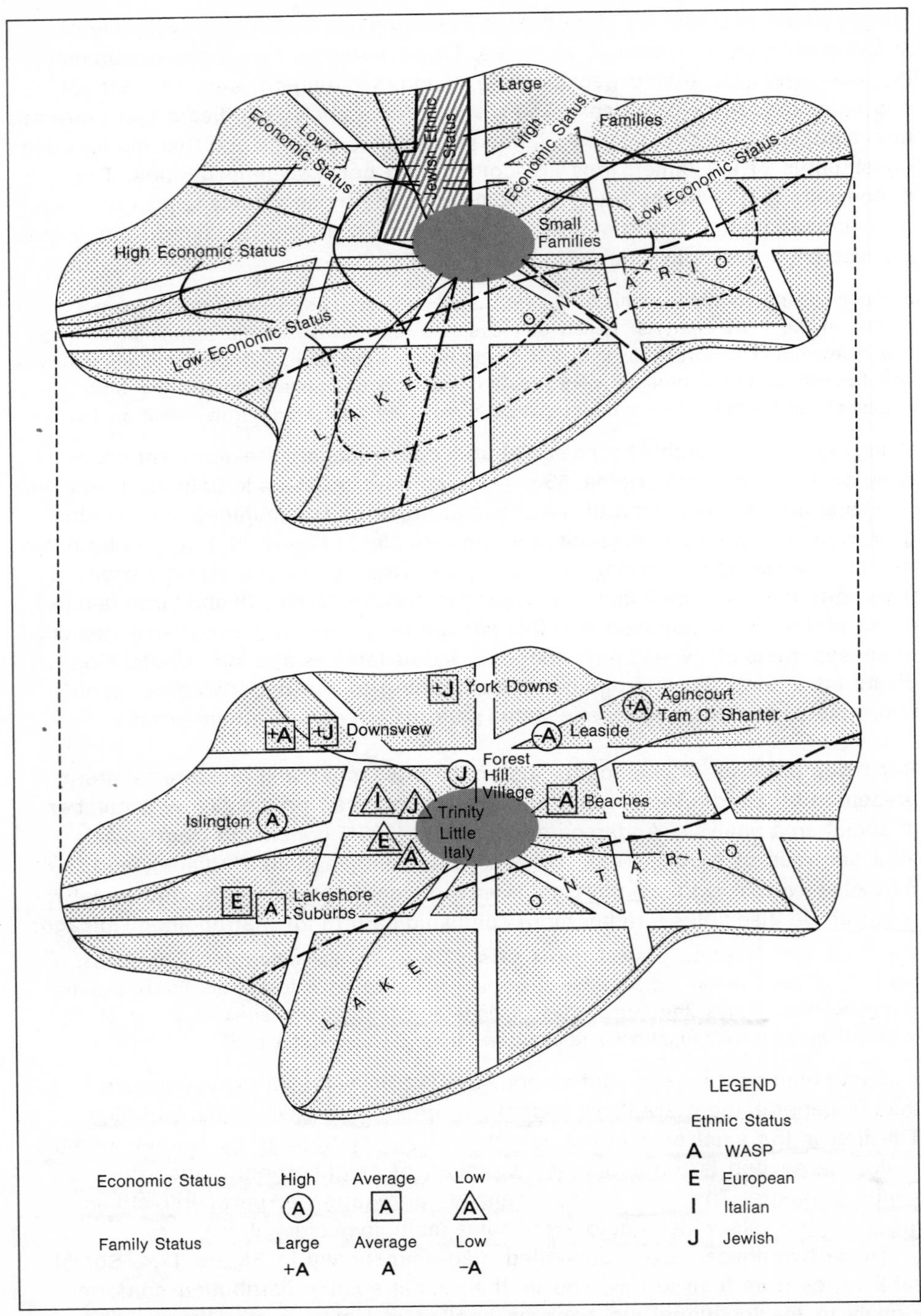

FIG. 11.3. "COMMUNITIES" IN METROPOLITAN TORONTO. (*Source:* After Murdie, 1969, Fig. 29.)

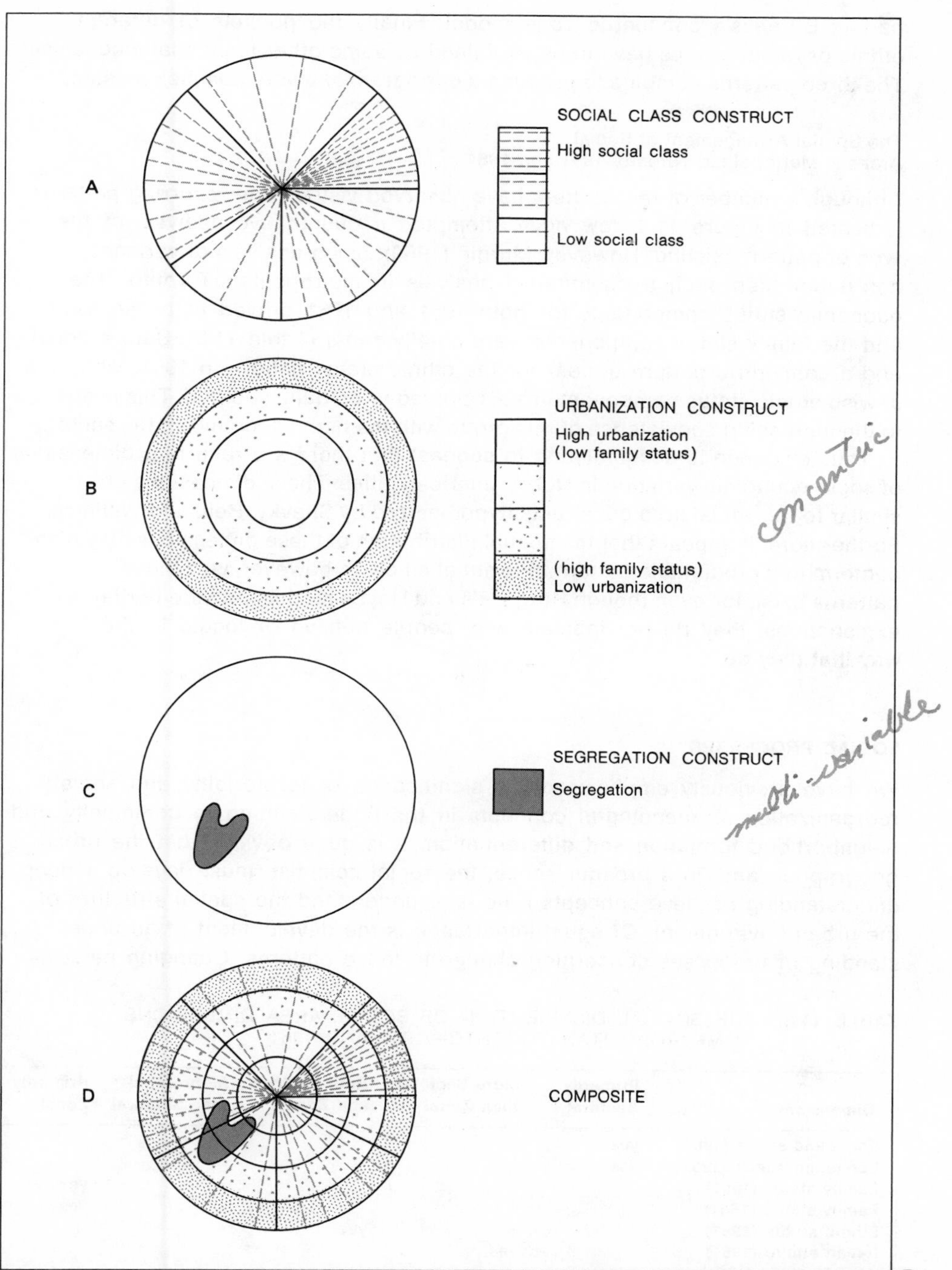

FIG. 11.4. AN IDEALIZED SPATIAL ARRANGEMENT OF INDEXES OF (A) SOCIAL CLASS, (B) FAMILY STATUS, (C) SEGREGATION, AND (D) A COMPOSITE VIEW OF THE SPATIAL VARIATION IN SOCIO-ECONOMIC STRUCTURE.

part in Burgess's concentric zone model. Finally the pockets of different ethnic or racial groups have to be explained by some other locational mechanism. The three patterns combine to produce a cartogram of a very complex mosaic.

The Spatial Arrangement of Social Areas in Metropolitan Toronto, 1951 and 1961

Although a number of researchers have observed visually the recurring patterns indicated in Figure 11.4, few have attempted a quantitative analysis of the type of pattern existing. However, Murdie (1969), using analysis of variance, has undertaken such a quantitative analysis in metropolitan Toronto. The economic status components for both 1951 and 1961 proved to be sectoral, and the family status components were chiefly zonal (Table 11.3). Both a zonal and a concentric pattern appear for the ethnic status pattern in 1951, while the Jewish ethnic status component in 1961 proved to be quite sectoral. This is due to the increasing coexistence of this group with the high economic status sector.

Thus evidence is accumulating to suggest that there are recurring dimensions of socio-economic variation in North American cities. These dimensions are similar to the social area constructs hypothesized by Shevky, Bell, and Williams. Furthermore, it appears that the spatial distribution of these dimensions may also conform to a predictable pattern. It is not at all clear, however, why these patterns exist, for even though Burgess's and Hoyt's models provide partial explanations, they do not indicate why people behave or locate in the way that they do.

SOCIAL PROCESSES

We have previously emphasized the significance of territoriality and social reorganization as meaningful concepts in the understanding of community and neighborhood formation and differentiation. It is quite obvious that the urban geographer, and, in a broader sense, the social scientist, must develop a deep understanding of these concepts if he is to understand the spatial structure of the urban environment. Of equal importance is the development of an understanding of processes concerning change in these patterns. Changing patterns

TABLE 11.3. THE SPATIAL DISTRIBUTION OF SOCIAL AREA DIMENSIONS IN METROPOLITAN TORONTO—1951 AND 1961

Dimension	Primarily Sectoral	More Sectoral than Zonal	Both Sectoral and Zonal	More Zonal than Sectoral	Primarily Zonal
Economic status (1961)	yes				
Economic status (1951)	yes				
Family status (1951)					yes
Family status (1961)					yes
Ethnic status (1951)			yes		
Italian ethnic (1961)		yes			
Jewish ethnic (1961)	yes				

Source: Murdie (1969), p. 164.

occur due to the changing socio-economic characteristics of the population of urban areas. Generally, there are two ways in which this change can occur: either through a change in the people themselves, or through a displacement procedure.

INVASION—SUCCESSION—DOMINANCE

One of the earliest, and most enduring, models concerning change has its roots in plant and animal ecology. In this model the process begins with a particular plant or animal occupying a given space or territory. An invasion then occurs with the influx of a species foreign to the area; and if this invasion is successful, the species will eventually dominate the territory. This succession

> . . . has its beginning on a frontier, an area of instability; wave after wave pushes on relentlessly until some form or system of organization has evolved that can maintain itself against external and internal attack (Ford, 1950, p. 156).

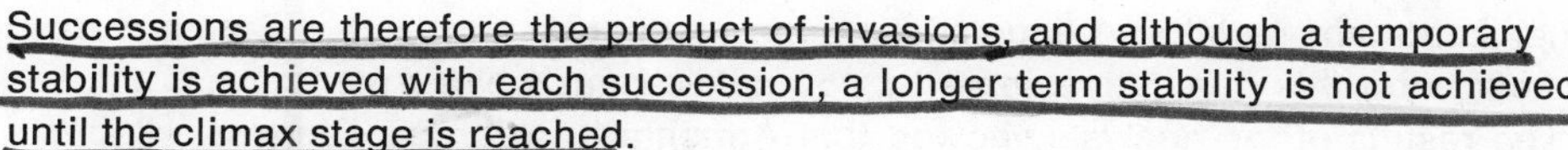

Successions are therefore the product of invasions, and although a temporary stability is achieved with each succession, a longer term stability is not achieved until the climax stage is reached.

This ecological process can be regarded as an analogy for social change if the plant ecologist's concept of an ultimate climax stage is disregarded. McKenzie (Park, et al., 1925, p. 74) suggests that intracommunity invasions can be grouped into two main classes: those involving land use change, and those involving change in type of occupant. Land use changes involve the transference of general uses, such as the replacement of a residential area by an industrial or business use. Changes of this type can usually only occur through rezoning. Occupancy changes refer in particular to the replacement of one type of residential group by another. The degree to which it is noticeable that a particular residential group is replacing another depends on the social distance separating them.

Social distance *Social distance* is a concept referring to the degree of separation between individuals, families, or groups. When applied to communities or neighborhoods, it refers to the way in which one community group or another perceive each other. This perception involves a host of factors: economic, social, and psychological. If the social distance between groups or neighborhoods is large, then it will be difficult for members of the one group to be assimilated in the other. If the social distance is great, and one group is trying to occupy the territory of another, then the change is noticeable and an invasion can be thought to be occurring. In situations where the social distance is not great, communities merge and there is little notion of replacement.

The measurement of social distance

As the concept of social distance involves numerous perceptive features, it has proved very difficult to actually measure the social distance between groups. An

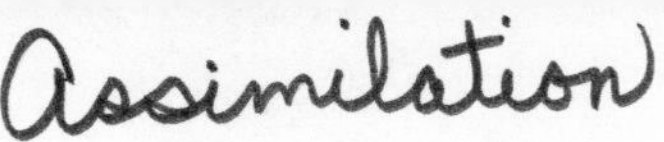

early attempt was undertaken by Bogardus (1926), who analyzed the perception by native-born white Americans of other ethnic and linguistic groups in the United States in the 1920s. He hypothesized the following rank order of social relations as a scale for measuring the perception by the native-born white American group of the other groups:

1. To admit to close kinship by marriage
2. To have as friends
3. To have as neighbors on the same street
4. To admit as members of one's occupation within one's country
5. To admit as citizens of one's country
6. To admit as visitors only to one's country
7. To exclude entirely from one's country

Other important racial and linguistic groups residing in the United States were ranked along this qualitative scale by 450 native-born white Americans.

The results of the analysis showed that Armenians, Negroes, Chinese, Hindus, and Turks were usually put in categories 6 and 7, while the English, French, Norwegian, and Scottish groups were generally put in categories 1 to 5. Thus, the first group is socially rather distant from the native-born white American majority, whereas the latter group is a great deal closer. Assimilation therefore is rather more difficult for the former group than for the latter. It is, however, to be remembered that social distance varies within groups and geographically. Also, Bogardus analyzed the perception of a number of groups by one, not the way in which each group perceived each other.

Conditions initiating invasions Invasions can occur as a result of many conditions. Probably one of the most important relates to changes in forms and routes of transportation. New transportation arteries affect accessibility for the entire urban area, and their local impact can be quite dramatic. For example, Hoch (1957) indicates that the Edens Expressway in Chicago has had a positive effect on land values on areas bordering the route. On the other hand, declining or blighted transportation arteries can adversely affect the surrounding area. Thus, obsolescence itself is also a debilitating factor that can change the entire image of a community or neighborhood and create opportunities for the invasion of a new occupational group or land use. On the other hand, the construction of new buildings or the redevelopment of an area can result in upgrading, which also provides a stimulus for invasion.

Some neighborhood invasions are created by real estate promoters who can change the image of an area simply by good advertising and the emphasis of a few local features. One of the most notorious examples of the working of this mechanism is "block-busting." This procedure requires a situation where one particular group is living in a confined segregated area in which the demand for housing greatly exceeds the supply. Once sufficient piling-up has occurred, the demand for new living space becomes so obvious and great that promoters can take advantage of the prejudices of the peripheral nonsegregated group by scaring it into panic selling. These properties are then purchased cheaply by speculators and renters, who subdivide the property and exploit the intense demand of the segregated group by greatly increasing unit space rents.

Conditions expressing succession Succession can therefore be expressed in many forms, such as:

1. Land ownership and value
2. The appearance of residential structures, involving either rebuilding or renovation
3. Transportation systems, particularly where one type of system replaces another, or where a particular system becomes blighted
4. Media of communication, particularly newspapers, radio, and television
5. Occupational groups
6. Business, industrial, commercial, and financial enterprises
7. Religious institutions and groups; and
8. Cultural or ethnic groups

Often a great deal of residual friction may occur if one particular group succeeds another in one aspect but fails to dominate in another. For example, one ethnic group may replace another, but the ownership of the buildings and media of communication may remain in the hands of the former. In this kind of situation the friction can be explosive, particularly if the succeeding group feels exploited in any way.

SEGREGATION

Lieberson (1963) suggests that one would expect residential segregation under two sets of circumstances. First, if a group is of an undesirable status, then the group will be involuntarily segregated. Secondly, voluntary segregation will occur if ". . . proximity to members of the same group facilitates adjustment to the conditions of settlement in a new country or if members of an ethnic group simply view the residential proximity of members from the same group as desirable" (Lieberson, 1963, p. 5). In the first instance the process of segregation involves, in the North American context, "ghettoization," and in the second some form of grouping due to sentiment and symbolism.

Ghettos Ghettos are common features of American urban life, for a vast majority of Negroes, Puerto Ricans, and Mexican Indians (Chicanos) are forced by a variety of pressures to reside in restricted areas where they are dominant (Taueber and Taueber, 1965). Morrill (1965B) suggests that it would be more accurate to state that almost every urban area, whatever the size, that has a considerable proportion of nonwhite inhabitants has a nonwhite ghetto. The term *ghetto* originally referred to the Jewish ghettos of eastern and southern Europe. In the cities of eastern Europe the Jewish area was not only distinct from the rest of the city but, ultimately, physically contained by a wall built to confine the Jews to their defined area.

As applied to North America, a *ghetto* is a spatially contiguous area of the urban landscape in which the inhabitants have particular social, economic, ethnic, or cultural attributes that distinguish them from the majority of the inhabitants of the country in which they reside. Because of these differentiating characteristics, the inhabitants are, by and large, not permitted by the majority to reside beyond this well-defined area even if they wished, unless these differentiating attributes change sufficiently for them to be accepted (Rose, 1970). The ghetto is thus a result of external pressure rather than internal coherence. With the passing of time, however, certain ghettos may well develop a vibrant culture and an internal coherence which sustains the community to such an extent that they would not wish to leave the ghetto even if they could.

This latter aspect of ghetto development is being reinforced as a result of the continuous deprivation, isolation, and exploitation of the black community. Black militants, who are frequently supported by the less militant, are stressing independence rather than integration, and the Martin Luther King concept of nonviolence is being replaced by that of self-defense. Integration proposals are being frequently viewed by the black community as a further, but subtle, development of the white community's inherent racist sentiments. As a consequence, black people ". . . are becoming increasingly unwilling to accept the assumptions of white culture, white values, and white power" (Skolnick, 1969, p. xxii). If the white community and power structure fails to overhaul its attitudes and procedures, which in many cases unwittingly give a racist impression, then the black ghetto will increasingly become an alienated and separate nation within North America (Kain and Persky, 1969).

Sentiment and symbolism Firey (1945) suggests that two other conditions also result in clusters of particular ethnic groups, or members of a certain socio-economic class: symbolism and sentiment. Symbolic features are described by Firey as being of particular importance when related to historic and aesthetic attributes. Beacon Hill in Boston and Society Hill in Philadelphia are good examples of this. Both areas are inhabited by high-income individuals who are consciously attempting to preserve the colonial and early American heritage of these areas. This end is achieved in the Beacon Hill district by strong local ordinances and the restricting of property sales to high-income, socially acceptable families who will preserve the atmosphere of their properties and the community.

The second condition involves sentiments that are often proscribed by the inhabitants of an area to the particular locale. Firey described this condition in great detail with respect to the Italian section of Boston's North End in 1940, a situation that resembles closely that of the Eastern European ethnic groups in Winnipeg in 1960. This group consists particularly of first generation immigrants who live together in the North End in order to preserve family and group cultural characteristics. So significant is the family in the Italian milieu that it is not uncommon to find a building completely occupied by one extended family of grandparents, their children, their children's children, and so forth. The strength of the family lies therefore in its size and joint economic power. Frequently, apartments owned by Italians are rented to their kin in order to keep the family in close proximity. Subsequent generations, however, become assimilated into the North American system and may move away from the area, leaving only the middle-aged and elderly behind.

Slums One of the characteristics of ghettos and some segregated communities is that many of their inhabitants live in slums. In a narrow sense, the term *slum* refers to a housing condition characterized by dilapidated conditions, overcrowding, filth, and vermin. In a broader sense, however, the slum is a "genuine social community in the culture of poverty with all of the institutions of support and adjustment and accommodation new urban migrants as well as low-income groups need" (Wingo, 1966, p. 145). Thus, the fact that ghettos contain slums, and that slums are particularly associated with the zone of deterioration encircling the central business district, is not surprising, for the slum is the home of the poor and the stranger. The function of a slum, then, is to house these persons until they are absorbed into city life. This assimilation should be possible when the poor person has attained sufficient skills to achieve a higher wage level, and when the stranger has accepted the culture and behavior patterns of the urban dwellers, and is thus employable.

Stokes (1962) presents a simple model that attempts to sort out the variables that are thought to be determinants of slums and the culture of poverty (Lewis, 1966). These variables can be combined to provide a classification of slums, which in turn can be used to describe the complexity of public policy in this area. Stokes discerns two main groups of slum dwellers in terms of their psychological attitude toward the possibility of economic improvement. One group is the slum dweller who has hope; he thinks that he can better himself and consequently he is employable. The second group is the slum dweller of despair, who has a negative estimate of the outcome of an attempt at economic improvement. This feeling of despair can of course be brought about by a number of conditions—continuous failure, old age, and so on.

Apart, though intercorrelated with these psychological attitudes, are the socio-economic conditions of the slum dweller. These conditions lead, in this simple model, to a postulate of the existence of an escalator class and a nonescalator class. An escalator group can move upward if it has the psychological attitude to do so. A nonescalator group is denied in some way the privilege of escalation, either because of a caste, race, religion, color, or some other discriminating aspect.

It is therefore possible to develop a simple classification of slums based on these psychological and socio-economic variables. This classification is presented as a 2 × 2 matrix in Table 11.4, which identifies the following:

A—slums of hope consisting of escalator classes

B—slums of despair consisting of escalator classes

C—slums of hope consisting of nonescalator classes
D—slums of despair consisting of nonescalator classes.

The suggestion is that a different strategy is necessary for each case. National policies concerning economic growth, equal opportunity, and minimum housing standards are basic prerequisites for a war-on-slums policy. Local area programs are necessary for each different type of slum condition, particularly the B and D types.

SOCIAL SPACE AND LOCATIONAL SPACE

Factors involved in the individual's or family's locational decision therefore determines in aggregate the social geography of urban areas. Conceptually, Rees (1968) defines three elements related to the process, the first of which relates the decision-making unit to its position in social space. The axes of this space (Fig. 11.5) are socio-economic status and stage in the life cycle which,

TABLE 11.4. A CLASSIFICATION OF SLUMS

SLUMS **CLASSES**	**HOPE**	**DESPAIR**
ESCALATOR	A. Rate of absorption depends on the growth of employment opportunties in the area. If the number of jobseekers is greatly in excess of available positions, then the surplus in this group will collect in slums. Thus steady national economic growth and expanding job opportunities will help hold this group to a minimum.	B. Can be regarded in most cases as a surplus that has lost hope. It may, for example, have been unemployed too long and lost any hope for economic betterment. Burgeoning job opportunities will not necessarily solve the problem of this group, for a degree of social reconstruction may be required along with job retraining. It is important, however, to prevent the feeling of despair being imparted to the younger generation of this group.
NONESCALATOR	C. This group has hope of economic improvement, but there is a barrier that has to be overcome. If the barrier is linguistic, they must learn a new language, but racial, ethnic, and religious barriers are not so easily overcome. However, if the barrier can be broken down, this group will move into Group A and will be assimilated during the process of economic growth.	D. This is the most difficult slum type of all, as the problem will not pass away even if the barrier is dismantled and decent jobs are available. It is difficult to envisage any other policy than "grass-roots" social, economic, and cultural reconstruction, along with a growing national economy, as a strategy for tackling the problems of this group. Concomitantly there must be a policy that prevents a slum with these characteristics being formed in the future. Many sections of black ghettos consist of Group D type; and a recession, along with a failure to implement equal employment laws, will only swell the numbers found in this category.

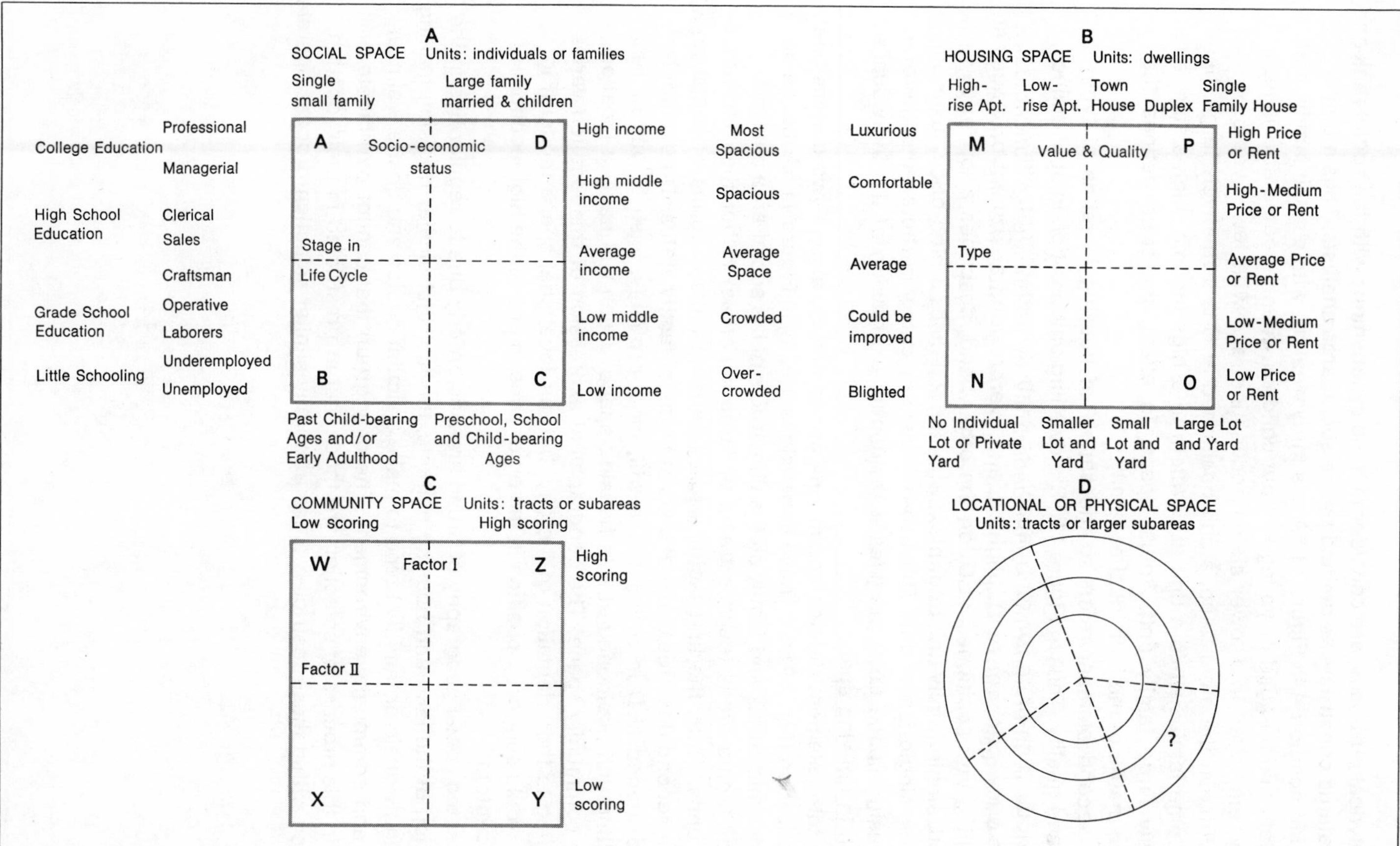

FIG. 11.5. THE DECISION PROCESS AND SOCIAL AREAS. (*Source:* Rees, 1968, Fig. 4.)

for analytical purposes, are considered to be synonymous with the social rank and family-status constructs as defined by the social area analysts. Thus a unit located in position *A* in Figure 11.5A is a fairly wealthy, with a small family, and either late middle-aged or young without children. A unit located at *B* is less wealthy, employed in a lower status occupation, and with fewer years of education. On the other hand, a unit positioned at *C* is a relatively large, but low-income family, while a unit at *D* refers to a high-income, high-status, and relatively large family unit. Social space, in effect, therefore defines the demand matrix of the individual or family.

The second element refers to the supply of housing in terms of type, value, and quality. Thus in Figure 11.5B a dwelling unit positioned at *M* defines a luxurious, high-price (or rent), spacious, high-rise apartment; whereas *N* defines a low-price (or rent), blighted, and overcrowded apartment or tenement. A dwelling unit positioned at *O,* on the other hand, describes a low-price, blighted, single-family unit or duplex; whereas *P* defines a high-price, luxurious, spacious, single-family unit. This two-dimensional category represents, therefore, the housing space for it provides a residential expression of the individual's position in housing space.

The third element defines community space and is, also, a two-dimensional categorization (Fig. 11.5C). These dimensions are, as in Figure 11.5A, based on the economic status and family status constructs of the social-area analysts, but they locate areas (census tracts or large subareas) rather than individual family units. Thus, the first factor refers to spatial units in terms of social rank, and the second describes spatial units in terms of family status. Thus a family unit positioned at *D* in social space will, most probably, wish to buy or rent a dwelling unit positioned at *P* in housing space, which will imply a location at *Z* in community space. The geographical expression of this location varies according to the orientation of the city, but our locational space model (Fig. 11.5D) would suggest a position in the outer zone in one of the high-economic status sectors.

Thus, the social geography of urban areas is orderly due to regularities in the operation of the land and housing markets, the fact that similar decision-making units (individuals or families) tend to make a similar choice and desire a similar social and community environment. The only group that cannot participate freely in this process of selection are those that are restricted in their location, but even within these restricted areas a roughly similar selection process operates.

“THE LOCATION OF COMMERCIAL USES”

Central places, it was noted in Chapter 7, are smaller settlements whose primary function is the provision of goods and services to consumers residing in areas surrounding them. As settlements get larger and the importance of the central-place function diminishes, the supply of goods and services to their resident population becomes increasingly more important. In order to service this population as efficiently as possible, commercial activities are spatially distributed within cities in general agreement with the distribution of population. In this chapter we will discuss the intraurban pattern of commercial activities and examine some of the regularities that are apparent in the commercial structure of cities.

THE IMPORTANCE OF COMMERCIAL ACTIVITIES

Commercial activities are not great users of land within cities. Figures presented in Chapter 9 indicated that they accounted on an average for only about 5 percent of the developed urban land area. In the city of Chicago in 1962, for example, only 9 out of the city's 224 square miles were devoted to commercial uses. However unimpressive this may seem, the layout of commercial land use is such that business is brought virtually into every neighborhood in cities. In Chicago, 500 miles of continuous commercial frontage abut the section, half-section, and radial streets. A further 25 miles are scattered among predominantly residential neighborhoods, while another 30 miles of frontage make up the larger shopping centers at important street intersections, not to mention the frontage of the innumerable smaller shopping centers located at minor street corners and hidden away in the middle of residential areas.

Although not an impressive user of land in the aggregate, commercial land uses are important in other respects. A sizable proportion of the total building space in cities is normally used by commercial activities. They are important generators of traffic flow within the urban area, and it is on trips to commercial land use that urban dwellers make most of their expenditures. It has been estimated that in Chicago, for example, over 16 percent of the city's total building space is used up by wholesale, retail, and service activities; that 28 percent (930 thousand out of 3.28 million) of all vehicular trips and 25 percent (1.46 out of 5.77 million) of all individual vehicular trips on an average weekday end on commercial land; and that on these trips to commercial land uses, Chicagoans make about 60 percent of their total consumer expenditures (Berry, 1963).

ELEMENTS OF COMMERCIAL STRUCTURE

The results from studies of the commercial structure of cities during the past quarter century suggest that the urban business complex can be disaggregated into three major elements or conformations. In turn, a number of subtypes within each of the major conformations can be recognized. A composite picture of these is presented in Figure 12.1. This classification is based on analysis of the locational requirements of the different business types within the urban area; that is, on the analysis of the functional

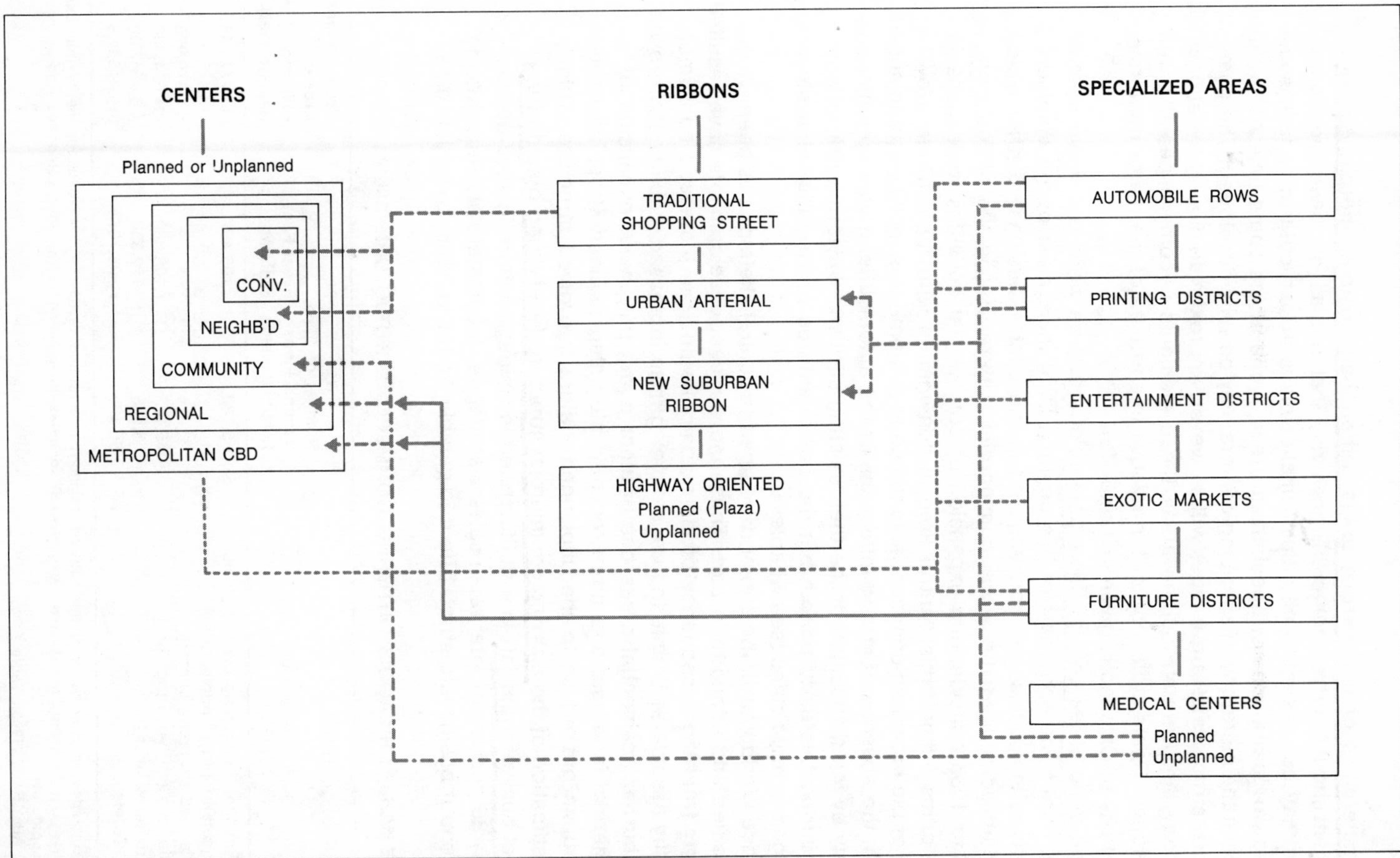

FIG. 12.1. MAJOR COMPONENTS OF THE URBAN BUSINESS PATTERN. (*Source:* Berry, 1963, Table 2.)

characteristics of commercial areas rather than on their morphology or form. It should be remembered, however, that not all of these functional types may be present in all cities. Smaller cities in particular may lack some of the various ribbons or specialized areas, while at the same time not all the levels in the hierarchy of shopping centers may be fully developed. The commercial structure of larger cities will, however, approximate closely the suggested typology, and in metropolitan areas these elements become especially well developed. Some indication of the relative importance of the major conformations in the city of Chicago is given in Table 12.1.

The general features of this commercial structure were laid down in most cities during the early part of this century. Until then, most of the commercial activity within cities was concentrated in the central business district which, as a result, dominated the urban commercial pattern. But in the period from 1900 to 1935 considerable expansion of commercial activities took place in most cities outside this central area in conjunction with rapid urban growth. Most of the growth of commercial land use at this time was, however, unplanned; and in the absence of strong influences of the automobile, it was conditioned largely by the disposition of the then existing surface transit network. It was also during this early period that the basic features of the land-value surface emerged in most cities (see Chapter 9).

Since World War II, the earlier developed structural skeleton has been intensified and added to in part. These more recent developments have resulted directly from the ascendancy of the automobile and the increased consumer mobility associated with it. In turn, stemming from increased mobility, the growth of suburban residential areas has brought about peripheral expansion of commercial land use; and more recently integrated planned shopping centers have been grafted on to the unplanned, naturally evolved structure. This intensification of the outlying commercial structure (everything outside the central business district) is well illustrated in Chicago, where in 1958 approximately 85 percent of total retail sales were made in commercial areas outside the central business district. The comparable figure in 1935, by which time

TABLE 12.1. CHICAGO'S OUTLYING COMMERCIAL STRUCTURE, 1961[a]

Type	Number of Ground Floor Establishments	Front Feet of Buildings	Ground Floor Area of Buildings (square feet)
1. Unplanned shopping centers (including small isolated nucleations)	5,782	165,497	14,777,145
2. Planned shopping centers	214	—	879,970
3. Ribbons (all types together)	45,172	1,108,680	91,074,000
4. Scattered uses	3,965	122,530	8,484,700
Totals	55,133	1,396,707	115,215,815

[a] Table includes only elements of the outlying commercial structure of the ctiy. No data for the central business district is included; the data for the specialized areas is included in the four categories and is not shown separately.

Source: After Berry (1963), Table 1.

the main features of outlying structure were well established, was about three-quarters of total retail sales. However, at the same time the post-war period was also one of emerging problems and strains on the existing structure. This has been associated in part with the continued outward growth of many urban areas, and in part with the concomitant decline of the older, inner parts of cities. As yet, however, the basic elements of the urban commercial structure have been little modified by this, although pressure for change is undoubtedly building up.

The basic elements of the land value surface within urban areas had jelled in most cities by the 1930s. Since that time there has been only little alteration of its general features although changes in transport technology have brought about marked change in particular instances. The peak value intersection and the disposition of the ridges of higher values along main arteries and minor peaks of value at the intersections of these are today very much as they were twenty-five years ago. Because of the need by most commercial uses for good accessibility to that part of the urban market served, a well-marked relationship appears to exist between the elements of commercial structure and these general features of the land-value surface. Generally the ridges of higher value are occupied by the various kinds of ribbon developments, while the minor peaks on the surface are associated with the more specialized retail and service businesses comprising the outlying shopping centers. As was pointed out in Chapter 9, the highest point on the surface of land values corresponds to the central business district and the very specialized and diverse commercial activities found in it. Moreover the general tendency is for high-level centers in the hierarchy to be associated with minor peaks of higher value. But it should be remembered that this relationship is often blurred by the distorting influences of distance within the urban area.

SPECIALIZED AREAS

Specialized areas is the name given to recognizable clusters of establishments of the same business type or of functionally interrelated business types within the urban area. They are usually freestanding in location, although they may be present in incipient form within larger outlying shopping centers and well developed within the central business district (see Chapter 13). The dominant locational factor for this aspect of the commercial structure is accessibility to the portion of the urban market served. Hence it is not uncommon to find specialized areas established on major arterials within the urban area (i.e. automobile rows) or at points of focus within the public transport system (i.e. medical centers). Specialized areas normally have "just growed like Topsy" at points within cities, hence are mainly unplanned, although recently some planned concentrations have emerged, especially in connection with the provision of medical facilities.

Specialized areas are of many diverse kinds, although the one most frequently encountered within cities is the automobile row. These rows are strung out along the main section and radial streets within urban areas as is, for example, indicated for Chicago in Figure 12.2A. They comprise contiguous strings of new and used automobile dealers and facilities for parts, repairs, and servicing. Other types of specialized areas that have been identified within the city of Chicago—and which are probably typical of other larger cities —include (1) medical districts comprising offices of doctors, dentists, and related medical facilities. The older, unplanned medical districts are often located at the upper-floor level within the outlying shopping centers, although in recent years the tendency has been for these to be either replaced or supplemented by newer, planned office accommodations away from shopping centers but at accessible locations near to them; (2) printing districts consisting of clusters of establishments performing printing and allied business services. These may not be associated with any particular sets of locations within the urban area although they are commonly distinguishing features in the area adjacent to the central business district where they are well placed to serve the demand generated from the concentrations of various office functions there; (3) household-furnishing districts comprising concentrations of furniture, household appliances, and related stores. The pattern of these in Chicago is presented in Figure 12.2B. If the location of this type of specialized area within

FIG. 12.2. SPECIALIZED COMMERCIAL AREAS IN THE CITY OF CHICAGO: (A) AUTOMOBILE ROWS AND (B) MAJOR "INDEPENDENTS" AND FURNITURE DISTRICTS. (*Source:* Berry, 1963, Figs. 17 and 18.)

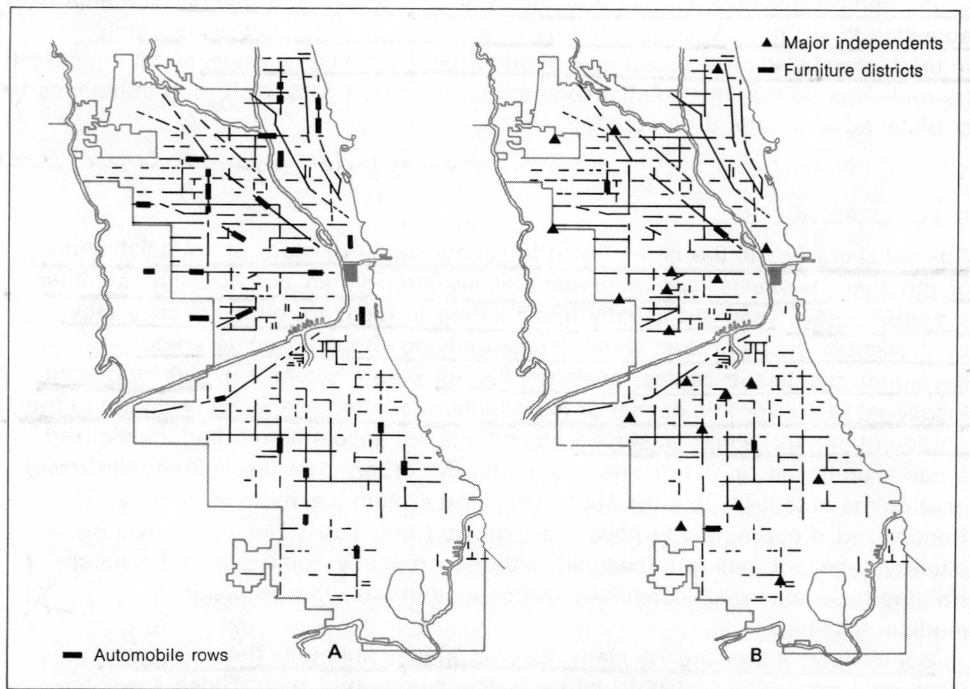

the city of Chicago is at all typical of the general location of this type within cities, as it most probably is, it occupies locations close to the larger outlying shopping centers. These shopping centers are usually within one-half mile of the specialized areas at sites outside of the main land value cone, where they can afford to pay the lower rents for the generally larger amounts of space needed. Although incipient clusters of furniture stores and allied activities have a tendency to develop within the larger outlying shopping centers, these are generally small scale and occur on low-value land within these centers.

Also included in Figure 12.2B are the major large, independent, and discount stores found today within most cities. These are well distributed within Chicago in accordance with the distribution of population. They are normally situated at locations away from other elements of the business pattern, especially from the shopping centers to which they offer, in some cases, serious competition. Although these do not constitute specialized areas in the true sense of the definition, they are distinctive, highly specialized features of the contemporary urban commercial scene and represent the trend to large-scale economies in modern retailing. Generally, these business types are found at arterial locations within urban areas for they depend on automobile shopping. They are freestanding because the wide range of goods offered at them permits one-stop shopping visits and does not, therefore, necessitate linkages with other business types nearby.

Although many other types of specialized areas may be thought of—for example, the entertainment districts and exotic markets (such as Maxwell Street in Chicago or Grant Avenue in San Francisco) listed in Figure 12.1—they all have one general feature in common regardless of specific functional type; namely, a concentration of establishments held together by close linkages between each other. They represent therefore the locational effects of the forces of scale economies, economies which—with the exception of the large independents—are external to individual establishments. By clustering together in this way, business types are able to take advantage of economies of operation that would be denied them if they were located apart. Some savings may result from the nature of comparative shopping trips as in the case of the automobile rows and furniture districts, or they may be the more usual kinds of savings associated with external economies in advertising and the sharing of common facilities.

THE RIBBONS

Ribbons, the second major element in the commercial structure of urban areas, are perhaps the most noticeable since their constituents form the backdrop to most well-traveled routes through cities. Business types that have a tendency to locate in one or other of the types of ribbons are those that need a certain minimum degree of accessibility to the market served. They do not, however, require sites of maximum centrality within urban areas and consequently can survive at locations along major arteries and urban highways. Although several different types of ribbons can be recognized, it is important to remember that the character of these is repeated from one part of the city to another. For the most part, the typical functions of ribbons is to serve demands originating on the highways or to cater to one-stop, home-based shopping trips (Table 12.2). As such they can be thought of as concentrations of commercial activities at common locations, but between which there is little if any functional interlinkage (Berry, 1959).

Highway-oriented ribbons Highway-oriented ribbons have often been described as natural strip developments along major highways within urban areas. The business types located in this kind of ribbon truly serve demands originating on the highways themselves. Generally the greater the volume of traffic on the highway, the more important it is as a generator of demand, and consequently the greater the density of commercial development along it. For the most part, these ribbons are uncontrolled developments; although along some of the

TABLE 12.2. SELECTED FUNCTIONS TYPICAL OF VARIOUS TYPES OF RIBBONS

Functions	District type
Highway-Oriented Ribbons	
Gas stations Restaurants Motels Fruit and produce stands	(Automobile service districts)
Urban Arterials	
Building services and supplies Lumberyards Miscellaneous repairs Radio-TV sales and repairs	(Space-consuming service districts)
Automobile repairs Bars Shoe repairs Furniture Automobile accessories Appliances Fuel dealers Gift and novelty stores Food lockers Florists	(Urban-arterial oriented)
Traditional Shopping Streets	
Groceries Laundromats Bakeries Restaurants Personal services	(Neighborhood streets)
Missions Second-hand stores Bars and liquor stores Rooming houses	(Skid Rows)

Source: Berry (1959), Table 1.

newer intraurban highways, service plazas of a planned nature have been constructed. Functions typical of the highway-oriented ribbons include gasoline and service stations, restaurants and drive-ins, ice-cream parlors, motels, and fruit and vegetable stands. These are essentially freestanding establishments between which there is very little functional linkage, which cater essentially to one-stop shopping trips originating from the transient market on the highways.

Urban arterials Functions generally associated with the urban-arterial ribbon development include things such as automobile repair shops, furniture and appliance stores, office-equipment sales, funeral parlors, lumberyards and fuel dealers, and a variety of building and household supplies, electrical repair services, plumbing establishments, and radio-television repairs and services. These types have two general characteristics: (1) they are for the most part large consumers of space, and (2) they are associated with an infrequent demand calling for an occasional special-purpose trip or even a "home call." As a result of either or both of these characteristics, these activities need locations offering reasonable access to large portions of the urban market. However, they are generally assumed unable to pay the high rents for sites within the shopping centers at the intersections of the major urban arterials. Consequently they function best outside the nucleated business centers where land values, and hence site rents, are generally lower. In many cases they form a continuation of commercial property along arterials between shopping centers. They exist because many different types of business seek out similar arterial locations for reasons of accessibility. However, as is the case for the functions typical of the highway-oriented ribbons, despite their common locations urban-arterial ribbons function independently of each other. There is normally little linkage between the different business types, which consequently can perhaps be best described as freestanding with common arterial locations.

New suburban ribbons New suburban ribbons are included largely for the sake of completeness, although their functional structure does differ somewhat from that of the two types of ribbons mentioned so far. They are more recent developments associated particularly with postwar suburbanization. As such they are typically found in the newer, peripheral parts of urban areas and especially in suburbs adjacent to central cities. Their functional character is derived from the inclusion of more exotic uses, catering to demands from new residential areas, along with business types that are typical of the urban arterial ribbons discussed above. Hence, more business types of the drive-in variety (i.e., banks, restaurants, and so on) are included in this variety of ribbon development.

Traditional shopping streets Traditional shopping streets are distinctive features of the older parts of North American cities. They should be thought of as ribbon developments only in the sense of being morphologically similar to the other ribbon types. In functional structure, the traditional shopping streets are similar to the lower level shopping centers. Typical business types in them include

groceries, drugstores, laundries and laundromats, beauty salons, and barber shops. As such, they constitute small clusters of low-order convenience goods and services that are interjected into the arterial ribbons at minor street intersections. In older parts of cities, and especially near the CBD, many of these assume the form of skid rows. Thus although their businesses share common locations with those of other ribbons, they differ in that they cater to home-based trips, which may be of a multiple-purpose nature. Hence there is more linkage between business types in these kinds of ribbon developments than in any of the others.

Although the different types of ribbon development are associated with different locations within urban areas, it is not unusual to find them intertwined within any particular city. Notwithstanding this, however, it has been suggested that a clear differentiation exists between ribbons that are adjacent to shopping centers and those that are isolated within the urban area. The former kind constitutes a frame around the shopping centers to which they adjoin; the latter are separated from them and are more or less freestanding. This difference in location is reflected in a difference in functional structure and size. For example, in investigating these types in Chicago, it was found that sample quarter-mile ribbons abutting shopping centers had on an average 91 establishments, 33 different business types, occupied 2250 front feet, and had a ground-floor area of 175,000 square feet. Isolated quarter-mile ribbons on the other hand contained on an average only 27 business types occupying 55 establishments, accounted for only 1670 feet fronting on the street, and had a ground-floor area of 130,000 square feet. In the ribbons close to shopping centers most of the activities of the ribbon types discussed above are represented, and particularly those typical of the urban arterials. In fact it is these that are mainly responsible for the intensification of ribbon development close to the shopping centers (Berry, 1963, p. 80). By comparison, the isolated ribbons in Chicago were found to be far more devoted to stretches of convenience businesses in association with highway-oriented activities and to restaurants, bars, liquor stores, and so on, than the adjacent ribbons. The service uses so typical of the arterials are noticeably absent from these less intensive ribbon developments.

THE NUCLEATIONS

The third major conformation in the commercial structure of cities comprises the various types of nucleated shopping centers. These consist of clusters of retail and service activities at important street intersections within the urban area. They usually constitute foci at the intersection of two or more ribbon developments, where high vehicular and pedestrian traffic intensity provides the focus for growth. On primary streets they may arise at intervals within ribbon developments; while in some cases, and especially the smaller centers, they may string out as local shopping streets as noted above. But regardless of their specific location, the nucleated centers are associated with high degrees of centrality within the urban transportation system, which is reflected in the

locational correlation between them and the peaks of higher land values at street intersections within the urban area.

Shopping centers in the urban area are the equivalent of the central places in predominantly rural areas. As such, it is generally agreed that they form a hierarchy comparable to that found in rural areas and discussed in Chapter 7. Consequently the same structural features of hierarchical organization are present, and the same general forces giving rise to hierarchical organization operate (Getis, 1963). However, because of the higher density of population in urban areas and the marked variation in levels of demand associated with differences in the social structure of cities, the hierarchy of urban shopping centers differs in some respects from its rural counterpart. These differences include the types of goods and services provided from the different centers, the spacing of centers within the urban area, and the size of trade areas served by them.

The hierarchy of shopping centers in cities is dominated by the central business district. This contains many different kinds of commercial functions including concentrations of offices and administrative buildings, warehouses, entertainments; but particularly important is the major concentration of retailing there. It is this element of the central business district that constitutes the highest level in the hierarchy of shopping centers within urban areas. Below the central business district there are at least four levels of centers. In order of decreasing size these are (1) regional centers, (2) community centers, (3) neighborhood centers, and (4) isolated store-clusters. It should be remembered, however, that the number of levels in the hierarchy depends very much on the size of the urban area. Thus in smaller cities the central business district itself may be only functionally equivalent to the higher level regional centers typical of larger cities, and the levels below this will be adjusted downward accordingly. However, within larger cities and especially within metropolitan areas, the four levels of outlying business centers indicated in Figure 12.1 are normally a very clearly established element in urban commercial structure. Because the CBD and outlying shopping centers are in some ways the most important aspects of urban service provision, they will be discussed separately in the following sections.

THE CENTRAL BUSINESS DISTRICT

The CBD is the largest single concentration of commercial activity within urban areas. Not surprisingly, it has been studied extensively from a wide variety of viewpoints; and geographers have long regarded it as a rather special region within cities for analysis. Yet despite the attention that has been focused on the CBD, there is still today little agreement as to what constitutes the central business district of a city, and hence where its boundaries should be drawn. The central district, central region, city center, central area, the 100 percent zone, or simply downtown—these are but some of the many terms used to refer vaguely to the heart of the city.

Regardless of this multiplicity in terminology, most people are familiar with the characteristic features of the downtown area. It is the area of greatest concentration and variety of retailing in the city; the tight cluster of the city's tallest buildings there gives rise especially to the distinctive skyline of North American cities; and it is the largest single focus of vehicular and pedestrian traffic in cities. The functions located in the CBD serve not only the local urban community but also the people living in the surrounding areas, and often even the wider regional and national scene. Concentration would appear to be its single and most visible distinguishing characteristic; and consistent with the intensity of land use there, land values reach disproportionately higher levels than those prevailing in the rest of the urban area. The highest land values in the city are found at the peak land value intersection within the CBD. It is these features that the U.S. Bureau of the Census has in mind in defining the CBD as comprising one or more tracts in the central parts of cities that constitute "an area of very high land valuation, an area characterized by a high concentration of retail businesses, offices, theaters, hotels, and service businesses, and an area of high traffic flow."

THE CORE-FRAME CONCEPT

Cursory examination of the central area of a city brings out the fact that it is far from homogeneous in structure. In particular, there is a marked variation in intensity of land use between its innermost and outermost parts. This change in the intensity of land use is at the same time associated with a change in the types of activities carried on within the central area. Differences in the intensity and in the types of use in the CBD are what underlie the recognition of its two component parts—the inner core area and the surrounding frame (Horwood and Boyce, 1959). The distinction between these two areas is presented diagrammatically in Figure 12.3. The boundary separating them is difficult to determine exactly, and the one should be thought of as gradually merging into the other. The frame, moreover, overlaps the area that has been described as the "middle zone" or "Gray Area" in models of urban structure (see Chapter 9).

The core of the CBD The general properties of the core of the CBD are presented in Table 12.3. This is the area within the CBD used with greatest intensity, largely devoted to offices and retail trade. Epigrammatically it can be thought of as being devoted to "people, parcels, and paper work." It is characterized by multistoried buildings that reflect the tendency for vertical as opposed to horizontal expansion. Walking distances are critical in restricting the spread of the core, and great reliance is placed on the elevator for interaction within it. The highest retail sales density per unit ground area in the urban area occurs here. In addition, it is the focus of convergence for mass transit systems, and the area of highest density of daytime population within the city. Of particular importance are the specialized retail and office activities found here. In many respects the core is the heart of the decision-making machinery for the entire urban business community.

Core + Frame of the CBD

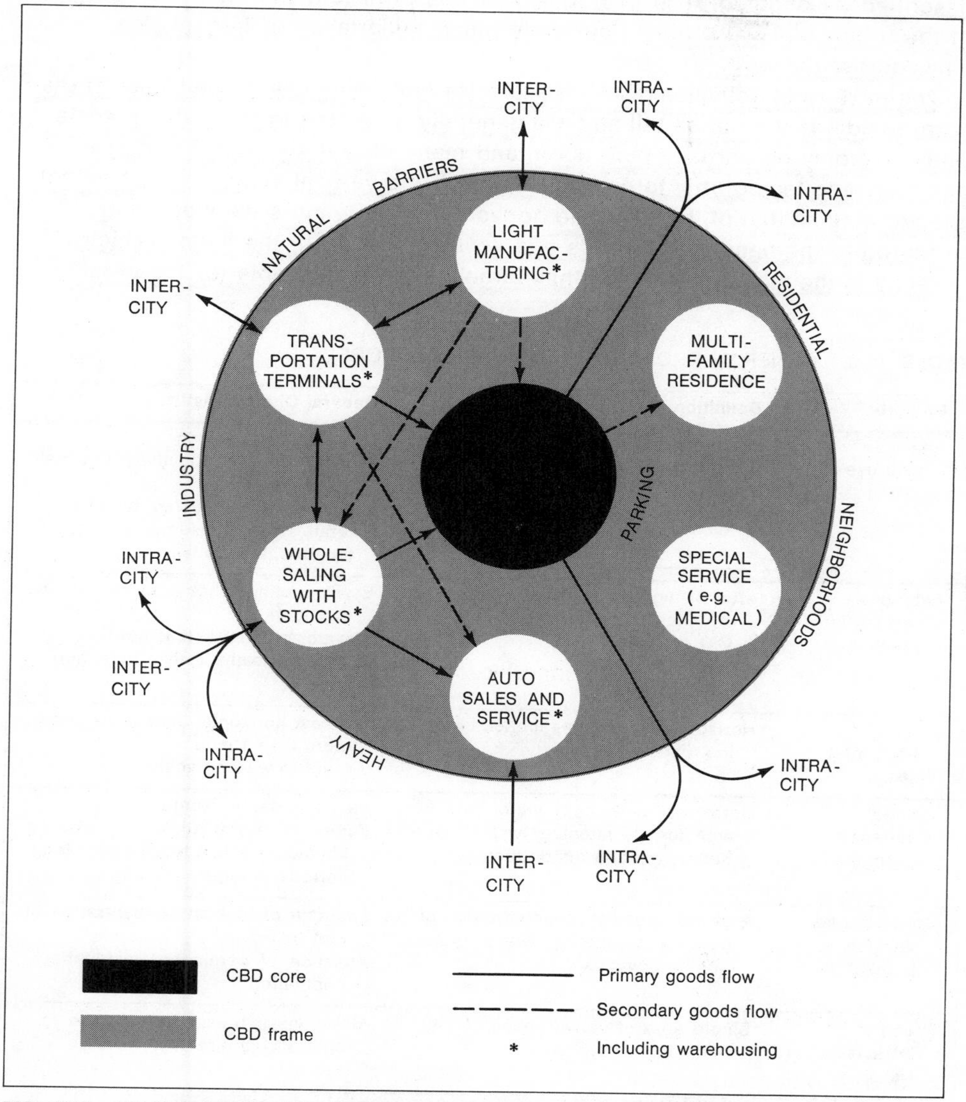

FIG. 12.3. DIAGRAMMATIC REPRESENTATION OF THE CORE-FRAME CONCEPT. (*Source:* Horwood and Boyce, 1959, Fig. 2.6.)

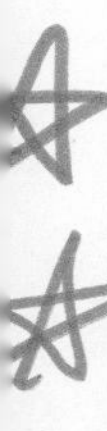

The frame of the CBD The frame is an area of mixed land use surrounding the inner core. Its general properties are listed in Table 12.4. Typical activities include business services, wholesaling with stocks, warehousing, light manufacturing, and various kinds of transport facilities, such as trucking and intercity transportation terminals. Intermingled with these are low-quality residences, especially aging multifamily houses, tenements, and transient rooming houses. The general character that such an admixture of land uses gives rise to can best be described as blighted. It is this zone that has furnished the sites for many of the urban renewal projects currently being undertaken in larger, older cities across the land.

The mixture of activities gives rise to a less intensive use of land than in the core. Buildings are not so tall and are generally restricted to the walk-up scale. Sites may only be partially built upon, and many vacant sites exist that are often devoted temporarily to parking. Although the vertical scale may not be so exaggerated as that of the core, the horizontal scale is more extended and is geared to the handling of goods and accommodation of the motor vehicle. In fact it is the motor vehicle that has largely been responsible for the creation

TABLE 12.3. GENERAL PROPERTIES OF THE CBD CORE

Property	Definition	General Characteristics
Intensive land use	Area of most intensive land use and highest concentration of social and economic activities within metropolitan complex	Multistoried buildings Highest retail productivity per unit ground area Land use characterized by offices, retail sales, consumer services, theaters, and banks
Extended vertical scale	Area of highest buildings within metropolitan complex	Easily distinguishable by aerial observation Elevator personnel linkages Grows vertically, rather than horizontally
Limited horizontal scale	Horizontal dimensions limited by walking distance scale	Greatest horizontal dimension rarely more than 1 mile Geared to walking scale
Limited horizontal change	Horizontal movement minor and not significantly affected by metropolitan population distribution	Very gradual horizontal change Zones of assimilation and discard limited to a few blocks over long periods of time
Concentrated daytime population	Area of greatest concentration of daytime population within metropolitan complex	Location of highest concentration of foot traffic Absence of permanent residential population
Focus of intracity mass transit	Single area of convergence of city mass transit system	Major mass transit interchange location for entire city
Center of specialized functions	Focus of headquarters offices for business, government, and industrial activities	Extensive use of office space for executive and policy-making functions Center of specialized professional and business services
Internally conditioned boundaries	Excluding natural barriers, CBD boundaries confined only by pedestrian scale of distance	Pedestrian and personnel linkages between establishments govern horizontal expansion Dependency on mass transit inhibits expansion

Source: Horwood and Boyce (1959), Table 2–1.

TABLE 12.4. GENERAL PROPERTIES OF THE CBD FRAME

Property	Definition	General Characteristics
Semi-intensive land use	Area of most intensive nonretail land use outside CBD core	Building height geared to walk-up scale Site only partially built on
Prominent functional subregions	Area of observable nodes of land utilization surrounding CBD core	Subfoci characterized mainly by wholesaling with stocks, warehousing, off-street parking, automobile sales and services, multifamily dwellings, intercity transportation terminals and facilities, light manufacturing, and some institutional uses
Extended horizontal scale	Horizontal scale geared to accommodation of motor vehicles and to handling of goods	Most establishments have off-street parking and docking facilities Movements between establishments vehicular
Unlinked functional subregions	Activity nodes essentially linked to areas outside CBD frame, except transportation terminals	Important establishments have linkages to CBD core (e.g., intercity transportation terminals, warehousing) and to outlying urban regions (e.g., wholesale distribution to suburban shopping areas and to service industries)
Externally conditioned boundaries	Boundaries affected by natural barriers and presence of large homogeneous areas with distinguishable internal linkages (e.g., residential areas with schools, shopping, and community facilities)	Commercial uses generally limited to flat land Growth tends to extend into areas of dilapidated housing CBD frame uses fill in interstices of central focus of highway and rail transportation routes

Source: Horwood and Boyce (1959), Table 2–11.

of the frame in that it brought with it greater locational freedom for a wide range of commercial activities and business services. Hence many activities were able to take advantage of inner locations close to the core of the CBD, but for which site rents are appreciably lower.

Subfoci are well developed in the frame; but unlike those typical of the core, they are not characterized by well-developed functional interlinkages. They are, for the most part, oriented outward to the rest of the urban area and beyond. Some of the uses within the frame, however, have important linkages with complementary activities in the core. This is particularly true of warehousing, a wide range of business services such as printing, and of course the facilities that transport people and goods to and from the concentration of activities in the core. Thus, although the core and the frame are two distinct and independent functional areas, they do not stand entirely apart; they are to a certain extent integrated functionally.

The difference in the intensity of use between the core and frame of the CBD is clearly illustrated in Figure 12.4. Intensity of use is measured by retail sales

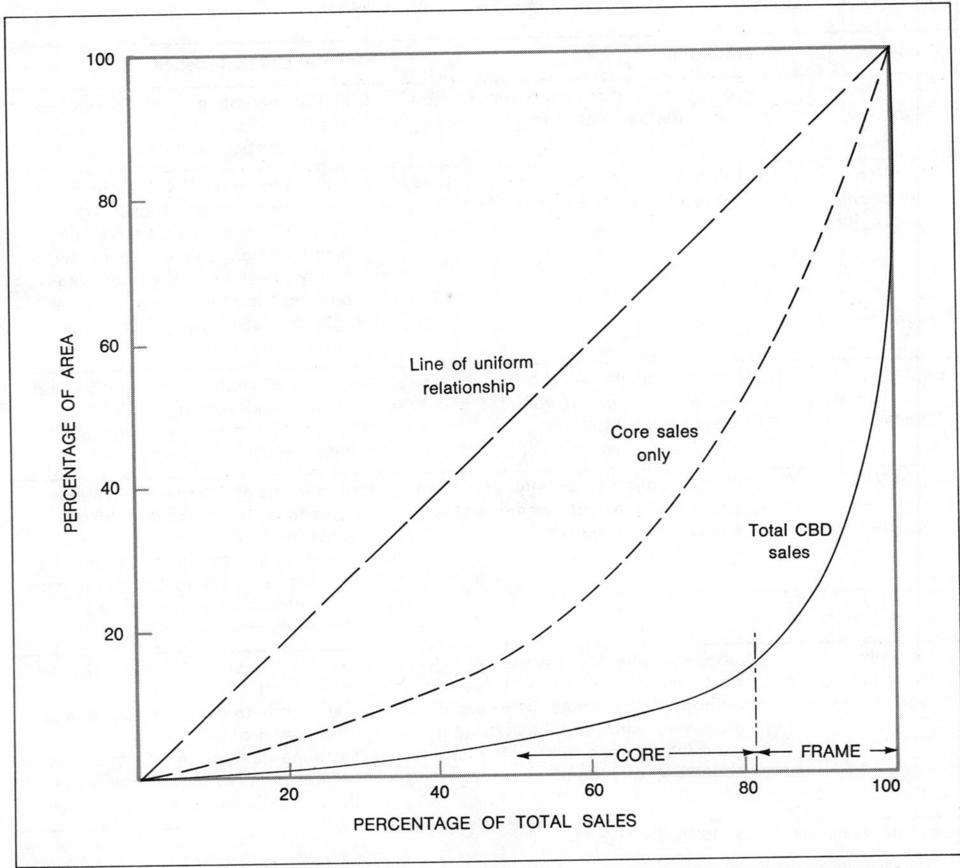

FIG. 12.4. SALES VOLUMES IN THE CORE AND FRAME OF THE CBD OF PHILADELPHIA, 1949. (*Source:* After Horwood and Boyce, 1959, Fig. 2.3.)

per city block, and the data refers to the CBD of Philadelphia in 1949. On the graph, a uniform distribution of sales within the CBD—if for example 50 percent of the sales occurred on 50 percent of the land area—would be represented by a straight line at an angle of 45 degrees as shown. Deviation from this diagonal indicates the extent to which concentration of sales takes place. Two curves are illustrated on the graph, one for the total sales within the Philadelphia CBD ($671 million in 1949) and the other for sales within its core. Both curves depart significantly from the diagonal. Total sales are shown to be extremely concentrated within the core of the CBD. Although this only accounted for 15.2 percent of the total CBD area, as much as 81 percent of total sales occurred there. The second curve indicates the more uniform distribution of sales within the core itself, although it is interesting to note that even here over two-thirds of the sales are generated on only about one-third of its area—an aspect of the internal structure of the CBD that is taken up in the following chapter.

DELIMITING THE CBD

The problem of delimiting the boundary of the CBD is, as is true for all regional studies, a difficult one because the edge of the central business district is a zone of transition. Admittedly, sharp breaks may occur around the CBDs of some cities whenever large obstacles such as parks, clusters of government buildings, or extensive railroad facilities prevent horizontal expansion. These are exceptional cases, however, and variation from one city to another prohibits their use as a basis for any standardized delimitation procedure. Largely because of this, the criteria used to delimit the CBD of individual cities has been a matter of local judgment set within the context of local problems.

It is therefore not surprising to find that a wide variety of measures have in the past been used in determining the boundary of the CBD. These include land values, trade figures, population distribution, building heights, traffic flows, and pedestrian counts, and several indexes based on land use. Regardless of the particular index used, however, it will be represented by a surface of intensity that declines with distance from a maximum somewhere within the core to a minimum at the outermost boundary of the frame.

THE CENTRAL BUSINESS INDEX METHOD

The CB Index method, proposed by Murphy and Vance (1954A) is generally recognized as a useful method of delimiting the CBD, especially for comparative purposes. The method rests on the analysis of detailed land-use mapping of all uses in the central areas of cities within which the true CBD is thought to lie. The city block is used as the basic areal unit, and two indexes (the Central Business Height Index and the Central Business Intensity Index) are calculated for each block from the land-use data. Calculation of these indexes, however, requires an initial classification of land uses into CBD and non-CBD types. The distinction used by Murphy and Vance was quite arbitrary and is shown in Table 12.5.

TABLE 12.5. NONCENTRAL BUSINESS DISTRICT USES[a]

Permanent residences (including apartment houses and rooming houses)
Government and public (including parks and public schools, as well as establishments carrying out city, county, state, and federal government functions)
Organizational institutions (churches, colleges, fraternal orders, etc.)
Industrial establishments (except for newspapers)
Wholesaling
Vacant buildings and stores
Vacant lots
Commercial storage and warehousing
Railroad tracks and switching yards

[a] All other uses are considered as CBD uses.
Source: Murphy and Vance, Jr. (1954A), Table 2.

The central business height index The CB Height Index (CBHI) is simply obtained by dividing the total floor area occupied by CBD uses in each block by the total ground-floor area of the block. The figure obtained in this way can be thought of as an indication of the number of floors of CBD use that would exist in the block if these uses were spread evenly over it. For example, if a block has a CBHI of 2.5, the amount of floor space devoted to CBD uses would be enough to cover the entire block with the equivalent of two and one half stories. In reality of course this amount of CBD floor space might be concentrated in a part of the block only, the rest of it being devoted to non-CBD uses. The shortcoming of this index is that it fails to take into account the proportion of the total floor area of the block devoted to CBD uses.

The central business intensity index To overcome this shortcoming a second index was developed. It is obtained by dividing the total floor area in the block devoted to CBD uses by the total floor area of the block itself. When multiplied by 100, the central business intensity index (CBII) represents the percentage of the total floor area (all floors combined) devoted to CBD uses.

These two indexes can be thought of as the coordinates that locate each block within a two-dimensional classification space. This is shown in Figure 12.5.

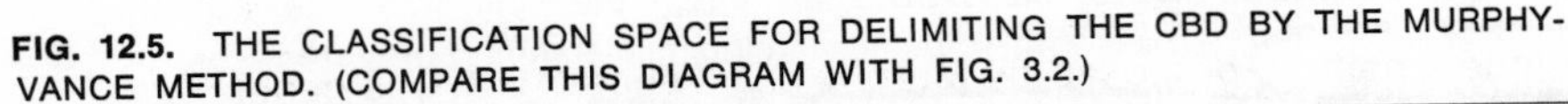

FIG. 12.5. THE CLASSIFICATION SPACE FOR DELIMITING THE CBD BY THE MURPHY-VANCE METHOD. (COMPARE THIS DIAGRAM WITH FIG. 3.2.)

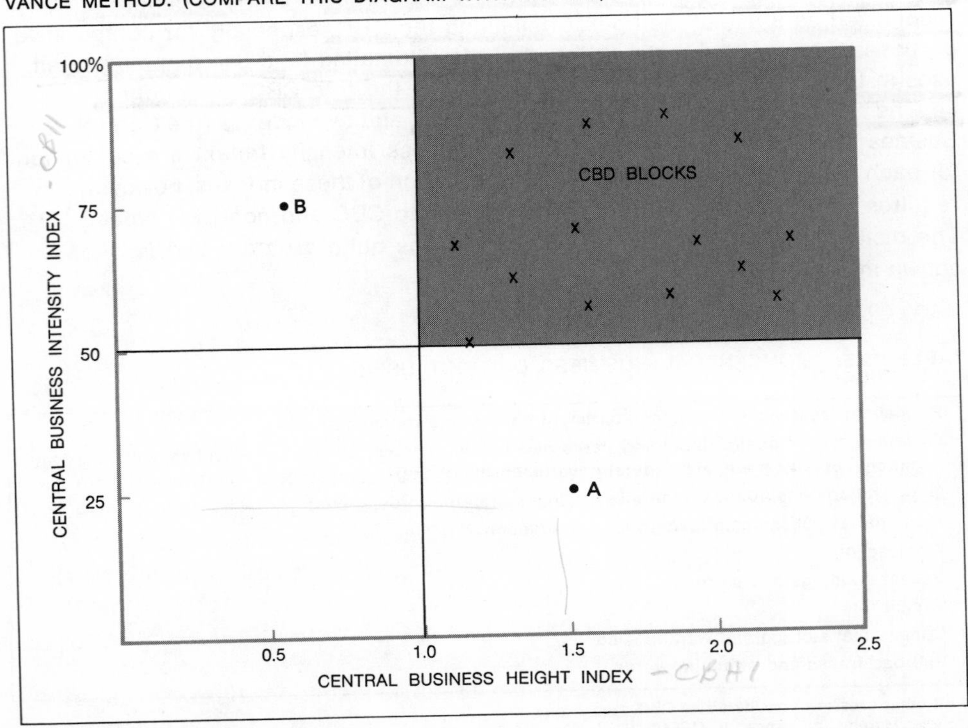

For example, on the graph point *A* represents a block for which the CBHI and CBII values are 1.5 and 25 percent respectively; similarly, point *B* represents a block with values of 0.5 and 75 percent. Murphy and Vance decided arbitrarily that for a block to be classified as forming part of the CBD, it should have a CBHI value of at least 1.0, and a CBII value of at least 50 percent. According to this definition, the CBD would include all the blocks falling within the upper right-hand shaded quadrant on the graph.

To apply the method meaningfully it was found necessary, however, to include blocks as part of the CBD even thought they did not have large enough CBHI or CBII indexes. For these blocks the following set of rules applied (Murphy and Vance, 1954A, p. 219):

1. The block must be part of a contiguous group surrounding the peak land-value intersections. Even though a block touches the others only at one corner, it is considered contiguous.

2. A block that does not reach the required index values, but is surrounded by blocks that do, is considered part of the central business district.

3. A block completely occupied by the buildings and grounds of a city hall or other municipal office building, a municipal auditorium, city police or fire department headquarters, or a central post office is included within the central business district if it is adjacent to (or contiguous with) blocks meeting the standard requirements. . . . In no instance should such government buildings . . . result in the extension of the central business district for more than one block beyond normal central business district blocks.

4. If the structures mentioned in Rule 3 occupy only part of a block that is contiguous with other central business district blocks and if the inclusion of these establishments as central business would bring the two indices of the block to the required totals, then the block is considered part of the central business district.

The application of the Central Business Index method for the delimitation of the CBD of Tulsa, Oklahoma, is illustrated in Figure 12.6. The boundary shown is based on the two indexes and the set of rules listed above.

Assessment of the method It should be remembered that the boundary resulting from the application of this method does not represent *the* boundary of the CBD but only an approximation to it; but it is most probably a fair approximation. The main advantages of the method lie in its simplicity and particularly its standardized approach to delimitation, which is essential if comparisons are to be made between central business districts. Its main disadvantages stem from the elements of subjectivity inherent in the selection of values for the indexes and in the classification of central business uses, for a different boundary would result if lower or higher values for the CBHI and CBII were to be used and if a different set of activities were defined as central business uses. The classification of uses excludes, for example, some of the functions listed as typical of the frame of the CBD. Consequently the boundary resulting from the method

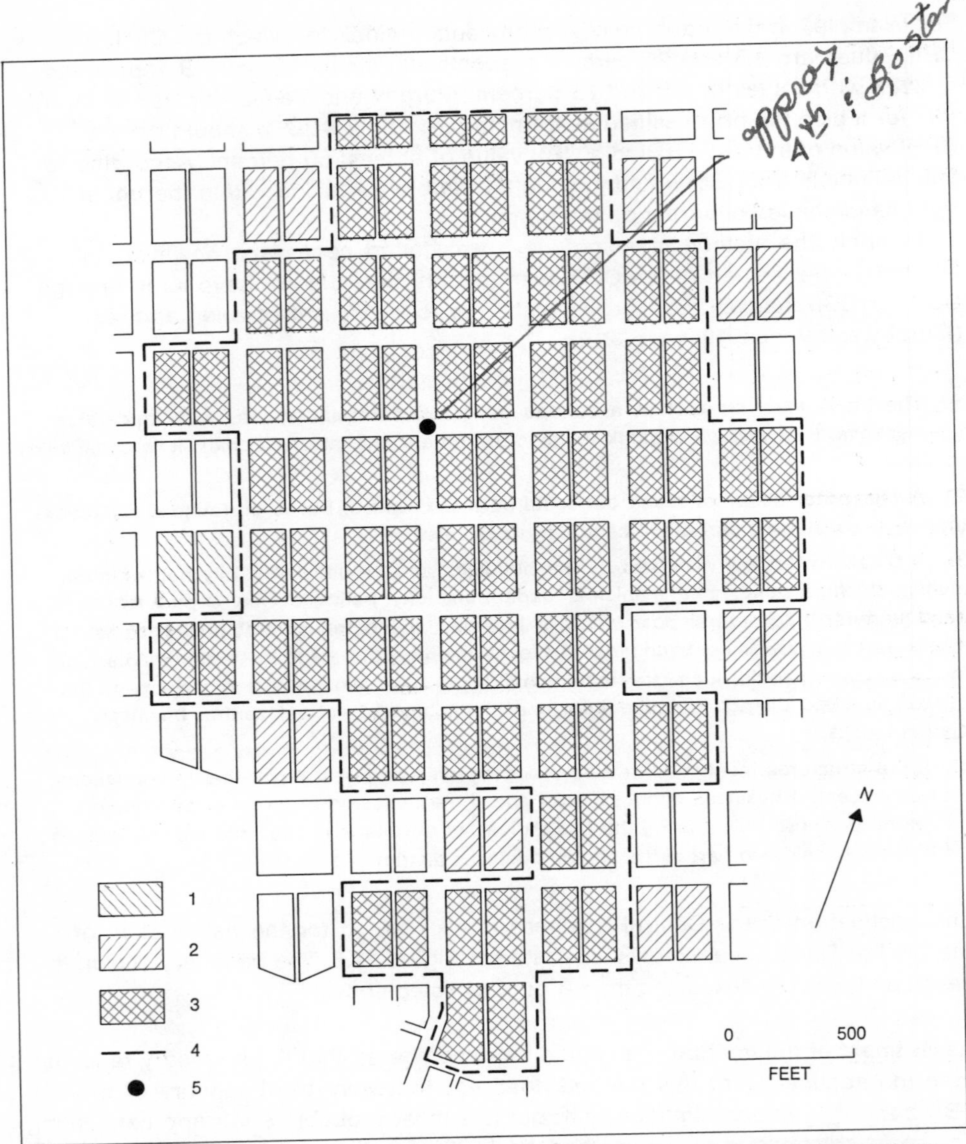

FIG. 12.6. THE CBD OF TULSA, OKLAHOMA, DELIMITED BY THE MURPHY-VANCE METHOD. ON THE MAP, THE SHADING IS AS FOLLOWS: (1) CENTRAL BUSINESS HEIGHT INDEX (CBHI) OF 1.0 OR MORE, (2) CENTRAL BUSINESS INTENSITY INDEX (CBII) OF 50.0 PERCENT OR MORE, (3) CBHI OF 1.0 OR MORE *AND* CBII OF 50.0 PERCENT OR MORE, (4) BOUNDARY OF THE CBD, AND (5) PEAK LAND VALUE INTERSECTION. (*Source:* Murphy and Vance, 1954A, Fig. 12.)

will generally fall short of the outer limit of the frame, but it will include more than just the core alone.

It was this shortcoming of the method as used by Murphy and Vance that has prompted others to attempt refinements of it. The work of Davies (1960) is particularly worthy of mention in that he recognized the need for distinguishing between the core and the frame of the CBD in the drawing of boundaries. In a study of the CBD of Capetown he decided to use a value of 4 instead of 1 for the CBHI, and a value of 80 percent instead of 50 percent for the CBII, which together with a more refined classification of central business uses he claimed would give a satisfactory delimitation of the core of the CBD.

CHARACTERISTICS OF CENTRAL BUSINESS DISTRICTS

The central business index method was used by Murphy and Vance to delimit the boundaries of the CBDs of nine medium-sized cities. Although each CBD can be expected to differ in its particular features, the results of comparative study enable some broad generalizations to be made about the size and land use structure of the CBD (Murphy and Vance, 1954B).

Size characteristics Selected size characteristics of the nine central business districts are listed in Table 12.6. The most noticeable feature in the table is the considerable variation in the size of the CBD between the nine cities. Using the figures in column 5 of the table, CBD's vary in size from 75.5 acres in Mobile to 207.7 acres in Tulsa; the average size based on this measure is indicated as 120 acres. Variation in the size of individual CBD's can only be understood from detailed study of their historical development and local conditions. However, it does appear that size is partly related to population of the incorporated city in which it is located, although there does not appear to be any regular relationship between CBD size and population of either

TABLE 12.6. SELECTED SIZE CHARACTERISTICS FOR NINE CENTRAL BUSINESS DISTRICTS

Place (1)	Population Size 1950[a] (000's) (2)	Acreages in CBD: Total Floor Space (3)	Acreages in CBD: Ground-Floor Area (4)	Central Business Floor Space (acres) (5)	Indexes[b]: CBHI (6)	Indexes[b]: CBII (7)
Grand Rapids, Mich.	277	195.5	58.9	142.5	2.4	72.9
Salt Lake City, Utah	277	255.4	120.8	186.4	1.5	73.0
Worcester, Mass.	219	176.7	59.6	120.0	2.0	67.9
Phoenix, Ariz.	216	138.8	76.8	113.8	1.5	82.0
Sacramento, Calif.	212	228.4	108.8	167.0	1.5	73.1
Tulsa, Okla.	206	251.8	79.8	207.7	2.6	82.5
Mobile, Ala.	183	107.1	50.4	75.5	1.5	70.5
Tacoma, Wash.	168	122.4	52.4	98.6	1.9	80.5
Roanoke, Va.	107	124.5	53.3	103.1	1.9	82.8
Average (median)	212	176.7	59.6	120.0	1.9	73.1

[a] Population figure for the urbanized area, 1950.
[b] The CBHI is calculated by dividing the total floor space devoted to central business uses (column 5) by the total ground-floor space (column 4); the CBII is obtained by dividing the total floor space devoted to central business uses (column 5) by the total CBD floor space (column 3).
Source: Murphy and Vance, Jr. (1954B), after Table 1.

the local SMSA, the city's trade area, or the population of the urbanized area in which it is located.

Land use characteristics The variation in the size of the CBD is paralleled by considerable variation in structure. Table 12.7 shows the proportion of total central business district floor space devoted to the main categories of land use for the average of the nine CBD's. The importance of the service-financial-office-use category is clearly revealed, and this category occupies about 44 percent of total floor space. Retailing ranks second (32 percent), and noncentral uses rank third (24 percent) as users of the CBD floor space. Considerable variation is also shown to exist between different land use types within each of the three major categories.

Figure 12.7 shows the same data graphically as well as the comparable breakdown for each of the nine CBD's separately. Considerable variation is shown to exist in the proportion of each CBD devoted to the three main categories and their subtypes. Roanoke, Tulsa, and Phoenix have the smallest proportions of noncentral uses. All three cities are relatively young; and by the time they were built, there was little demand for space in the CBD except for true central uses. Conversely, nearly one-third of the CBD of Worcester is devoted to noncentral uses, particularly to public and organizational uses. Variation in the proportion of the CBD devoted to the other two categories is also marked and

TABLE 12.7. LAND USE CHARACTERISTICS OF AN AVERAGE CBD[a]

Central Uses	Proportion of the Total Floor Space in CBD	Total Space in Category
Service-Financial-Office Uses	44.0 percent	100.0 percent
General offices	12.7	29.0
Transient residences	11.7	27.0
Parking	7.0	16.0
Headquarters offices	5.0	11.0
Service trades	4.0	9.0
Financial	3.0	7.0
Transportation	0.6	1.0
Retail Business	32.0 percent	100.0 percent
Variety	9.4	29.0
Household	5.3	17.0
Miscellaneous	5.3	17.0
Clothing	4.2	13.0
Foodstuffs	3.9	12.0
Automotive	3.9	12.0
Noncentral Uses	24.0 percent	100.0 percent
Public-organizational	11.7	49.0
Vacant	5.5	23.0
Residential	3.5	14.0
Wholesale	1.8	8.0
Industrial	1.5	6.0

[a] Average for the nine central business districts listed in Table 12.6.
Source: After Murphy and Vance, Jr. (1954B), Figure 25.

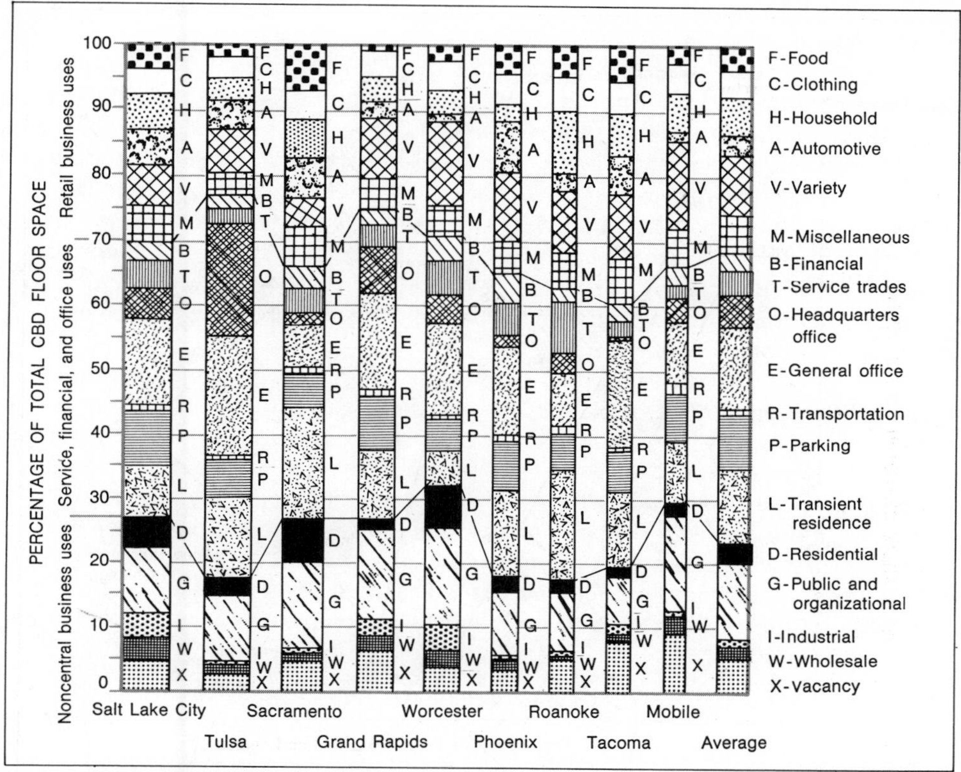

FIG. 12.7. THE PROPORTION OF THE TOTAL FLOOR SPACE DEVOTED TO MAJOR LAND USE CATEGORIES IN NINE CENTRAL BUSINESS DISTRICTS. (*Source:* Murphy and Vance, 1954B, Fig. 25.)

can only be understood from detailed study of the individual cities themselves. In part, the land use structure reflects the functional specialization and hinterland characteristics of each city.

OUTLYING SHOPPING CENTERS

That the outlying shopping centers within cities are consistently related to the hierarchy of central places in rural areas is shown in Figure 12.8. Centers within the urban area form part of the overall systematic relationship between trade areas, population served, levels in the hierarchy, and the density of population. Differences in the structure of the hierarchy within urban areas may, however, be expected on account of much higher densities of demand there. Because of the more extreme market condition in urban areas (1) business types are able to enter the hierarchy at lower levels than in rural areas; (2) the higher density and diversity of demand makes possible a far greater degree of

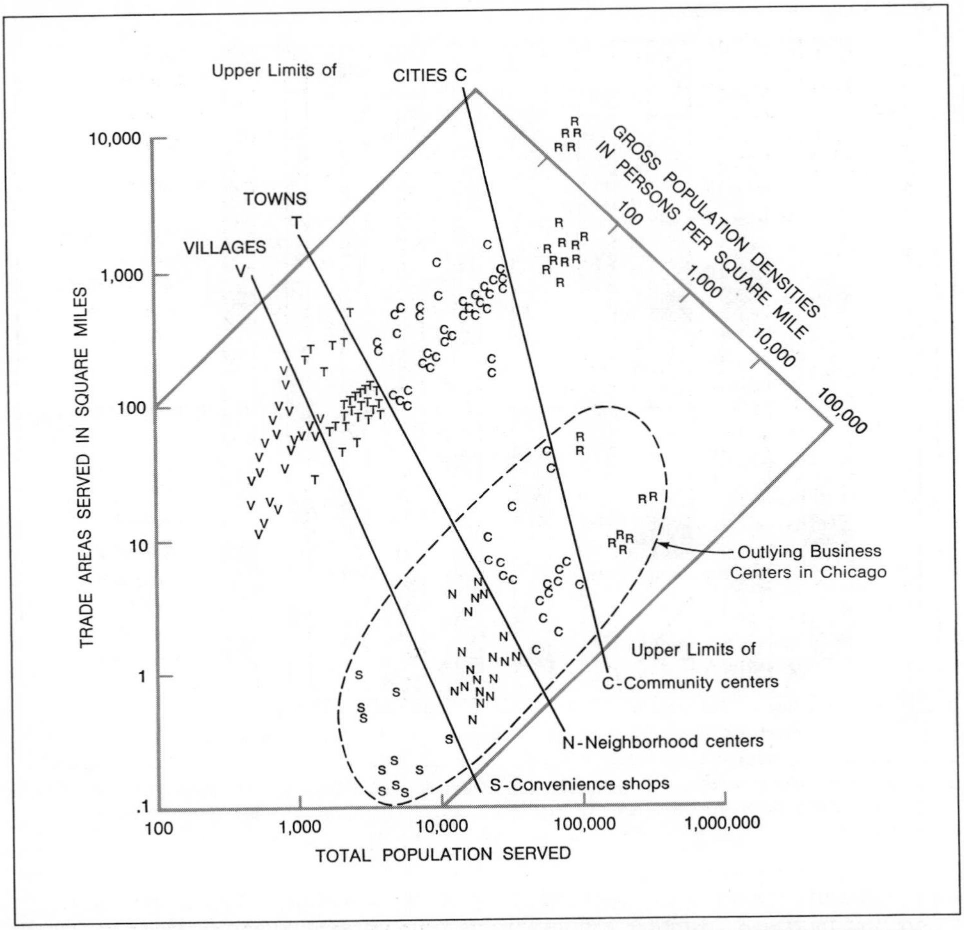

FIG. 12.8. SYSTEMATIC VARIATIONS IN THE HIERARCHY OF URBAN SHOPPING CENTERS AND RURAL CENTRAL PLACES. (*Source:* Berry, 1967A, Fig. 2–9.)

specialization between establishments of the same type, and this tendency increases with the population size of cities; and (3) the urban market is considerably more diversified on account of marked differences in the socio-economic characteristics and ethnic groupings between various parts of the city. The effect of these conditions is to make centers at any given level in the urban hierarchy considerably more complex and less rigid in their functional structure than those at comparable levels in the rural central place system. A general impression of the functional structure of the different level outlying shopping centers is given in Table 12.8. Centers at the two lowest levels are essentially of the convenience type.

The street-corner developments constitute the most ubiquitous element of the pattern of nucleated centers; consequently they are scattered throughout

TABLE 12.8. A REPRESENTATIVE SAMPLE OF BUSINESS TYPES TYPICAL OF OUTLYING SHOPPING CENTERS

Street corner
- General stores
- Groceries
- Drugstores

Neighborhood
- Supermarkets
- Bakeries
- Barber shops and beauty salons
- Laundries—laundromats

Community centers
- Variety stores
- Clothing stores
- General furniture stores
- Florists
- Jewelers
- Real estate agents
- Banks

Regional centers
- Department stores
- Shoe stores
- Camera shops
- Sporting goods stores
- Other more specialized types (i.e. music stores)
- Professional services

Source: After Berry (1959), Table 1.

residential neighborhoods to ensure maximum accessibility to consumers residing within a two- or three-block radius of the cluster. They normally comprise from one to four business types of the lowest threshold types, and the grocer-drugstore combination is most common.

Neighborhood centers are characterized by the addition of higher threshold convenience types, which supply the major necessities to consumers living in local areas of the city. Grocery stores, small supermarkets, laundries and dry cleaners, barber and beauty shops, and perhaps small restaurants are the most usual business types represented.

Centers at the higher levels in the hierarchy are distinguished by their shopping goods, which are added to the convenience functions of the lower-level centers. In addition they provide a range of personal, professional, and business

TABLE 12.9. AVERAGE SIZE CHARACTERISTICS OF UNPLANNED SHOPPING

Level of Center	Number	Ground-Floor Establish-ments	Business Types
Major regional centers	4	196	60
Shopping goods centers	14	114	43
Community centers	25	73	37
Neighborhood centers	21	41	25

[a] The median is used as the average for all characteristics.
Source: Berry (1963), from data presented in Table 6.

services. Community centers provide the less specialized shopping goods, such as variety and clothing stores, small furniture and appliance stores, florists, jewelers, and in many cases a post office. Supplementing these are a range of more ubiquitous services and entertainment facilities.

The highest level regional centers are set above the community centers not so much by the types of business they perform as by the number and variety of activities they provide for large segments of the urban area. Increased specialization of business types thus becomes the keynote at this level.

As indicated in Figure 12.1, outlying shopping centers may be either planned or unplanned. Most of the older centers within central cities are of the unplanned sort and have grown up around major street intersections. But in the more recently developed suburbs, and also in those parts of central cities that have undergone redevelopment within the past decade, shopping centers are increasingly planned on a unitary, integrated basis. Planning, however, affects largely the design of centers, and to a lesser extent their location, and has little effect on their functional structure. Hence both planned and unplanned centers at any given level in the hierarchy may be expected to provide essentially the same kinds of retail and service businesses. Planned centers do differ in their structural characteristics, however, as will be indicated below.

Regardless of whether centers are planned or unplanned, they share the same degrees of centrality within urban areas. By clustering together at discrete locations, business types are able to capitalize on the tendency of consumers to make single, home-based trips, shopping from store to store within centers for the bundle of goods they expect to be offered by them. Functions at any one level are thus linked together into nucleations by the desire of consumers to visit several establishments on a single shopping trip.

THE HIERARCHY OF SHOPPING CENTERS IN THE CITY OF CHICAGO

Specific details of the structure of outlying shopping centers can best be illustrated by a study of outlying shopping centers undertaken in the city of Chicago (Berry, 1963). In this study the structural characteristics of 64 outlying

CENTERS IN THE CITY OF CHICAGO, 1961[a]

Ground-Floor Area (square feet)	Front Feet	Estimated Sales[b] ($ millions)
566,627	6,562	60
314,693	3,170	32
161,250	2,075	25
90,125	1,200	18

[b] Sales data, obtained from a special tabulation of the Census of Business, 1958, do not relate exactly to the centers as they were delimited in the study but to a group of census tracts most closely approximating them.

shopping centers were analyzed using factor analysis. The resulting typology indicated that a four-tier hierarchy existed within the city limits. The distribution of these centers within the city is shown in Figure 12.9. The basic size characteristics of an average center at each of the four levels are presented in Table 12.9. The general features are consistent with what was discussed regarding the rural central place hierarchy in Chapter 7. Low-level centers are more

ubiquitous in the urban area than high-level centers, although from the table this is apparently not the case for the neighborhood centers. This discrepancy results from the way in which shopping centers were identified in the Chicago study. From the relationship previously noted between the location of shopping centers and the minor land value peakings within the city, only those retail clusters with peak land values of more than $750 per front-foot were selected. Consequently, many of the smaller neighborhood centers, and all of the street-corner developments were omitted from the analysis. Had these been included, then the regularity would have been as expected from the nature of hierarchies.

The other features of the table are much as expected. High-level centers have more business types, more establishments, account for greater frontages, and occupy larger ground-floor areas than low-level centers. Sales generated at each level follow the same general sequence, and data showing numbers of persons employed, size of trade area, and number of shopping trips would tend to emphasize the regularity with size of center.

Table 12.10 indicates the way in which functions most typical of each level enter into the hierarchy. The difference between the essentially convenience-goods nature of the neighborhood center and to a lesser extent the community center is clearly revealed. The shopping-goods centers and major regional centers are particularly characterized by the addition of shopping goods.

Centers at each higher level in the hierarchy perform all the functions of the lower-level centers in addition to a set of high-threshold, more specialized types, which set them above the low-level centers in the hierarchy. However, because of the greater opportunities within the urban area for remaining in business, it is not uncommon to find some high-threshold types in lower level centers. This gives rise to rather more complex functional patterns at centers in cities than those typical of rural areas. Comparison of Table 12.10 and Table 7.5 will give

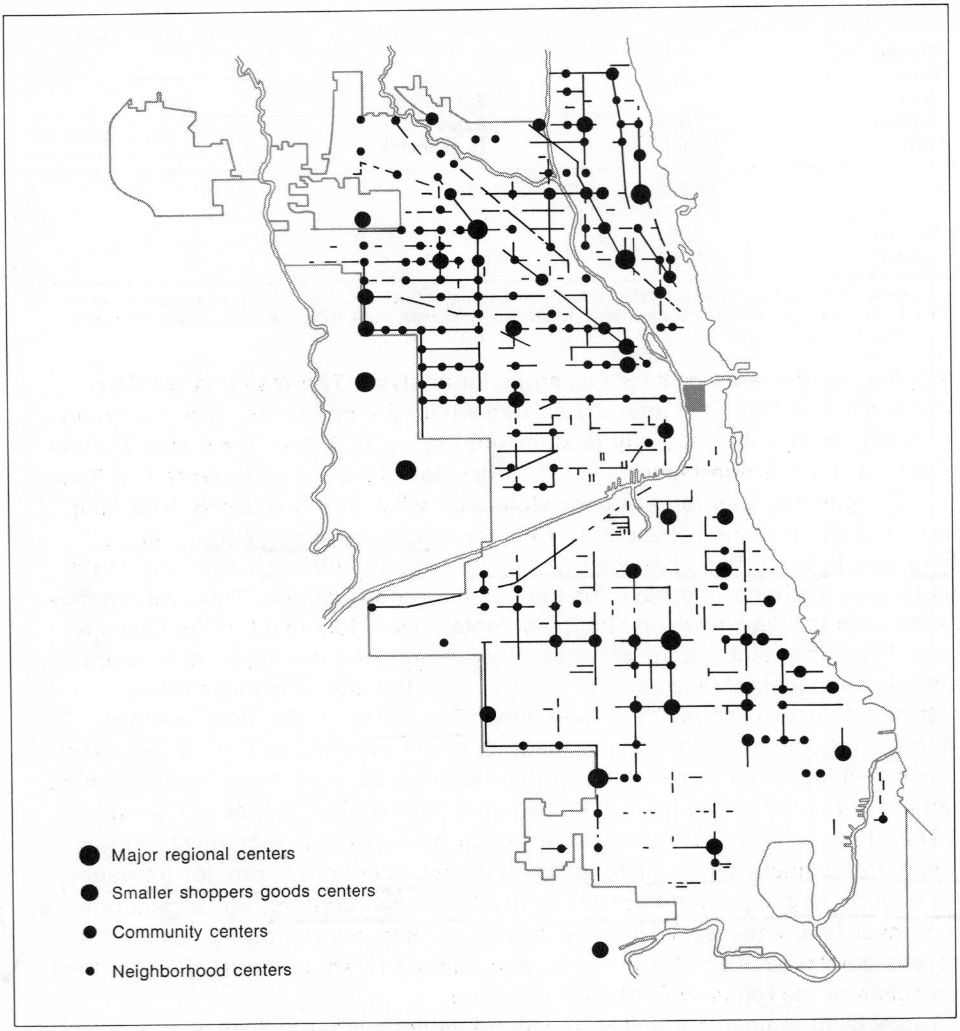

Major regional centers
Smaller shoppers goods centers
Community centers
Neighborhood centers

FIG. 12.9. THE HIERARCHY OF SHOPPING CENTERS IN THE CITY OF CHICAGO. (*Source:* Berry, 1963, Fig. 10.)

some idea of how certain functions enter centers at lower levels in urban areas than in rural central places.

Planned centers in Chicago Nine of the largest planned centers within the Chicago city limits and a number of larger planned centers in suburbs immediately adjacent to the city were also included in the analysis. Using the same method of classification, a similar four-tier hierarchical arrangement was also indicated for them. However, some noticeable differences exist between the planned

TABLE 12.10. ORDER OF ENTRY OF FUNCTIONS IN THE HIERARCHY OF UNPLANNED CENTERS IN THE CITY OF CHICAGO, 1961

	Centers			
	Neighborhood	**Community**	**Shopping Goods**	**Major Regional**
	Groceries	Supermarket	Supermarket	Supermarket
Core neighborhood functions	Variety stores Men's and boys' clothing Women's clothes Eating places Drinking places Drugstores Liquor stores Jewelry Currency exchanges Laundries Beauty shops Barber shops	Yes	Yes	Yes
Functions added at the community level		Hardware Department stores Candy stores Bakeries Family shoes Furniture Radio-TV Real estate agents Physicians Optometrists	Yes	Yes
Functions added at smaller shopping-goods centers			Butchers Millinery Children's wear Men's shoes Women's shoes Appliances Music stores Gift and novelty stores Banks Movies Dentists	Yes
Functions performed only by major regional centers				Hosiery Family clothing stores Custom tailors Drapery stores Miscellaneous home furnishings Stationers Florists Camera stores

Source: Berry (1963), Table 19.

centers and their unplanned equivalents. Apart from the obvious differences in their architectural features, the planned centers are generally smaller in content and structure. They offer fewer business types, have fewer establishments, which are however normally larger in size than those in unplanned centers, and have smaller ground-floor areas than their unplanned counterparts at the same levels.

Major planned regional centers contain an average of between 50 and 70 establishments, have about 40 business types, and occupy ground-floor areas exceeding 400,000 square feet. Planned shopping-goods centers have between 30 and 40 stores, 25–30 functions, and ground-floor areas of 150,000 square feet. The comparable figures for the community- and neighborhood-level centers are respectively 25 establishments, 20 business types, and 100,000 square feet of floor space, and 17, 15, and 50,000 square feet.

The implication from these figures is that, at any given level in the hierarchy, planned centers provide fewer business types than unplanned centers; yet above it was stated that planning had little effect upon the functional structure of shopping centers. What happens is that the same core functions at each level are provided but many of the peripheral uses are absent. Thus in planned shopping-goods centers—and to a lesser extent in the major planned regional centers—the peripheral uses such as army and navy stores, furniture stores, bars, liquor stores, insurance agents, and movie houses typical of the unplanned centers at this level are missing. In addition, planned centers normally do not have any extensive upper-floor uses. Hence the upper-floor medical-dental complex, common at larger unplanned centers, is not represented, unless specific provision has been made in planning the center for a professional office building.

The same may be said for the planned community and neighborhood centers. At the former, the doctor-dentist-lawyer complex found at the upper floors of unplanned centers is missing, as are such business types as bars, liquor stores, radio-TV sales and repair, and so on. On the other hand, planned community centers tend to offer certain shopping goods not found at the unplanned centers, including junior department stores, gift and card shops, and certain of the clothing functions. Neighborhood centers are much the same whether planned or unplanned, although the newer ones usually have supermarkets instead of grocery stores and often provide a gas station and laundromat—functions noted as typical of the ribbons in unplanned areas of the city.

The reduction in number of business types at planned centers is related to the reduced number of establishments at them, for shopping-center developers seek to restrict competition between stores within the center by controlling the amount of functional duplication. Hence there is usually only one establishment of a given business type at each planned center, although at the larger centers the amount of duplication increases to cater adequately to the larger number of consumers who visit them. The generally larger size of establishments reflects the technological changes currently taking place in retailing toward larger economies of scale, especially in such functions as drugstores, supermarkets, variety stores, and so on. Elimination of duplication together with these trends in retailing results in the tendency for larger store sizes in planned centers.

The effects of income differences on the hierarchy We have observed in the previous chapter that one of the distinguishing features of a large urban area is the considerable variation in socio-economic conditions between its various parts. At least a simple distinction can be made in most cities between areas of high and middle income and those with low incomes. When these areas occupy considerable portions of cities, as they do in the larger metropolitan areas, the differences in purchasing power, and related to this the nature of demands, may be expected to influence the structure and functional components of shopping centers in them. This is certainly the case in Chicago, where low-income neighborhoods occupy an extensive part of the city.

Accordingly unplanned shopping centers occur in different ways in the low-income parts of the city than they do in the high-income areas. In the high-income parts of the city, shopping goods are provided by major regional centers located at strategic points and by the smaller shopping-goods centers located around the edges of the trade areas of the larger centers. Convenience goods are provided by the high-level community centers and smaller neighborhood centers. In contrast to this normal development, Table 12.11 indicates that low-income neighborhoods lack both the highest level major regional centers and also for the most part the community-level centers, but have a greater proportion of the low-level neighborhood centers. Consequently in these areas the hierarchy is simpler and comprises essentially only two levels: the smaller shopping-goods centers that provide most of the shopping goods required by the low-income consumers and a larger number of neighborhood centers that provide the basic necessities. The effect of the lower incomes, therefore, is to eliminate the larger centers providing greater varieties of goods, more specialized stores, and greater opportunities for a full range of shopping choice.

The effect of the lower incomes is not only confined to the types of shopping centers located in the different socio-economic areas of the city. It also underlies some considerable changes in their structural characteristics. For example, the shopping-goods centers in the low-income areas are noticeably smaller than their counterparts in the high-income areas. In the former case they have on average 40 business types, 100 establishments, about 3,100 feet of street frontage, and occupy a little less than 300,000 square feet of building area. In contrast, the latter perform on an average 54 different functions, have

TABLE 12.11. DIFFERENCES IN THE OCCURRENCE OF CENTERS IN AREAS OF THE CITY OF CHICAGO

Class of Center	Area Served: High Income	Area Served: Low Income
Major regional	4	—
Smaller shopping-goods centers	5	9
Community centers	22	3
Neighborhood centers	7	14
Totals	38	26

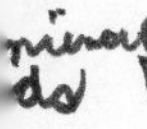

Source: Berry (1963), Table B1.

an additional three or four business types at upper floors, 150 ground-floor establishments covering 330,000 square feet of ground-floor building space, and account for a frontage of over 3,600 feet.

Although there appears to be little difference in the size of the community-level centers in the two areas, there is a considerable difference at the neighborhood level, for in the low-income part of the city, the neighborhood centers are the largest centers exclusively concerned with selling convenience goods. In line with this more important role, centers at this level are slightly larger in the low-income areas than their equivalents in the high-income parts of the city. Thus they perform 28 types of business as opposed to 25 business types in the high-income areas; have 55 as against 40 stores; occupy 125,000 square feet of ground-floor areas opposed to only 75,000 square feet in high-income areas; and account for frontages of 1,500 feet as opposed to about 1,000 feet.

Another important difference between centers in the two areas relates to the size of establishments at centers. In the centers serving the low-income parts of the city, establishments tend on an average to be larger than those at centers in the high-income areas. This is especially true for such functions as army and navy stores, men's and women's clothing stores, millinery shops, family shoe stores, furniture stores, radio-TV stores, and liquor stores. Several reasons may be offered for this tendency. First, lower rents within centers coupled with greater availability of space enable individual stores to operate on a less-rent intensive basis. Second, demand is lacking for the smaller specialized stores, so that fewer larger stores offering a more general bundle of goods provide the goods and services provided. Third, many of the retail properties in the older parts of the city were laid out on a larger scale than those in the relatively newer parts of the city.

Lastly, lower levels of demand result in greater duplication rates at centers in the low-income areas. As areas have undergone transition from high- to low-income levels, the more specialized functions in the centers have been unable to stay in business and so have left. The space that they left behind is eventually taken over by more ubiquitous functions, which were previously located in the ribbons. In this way the centers are able to remain full, but with substantial duplication of the low-threshold functions. However, as incomes continue to fall and trade areas shrink, so the number of business types is reduced at centers, resulting in high vacancy rates and eventually in occupation of former retail property by alien uses.

STRUCTURAL RELATIONSHIPS IN THE URBAN HIERARCHY

It is reasonable to assume that the number and types of retail service activities in urban areas are constantly being pushed and pulled toward an equilibrium situation; that is, to a high level of adjustment to the demands of the consumers served. But this state of balance is hard to reach because the supply of, and demands for, goods is constantly changing. However, at any given stage in the evolution of the hierarchy of shopping centers, an approximation to the equilibrium conditions might be expected to occur even if perfect development is never obtained. Certain areas of the city will have more or less retail and service activities because people and their incomes are more mobile than retail and service businesses.

This idea of a tendency toward equilibrium was, of course, implied by the regularities noted in the structure of the central place hierarchy and discussed in Chapter 7. Because the same underlying mechanism, leading to the formation of a hierarchical structure, operates in the case of shopping centers within urban areas, it is to be expected that analogous kinds of regularities will be characteristic of the hierarchy of shopping centers as well. The essential features of the structural relationships in the urban case can be outlined as follows. The total sales of a center ($) in the hierarchy will depend on the total population served by it (*P*). In turn, the number of business types (*BT*) it provides will depend on its total sales; the larger the total sales of a center, the more business types it should provide. Since high-level centers have more business types and establishments—and these occupy a larger floor area—than lower level centers, it can also be argued that the number of establishments (*E*) at a center will be related in some way to its number of business types. It follows from this that variation in the ground-floor area (*G*) at shopping centers will generally depend on the number of establishments, other things being equal (Berry, 1963).

The chain of relationships can be represented symbolically by the following set of functional relations:

$$\$ = f_1(P) \qquad \text{equations (1)}$$
$$BT = f_2(\$) \qquad (2)$$
$$E = f_3(BT) \qquad (3)$$
$$G = f_4(E) \qquad (4)$$

The structural equations will hold separately for the hierarchy in high- and low-income parts of the city, for in this way marked variations in level of demand (income) are held constant. The exact forms of these relationships for the hierarchy in Chicago are listed in Table 12.12, for the planned centers, and for the unplanned centers in both the high- and low-income areas of the city.

The correlation coefficients for the relationships between variables in the high-income part of the city (Table 12.12, Part A) indicates the close agreement to equilibrium conditions found there. But in contrast to this, the equivalent relationships in the low-income areas are considerably less well developed (Table 12.12 Part B). In each case the correlation coefficients are smaller than those in the high-income area, indicating the lower level of adjustment in the retail structure in the poorer part of the city. Table 12.12C gives the same relationships for the planned centers, which are typified by lower correlations than the equivalent unplanned centers in the high-income areas. Planned centers are less commonly found in the poorer areas of cities except where they form part of redevelopment schemes.

TABLE 12.12. STRUCTURAL EQUATIONS FOR SHOPPING CENTERS IN CITY OF CHICAGO

Equation	Correlation[a]
(A) Unplanned Centers in the High-Income Areas	
1. $\$ = 18{,}652{,}558 + 145(P)$	0.630
2. $BT = -201.8 + 32.48(\text{Log } \$)$	0.715
3. $\text{Log } E = 1.111 + 0.020(BT)$	0.956
4. $\text{Log } G = 3.268 + 1.043(\text{Log } E)$	0.932
(B) Unplanned Centers in the Low-Income Areas[b]	
1 & 2. $BT = -32.7 + 13.161(\text{Log } P)$	0.467
3. $\text{Log } E = 1.242 + .018(BT)$	0.830
4. $\text{Log } G = 3.145 + 1.126(\text{Log } E)$	0.910
(C) Planned Centers	
2. $BT = -83 + 14.848(\text{Log } \$)$	0.640
3. $\text{Log } E = .843 + .0263(BT)$	0.948
4. $\text{Log } G = 3.261 + 1.2567(\text{Log } E)$	0.922

[a] The Pearson Product Moment correlation coefficient is used. The closer the value of this is to 1.0, the higher the degree of correlation.
[b] Equations 1 and 2 are combined in the lower income areas on account of the lack of sales data.
Source: Berry (1963), from Tables 49–51.

The fact that a considerable part of the commercial structure of Chicago, like that of other cities, is not in equilibrium is a reflection of the processes of change going on in cities. Changes in the commercial structure of cities in North America are currently being influenced by factors such as (1) the increased mobility associated with the automobile and the more complicated shopping patterns it brings about, (2) changing purchasing levels and tastes associated with rising incomes, (3) the increasing tendency to control commercial developments through the zoning mechanism, which if anything tends to reinforce the trend toward larger, integrated centers, (4) changes in the technology of retailing itself with its emphasis on increasingly large-scale operations, and (5) the actual physical changes associated with urban renewal. Because of these kinds of influences, the commercial structure of cities is in a constant state of flux, even though in part it may exhibit the characteristics of short-term stability and equilibrium.

13

Shopping centers, ribbons, and specialized areas have a spatial extent and constitute small uniform regions suitable for analysis at a more elemental level. These conformations have been treated in the previous chapter as if they were

points on maps and graphs, and differences between their functional structure have been stressed at an aggregated level. In this chapter we are particularly concerned with some aspects of the internal structure of these conformations. Of particular interest are the differences in the location of business types within commercial areas and the small-scale land use patterns to which these differences give rise. These patterns may be found to some extent in all retail conformations, but distinctive arrangements of business types are most noticeable within shopping centers, and especially within the older unplanned ones. It is at these that the economic forces influencing the intensity of land use discussed in Chapter 9 operate unhindered by social, political, and architectural (in the case of newer planned shopping centers) constraints to give rise to significant land value–land use relationships. These relationships may be particularly well developed at the larger outlying shopping centers but reach their optimum within the CBD, where they result in well-ordered arrangements of commercial activities. The ensuing discussion is therefore concerned with a description and analysis of the arrangement of commercial and business activities within the CBD and outlying shopping centers.

CBD LAND VALUES AND LAND USE

As the area of most intensive commercial land use within cities, the CBD is associated with a disproportionately higher level of land values than the rest of the urban area it dominates. Although the average level of land values is high, actual values vary considerably between locations within the central district. They reach a maximum at what is called the peak-value intersection (the PVI)—the street intersection within the CBD at which intensity of land use is greatest. This intersection may, but normally does not, coincide with the geometrical center of the CBD. Away from this maximum at the PVI, values decrease with distance in all directions. So marked is this decline that at the edge of the CBD values are generally only about 5 percent of that at the PVI.

GRADIENTS

The land value gradient within the CBD is concave but does not, however, assume the form of a smooth curve. Rather it is stepped in character, indicating that the surface of values is discontinuous. Normally there is a very steep drop in values within a short distance from the PVI, but thereafter the decline is more gradual. Hence, land values decrease with distance away from the PVI but at a decreasing rate. Neither is the gradient symmetrical about the PVI. Land values decline more sharply in some directions than in others. Usually this decline is less rapid along the longitudinal axis of the CBD than in the direction at right angles to it.

These features of the land value surface within the CBD are shown for the small city of Dubuque, Iowa, in Figure 13.1. The gradients represent slices across the CBD in a north-south and east-west direction intersecting at the PVI. On the

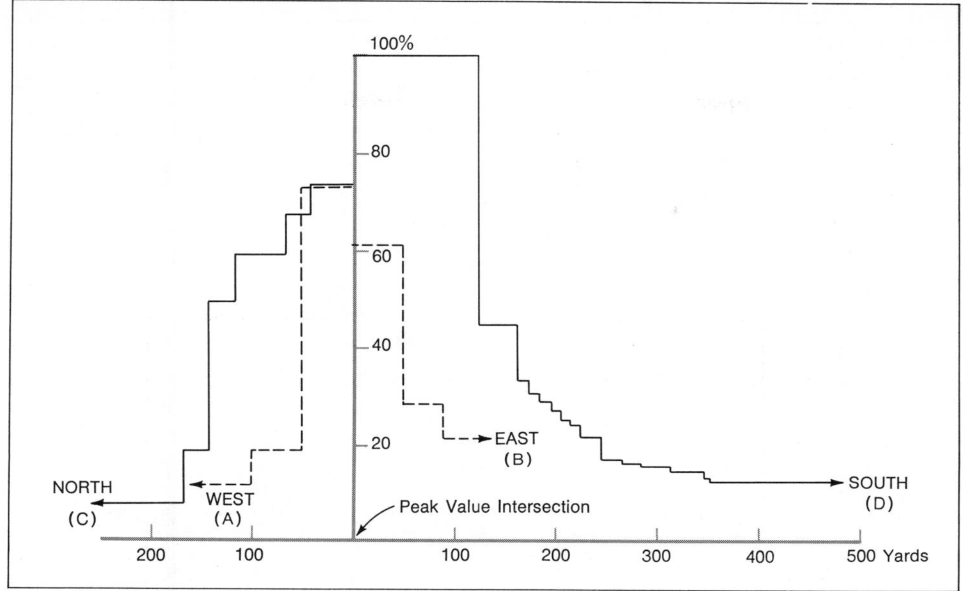

FIG. 13.1. LAND VALUE GRADIENTS IN THE CBD, DUBUQUE, IOWA, 1960.

graphs, actual land values expressed as dollars per front-foot have been translated into percentages of the value at the PVI—the 100 percent value. The north-south gradient along the main axis of the CBD is notably higher than that cutting across the CBD in the east-west direction at comparable distances from the PVI. Note also the steepness of the decline in values; there is a very marked drop-off in values within a short distance from the PVI in the east-west direction, and there is an even more pronounced decline in the gradient toward the west. Conversely it is as though the gradients have been stretched out along the north-south axis of the CBD. If anything, along this section, values appear to decline more rapidly with distance in the northerly direction. Regardless of these minor directional variations of the land value surface the dominant aspect of the relationship is clearly shown: there is a marked decline in value in all directions within relatively short distances of the PVI.

The directional differences in the nature of the gradients of value within the CBD are of course related to its shape. In Dubuque, the CBD delimited by the Murphy-Vance index method is rectangular in shape as shown in Figure 13.2. It is elongated along Main Street, which runs north-south and extends for only one, at most two, blocks at right angles to this axis in an east-west direction. Differences in the general value levels and rates of decline in land values, and concomitantly the intensity of land use, are accounted for by a complex set of local conditions in the historical evolution of the downtown area of individual cities. Regardless of these individual peculiarities, however, the general features of the land value surface described are typical of the pattern within all CBD's.

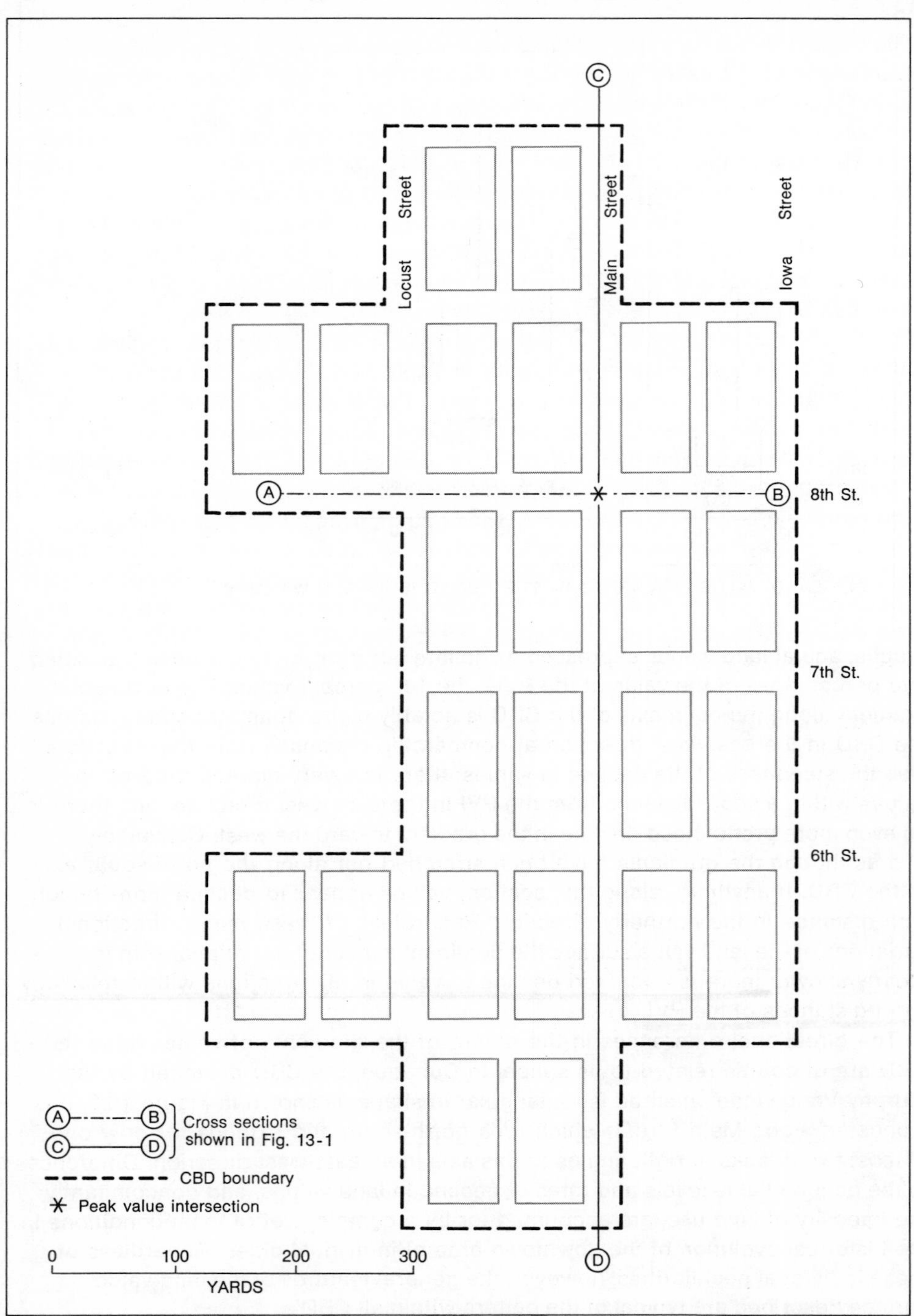

FIG. 13.2. THE DUBUQUE, IOWA, CBD DELIMITED BY THE MURPHY-VANCE METHOD.

SURFACES

The discontinuous nature of the land value surface indicated by the stepped characteristic of the value gradients for the CBD of Dubuque is shown in map form in Figure 13.7. This surface has two marked features. First, there is a very small core area immediately adjacent to the PVI comprising locations with values as high as approximately 75 percent of the peak value. This innermost area stands in contrast to the rest of the CBD, which is characterized by values below this level. Second, most locations in the downtown area have values less than about 25 percent of the peak value. From our understanding of the relationships between intensity of land use and land values, we might expect from this that the greater part of the CBD is associated with a relatively low level of use intensity.

That this picture is typical of land value patterns in the CBD's of the medium- and small-sized cities is indicated by the data in Table 13.1. These data show the amount of land associated with various levels of land value in six of the CBD's investigated by Murphy and Vance and discussed in the previous chapter. The difference between the small inner hard-core area of high values and the generally low level of the value surface for the greater part of the CBD is clearly indicated by the figures in column 2 of the table. These figures represent percentages of the total land area in the different value classes for all six CBD's combined. Just over 1 percent of the total area is associated with values as high as 90 percent of the peak value. In marked contrast to this, just over 40 percent of the total area in the six downtown districts has land values of less than 10 percent of that at the peak-value intersection. Perhaps the most significant aspect of the land value pattern illustrated by these figures is that approximately nine-tenths of the total area of these six CBD's consists of land values of less than 50 percent of the peak value.

LAND USE

In Chapter 9 a direct relationship was suggested between the surfaces of land values and land use. The implication of this is that low-value sites are generally 

TABLE 13.1. LAND VALUES AND AREAS WITHIN SIX CENTRAL BUSINESS DISTRICTS[a]

Values as a Percentage of the Peak Lot	**(1) Total Area in Acres Within Six CBD's Combined**	**(2) Percentage of the Total Area Within the Six CBD's**	**(3) Mean Area in Acres Within Each Land Value Class**
100.0–90.0	4.07	1.16	0.68
90.0–70.0	6.57	1.88	1.10
70.0–50.0	16.20	4.63	2.70
50.0–30.0	33.45	9.80 }	5.58
30.0–10.0	134.83	38.60 } 92.34%	22.48
Less than 10.0	153.58	43.94 }	43.61

[a] The six central business districts are those at Phoenix, Sacramento, Grand Rapids (Mich.), Tacoma (Wash.), Salt Lake City, and Worcester (Mass.).
Source: After Murphy, et al. (1955), Table 1.

not so intensively used as high-value sites. Since in the CBD the high-value sites occupy central locations around the PVI, the intensity of use should reach its highest level there and should decrease with distance outward to the edge of the CBD. The change in use intensity is brought about by changes in the type of activities at different locations. This was illustrated in the discussion of elementary land-use theory in Chapter 9. From this kind of argument it is expected that an analogous kind of pattern will be typical of the distribution of commercial activities around the PVI within the CBD.

Evidence suggesting this to be the case has been presented by Murphy and Vance (1955) in their study of the internal structure of eight CBD's. In their analysis, a grid with 100-yard divisions centered on the PVI was superimposed over the innermost part of each CBD. The proportion of each zone devoted to various activities was then calculated and used to compare the land use pattern at different distances from the PVI.

The application of this framework to the CBD of Tulsa, Okla., is given in Figure 13.3. Zone 1 is the area immediately surrounding the PVI itself and includes all frontages bordering streets radiating outward up to a distance of 100 yards. Zone 2 includes all frontages between 100–200 yards from the PVI, while zones 3 and 4 include frontages between 200–300 and 300–400 yards respectively from the peak-value intersection. Because Murphy and Vance did not extend the grid beyond a distance of 400 yards from the PVI, only a small proportion of the total CBD area was included in the analysis. For the example shown in Figure 13.3, only about 60 percent of the total ground-floor area is included within the outer boundary of the 400-yard zone. But this area contains the most intensively used part of the CBD.

Variation in the proportions of each of the four zones devoted to three main categories of land use (retail business, offices, and noncentral users) are presented in Figure 13.4. In the diagrams the total area of each zone is represented by the vertical column, and this is divided into percentages on the vertical (the *Y*) axis. The bar graphs shown are based on the average land use pattern for eight CBD's. Separate graphs are given for (A) the average of all floors combined, (B) for first floor, and (C) for all upper floors combined.

All floors by zones The zone immediately surrounding the PVI represents the quintessence of the characteristics that are associated with the core of the CBD. This is the area of greatest concentration of vehicular and pedestrian traffic. It includes the inner core of highest land values arising from the extremely intense level of competition for the use of land, and this is where we should normally expect to find the tallest buildings in the downtown area. It is perhaps not surprising to find that this innermost zone is dominated by various retail business uses, which account for about 55 percent of the total floor space (Fig. 13.4A). Offices are the second most important users of land in this zone and occupy about one-third of available space there. As expected, the activities classified by Murphy and Vance as noncentral uses are only poorly represented and account for just under 12 percent of the total area of the first zone.

Beyond this first zone there is a regular change in the proportion of the total

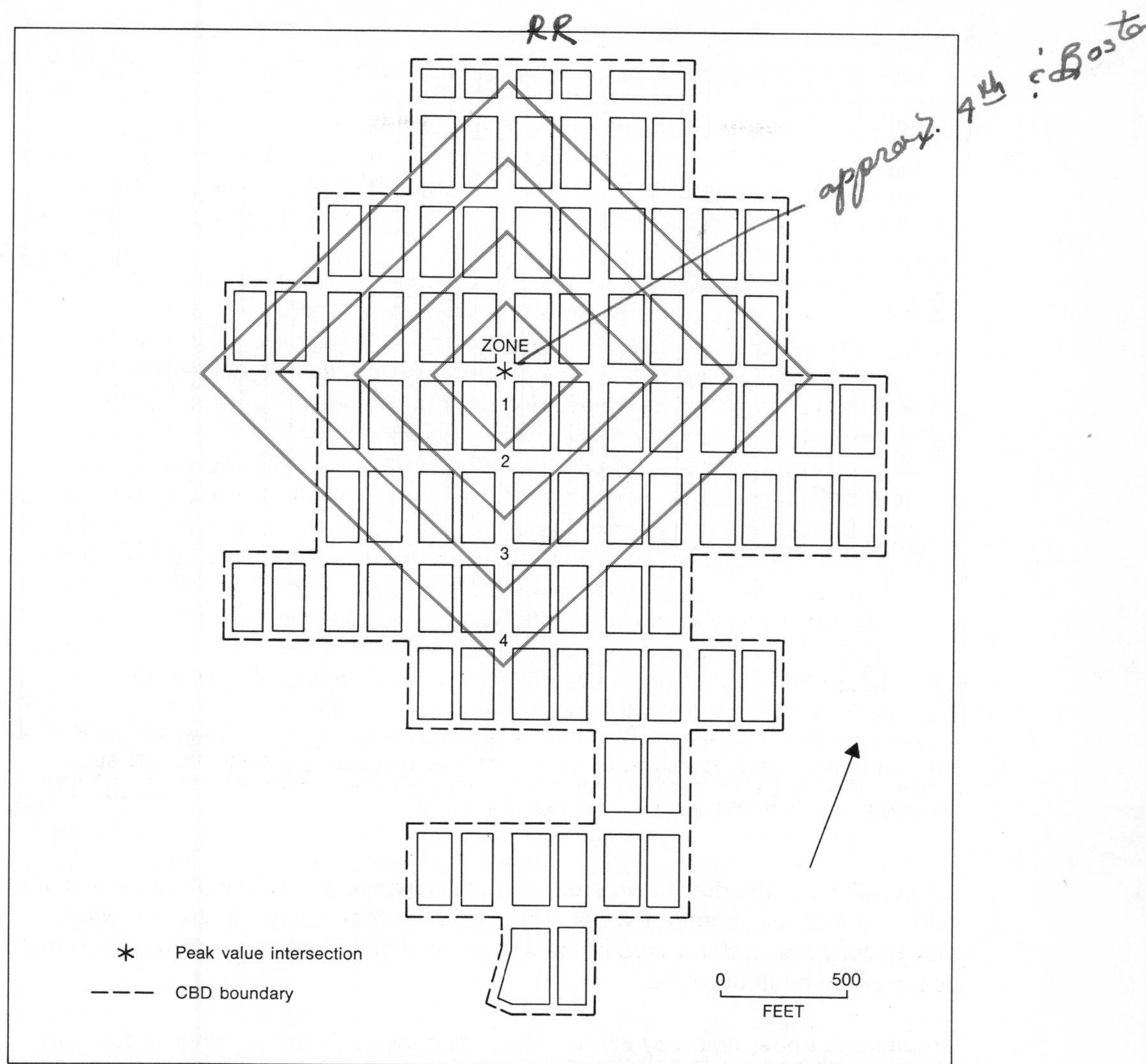

FIG. 13.3. THE "100-YARD GRID" SUPERIMPOSED ON THE CBD OF TULSA, OKLAHOMA.

area devoted to each of the three sets of activities. Most significant is the marked decrease in the proportion devoted to retail business as distance increases away from the PVI. In the outermost zone, only about a quarter of the total area is devoted to retailing, and there it becomes the least important of the three main types of activity. This reduction in the area devoted to retail uses in the outermost zones is counterbalanced by the increased importance of both office functions and noncentral uses. Offices are well represented in all the zones beyond the first, and in zones 3 and 4 account for about half of the available floor area where they become the dominant use. Although noncentral uses are more important toward

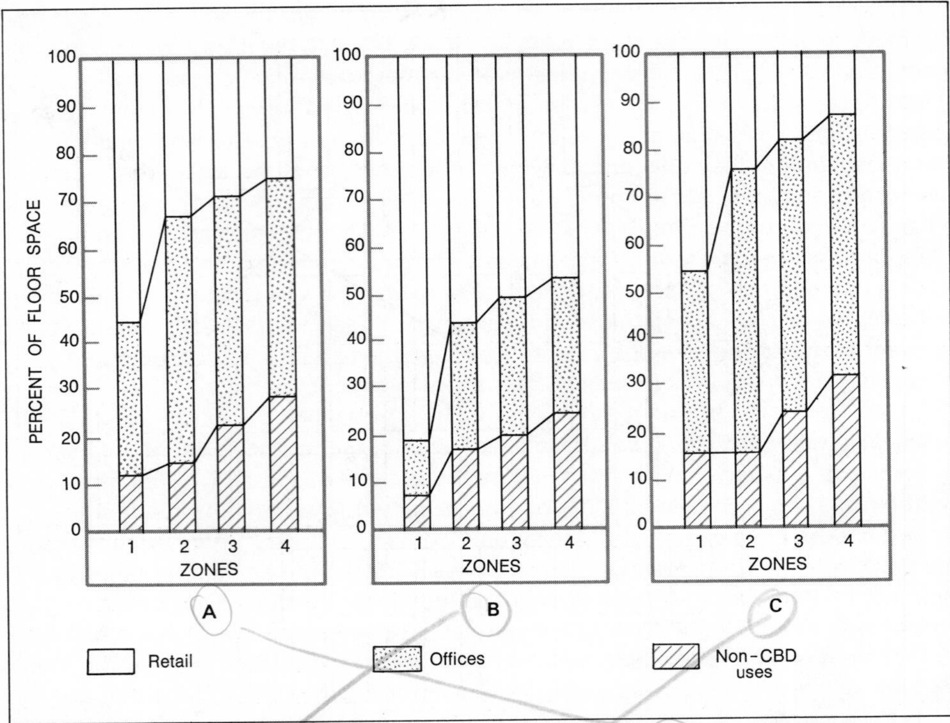

FIG. 13.4. LAND USES BY DISTANCE ZONES WITHIN THE CBD: (A) AVERAGE FOR ALL FLOORS COMBINED, (B) FIRST FLOOR USES, AND (C) AVERAGE FOR ALL UPPER FLOORS COMBINED. (*Source:* After Murphy, et al., 1955, Fig. 3.)

the periphery of the downtown area, they are nowhere a very important user of land within its first four hundred yards. They are best represented in zone 4 where they occupy just under a third of the space—a slightly higher proportion than that occupied by retail business.

Ground and upper floors by zones By combining all floors together in this way, however, interesting patterns in the vertical distribution of the three main types of land use are covered up. Figure 13.4B shows the arrangement of uses at the ground-floor level only. The intensive use of street-level frontage by retail businesses is clearly shown in this diagram. This set of activities dominates in all four zones; in the innermost area it accounts for as much as 82 percent of the total ground-floor area. Even in zone 4 retail business occupies just under half of the available frontage. The noncentral uses are poorly represented at this level and reach their maximum representation in the outermost zone where they account for about a quarter of the ground-floor space. The remainder of the available space at ground-floor level is devoted to office uses, which become particularly important in zones 3 and 4 where they account for one-third of all ground-floor property.

The use of upper-floor space (all upper floors combined) is much as might be intuitively expected in that office functions are by far the most important users of space (Fig. 13.4C). This is especially true in the three outermost zones where offices account for well over one-half of the available floor space. Noncentral uses become slightly more important at the upper floor than at ground level, but even in outermost zone 4, they only account for about one-third of the total area. Retail business is dominant at the upper-floor level only in zone 1, where its importance is halved in comparison to what it is at street level. The 45.5 percent of combined upper-floor space devoted to retail business in this innermost zone most probably reflects the multistory department and variety stores that are typical retail functions in the high-value area immediately adjacent to the peak intersection. Outside this compact area very little upper-floor space is devoted to retailing and in zone 4, this activity accounts for less than 15 percent of total floor space.

Tulsa, Okla.: an example The above description of the arrangement of land uses presents the average picture of the internal structure of the CBD. The specific patterns within any individual CBD can be expected to differ in its particulars for two important reasons. First, individual functions will vary in importance from one CBD to another; and second, because the CBD is the commercial heart of the city, it will reflect in a general way the functional specialization of its surrounding urban area. Figure 13.5 illustrates how these considerations affect the arrangement of land uses within the innermost part of the CBD at Tulsa, Okla. The diagram is directly comparable with that given in Figure 13.4, except that the three main classes of activity have been further subdivided into more specific types of uses in the graph showing the pattern at the ground-floor level (Fig. 13.5B).

The pattern shown in Figure 13.5A is very similar to the average for all floors combined by zones discussed above. The most noticeable difference in Tulsa is the greater proportion of floor space devoted to office uses. In all, offices account for more than one-third of the total floor space in Tulsa's CBD. In zone 2, where Tulsa's tallest buildings occur, offices account for as much as 78 percent of the combined floor space. As was the case for the average of the nine CBDs, retail business is most important in the innermost zone in Tulsa. The proportion of floor space devoted to this activity declines, however, very steeply as distance increases away from the peak intersection; and in zone 4 it amounts to only about 12 percent. Noncentral uses are virtually absent from the innermost two zones here; they occupy about 27 percent of the space in zone 3, and just under a fifth of the combined floor area in zone 4.

The dominance of offices in the CBD of Tulsa partly reflects the history of the city as a commercial focus and partly the functional role the city has assumed more recently for the surrounding area. Tulsa is a relatively young city. Like many cities, it developed as a product of the railroad era; but its rapid growth resulted from the development of the nearby midcontinent oilfield. It was built primarily as an office center serving the oilfield interests, and for a number of years it has been a major headquarters for many kinds of prospecting, refining, and sales

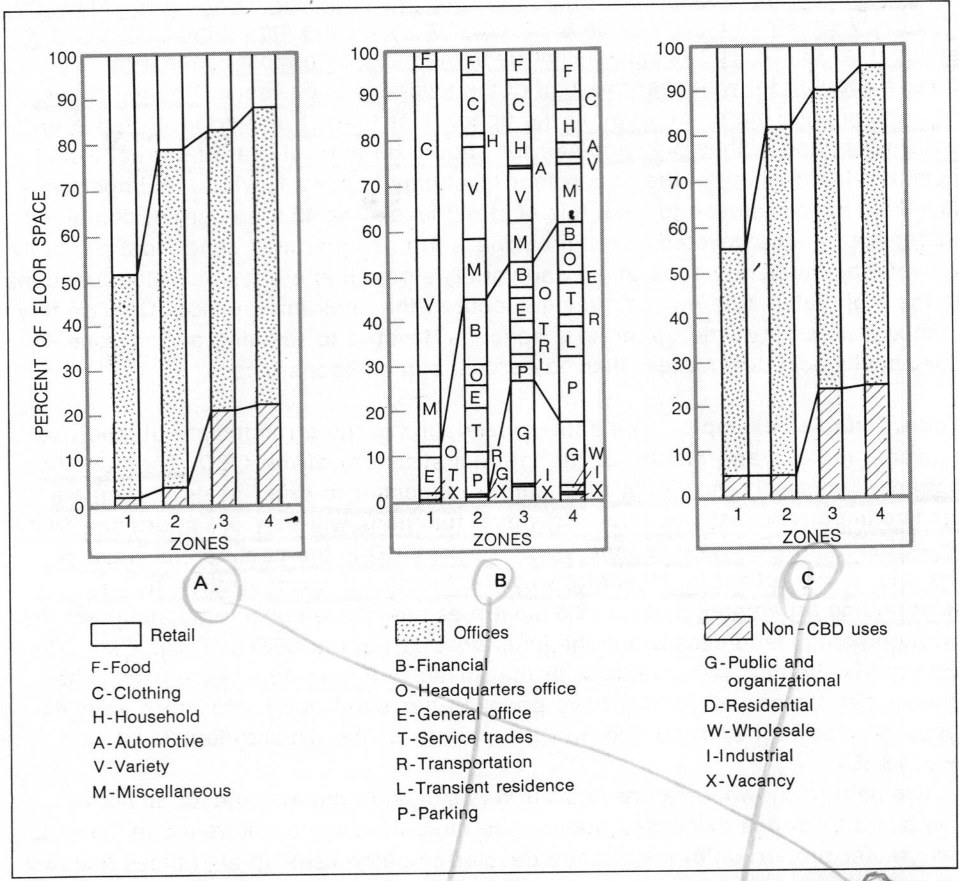

FIG. 13.5. LAND USES BY DISTANCE ZONES WITHIN THE CBD, TULSA, OKLAHOMA: (A) AVERAGE FOR ALL FLOORS COMBINED, (B) FIRST FLOOR USES, AND (C) AVERAGE FOR ALL UPPER FLOORS COMBINED. (*Source:* After Murphy, et al., 1955, Fig. 10.)

operations. In fact, about 18 percent of the total CBD floor space is devoted to central and regional offices of these oilfield-oriented activities. Moreover, the petroleum industry and the services it requires undoubtedly go a long way toward explaining why another 18 percent of total floor space is devoted to general offices. It is not surprising, then, to find that Tulsa had the highest and most modern buildings, the highest proportion of floor space devoted to offices uses, and the lowest vacancy rate of all nine CBD's studied by Murphy and Vance.

Although offices and retail businesses are major uses in this CBD, they differ in their locations within it. Figure 13.5C shows that offices tend to concentrate on the upper-floor level in all four zones, while Figure 13.5B indicates the dominance of retail businesses at the ground-floor level, and especially in the innermost zone, where it accounts for 87 percent of the total floor space. Closer inspection of Figure 13.5B reveals considerable variation in the distribution of the different retail business types within the CBD. Some types occur in all of the zones but with varying degree of concentration, others are distinguished by their absence from some zones and presence in others.

In generalizing the picture portrayed by the graphs, the innermost zones (1 and 2) are clearly the area of clothing and variety stores. In zone 1, these types account for over three-quarters of the total retailing floor space. However, as distance away from the PVI increases, these types become less important as space is taken over by other retail types. Thus locations in zones 2 and 3 are important for food, miscellaneous, and household-goods stores. The distinguishing characteristic of the outermost zone is its mixture of retail types. This is reflected by the importance of the miscellaneous category there, which alone accounts for 13 percent of the retailing floor space. Food, household goods, and automotive stores all attain their greatest concentration at these more distant locations.

These patterns of commercial land use are of course generalizations of specific spatial distributions of activities within the CBD. Some of the actual distributions are shown in Figure 13.6. Clearly there is considerable order to the arrangement of different business types—an order that certainly appears to be based on distance from the peak value intersection. The extreme level of concentration of clothing and variety stores in the immediate vicinity of the PVI noted in the graphical analysis is clearly shown on the map. This pattern is perhaps best described as linear and reflects the concentration of this set of activities along the main thoroughfare of the CBD. In contrast to this, automotive stores and transient residences show a marked tendency to be located toward the periphery of the downtown area. A second interesting feature of these patterns is the marked clustering of these types at various parts of the peripheral zone. This was noted in the case of automobile showrooms in the last chapter, where they were identified as one of the types of commercial activity which, for a number of reasons, tend to congregate together to form specialized areas. Offices, on the other hand, seem to be located at the ground-floor level at locations intermediate to these extremes. For the most part, offices are dispersed at locations just outside the innermost area of intensive clothing and variety store retailing. Although the distribution shown for this activity contains a peripheral element, this is by no means as strong nor as typical as it is for certain other activities.

THE RELATIONSHIP BETWEEN LAND VALUES AND LAND USE

It is clear from the discussion so far that both land values and the locational patterns of different activities are related to distance from the PVI within the CBD. One of the major shortcomings of the 100-yard zone method used by Murphy and Vance in their analysis of the internal structure of the CBD is that it does not permit explicit recognition of the relationship between these two patterns. The simplicity of the method is offset by its more serious limitations arising from the rigid, geometrical nature of the grid. It is insensitive to variation in the size and in the shape of the CBD and hence to the marked distance and directional variation in the pattern of land values and associated patterns of land use.

The shortcomings are vividly revealed when the 100-yard zones are superimposed on the pattern of land values, as is done in Figure 13.7 for the CBD of Dubuque. Because of the elongated shape and restricted size of this downtown area, the first 100-yard zone from the PVI extends to the edge of the CBD in all directions except to the south. As a result it contains locations that differ

FIG. 13.6. DISTRIBUTION OF SELECTED BUSINESS TYPES WITHIN THE CBD OF TULSA, OKLAHOMA. (*Source:* Murphy, et al., 1955, Figs. 12 and 15.)

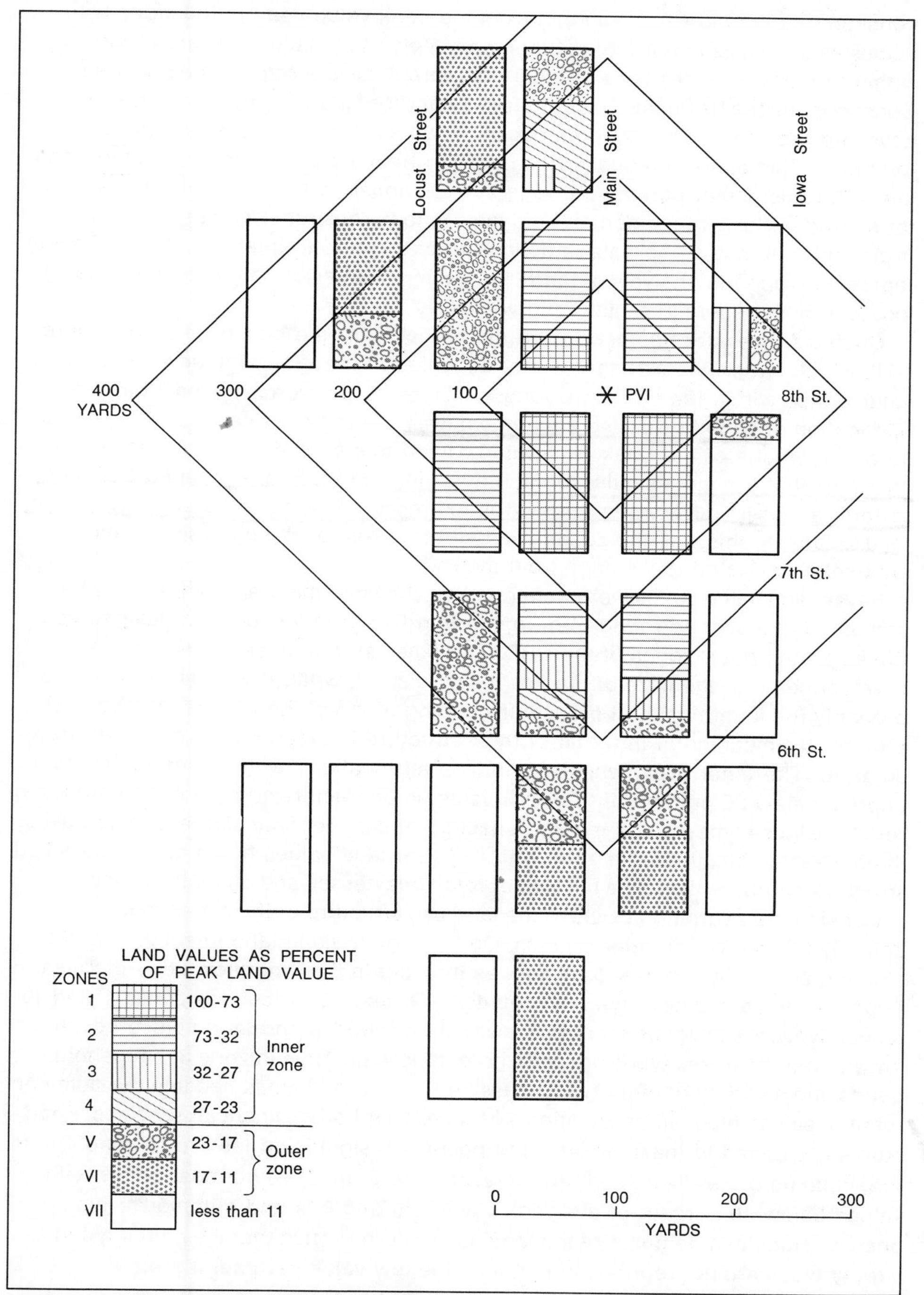

FIG. 13.7. THE "100-YARD GRID" SUPERIMPOSED ON THE CBD OF DUBUQUE, IOWA.

by Murphy & Vance

considerably in land value, ranging from the peak value itself to locations with values as low as 32 percent of it. Similar diversity to the land value structure within the first 100-yard zone is clearly apparent for the other zones as well. Consequently the use of such a rigid framework for land use analysis tends to cover up the real locational patterns of activities within the CBD by grouping together in the same zone uses that ought to be separated from each other, and separating uses that perhaps go together. Obviously a more flexible framework for analyzing the arrangement of land uses is to be desired. Despite the general argument that land value data is difficult to obtain and to interpret, it would seem logical to place the analysis of land use within a framework of zones comprising locations with generally similar land values.

Such a framework has been used as the basis for the construction of Figure 13.8, which shows the arrangement of activities at the ground-floor level by land-value zones within the CBD of Dubuque. These zones were derived from the application of a method called *linkage analysis* to the front-foot values expressed as a percentage of the peak land value. Using this simple grouping procedure, locations that are most similar to each other in land value are grouped together to form a class, which when mapped is expressed spatially as a zone of similar land values. In this way the zones used as the basis for the analysis of land use are explicitly related to distance from the PVI.

Seven land value zones were generated as shown in the graph. These may be combined in a second round of grouping into two broader regions, designated as the inner and outer zones of the CBD. The inner area may be thought of as corresponding to the core of the downtown district, while the outer area is most probably the innermost part of the surrounding frame of the CBD. That these two regions are meaningful in terms of their structure is clearly apparent from the diagram. The inner area, which comprises all locations with values higher than approximately 25 percent of the peak value, is characterized by a concentration of retail business types and a marked absence of service, financial, and office uses. In contrast to this, the outer zone with its lower land values has a more diversified structure characterized by a mixture of retail businesses and office functions.

Considerable variation exists in the land use structure of the zones that comprise these two broader regions. On the higher-value land in zones 1 and 2, clothing and variety stores dominate, as they did in the innermost zone in Tulsa. Together these business types account for 80 and 65 percent of zones 1 and 2, respectively. As distance increases away from the PVI, and land values become lower, other business types become more important. Thus in zone 3, household goods and a variety of other types classified as miscellaneous become the dominant retail business types in association with banks and other financial services. Food stores are added to these activities to become a significant feature of zone 4, and they dominate the diversified structure of zone 5. In the outermost zones with values below 16 percent of the peak value, parking lots and automotive types become significant features of the land use pattern. Notice that the clothing and variety types are not represented at all in the low-value peripheral area of the CBD in Dubuque.

retail businesses & office functions

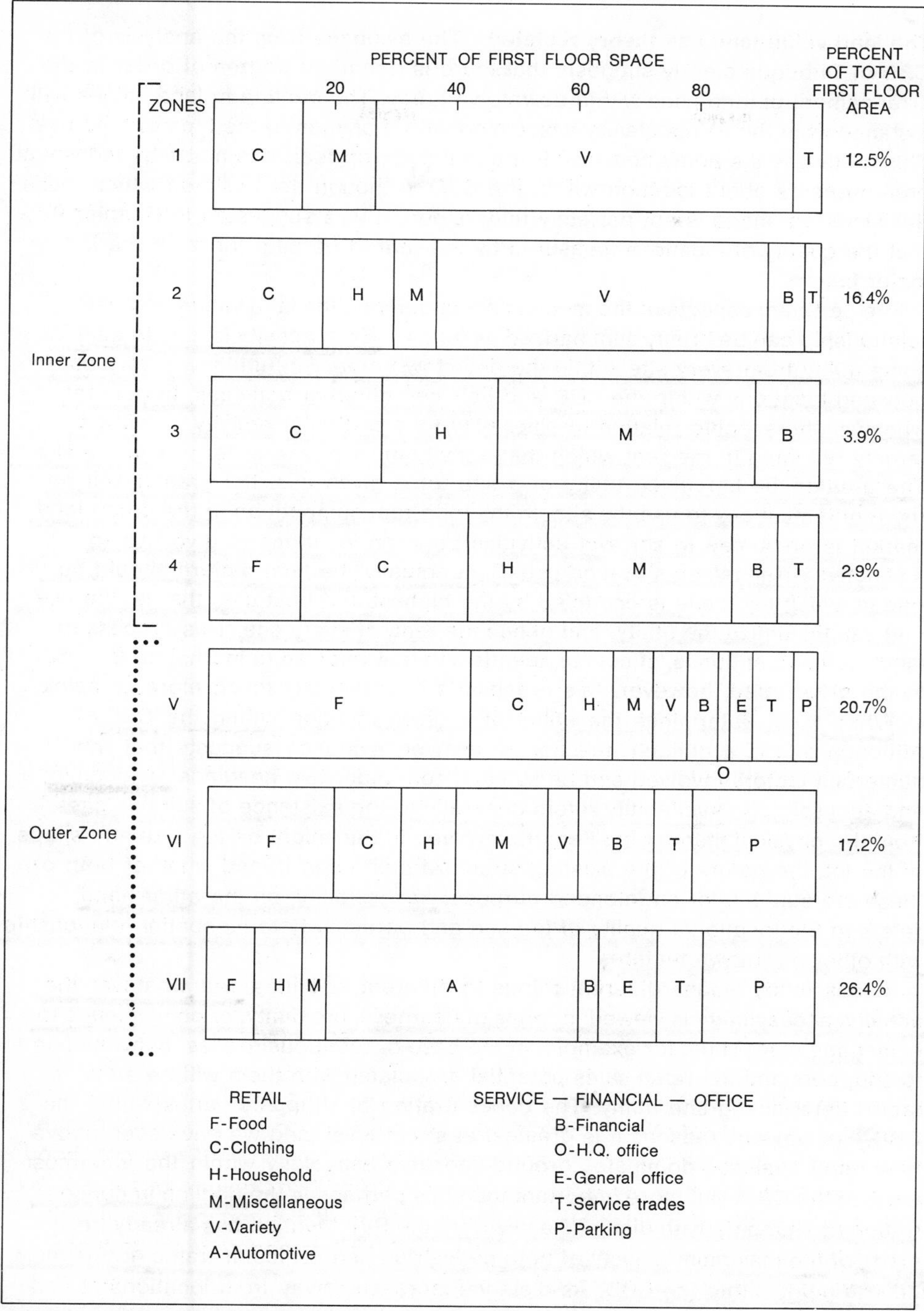

FIG. 13.8. FIRST FLOOR LAND USE BY LAND VALUE ZONES WITHIN THE CBD OF DUBUQUE, IOWA. THE SEVEN LAND VALUE ZONES ARE SHOWN IN FIG. 13.7.

The land value-land use theory restated The evidence from the analysis of the CBD of Dubuque clearly suggests that there is a marked degree of order in the arrangement of land uses within downtown areas. The decline in land values with distance from the PVI is clearly associated with a change in the type of land use. This pattern is the combined result of a multitude of decisions made by individual entrepreneurs about location within the CBD. Although the basis on which these decisions are made is not perfectly understood, it was suggested in Chapter 9 that the quality of locations measured by the rent to be paid for their use is a major factor.

The pertinent aspects of the mechanism underlying the land value-land use relationship can be briefly summarized as follows. Each activity is able to gain some utility from every site within the downtown area. Site utility will vary both between locations within the CBD and between different activities. In general, whatever the specific relation of site utility to a particular activity, it will be largely reflected in the rent which that activity must pay in order to use the site. The greater the perceived utility of a site for a given use, the greater will be the rent it must pay to use the site. In the long run, competition in the urban land market is presumed to sort out activities between locations to give rise to distinctive arrangements of land use. Conceptually the final pattern should be one in which each site is occupied by the highest and best use; that is, the use that can maximize the utility, and hence the rent, of every site. This process of land use competition is, of course, identical to that referred to in Chapter 9. In the urban area, however, this process is operationally much more complex.

What, then, determines the utility of a given location within the CBD? Although this is a difficult question to answer, evidence suggests that the numerous factors involved can be summarized under two headings: availability and accessibility. Availability refers generally to the existence of suitable sites from the physical standpoint. Factors involved in this might be the size and shape of the lot, the nature of the existing structure built upon it, and whether both of these are suitable for an intended purpose. Accessibility, on the other hand, refers to the locational quality of the site and particularly to its spatial relationship with other downtown features.

Accessibility means different things to different activities. But whatever the activity, accessibility is viewed in terms of nearness, proximity, or convenience to something else. Thus, for example, in the case of retail businesses, convenience to shoppers and the retail sales potential associated with them will be a major factor determining site utility. The concentration of shoppers varies within the CBD. For obvious reasons it is greatest at street level, and we have seen above how retail business dominates ground-floor use especially within the innermost parts of the CBD. But more important than this perhaps is the decline in concentration of shoppers with distance away from the PVI. Mention has already been made of the maximum density of both pedestrian and vehicular traffic at this most central point within the CBD. As distance increases away from locations at and around the PVI, the concentration of shoppers, and presumably therefore sales potential, declines. It is to be expected, therefore, that strong centripetal forces operate in the location of retail businesses, pulling them toward the innermost part of the downtown area. Competition for site use is intensified, and rents become high there.

Not all types of retail business have the same ability to pay high rents for the use of the more central sites in the CBD. Rent paying ability depends very much on sales turnover and markup. Because of this, certain uses are able to outbid all others for the most desired sites; in the analysis of Dubuque's CBD, the evidence suggests that the clothing and variety department store types are most able to acquire the prime sites adjacent to the PVI. Other uses are forced to occupy sites at increasingly greater distances from it.

At the same time we might imagine a set of opposing centrifugal forces acting within the CBD that tend to pull some kinds of activities toward the periphery of the downtown area. These forces are largely related to the space demands of different activities. For example, furniture stores need larger floor areas for display purposes than do most food stores or clothing stores. The same is true for new and used automobile showrooms. Moreover, these kinds of activity probably have lower retail sales turnover than, say, department stores. Consequently they are pulled toward the periphery of the CBD where rents per unit area are lower and where they are able to outbid other activities for the use of land. It is in this way that the general factors of availability and accessibility are interrelated to give rise to well-ordered patterns in the distribution of retail and other commercial activities within central business districts.

SPECIALIZED AREAS

Thus far the discussion has focused on patterns within the central business districts of small- and medium-sized cities. At this scale, distinct relationships between the location of different commercial activities and distance (measured in terms of land values) are a prominent feature of their internal structure. Similar relationships also underlie the internal structure of the downtown areas of larger cities. However, because of the larger spatial dimension and greater functional complexity of the CBD in large cities, these relationships may not initially be as clearly apparent. One of the reasons for this is that functional specialization becomes a distinctive feature of the land use pattern in large CBDs. These specialized areas are superimposed on the underlying distance regularities which, as a result, may become blurred.

Two general types of specialized areas may be recognized within central business districts. First there are what may be called *functional areas* that consist of local concentrations of different business activities which are functionally interrelated with each other. Second, tiny *clusters* develop comprising different establishments of the same business types. These are generally small-scale concentrations and may develop within the larger functional areas. Both types are examples at different scales of the effects of the forces of agglomeration discussed in Chapter 14.

Examples of some functional areas in the CBD of Chicago are presented in Figure 13.9. The area shown on the map includes both the core, the Loop in Chicago, and the frame of the central business district. At this scale retail business emerges as one of the many different functional areas in the CBD core. Other examples in the core might be financial districts, theater districts, and medical centers. In the surrounding frame, separate districts devoted to wholesaling, transportation facilities, warehousing, and small manufacturing and service industries (e.g., printing) may emerge as functional areas. In some cases this kind of areal specialization may extend over several city blocks; in others a particular set of activities may be concentrated on a particular street in the CBD; in still others the functional area may be contained within a specific block. Many of them are so strongly developed and important to the urban, even national community, that the districts or streets in which they are located have become household names. For example, to take a rather special case, many of the functional areas of Manhattan are known throughout America, even the world; Wall Street is synonymous with the financial community there; Park Avenue with the headquarter offices of many of America's largest corporations;

FIG. 13.9. FUNCTIONAL AREAS WITHIN THE CBD OF CHICAGO. (*Source:* Berry, 1967A, Fig. 2–23.)

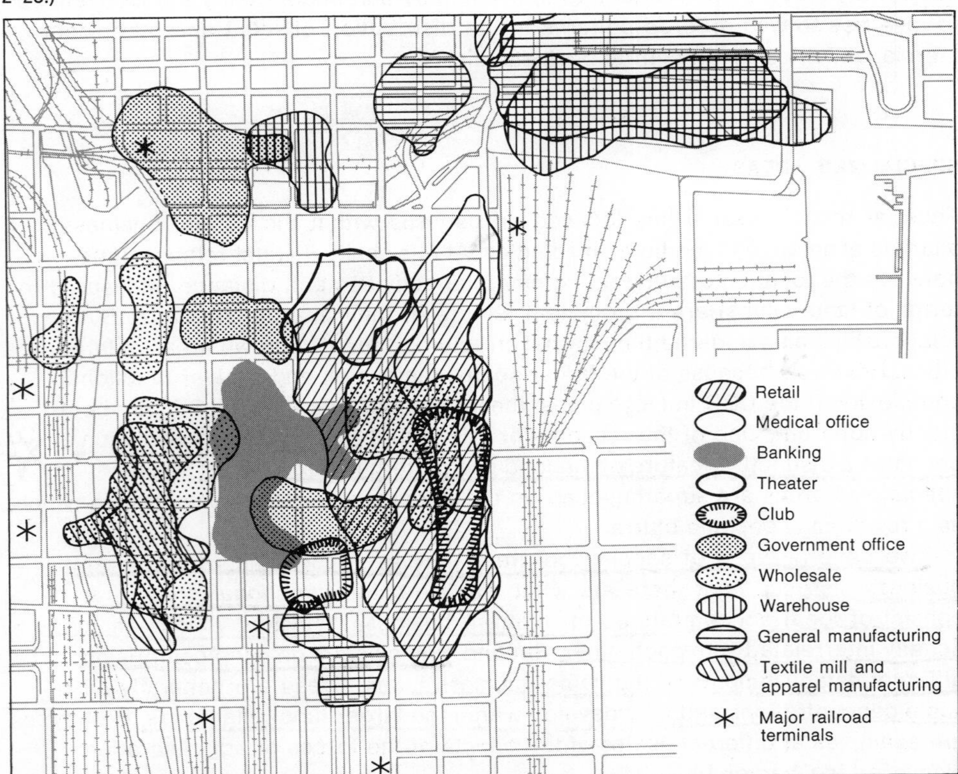

Madison Avenue goes with advertising agencies; and Fifth Avenue is associated with high-quality retailing.

Examples of clusters of similar types of activities are perhaps best developed within the retailing area of large CBDs. Thus a characteristic feature of these is the marked concentrations on certain streets or blocks of activities such as clothing stores, shoe stores, and furniture and automobile showrooms (Getis and Getis, 1968). Similar clusters of services and entertainments may develop, as for example of theaters (Broadway in Manhattan), legal offices, restaurants, and so on. In some cases these may overlap with each other to give rise to more complex kinds of specialized areas.

Although specialized areas may be best developed within the CBD's of larger cities, they are by no means absent from the smaller downtown areas. However, at this smaller scale they may only be incipient developments lacking any distinct spatial extent. Certainly at this scale clothing stores tend to cluster together and usually in conjunction with the larger department stores. An example of the more weakly developed specialized areas, which may be observed generally within smaller CBDs, is given for the city of New Brunswick, N.J., in Figure 13.10. The area shown on the map includes more than the CBD proper, which if delimited

FIG. 13.10. INCIPIENT FUNCTIONAL AREAS WITHIN THE CBD OF NEW BRUNSWICK, NEW JERSEY.

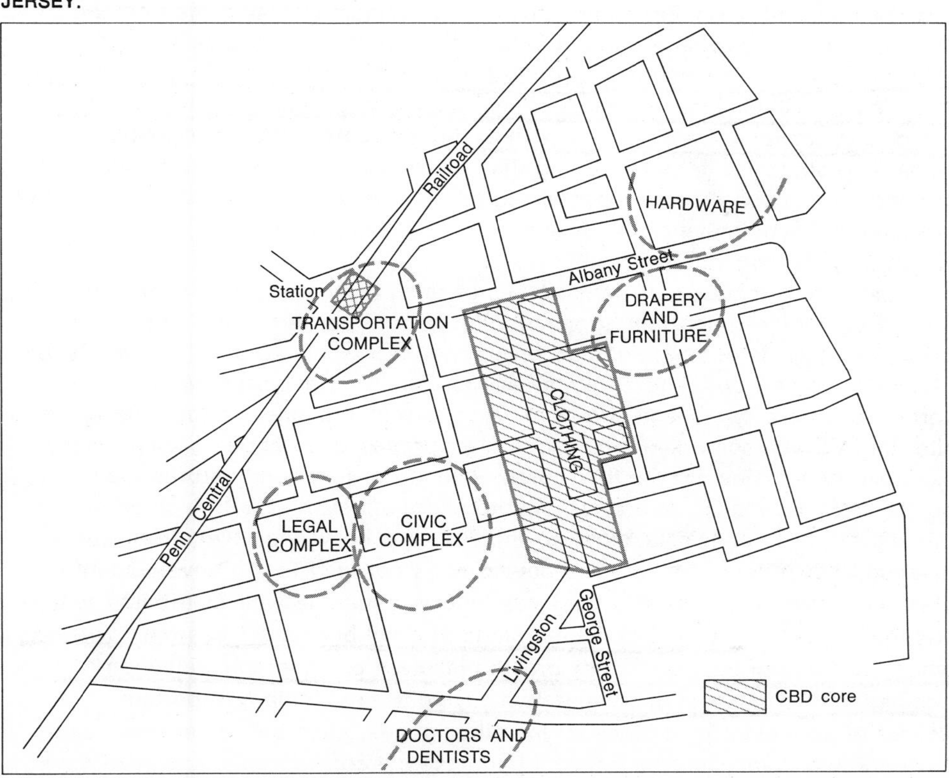

by the Murphy and Vance index method would most probably extend only for one block, perhaps two blocks, along George Street, the central axis. Weak concentrations of hardware stores, household-goods stores, and clothing stores can be clearly delimited here. In the vicinity of the railroad station a small complex of transportation-oriented activities has developed including hotels, eating places, the bus station, and a variety of dingy entertainment activities. Perhaps the best examples of specialized areas in this CBD are the tight cluster of legal services adjacent to the group of civic buildings, especially the Middlesex County courthouse, with which they are functionally linked, and the more recently developing concentration of professional offices, especially of doctors and dentists, at the edge of the CBD along Livingston Avenue.

The distribution of specialized areas within the CBD does not necessarily bear any relationship to distance from the PVI. This is because they develop from a separate set of forces than those embodied in the land value-land use relationship discussed above. Specialized areas result from the forces of agglomeration generally founded upon the external economies of scale made possible when functionally interrelated activities are located in close juxtaposition with one another. For some activities these economies may stem from the sharing of common facilities; for example, this is often the case in medical centers where patients may be referred to specialists in the complex or use is made of a central X ray facility, and so on. For other activities the economies may come from the possibility for face-to-face contact with other functions in the cluster. The important point to remember is that the economies are external to the individual activities or establishments, and savings are made by being part of a larger complex of similar or interrelated activities. In this context, then, accessibility takes on a slightly different meaning than nearness to the PVI. For activities forming the various types of specialized areas, it is the accessibility or proximity to similar kinds of activities that is important and which determines site utility and eventually land value.

In the case of clusters of similar types of retail businesses within the broader retail area another important agglomerating factor operates. This is related to the different kinds of shopping and buying habits associated with different types of goods and services. These habits have an important effect on the location of certain business types and are to a large extent responsible for differences in site utility. Thus, some kinds of goods are purchased on impulse such as, for example, chocolates. Hence it is not uncommon to find candy stores located at points that truly maximize accessibility to shoppers in the CBD, such as near transportation terminals or close to the PVI. We know, however, from our everyday experience that impulse buying does not lead to the development of clusters of candy stores; this business type is generally well distributed within shopping centers. Clusters of similar kinds of retail business types only develop when purchase of the goods they provide involves considerable selection and comparison. This aspect of comparative buying is a particularly important aspect of shopping for clothes or for other goods, such as automobiles and furniture, which involve less frequent purchase but considerable outlays of money.

For these kinds of goods, shoppers usually want to shop around from one store to another in order to compare prices, style, and quality before making the final purchase.

It is this feature of shopping around which, it is argued, results in the clustering together of similar types of retail businesses. For in shopping around the customer, if obeying the principle of least effort, will want to minimize his time and effort on the shopping trip. At the same time, the astute entrepreneur will realize that it is to his advantage to ensure that his goods are included in the selection and comparison process. It is to his advantage to locate close, even next door, to other stores offering similar kinds of goods. Over the long run, small clusters of, for example, clothing or shoe stores may build up within the downtown retail area. In the case of these business types, accessibility does not only relate to the general concentration of shoppers in the immediate vicinity of the PVI, but also to other establishments of the same kind. Site utility is greater within the cluster than outside it, and hence higher rents must be paid for site use. If these higher rents represent a savings in transportation costs as implied in Chapter 9, it is in terms of the shoppers' time and effort involved in comparative buying. Hence, the formulation at this microscopic level is consistent with the general model for land values presented above.

OUTLYING SHOPPING CENTERS

Despite the smaller size and less complex functional structure of outlying shopping centers, a certain measure of order in the arrangement of different business types appears to be a characteristic feature of their internal structure. Although the regularities with distance are not usually so readily apparent in the lower order unplanned neighborhood and community-level centers, they become an important feature in the internal structure of the regional level centers. Distinctive patterns in the arrangement of the different land uses within planned shopping centers are more difficult to recognize because the natural locational forces are constrained by architectural controls.

REGIONAL LEVEL CENTERS

Unplanned centers at the regional level in the hierarchy are large enough and functionally complex enough for the development of considerable variation of the land values within them. Moreover, distances from the PVI to the edge of the center are great enough to allow for considerable choice of location within them. Because of this, the land value-land use relationships based on distance may develop. This size of center is really too small to permit the development of specialized areas, although contiguity in the location of establishments of the same retail business type may be noted. Incipient clusters of similar types are most noticeable at these centers at the upper-floor level, and especially in the limited area of taller buildings immediately around the

PVI where, for example, small service and medical offices may congregate.

Aspects of the internal structure of large outlying business centers are well illustrated in the largest regional level center in the city of Chicago. In 1962 it contained 61 different business types occupying a ground-floor area of 18.3 acres. This makes it approximately one-quarter the size of the CBD of Tulsa shown in Figure 13.3. The combined frontage of its 253 establishments totaled 8,055 feet on 63rd and Halsted Streets, around which the center has a cruciform plan as shown in Figure 13.11. The intersection of these streets is the PVI of the center where values reach a maximum of $7,000 per front foot. From this peak values decline rapidly over a relatively short distance to the edge of the center where they are only $200 a front foot—the general level of land values along the adjoining ribbons (Fig. 13.11).

Differences between business types in average front-foot land values within the center are indicated for a sample of types in Table 13.2. In general, the pattern is similar to that already noted within the CBD. Limited price variety stores, department stores, women's clothes, and shoe stores have the highest average values reflecting the tendency for them to be located close to the PVI, in conjunction with the maximum concentration of shoppers. In contrast, the lower average values associated with furniture stores, laundromats, and beauty salons indicate the tendency for these types to be located toward the periphery of the center. But as columns 3 and 4 of the table indicate, these averages do not tell the complete story. There is a range in values for many of the types,

FIG. 13.11. LAND VALUE PROFILES FOR THE REGIONAL LEVEL SHOPPING CENTER AT 63rd AND HALSTED, CITY OF CHICAGO. (*Source:* Berry and Tennant, 1963, p. 2.)

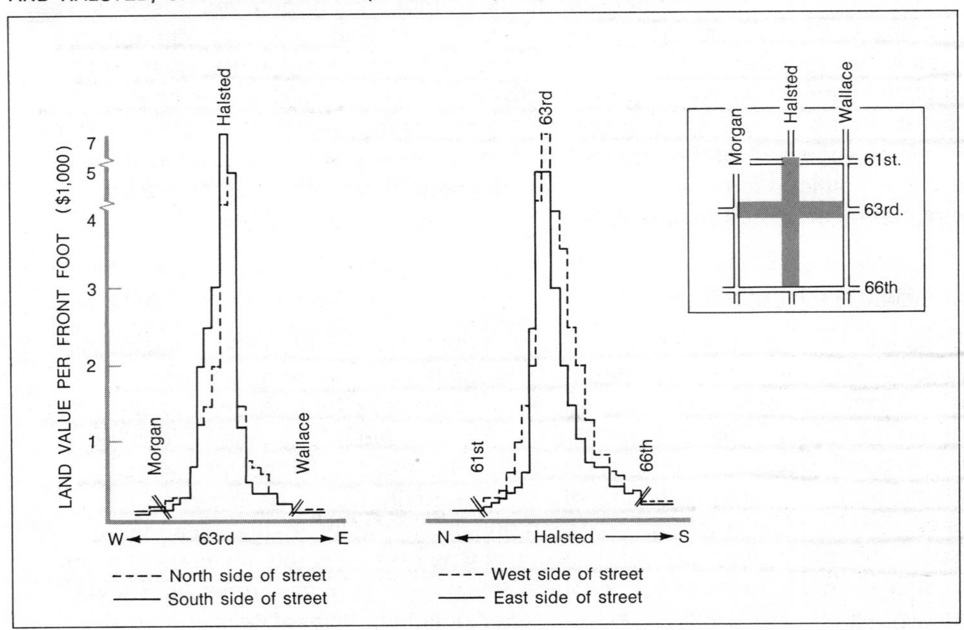

TABLE 13.2. LAND VALUES FOR SELECTED BUSINESS TYPES IN THE REGIONAL SHOPPING CENTER AT 63RD AND HALSTED STREETS, CHICAGO

Business Type	Number of Establishments	Average Front-Foot Land Value	Range in Value		V Coefficient[a]
			High	Low	
Limited price variety stores	3	$3,066	$7,000	$ 700	2.1
Department stores	3	2,575	5,000	2,500	0.9
Women's shoes	7	2,428	4,000	1,000	1.2
Women's clothing	16	2,218	5,000	500	2.0
Jewelers	12	1,731	3,500	200	1.8
Drugstores	4	1,525	4,200	300	2.5
Family shoes	11	1,500	3,500	300	2.1
Men's clothing	9	1,333	3,000	450	1.9
Eating places	15	865	3,000	200	3.2
Furniture stores	11	722	2,000	350	2.3
Laundromats	4	306	400	250	0.5
Beauty shops	5	280	400	225	0.6

[a] Obtained by dividing the standard deviation by the arithmetic mean.
Source: After Berry and Tennant (1963), p. 3.

indicating their considerable variation in location within the center. The extent of this variation in location is summarized by the *V*-coefficient in the final column of the table. The low values for department stores, laundromats, and beauty salons reflect the tendency for concentraton of these types. Department stores cluster in the inner area of high-value land; and the two service types, on low-value land at the periphery. In contrast to these, eating places have a very high coefficient of variation that reflects considerable scatter of this type within the center. To a lesser extent, this is also the case for drugstores, family shoes, variety stores, and women's clothing stores.

A MODEL OF THE INTERNAL STRUCTURE OF SHOPPING CENTERS

The relationship between land values and the location of business types suggests that land use patterns within shopping centers are consistent with the general theory of tertiary activity developed in Chapter 7. The structural features of the hierarchy of centers are translated into spatial patterns within the different level centers. Business types are allocated to different levels in the hierarchy according to their threshold size; high-threshold types are found only at high-level centers, while low-threshold types occur at all levels. If threshold size is directly related to rent paying ability, then the same allocation process possibly operates within the different level centers to give rise to well-developed patterns. According to this hypothesis, high-order business types would tend to be located at high-value locations close to the PVI, while low-threshold types would be displaced outward onto low-value land.

The hypothesis of a direct relationship between threshold size and land value is intuitively appealing but difficult to establish. Evidence recently presented suggests that there tends to be a general relationship between the two variables (Garner, 1966). The argument can be simplified as follows: High-order business types require locations with high degrees of centrality within the overall urban commercial complex. Centrality is measured in terms of accessibility to consumers. Within shopping centers, centrality may be thought of in terms of accessibility to the local concentration of shoppers. We have already noted above that the density of shoppers within centers declines with distance from PVI. This is illustrated in Figure 13.12A for a section along Ashland Avenue in Chicago. Note how the density of pedestrians drops off sharply from the two main business intersections at 63rd and 79th Streets. The differences in desirability of sites within centers which arises from these differences in pedestrian traffic are great enough to result in marked variation in land values. As shown in Figure 13.12B, the decline in land values around the two intersections mirrors the pattern of consumers walking along the street. High-threshold business types can, then, ensure maximum centrality within centers if they gravitate toward the peak-value intersection where site utility is greatest for them, and where they can best satisfy their thresholds. But to do so, of course, they must pay higher rents. Low-threshold types will not generally be able to compete with these high-order business types for the use of these prize locations and will be pushed farther out onto low-value locations.

The hypothetical pattern in the internal structure of outlying business centers, which this argument gives rise to, is formalized in Figure 13.13 for the three levels of centers. The innermost sites with their high land values are occupied by the set of high-threshold functions that are typical of the given level of centers. Thus within community centers, these functions are the high-threshold community-level functions, while at the regional centers they are the higher-threshold regional-level functions. Business types typical of each low-level center in the hierarchy

FIG. 13.12. PEDESTRIAN COUNTS (A) AND LAND VALUE PROFILES (B) ALONG A PART OF ASHLAND AVENUE, CITY OF CHICAGO. (*Source:* Berry, 1967A, Fig. 2–21.)

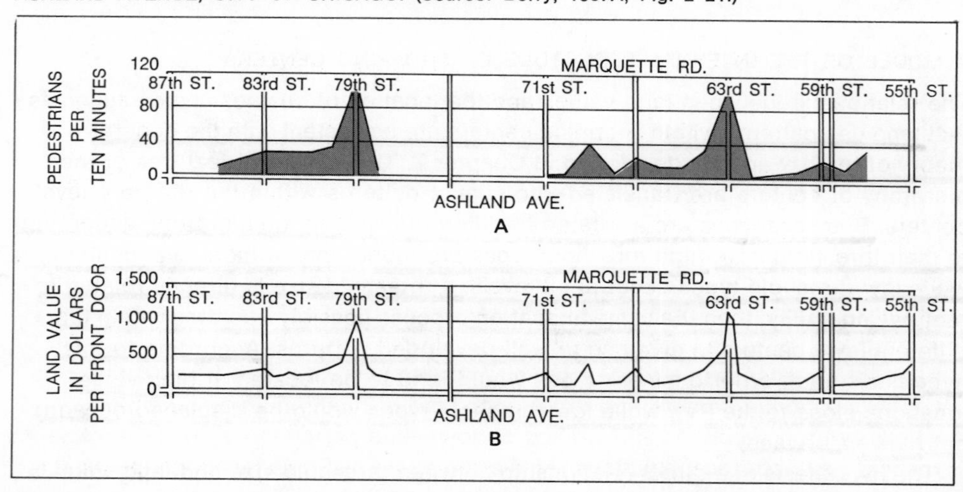

Site utility is greatest at PVI

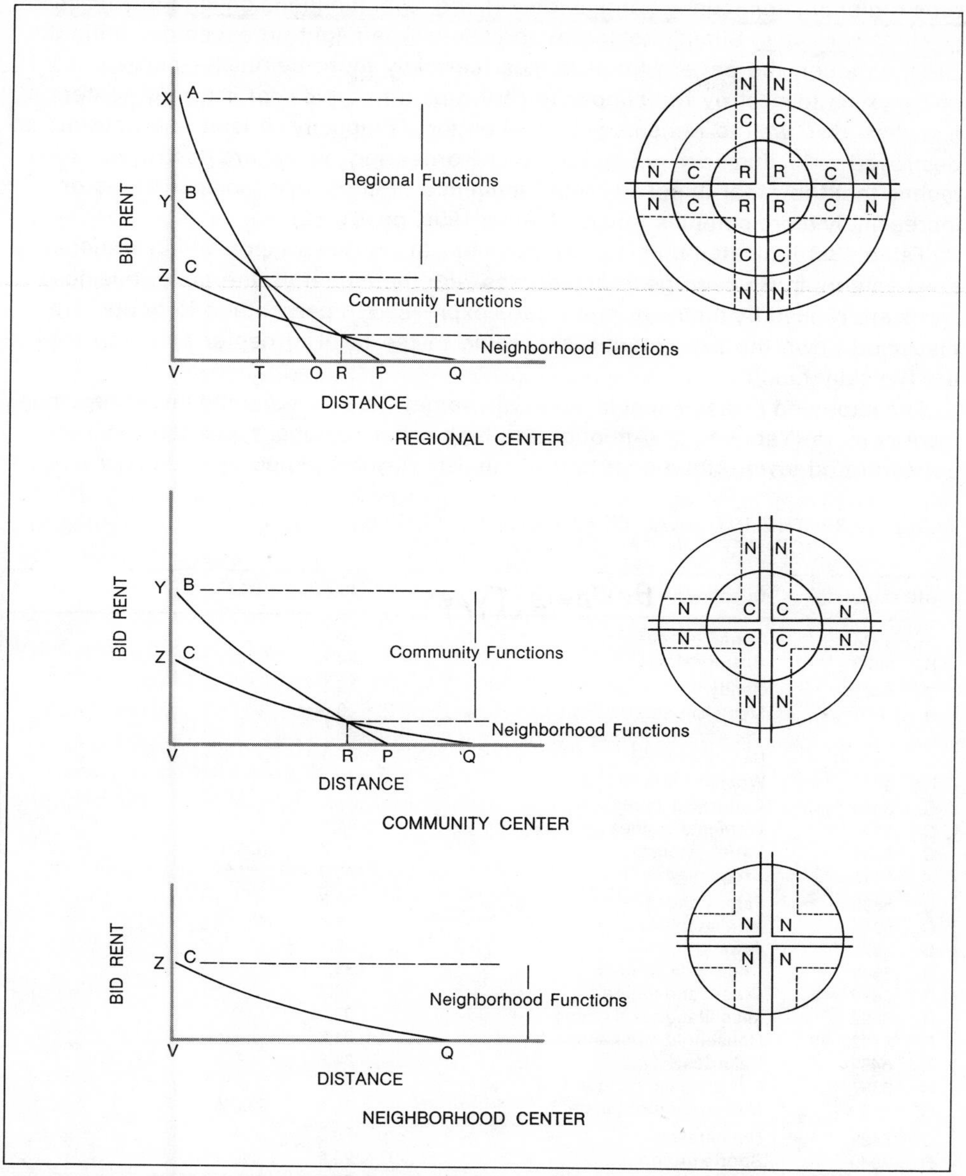

FIG. 13.13. HYPOTHETICAL PATTERNS OF THE INTERNAL STRUCTURE OF REGIONAL, COMMUNITY, AND NEIGHBORHOOD LEVEL SHOPPING CENTERS. (*Source:* Garner, 1966, Fig. 20.)

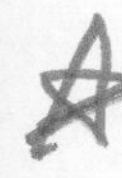

are located at successively low-value sites consistent with their lower thresholds. Thus in community centers, the inner-core area of high values is occupied by community-level functions surrounded on low-value peripheral sites by the low-threshold neighborhood functions. At the regional level, the locational sequence runs regional-, community-, and neighborhood-level functions on land of successively lower value. Similar zoning by threshold type might be expected within the CBD, although the pattern there is most certainly more complex—perhaps so complex as to destroy the simplicity of the pattern typical of outlying centers. It is, however, well to remember that when the "simplicity of land use patterns is destroyed . . . this does not mean that the order and system are destroyed. It means that the order imposed by the influence of economic distance takes on increasingly more complex forms." (Dunn, 1954, pp. 61–62).

Table 13.3 indicates that the arrangement of business types within regional-level centers in Chicago generally agrees with the model. In the table, business types are ranked by their average values expressed in percentage form and are classified down the right margin according to the level of center at which they are typically found.

The expected arrangement is, however, somewhat blurred at the larger regional-level centers (Table 13.3). Although the high-order regional types tend to be concentrated toward the upper part of the list, they are joined by low-order types.

TABLE 13.3. THE INTERNAL STRUCTURE OF REGIONAL CENTERS IN THE CITY OF CHICAGO

SIC Code		Description	Percent Value	
R	5634	Apparel accessory	56.2	
R	5633	Hosiery stores	53.7	50.0%
C	5441	Candy	49.1	
R	5662	Men's shoes	49.0	
C	5311	Department stores	48.7	
C	5651	Family clothes	44.1	
R	5663	Women's shoes	43.7	
R	5664	Children's shoes	41.7	
C	5621	Women's clothes	41.3	
C	5331	Variety stores	41.3	
N	5912	Drugstores	40.8	40.0%
C	5665	Family shoes	39.3	
C	5612	Men's clothes	38.4	
C	5971	Jewelers	35.3	
R	5641	Children's clothes	32.7	
R	5632	Corset and lingerie	32.5	
R	5699	Miscellaneous clothing	32.0	
R	5722	Household appliances	31.8	
N	5462	Bakeries	31.8	
N	605	Currency exchanges	30.9	
C	783	Motion-picture theaters	30.5	30.0%
C	5499	Delicatessen	28.8	
R	7949	Sports promoters	28.2	
N	5812	Eating places	28.0	
C	60	Banks	27.6	
C	5732	Radio & television	26.2	
C	6159	Loan offices	25.8	
R	5631	Millinery stores	25.3	
N	8099	Optometrists	25.1	
R	5996	Camera stores	25.1	
C	5997	Gift and novelty	24.5	

Neighborhood-level types are not all concentrated at the lower end of the list as we might expect; neither are all the community-level types placed between those in the middle of the table. There appears to be considerable scatter of the different groups of activities through the list. Of the many factors responsible for these distortions two are of particular importance: space demands and product differentiation.

Space demands In discussing patterns in the CBD, it was noted that business types that need large amounts of space tend to be located at peripheral sites where they can afford it. This factor is not taken into account in the model. It is, however, clear from Figure 13.14 that a strong correlation exists between average front-foot land value and the average size of stores for a sample of business types in the regional center at 63rd and Halsted Streets in Chicago. Candy stores are generally small in size and are associated with high-average land values consistent with the tendency for them to locate as close to the PVI as possible, where they can tempt the large numbers of shoppers into buying on impulse. In contrast the high-order

TABLE 13.3. (Continued)

SIC Code		Description	Percent Value	
R	64	Insurance	24.1	
C	7631	Watch repairs	24.0	
N	5251	Hardware	23.5	
C	5712	Furniture	23.4	
N	5411	Grocers	22.8	
R	5713	China and glassware	22.4	
N	5422	Meat markets	22.2	
C	5921	Liquor stores	22.1	
N	801	Medical services	22.1	
R	5952	Sporting-goods stores	21.9	
C	5392	Army and navy stores	21.5	
R	7221	Photographers	20.5	
N	65	Real estate agents	20.1	20.0%
R	5714	Drapery stores	19.8	
C	5733	Music stores	19.6	
N	5813	Bars	19.6	
N	7231	Beauty shops	19.3	
N	10	Supermarkets	19.0	
N	7211	Dry cleaners	18.9	
N	7241	Barbers	18.3	
C	5943	Stationery stores	18.3	
N	7215	Laundromats	17.7	
C	5231	Paint and glass stores	17.7	
R	5715	Floor covering	15.1	
N	7251	Shoe repairs	14.7	
R	5719	Miscellaneous furnishing	14.5	
N	5423	Fish and sea foods	14.2	
C	5992	Florists	13.9	

Note: R, C, and N indicate regional-, community-, and neighborhood-level functions, respectively.

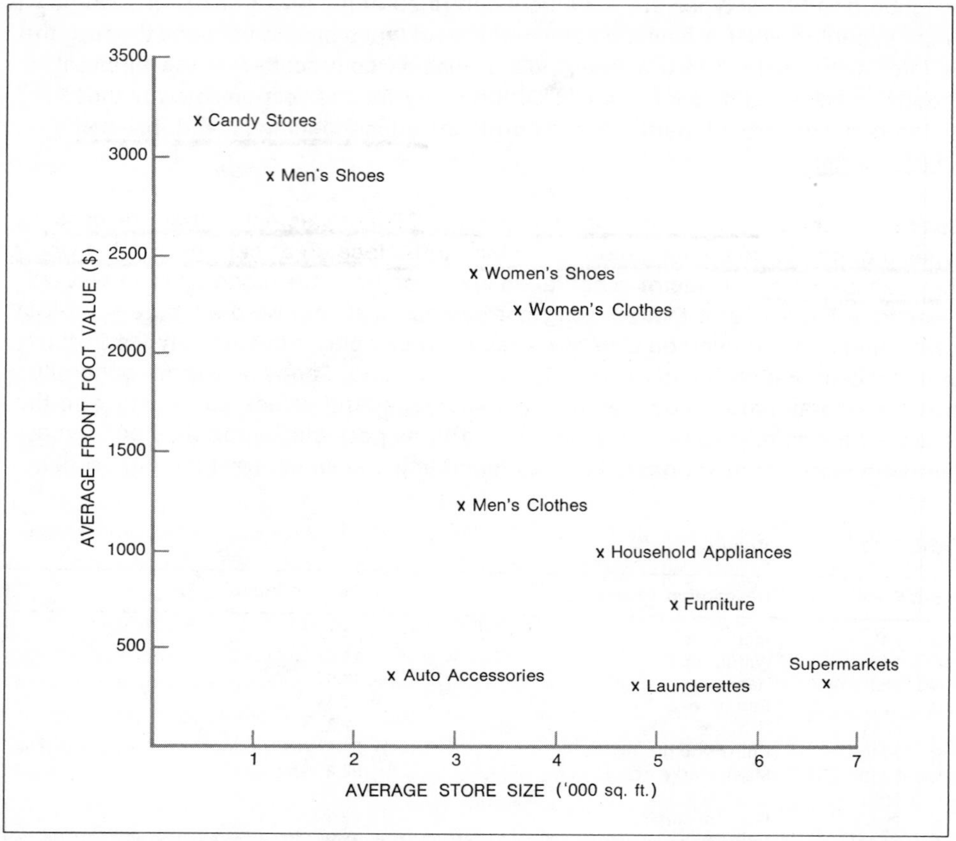

FIG. 13.14. RELATIONSHIP BETWEEN AVERAGE FRONT FOOT LAND VALUES AND STORE SIZE FOR SELECTED BUSINESS TYPES IN THE 63rd AND HALSTED REGIONAL LEVEL SHOPPING CENTER, CITY OF CHICAGO. (*Source:* From data in Berry and Tennant, 1963, p. 3.)

furniture and household-appliance stores with their larger showroom space tend to be pushed outward onto the low-value land consistent with the comparative buying associated with the goods they sell.

Product differentiation Product differentiation refers to qualitative differences between establishments selling the same type of goods. Our methods of classification implicitly assume that all men's clothing stores or supermarkets are identical in the nature of the goods they sell—that they are all of the same quality. In reality, however, the competitive nature of retailing tends to bring about a variety of tangible (e.g., price) and intangible (e.g., level of service) differences between individual establishments of the same business type. When these differences affect the cost structure of establishments, they are reflected in threshold size. Thus each establishment can be thought of as having its own threshold size. As a result there is a range of threshold sizes reflecting the product differentiation between establishments of the same business type, and in turn a considerable variation in rent paying ability and hence location within centers. The average figures in the tables mask this variation and, because of the way they are calculated, may even result in the upward and downward movement within the table to give rise to apparent distortions to the regularity.

CHANGES IN LAND USE PATTERNS

Patterns within shopping centers result from the operation of complex, and often conflicting, sets of locational forces. The nature of these forces, however, is constantly changing with time. Hence order in the internal structure of the CBD and outlying shopping centers may not ever be perfectly developed, because the arrangement of land uses is in a constant state of flux. The observed patterns are only temporary for many anomalies indicate that the present distribution is merely temporary, as a result of complex causes in a constant state of flux. The present distribution is only a stage, not even a stable one, in an evolution whose progress we cannot completely understand. Some of its causes are permanent, some no longer active, others are just beginning to function.

Changes in land use patterns may be observed in two ways: (1) as changes taking place over a wide area, and (2) as changes taking place at a given location. The first appears as a gradual shift of activities among available locations and is perhaps more typical of changes taking place within the CBD, and especially within the larger ones. Evidence of such shifts is well documented, for example within the CBD of Manhattan. It may involve the shift of an entire retail area, for example, or theater district, or a particular kind of wholesaling concentration. In Manhattan, for example, the main retail area today is centered in midtown, whereas in the past it was located farther to the south. Alternatively changes of this type may take the form of new centers growing up at some distance from the old. For example, this is the case in Manhattan, where a new office concentration has grown up in midtown to complement an earlier concentration downtown. The second type of change is implicit in the first and is observed as a succession of different kinds of use at the same location—either an individual site, a single building, or even a particular block. These changes are generally referred to as the *sequent occupance* of a location, and this is particularly common in older buildings downtown. This kind of change is perhaps more characteristic of changes within outlying business centers. As a result of these changes, there is always a mixture of related and unrelated activities at each zone within shopping centers.

In addition to changes of this sort, evidence suggests that the CBD itself is not stable through time, but that its boundaries shift gradually. The CBD expands in one direction and contracts in another, usually the opposite direction. The front on which the CBD is advancing has been called the "zone of assimilation;" the retreating front called the "zone of discard." Evidence of these two types of zone are given in Figure 13.15 for some of the CBD's studied by Murphy and Vance.

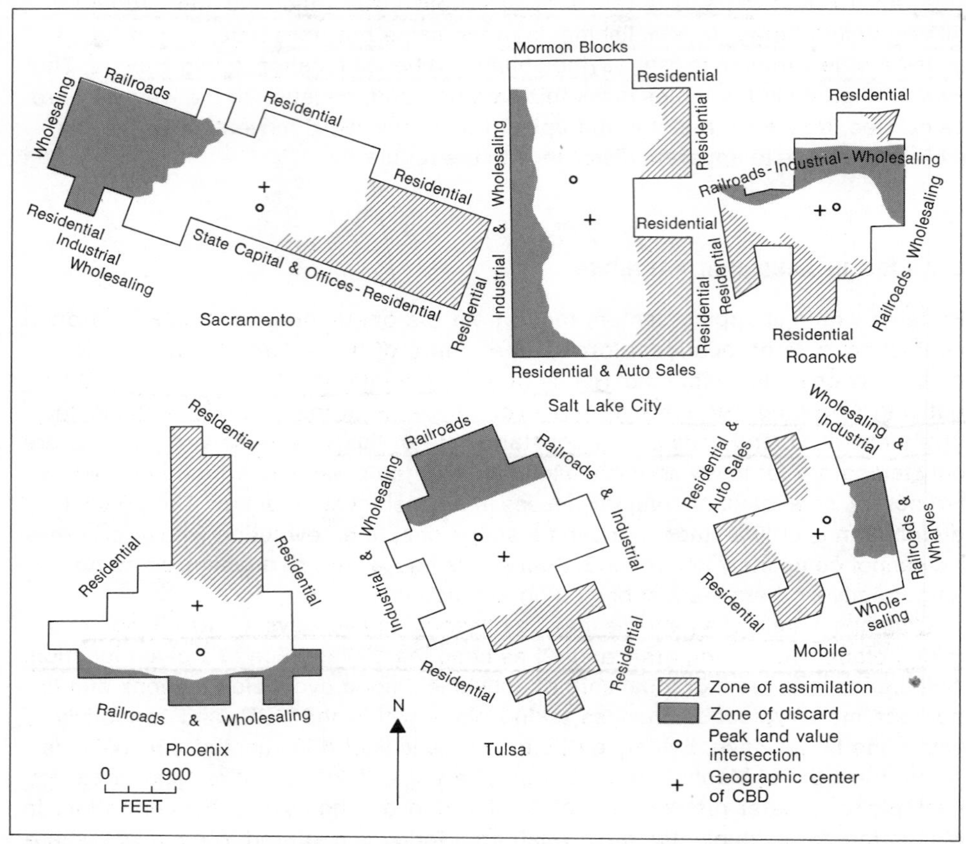

FIG. 13.15. ZONES OF DISCARD AND ASSIMILATION IN SELECTED CENTRAL BUSINESS DISTRICTS. (*Source:* After Murphy, et al., 1955, Fig. 16.)

Although exact reasons for this gradual shift are not at all clear, it does appear as though some kind of push-pull mechanism operates, inasmuch as the zone of discard appears to reflect the repelling influences of industrial and deteriorated residential property in the frame while the zone of assimilation reflects the attraction toward better residential areas. Accompanying this gradual change in the areal extent of the CBD, the peak intersection alters its location over time in the direction of the advancing front. This is a more gradual process on account of the heavy investment of buildings and enterprises at the existing PVI. But over time as newer buildings are erected at sites near to the existing PVI, and as the pull of activities locating in them gains momentum, so adjustments in site utility take place resulting in gradual change in the land value pattern.

The zones of discard and assimilation represent an invasion-succession process. Activities that were characteristic of a former pattern are gradually replaced by a new and different set of activities. Murphy and Vance (1955) postulate that invading activities in the zone of assimilation include specialty shops, automobile showrooms, drive-ins, banks, headquarter offices, and newer hotels.

In contrast, the zone of discard is invaded by poorer types of activities catering to the lower levels of demand in the adjacent areas of deteriorating residences (the transition zone). Functions typical of this area include pawnshops, cheap family-clothing stores, bars, low-grade eating places, and a wide variety of small food and second-hand stores. In some cases, incipient skid rows may develop in the near blighted environment of this depressed area. The contraction of commercial activity in this part of the CBD normally gives rise to a level of vacant stores and office buildings, many of which may be in a severely deteriorated condition. It is not uncommon for these vacant properties to be utilized eventually by activities for which they were never originally designed. Thus store-front churches, "chicken farms," and even store-front residences are commonly distinctive features—features that are characteristic of a well-advanced state of commercial blight.

These features may also be typical of certain outlying business centers as they contract in the face of competition from newer suburban shopping centers or from a reduction in purchasing power resulting from changes in the social structure of their immediate market areas.

Thus a certain measure of order is evident in land use patterns within retail nucleations. Order in internal structure is never perfectly attained, however, because of a constant change in the importance of different locational forces. Land use patterns are consequently in a state of constant flux. The array of activities found within shopping centers results from the continuance of previous patterns and the active formation of new groupings of businesses, and occasionally of altogether new types of activity. Despite the general inertia characteristic of many activities within centers, the shifting of activities among alternative locations is always going on.

zones of discard & assimilation represent an invasion - succession process.

"THE LOCATION OF MANUFACTURING"

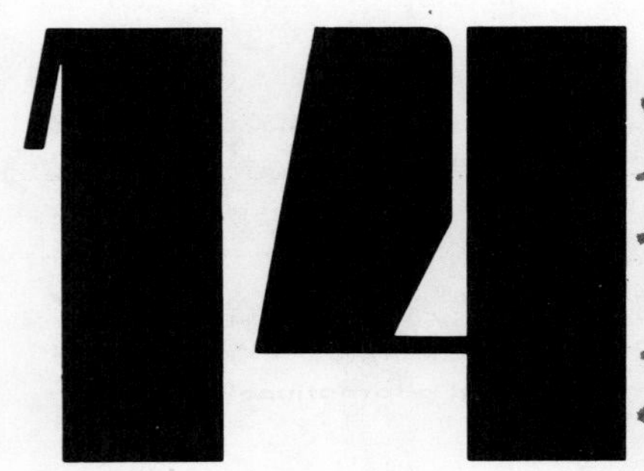

Although manufacturing land occupies a small proportion of total urban land, it contains a very important aspect of the urban economy, for on this land are located production facilities that provide employment for a large proportion of a city's labor force (see Fig. 14.1 and Table 9.1). For example in the Pittsburgh region, although manufacturing production facilities occupy less than 15 of the region's 4487 square miles, on an average workday more than one-third of the region's work force pours into this area and the activities of these industries generate more than two-fifths of the total earned income of the region (Lowry, 1963, p. 60). It is therefore extremely important to develop an understanding of the factors influencing the location of industry within urban areas, for these manufacturing activities are centers of a large proportion of total urban economic activity.

Many studies of the manufacturing structure of cities have been made, yet the geographic literature is rather sparse on the subject of industrial location models at the urban level (Hamilton, 1967, p. 412; Rowlands, 1959, pp. 15–16). While general industrial location theory can be used to indicate fairly well the metropolitan area in which a firm can best locate, it provides a less adequate framework for indicating where, in an urban area, industry should be situated (Goldberg, 1970). There is, in fact, an important difference in scale, for the problem of manufacturing location within an urban area becomes that of choosing a particular site. Thus Kitagawa and Bogue distinguish between location theory as a framework to place a factory at a given metropolitan area and site considerations to locate the industry within the metropolitan area (Kitagawa and Bogue, 1955, p. 127). The problem that arises in a discussion of site considerations is that it is difficult to express them in terms of a general model of the intraurban location of manufacturing. However, an attempt will be made in this chapter to provide a framework for such a model, though before this can be presented it is necessary to have some discussion of factors influencing site selection in both a spatial and historical framework.

LOCATIONAL REQUIREMENTS OF MANUFACTURING PLANTS

Factors determining where in an urban area a manufacturing concern can most profitably operate fall mainly into three broad groups (Lowry, 1963, p. 63):

1. Characteristics of the site itself, including such buildings as may be already on it when it is being considered as a location
2. Characteristics of the neighborhood or immediate surroundings of the site
3. Accessibility characteristics, such as access to customers, suppliers, and labor

Although it is assumed that manufacturing concerns will seek the most profitable location, it must be remembered that this consideration comes up when the location is being sought. Furthermore, it is possible that for many concerns "profitable" really means "survival," particularly for new firms just starting. Indeed it should be noted that " . . . most human decision making, whether individual or organizational, is concerned with the discovery and selection of satisfactory alternatives; only in exceptional cases is it concerned with . . . optimal alternatives" (March and Simon, 1958, pp. 140–141).

At this juncture it is also necessary to distinguish between plants and firms, for the locational requirements may well be affected by this distinction. A *firm* is regarded as an independent entity, either publicly or privately owned; and in much of the industrial location literature, it is synonymous to the entrepreneur. A *plant* is a manufacturing unit (establishment) located on a particular site. Thus a firm can consist of one or many plants. In the latter case, the plants may be distributed at many locations that may be adjacent or dispersed throughout an urban area or over a very large area (such as a country, continent, or the world). In the situation where a firm consists of many plants, the important locational distinction is that the firm may be seeking to maximize or obtain satisfactory profits from the combination of plants, not from a single plant. Furthermore for firms with a large number of plants, this maximization procedure is with respect not only to the short term but the long term as well. Thus a firm with many plants may have a number running at a loss if the potential long-term prospects at those particular locations deem the investment to be sound. As much of the following discussion is with respect to plants, this important distinction must be borne in mind.

SITE CHARACTERISTICS

Firms or plants may seek sites with particular characteristics. For example a few may desire a particular type of water that requires a well at a particular site, others may use mineral materials derived from a particular site. In this latter case the weight-loss principle is obviously the determining factor. However, in general terms, the site characteristics of importance to most plants concern the amount, flatness, and cost of the land, and the type of building found upon it.

Physical and cost characteristics The amount of level land available and its cost are two of the most important factors determining the location of a plant within an urban area. Some types of industry require large quantities of fairly level land, for the production process may be of the conveyor-belt or integrated type. For this type of industry the employment density of the site is fairly low. Table 14.1 lists the ten largest users of industrial land in the Pittsburgh region and the site employment density for each manufacturing type. The largest users of space are the iron and steel, railroad equipment, electrical-industrial apparatus, and metal can industries, for in all of these the employment- density ratio is very low. Thus it is clear that industries requiring large amounts of space per plant and per employee usually locate only in those areas where land is cheap and not in general demand. On the other hand, industries requiring relatively little space per plant and per employee could locate in the more intensely developed parts of urban areas.

Land Cost

Our discussion of land values in Chapter 9 suggested that the cost of land at the edge of the city is generally less than that within the city, and a great deal less than that at the center of the city. The cost of a site is further increased for the purchaser

TABLE 14.1. AVERAGE SITE AREA IN USE AND EMPLOYMENT DENSITY BY MANUFACTURING ESTABLISHMENTS, PITTSBURGH REGION, 1960–61

SIC Code	Industry Type	Employment Density (persons per 1,000 sq. ft.)	Average Site Area in Use (in millions sq. ft.)
331	Blast furnaces, iron and steel works, rolling mills	2.2	13.5
291	Petroleum refining	14.3	3.2
282	Plastics materials, etc.	6.1	3.1
325	Structural clay products	49.8	2.9
374	Railroad equipment	1.1	1.9
373	Ship and boat building	4.1	1.7
321	Flat glass	3.5	1.7
362	Electrical-industrial apparatus	1.0	1.3
341	Metal cans	0.9	0.9
329	Abrasives, asbestos, etc.	14.9	0.6

Source: Lowry (1963B), p. 65.

if he has to buy a building that has been erected previously on the lot. Thus an industrialist who wishes to buy land per se is usually looking for vacant serviced lots. The serviced aspect is particularly important, for the provision of water, electricity, sewage, and access routes are an expensive overhead. The evidence available indicates that the price of industrial land varies according to the degree to which it is serviced and the size of the lot, as well as its location within the urban area. Bearing these details in mind, Stuart (1968, p. 37) suggests that the average price of industrial land within the city of Roanoke, Va., in 1964 (population 160,000) was $6,000 per acre, compared with $4,200 per acre in the suburban ring and suggests that the difference between city prices and suburban prices is greater in larger urban areas.

Buildings Some types of manufacturing establishments seldom have a plant specifically designed for their purpose, but prefer to rent or lease floor space in existing buildings. Rental buildings or loft space are attractive for those enterprises with uncertain futures and particularly for those not using heavy equipment or materials, who are thus able to use secondhand space. Vacant space of this type is most plentiful around the CBD, and it is common to find numerous small firms clustered together in the frame of the CBD.

The types of industries located in this kind of premise are usually those that have some functional link with CBD activities. Lowry (1963, p. 64) indicates that the following are typical of this group in the Pittsburgh area:

Service industries to the printing trades
Ophthalmic goods
Jewelry, silverware, and plated ware
Costume jewelry, costume novelties, etc.
Publishing and printing of periodicals
Photographic equipment and supplies

Men's and boys' furnishings, etc.
Miscellaneous apparel and accessories
Manufacture of manifold business forms
Miscellaneous manufacturing industries
Miscellaneous plastics products
Pens, pencils, etc.

From the above list it can be observed that printing and publishing activities in general, and the clothing industries (including accessories) are the two dominant groups. In most urban areas the total employment in these industries is relatively small, but in the large metropolises these industries are extremely important as they form a vital adjunct to the regional office and service activities located in the core of the CBD.

Taxes Another important factor influencing the location of industry that involves land, buildings, and profits are taxes (Due, 1961). The importance of differential taxation rates between central cities and suburban areas has been emphasized by Campbell (1958), who indicates that 14 percent of factories leaving New York City between 1947 and 1955 gave taxes as their prime reason for doing so, and for another 25 percent taxes were a secondary factor. State differences in industrial taxation in the New York region have also been emphasized by Hoover and Vernon (1959, pp. 55–60). Prior to 1958, New York City had both a corporate tax and a tax on gross receipts, while New Jersey had only a property tax. New Jersey, therefore, was favored as a location by firms with high profits and low property requirements, while New York attracted firms with low profits and high property needs.

Tax differentials are therefore an important economic aspect of the locational decision, though they usually represent only a very small component of the total costs or expenditures of most manufacturing firms. However, it seems to be the manufacturer's perception of taxes that is important, for although they may form a small proportion of his costs they nevertheless loom large in his decision-making matrix (Williams, 1967). This may be because low taxes are synonymous with freedom in the entrepreneur's mind. Nevertheless the higher taxes on land and buildings, as well as business taxes, in central cities do seem to have an effect on the location of firms and plants.

NEIGHBORHOOD CHARACTERISTICS

Much industrial activity is noisy and dirty, and these characteristics give rise to air and water pollution and blight. Although industry is but one cause of air pollution, the local effect of a particular plant or group of plants can be quite overwhelming. This is because man in his industrial life uses the air as a sewer, into which he discharges dust, soot, ash, and gaseous chemical effluents. One of the most devastating examples of this latter kind of pollution exists in and around Sudbury, Ont., where sulphurous and nitrous fumes have completely destroyed the vegetation of an area of many hundreds of square miles. Local air pollution can therefore be a deterrent to other industries, particularly the clean light industries that use electricity. As these industries are usually modern and fast growing and thus welcomed by most communities as a desired addition to the urban economy, any local factor discouraging their location has severe repercussions.

Some industrial activity also results in neighborhood frictional blight. It is evident in most urban areas that the "incompatibility of manufacturing with most other land uses has contributed to the formation of industrial clusters within which neighbors are not overly critical" (Lowry, 1963, p. 66). This clustering of plants has been made formal in most urban areas by zoning ordinances. But the potential use of land bordering these industrial zones is limited, and the demand for such land is relatively low. Consequently inexpensive and low-rent residential structures, occupied by low-income families, usually are found in these areas. However, since the advent of electricity and natural gas as sources of industrial energy, it is possible for some plants to conduct their operations intermingled with other land users, and in many cases commercial despoilation is greater than that of the modern industrial plant.

It may be suggested that although neighborhood characteristics may not now play a major role in the selection by industrialists of manufacturing sites, it is almost certain that their importance will increase as other locational constraints are eased. A major reason for this expectation is derived from the fact that the proportion of female, professional, and highly skilled workers in the manufacturing labor force is continually increasing. In order to recruit and retain these people as employees, industrialists will be forced to pay attention to the environment surrounding the plant. Thus, the availability of labor, as an input material to the firm, may well be determined in part by the characteristics of the neighborhood.

ACCESSIBILITY

In Chapter 6 we have emphasized the effect of accessibility on the location of manufacturing between urban centers. In this section we are concerned with the effect of accessibility on the location of industry within urban areas. The term *accessibility* in this context covers a number of factors influencing location decisions. Generally, these include accessibility to materials, accessibility to labor supply, and accessibility to markets. These factors, taken together, are commonly considered to be the most important influences on location decisions.

Accessibility to material inputs The sensitivity of a plant to accessibility to materials is related to the weight-loss and bulk of the input concerned. Many fuel inputs are very bulky and incur weight-loss in the manufacturing process; and, as a consequence, plants requiring this kind of input tend to locate adjacent to the cheapest means of transportation available. This is either water or rail, with water transportation usually being the cheaper, particularly if the commodity has to be hauled over long distances. For example in Pittsburgh the iron and steel industry has a vast intake of coal and iron, and shipments of these commodities are twice the weight of outbound product commodities. Thus these, and a few other heavy industries, depend on cheap barge transportation; and they locate along the navigable waterways in the Pittsburgh area. Table 14.2 indicates for these industries the high weekly tonnage of inbound shipments by barge, which contrasts sharply to the general absence of outbound shipments using water transportation.

If good water transportation is not available, rail is usually used, particularly as it is the most preferred form of shipment for the outbound products of industries with high weight-loss material inputs. Those industries with low weight-loss material inputs are obviously less tied to cheap transportation facilities and are, therefore, able to use either rail or truck transportation. In the latter case the industry has a high degree of locational freedom, and plants can be established with a minimal consideration of accessibility to material inputs.

Accessibility to labor The effect of labor differentials within urban areas on the location of industry is partly related to city size. In small urban areas labor differentials are relatively unimportant, but in large urban areas they may be extremely important for certain industries. This is most particularly the case for light manufacturing industries employing large numbers of low-wage, unskilled married female labor, for married women generally have a much more restricted commuting range than men. Industries that fall into this category are those concerned with canning and preserving, confectionery, electric measuring instruments and test equipment, and household appliances.

Some industries locate within certain areas because of particular skills. This is especially true of the clothing trades in large metropolitan areas where certain groups have developed traditional skills in needlework, cutting, and designing. For

TABLE 14.2. PRINCIPAL MANUFACTURING INDUSTRIES IN THE PITTSBURGH REGION USING WATER TRANSPORTATION (RANK ORDERED BY TOTAL VOLUME)

	Average Weekly Tonnage of Barge Shipment per 100 Employees		
Industry	**Total**	**Inbound**	**Outbound**
1. Blast furnaces and steelworks	250	220	30
2. Producers of lubricating oils and greases	2,294	2,294	0
3. Producers of ready-mixed concrete	1,555	1,111	444
4. Producers of paving mixtures and blocks	1,510	1,483	27
5. Producers of ground or otherwise treated minerals and earths	470	470	0
6. Petroleum refining	305	305	0
7. Producers of plastics materials, etc.	199	193	6
8. Zinc smelting and refining	n.d.	n.d.	n.d.
9. Cement, hydraulic	74	7	67
10. Industrial inorganic chemicals n.e.c.	34	34	0

n.d.: Figures not disclosed to avoid revealing information of individual operations.
Source: Lowry (1963B), p. 67.

example Kenyon (1964, p. 163) notes that the great growth of the apparel industry in New York City in the 1880s is related in part to the arrival of thousands of Jewish immigrants from Eastern Europe who, in reality, initiated the needle trades in New York. The high level of skills introduced by these people was extremely important in making New York City the center of the clothing industry in North America; and the dominant influence of this group continues today.

Unionization also seems to be a factor influencing the locational decision of some firms, particularly with respect to suburban and central city locations. Stuart (1968, p. 31) notes that some nonunion plants in Roanoke, Va., chose suburban sites so as to place a distance barrier between themselves and the unionized plants in the central city. This is particularly true if the company is labor intensive and is using low-wage workers. It is interesting in this regard to note that some unions are recognizing this trend and, in the case of the International Ladies Garment Workers Union in New York City, are trying to protect the job opportunities of their members by pursuing only reasonable wage demands (Helfgott, 1959, p. 88). It would obviously be a hazard to the unions if union companies decreased in employment while nonunion companies increased their employment.

Accessibility to markets There are two aspects of the marketing process that are of interest to the urban geographer. The first involves the destination of the product, and the second involves the geographic range of the sales. In Chapter 6 we have observed that in any economy goods can be produced and purchased by each industrial group. In a closed, urban system the flows all occur within one area; but in an open system, where all urban areas are linked, goods can flow between urban areas as well as within an urban area. Thus the geographic range of sales of a plant may be local or worldwide.

Interindustry Linkages

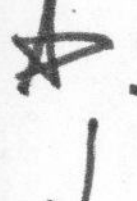

The flow of a product from one industrial group to another gives rise to interindustry linkages. In these cases the output of one firm forms the input of another. Thus is would be logical to expect that firms with a high degree of interdependency would, other things being equal, tend to cluster within an urban area. However, the effect of interindustry linkages on location is difficult to determine. In Roanoke, Va., the only case of within-city interindustry linkage occurs with respect to frame makers and box fabricators supplying local furniture-making establishments. As these plants are located at relatively great distances from each other, the effect of interindustry linkage does not appear to be great. Karaska (1966, pp. 80–96) uses input-output methodology to estimate the degree to which certain industries in Philadelphia are linked, but he does not determine the degree to which highly linked industries are also spatially associated.

The Geographic Range of Markets

The geographic range of sales of most plants is usually very wide, and for a few it may be worldwide. For example in a study pertaining to a few small towns in southern Ontario, it is estimated that only 1.56 percent of the outputs of manufacturing industries were sold locally, 21.78 percent were sold to metropolitan Toronto, 30.93 percent to the rest of Ontario, 33.71 percent to the rest of Canada, 9.96 percent to the United States, and 2.06 percent to the rest of the world (Yeates and Lloyd, 1970, p. 28). The total population of the local area referred to in this case is only 100,000 persons, and one would expect that as the population of an area increased the proportion of local sales would also increase.

Industries that serve a local area have been referred to in Chapter 5 as non-basic industries. They are usually those in which the product is perishable, bulky, or custom-made, and in which small scale operation is practical. Plants of this type include those concerned with bottled beverages, dairy products, baked goods, commercial printing, ready-mixed concrete and concrete products, and so forth. In Pittsburgh this type of industry usually sells greater than 70 percent of its output to the local region, whereas the electrical industries commonly sell less than 20 percent of their output to the local area (Table 14.3). Furthermore, it is interesting to note from Table 14.3 that industries making the greatest use of rail transportation are those that ship most of their output beyond the local Pittsburgh region. We have previously noted that the type of transportation used depends a great deal on the weight-loss incurred; consequently some industries use water for the transportation of inputs and rail for outputs. Examples of these are plants classified as blast furnaces, steel works, and rolling mills.

It is in this context of transportation that the contrast between suburban and city plants is most outstanding. Plants located within the city tend to make use of rail transportation much more than plants in suburban locations, which tend to transport by truck. These differences are detailed in Table 14.4 for Roanoke, Va., the contrasts being particularly evident if comparisons are made with the total shipment pattern for the metropolitan area. Furthermore, the table indicates that whereas there is a great difference between the proportion of materials moved into and from the city by rail, this difference is very minor in the suburban ring.

THE SPATIAL EVOLUTION OF MANUFACTURING

In terms of contemporary transportation facilities and communications media, it would seem that a manufacturer is fairly free to locate in any part of an urban area, provided that land in sufficient quantities is available. Thus any pattern of industry observed in the present, such as that for Minneapolis–St. Paul (Fig. 14.1), has to be perceived as a product of differential locational forces prevailing in the past, some of which are no longer of importance. Noting the apparent confusion and geographic chaos in the distribution of manufacturing in the modern city, Pred comments that

> . . . beneath this superficial disorder and confusion, certain spatial regularities can be discerned if the structure of metropolitan manufacturing is viewed in terms of its evolution, the local friction of distance, and broad industrial categories which express similar locational tendencies (Pred, 1964, p. 165).

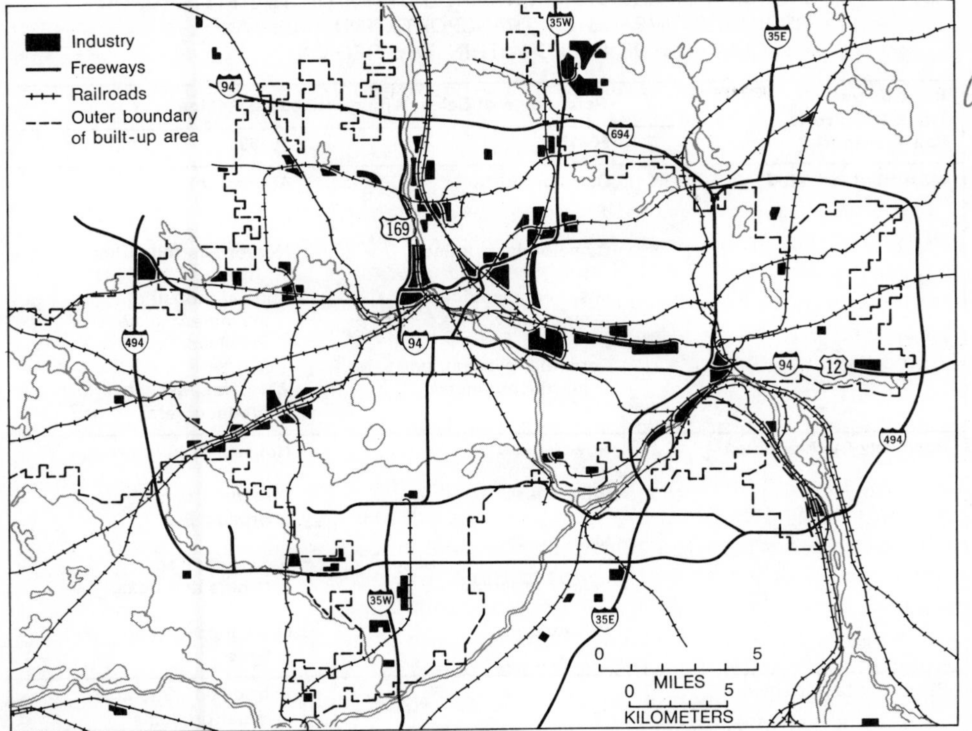

FIG. 14.1. THE DISTRIBUTION OF INDUSTRIAL LAND USES IN MINNEAPOLIS–ST. PAUL, MINNESOTA, 1970. (*Source: Focus* (published by the American Geographical Society of New York), 1970, after Map 1.)

This evolution can be expressed in terms of technological change in the organization of manufacturing industry and major transportation innovations, both of which interwine historically to constrain locational patterns. These can be classified as (1) the pattern before the Industrial Revolution, (2) the early Industrial Revolution waterway era, (3) the middle Industrial Revolution railway era, and (4) the late Industrial Revolution highway era. In each of these eras certain locational forces tended to predominate, but no one locational force is exclusive to any particular era.

PREINDUSTRIAL REVOLUTION

In the colonial or preindustrial era in North America, the population of towns was very small, and the manufacturing that took place usually occurred within an area corresponding today to the center of the metropolis. This area usually corresponded to a zone adjacent to a waterfront, for nearly all colonial towns were located with respect to river and sea transportation. The preeminence of the waterfront as a manufacturing area derived from the fact that in every colonial

TABLE 14.3. PRINCIPAL MANUFACTURING INDUSTRIES OF THE PITTSBURGH REGION, BY MEANS OF TRANSPORTATION USED AND PERCENTAGE OF SALES WITHIN THE REGION

Rank in Use of Truck Relative to Rail Transport	Percentage of Sales Within Pittsburgh Region	
	70–100	35–69
Most truck-oriented	Dairy products	Apparel, etc.[a]
	Commercial printing[a]	Nonferrous foundries
	Misc. nonelectrical machinery	Special industrial machinery, except metal-working
	Concrete, gypsum, and plaster products[b]	Abrasives, asbestos products, etc.
Relatively truck-oriented	Newspapers	Household furniture
	Beverages[a]	Structural clay products[b]
	Meat products	Paperboard containers and boxes
	Bakery products	Misc. food preparations
	Millwork, etc.	
Relatively rail-oriented		Fabricated structural metal products[b]
		Metal-working machinery and equipment
Most rail-oriented		

[a] Indicates industries reporting largest use of air freight or express relative to employment.
[b] Indicates industries reporting significant use of water transportation.
Source: Lowry (1963A), p. 69.

20–34	10–19	0–9
General industrial machinery Heating apparatus and plumbing fixtures	Metal stampings	Instruments for measuring, etc.[a]
Construction, mining, and materials-handling machinery	Paints, etc.[a] Electric lighting and wiring equipment	
Screw-machine products Misc. fabricated metal products Nonferrous metals rolling, etc.[b] Industrial chemicals[b] Plastic and rubber products	Ship and boat building and repairing Plastics materials[b] Misc. primary metals industries	Electrical industrial apparatus[a] Electric transmission and distribution equipment
Iron and steel foundries	Pottery, etc. Cutlery, hand tools, etc. Misc. products of petroleum and coal[b] Motor vehicles and equipment Blast furnaces, steel works, and rolling mills[b]	Pressed and blown glass Flat glass Canning and preserving[a] Petroleum refining Railroad equipment Metal cans

TABLE 14.4. CONTRASTS IN TRANSPORTATION MODES USED BETWEEN THE CITY AND SUBURBAN RING, ROANOKE, SMSA, 1964

	Percent Materials Moved In			Percent Product Moved Out		
Zone	**Rail**	**Truck**	**Air**	**Rail**	**Truck**	**Air**
City	32.7	66.9	0.4	23.1	74.9	2.0
Suburban ring	16.4	82.4	1.2	15.4	82.1	2.5
SMSA total	25.5	73.8	0.7	19.7	78.1	2.2

Source: Stuart (1968), p. 31.

town the principal industries were those concerned with shipbuilding and the preparation of provisions or naval stores for export (Bridenbaugh, 1950). Thus shipbuilding was early established as the chief waterfront activity in seventeenth century Boston, New York, and Philadelphia; and it was even of importance in centers founded later in nonmaritime locations, such as Pittsburgh and Cleveland.

The types of activity undertaken usually occurred in small workshops, which were often the place of residence as well as the place of work. These workshops clustered around the waterfront and the incipient commercial and retail centers, all of which vied for the best business locations. Eventually, in some towns, the commercial and retail centers grew to sufficient proportions to make it possible for local manufacturers to produce for these local businesses. In this way small clothing establishments, weavers' shops, and leather-working plants grew to provide goods for the quasi CBD as well as the waterfront. Thus, with urban growth, manufacturing activity can be regarded as being located with respect to the CBD and the waterfront. As these areas were often juxtaposed, the spatial differentiation of manufacturing location was not immediately obvious, but in time this distinction became extremely important.

THE EARLY INDUSTRIAL REVOLUTION

The early nineteenth century development and spread of settlement in North America followed very closely the pattern of waterways, for the river systems had an obvious advantage over muddy roads and rutted tracks. This advantage was reflected by the choice of manufacturing to locate along waterway sites and, for example, is one reason for the location of various industrial enterprises along the forked branches of the Chicago River (Solzman, 1966, p. 16). Thus the advantages of the waterfront in maritime urban locations were paralleled by settlements in the interior, many of which were located with respect to water transportation.

Technological innovations and expanding markets resulted, however, in a greater complexity and proliferation of manufacturing which, in the American experience, ". . . became apparent with the introduction of the factory system, power-driven machinery, interchangeable parts, and other mass-production techniques during the later eighteenth and early nineteenth centuries" (Pred,

1964, p. 167). The power source was frequently water, particularly with respect to wool and textile mills, and this requirement ". . . often dictated location at rural waterfall sites, such as in Waltham, Mass., and in Paterson, N.J. . . ." (Pred, 1964, p. 167), locations that have since become industrial areas within the Boston and New York metropolitan areas. A further aspect of this changing technology is that water became not only important for transportation and as a power source, but also as a material input to the production process. Thus for those industries using large quantities of water, waterway locations were extremely important. In this regard, most of the blast furnaces in operation by 1825 in the Pittsburgh area had riverside locations outside the city and formed industrial nucleations as the city grew in response to the burgeoning urban economy.

Thus water sites were extremely important areas for the early development of manufacturing, and their importance has continued through to today. However, it is possible that ". . . in giving due weight to the necessity for water in industrial processes we have overemphasized its strategic importance in industrial location" (White, 1960). This overemphasis may well have resulted from the continuing expansion of manufacturing at the center of the city for "the factory system was a city development" (Taylor, 1951, p. 233). We have previously noted that these industries were often juxtaposed with waterfront locations, and so in many instances it is difficult to determine whether CBD industrial expansion or waterway industrial expansion was the primary growth trend. Furthermore the limited physical mobility of the working force constrained industry to locate in the central part of the city.

THE MIDDLE INDUSTRIAL REVOLUTION

The rapid development of the North American railroad network in the middle and late nineteenth century reinforced the advantages of central areas in most urban concentrations. This was particularly due to the fact that the railroad companies established their terminals either within the CBD or as close to the CBD as possible, and these terminals became break-of-bulk points that offered direct access to a large geographic supply and market area. Thus a mélange of wholesaling and manufacturing establishments became located around rail terminals which, in the process of serving each other, developed a complex network of commodity and information flows. Pred (1964, pp. 167–168) notes that the "railroad was particularly influential in the evolution of the manufacturing districts near the core of midwestern metropolises; e.g., by the 1870s "The Flats" of Cleveland and the Union Stockyards of Chicago were prominent features in their respective urban landscapes."

The innovation of new manufacturing technology continued to increase at an exponential rate through the nineteenth century. In terms of the demand for space, this was reflected particularly in the increasing scale of operation of factories that continually required more land on which to expand. Small factories could not realize the efficiencies of production gained by the larger factories, and many were forced to amalgamate or close down in the face of increased competition. The larger factories could not find enough cheap space in the traditional railroad terminal or waterfront locations, and thus they were forced to decentralize. This decentralization was not possible without innovations in public transportation (detailed in Chapter 8) which permitted the urban area to spread, and without the provision of cheap industrial land, particularly by railroad companies.

Belt-line railroads As the private-enterprise-constructed railroad system in North America continued its development during the latter part of the nineteenth century, the trunk-line railroad companies realized that the interchange of rolling stock between systems was essential for the continued expansion of the industry. This need was particularly noticeable within large urban areas, where many different companies might operate lines and share terminal facilities. It was to serve this need that belt-line railroads were established, along with classification yards, either by a consortium of railroad companies or by independent operators. The belt-line railroad could only stay in business if it offered multichange facilities that were cheaper than single-stage transfers between trunk-line companies. In order to offer cheap facilities and additional traffic inducements, the belt-line railroads also encouraged industry to locate along their tracks and adjacent to their classification yards.

The Chicago Belt-Line Railroad

A classic case of belt-line railroad manufacturing location is in Chicago. The Belt Railroad Company (BRC) began industrial promotion almost from the day it was opened for traffic in the 1880s (Pinkepank, 1966). The inducements were similar to those offered by the trunk lines to industry locating along their tracks: cheap land and direct rail access. However, the BRC inducements were greater in that they offered freedom of access to all of Chicago's trunk-line railroads, and thus an industry would be free to use the facilities of trunk-line companies that offered the most favorable rates. The plentiful supply of cheap, transportation-serviced land was particularly important for those industries that could not obtain land for new plants, or expansions, near the center of the city.

In fact, up to the 1880s manufacturing in Chicago had concentrated around the Chicago River near the present Loop (CBD) district.

> This area soon became crowded, and the Chicago River itself would not accommodate the larger lakeboats. The mouth of the Calumet River arose as a rival to the downtown area for industrial location, and BRC was active in promoting this new industrial site, since the Calumet district was on BRC rails (Pinkepank, 1966, p. 40).

The largest industrial district promoted by BRC, however, is the Clearing Industrial District adjacent to Clearing Yard, which is operated by BRC. This city of factories was developed by a land syndicate in the 1920s and 1930s as a planned industrial community, with its own street, water, and sewerage services.

Thus the decentralization of manufacturing began during the latter half of the nineteenth century and is directly related to transportation innovations and changing technology, which increased the scale and diversity of manufacturing in growing urban areas. However, the rate of decentralization was limited by the general lack of low-cost urban transit facilities, which kept many manufacturers close to the traditional work and residential areas around the CBD. For example, as late as 1910, 75 percent of the manufacturing employment in Manhattan was in the small area south of 14th Street (Pratt, 1911, p. 188). This pattern of downtown manufacturing concentration was not noticeably broken until the advent of mass public transportation, the internal combustion engine, the truck, the highway, and the widespread use of electricity for power in manufacturing.

These are some of the features that are characteristic of the late Industrial Revolution.

THE LATE INDUSTRIAL REVOLUTION

know changes to p. 391

Although there is no degree of uniformity in the rate of decentralization of industry within urban areas, nevertheless the present century has witnessed a general centrifugal movement of manufacturing activity (Colby, 1933; Moses and Williamson, 1967). For example, for the period 1939 to 1947, the Standard Metropolitan Areas of thirteen economic regions in the United States showed extensive suburbanization in three regions, and no consistency of change in the other seven (Kitagawa and Bogue, 1955, p. 32). This lack of uniformity appears to be partly a function of time, for in some urban areas decentralization began earlier than in others. Weber (1899, p. 202), for example, notes decentralization tendencies in New York City before the turn of the present century, though Chinitz indicates quite clearly that this decline is relative (Table 14.5). Whereas the proportion of manufacturing employment in Manhattan declined, particularly between 1889 and 1919, total employment in Manhattan continued to increase. The great growth in manufacturing employment has been in the counties adjacent to New York City but within the metropolitan area.

The time element in decentralization can be illustrated specifically with respect to Philadelphia (Institute for Urban Studies, 1956, p. 52) and Chicago (Department of City Planning, 1961, p. 2). Within the city of Philadelphia manufacturing employment increased by 52,502 between 1940 and 1954, whereas employment in Chicago decreased by 66,500 between 1947 and 1957, a roughly similar period. At the periphery of these cities (within the metropolitan region of each, but outside their respective city boundaries), manufacturing employment increased by only 63,714 in Philadelphia compared with 92,200 in Chicago. The difference between these two cities seems to be temporal, however, for since 1951 the exodus of employment from Philadelphia has been increasing, whereas that from Chicago has remained relatively constant.

Forces of change Thus far we have discussed intraurban location in terms of the competitive advantages of various areas, particularly with respect to transporta-

TABLE 14.5. THE CHANGING DISTRIBUTION OF PRODUCTION WORKERS IN THE NEW YORK METROPOLITAN REGION, 1869, 1889, 1919, AND 1956

Year	Number of Employees (thousands)	Manhattan		Rest of What Is Now New York City	
		Number	Percent	Number	Percent
1869	240.3	131.4	54.7	22.1	9.2
1889	683.0	356.5	52.2	122.9	18.0
1919	1,158.6	387.0	33.2	250.4	21.6
1956	1,483.3	376.8	25.4	327.8	22.1

Source: Chinitz (1960), p. 131.

tion facilities and the availability of space. Kitagawa and Bogue list numerous factors of a centrifugal (Table 14.6) and centripetal (Table 14.7) nature that can result in a decentralization or centralization of industry in particular urban areas. However, although all of these forces can be regarded as extremely relevant in particular situations, one factor that has strong spatial implications is the continuing changing nature of industry itself.

Innovation and Uncertainty

Innovation implies uncertainty with respect to all phases of production and marketing (Hund, 1959, p. 313). These uncertainties force newly established firms to keep their capital outlays at a minimum and to direct their sales efforts toward large concentrated markets where advertising costs can be minimized. Although the per capita probability of acceptance of an innovation may be equal for all persons, nevertheless the total probability of acceptance in a large urban area will be greater than in a small area. Furthermore, it may well be possible that large urban areas have a higher per capita probability of acceptance of new innovations than small urban areas, for the inhabitants may have become conditioned through time to accept new things because they are more frequently exposed to them. Uncertainty in production techniques tends to result in firms locating toward the center of urban areas where there is the greatest concentration of other small firms and rentable space. In these areas firms can expand and contract fairly easily, can gain a degree of security through accepting contracted work, and can subcontract work if they are going through a successful period. Also, it is in these central areas that labor is cheapest and easiest to hire and lay off.

All these aspects of central locations that reduce the penalties of innovation cannot be incorporated into the accounting structure of the firm. The entrepreneur realizes the advantages of these central locations in a perceptual sense, but he cannot estimate in monetary terms the economies derived from these advantages. Economies of this type are commonly referred to as external economies and are generally defined as a favorable effect on one or more persons or firms that results from the actions of other persons or firms. External diseconomies are the opposite: they refer to the harm done to individuals or

Other New York Counties and Fairfield		New Jersey Counties	
Number	Percent	Number	Percent
36.8	15.3	50.0	20.8
69.7	10.2	124.9	19.6
133.4	11.6	387.8	33.6
247.7	16.7	531.0	35.8

firms by the actions of others. Thus in cases of uncertainty, the external economies that can be derived from central locations are extremely important factors influencing the firm to locate around the CBD.

If the firm is successful with respect to both sales and production techniques, then the degree of uncertainty is reduced. The firm will now be able to raise capital more easily in the money market and will be able to reduce costs by large-scale production. The required increased scale of production can often only be achieved by more space and buildings constructed specifically to house the production process that has been developed (Kenyon, 1960). Thus the firm is now free to locate in areas other than the "incubator" of the central part of the city. Consequently as uncertainty is reduced, the location horizons of the firm expand.

The types of firms that are involved in the process outlined above are essentially those involved with the high-growth industries. These are industries involved with plastics, communications equipment, motor vehicles, and electrical goods of all kinds. All of these industries are spatially flexible, for they are not tied to any one mode of transportation; and they use electrical machinery in their production processes. Thus the construction of highways has facilitated the outward movement of firms of this type.

Industrial parks One of the more recent developments in North America are industrial districts or industrial parks (Wrigley, 1947). Although they were first developed in North America in conjunction with railroads, they are now commonly associated with freeways and are especially located near the interchanges of freeways.

An "organized" or "planned" industrial district is a tract of land which is subdivided and developed according to a comprehensive plan for the use of a community of industries, with streets, rail lead tracks, and utilities sold before sites are sold to prospective occupants (Pasma, 1955, p. 1).

Industrial parks have been developed in a number of urban areas for a variety of reasons. Industrial parks are often established as an antidote to the depressing appearance of established industries in old urban areas. Very

TABLE 14.6. CENTRIFUGAL FORCES IN INDUSTRIAL LOCATION

1. Topography—A central city located in hilly country with narrow valleys may have little land suitable for factory sites.
2. Late manufacturing development—Cities that have had little manufacturing and are now belatedly attracting factory development may have little room for such activities except beyond the city border.
3. Manufacturing type—Certain types of manufacturing, such as oil refineries, steel mills, meat-packing plants, and aircraft factories with test-flying fields, may create nuisances to such a degree that location beyond the city's boundaries is imperative.
4. Nonfocused transportation—Along a harbor front, navigable river, canal, or belt railroad, the advantages for manufacturing are spread out for a long distance.
5. Annexation difficulties—Some central cities are in sections of the country where annexation of surrounding land is essentially impossible.
6. Extensive highway transportation facilities—With well-designed freeways and other modern highway facilities, factory development is less restricted to the central city.
7. Government policy—Some metropolitan areas experienced much of their manufacturing growth with the development of plants during World War II and were thus subject to government policy of avoiding concentration.
8. Tax laws—In some metropolitan areas, manufacturing plants have been located outside the central city in order to avoid paying the high taxes of the city or taxes to both the city and the state.
9. Failure of former factories—As old manufacturing operations located in the central city die from obsolescence or other causes, their facilities and space are often converted to parking or other nonmanufacturing uses.
10. Zoning—Where the zoning ordinance of the central city fails to set aside enough land or large enough parcels of land for manufacturing, development in suburban areas is encouraged.
11. High land values in central city—The high costs of factory sites inside a city may result in industries locating just outside the city.
12. Satellite manufacturing cities—In some cases manufacturing may be highly concentrated in the central city and in one or two adjacent satellite cities that are not quite large enough to be classed as central cities but may have had their factories as long as the central city itself.
13. Promotion by railroads—In some standard metropolitan statistical areas, railroad companies have promoted manufacturing growth on sites strung out along their rights-of-way and therefore extending out of the city.
14. Rural labor force—In some instances a substantial rural and suburban labor force may tempt industrialists to move their factories to suburban locations.
15. Factory design and space requirements—The relatively large space needs of new factories for plant construction, parking facilities, etc., often favor a suburban location.
16. A single-industry city—When a city is essentially a single-industry city, new manufacturing may actually be discouraged by the dominant firm and may be forced to occupy suburban positions.

Source: Modified from the list in: Kitagawa and Bogue (1955), pp. 121–123.

often it is hoped that these parks will attract new industry to the town, and for this purpose the park may well be equipped with standard factory shells that are rented at low cost. There are, therefore, many types of industrial parks, ranging from those developed by private companies, such as the Hershey Industrial Park in Hershey, Pa., and the National Cash Register Company in Dayton, O., to those established by municipalities. In some cases the parks are established as parks in the garden-city sense (Howard, 1945), while in many cases they are simply tracts of land at the edge of the city that have been zoned for industry and are partially serviced.

TABLE 14.7. CENTRIPETAL FORCES IN INDUSTRIAL LOCATION

1. Topography—In a hilly area the central city may contain the only land suitable for most types of manufacturing. Swamps and lowlands subject to flooding also may keep industry inside a city. Or, all of the waterfront area suitable for port activities and water-oriented industries may be inside the city's boundaries.
2. Utilities—Factories require water, sewage disposal, gas, electric power, and fire protection. These may be available only from the central city, which may be reluctant to provide facilities for suburban areas.
3. Early industrialization—Some cities founded as industrial centers grew up around factories, thus producing a centralized pattern of manufacturing.
4. Use of old buildings—Industry sometimes expands by taking over old warehouses or old factory buildings left by earlier industries. Such developments would result in centralization of manufacturing.
5. Growth through expansion of existing plants—In some standard metropolitan statistical areas most of the expansion of manufacturing volume has come about through expansion of old, well-established firms located in the central city.
6. Single-industry or single-firm towns—Where a single industry or single firm dominates manufacturing employment, it is often located within the city limits and is closely identified with the central city.
7. Zoning—The early adoption of a zoning program that made liberal provision for manufacturing has favored centralization in some cities.
8. Original area of city—Other things being equal, we should expect that a city whose boundary was liberally drawn to begin with would have a relatively low degree of suburbanization of manufacturing.
9. Annexation—Some states have liberal provisions by which central cities can annex adjacent territory. Such additions bring industries inside the city's boundaries, thus reducing the percentage of workers employed outside the central city or cities.
10. Type of manufacturing—Some types of manufacturing, such as jewelry and garment manufacture, seek a central location to be near other industries, near suppliers, or near a market.
11. Focused transportation—Where transportation facilities are highly focused upon the city but only limited outside the city's boundaries, industries are likely to be centralized.
12. Cheap labor from slum areas—In some large cities factories develop to use the cheap labor from slum areas at the edge of the central business district. This favors location of manufacturing within the city's central area.

Source: Modified from the list in: Kitagawa and Bogue (1955), pp. 123–124.

THE ELEMENTS OF INTRAMETROPOLITAN MANUFACTURING LOCATION

Having observed the way in which transportation and technological evolution have placed their stamp on the industrial pattern of North American cities, we must now interpret the entire industrial pattern of cities from a locational point of view. Chinitz has defined industrial plants as (1) those serving markets that are predominantly local, (2) those serving markets of national extent, and (3) those plants localized by external economy considerations (Chinitz, 1960, pp. 129–157). All of these categories can, of course, be subdivided, but the basic aspect of the classification is that each has particular, though not exclusive, locational tendencies. Using this approach as a basis, Pred (1964, p. 174) has grouped metropolitan manufacturing into ". . . seven flexible types, each of which . . . should be characterized by distributional patterns with a unique set of attributes . . ." though within each type a random element may well be present. These are (1) ubiquitous manufacturing industries concentrated near the CBD, (2) centrally located communication-economy industries, (3) local market industries with local raw material sources, (4) nonlocal market industries with high-value products, (5) noncentrally located communication-economy industries, (6) nonlocal market industries on the waterfront, and (7) manufacturing industries oriented toward national markets.

UBIQUITOUS MANUFACTURING INDUSTRIES CONCENTRATED NEAR THE CBD

Industries are classified as ubiquitous because their market area is coextensive with, or part of, the metropolis in which they are located. They are concentrated near the edge of the CBD partly because they are intricately linked with wholesaling firms in the wholesaling district, and partly because they wish to minimize distribution costs to the entire urban area. The industries in this group are usually associated with food processing in one way or another, as the old warehousing and multistory factory buildings located in this area are particularly useful for the storage of both raw materials and finished products.

CENTRALLY LOCATED COMMUNICATION-ECONOMY INDUSTRIES

Industries grouped in this category have a particular need to realize the external economies of face-to-face communication with the purchaser immediately prior to manufacturing. In this case, as the purchasers are located usually within the CBD, the industries have to locate as close as possible to this area. Industries found within this group, such as the job-printing and garment industries, are usually composed of small plants that are prepared to pay relatively high rents for central locations. These high rents are, of course, merely a small part of the costs of central locations, for in addition to these are the costs of ". . . congestion on the streets, and the higher cost of handling freight at the plant because of inadequate facilities" (Chinitz, 1960, p. 42). External economies, other than communication, offset these costs through advantages such as centrally located freight-forwarding agencies, communal warehousing facilities, and unionized labor pools which permit the individual plant to have a flexible working force.

LOCAL MARKET INDUSTRIES WITH LOCAL RAW MATERIAL SOURCES

The manufacturing industries grouped in the category of those with local raw material sources include (1) those whose chief raw material is fairly ubiquitous, such as ice manufacturing and the concrete brick and block industries; (2) those whose raw materials are the by-product(s) of local manufacturing industries, such as those using the by-products of petroleum refining; and (3) those industries that process locally produced semimanufactured goods, such as the metal-plate and polishing industry. Industries in each of these categories are found dispersed over the entire urban area, for the fact that all input assembly and product distribution takes place within the urban area means that truck haulage is the chief means of transportation. Furthermore, as trucking has been ". . . one of the most powerful of several propulsive forces uprooting industry from its established locations within the congested core of the metropolitan area" (Fellman, 1950, p. 77), industries in this category tend to be noncentrally located.

NONLOCAL MARKET INDUSTRIES WITH HIGH-VALUE PRODUCTS

Industries manufacturing high-value products are oriented toward truck or air-freight transportation rather than rail or waterway facilities. As a consequence they too are dispersed in locations around the urban area, particularly in those metropolises criss-crossed by freeways such as Los Angeles where ". . . many industries have found that they can operate efficiently at greater distances from the heart of the city" (Kitagawa and Bogue, 1955, p. 97). Industries with high-value added products include the high-value added machinery and chemical industries, such as computer and drug manufacturing firms. Chinitz (1960, p. 149) notes that small plants in this group may locate centrally for external accessibility purposes, but Pred (1964, p. 177) emphasizes that the locational pattern of these small firms tends to be deemphasized by the apparent modern distribution of the larger factories within this group.

NONCENTRALLY LOCATED COMMUNICATION-ECONOMY INDUSTRIES

The manufacturing industries in the fifth group embrace those firms that tend to cluster in noncentral locations in order to realize external economies of communication, particularly with respect to innovations and possible contracts. Such industries are generally highly scientific or technical, and they do not cluster in order to be close to their purchasers but to observe each other's activities and progress. A typical example of a concentration of this type is along Route 128 around Boston, adjacent to which are located many electronic, research, and technical consulting firms. Similar clustering is observed by Pred (1964, p. 178) in San Francisco, with respect to the electronic components industry, and it is to be noted that both these locations are adjacent to prominent urban highways.

NONLOCAL MARKET INDUSTRIES ON THE WATERFRONT

Many industries in the sixth group are very transportation conscious, because the weight loss incurred in manufacturing or the orientation of markets of firms in this category are vital considerations. Industries in this group are those involved with petroleum refining, sugar refining, and others that use nonlocal water-carried materials. Obviously the shipbuilding and repairing industry is also constrained to waterfront areas. It is to be noted that not all waterfront industries use the waterfront; in many cases they happen to be there for other reasons.

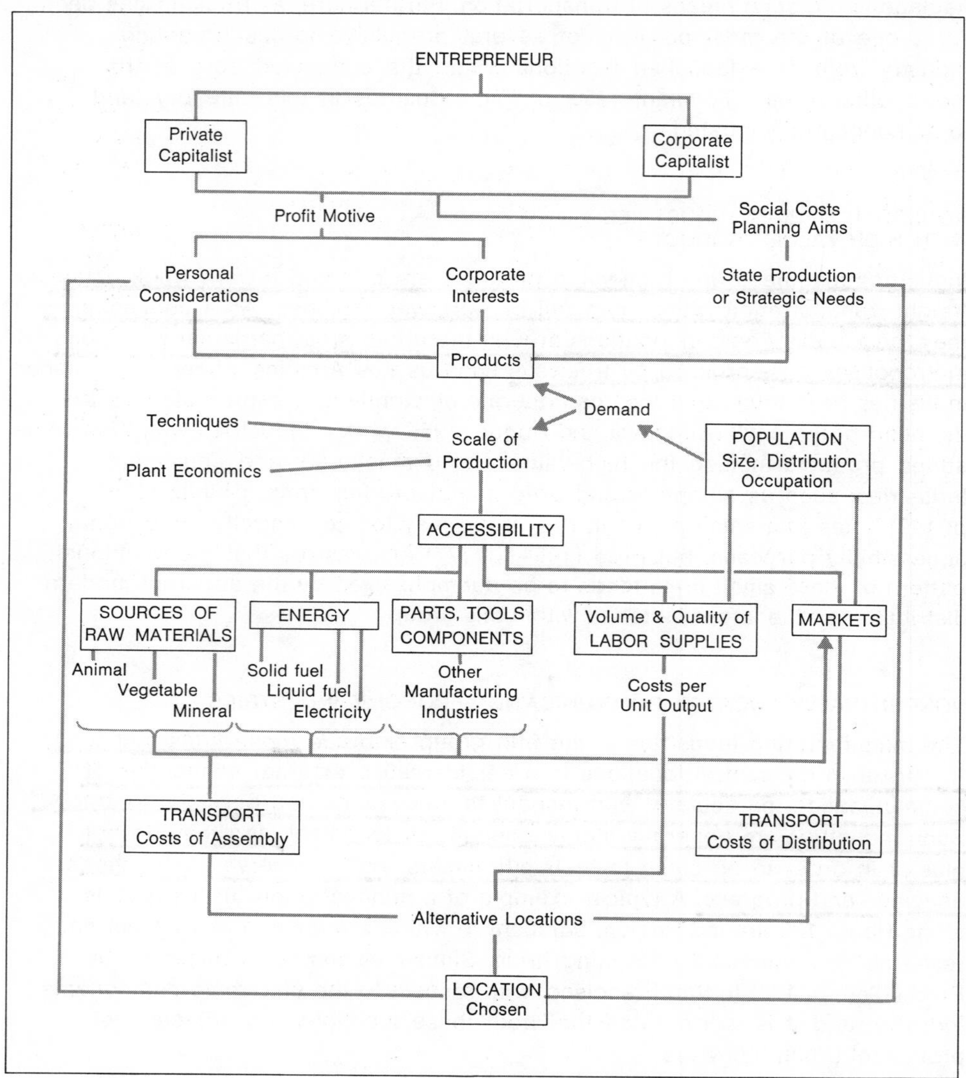

FIG. 14.2. A MODEL OF THE FACTORS INFLUENCING INDUSTRIAL LOCATION DECISIONS IN NORTH AMERICA. (*Source:* After Hamilton, 1967, Fig. 10–1.)

Indeed, it is observable that many manufacturing firms occupy waterfront property who do not use the waterway for transportation.

MANUFACTURING INDUSTRIES ORIENTED TOWARD NATIONAL MARKETS

Group seven consists of those industries, such as iron and steel and motor-vehicle manufacturing, that have extensive national market areas and are greatly influenced by high transport rates on their bulky finished products. In order to be close to their national markets and to facilitate transportation without too many railroad transfers, these industries tend to locate on the side of the metropolis facing the greatest proportion of the national market. Because these industries have large space requirements, they are located at some distance from the center of the city; but their labor requirements constrain their location to the vicinity of good highways as well as rail facilities.

Thus the pattern of intraurban industrial location is a product of myriad decisions, the bases of which vary in time and space. Change in the structure and organization of manufacturing through time, the continuing technological revolution, change in consumer preferences, change in governments and laws, all these factors, and many others, have contributed to the spatial arrangement of industry within urban areas that the geographer can describe but finds difficult to explain. The complexity of Hamilton's (1967, p. 365) industrial location decision model (Fig. 14.2) illustrates the problem very well, for to each of the decisions should be attached a probability statement that varies not only for every entrepreneur, but also for each entrepreneur in time. However, the locational approach has permitted us to analyze the observed spatial regularities, for the sum total of many individual and often conflicting decisions does appear to be economically rational.

INTRAURBAN MOVEMENTS

Modern intraurban travel involves a variety of modes that developed at different periods in time. Though some modes of travel are declining while others are increasing in importance, the modal picture at any given period in time involves an

urban transportation system of great variety. This system involves the suburban railroad, the subway or elevated rapid transit, buses, the automobile, trucks, taxis, and walking. Information based on origin and destination surveys in Chicago, Washington, D.C., and Detroit suggests the automobile accounts for between 74 and 82 percent of total vehicle trips within the city, that trucks account for between 10 and 13 percent, and that taxis account for between 1 and 3 percent (Table 15.1). Information concerning vehicle trips for other modes is lacking.

The relative importance of these modes can, however, be gauged with respect to the movement of persons within urban areas (person trips). From Table 15.2 it can be observed that for the three large urban areas of Chicago, Washington, and Detroit, automobile drivers made up the great majority of all person trips. As automobile passengers contribute the second largest proportion, total

TABLE 15.1. THE RELATIVE IMPORTANCE OF DIFFERENT TYPES OF VEHICLE TRIPS

Mode		Percent of Total Trips
Automobiles	resident, internal	74–82%
	resident, external	2–6
	nonresident	2–9
Buses		unknown
Trucks	internal	10–13
	external	1–2
	through	0–1
Taxis		1–3

Source: Martin, et al. (1961), p. 23.

TABLE 15.2. THE RELATIVE IMPORTANCE OF DIFFERENT TYPES OF PERSON TRIPS

Type of Person Trip		Percent of Total Trips
Automobile drivers	resident, internal	41–53%
	resident, external	1–4
	nonresident	1–8
Automobile passengers	resident, internal	22–26
	resident, external	1–4
	nonresident	1–4
Bus		15–20
Subway—elevated rail rapid transit		5
Commuter railroad		3
Walk		unknown

Source: Martin, et al. (1961), p. 23.

automobile trips comprise about three-quarters of all person trips. Buses account for between 15 and 20 percent, and rail rapid transit and the commuter railroad account for only 8 percent between them.

THE MOVEMENT OF PEOPLE

It is evident from the preceding discussion that although person and vehicular travel can be discussed separately, neither can be regarded as mutually exclusive for both overlap each other. As approximately 75 percent of person travel is also included within vehicular travel, it can be concluded that person trips comprise the greater part of the total traffic within urban areas. The volume of this traffic is staggering. The average daily number of person trips regardless of origin in the Chicago area (C.A.T.S., 1959, p. 29) in 1956 (population 5.17 million) totaled 10.5 million, and in the Toronto area (M.T.A.R.T.S., 1966, p. 52) in 1964 (population 2.7 million) the average daily trip volume was approximately 4 million. These trips involve a number of origins and destinations and can occur at any time throughout the day.

THE COMPONENTS OF URBAN TRAVEL

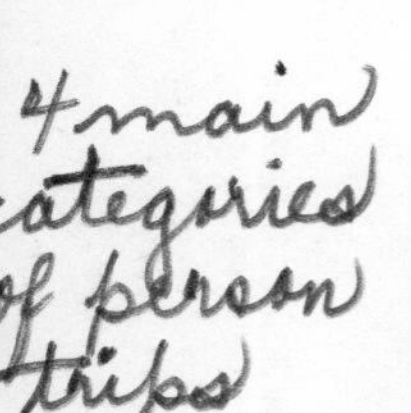

Person trips are undertaken for a variety of purposes and involve a multitude of origins and destinations. Commonly, these can be grouped into four main categories: (1) trips to and from home, (2) trips to and from work, (3) social and recreational trips, and (4) trips for shopping, school, and personal business purposes. A diagrammatic representation of the flow pattern involving these four categories is presented in Figure 15.1, which uses data derived from the Metropolitan Toronto and Region Transportation Study.

Figure 15.1 indicates that nearly all trips in the Toronto area involve the home as either an origin or destination. One-half of all trips involve home to work and return, and another very large proportion involves home to shops and schools and return. It is estimated that school trips, which can be repetitive in a day, exceed the proportion of work trips; but the Toronto data includes only school trips made in a vehicle. Thus shopping trips are very large in number. Nearly 17 percent of all trips involve the home and some social or recreational destination and return. Although the home is the origin and destination of nearly all the person trips, a number (almost 10 percent) do not. These are usually three-stage trips—such as home–work–shopping–home—and can include a few involving all four categories.

This type of daily flow pattern can be examined in more detail by using information for Chicago. Table 15.3 presents the proportions of total traffic in an average weekday in 1956 that can be allocated to 64 possible combinations of trip purposes. In the aggregate 43.3 percent of the total 9.9 million internal person trips originated at the home, and a further 43.5 percent ended at home. Most of these trips were single purpose, the dominant flow being home–work (16.6 percent) and work–home (15.9 percent). Another quite large flow involves

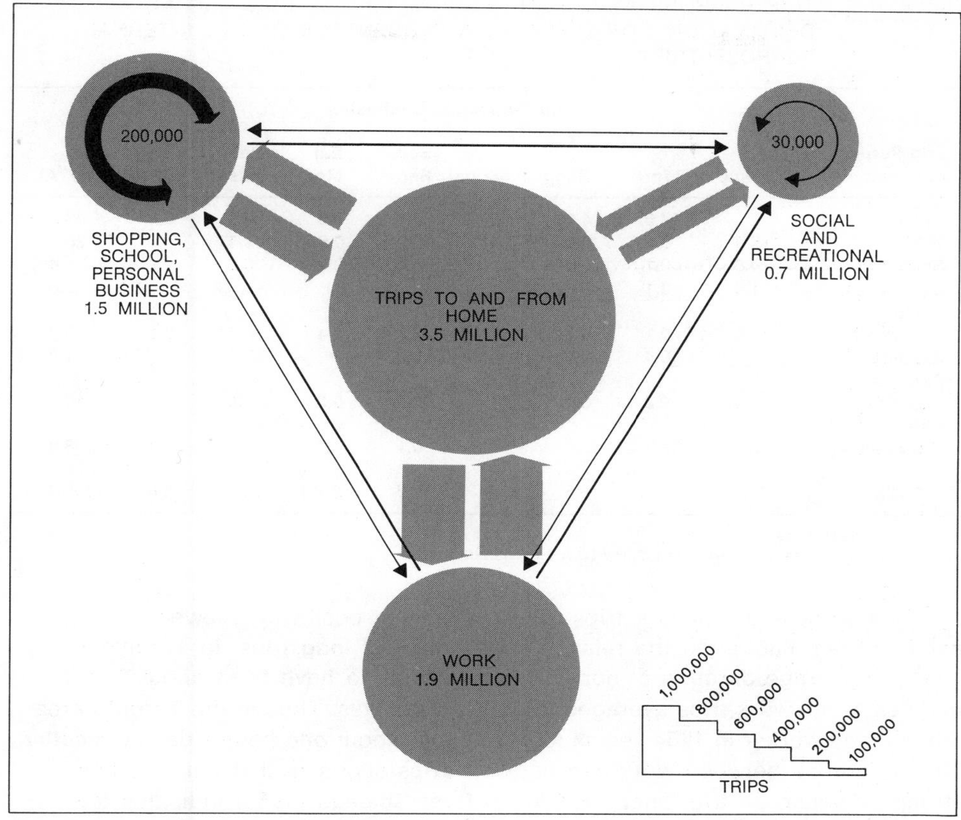

FIG. 15.1. THE PREDOMINANCE OF HOME-BASED TRIPS WITHIN URBAN AREAS. (*Source:* The Queen's Printer, Toronto M.T.A.R.T.S., 1966, Fig. 40.)

home–social–recreational (9.3 percent) and social–recreational–home (10.4 percent). A reasonably large flow involves shopping and general personal business activities, while all other flows are small in magnitude. The number of triangular trips seems to be very few. Slightly more trips go to work than come home directly from work, while slightly more trips return to home from shopping than go to shop from home. Thus, though a number of flows are triangular trips, such as home–work–shop–home, the proportion is very small, probably about 5 percent. This fact of directional symmetry permits the transportation planner to deal with trips in one direction only, for he can be fairly confident that over a 24-hour period directional travel on individual streets is equal, with outward and returning movements balancing one another.

Time–distance variations A second general feature of these person trips is that their length varies according to their purpose. Figure 15.2 presents a highly aggregated view of the difference in trip length (measured in minutes)

TABLE 15.3. TRIP PURPOSE AT ORIGIN RELATED TO TRIP PURPOSE AT DESTINATION EXPRESSED AS A PERCENTAGE OF ALL INTERNAL PURPOSE TRIPS

	Trip Purpose at Destination								
Trip Purpose at Origin	**Home**	**Work**	**Shop**	**School**	**Soc–Rec**	**Eat Meal**	**Pers. Bus.**	**Serve Pass.**	**TOTAL**
Home		16.6	4.1	1.7	9.3	0.8	7.6	3.2	43.3
Work	15.9	3.1	0.2	0.1	0.2	0.5	0.4		20.4
Shop	4.3	0.1	0.5		0.2	0.1	0.2		5.4
School	1.6	0.1		0.1					1.8
Social—recreation	10.4	0.1	0.2		1.6	0.4	0.4	0.1	13.2
Eat meal	1.0	0.4	0.1		0.2		0.1		1.8
Personal business	6.9	0.2	0.4		1.0	0.2	1.5		10.3
Serve passenger*	3.4				0.1			0.3	3.8
TOTAL	43.5	20.6	5.5	1.8	12.7	2.1	10.2	3.6	100.0

* Includes "ride" trips.
Source: Chicago Area Transportation Study (C.A.T.S., 1959), p. 37.

between work and nonwork trips. The polygon is positively skewed, the extended tail illustrating the relative infrequency of long trips. In Toronto in 1964 the average duration of nonwork trips seems to have been about 21.4 minutes, while work trips averaged about 27.8 minutes. Thus in the Toronto area the average worker in 1964 seems to have spent about one hour a day commuting. This difference between work and nonwork trips suggests that purpose has a strong influence on trip length. Evidence from Chicago (1956) indicates that shopping trips are usually short, averaging about 2.8 miles in length, and that the longest trips are made to work, with an average length of 5.3 miles (C.A.T.S., 1959, p. 38).

The form of travel or mode, like person trips, also vary by length. These variations are illustrated in Table 15.4 where the average length of each person trip by mode is estimated from the total miles of travel for each mode. The average

TABLE 15.4. AVERAGE INTERNAL PERSON TRIP LENGTH (AIRLINE) BY MODE

Mode of Travel	Person Trips	Miles of Person Travel	Average Length[a]
Auto driver	4,810,886	18,878,000	3.9
Auto passenger	2,706,114	9,593,000	3.5
Suburban R.R.	248,851	3,300,000	13.3
Subway—elevated	479,780	3,444,000	7.2
Bus	1,686,007	6,112,000	3.6
TOTAL	9,931,638	41,327,000	4.2

[a] Airline miles.
Source: Chicago Area Transportation Study (C.A.T.S., 1959), p. 47.

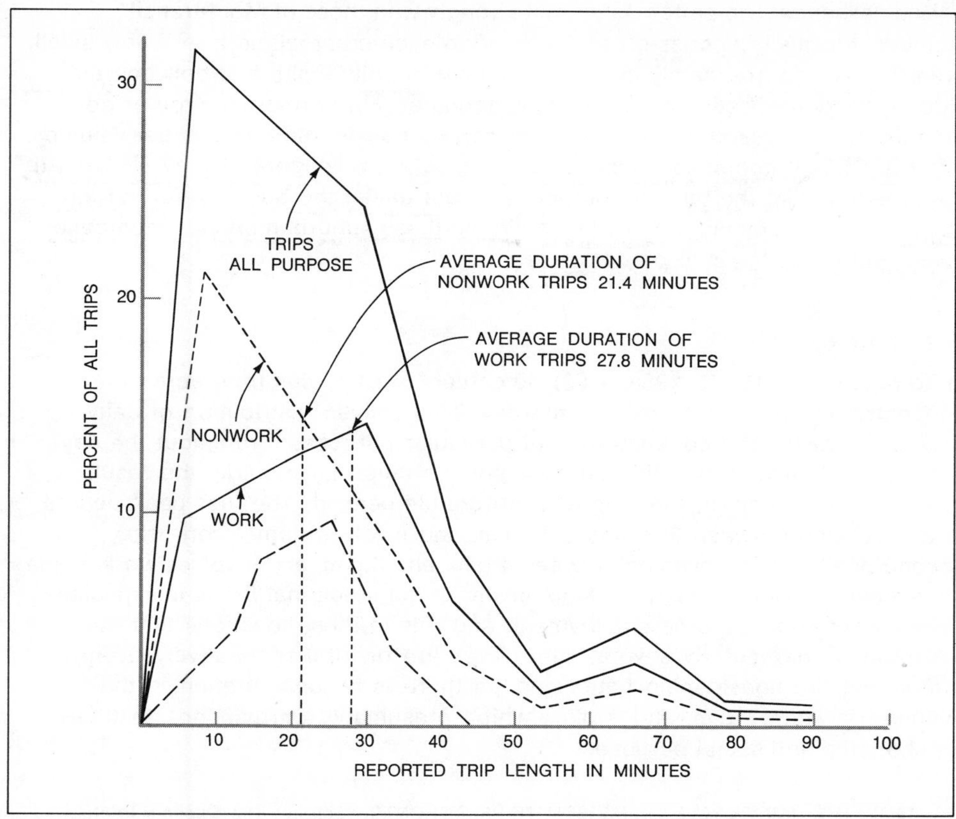

FIG. 15.2. FREQUENCY DISTRIBUTIONS OF ALL-PURPOSE, NONWORK, AND WORK TRIP LENGTHS, TORONTO. (*Source:* The Queen's Printer, Toronto, M.T.A.R.T.S., 1966, Fig. 42.)

length of each trip in Chicago in 1956 is estimated as 4.2 miles, and the average length of trips on three of the modes is less than this. The shortest trips of all are made by auto passengers, followed by bus passengers and auto drivers. The longest trips of all are made by suburban railroad users who average about 13.3 miles per trip. As most of these trips are work trips, it can be concluded that suburban railroad users commute, on the average, about 27 miles per day.

Travel pattern variations These variations in modal trip length and frequency imply great variations in travel patterns. Rapid-transit facilities, such as the suburban railroad and elevated-subway facilities focus dramatically on the CBD. Although these rapid-transit facilities represent a small proportion of all person trips (in Chicago, less than one-twelfth) they nevertheless comprise the great majority of all trips to the CBD (in Chicago, over 45 percent). As the lengths of these trips tends to be long and focused on a single area, there is a strong radial pattern. This radial pattern is emphasized by the location of the transportation facilities along corridors of intense land usage.

Bus passenger trip patterns contrast strongly with those of rapid-transit facilities, for bus trips criss-cross and overlap each other within a relatively small area. The routes are mainly located within central city limits and between the older, more densely settled suburban communities. Furthermore the routes do not tend to be focused, though buses do carry a considerable passenger volume into the CBD. Automobile drivers and automobile passengers display similar trip patterns that, like the bus, are nonfocused, but unlike the bus, spread out into suburban areas beyond the city limits. Within these suburban areas, automobile passenger traffic tends to predominate.

THE DAILY CYCLE

In Toronto (M.T.A.R.T.S., 1966, p. 53), 40 percent of all person trips were concentrated within four hours of the day. This uneven distribution of daily trips is the result of a concentration of particular purposes throughout the day. Figure 15.3 indicates that this purpose concentration is primarily the result of work trips, which, in the diagram, are double-peaked. The first peak occurs in the morning between 6:30 and 8:30 a.m. and involves home–work trips. The second peak is in the evening between 4 p.m. and 6 p.m. and involves work–home movements. This twice daily peaking, involving unidirectional flows, is especially severe near areas of large employment; and it is in these locations that the rush hour is particularly severe. Other trips are distributed relatively evenly throughout the nonsleeping hours, though there is a concentration in the evening between 7 p.m. and 9 p.m., which presumably corresponds to travel for shopping and social purposes.

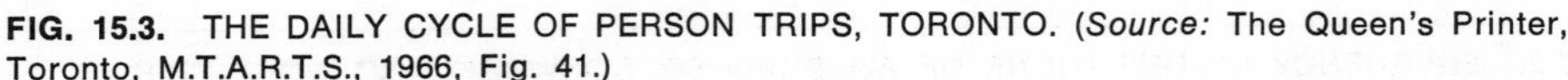

FIG. 15.3. THE DAILY CYCLE OF PERSON TRIPS, TORONTO. (*Source:* The Queen's Printer, Toronto, M.T.A.R.T.S., 1966, Fig. 41.)

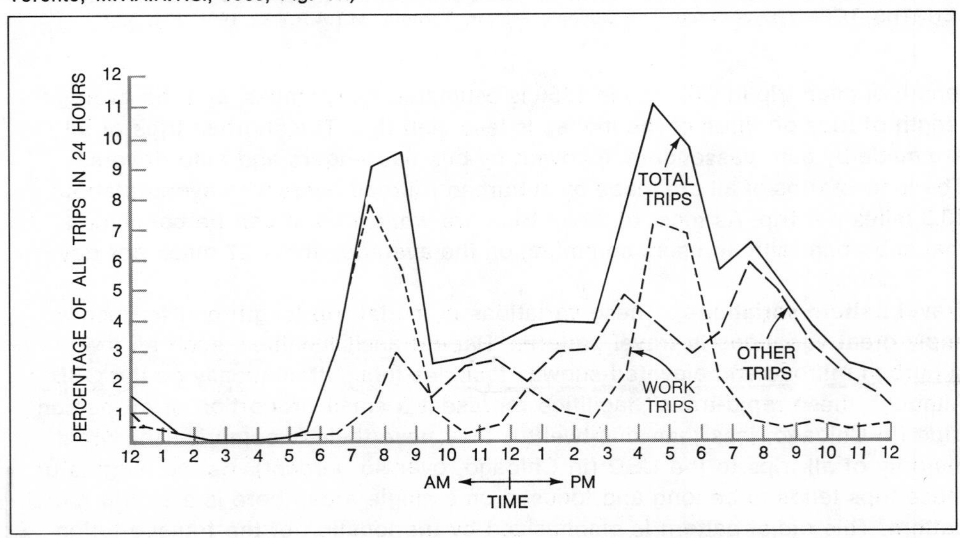

In the same way that person trips are concentrated in certain hours of the day, so is the demand for various modes of travel concentrated in certain hours. Some modes, in fact, are in much greater demand at certain times of the day than others. This is well documented in Figure 15.4, which presents the hourly percentages of total daily trip volume for five modes of travel on an average weekday in Chicago in 1956. The demand for travel which, we have seen, is satisfied (within limits) by a transportation system consisting of a rapid-transit system, a system of buses, and a road network system for automobiles, has a counterpoint in time consisting of a layering of service patterns. In Figure 15.4 automobile travel is the base, its use being spread relatively evenly throughout the day, though there is a definite concentration of use in the morning and evening rush hours. Buses have much sharper peaks, and in the subway-elevated and suburban railroad systems the peaking of activity is even more dramatically evident. We shall observe in a later chapter that this peaking of activity is basically the most difficult problem concerning the provision of mass transportation facilities.

FLUID FIELDS

This double peaking of traffic-flow intensity during an average weekday is also apparent where the hourly distribution of internal person trips is examined by trip purpose. The data presented in Figure 15.5 indicates that in Chicago in 1956 the purpose of travel varied throughout the day. In fact there appear to be

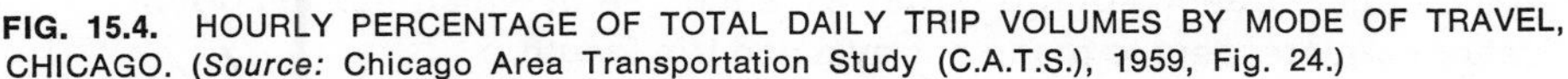
FIG. 15.4. HOURLY PERCENTAGE OF TOTAL DAILY TRIP VOLUMES BY MODE OF TRAVEL, CHICAGO. (*Source:* Chicago Area Transportation Study (C.A.T.S.), 1959, Fig. 24.)

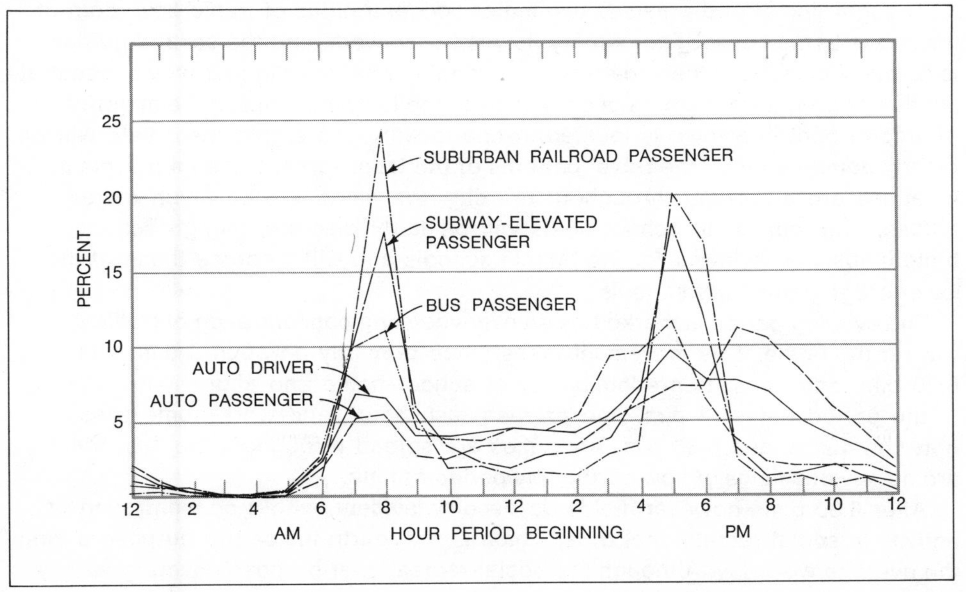

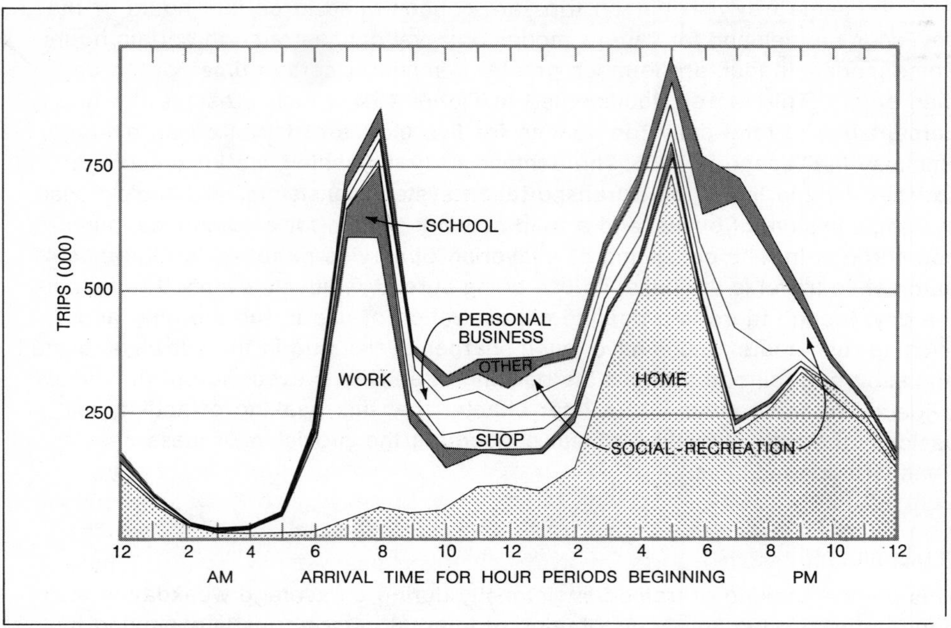

FIG. 15.5. HOURLY DISTRIBUTION OF INTERNAL PERSON TRIPS BY TRIP PURPOSE, CHICAGO. (*Source:* Chicago Area Transportation Study (C.A.T.S.), 1959, Fig. 15.)

four major concentrations of trip purposes, each one of which has important implications with respect to mode of travel and trip length.

The morning period presents two major concentrations of traffic flow, both of which are home based. The primary flow is home–work, and the secondary flow is home–school. Both these patterns are nodal in character in that they concentrate the flow toward a few centers of employment and learning. Thus, if the majority of employment in a town is located in one locality, the employment field will be clearly demarcated by the travel patterns of the labor force. If the employment locations are dispersed throughout the city, the fields will be much more diffuse. The journey to school fields will be fairly discrete, though school hinterlands will be larger for the largest schools and will embrace those of the lower order elementary schools.

The evening period is marked by an overwhelming concentration of traffic toward the home. This movement takes place primarily between 3 p.m. and 6:30 p.m. and consists predominantly of school–home and shop–home trips in the period before 4 p.m. (the prerush rush hour), and work–home trips between 4 p.m. and 6:30 p.m. As homes are spread throughout the city, there are no obvious fields of flow during this period of time.

After 6:30 p.m., however, fields do become evident, with a concentration of activity in social-recreational trips, which is the fourth major trip purpose during the average weekday. Although the social-recreational purpose covers a variety of trips, the concentration of entertainment and retail activities within certain areas does imply a focusing of traffic to these nodes. Furthermore, whereas the three earlier concentrations involve a variety of transportation modes, this particular activity tends to be much more automobile dominant.

Thus the temporal variation in internal person-trip volume is matched spatially by a fluid pattern of traffic fields. The ever-changing nature and modal composition of these fields reflect the daily cycle of human activity within urban areas, and it is this changing activity which is the life blood and purpose of urban life. In the ensuing sections we will specifically examine work and shopping trips, as these are the basic components of urban travel.

THE JOURNEY TO WORK

The daily journey to work is not only an important area of study because of its magnitude; it is also important because it is a common experience of many people (Liepman, 1944, p. 1). The fact that the journey to work is an experience should not be lost in any mechanistic discussion of its spatial ramifications. Commuting takes time, and to many people this is time wasted in a life of finite length. To others it is not merely that time is wasted, that so many hours are lost in the day, it is the general nervous fatigue of daily travel that is most difficult to withstand. In fact it could be suggested that it is the mass ebb and flow of human beings in packed public transportation facilities and overcrowded highways that makes for much of the depersonalization of everyday life. Thus any changes in the journey-to-work patterns, trip lengths, and modes of travel are important to catalog and understand.

JOURNEY-TO-WORK PATTERNS

Although the greatest area of employment concentration is in the CBD, we have observed that employment locations are widely dispersed throughout the city. In fact we have observed that a general outmigration of employment opportunities has taken place in recent years and that this outmigration shows no sign of abating. Thus it is imperative to have some knowledge of the changing journey-to-work patterns associated with this outmigration. The information available, however, is limited and confined to a series of snapshots at a given point in time (Taaffe, et al., 1963, pp. 8–35).

These snapshots are presented in five maps (Fig. 15.6) based on data collected by the Chicago Area Transportation Study in the spring and summer of 1956. The dots on the maps relate to grid cells a half-mile square, and the dots indicate whether one or more commuters traveling to a particular employment location originated in that cell. Thus the visual impression gained from the dot maps overstates the degree of dispersion of the journey-to-work patterns, since it could be expected that the number of commuters in half-mile square grid cells close to employment locations would be considerably greater than from other

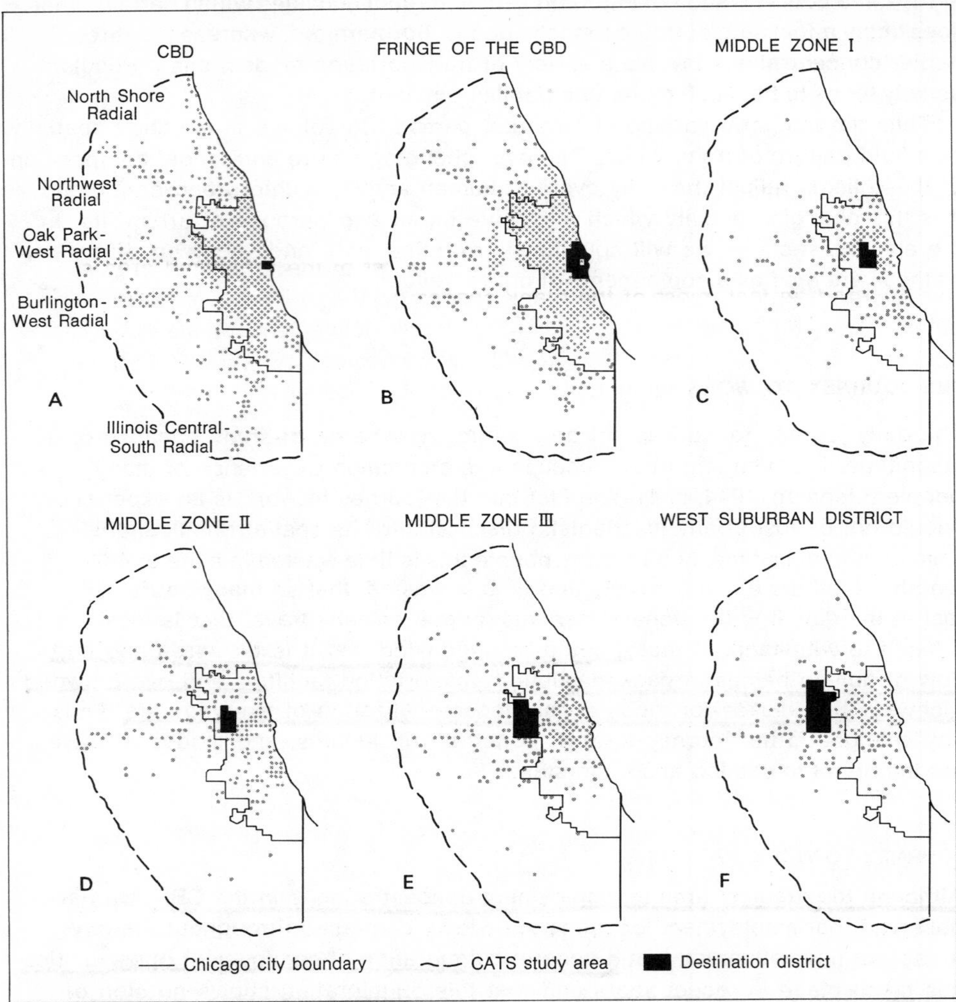

FIG. 15.6. ORIGINS OF COMMUTERS TO SELECTED WORK PLACE ZONES, CHICAGO REGION, 1956. (*Source:* Taaffe, Garner, and Yeates, 1963, Fig. III–3.)

cells farther away. Bearing that consideration in mind, however, it is possible to compare the change in dispersion pattern of commuters to different destination districts within the same sector in a traverse from the CBD to the periphery.

A sectoral traverse: Chicago The six maps displayed in Figure 15.6 indicate the origin cells of work trips to six employment areas in the western sector of Chicago in 1956. These employment areas are:

1. The central business district
2. The fringe of the central business district

3. Three areas in the middle zone or grey area (see Fig. 9.12)
middle zone I
middle zone II
middle zone III

4. The west suburban district, which is part of the peripheral ring

The CBD Commuter Pattern

Figure 15.6A shows the distribution of the commuter origin cells for work trips to the central business district. The dots cover most of the urbanized area of Chicago, and, in fact, most of the blank spaces on the map represent nonresidential areas. All of the radial suburbs are clearly delineated, for the suburban population is able to use both the rail and highway routes along these fingers. Thus rail and highway commuting to the CBD are both dominant.

The Fringe of the CBD Commuter Pattern

The second zone corresponds roughly to the fringe of the CBD area as delimited and discussed in Chapter 9. This destination area has a journey-to-work pattern (Fig. 15.6B) which is roughly similar to that for the CBD. The radials are well defined, though the intensity of the dot pattern is not quite so great as that for the CBD pattern. Within the city of Chicago almost every cell is the origin of at least one commuter to this zone, and the pattern seems to be even more intense than that for the CBD. Thus though Figures 15.6A and 15.6B are very similar, there is a minor difference in that the fringe of the CBD pattern tends to be less dispersed.

The Middle-Zone Commuter Pattern

The greatest change in commuting patterns occurs for origin cells in the middle-zone employment areas (Fig. 15.6C, D, E). The first of these maps (Fig. 15.6C) presents a pattern to a middle-zone destination district that is at the edge of the fringe of the CBD. The pattern illustrates that in this zone the advantages of the concentration of transportation facilities at the CBD have been lost, particularly in those areas and radials that are not within the western sector. There are very few origin cells in the northern and southern suburban radials; and the city itself is considerably less thoroughly covered with origin cells, particularly to the north and south of the destination district. Although relative concentrations are difficult to discern in these maps because magnitudes are ignored, it is possible to note that the Figure 15.6C pattern is less dispersed than that for the CBD.

Essentially the same pattern prevails as the destination areas move outward in the middle zone of the western sector. The origin cells for commuters to middle zone II (Fig. 15.6D) and middle zone III (Fig. 15.6E) are not so dispersed as those for the CBD though the location of commuters along more than one radial becomes evident. This is particularly true for two other western radials—the Burlington–West Radial and the Northwest Radial. Furthermore the concentration of employment cells in the western sector of the city is greater. Thus the adjacent area in the city becomes rather more important as a source of commuters to middle zone III.

The West Suburban District Pattern

The changes observed through the middle zone are repeated in the west suburban district pattern (Fig. 15.6F), which is part of the peripheral ring. The adjacent radial (the Oak Park–West Radial) and the adjacent area within the western sector in the city are particularly important, but the areas to the north and south are barely represented. Furthermore it is interesting to note that the Burlington–West Radial and the Northwest Radial are less well represented as origin areas for commuters to this peripheral location than for employment districts in the middle zone.

Thus the sectoral traverse indicates that for employment districts farther away from the center of the city the frictional effect of distance is greater. This increasing friction of distance, which has also been noted elsewhere (Reinemann, 1955, pp. 100–105; Hoover and Vernon, 1959, p. 145; Burtt, 1961), is due to the lack of a concentration of transportation facilities in these areas compared with the concentration of transport facilities at the center of the city. Table 15.5 indicates that approximately 84 percent of the west suburban commuters drive or are driven to work, whereas only 30 percent of the CBD commuters use these modes. On the one hand, mass transit facilities account for almost 70 percent of the commuters entering the CBD as opposed to less than 10 percent for the west suburban district. This contrast suggests that the mass transit modes facilitate much longer work trips to the center of the city, and that their concentration in the CBD permits a wide dispersion of commuters.

THE COMPONENTS OF THE JOURNEY-TO-WORK PATTERNS

The discussion of the various journey-to-work patterns of different employment areas in the preceding section emphasizes that the dispersion of the patterns decreases toward the periphery. These patterns are, however, aggregates of

TABLE 15.5. MODE OF COMMUTER TRANSPORTATION TO THE CBD AND WEST SUBURBAN DISTRICTS, CHICAGO, 1956

Mode	**CBD (percent)**	**West Suburban (percent)**
Auto drive	24.4	65.4
Auto passenger	5.7	18.3
Railroad	16.6	0.7
Elevated—subway	24.4	1.3
Bus	28.4	7.4
Walk to work	—	6.2

Note: The modes "taxi" and "at home" are missing.
Source: Taaffe, et al. (1963), p. 9.

individuals and families who locate according to a variety of criteria. These criteria have been discussed in detail in Chapters 10 and 11 but they also provide an important framework for an appreciation of the components of commuting fields. These components include transportation and distance, race, sex, and occupation and income.

Transportation and distance There is little doubt that one of the factors influencing the dispersion of the commuting field is distance (Lapin, 1964, pp. 123–140; Wolforth, 1965; Duncan and Duncan, 1960, p. 41), the perception of which is strongly influenced by the alternative modes of transportation available. Commuting by automobile along expressways and freeways is easier than along congested urban arterials, and riding the commuter railroad can be quite a pleasurable experience. Lansing (1966, p. 99) notes from a sample interview of drivers that 53 percent enjoyed the journey to work, 34 percent didn't care one way or the other, and only 13 percent expressed dislike of it. He suggests, however, that there is a limit for quite a large proportion, as 36 percent indicated a definite maximum time for the journey to work beyond which commuting would be time lost (Lansing, 1966, p. 74).

It is interesting to consider the factors that might influence this threshold time limit for, intuitively, one would suggest that through time this threshold limit is increasing. Undoubtedly technological changes in urban transportation have had a great effect, for ultimately the result has been to make intraurban movement less arduous. A more important facet, however, may probably be that the provision of new housing stock is much greater at the periphery of urban areas than elsewhere (Meyer, et al., 1965, pp. 119–130). Thus the head of the household has become willing to offset better living conditions against an increase in time spent in the daily journey to work. Undoubtedly the general reduction in the hourly length of the working week has had an important effect on this kind of decision.

Occupation and income As the higher incomes and the higher status occupations tend to live farther from the center of the city, it could be expected that the length of the journey to work for these groups would be greater than for others. Table 15.6 presents information that supports this contention with respect to commuting to the CBD of Chicago in 1956. The trip lengths are measured in airline miles, and the median distances only are listed. Thus 50 percent of the workers classified as proprietors and managers traveled 8.7 airline miles or more to their employment in the CBD, and 50 percent traveled less than this. The occupational groups are ranked in descending order of occupational class; and the median miles tend to decrease as the class of occupation decreases. It is noticeable, however, that there is no such regular arrangement of commuting distances by occupational class at the periphery of the city.

This apparent difference between CBD and non-CBD commuting lengths may account for the inconsistencies noted by Lansing (1966, p. 90) in the literature concerning this problem. For example, Lapin (1964, p. 100) suggests that the

TABLE 15.6. COMPARISON OF MEDIAN TRAVEL DISTANCES OF VARIOUS OCCUPATIONAL GROUPS TO THE CBD AND WEST SUBURBAN DISTRICT, CHICAGO, 1956

	Median Miles	
Occupational Group	**CBD**	**West Suburban**
Professionals and technicians	8.5	3.9
Managers and proprietors	8.7	4.0
Clerical and kindred workers	7.2	2.2
Sales workers	7.6	2.8
Craftsmen	6.2	4.7
Operatives and kindred workers	4.9	3.0
Service workers	5.1	1.4
Laborers	3.9	3.6

Source: Taaffe, et al. (1963), p. 88.

work trips for middle-income clerical, sales, and blue-collar workers are relatively long, while Lowry (1963, p. 153) and Duncan (1956, pp. 48–56) both support the contention that higher income persons live farther away from their job locations. Thus the decentralization of employment opportunities discussed specifically with respect to manufacturing in Chapter 14 and commercial activities in Chapter 12 necessitates a continuous reassessment of the influence of occupation and income on the journey to work (Simmons, 1968, p. 647).

Race Residential segregation obviously distorts the work-trip length preference of nonwhite commuters and makes this group a separate component of the aggregate commuting pattern (Taaffe, et al., 1963, p. 63). In one sense residential segregation limits the range of employment opportunities of nonwhite workers, for the direction of public transit or radial highways may restrict travel in certain directions. For example, whereas 14 percent of all CBD commuters in Chicago in 1956 were nonwhite, only 6 percent of the commuters to the west suburban district were nonwhite. Whether this is due to the lack of industries requiring low-wage labor, or the lack of low-wage labor discouraging the location of industry of this type is not clear. It is clear, however, that residential segregation does result in race forming a separate and distinct component of the journey-to-work pattern (Kain, 1968). This component obviously suffers tremendous disadvantages as new industry is increasingly being located beyond the central city.

Sex There seem to be significant differences in the commuting patterns of male and female workers. In 1956, of the commuters to the Chicago CBD, 68 percent were male and 32 percent, female, whereas 77 percent of the west suburban district commuters were male and only 23 percent, female (Taaffe, et al., 1963, p. 63). This tendency for a lower percent of female workers in peripheral employment centers seems to be fairly well established in other studies as well (Reinemann, 1955; Hoover and Vernon, 1959; Burtt, 1961).

There are, perhaps, two main reasons for the apparent concentration of female employment in the CBD: the need for the private automobile for peripheral-area employment, and the relative attraction of CBD amenities. Automobiles are not always available to female workers. Many young unmarried women do not own automobiles, chiefly because clerical work and service activities (the chief sources of female employment) generally pay low wages. In addition the American dating system requires that the automobile be provided by the male, not the female of the species. Married women are often without an automobile because their husbands use the family car for their own commuting. Thus low-cost public transportation facilities concentrate the direction of female commuting to the center of the city.

In addition to these fundamental economic advantages of the CBD for women are the attractions of the bright lights and greater array of shopping, social, cultural, and recreational amenities of the downtown area, particularly for single women. Not to be discounted is the real (or imaginary) function of the CBD as a marriage market. In fact Burtt quotes an example of a downtown Boston firm that carefully recruited its female help from the suburban area to which it was about to relocate. When the relocation took place, however, many of the girls resigned and went to work for another downtown firm even though every effort was made to keep them with the company (Burtt, 1961, p. 18). Thus, it is not surprising that the average length of commuter trips to the CBD by females is slightly longer than that for males, though for the urban area as a whole it is less.

A MODEL OF A JOURNEY-TO-WORK TRIP LENGTH

We have observed that the journey-to-work trip length can be measured in a number of ways—time, distance, airline distance, cost, and so forth. For the development of a journey-to-work model, Kain uses elapsed time; that is, the actual time spent by a person in commuting from his home to his place of work (Kain, 1962, pp. 40–47). The data relates to Detroit and is based on information received from interviews of a stratified random sample of households of the white work force conducted in 1953, which has been aggregated to 254 work-place zones.

The hypotheses The statement developed by Kain for use in a larger multiple-equation model of household locational and trip-making behavior is expressed in equation form as follows:

$$ET_j = \alpha + b_1SR_j + b_2MP_j + b_3Y_j + b_4P_j + b_5SW_j + b_6PT_j \qquad (15.1)$$

where, ET_j = mean elapsed time in hours and tenths spent by the workers of the jth work-place zone in reaching work

SR_j = percentage of the jth zone's workers residing in single-family residential units

MP_j = proportion of the workers in the jth zone that are male

Y_j = mean income of the jth work zone

P_j = a proxy variable for the price of residential space for workers in each zone, calculated as 11.5 minus the airline distance from the CBD, where 11.0 is the maximum distance. The location rent curve implied by this statement is presented in diagrammatic form in Figure 15.7, though the values will increase with distance rather than decrease

$SW_j =$ percentage of the workers of the jth work-place zone belonging to families that have a single wage earner

$PT_j =$ the proportion of the workers of the jth work-place zone that use public transit.

and, α, b_1, . . . , b_6 are empirically determined constants.

The hypotheses developed by Kain are quite consistent with our preceding discussion, and can be listed as follows:

1. Work-trip length is positively correlated with the proportion of workers living in single-family dwelling units. The rationale for this is that the worker offsets greater time spent in getting to work against the advantages of single-family residential locations.

2. The average length of the journey to work should be greater in those zones that have a high proportion of male workers. We have noted that female trips to the CBD have a tendency to be longer than male trips, but that for the whole urban area they are shorter. Kain contends that the reason for this is that the labor-force attachment of women is generally weaker than that for men. This is because working women often belong to families that have low space preferences, and more than a single wage earner.

3. If, in the multiple-regression model, the effect of residential space consumption (SR_j), the price of residential space (P_j), and transit usage (PT_j) are held constant, then it could be expected that higher income

FIG. 15.7. IDEALIZED LOCATION RENTS FOR WORK PLACES AT VARIOUS DISTANCES FROM THE CBD. (*Source:* Kain, 1962, Fig. 2.)

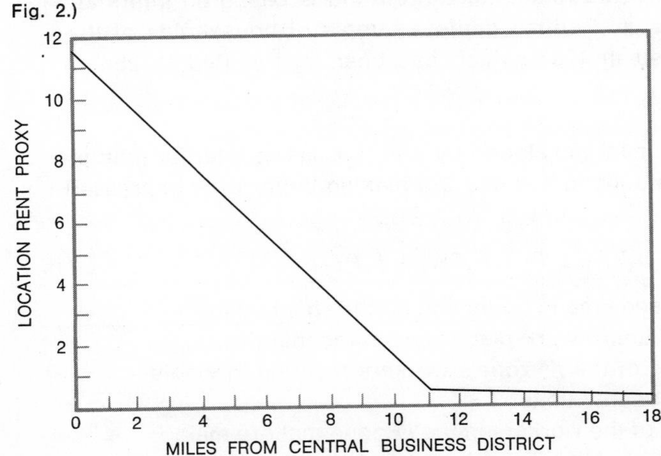

households would make shorter work trips in terms of elapsed time. This is because higher income households can afford to use higher speed modes of transportation which also cost more.

4. The proxy location-rent variable should be positively correlated with trip length. This is because "workers would make longer journeys-to-work at every level of space consumption as the price of residential space increased, since the savings in location rents would be great enough to make longer journeys-to-work economically rational" (Kain, 1962, p. 45).

5. Zones with large proportions of families having a single wage earner should have greater time spent in the journey to work.

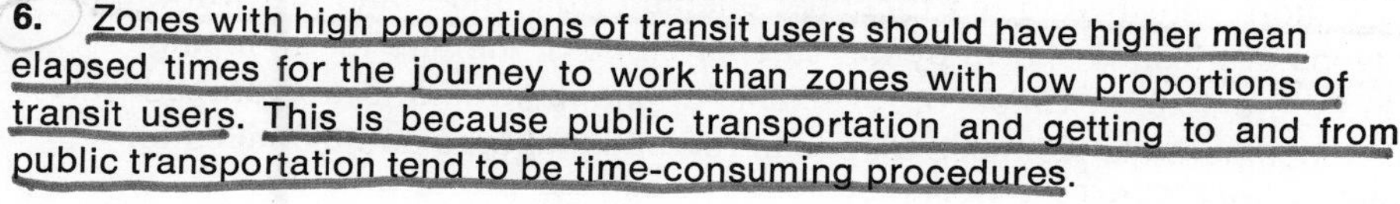

6. Zones with high proportions of transit users should have higher mean elapsed times for the journey to work than zones with low proportions of transit users. This is because public transportation and getting to and from public transportation tend to be time-consuming procedures.

The results Table 15.7 gives the coefficient of multiple determination (R^2) for Equation 15.1. The regression equation explains 65 percent of the total variation in the dependent variable, which is mean elapsed journey-to-work time. The standard error of estimate of the regression equation is quite small, so the results can be viewed with a degree of confidence. Also presented in Table 15.7 are the regression coefficients pertaining to the independent variables and their standard errors. These indicate that all the regression coefficients, except the one pertaining to single-family residence (SR_j), can be regarded as significantly different from zero at the 0.05 percent confidence level.

The signs of the regression coefficients for the proportion using public transit, the proportion male, and the location-rent proxy are all positive. These all conform to the hypothesized relationships. The negative signs of the regression coefficients pertaining to the income and single wage-earner variables also behave as expected. Thus the multivariable model, expressed in Equation 15.1 and empirically examined with sample data from Detroit, combines in a rather interesting way many of the factors that we have discussed as influences of journey-to-work trip lengths. It can, however, be readily appreciated that the model provides only a partial statement of a very complex situation.

TABLE 15.7. ESTIMATED COEFFICIENT OF DETERMINATION, REGRESSION COEFFICIENTS, AND STANDARD ERRORS FOR EQUATION 15.1

Variable	*SR*	*MP*	*Y*	*P*	*SW*	*PT*
Regression coefficient	−.0006	.0020	−.0010	.006	−.0006	.0040
Standard error	.0004	.0004	.0005	.002	.0003	.0005
Coefficient of determination	0.65	Intercept	.304	Standard error of estimate		.06

Source: Kain (1962), p. 46.

THE JOURNEY TO SHOP

Shopping trips differ from the journey to work in the following important ways:

1. They account for only a small part of the total pattern of urban movement. Whereas, for example, journeys to work account for about 20 percent of the total person trips by destination in Chicago, shopping trips account for only 5.5 percent of the total (see Table 15.3). Evidence suggests that for other urban areas shopping trips average about 8.5 percent of total trips and that there is relatively little variation between cities of different size (Garrison, et al., 1959, p. 200).

2. They are typically much shorter in terms of time and distance. Shopping trips are more sensitive to the frictional effects of distance than are work and other types of trips, as shown by the steeper slope of the line for shopping trips in Figure 15.8. In Chicago, for example, shopping journeys averaged only 2.8 miles compared to 4.3 miles for social-recreational trips and 5.3 miles for journeys to work (C.A.T.S., 1959).

3. They are much less regular in time and space. The marked concentration of commuting flow during the morning and evening rush hours is not typical of shopping patterns, which for the most part occur fairly evenly throughout the day, and particularly in the period 10 a.m. to 2 p.m. The intensity of shopping may increase to give minor peaks at suburban centers between 3 and 6 p.m., while Fridays and Saturdays are generally more important shopping days during the week (Vorhees, et al., 1955).

Unlike commuting, which takes place between the same set of origins and destinations each day, shopping trips are spatially more dispersed. The distance and direction traveled from day to day varies depending on the specific demands to be satisfied. Thus on some days consumers may undertake major shopping excursions to the more widely spaced higher level centers, on others only short trips may be made to purchase convenience goods from local centers, and occasionally a longer trip may be made to the CBD. The wide range of shopping opportunities within the urban area, coupled with the varying frequency, nature, and intensity of demand for different goods and services, give rise to very flexible patterns of shopping journeys.

TYPES OF SHOPPING TRIP

Shopping trips can be classified in a number of different ways; for example, by type of good(s) purchased (the distinction between convenience goods and shopping goods is particularly important in this respect), by mode of travel, and so on, depending on the purpose of study. For general purposes it is important to distinguish between the following three types of shopping trips:

1. *Single-purpose trips*, during which a stop is made at one kind of retail or service establishment on a trip that starts and ends at the same location, usually the home. They are the most frequently undertaken type of shopping trip and are particularly important in the purchase of convenience items (e.g.,

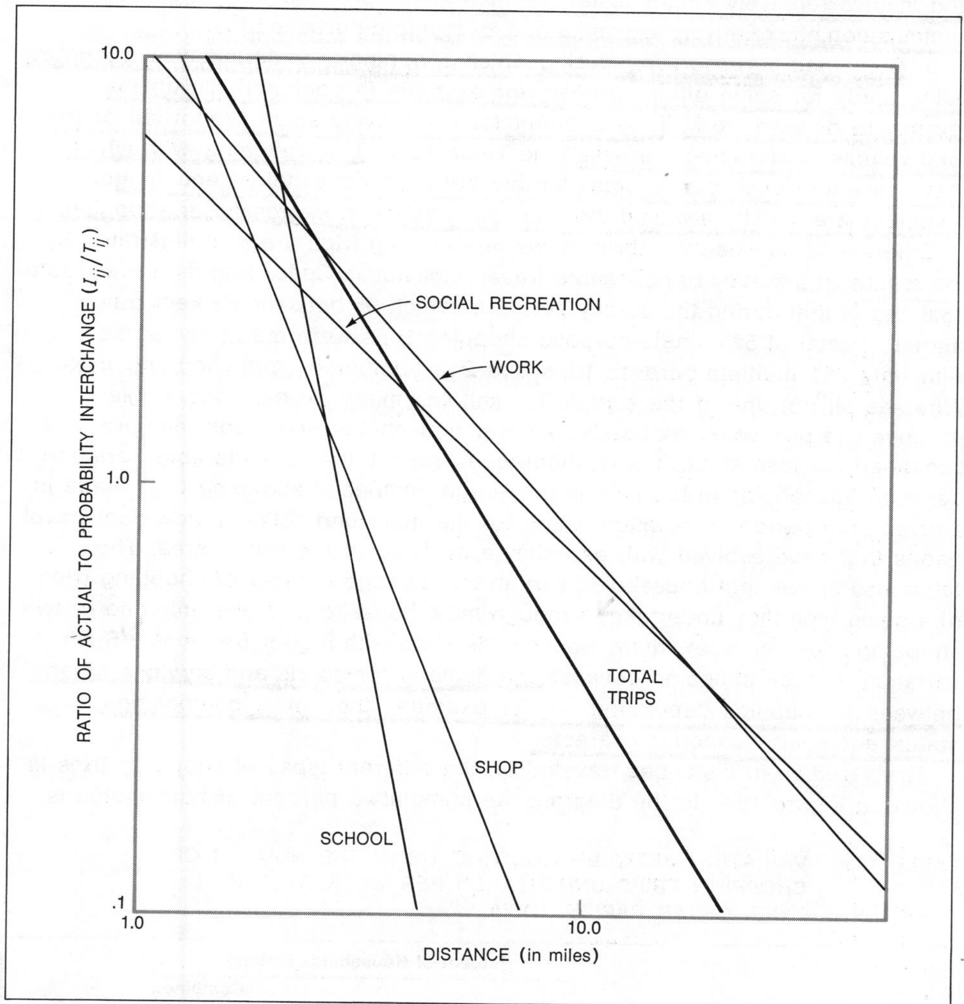

FIG. 15.8. THE FRICTION OF DISTANCE VARIES DEPENDING ON TRIP PURPOSE. (*Source:* Carroll and Bevis, 1957, Fig. 5.)

groceries). Normally they are characterized by a visit to only one establishment; but when comparison buying is associated with the good in question, a number of different establishments of the same type may be visited. Distance minimization is often an important influence on this kind of trip, hence the distances involved are normally relatively short.

2. *Multiple-purpose trips,* during which stops are made at more than one kind of retail and/or service establishment, and hence a variety of different goods are purchased on the same trip. They are especially important in connection with visits to larger business centers. In general they are less frequently undertaken

and involve relatively longer distances than single-purpose trips. Distance minimization has relatively less influence for multiple-purpose trips.

3. *Combined-purpose trips*, during which shopping is undertaken or a journey being made for some other purpose, for example in conjunction with the journey to or from work. They account for a relatively small proportion of the total volume of shopping journeys (see Table 15.3). The frequency with which they are undertaken varies considerably between households, and longer distances are usually involved than for journeys made expressly for shopping.

Differences between the three types of shopping trips are well illustrated by the results of a survey of household travel behavior in Cedar Rapids, Iowa. Table 15.8 shows that during the 30-day period in which 95 households kept travel diaries, a total of 524 single-purpose shopping trips were made compared with only 251 multiple-purpose trips and 242 combined work-shopping trips. Whereas all but one of the sample households made at least one single-purpose trip per week, successively fewer households undertook multiple- and combined-purpose trips. These differences reflect the considerable variation between households in the type and average number of shopping trips made in a given time period, a variation which for the most part reflects individual travel habits that have evolved with experience of living in the urban area. The table also shows that households vary in the average number of shopping trips of a given type they undertake. Although most households make only one or two shopping trips per week, many households shop with higher frequency. Such variation is to be expected because the demand for goods and services differs between households depending on, for example, their size, composition, status, and socio-economic character.

The variation in distances traveled on the different types of shopping trips is shown in Figure 15.9. In the diagram the cumulative percent of households is

TABLE 15.8. VARIATION BETWEEN HOUSEHOLDS IN THE NUMBER OF SHOPPING TRIPS UNDERTAKEN PER WEEK BY TRIP TYPE, CEDAR RAPIDS, IOWA

	Percent of Households Making		
Average Number of Trips per Week	**Single-Purpose Trips**	**Multiple-Purpose Trips**	**Combined Work-Shop Trips**
1	31.8	41.9	35.4
2	24.5	33.8	25.0
3	14.8	13.5	10.4
4	9.6	5.4	8.3
5	7.5	4.0	12.5
6	4.3	1.4	4.2
more than 6	7.5	–	4.2
Total households	94	74	48
Total number of trips	524	251	242
Mean trips per household	5.6	3.4	5.0

Source: Garrison, et al. (1959), based on figure 11–6.

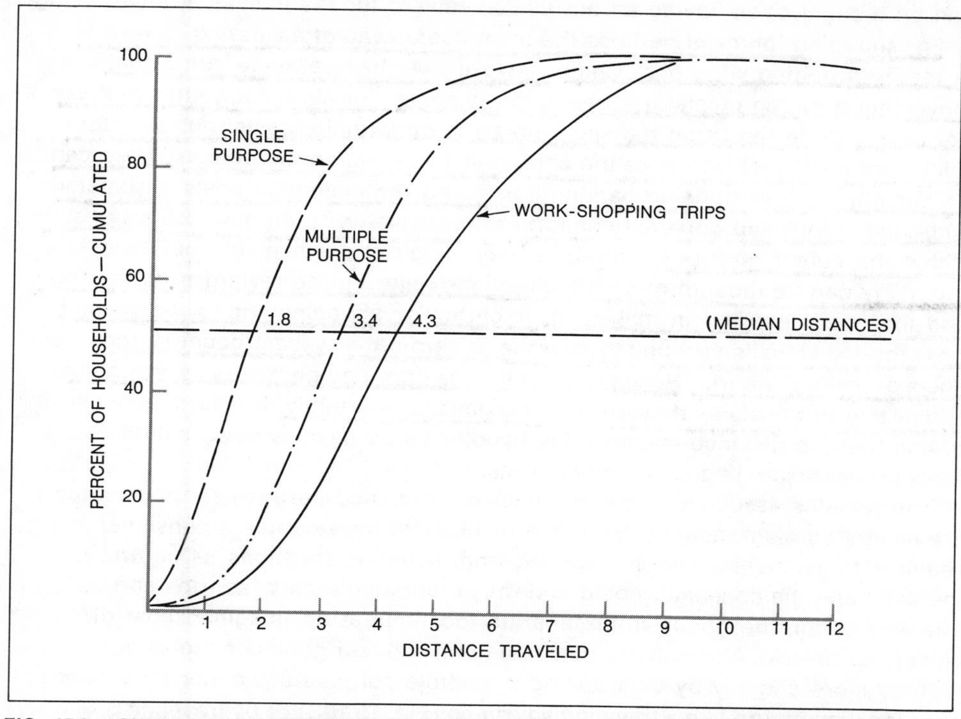

FIG. 15.9. CUMULATIVE DISTRIBUTIONS OF DISTANCES TRAVELED ON DIFFERENT TYPES OF SHOPPING TRIPS. (*Source:* After Garrison, et al., 1959, Fig. 11.5.)

plotted against average length of journey according to trip type. The longer distances typical of multiple-purpose trips are indicated by the fact that the curve for this type of trip lies wholly to the right of that for single-purpose trips. Similarly, combined work-shopping trips are shown to be longer than the others. Half of the sample households traveled distances of less than 1.8 miles on single-purpose trips compared to 3.4 miles and 4.3 miles on multiple-purpose and combined work-shopping trips respectively. Variations above and below the median distances reflect in large part differences between households, particularly in their income levels and mobility. Generally, consumers from higher-income households will travel farther for shopping purposes than consumers of lower economic levels. This is expected partly on the basis that the demands of individuals of higher economic levels are generally greater, and partly on the basis that they have better means of transportation at their disposal and therefore can experience somewhat lower shopping travel costs than individuals from lower-income groups (Huff, 1961).

THE NOTION OF TRIP UTILITY

For the consumer, the distinction between these three types of shopping trip is largely a matter of the differences in trip utility associated with them. Any trip can be thought of as having an associated reward for the individual undertaking it. For shopping journeys perhaps the most useful way of assessing reward is in terms of getting what one wants. However, we have already noted that movement between points in space involves costs. For shopping journeys these not only include the usual transportation and opportunity costs, but also the additional costs incurred once the consumer has reached the center. These can be thought of as comprising parking costs, and the intangible costs associated with time, effort, and personal comfort that are related to the level of congestion within the center and its stores. In a very simple way, then, the notion of *trip utility* can be thought of as the difference between the reward from the trip and the costs incurred in making it. A particular shopping trip is worthwhile from the individual's viewpoint when the rewards are at least equal to the costs of making the trip. Hence consumers may not be concerned as much with minimizing trip costs as they are with maximizing trip utility. It is largely because of this that the distance-minimization hypothesis by itself is not a sufficient basis for understanding shopping patterns.

The benefits associated with multiple- or combined-purpose shopping trips are illustrated diagrammatically in Figure 15.10. In the example a consumer requires four different goods available from separate locations as shown. On the one hand the consumer could undertake four single-purpose trips and in this way obtain the goods from separate locations at an imagined cost of 10 units (Fig. 15.10A). Alternatively he could obtain all four goods on the same journey more cheaply by undertaking a multiple-purpose trip either by visiting each location in turn like a traveling salesman (Fig. 15.10B) or by traveling to a larger center where all four goods are found in association (Fig. 15.10C). Clearly the multiple-purpose trip is a strategy that is likely to yield higher shopping trip utilities because the effort or cost of travel is spread over a number of different goods to result in lower per unit costs. The potential savings from multiple-purpose trips are such that consumers will often travel much longer

FIG. 15.10. DIAGRAMMATIC REPRESENTATION OF THE COSTS OF DIFFERENT TYPES OF SHOPPING TRIPS: (A) SINGLE-PURPOSE TRIPS, (B) "TRAVELING SALESMAN" MULTIPLE-PURPOSE TRIPS, AND (C) REGULAR MULTIPLE-PURPOSE TRIPS.

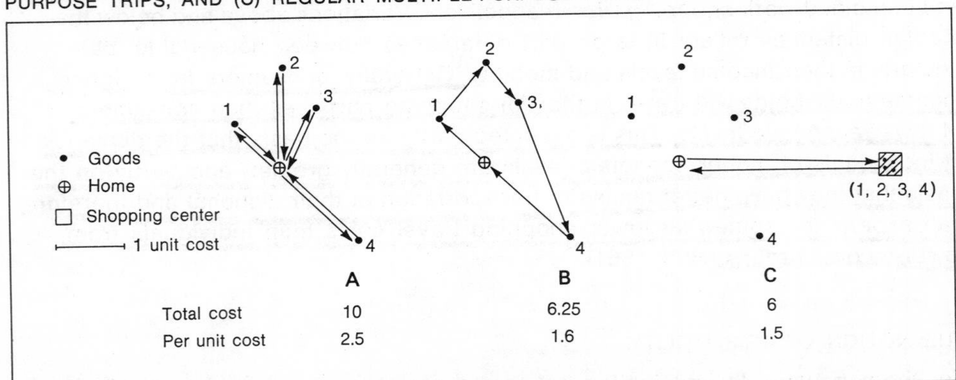

distances than necessary to larger centers where the goods and services they require can be obtained together.

THE INFLUENCE OF RETAIL STRUCTURE

That the shopping patterns of urban residents should be affected by the distribution of business types within the city follows from the discussion of the urban commercial structure in Chapter 12. There it was noted that business types occur in the landscape more or less frequently depending on their threshold requirements. This in turn results in their being more or less ubiquitously distributed within the urban area. Thus lower-order convenience types are widely scattered throughout the urban area in close correspondence with the density and distribution of population, while higher-order types needing higher centrality tend to be concentrated at increasingly fewer locations. Some very specialized types with very large threshold requirements may only occur downtown. Because of this, the average distances separating consumers from an establishment of a given business type tend to increase directly with its order in the hierarchy of centers.

The result is that consumers need only travel relatively short average distances to acquire frequently demanded, lower-order goods but are more or less obliged to travel longer average distances to obtain the less frequently demanded, higher-order shopping goods and more specialized services. Data from the survey of household travel behavior in Cedar Rapids, Iowa, shown in Table 15.9 indicates this to be generally true for single-purpose trips, but less so for multiple-purpose trips. On these, longer distances are traveled to purchase the

TABLE 15.9. AVERAGE DISTANCES TRAVELED TO SHOP FOR DIFFERENT ORDER GOODS AND SERVICES BY TYPE OF SHOPPING TRIP, CEDAR RAPIDS, IOWA

Business Types	(1) Total Number of Trips	(2)[a] Average Distance	(3) Number of Single-Purpose Trips	(4)[a] Average Distance	(5)[b] Number of Multiple-Purpose Trips	(6)[a] Average Distance
Grocery stores	264	1.9	157	0.5	107	4.1
Beauty salons	17	4.0	4	0.7	13	5.0
Bakeries	34	3.3	5	0.9	29	3.6
Drugstores	160	3.0	57	1.1	103	4.1
Barbers	18	3.6	5	1.7	13	4.4
Appliances	12	4.9	2	1.7	10	5.6
Banks	62	5.0	6	2.1	56	5.2
Furniture stores	18	3.5	3	2.4	15	3.7
Dentists	13	3.0	6	2.4	7	3.4
Clothes stores	52	4.6	4	2.5	48	4.7
Theaters	108	4.4	67	2.9	41	3.4
Department stores	151	4.7	11	3.0	140	4.1

[a] Average distances in miles are for round-trip journeys.
[b] Multiple-purpose trips include multiple-purpose shopping trips and all other combined purpose shopping trips.
Source: Garrison, et al. (1959), after Table 11-VIII).

same set of goods, and this is particularly noticeable for convenience goods. An important effect of the multiple-purpose trips is, therefore, to blur the distance relationships between buyers and sellers which is implicit in the spatial distribution of business types. When trips of all kinds are grouped together, the average distances traveled to obtain different order goods and services range from 1.9 miles for groceries to 4.7 miles for visits to department stores. Similar aggregate relationships are evident in other cities, for example in Detroit, where the average distances traveled to grocery stores and department stores were 2.0 and 4.8 miles with elapsed journey times of 8.9 and 22.8 minutes respectively (Detroit Metropolitan Area Traffic Study, 1955). This kind of evidence suggests that the spatial patterns explicit in the commercial structure of cities operate to give rise to fairly regular distance relationships in aggregate patterns of consumer behavior from city to city, often despite marked differences in their population size and areal extent.

BEHAVIOR-SPACE PERCEPTION

Shopping trips are the result of a consumer decision process. Although we do not know very much about the way consumers in fact make their decisions, they are undoubtedly influenced by distance and travel costs. For a more complete understanding of shopping patterns we must, however, consider other factors. Particularly important among these are the so-called socio-psychological factors affecting spatial behavior. Unlike the rational economic man so important in our abstract conceptual arguments, the real-world consumer does not have perfect knowledge about the city's commercial structure. Rather, his knowledge is imperfect and is restricted at any given time to the opportunities for shopping he has learned about from his experience of living in the urban area. It is this part of the retail structure that constitutes his behavior space. Each consumer can be thought of as having his own, highly personalized behavior space, the extent of which will depend primarily on his level of mobility and attitude to space.

The way in which the consumer operates within his behavior space depends on his perception of the opportunities it contains for the satisfaction of a given need. This perception can be thought of as comprising two sets of images, those pertaining to the contents of the space and those relating to the ease of movement within it. Both of these will be conditioned by the individual's value system, which is influenced by things such as income level, age, sex, race, occupation, and educational level, besides such intangible qualities as his ethical and moral code, personality, and mental synthesizing abilities (Huff, 1960). The way in which these are interrelated to give rise to shopping patterns is suggested in Figure 15.11. Although the value system, and hence the images consumers have of the retail structure, will be in part idiosyncratic, the scanty evidence available to date suggests that a certain proportion of these images are common to groups of individuals (Lynch, 1960). Because of this it is possible to make meaningful generalizations about the shopping patterns of, for example, high- or low-income groups, young and old shoppers, and so on.

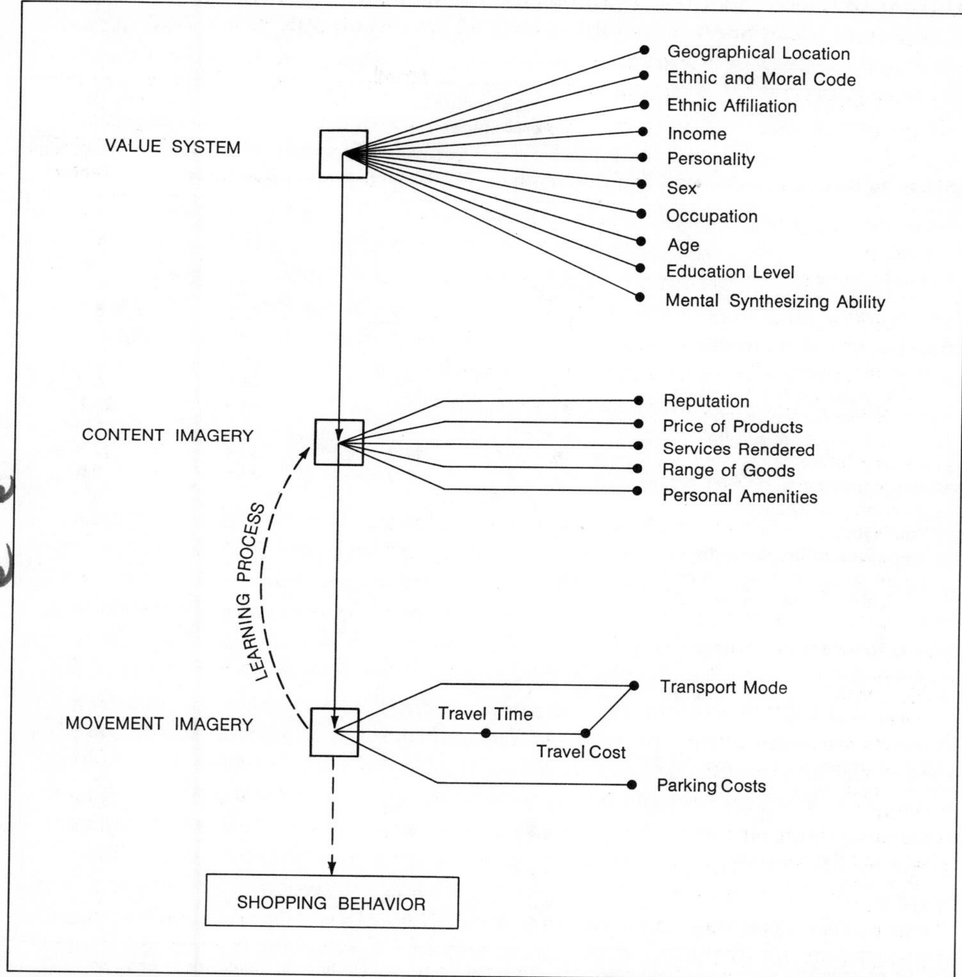

FIG. 15.11. SUGGESTED RELATIONSHIPS BETWEEN CONSUMER IMAGES AND SHOPPING BEHAVIOR. (*Source:* Huff, 1960, Fig. 6.)

Content imagery Content imagery is related to the value the consumer attaches to the various shopping areas and individual establishments comprising his behavior space. It is presumably on the basis of these value images that consumers express preferences for some shopping areas over others, or for the goods of one retailer over those of another. The perceived differences between shopping centers appear to be related to things such as level of discomfort experienced while shopping, the general attractiveness of the center, and the quality and choice of goods offered there (Jonassen, 1955). It is partly on the basis of these attitudes that many consumers choose to shop at newer, planned shopping centers instead of at the older, unplanned ones. Table 15.10, which shows the

TABLE 15.10. ATTITUDES OF CONSUMERS TO SHOPPING DOWNTOWN AND AT SUBURBAN SHOPPING CENTERS IN COLUMBUS, OHIO, AND HOUSTON, TEXAS

	Columbus Percentages for		Houston Percentages for	
Shopping Satisfaction Factors	**Downtown**	**Suburban Centers**	**Downtown**	**Suburban Centers**
Greater variety of styles and sizes	86.3	2.3	87.6	4.0
Greater variety and range of prices and quality	81.1	1.7	83.1	5.0
More bargain sales	65.5	2.7	70.8	6.7
Best place to meet friends from other parts of the city for a shopping trip together	66.9	11.5	65.1	16.0
Better places to eat lunch	61.3	7.9	49.0	26.7
More convenient to public transportation	52.5	14.2	44.4	17.8
Cheaper prices	46.6	7.9	51.5	8.6
Goods more attractively displayed	44.1	16.3	67.9	6.5
Better place to combine different kinds of shopping and other things one may want to do	56.3	29.7	72.3	20.6
Easier to establish a charge account	30.1	5.2	33.5	7.3
Better place for a little outing away from home	38.5	33.2	50.2	28.5
The right people shop there	10.3	21.5	15.3	15.5
Cost of transportation less	15.7	59.3	4.0	72.4
Keep open more convenient hours	16.3	62.6	9.1	51.6
Less walking required	16.3	69.9	13.6	72.4
Easier to take children shopping	2.5	47.6	1.6	60.9
Less tiring	9.3	75.0	9.0	75.4
Takes less time to get there	12.3	78.9	9.6	78.8

Note: Percentages for each city do not equal 100 percent since two other choices, "undecided" and "no concern," are not shown.
Source: Jonassen (1955), after Table 20.

results of attitude surveys among shoppers in Columbus, Ohio, and Houston, Texas, suggests some of the ways in which consumers perceive differences between suburban shopping centers and downtown.

Images of particular retail or service outlets are based on things like the breadth of merchandise offered, price, personal amenities, window display, services rendered, and the store's reputation (Garner, 1969). Thus, although a consumer may be aware of a number of centers and specific retail/service establishments of a given type, on the basis of his content imagery he may consider some of them unsuitable for the satisfaction of his own particular needs and wants. These will be disregarded, and consequently we can think of his shopping activities as being restricted to those alternatives for which he has well-developed preferences. If the wants cannot be satisfied by searching among these, the consumer may then extend his shopping activity to other stores for which at the time his awareness and preferences are not so well developed.

Movement imagery Movement imagery relates to the images consumers have of the relative location of centers and stores and the difficulties of undertaking shopping journeys to them. A significant factor in these is the way in which distance between home and shop is perceived, and it is largely on the basis of this that the concept of accessibility takes on a specific meaning in the shopping context. The perception of distance depends on a number of factors, including the means of travel available, relative travel time and costs, and time available for undertaking the journey. It will also depend on the way barriers to movement are perceived within the urban area. These may be formed either by natural features, such as rivers, which can only be bridged at certain points, or man-made features, such as large areas of industrial land use and railroad tracks. Increasingly important, however, are the perceived barriers to movement arising from the social and ethnic structure of the urban area. The result of these barriers, both real and perceived, is to divide the city effectively into cells, as shown for example in Figure 15.12. Unfortunately, and to an increasing extent in the larger cities, these tend to constrain the behavior space of many individuals, not only for shopping but for other activities as well. On the basis of his movement imagery, therefore, the consumer may further discriminate between otherwise acceptable shopping opportunities and in this way reduce still further the set for which he develops well-formed preferences.

An immediate effect of the consumer's content and movement imagery is that it gives rise to highly individualistic shopping patterns within the urban area in which the importance of distance minimization may be still further reduced. This is particularly important in connection with the purchase of shopping goods and may even be characteristic of trips for lower-order convenience items. For example, in a survey of shopping habits in Christchurch, New Zealand, it was found that for purchases of groceries, meat, and vegetables only 63.1, 66.4, and 52.1 percent respectively of the total families interviewed habitually frequented their nearest stores for these goods (Clark, 1968). Table 15.11 clearly shows that many consumers travel considerably farther on shopping trips than they need to from a purely distance-minimization standpoint. Although the pattern revealed by this particular data cannot be interpreted solely on the basis of behavior space perception, consumer preferences and movement imagery are likely important factors in accounting for the discrepancy between the two sets of distance figures.

THE LEARNING PROCESS

The consumer's imagery of the retail structure is a potent factor affecting his shopping patterns. These images are not, however, static but are continually

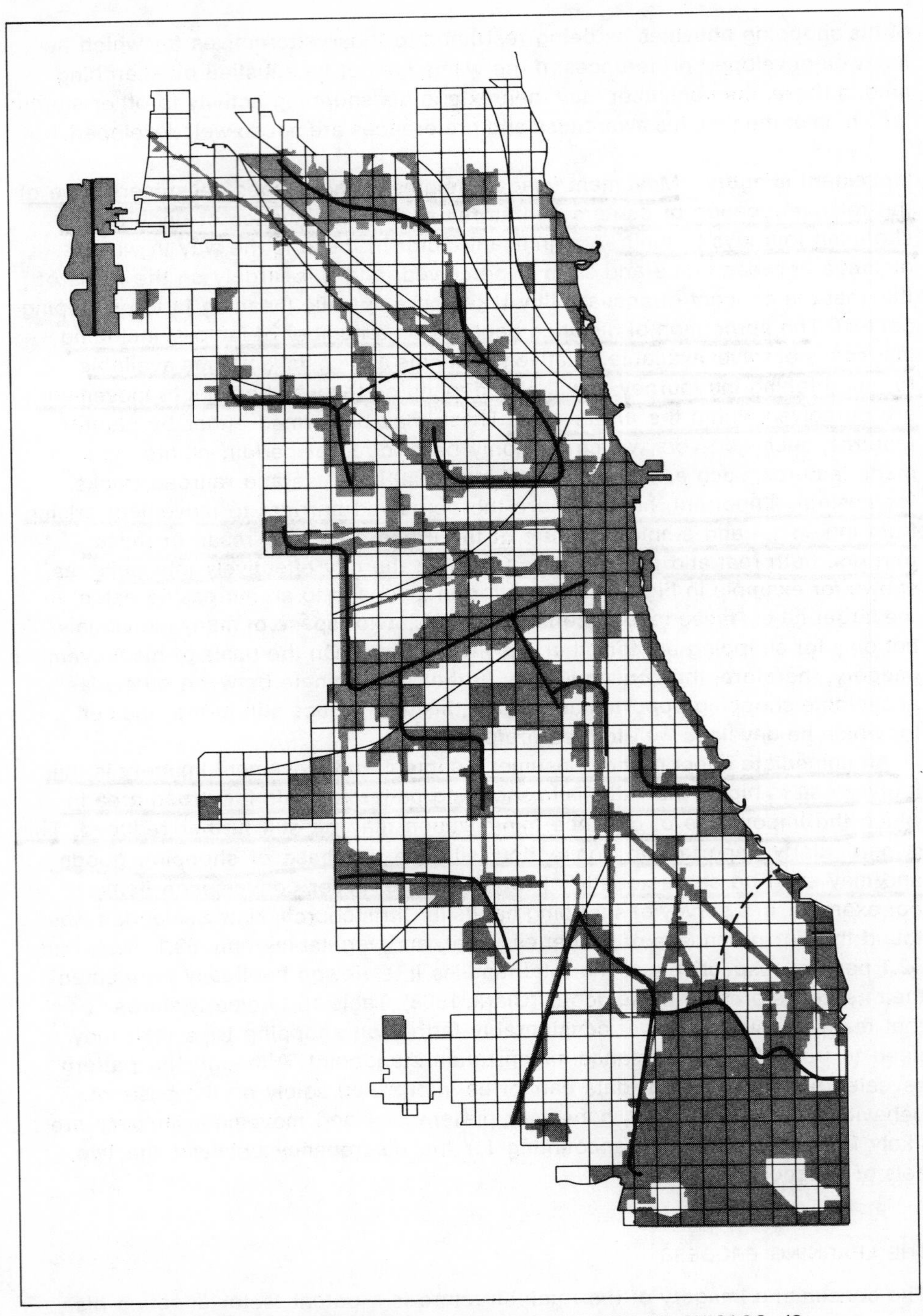

FIG. 15.12. BARRIERS TO CONSUMER MOVEMENT IN THE CITY OF CHICAGO. (*Source:* Berry, 1963, Fig. 14.)

TABLE 15.11. DIFFERENCES BETWEEN LENGTH OF SHOPPING TRIPS AND DISTANCE TO THE NEAREST ESTABLISHMENT FOR SELECTED GOODS

	Distances in Miles to			
	Center Visited		Nearest Center	
	Mean	S.D.	Mean	S.D.
Canterbury, N.Z.				
Groceries	.71	1.21	.23	.15
Vegetables	.95	1.12	.31	.18
Meats	.70	0.99	.29	.20
Cedar Rapids, Iowa				
Groceries	.60	–	.19	–
Supermarket	.78	–	.70	–
Clothing	1.30	–	1.23	–
Restaurant	1.65	–	0.32	–

Source: Clark (1968), Table 5, p. 393 and Marble and Bowlby (1968), Table 1, p. 62.

changing through time as the consumer develops greater awareness of the urban area. The consumer experiences a learning process. There is a continuous input of sensory information from the urban environment; however, not all of this is stored ad infinitum—or until it may be needed. Much of it may be rejected at once as being irrelevant or because it contributes nothing new to the images already developed. The rest makes its mark, impresses, and is incorporated into the individual's behavior space perception. Thus, although aggregate shopping patterns may be fairly stable over periods of time, the patterns for many individuals may be subject to continual adjustment and change through time.

A number of factors are involved in the learning process. Two important ones are the length of residence in an area and the changes taking place in the urban retail structure referred to in Chapter 12. That length of residence in an area affects the individual's behavior space is obvious and can perhaps best be illustrated by what happens when people migrate into an urban area, or move from one part of it to another. Newcomers to the city must learn about the shopping opportunities from scratch. The rate at which they learn will vary from individual to individual and may be largely influenced by the value system. For these people, the more distant, larger centers with their greater number of establishments and functions will be particularly attractive in the early stages, since the probability of getting what they want will be highest at them. People relocating within a different area of the same city will already be familiar with parts of its retail structure, but they will most probably have to learn about the new opportunities in the local area. Oldtimers in the city can be expected to have fairly well-established images developed during their longer period of familiarity with the city. Hence individuals can be expected to be in different stages of the learning process. This can be thought of as another important factor influencing their particular behavior spaces and shopping patterns. That changes in the city's retail structure will also influence the learning process is equally self-evident. New stores are continually being added to the retail structure; old and familiar elements are forever disappearing, either under the bulldozer or because of changes in function, even management. Whole shopping areas change their character, particularly when there is invasion of the surrounding neighborhood by different social and ethnic groups; and consequently they may not continue to offer the same kind of opportunities for shopping to the traditional clientele (Pred, 1963). In the postwar period entirely new shopping centers have been added, particularly in the newer suburban growth areas.

These ongoing changes in the retail structure will influence the images held by consumers and will bring about changes in them through time. The result is that behavior space perception is subject to varying degrees of modification, which will be reflected in individual, and in some cases aggregate, shopping patterns.

TRADE AREAS

Shopping journeys undertaken by consumers from dispersed origins tend to focus on specific retail/service establishments or shopping areas. They consequently involve a centripetal element that gives rise to trade areas. Unlike the comparable areas associated with rural service centers, those for shopping centers within the city are considerably more complex. In the densely built-up urban areas, consumers have a much greater range of alternative shopping opportunities available to them within the maximum distances they are prepared to travel. Although they may have well-developed preferences for certain of these, they visit none exclusively but rather will visit many of them at some time or other in the course of their shopping behavior.

In this way consumers can be thought to have probabilities of visiting the different centers. The probability of visiting a given center will be influenced by the consumer's content and movement imagery, and consequently they are difficult to determine empirically. It has been shown, however, that a useful approximation to the probabilistic nature of trade areas can be obtained on the basis of center size and distance (Huff, 1963). A hypothetical example of the trade areas for three centers is shown in Figure 15.13. The overlapping influence of different shopping centers, the break-points between centers (which occur where the contours of equal probability intersect), and the general decline of center influence with distance are clearly shown. The latter is well illustrated from the results of a study of regional shopping centers in the San Francisco Bay area, where it was found that although 17 percent of the customers come from over 10 miles away, one-half of the customers live within 3 miles of the center visited (Vance, 1962).

Despite this probabilistic nature of trade areas, it is still very useful to indicate their size and shape in a more general way to show the dominant area served by a shopping center. An example is given in Figure 15.14. The trade-area boundaries shown on the maps include about 80 percent of the centers' regular customers. The resulting patterns indicate quite clearly the hierarchical nature of the shopping centers discussed in Chapter 12 and the nesting of trade areas

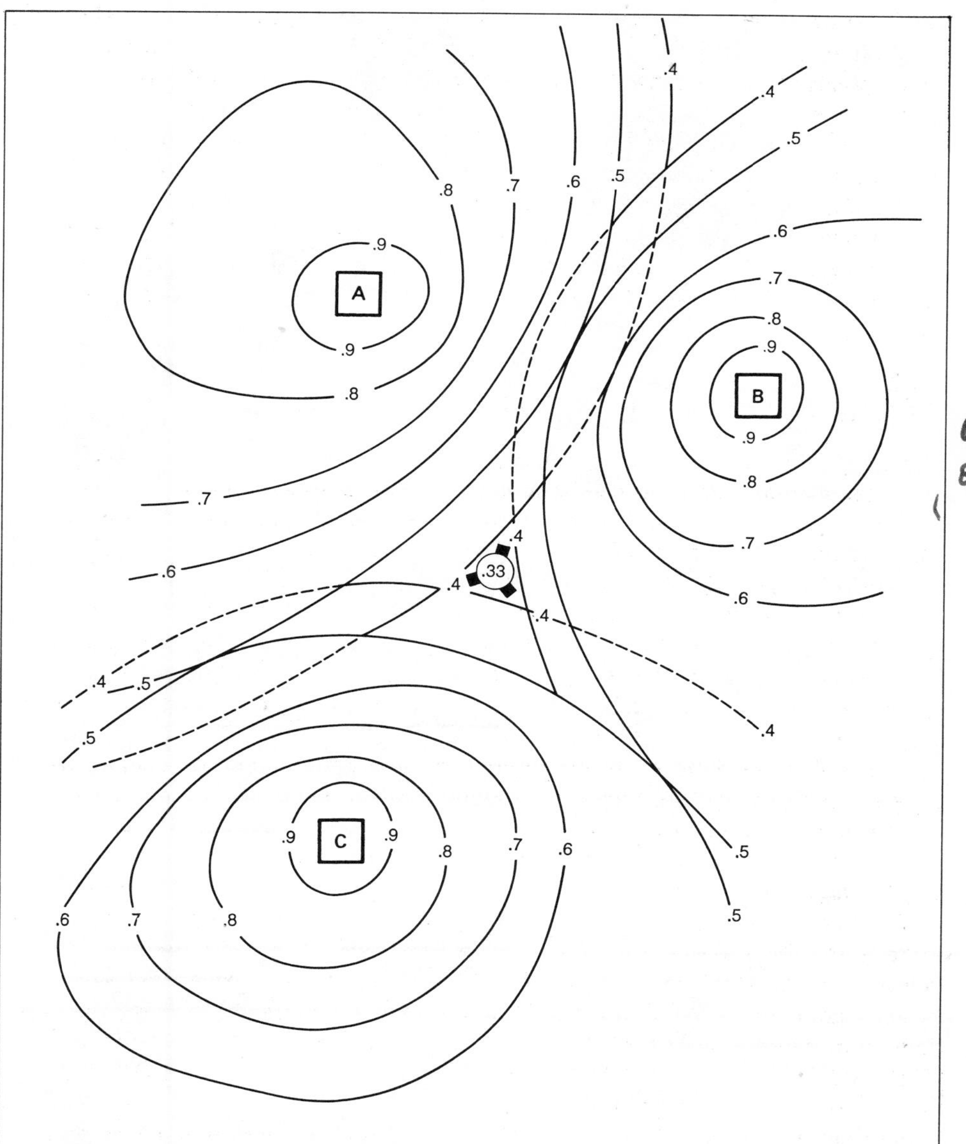

FIG. 15.13. PROBABILITY CONTOURS FOR CONSUMERS SHOPPING IN THREE CENTERS. (*Source:* Berry, 1967A, Fig. 2.16.)

discussed in Chapter 7. The convenience-goods trade areas (Fig. 15.14A) are relatively small and form a mesh over the city. Boundaries overlap, especially in the more densely built-up parts of the city, and the size of the trade area appears to be generally related to the size of the center. At the higher order,

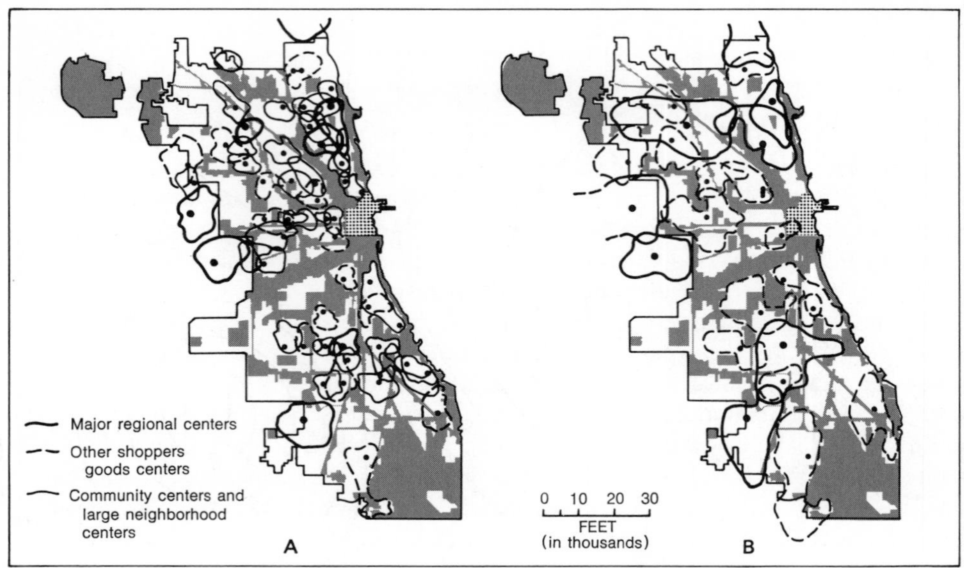

FIG. 15.14. SHOPPING TRADE AREAS IN CHICAGO: (A) CONVENIENCE GOODS TRADE AREAS AND (B) SHOPPERS' GOODS TRADE AREAS. (*Source:* Berry, 1963, Figs. 11 and 12.)

shopping-goods level, many of the smaller centers drop out, consistent with the notion of the hierarchy, and fewer larger centers dominate the trade-area pattern (Fig. 15.14B). The way in which the smaller trade areas nest within the larger ones is clearly revealed when the maps are superimposed. The patterns also indicate the influence of the barriers to movement, shown by the grey areas, on the size and shape of trade areas.

A SHOPPING MODEL

Most models used to describe and predict intraurban shopping patterns are direct descendants of the gravity model discussed in Chapter 4. As such, they deal with aggregate patterns of interaction between shopping areas and various residential zones in the city. They differ from the original Reilly (1931) formulation in three important respects: (1) movement for all kinds of goods is considered, (2) the interaction between a continuous distribution of population and shopping opportunities is described, and (3) the dependent variable is, initially at least, specified as a probability—thereby including the notion that consumers choose between many shopping centers. As developed by Lakshmanan and Hansen (1965) the probability that a consumer resident in zone i patronizes a center in zone j is given as:

$$P_{ij} = \frac{A_j^{\alpha}/d_{ij}^{\beta}}{\sum_{j=1}^{n} A_{j'}^{\alpha}/d_{ij}^{\beta}} \qquad (15.2)$$

in which

A_j is the attractiveness of shopping center located in zone *j*
d_{ij} is the distance between residential zone *i* and center *j*
α and β are empirically derived exponents.

When the right-hand side of the equation is multiplied by the total consumer retail expenditure in residential zone *i*, the model will estimate the total amount of consumer expenditure from that zone spent at center *j*. If the total population of residential zone *i* is multiplied by P_{ij}, the model will estimate the total number of consumers traveling from zone *i* to center *j*.

The above model states that the probability of a consumer traveling from zone *i* to shop at center *j* is (1) directly proportional to the size of shopping center at *j*, and (2) inversely proportional to (*a*) the distance between *i* and *j*, and (*b*) the competition from other centers (the expression in the denominator of Equation 15.2). For its application, the exponents in the equation must be estimated and the variables indexed. The first problem is essentially a technical one, but it is critical for the successful operation of the model, the effectiveness of which depends largely on the specific value given to the exponent of distance (β). The second problem is largely one of definition and is concerned with quantifying distance and the rather vague concept of the attractiveness of centers. Distance is usually measured by airline miles, although other measures such as driving time may be used. Attractiveness is a more difficult concept to handle, however, and most studies use some measure of size of shopping center for this. Size can be measured in a number of ways, including total floor area, number of functions or establishments, and total sales, if this is known.

The success of the model is normally measured by a correlation between observed flows and those generated from the model; and despite the simplicity of the equation, its application in planning studies has been highly satisfactory by this standard. In the Baltimore region for example, the correlation between shopping flows known to exist from an origin-destination study and those generated from the model was very high ($R^2 = 91\%$). Nevertheless, large discrepancies between observed and expected patterns may often result, and modifications to improve the model's efficiency are continually being suggested. Huff (1963) has suggested that the model be disaggregated by type of good to take into account the observation that consumers are prepared to travel longer distances for higher order, specialized commodities. More recently, the notion of competition between claimants at shopping centers has been introduced, and a modification of the distance variable to incorporate this into the model has been suggested. It is not difficult to think of other ways of making the model more realistic, but regardless of the refinements made, the results from using this kind of model will always be highly generalized because of its aggregative nature.

Thus the arrangement of commercial activities within the urban area affects intraurban movements in the same way as the location of work places affects the journey to work. Concomitantly, the predominance of trips for socio-recreational purposes, which take place primarily in the evening, are also affected in their direction and frequency by the arrangement of entertainment facilities in the urban area. Trips to local movie houses or bowling alleys are shorter and more frequent than those to theaters or night clubs located in downtown areas. Consequently, the movement concepts presented with respect to work and shopping trips are underlying forces determining most trips in urban areas.

THE URBAN DILEMMA

3

"ACCELERATING URBANIZATION"

During the present century the urban population of North America has increased at a much faster rate than that of the rural areas. As a consequence a far greater proportion of the total population of North America is now living in urban areas than even thirty years ago. From Table 2.1 it can be observed that the population of the United States was more than 50 percent urban by 1920. That of Canada passed the halfway mark between 1921 and 1931 (Stone, 1967, p. 29). In 1960 to 1961 it was estimated that the population of North America was about 70 percent urban, and that the rate of urbanization shows no sign of decreasing. Inasmuch as the population on the whole is growing continually this means, of course, that the total urban population is increasing at a rapid rate. In fact it is estimated that in 1960 135 million North Americans were living in urban areas (of 1,000 or more people) and that by 1980 this figure will have increased to approximately 190 million persons. Thus, in twenty years 55 million additional persons will have been accommodated within the urban realm of North America.

The proportion of urban dwellers, however, is not the same across North America. Some states and provinces have a higher proportion of urban dwellers than others. Figure 2.1 indicates that there is a distinct historical trend in the evolution of this pattern, with urbanization proceeding at a faster rate in the northeast industrial area of the United States and, it may be mentioned, the associated Great Lakes–St. Lawrence region of Canada. The maps in Figure 2.1 also illustrate the great dominance of urban areas in the population growth of the West Coast of the United States. This uneven distribution of urbanism of course implies that the problems of urban areas are not considered as important to the state and provincial legislatures of some states and provinces as in others.

This increasing urbanization and the spatial variation in the proportion of urban dwellers have accentuated a number of problems such as government, water and air pollution, blight, crime, congestion, and so forth, that have been accumulating at a rapid rate over the past eight decades (Bollens and Schmandt, 1965, p. 245–273). One of the most dramatic of these problems concerns the alienated Negroes of North America, the majority of whom are located in large urban areas in blighted ghettos. As this problem has been referred to in previous chapters and is as much psychological as it is social and economic, we will not discuss it any further at this point except to suggest that, if it is not solved, urban living may well become meaningless. The problems that we will confine ourselves to at this juncture are among those directly related to the growing mass of urban areas and concern the way in which this mass affects urban government, transportation, and air pollution.

THE GOVERNMENT OF URBAN AREAS

Frequently we have alluded to the problems of governing urban areas. These problems have been observed with respect to many facets of urban life; and consequently urban government warrants some discussion of its own. Berry and Meltzer (1967, p. 1) in fact regard the problems of urban area government as paramount, and they suggest that this is because ". . . the organic socio-economic city is out of phase with the political organization by which it is supposed to be governed." The problems arising from rapid social and economic change are proliferating at so rapid a rate that the administrative structure is unable in many cases to understand them, let alone cope with them. This inability is partially related to the historic development and present structure of urban political government in North America as well as the general complexity of the social and economic problems themselves.

THE DEVELOPMENT OF URBAN GOVERNMENT

Before 1910 local government did not appear to be a very important aspect of the urban scene. This was largely because the government played a relatively unimportant part in the economic affairs of the city, for urban areas employed few people and had relatively low budgets. As a consequence, there was very little desire on the part of the inhabitants of urban areas to participate in local area government; and this was, therefore, relegated to those individuals who were prepared to undertake the administration of the developing urban areas. In many instances these individuals were prepared to undertake the responsibilities in order to attain the rewards that could be derived from positions of power. This power was maintained in a comparatively democratic system through the judicious deployment of patronage, influence, and bribes.

For example in New York this was the heyday of Tammany Hall, the leaders of which tended to regard the direction of the city as a personal commercial venture and ". . . the style of the time was to regard government programs as sources for exploitation and plunder" (Wood, 1961, p. 5). The support of private enterprise was of course vital to the preservation of this system; and, in turn, many private enterprises found it necessary to cooperate with the system in order to obtain licenses and other necessary papers for the continuation of their ventures. The support of the mass of the electorate was also maintained through paternalistic procedures. For example, there was the moral association of the local government with such "all-American" activities as Thanksgiving Day through its sponsorship of mass parties and rallies at which free barbecued beef, beer, and entertainment were dispensed.

At this time, therefore, it was not considered that local government, or for that matter national government, should guide and stimulate the development of the urban area. Although a body of laws had been growing concerned with restricting the rights of private property, particularly those involved with offensive trades and industries in residential areas, these laws were often minimally enforced and frequently ignored. In fact the laissez-faire doctrine as applied to government of any form was ". . . the less government the better," and, as enunciated in President Grover Cleveland's *Second Inaugural Address* it was generally considered quite proper that while "the people should patriotically and cheerfully support their government, its functions do not include the support of the people." Thus the role of local government in the economic life of the city was limited and frequently dictatorial and paternalistic.

A period of change From 1910 to 1935 a great change took place in the powers of local government and a concomitant change in the attitudes of the civil servants and electors in the urban community toward local government. However, although most people could perceive that changes were in fact taking place, it was often very difficult to determine the exact directions involved; furthermore the pace of change varied from one urban area to another. These changes were associated with the rapidly growing urban environment.

Wood (1961, p. 9) indicates that the period between 1910 and 1935 was a period of great growth in governmental activities because the associated "changes in the nation's economy and technology translated themselves into more public expenditures, more taxes, more governmental intervention." We have previously observed the fact that it was during this time that the automobile became of widespread use in urban areas and wrought its great impact on urban structure and urban form. Thus more and more highways were required, newer suburbs were constructed, more and more sanitary, electrical, and water facilities were demanded, and many of these facilities came under the supervision of public administration. Furthermore, the general rising level of incomes and expectations resulted in a greater demand for schools and hospitals; and local governments were increasingly being forced by the electorate to encourage and prompt the private sector to help provide these facilities. In some cases, particularly with respect to utilities, local government had to assume their management.

The chief stimulus for change, however, was the Great Depression, which according to Wood (1961, p. 9) ". . . shattered established procedures for government action." The economic collapse increased the demand by the electorate for positive action by all levels of government to alleviate the crisis. These pressures were felt most acutely at the local government level, and so it was here that the inherent weakness of local government became most apparent. This weakness was not only expressed in terms of the administrative machinery and the talent of the civil servants employed but also by their financial structure. Unfortunately most local governments were in a relatively weak financial position, for the investments incurred in response to advances in transportation technology and the desire for better health, education, and welfare had been financed through local government expenditures that had necessitated large-scale borrowing. In fact, between 1913 and the early 1930s the interest payments of loans to local government in the United States rose from $167 million a year to $1.5 billion a year. It was as a result of these weaknesses that the actions of the federal government in Washington had to be extended in order to alleviate the ever-increasing problems, for the financial power of local governments was severely limited.

LOCAL GOVERNMENT TODAY

Since World War II the efforts of local governments have been directed toward trying to develop machinery and procedures for dealing with problems of the growing urban areas. All local governments have assumed a wider array of responsibilities with respect to their local areas and, concomitantly, local government expenditures have been increasing rapidly. As a consequence, the sheer economic impact of local government activities on their urban areas is extremely important, as well as their efforts to alleviate and cater to the demands of the growing urban areas. The ever-expanding role of local governments has resulted in the development of a number of problems, three of which are of major importance and concern. One involves the methods by which local governments obtain their finances; a second involves methods by which the inhabitants of local areas participate and control the actions of their local government through the electoral process; and a third refers to the fragmentation of governments of contiguous urban areas. This latter problem is referred to in detail in the ensuing chapter concerning megalopolis.

The financing of urban areas One of the chief reasons why many local governments are in deep trouble is that they do not have the necessary income to undertake the range and level of expenditures that the electorate seems to demand. The chief problem here lies in the ways in which local governments are able to obtain their income. The income of governments at any level is obtained from taxes that are, in general, levied on two major sources, property and income. In the United States and Canada, urban areas have limited powers of taxation. At the most these range from taxes on various types of property, sales, and wages (though not total earnings). All of these are essentially regressive taxes—they hit the poorer harder than the wealthier families.

But, the desires and necessities of urban areas are a great deal more complex than those of rural areas, and they demand a great deal more local government expenditure. However, as most state legislatures and provincial governments have tended to be rather more rural oriented than urban oriented in recent decades, the state and provincial governments have been loath to pass taxation rights to urban areas based on income. Thus urban areas have in most instances been left to raise the greatest proportion of their finances through the agrarian accepted measure of the property tax. In fact, former U.S. Senator Joseph S. Clark suggests that "roughly seven out of every eight local tax dollars are still collected from the real property tax" (Berry and Meltzer, 1967, p. 40).

Taxes levied on property are of course a good and sound measure of taxation as long as property itself is a true measure of an individual's or family's wealth. But increasingly throughout North America this is not so, particularly when taxes are also imposed on income at the state or provincial and central government levels. In these circumstances it is often contended that it is the middle class and particularly the lower middle-class home owner who bears proportionately by far the heaviest rate of taxation. As a consequence, in many urban areas it is the middle-class vote that is perpetually rejecting new school bond issues and any other new expenditure that might cause an increase in the taxes to be derived from property.

It would seem that the best solution to this problem is not through an increase in property taxes or through introducing or increasing any other form of indirect regressive taxation (such as sales taxes) but to derive all revenues from taxes on income and earnings. These monies should probably be collected at one place and then allocated to the federal, state, and local government areas. The finances could then be administered by the local urban areas according to the needs of that particular metropolis. This procedure will of course involve a complete revision of all laws and structures concerning taxation, but this appears to be very necessary in the face of the current financial difficulties facing the urban areas, which will soon house 80 percent of the population of North America.

Forms of urban government Another problem facing the urban areas of North America is the variation and complexity of local government structures. These structures are very often so complex that many voters usually find it very hard to understand exactly what is going on in a municipal election, particularly if they have recently moved from one urban area to another. Adrian (1961, pp. 197–231) suggests that there are three basic forms of city government in the United States: (1) the mayor-council, (2) the commission, and (3) the council-manager, as well as the representative town meeting often found in New England. As no two cities have exactly the same form and structure of urban government, these three types are, of course, basic generalizations.

The Mayor-Council Form of Government

At the two extremes of a continuum of urban areas containing the mayor-council form of government are the strong and the weak mayor-councils. The strong mayor-council form calls for the direct election of the mayor and the council by the electorate and the appointment by the mayor of the department heads. The direct election of the mayor alone thus gives him a power base and a mandate to proceed with the philosophy or policies enunciated during the election. Boston and Cleveland are examples of urban areas at this extreme. In this situation the mayor is responsible for all policy decisions, though they have to be ratified by an elected council. In effect he acts in a similar fashion to the President of the United States.

The weak mayor-council system involves the election of not only the mayor and the council but also a wide array of department heads such as a controller, a clerk, a treasurer, an assessor, a city engineer, a health officer, a city attorney, and so forth. Many cities elect just a few of these, such as San Francisco, which elects an attorney, a treasurer, an assessor, as well as the mayor and the council. This of course results in a diffusion of powers and responsibility, for the winner of one office may well have an entirely different political philosophy than the winner of another. Probably the best examples of weak mayor-council systems in North America are Milwaukee and Los Angeles.

The Commission Plan

The commission plan was first introduced in 1900 in Galveston, Tex. The plan calls for the direct election of a committee of commissioners, each of whom serves individually as the head of one of the city's administrative departments; and collectively they form the policy-making council for the city. There is, therefore, no separation of powers as between the council and a mayor, for the commission performs both the legislative and executive functions. In 1960 there were 309 commission-governed cities in the United States, but those that had existed in Canada had by that time adopted a different form of urban government. This plan has largely been superseded in favor of a strong mayor plan or the council-manager plan.

The Council-Manager Plan

The council-manager plan has been spreading with great speed among urban areas in North America. It is probably the simplest form of democratic urban government yet devised, and has proved particularly useful for the multitude of medium-sized urban areas throughout North America. The basic form of the manager-plan model involves ". . . a council of laymen responsible for policy making and a professional administration under a chief administrator responsible to the council" (Adrian, 1961, p. 221). The council is usually elected for staggered terms. They employ the manager, who in turn hires the administrative staff. The manager is directly responsible to the council. Although this, along with all other human institutions, exhibits imperfections, nevertheless it appears that the relative efficiency and simplicity of its operation is appreciated. It is estimated that approximately 1,700 cities had managers in the United States and Canada in the mid-1960s.

LOCAL GOVERNMENT DECISION MAKING

The rapid expansion of the economic power of the government sector in North America has brought into sharp focus the fact that government decision making is radically different from that undertaken in the private sector. In the first place ". . . the basic unit of decision making is not the individual producer or consumer; it is the group formally or informally organized." Secondly, ". . . the mechanism through which resources are obtained and expenditures made is not the price mechanism of the marketplace but the budgetary process." Thirdly, ". . . the products provided by government are public products; that is, theoretically they are always indivisible among persons, and practically, they are frequently so" (Wood, 1961, p. 19).

Although individuals vote in an election, they cannot be consulted at all times concerning the myriad of minor policy decisions that have to be undertaken by local governments. These expressions of opinion on issues are obtained from a number of individuals whom the local government respects as representing the will and opinion of aggregates of electors or groups. In urban areas these groups are often aggregated into institutions such as churches, banks, or labor unions, and frequently into spatially coherent groups such as ethnic blocks and their neighborhood units. Thus the degree to which a particular view is taken into account in the decision-making process depends to a large extent on the vigor with which the spokesman for a group presents the perceived attitude of the group. It is therefore not suprising that, if a group considers itself not well represented in the decision-making process, it may attempt to create a situation such that its opinions have to be recognized.

Although these groups come into play at all levels and in all kinds of urban decision making, one area in which their opinions are of particular importance is with respect to the urban budget. The urban budget involves the allocation of funds among the various needs of the urban area, and it is not so much an allocation based on calculated needs and benefits but ". . . on a system of preferences filtered through group representation" (Wood, 1961, p. 20). In fact allocations are very often based on compromises and estimates of what will minimally satisfy a group's expectations. If costs have to exceed revenues in order to meet these minimal expectations, then they are allowed to do so; and the difference accumulates as the public debt.

If the individual elector is not satisfied with the returns that he receives from his taxes, then he has a number of alternatives open to him, the most common of which is to vote for some other party or person at the next election. If individual groups are not satisfied with their treatment from the urban government, then they also can help to organize a reversal in the next election or organize public outcries of condemnation. In the last resort an effective political weapon may be to threaten revolution, but this may well be self-defeating as it can result in an adverse reaction from other groups.

Thus the government of urban areas is exceedingly complex, and its economic power in recent decades has so increased that this complexity often gives the appearance of confusion. Essentially what is needed is a reorganization of local government, spatially, structurally, and financially. In spatial terms the proliferation of local governments could be reduced by redefining government areas to coincide with their true functional or economic boundaries. In structural terms it would be far easier for the electorate to understand a system that is comparable from one urban area to another. Comparability does not of course imply that all structures should be exactly the same. Finally, the most pressing need involving financial stability depends on an extension of the use of graduated taxation based on income and profits and on the abolition of the property tax and regressive sales tax.

THE URBAN TRANSPORTATION PROBLEM

For most individuals living within urban areas, the urban transportation problem is the major and continuing source of frustration. This frustration is directed in particular toward the automobile, for it is this means of transportation that promises the greatest freedom and excitement, but instead offers a major constraint. The result has been on the one hand passionate outcries against the further proliferation of use of automobiles and the construction of highways, while on the other hand the per capita use of automobiles has been steadily increasing. These passionate outcries often assume an emotional tone:

In short, the American has sacrificed his life as a whole to the motorcar, like someone who, demented with passion, wrecks his home in order to lavish his income on a capricious mistress, who promises the life he can only occasionally enjoy (Mumford, 1963, p. 235).

Less emotionally, but in more specific terms, it is often considered that ". . . the price being paid for the privacy and convenience provided by the automobile is enormous" (Hamilton and Nance, 1969, p. 19). This price includes congestion, high accident rates, air pollution, the dominance of the city by expressways and freeways, and urban sprawl. However, it may well be that we ". . . blame automobiles for too much" (Jacobs, 1961, p. 338), and what is really needed is a clear assessment of urban transportation requirements and trends. To do this we must of course discount one element in all the automobile passion, and that is the advertising-induced perception of it as a fountain of youth, a sex symbol, or a surrogate for power.

Two elements of transportation are available for the movement of cargo (people or goods) around urban areas. One element involves private transportation facilities such as automobiles, trucks, and self-locomotion on foot. The second element, public transportation, is available in a variety of forms such as taxis, buses, or rapid transit. We have previously observed how these facilities are used in the modern North American city and that even when public transportation was dominant there was a tendency for the decentralization of the population. This decentralization has as much to do with the desire for larger living space and more modern housing as anything else. Previous discussion has also indicated that there are two major constituents of the daily flow of people within urban areas. One is the peak travel and the other is the off-peak travel, and the solution to the transportation problem lies in an assessment of both these components.

OFF-PEAK TRAVEL

Off-peak travel involves the greatest number of hours in the day. The people involved in this movement are usually concerned with a wide variety of activities such as shopping or social visiting. With the dispersal of the urban population and the decentralization of many urban activities, the origins and destinations of these trips appear to be extremely dispersed, and as a consequence it can be argued that the best means of transportation available is the automobile. This contention is reinforced by an analysis of personal preferences, which indicate that even when there is public transportation available there is a much greater tendency to use a private means of transportation. Furthermore, it appears that movement around urban areas during these off-peak hours is not really all that difficult. Even in large urban areas, such as Los Angeles, it is quite possible for people to move from one part of the city to another in quite a short space of time using the automobile and freeways.

The only problem that emerges during these off-peak hours involves the provision of parking space in areas where the destinations of many individuals are concentrated. Parking, however, appears to be a necessity for which individuals in an affluent society, such as that in North America, are prepared to pay; and if necessary, to pay quite high rates. Those individuals who cannot afford to pay high rates simply do not frequent or visit only occasionally those areas in which parking is expensive. If business does find that high parking rates reduce the level of demand for its services, then it will have to subsidize the parking or persuade the local government that it is a social good to provide free public parking subsidized through taxes. Furthermore, if the residents of an urban area consider that adequate parking should be provided, and that it should be free, then they too can persuade the local government to provide these facilities.

PEAK TRAVEL

Urban transportation becomes a problem when rush-hour traffic occurs. We have previously noted that this rush-hour traffic occurs for approximately five hours in any given day, and it consists of individuals going to and from work. The problem becomes particularly acute in those areas where there are a large number of work places concentrated in a few locations. Under these conditions the desire of many individuals to use automobiles results in severe congestion on highways and traffic jams of mammoth proportions on the periphery of large central business areas.

It could be considered that an urban area with severe traffic jams has three choices. The first is to permit traffic jams to continue; that is, do nothing. The second is to build more highways, so that there is enough space for vehicles to enter and leave places of work. The third condition is to provide some other means of transportation that will cater to the vast number of individuals that need to be moved.

Do nothing The first alternative, that is "do nothing," has as many repercussions as doing something. For example if nothing is done, the electorate may become so frustrated as to demand reform and vote against the administrative structure that it considers responsible for the situation. The economic impact may also be dramatic, for continuous overcrowding could well cause a stagnation of activity in the area concerned because people will refuse to work and firms to locate or expand within the congested area. Thus the "do nothing" alternative is a negative attitude, and in a philosophical sense is antiurban in that the chief function of urban areas is to encourage and promote contact between people.

Private transportation only The second alternative involves the assumption that people do not want to use public transportation at all. The question that arises then concerns the possibility of building enough freeway and highway space to cater to rush-hour automobile traffic without there being severe jams and long delays. If areas of employment are dispersed, this may well be a solution, though of course it is an expensive solution, particularly when rights-of-way have to be obtained. If people really wish to use their automobiles to go to and from work, it would seem reasonable—given modern construction techniques—to build double-deck and triple-deck expressways (or freeways) in dispersed urban areas such as Los Angeles.

Urban areas with great concentrations of employment in particular locations, such as in central business areas, cannot, however, adopt a private transportation solution because there would be no way possible of building enough freeway space. The question that arises then concerns the degree to which this heavy traffic can be handled while still using as much private transportation as possible.

Personal Transit

One private system recently proposed is called *Personal Transit* which, in effect, operates like a railroad but transports individuals or groups to stations of their own selection. The vehicles used for this transportation are similar to automobiles, but they are electrically propelled and run on tracks called *guideways,* which seem to be rather similar in concept to those used in Autopia in Disneyland. It is envisaged that "the passenger will enter a waiting car at a station, touch his destination on a keyboard and then be carried to the designated station with no further action on his part" (Hamilton and Nance, 1969, p. 21). As the guideways would be designed to carry both private automobiles and public transit cars, it would be possible to extend the system out to the suburbs and control the entire flow and speed through the use of computer controlled flow mechanisms.

For the suburbs it is suggested that individuals could be taken to the guideway stations by using the dial-a-bus system, which would in effect be a large taxi that could be called to a person's home by dialing the rapid-transit station. As the calls come in, a computer would continually optimize the route pattern of the buses in the system. For short-distance travel in high density central areas, the best mode of transportation probably would be on foot or moving sidewalks. This would greatly speed up the flow and reduce the density of traffic and eliminate the need for taxis and buses for short-distance travel. It is suggested that people could be encouraged to use the public transit capsules by charging exorbitantly high amounts to private automobiles using the guideway system and for parking.

Public and private transportation The third alternative is to use public transportation, for this involves the use of facilities that are capable of moving vast numbers of people within very limited spaces and in a short space of time. There are several difficulties, however, that emerge in the use of these systems in North America. The first is that some urban areas that have not developed public transit systems, and particularly mass transit systems, find it very expensive to adopt their use once the urban area has reached sizable proportions. For example, Los Angeles considered spending $2.5 billion on a rapid-transit commuter-railroad system that was rejected by the electorate. Furthermore, it is questionable that such expenditures are justified in large decentralizing urban areas, particularly when the private transit system previously mentioned may well be much less costly to institute. For those urban areas that have mass transit systems, it may well be worthwhile to consider renovating and modernizing these systems out of public funds in order to make them more efficient for modern purposes.

One of the reasons why these systems have to be modernized is that they are considered by the vast majority of individuals to be an inferior form of transportation and are therefore used only when the automobile alternative proves for some reason or another to be impossible. If highways are not constructed to serve areas of dense employment and mass transit facilities are available, then mass transit becomes the only alternative; but this alternative is really the same as the first, the drawbacks of which we have already discussed.

Thus for those urban areas that have mass transit, the aim should be to improve the service, make it more comfortable, and to try to raise it from being an inferior good to being one that is comparable with using the automobile. In the first instance public transit will have to be made more personal, more pleasing and physically safe for travel. But unfortunately, even if this were accomplished, the problem remains that some people dislike traveling with individuals that they consider to be of a lower socio-economic status or of a different ethnic group or color. This latter problem can only be solved through time and really involves the reeducation of the urban population to perceive public transit in a favorable light. Of course elements of personal transit can also be incorporated, such as the dial-a-bus system in the suburbs, which will also help to overcome the refusal of most North Americans to walk more than three blocks.

It therefore seems highly desirable to have a mixture of both public and private transportation within any urban area. This can be viewed as not only an economic-optimum solution but also as a social-optimum solution. Many people in the urban community cannot for some reason or another drive or own automobiles, such as the elderly, schoolchildren, unemployed, and so forth, and these people simply must be provided with a rational alternative. If no alternative is provided, then, in terms of social welfare, some form of private transportation should be provided for them; otherwise a large segment of the urban population will be prevented from moving around the urban area. There have been many designs for the solution of urban transportation problems in different cities, all of which involve the outlay of large sums of money; but in no case are the sums of money excessive when compared with other expenditures by central governments (such as defense).

AIR POLLUTION

On the average, each person uses about 15,000 quarts of air per day. This is ten times the weight of food and water consumed daily by the average person, and it is therefore rather surprising that mass concern and legislative action concerning the control of air pollution is rather recent. Legislation concerning the purification of drinking water and the adulteration of food precede that for air by a number of decades. As a result it has taken catastrophic events of dramatic proportions to publicize the need for cleaner air. This is because people get used to normal air pollution, and the effects of many abnormal incidents of air pollution are never recorded.

One case in America that has been recorded and is cited in many reports of the U.S. Department of Health, Education and Welfare is that of Donora, Pa., a town of some 14,000 people located in a deep valley about 30 miles south of Pittsburgh (Heimann, 1967, pp. 4–5). On the morning of October 27, 1948, the residents of Donora arose to find themselves enveloped in a fog resulting from a temperature inversion. Fogs are not unusual to this area, but this particular fog was quite intense and lasted for four days until the afternoon of October 31. In that period of time there were 17 deaths in a community that normally experienced an average of 2 deaths in an equivalent period at that time of the year. Many persons became ill, experiencing soreness of throat, chest constriction, headache, breathlessness, a burning sensation of the eyes, lacrimation, vomiting, and so on. Elderly individuals proved to be particularly susceptible to this abnormal air pollution, and subsequent autopsies showed acute lung irritation.

Events of this kind are not uncommon in the memories of most urban dwellers, but rarely have they been so carefully recorded and their cause so directly established. However, although it is the eight times above normal death rate that wins headlines and prompts responsible individuals to act, it is the continuing normal despoilation of our air that is of primary concern. It is sad that many of the inhabitants of Los Angeles have become used to being unable to see the hills around them and have accepted watering eyes as part of everyday urban living.

THE SOURCES OF AIR POLLUTION

Pollutants present in the air are normally divided into two categories—primary and secondary. Primary pollutants are those emitted directly from identifiable sources, while secondary pollutants are the result of the interaction of two or more primary components, or the reaction of primary components with normal constituents in the atmosphere. Thus if man is to control air pollution, the source of the primary pollutant must be identified.

Natural air pollution The major sources of air pollutants are man and the natural physical environment (Table 16.1). Man can do very little to control the regular and irregular flow of pollutants derived from volcanoes, breaking seas, and plant pollen, but he can diminish the dust content of the atmosphere derived from windstorms and fires. The construction of roads and buildings in semiarid areas usually results in a removal of the natural vegetation cover, which is difficult to replace. The result is often widespread wind erosion and dust storms. Forest and brush fires are even more hazardous to the atmosphere, for they lay waste to an area for a considerable period of time.

TABLE 16.1. THE SOURCE OF PRIMARY POLLUTANTS

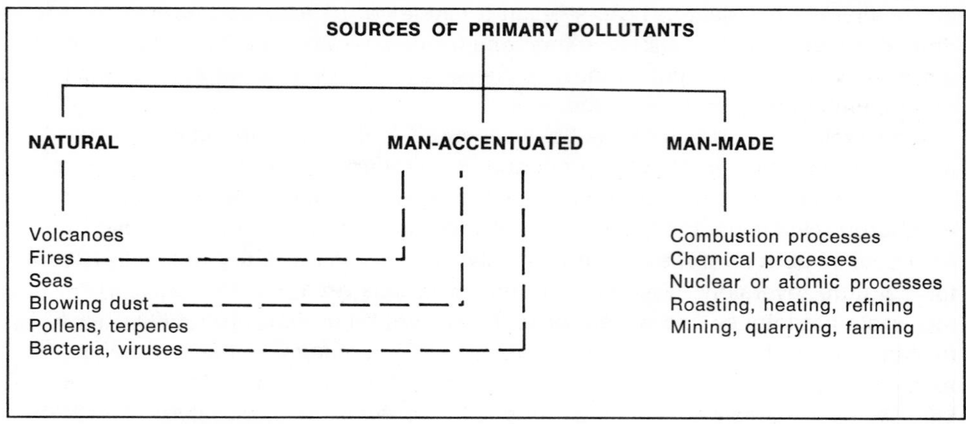

Source: Bryson and Kutzbach (1968), p. 9.

Man-made air pollution Combustion processes are a major source of primary pollutants of both the particle and gaseous variety. The most common forms of particle pollution in urban areas are ash and soot, pollutants that are easily visible for they soil buildings, plants, and people and provide obvious obstructions to sunlight. Very small particles have important secondary effects on the climate of urban areas, for they can act as nuclei for the condensation of atmospheric water vapor, thus causing a further decrease in visibility through mists and fogs. It would therefore appear that urban areas significantly affect their own climates, particularly with respect to fogs (Table 16.2).

Gaseous pollutants are also derived from the combustion of fuels, particularly coal and fuel oil. These gases are primarily sulphur dioxide and various nitrogen oxides, which, by themselves, are fairly harmless though they can and do accelerate erosion and wear when combined with moisture. It is, however, the secondary reaction of these gases with other pollutants in the atmosphere that gives rise to the two best-known types of air pollution. Colloquially, these can be referred to as the "London (England) type" and the "Los Angeles type."

TABLE 16.2. CLIMATIC CHANGES PRODUCED BY CITIES

Climatic element	Comparison with Rural Environs
Clouds	5–10% more
Fog, winter	100% more
Fog, summer	30% more
Precipitation	
total amount	5–10% more
days with 0.2 in. (or less)	10% more

Source: Data from Landsberg (1962), tabulated in Bryson and Kutzbach (1968), p. 11.

The "London Type" of Air Pollution

The London type of air pollution is common to many cities that still have a nineteenth century form of industry and domestic heating, using coal as the energy base. Coal combustion generates quantities of sulphur dioxide, which reacts to form sulphur trioxide in the atmosphere. The sulphur trioxide combines with droplets of water vapor to produce small droplets of sulphuric acid around minute particles of dust and ash. In humid conditions these droplets produce haze and fog and, when they are coated with an oily film of other pollutants, they produce the "pea-soup" fogs for which the London area is infamous. Apart from a reduction in visibility to such an extent that on occasions one cannot see one's outstretched hand, these acid water droplets are an irritant to the bronchial tubes and are highly corrosive.

The "Los Angeles Type" of Air Pollution

The Los Angeles type (or the oxidation type) of air pollution is directly related to the widespread use of the internal combustion engine, which, even in its modern form, incurs a loss of about 15 percent in fuel energy. Haagen-Smit (1964, p. 7) suggests that this represents an annual loss of about $3 billion, which can be interpreted as excess use of $3 billion worth of energy fuel. Through this loss the internal combustion engine releases large amounts of nitrogen oxides and hydrocarbons which, together with other pollutants, incur a photochemical reaction in sunlight to produce smog. From Figure 16.1 it can be observed that one of the key elements in this reaction is the group of hydrocarbons. Smog obscures views, damages plants, irritates eyes and throats, has an unpleasant odor, increases corrosion, and may well adversely affect health.

Thus it would appear that the principal man-made causes of air pollution are:

1. Heavy industry, such as iron and zinc smelting and steel manufacturing, which produce dust, and iron, zinc, and copper oxides
2. The internal combustion engine, which produces nitrogen dioxides and a variety of hydrocarbons

FIG. 16.1. THE LOS ANGELES TYPE OF AIR POLLUTION. (*Source:* Haagen-Smit, 1964, p. 30.)

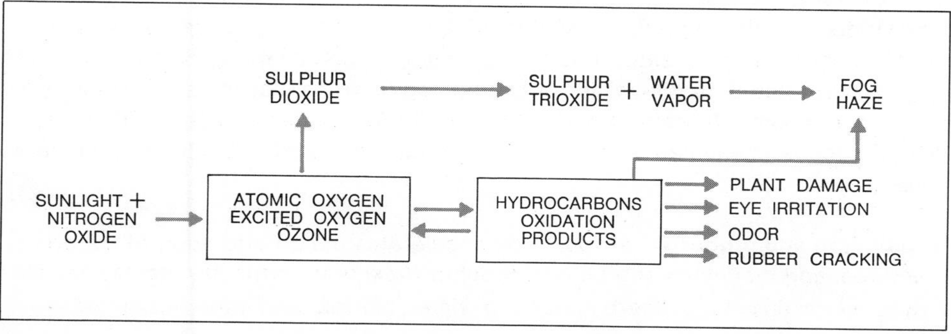

3. General coal combustion, which in some areas adds greatly to the quantity of suspended particles in the atmosphere

4. Petroleum refining, which produces hydrocarbons and suspended oily particulates

Thus the causes and the sources of much urban air pollution are well known.

THE EFFECTS OF AIR POLLUTION

We have previously referred to some of the effects of air pollution, particularly those effects that are dramatic and evident to the urban dweller. However, studies in Great Britain, Japan, and the U.S.S.R., as well as the United States have cataloged a variety of effects of normal everyday air pollution on health, agriculture, property, safety, and the weather. Some of these effects can be measured in financial terms, others have to be viewed in a nonmonetary or aesthetic sense.

Air pollution and health The major effect of air pollution may well be on health. The cost of illness, decreased strength, and a shortened lifespan cannot be measured in dollars, but there is sufficient evidence to indicate that normal air pollution does adversely affect man's health. In particular there is strong evidence to suggest that air pollution is associated with (1) acute nonspecific upper respiratory disease, (2) chronic bronchitis, (3) chronic constrictive ventilatory disease, (4) pulmonary emphysema, (5) bronchial asthma, and (6) lung cancer. There are many other diseases or illnesses, which may also be associated with air pollution, but the evidence is slim in this respect.

Air pollution and agriculture The effects of air pollution on agriculture vary according to the variety of plants and the mix of pollutants in the atmosphere. Some of the classic cases occur with respect to sulphur dioxide at Copper Hill, Tenn., and in the state of Washington from the smelter at Trail, British Columbia. Ozone has been found to affect grape leaves in California, tobacco leaves in the eastern part of the United States, and has injured spinach, alfalfa, rye, barley, orchard grass, tobacco, petunias, radishes, clover, beans, parsley, and so forth in New Jersey.

Fluorides, which are primarily of industrial origin, have also caused extensive damage, particularly to cattle foraging on fluoride contaminated vegetation. Hydrogen fluoride in particular is very damaging to crops, particularly corn and peaches. Economic losses from air pollution on agriculture are very difficult to measure, the best estimate available being around hundreds of millions of dollars a year.

Air pollution and property Air pollution accelerates the deterioration of materials, structures, and machines of all kinds. Sulphur dioxide in particular attacks metals and converts limestone, marble, roofing slate, mortar, and other carbonates containing stone to water soluble sulphates, which can then be leached away by rain. Dust and ash settles on buildings and enters all structures, including homes, and has to be continually removed if the property value is to be maintained. Ozone in smog causes excessive cracking in rubber, as well as deteriorating dyes, fabrics, and other synthetic material. The total cost of this type of pollution, including its depreciating effect on property values, is estimated to be about $65 per person per year, which, in the United States, represents an annual cost of over $11 billion.

The effect of normal air pollution on urban areas in North America is therefore very high. Dramatic accidents involving instances of rapidly recurring fogs on highways and airline landing lanes are well documented. More difficult to estimate is the aesthetic and psychological effect of air pollution on man. No real permanent health effects have been demonstrated from smog-induced stinging and tearing of the eyes, but there is no doubt that it is uncomfortable and disturbing. Dirty buildings, smog-filled skies, dying flowers, and rapidly depreciating property values certainly detract from the variety of pleasures of urban living.

SOLUTIONS TO AIR POLLUTION

The two major causes of urban air pollution therefore appear to be industry and automobiles. Pollution from both these sources can be controlled if sufficient emphasis is placed on legislative controls and preventative measures. Before 1940, Pittsburgh was a classic case of a city polluted by industrial wastes (Friedlander, 1965, pp. 13–14). For forty years Pittsburgh had relied upon the self control efforts of industry to solve the problem, but the results of self regulation were negligible. As a result Pittsburgh adopted city and county ordinances against air pollution from industry and domestic sources, and the results are outstanding. In 1965 the average sootfall in Pittsburgh was only 30 tons per square mile per month, compared with 60 tons per square mile per month in New York City.

The methods used to achieve this reduction in air pollution were undoubtedly costly to the operators. Smoke-control devices (such as the electrostatic precipitator) had to be installed on industrial stacks, and home owners had to use smokeless fuels or install gas or oil furnaces. With the exception of installations in private residences, all fuel-burning equipment is subject to periodic inspection by the local bureau of air pollution control.

Pollution in Pittsburgh has therefore been controlled by strong local action, but pollution control from industry in other areas has not been introduced as effectively. For example, the Chicago area has been plagued by a continuous barrage of soot and smoke from the steel mills of Hammond and Gary, which are located 15 miles to the south in northern Indiana. On many days of the year the sky in this area is black and the sootfall tremendous. The present average monthly sootfall is 43 tons per square mile; but on many days of the year when the smoke from steel mills is wafted in the direction of Chicago, the rate of sootfall is three to four times greater. Although the steel producers in the Calumet region of Chicago are installing $50 million worth of control equipment, the steel mills of Northern

Indiana cannot be coerced in the same way, for they are in another state. Thus cases of interregional and interstate air pollution can only be effectively controlled by federal action.

The contribution of automobiles to air pollution has been shown to be quite large, particularly with respect to the formation of smog. The key elements emitted by automobiles in this case are nitrogen oxides and unburned hydrocarbons. So far state laws, for example, those in California, have been concerned with eliminating the amount of unburned carbons by requiring the addition of a few simple devices (such as afterburners) to cars. The problem of nitrogen oxide emission has not, however, been tackled, though further engine modifications could radically reduce the emission of this pollutant as well. Figure 16.2 indicates how this combined approach could radically reduce smog to a fairly tolerable level. There is little doubt that, if the automobile industry were prepared to spend a fraction of the amount on engine modifications that it spends on advertising to reduce those emissions, the problem of urban air pollution would be greatly reduced, though not eliminated.

Thus urban air pollution exists because man insists on treating the atmosphere as a sewer. The question, of course, arises concerning whether people are prepared to pay to have clean air. In many cases it appears that man is prepared to accept dirty air as part of the price of urban living, and it may well be that after a while he gets used to it. It must be remembered, however, that air pollution, though at its greatest in urban areas is really a global problem. We all breathe air from the atmosphere, and as the population of the world expands it is a finite resource that is being consumed and polluted at an ever-increasing rate.

FIG. 16.2. AIR POLLUTION IN LOS ANGELES. THE SCALE OF SMOG LEVELS ON THE *Y*-AXIS IS A RATIO WITH RESPECT TO THE 1947 LEVEL WHICH EQUALS 1; 2 IS TWICE THE 1947 LEVEL, AND 3 IS THREE TIMES THE 1947 LEVEL. ON THE GRAPH, (1) INDICATES THE PROJECTED SMOG POLLUTION LEVEL WITHOUT ANY NEW CONTROLS, (2) INDICATES THE PROJECTED SMOG LEVEL WITH ONLY HYDROCARBON CONTROLS, AND (3) INDICATES THE EXPECTED SMOG LEVEL WITH BOTH HYDROCARBON AND NITROGEN OXIDE CONTROLS. (*Source:* Haagen-Smit, 1964, p. 28.)

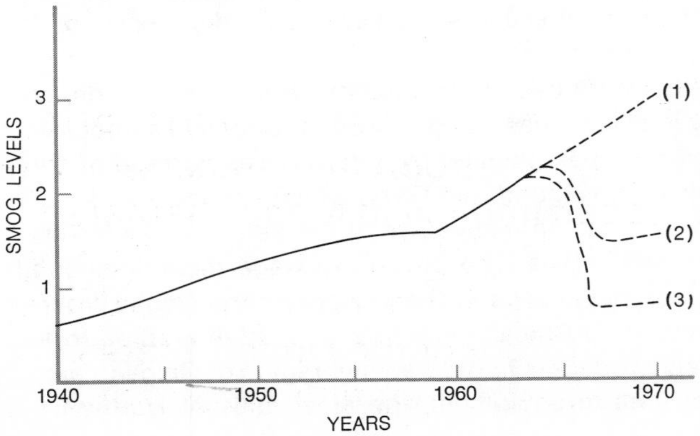

“MEGALOPOLIS AND POLITICAL FRAGMENTATION”

The trend toward the growth of large-scale metropolitan areas, which has been implicit in many chapters of this book, has reached its most extreme form along the northeast seaboard of the United States. Here, accelerating urbanization has resulted in an almost continuous urban, suburban, and exurban sprawl extending from New Hampshire southward to northern Virginia, and from the Atlantic Coast inland to the Appalachians. This is urban North America par excellence. No other part of North America has such high average densities over so wide an area. And no other urban concentration has a comparable role in the affairs of North America or even the rest of the world. As Gottmann (1961, p. 3) points out: "Here has been developed a kind of supremacy in politics, in economics, and possibly even in cultural activities, seldom before attained by an area of this size." To capture the very special significance of this mammoth urban region, Gottmann (1961) referred to it as *megalopolis*.

In using megalopolis in the title for this chapter, we do so more for what it symbolizes than for what it is. The term *megalopolis* has become, the world over, synonymous with urban growth of supermetropolitan proportions. For many people it conjures up the evils of large-scale urban growth; and there is no doubt that today many of society's most difficult problems are associated with, either directly or indirectly, with what is thought of as megalopolitan urban development. For many of these people, megalopolis is viewed as a cancer of the landscape and a menace to civilization.

But, for Gottmann, megalopolis meant something else. He saw the urbanized northeastern seaboard through more rose-colored glasses. For him, megalopolis was the "cradle of a new order in the organization of inhabited space," although he was the first to admit that the "new order" was—and still is—far from orderly. In this chapter, then, we will discuss some of the major characteristics of megalopolis, and use this area as a framework for continuing the discussion of selected problems associated with accelerating urbanization. For the most part, attention will be focused on problems at the regional rather than at the local scale.

THE DIMENSIONS OF MEGALOPOLIS

The area Gottmann delimited as megalopolis is outlined in Figure 17.1. Its main axis stretches nearly 600 miles from Massachusetts Bay in the north to the valley of the Potomac in the south. Varying in width between 30 and 100 miles, it extends over an area of more than 53,575 square miles, in which a population of about 37 millions was concentrated in 1960. Hence in megalopolis, about 20.0 percent of the total population of the coterminous United States is concentrated on 2 percent of its land area.

Within this area are five of America's largest metropolitan regions—Boston, New York, Philadelphia, Baltimore, and Washington—besides another dozen or so smaller ones ranging in population from 200,000 to 800,000. Although not a continuously built-up urban region, the overall intensity of urban development means that population densities are invariably high. In 1950 the average density was 596 persons per square mile. In New Jersey, population density had reached the high figure of 800 per square mile, the highest of any state in the nation. Outside of this area, in 1960 no other state could boast densities of more than

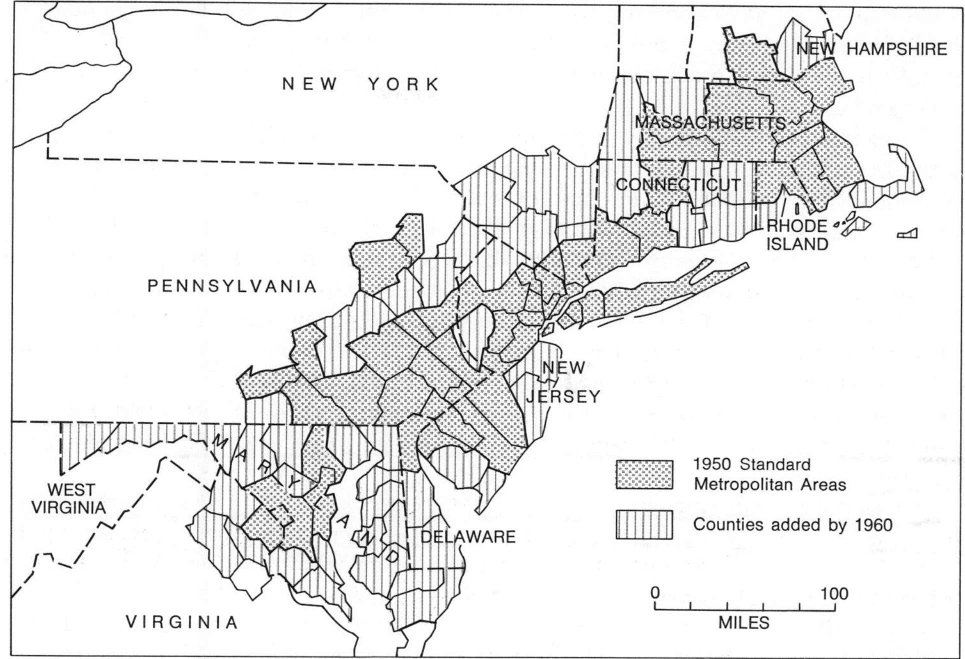

FIG. 17.1. MEGALOPOLIS AS DELIMITED BY GOTTMANN. (*Source:* Gottmann, 1961, Fig. 3.)

300 per square mile, and even in the rapidly developing urban parts of western California, in an area of comparable size, population densities only reached about 200 per square mile. There are in fact only one or two areas of comparable size in the whole world in which people live at such high levels of concentration.

This high level of concentration of population in megalopolis reflects the wealth of economic opportunity the region contains. It also reflects the advantages of an early start; this we noted in Chapter 2. For as the resources of the interior were opened up after 1800, so the fortunes of the larger cities on the northeastern seaboard grew bigger; and collectively they took over control of the greater part of the developing national economy. Here, then, is a supreme example of growth breeding growth. By 1950, megalopolis provided employment for 12.8 million people—about 23 percent of the total number of persons employed in the entire nation. As Gottmann (1961, p. 48) pointed out, there are not many nations in the whole world today with labor forces much larger than this.

The continually expanding labor market of the region has been supported and maintained despite the fact that the area is not exceptionally well endowed with either good agricultural resources or significant mineral deposits. From very early times, the labor market was oriented to employment in trading, servicing, and manufacturing. As such, the labor market has traditionally been geared toward the upper end of the spectrum of employment opportunities and has catered on the whole to the more highly skilled technical and professional workers.

White-collar jobs have generally been more important than blue-collar ones. As a result, per capita incomes are generally among the highest in the country; and megalopolis has for some time been the largest market in the United States for well-paid labor.

For example, in 1968 the average personal income of Americans was estimated to be $3,412. Sixteen states and Washington, D.C., had per capita incomes exceeding this national average, and of these, nine were wholly or partly within megalopolis as defined by Gottmann in 1960. In fact, New Hampshire is the only state partly included in megalopolis in which per capita incomes are below the average for the country as a whole. Hence, with such high per capita figures as $4,516 (Washington, D.C.), $3,907 (New Jersey), $4,133 (New York), and $3,796 (Massachusetts), the average per capita income for residents in megalopolis was in 1968 probably well over $3,750. The people of megalopolis are, on paper at least, without a doubt the richest group of 40 million people in the world. As a group they are also, on average, the best educated, best fed, best housed, and best serviced.

Megalopolis is also a center of power, wealth, and knowledge of unprecedented size. It is the nation's biggest concentration of decision-making activities. Although cities like Chicago, San Francisco, and Detroit are important policy-making centers at the regional level, and for certain specialized activities at the national scale, they are matched and even excelled, by cities like Boston, Philadelphia, and Baltimore in megalopolis. But no cities on the entire North American continent can match the supreme decision-making roles on both the political and economic sphere of Washington, D.C., and New York City. New York City alone comprises the largest concentration of financial power and industrial management the world has ever seen, which together with the banking, insurance, and corporation headquarters located in other major cities of the region makes the central axis of megalopolis "the financial and managerial Main Street of the modern world" (Gottmann, 1961, p. 54). This concentration becomes all the more impressive when we consider the concentration of managerial offices for advertising, publishing, the mass media, and the facilities devoted to scientific research, which are also located along the axis.

And yet in spite of this concentration of wealth, knowledge, technical know-how, and decision-making capacity, the metropolitan regions that make up megalopolis are bedeviled with a set of social, economic, and governmental problems of unprecedented magnitudes. Here, the scale of the problems associated with supermetropolitan growth have reached their climax; problems which, paradoxically, have stemmed from the rapid economic and social advances by which the distinctiveness of the region was created. The nature of these problems is now well documented and does not need lengthy discussion here. They are generally associated with deprivation, deterioration, congestion, and fragmentation—all of which for the most part stem directly or indirectly from the extreme levels of population concentration in the region.

Perhaps the most intractable of all these problems is that associated with deprivation and the social strains caused by the continuance of an undereducated, underskilled, underpaid, and underprivileged minority. Thus although in aggregate the people of megalopolis may be among the best paid, best fed, best housed, and best serviced in the world, there remain within the region large groups of people for whom living conditions fall far below the average. For these, perhaps the fundamental characteristic of the urban environment is that of deterioration, which is expressed most vividly spatially in the form of the ghetto and the slum. The problems of an aging and dilapidated housing stock, shortages of open space and adequate recreational facilities, and the general running-down of social facilities have reached extreme proportions in the older, central cities of the region, and particularly in New York City.

In part, the deterioration of a great deal of the urban environment in the central areas of the large megalopolitan cities is closely bound up with the problems arising from increasing congestion. This would appear to be one of the basic characteristics of megalopolis. It is expressed in a variety of ways ranging from high residential densities and overcrowding, traffic snarls on the ground and increasingly in the air, to overfilled parks and beaches. Although the problems associated with congestion are naturally greatest in the innermost parts of the metropolitan areas, it is becoming increasingly clear that this is also likely to emerge as a problem of serious proportions in the areas of sprawling suburbs.

It is largely in terms of the spread of suburbs that fragmentation has become a major problem in the region. For the decentralization of population outward from the core cities has meant a corresponding decentralization of government. The proliferation of local governmental entities and the resulting fragmentation of decision making are therefore two of the major characteristics of present-day metropolitan structure. These are problems because the public sector is increasingly relied upon to finance the provision of a wide range of urban services and to solve pressing urban problems. However, the very nature of many of these services and problems is such that, within an economically and socially integrated metropolitan community, they cannot be handled effectively by a proliferation of local governments acting in isolation. From the governmental point of view, the metropolitan whole should be very much more than the sum of its administrative parts. And because it is not, many of the pressing problems have become increasingly difficult to solve. This is particularly the case with those problems that can be thought of as being regional as distinct from purely local in scale.

FRAGMENTATION OF POLITICAL STRUCTURE

Although from a variety of standpoints megalopolis can be considered as forming a single, large uniform region, organizationally it is not. One reason for this is that it extends across the boundaries of ten states and the District of Columbia. Nested within these are 117 counties and many cities, all of which are endowed with the power to govern, and between which there has been a long tradition of non-cooperation. In fact, it could be argued that the competition between states and between the central cities they contain has been a major factor underlying the distinctive economic development of the region.

In addition to this political fragmentation, megalopolis is also fragmented to a marked degree economically. Despite the many strong and varied inter-relationships that bind together the various parts of the region, megalopolis is nevertheless characterized by a well-developed polynuclear structure. Economic, and to a lesser extent, social organization focuses on the five metropolitan centers. As a result, each of these forms a fairly distinct economic subsystem within the region as a whole. Hence the problem of political fragmentation can be discussed at two levels: at that of the metropolitan regions themselves, and at the higher level of the megalopolis that together they form. At present, it is the problems associated with the former metropolitan regions that are the most pressing and with which we will consequently be concerned here. And these problems are perhaps most vividly illustrated by, and certainly have been most extensively documented for, the largest of the metropolitan regions—that based on New York City.

THE NEW YORK METROPOLITAN REGION

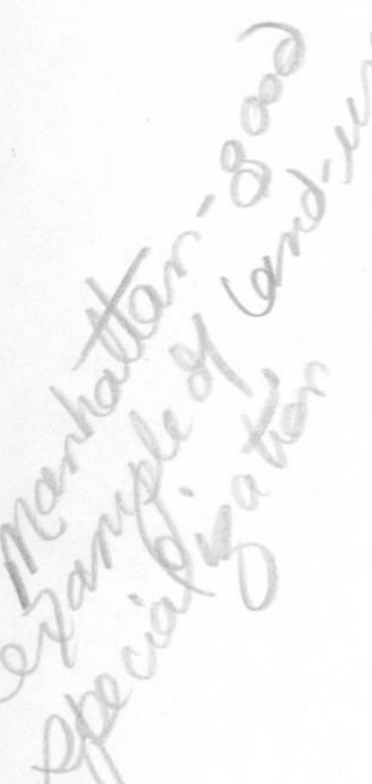

As long ago as 1922, a private organization—the Regional Plan Association of New York—was set up to study the social and economic problems of the New York region. Today, nearly fifty years later, this is still the only public or private body seriously concerned with studying the planning problems of America's largest metropolitan region. The metropolitan region as delimited by this organization is shown in Figure 17.2. It covers an area of 6,914 square miles and includes 22 counties in parts of three states. In 1960 this region had a population of 16,139,000, and it has been gaining in population at the rate of roughly 200,000 per year since 1950. Densities of population range from about 77,000 per square mile at the core of Manhattan to about 200 per square mile in the counties at the periphery. The overall density was, in 1960, 2,337 persons per square mile.

The boundaries of the region were delimited partly on the basis of commuting watersheds and partly by the way in which the outer parts of the region come under the influence of the center. In this way, then, the New York metropolitan region shown in Figure 17.2 is very much a functional whole—a huge social and economic complex centered essentially on the 9⅓ square miles comprising the CBD of Manhattan. This area, one about the same size as Kennedy International Airport, had a daily working population of 2,475,000—35 percent of all the employees in the region in 1956.

This high level of concentration of employment at the center of the region is just one reflection of a much broader feature of the metropolitan structure: land-use specialization. As the scale of urban growth increases, so specialization in the use of urban space becomes essential, and the opportunities for it to occur become greater. But the corollary of land use specialization is interdependence; the various specialized parts of the region become increasingly more intertwined and dependent on each other. The most obvious example of this interdependence is the daily flow of commuters from residential suburban communities to jobs in the central cities; but this is just one of a wide variety of kinds of interaction between the region's different parts.

Yet despite this natural trend toward increasing levels of social and economic

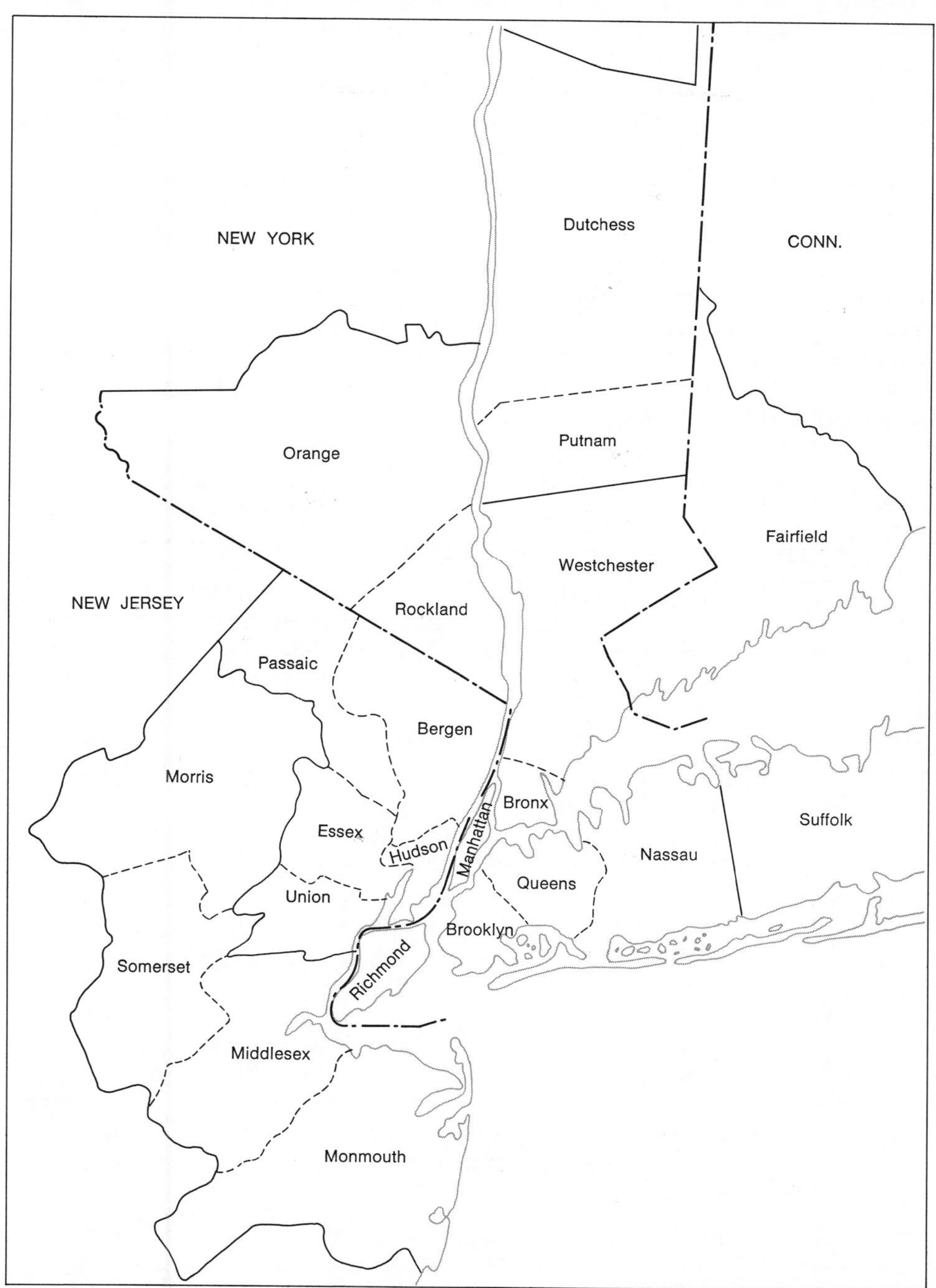

FIG. 17.2. THE NEW YORK METROPOLITAN REGION. (*Source:* Hoover and Vernon, 1959, Chart 3.)

interdependence within the region, the decisions concerning land use specialization, the responsibilities for maintaining law and order, of providing schools, water, and sewage systems, and the task of ensuring the continued well-being of the total urban environment remain gloriously or ridiculously fragmented. In concluding his intensive study of the political economy of the region, Wood (1961) came to the conclusion that here one could observe ". . . one of the great unnatural wonders of the world; that is, a governmental arrangement perhaps more complicated than any other that mankind has yet contrived or allowed to happen" (Wood, 1961, p. 1). He was of course referring to the fact that the metropolitan region governed itself in 1960 by means of 1,467 distinct political units, each one of which has its own power to raise and spend money in areas of jurisdiction which have developed more by chance than design. Although this state of political fragmentation can be defended on the grounds of continuing a democratic tradition of home rule, it can also be deplored as being hopelessly unsuited to the realities of modern metropolitan life.

The proliferation of local governments Government at the local level in this as in other metropolitan regions consists of two sorts; the elected governments of cities, counties, boroughs, towns, villages, and so on, and the ad-hoc special purpose bodies such as school, water, and fire districts. The latter usually represent unions of several local municipalities, and both sorts of governmental unit have jurisdiction over relatively small geographic areas. Hence at the local level, the decision-making apparatus is quite varied and extremely complicated. At the center is New York City and the five boroughs it comprises. Outside of this core to the north and east are the seven suburban counties of New York state plus Fairfield County in Connecticut. Together these included 866 different governmental entities. To the west and south, the nine counties in New Jersey include another 606 different local government units.

The powers and functions of these many different entities vary considerably from state to state, and especially between New York and New Jersey. In New York, there are no hard and fast rules concerning the functions local governments perform. Outside New York City, the counties generally have the major responsibilities over things such as tax assessment and collection, highways, the courts, public works, and planning programs. But where cities exist within county borders, as for example with Yonkers and White Plains in Westchester County, almost all functions are normally carried out by the local municipality. The towns and villages usually have more limited functions, an important one of which is their control over various aspects of zoning and land use. The functions of the different governmental units and the allocation of duties are far more regular in New Jersey. Here the county is generally less important and, subject to variations in population size, the boroughs, towns, villages, townships, and cities all perform roughly the same set of public services. Again, an important one of these is the control of land use.

The variations in functions that exist among the different kinds of political units in the region are naturally accompanied by other discrepancies. Differences in structure, population size, areal extent, tax and spending levels, and political tradition all add reinforcement to the pattern of political fragmentation. Moreover, since each body is as a rule more concerned with preserving its own autonomy than anything else—and quite understandably so—it is perhaps not surprising to find that the system does not generate common policies or programs for the benefit of the region as a whole.

Of course not all of the problems within metropolitan areas require region-wide policies and solutions. Many problems are of a purely local nature, and the existing system of local government is largely capable of handling them. It is important, therefore, to distinguish between the provision of local as distinct from regional or area-wide services. An attempt to do this is made in Table 17.1. Since it is impossible to draw a fast line between the two categories, the various functions and services have been ranked in the table on an impressionistic scale from most local to least local. There is of course nothing sacrosanct about this ranking, and as Bollens and Schmandt (1965) have pointed out, it should only be viewed as a rough approximation of the possible order that is useful for purposes of discussion.

Conflicting programs The need for region-wide policies within metropolitan areas thus becomes increasingly more urgent as one moves down the list of urban functions given in Table 17.1. But it is in connection with these that the friction and noncooperation between local governments is often most pronounced. As a result, major programs undertaken by local governments frequently tend to work against the interests of the wider region rather than in harmony with them. Of the many examples that could be chosen to illustrate this, that of the control (or perhaps better, the noncontrol) over land use is a good one to indicate the conflict of interests between local communities and the region. For

TABLE 17.1. RANK ORDER OF URBAN SERVICES ON THE BASIS OF THEIR LOCAL IMPORTANCE

	Rank	Function
	1	Fire protection
MOST LOCAL	2	Public education
	3	Refuse collection and disposal
	4	Libraries
	5	Police
	6	Health
	7	Urban renewal
	8	Housing
	9	Parks and recreation
	10	Public welfare
	11	Hospitals and medical care
	12	Transportation
	13	Planning
LEAST LOCAL	14	Water supply—sewage disposal
	15	Air pollution control

Source: Advisory Commission on Intergovernmental Relations (1963), p. 11.

as we noted in the previous chapter, property is one of the basic sources of community income. Since in this case property means land and the buildings placed upon it, it is land that becomes one of the basic resources for providing the revenue to pay for the ever-growing set of community services. Although property taxes are not the only means by which community revenue is generated, they are still in absolute terms one of the most important.

Hence one of the principal ways in which local governments can respond to their continually increasing financial difficulties is to use their powers of planning and zoning to develop the use of their land as advantageously as possible. In this context, it is the mix of residential, commercial, and industrial land uses that counts. Different types of land use demand different kinds of services and, at the same time, are capable of making different-sized contributions to the public purse. Thus, whereas commercial and industrial uses are often able to contribute in taxes two or three times the cost of services they receive, residential property of average standard pays only a fraction of the cost of public services it requires.

It is because of this that a community with a well-balanced land use pattern stands to gain most. The same holds true for the broader metropolitan region. The problem is, however, that this desirable mix of land uses must pertain to the total urban complex and not necessarily to each administrative part of it. Yet the financial structuring of urban areas more or less forces local communities to strive to achieve a kind of development that produces more in tax revenue than it costs in public services. And usually this can only be achieved by pursuing land use policies that counter those policies that should exist in the metropolitan area as an entity.

The power to guide growth through planning and zoning is, therefore, an extremely important instrument of local government. Unlike the manipulation of fiscal policies from which more immediate returns may often be obtained, the rewards from zoning practices may often, however, be a long time in coming. As a result, there exists a conflict of interests between the policies aimed at short-term gains for individual communities, and the much longer term gains for the complete region. For in the attempt to speed up the process whereby benefits are derived from the use of land, communities may make decisions that are in their immediate interests but run counter to the proper development of the wider urban environment. It is largely as a result of such decisions that, for example, islands of high-value residential property become surrounded by industrial sections, or "enclaves of industrial activity persist in areas apparently economically unsuitable for their location" (Wood, 1961, p. 76) to result in many irrationalities in the overall metropolitan land use pattern.

With this goal of attracting what are for them the most beneficial land uses, a kind of "beggar thy neighbor" policy has become a significant feature of much local government behavior in metropolitan areas. This is especially so in attempts to bolster sagging tax bases by attracting industry to a community. The inevitable community boosting and the often exaggerated claims of locational advantage and sense of political power that go with such strategies, have frequently led in the past to open hostility between neighboring areas. Thus, strong pressures build up to go it alone.

This strategy is well documented by the planning activities in the New Jersey portion of the metropolitan region, although similar examples could be taken at random from any of the metropolitan regions within megalopolis. Here, in New Jersey, where the tendency for a large number of fairly small governmental units prevails, and where the potential coordinating role of the county is restricted by its limited powers, a complete mixture of planning programs based on a proliferation of zoning ordinances has been developed. In many cases these are unrealistic; in others, simply impracticable. After a careful consideration of the multiplicity of planning reports in the area, each with its detailed summaries and predictions of land use, movement patterns, highway needs, and open space requirements, Wood (1961, p. 106) concluded that

> . . . the divergencies between the general forces of growth (in the region) and the particularistic response to these trends (in the counties) become apparent. Land use measures appear more and more designed to attract a certain business plant or to exclude residential houses which do not pay their way, or to capitalize on a windfall of an exclusive development which might come a municipality's way.

It is largely as a result of the community-centered form of behavior represented by these strategies that a segregation of resources and needs has emerged within metropolitan regions today. In general, the older central cities have the greatest financial needs, while many of the newer suburban developments have the resources. The irony is that these resources and the consequent well-being of the communities with them usually stem directly from the economic opportunities provided at locations within the central cities. But not all suburban communities are so lucky; and there are many that struggle to satisfy their extensive needs that they cannot finance without turning to outside sources of aid, such as the state or the federal government. The problem is no longer one between central cities and suburbs, but now "involves all units and their fiscal position in the metropolitan matrix" (Bollens and Schmandt, 1965, p. 367).

At the heart of the metropolitan land use problem is, then, the dilemma of local community finances. Toward a partial solution of this is the need to regulate the high degree of freedom of choice in the allocation of land for various uses and to reconcile the heretofore independent community actions. For it is becoming increasingly clear that the risks of inconsistent patterns of land use and community financing have become increasingly high in a system of fragmented government, which neglects the facts of interdependence within the total metropolitan community (Chinitz, 1965).

The solution to this problem obviously requires careful consideration. Clearly, there is a need to formulate some kind of region-wide public policy in which the control over land use is but one of the many important ingredients. It would appear, however, that little opportunity exists for this within the present system of local government. For within the New York metropolitan region as well as in many others

> Each government is preoccupied with its own problems, and collectively the governments are not prepared to formulate general policies for guiding economic development or to make generalized responses to the financial pressures generated by urbanization. They are neither in a position to establish and enforce public criteria for appropriate conditions of growth nor to provide public services that the private sector requires on a regionwide basis. By their organization, financing, and philosophy, they foreswear the opportunity for the exercise of these larger powers (Wood, 1961, p. 113).

TOWARD METROPOLITAN GOVERNMENT

Wood's conclusions from the study of the political economy of the New York metropolitan region are perhaps a little pessimistic and harsh in view of the increasing extent of intergovernment cooperation taking place in metropolitan areas. Nevertheless, the fact remains that much of this has not led to any drastic reduction in the scale of metropolitan problems, which still loom as large as ever. In fact, in view of the obvious difficulties created by the proliferation of local governments, the remarkable thing is that major disasters have, so far, been averted. The question remains, however, of how long they can be forestalled. As disruptible powers mount, it is clear that some kind of change in the governmental pattern is needed within metropolitan regions. To this end, some argue that public finances lie at the root of the problem. Given a rational distribution of funds, it is felt that the problem would sort itself out without any major change in governmental structure.

Although this may be true to a certain extent, it would most probably only result in a postponement of other crises. For the problem is not only one of the distribution of funds but also one of lack of coordination in the provision of region-wide services and facilities. It does not follow that an equable distribution of money would bring about cooperation in the way it is spent. Because of this, others argue that more fundamental changes in metropolitan government are needed to establish an administrative machinery capable of effectively mobilizing the metropolitan region's resources. These are the advocates of some form of metropolitan government. To this end a number of alternative strategies are open.

VOLUNTARY COOPERATION

The simplest approach to solving the problem of intercommunity needs is that of a voluntary association between local governments within the metropolitan regions. Since World War II this has been promoted by a variety of public and private bodies and organizations as an effective mechanism for solving problems without relinquishing local control. Voluntary cooperation is mainly viewed, then, as a defensive strategy against more thorough forms of government reorganization within metropolitan areas. Two forms of voluntary association may be recognized.

Service agreements The first of these associations relates to the provision of specific services and functions; for example, sewage disposal, flood control, libraries, parks and recreation, and so on. Variations of this theme include the provision of a service facility by one community which is shared with adjoining ones (such as water), the joint operation of a facility by two or more governments, and a more restricted kind of cooperation based on mutual aid during times of serious difficulties (e.g., fires). Municipalities have to date been the most numerous participants in these forms of interlocal cooperation—either in cooperation with each other or in association with higher levels of government, particularly the county. So far, this kind of approach has been most successful in the provision of services at the lower end of the spectrum in Table 17.1, such as libraries or public health facilities. It has not commonly been undertaken in the provision of common facilities such as water supply or sewage disposal.

Although such voluntary schemes as these are a step in the right direction, many are essentially temporary in nature. Frequently they amount to little more than a kind of stand-by arrangement between governments for mutual aid at times of crisis. The piecemeal nature of most service agreements means that they would have to be extensively operated throughout metropolitan regions if they were ever to become an effective solution to region-wide problems. Moreover, since they are founded for the most part on the provision of a service for money, many communities are unable to take advantage of the opportunities available because of their already inadequate financial resources. Consequently, this form of agreement appears to be better suited to the provision of local services than to region-wide facilities. It is judged by many as a weak approach to the problem of governmental reorganization (Bollens and Schmandt, 1965).

Metropolitan councils The second approach to voluntary cooperation is more recent and dates effectively from the mid-fifties. It is based on the formation of metropolitan councils. So far, seven of these have been created, including those in the metropolitan regions of Detroit, New York, Philadelphia, and the San Francisco Bay Area. The structure of these councils varies from one to the other, but in general they do not have any governmental powers. Rather they function as multipurpose advisory bodies to make recommendations concerning cooperation and coordination toward the solution of metropolitan problems.

Their main strength is the forum they provide for discussing problems and acting as a unified spokesman in these matters with branches of state and federal government, who are relied upon increasingly to finance suggested programs. However, they lack bite; and their real effectiveness is limited by their general lack of power. In fact for many this lack of power is their strong point. When, for example, some years ago an attempt was made to give the metropolitan regional council of New York a measure of power and some financial support through state legislation, there was some fierce opposition. Cries of plans "made in Moscow" were heard, and a real fear was expressed that the council would become a supergovernment. As a result, this particular council is now more palatable but less effective than ever.

GOVERNMENT

TWO-TIER APPROACHES

The weaknesses of the various forms of voluntary associations as approaches to solving metropolitan-wide problems has led recently to alternative schemes. These are based on the premise that local needs and services should be handled at the local level and that only certain kinds of broader, area-wide functions should be handled by various forms of metropolitan government. Hence schemes in this category are based on a two-tier arrangement in which the concept of federation is often an important one. Three types of two-tier approaches may be recognized.

Metropolitan districts The first of these approaches, the metropolitan districts, is the mildest of the three. Although they may operate over the entire metropolitan region or major parts of it, they are normally restricted in scope to the handling of one service or a very small number of activities. They have been most frequently established to provide area-wide coordination of sewage disposal and port facilities, although they commonly exist to look after airports, mass transit facilities, parks and recreational land, and water supply. Despite their restricted functional scope, and perhaps because of it, metropolitan districts have an impressive record for alleviating pressing metropolitan problems with which they are concerned.

This record is in part responsible for their relatively rapid spread, and in 1965 there were about 100 such districts in the United States (Bollens and Schmandt, 1965, p. 441). However, other factors in their widespread adoption have been the fact that they can be set up relatively simply and that they are not generally empowered to levy taxes. Most metropolitan districts are therefore profit-making concerns, which raise funds through tolls and service charges. As such their scope is restricted to those functions that can be made to pay—although the very nature of these is that they do not. Thus the Port of New York Authority has a greater amount of outstanding debt than most states. This restricted role is commonly the basis of arguments against the metropolitan district approach, for in being confined to only one function, a fragmented approach to the solution of metropolitan-wide problems is said to exist. Other arguments against them are that they are too remote from the people for whom they provide services and that in many cases they are not representative of the people and communities they serve. Despite these objections there is probably little doubt that metropolitan districts will continue to play a useful role in solving area-wide problems.

The comprehensive urban county plan The second important form of two-tier government, the comprehensive urban county plan, is based on the reallocation of certain functions from all municipalities to a county. In this way a kind of metropolitan government is created to look after area-wide problems while local service provision remains in the hands of existing local governments. Thus a certain measure of metropolitan control is obtained without the need to create yet another unit of government. However, although an attractive proposition on paper, it is restricted in application to those metropolitan areas that fall completely within the boundaries of a single county. Unfortunately most of the largest metropolitan regions include a number of counties.

Even where one-county metropolitan areas exist, this approach is often difficult to implement. Bollens and Schmandt (1965, pp. 455–456) list five major obstacles: the approach is not legally sanctioned in many states; for it to work effectively, existing county governments need extensive restructuring; the governing body is difficult to constitute; it is difficult to decide which functions should be assigned to the county government; and the financial powers of most counties are inadequate. In view of these difficulties, it is perhaps not surprising that the concept has become a reality in only one locality: metropolitan Miami in Dade County, Florida, where the one-county approach was adopted in 1957.

Federation The third variation of the two-tier approach, federation, is very similar to the one-county concept, and in fact in the case of one-county metropolitan areas the two are virtually indistinguishable. This approach can be almost considered, then, as an extension of the previous concept to regions consisting of more than one county. In this situation a new intercounty governmental unit is created to look after area-wide functions, while local municipalities are left in charge of local service provision. The idea of federation in metropolitan government has been an appealing one in the United States since the end of the nineteenth century. However, because of the many legal problems for its implementation, there have only been three serious attempts to federate: Boston (as early as 1896), Alameda County (Oakland, California), and Allegheny County (Pittsburgh)—all of which ended in failure. By the mid-fifties, interest in the approach had virtually vanished as attention shifted to the other two kinds of two-tier concepts.

Metropolitan Toronto: An Example

While interest in the idea of federation flagged in the United States, it was taken up in Canada where on January 1, 1954, this approach was adopted as the solution to the problems of rapid growth in the metropolitan Toronto region.

Events leading up to this decision began initially with the decision in 1912 of the City of Toronto to curtail its long-time policy of annexing adjacent territory when it became fairly well settled. The costs of providing services to the newly acquired areas had become too great. As the fringe areas continued to grow in population, so separate municipalities were established to cater to local needs. By 1930 thirteen such municipalities had been created, and these continued to grow in population size, so that by the outbreak of World War II several serious problems had emerged in the area. At the root of these was the familiar problem of community finances (Smallwood, 1963).

Although some municipalities had managed to attract a favorable mix of land uses, others had rapidly developed as dormitories for workers of the central city. For these the cost of providing community services rapidly became a major problem, and the quality of service provision deteriorated. This became acute with respect to education facilities, water supply, and sewage disposal. In an attempt to alleviate what had obviously become area-wide problems, the City of Toronto filed an application to the provincial government in 1950 calling for consolidation of the thirteen inner municipalities into a single governmental unit. The resulting metropolitan area created in 1954 is shown in Figure 17.3.

As a result of this plan, the Municipality of Metropolitan Toronto was established to perform area-wide functions including water supply, sewage disposal, property assessment, construction of arterial highways, parks, and planning. The original city and twelve suburbs were retained as local units to carry out functions not assigned to the metropolitan government, such as provision of local parks, libraries, fire protection, and various aspects of public health.

Since its inception, the new government has flourished and major accomplishments have been made on several fronts. In the areas of education, water supply, and sewage disposal, many of the earlier problems have been arrested; a metropolitan park district of many thousand acres has been established; an extensive expressway system has been launched; an attempt has been made to control air pollution; and a system of unified law enforcement has been implemented. Naturally, the new form of region-wide government is not without its critics, but despite some obvious failings on the part of the metropolitan council, notably in planning, it appears that in Toronto the metropolitan government concept is clearly established.

FIG. 17.3. THE MUNICIPALITY OF METROPOLITAN TORONTO.

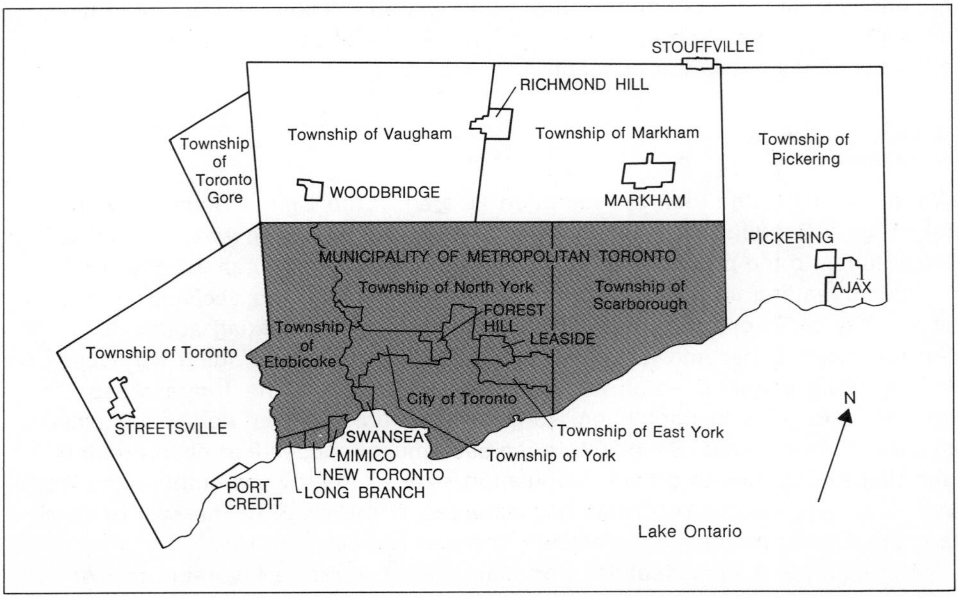

Thus, from our brief review of the various strategies open to advocates of metropolitan government reform, the two-tier approaches, and especially federation, are appealing. These offer a workable compromise between the politically impossible supergovernments controlling everything and the metropolitan councils controlling nothing. Their main value lies in the fact that they offer a new system that does not require the complete dissolution of the old. If they could be combined with some kind of direct sharing of tax revenues among communities as proposed by Chinitz (1965), then perhaps workable solutions to the problem of the proliferation of governments within metropolitan regions will be possible. For as long as local governments are forced to balance their books within their own boundaries it is unrealistic to expect them to surrender their parochial interests in favor of regionalism. However, regionalism must inevitably become a more important part of our thinking if, as Gottmann (1961) suggests, the new order in the organization of inhabited space is to be megalopolitan. For without greater concern for, and sacrifice in the interests of, the larger whole, the outlook for the urban future is very bleak indeed.

"THE URBAN FUTURE"

Our discussions concerning the urban geography of North American cities reveal a vast number of problems that need to be solved if society is to continue to develop meaningfully in the last few decades of the twentieth century. It is quite obvious that urban life will not be very meaningful if

1. The general standard of housing for everyone fails to increase
2. There are not equal opportunities and access to these opportunities for all in terms of education, medical services, and cultural and recreational amenities
3. The transportation system within urban areas continues to be congested
4. The quality of the environment continues to deteriorate through pollution, lack of adequate sewerage facilities, and so forth
5. General distrust and disillusionment as a result of the apparent outright rejection of humanistic values in some levels of government continues to express itself in increasing social unrest
6. Crime, particularly that of the organized variety, increases its hold on society.

Many of these conditions are interrelated to varying degrees, so what in fact is needed is a program to tackle some of these issues in a comprehensive manner (Advisory Committee . . . , 1968). Items 5 and 6 require a fundamental ethical change in society which is beyond the scope of an urban program but is, nevertheless, partly predicated upon it. Individual packages, such as urban renewal, metropolitan transportation studies, and special mortgage facilities for the lower incomes have attempted to ameliorate some of the problems; but they have in fact raised more issues than they have solved. Many of the principles and concepts discussed in the previous chapters will hopefully help lead us toward the development of a comprehensive program. In this concluding chapter we will limit ourselves to suggesting some basic spatial forms and structures and indicating the framework or assumptions that are the necessary constraining background of such a program.

PROGRAM ASSUMPTIONS

All programs are defined with certain assumptions in mind, and it is the duty of the programmer to state them clearly. In this particular case the assumptions fall into two major categories. The first category refers to assumptions concerning the continuation of present trends. The second category involves assumptions concerning individual tastes and technological innovation. Of course even in these latter cases the assumptions are based on perceived trends, but they are personal prognostications as much as soundly based projections.

CONTINUING TRENDS

One of the major assumptions concerning continuing trends is with respect to the increasing numbers of people to be found in urban areas. This is not, of course, a North American situation alone. At present the population of the world is about 60 percent rural and 40 percent urban, but according to Doxiadis

(1966, p. 75) this will change to about 95 percent urban and 5 percent rural in about one hundred years. This change, together with a projected increase in the world's population to between 6 and 7 billion by the year 2000 and more than 12 billion one hundred years from now, will mean that there will be a rapid expansion in urban areas. In fact, the much discussed world population explosion is being accompanied by an urban explosion of mammoth proportions. Thus any trends and assumptions involved in the development of an urban program in North America will be watched with great interest by the rest of the world.

Increasing urbanization Our first assumption, therefore, with respect to North America is that the urban explosion over the next few decades will be of dramatic proportions. The magnitudes of the changes over the last seventy years are indicated in Table 18.1, and these provide some factual bases for this prognostication. In terms of the actual growth of metropolitan areas, Table 18.1 lists the ten largest United States metropolises in 1910 and 1960 and makes a projection to the year 2000. In gross terms, the ten largest urban areas accounted for one-fifth of the U.S. population in 1910, one-fourth in 1960, and should account for one-third in 2000. The rapid growth of each metropolitan area is made possible by a great increase in size of the urban areas concerned.

The New York supermetropolitan area will still be the largest, but this, of course, will embrace the southern part of New York State, northeastern New Jersey, and southwestern Connecticut. A close second will be the Los Angeles area of southern California, which will have extended north to Santa Barbara, merged to the south with the northward thrusting San Diego, and extended in the east to San Bernardino and the desert fringe. Chicago and Detroit will exhibit similar growth, but not of such dramatic proportions as Los Angeles.

TABLE 18.1. TEN LARGEST METROPOLISES, UNITED STATES, 1910, 1960, AND 2000 (POPULATION DATA IN MILLIONS)

1910 Census Metropolitan Area	Pop.	1960 Census Standard Metropolitan Statistical Area	Pop.	2000 Projection Supermetropolitan Area	Pop.
New York	6.7	New York	10.7	New York	23.0
Chicago	2.5	Los Angeles	6.8	Los Angeles	20.0
Philadelphia	2.0	Chicago	6.2	Chicago	11.0
Boston	1.6	Philadelphia	4.3	Detroit	9.5
Pittsburgh	1.0	Detroit	3.8	Chesapeake and Potomac	9.5
St. Louis	0.8	San Francisco-Oakland	2.8	Delaware Valley	8.5
San Francisco-Oakland	0.7	Boston	2.6	San Francisco Bay	7.5
Baltimore	0.7	Pittsburgh	2.4	S. E. Florida	6.5
Cleveland	0.6	Washington	2.0	New England	6.5
Cincinnati	0.6	St. Louis	2.0	Cuyahoga Valley	5.0
Total	17.2		43.6		107.0
% of U.S.	19%		24%		33%

Source: Projection from Pickard (1959), p. 43.

A number of large metropolitan areas will have completely merged. The Chesapeake-Potomac supermetropolis consists of the merging of Washington and Baltimore; the Delaware Valley supermetropolis will be a combination of Philadelphia, Trenton, and Wilmington; present-day San Francisco-Oakland will expand to include San Jose; S. E. Florida City will include Miami-Palm Beach; the New England supermetropolis will cover most of eastern Massachusetts and Rhode Island; while the Cuyahoga Valley metropolitan area will be formed by the merging of Cleveland with Lorain, Elyria, and Akron. All of these supermetropolitan areas will be larger (except Cuyahoga Valley) than the standard statistical metropolitan area of Chicago in 1960.

The Urban Areas of North America in 2060

According to Doxiadis (1966, p. 112) the urban pattern of North America about one hundred years from now will consist of "some great concentrations of megalopolises interconnected by elongated strips of settlement along the major highways of the future." The macrogeographic aspects of this pattern are indicated in Figure 18.1, in which are outlined twelve major supermetropolitan areas. These are:

1. The northeastern Atlantic Seaboard—an area stretching from New Hampshire to North Carolina

2. Chipitts—the area stretching from Milwaukee through Chicago, Detroit, and Cleveland to Pittsburgh

3. Southern Ontario–St. Lawrence lowland surrounding the twin-growth areas of Toronto and Montreal

4. Ciloubustonis—consisting of an agglomeration of Cincinnati, Louisville, Columbus, Dayton, and Indianapolis

5. Minneapolis–Duluth in the upper Midwest

6. California—from Eureka to Tijuana, Mex.

7. The Puget Sound lowland—including Portland, Seattle, and Vancouver

8. Central Colorado—rapid growth being experienced in Denver, Colorado Springs, and Pueblo

9. Florida—covering the entire southern half of the Florida Peninsula and stretching north through Jacksonville to coastal Georgia

10. The coastal "Old South," including Baton Rouge, New Orleans, Mobile, and Pensacola

11. Houston–Dallas–Fort Worth in Texas

12. The mouth of the Rio Grande—incorporating a small area around Brownsville, Tex., but including a larger part of northeastern Mexico, in particular Monterey

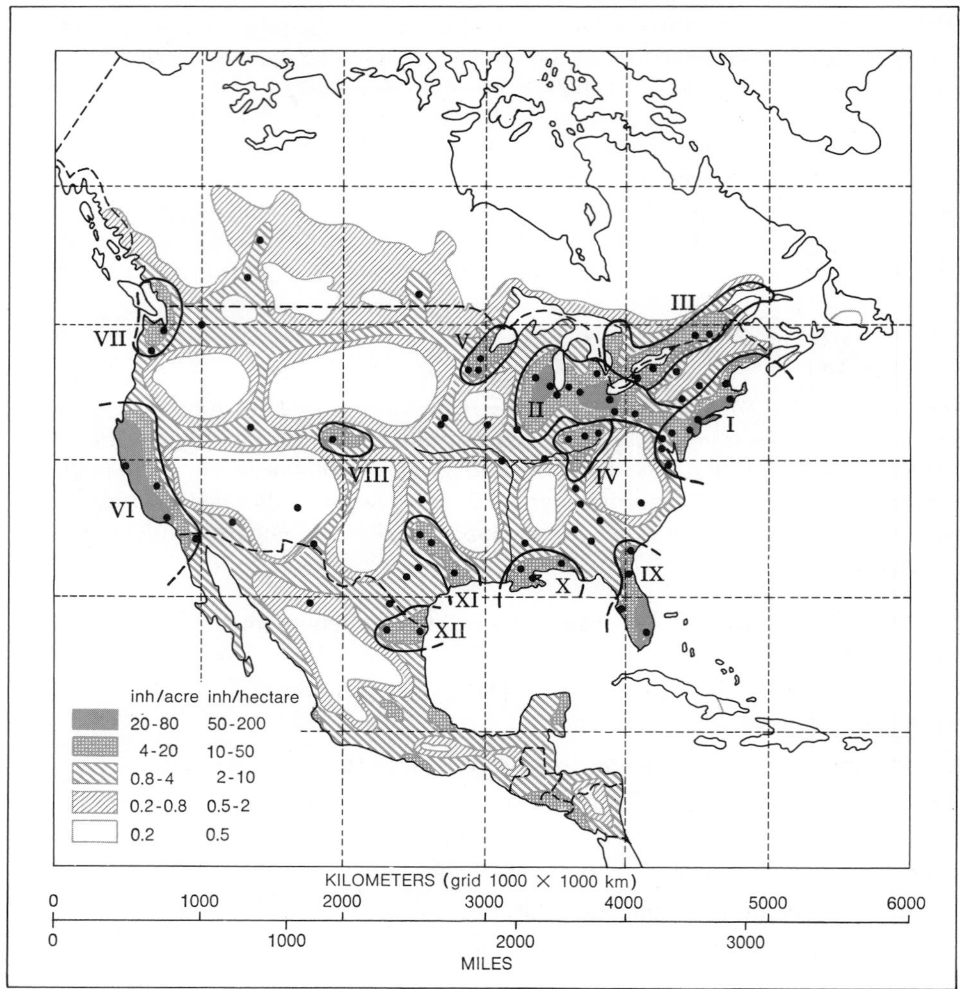

FIG. 18.1. A VIEW OF URBAN NORTH AMERICA, 2060. (*Source:* Doxiadis, 1966, Fig. 49.)

Thus the supermetropolitan areas of the industrial belt of North America will have merged to form a continuous urban area, but the greatest urban growth will be in the Southwest along the Gulf Coast and the Florida Peninsula.

Continuing economic growth A second major assumption is that the rapid rate of economic growth (on a per capita basis) experienced in the 1960s will continue through into the 1970s and beyond. Throughout the 1960s the rate of growth in the gross national product (GNP) in the United States and Canada varied between 4½ and 6 percent. The real average annual increase in GNP per capita in Canada between 1961 and 1968 was, in fact, 3.9 percent.

Short-term estimates predict that this rate of growth will continue to 1975, and it could be suggested that if certain factors are fulfilled this average rate of growth could exist for a much longer period. The factors influencing this growth are of both an economic and noneconomic nature.

Economic Factors Influencing Growth

It is generally considered that the long-term growth in productive capacity of an economy can be traced to two main sources:

> First, an increase in the quantity of productive resources which can be put to use in the economy; and second, an increase in the productivity of these resources stemming from improvements in their quality and in the efficiency of their use (Economic Council of Canada, 1964).

It is the interplay of these two factors that affects long-term growth potential. If productivity is held constant, and if the quantity of productive resources available for use and used increases, then an expansion in the productive capacity of an economy can occur. These productive resources include labor of all types and quality, and physical resources such as land, natural resources, buildings, equipment, and so forth.

On the other hand, if the quantity of productive resources available for use is held constant, an expansion in the productive capacity of an economy can occur if productivity increases. Increases in productivity are associated with improvements in the productive quality of the factors of production and improvements in the efficiency with which these factors of production are combined. The former are associated with facets such as improving the labor force through education and training or the development of better quality natural resources, while the latter are usually associated with improved technology, better management techniques, and increasing the scale of production. It has become clear among the advanced nations of the world that it is increases in productivity that account for the greater part of economic expansion.

Thus the assumption of continuing per capita economic growth is based primarily on the premise of increasing productivity much more than that of increasing the quantity of productive resources. Of course the population projections indicate that the labor force will continue to expand in numbers, but this implies a concomitant task to increase the quality of that factor of production. This can be achieved through education and the application of improved technology.

Noneconomic factors influencing growth Continuing economic growth also implies that the productive capacity of North America is not squandered by war or halted by calamitous economic events. There are many potential "little" wars occurring that could expand into a major conflagration, but since World War II such a catastrophe has been avoided. If a large war between the major powers, and therefore of global proportions, were to occur in the future, any comprehensive urban plan would be financially impossible; and at worst, any progress would be nullified, for a large proportion of the population of North America may not be alive, and large sections of the land surface may be uninhabitable.

Economic events are also influenced by crises of a psychological nature. The changes that are always occurring in society require continuous economic adjustment. The continuing United States balance-of-payments deficits in the 1960s led to widespread gold speculation, which caused minor crises of faith in the western economic system. Such a crisis could easily expand into a depression of some magnitude if the international currency situation collapses. Also racial problems and poverty in the United States could seriously disrupt the economy if revolution through violence becomes widespread. Events of this type can be regarded as random shocks to the economic system, though the seeds are present for all to see.

The changing goals of society One of the most important assumptions with respect to the development of a comprehensive urban policy involves the changing goals of society. Two events occurred that have influenced the collective action of most middle-aged and older inhabitants of the United States and Canada. These were the Great Depression and World War II. As a consequence, the highest priorities of the last two-and-a-half decades have been assigned to devising procedures to prevent a recurrence of events of this type. The colossal expenditures of the United States on defense and the establishment of complex social and economic machinery on a national (welfare and area development programs) and international (the International Monetary Fund) scale are examples of this.

It is, however, becoming apparent that though these programs are important they are not the overwhelming concern of over half of the population of North America that has not experienced these catastrophic events. Defense is and will still be important, but unquestioned praise and approval of defense expenditures will become a thing of the past. Alliances and prejudices established in the flurry of activity following World War II will also be questioned. But, more importantly, there will be a continuing development of a consensus on a different set of priorities, priorities that involve achievement goals (Economic Council of Canada, 1969, p. 171).

Basically, these achievement goals arise from the recognition that economic growth should provide more than material comforts and a degree of financial security. People are becoming increasingly aware that material comforts and financial security are really the means toward achieving something, and that something is really a better quality life. As man is becoming increasingly an urban dweller, this means for most people a better quality urban life. In fact, good planning is impossible without a clear specification of goals and priorities. Thus our assumption is that whereas society wishes to pursue goal objectives such as:

Aid to underdeveloped countries
Peace and stability (e.g., strong defense-offense system)
The creation of new knowledge (e.g., space program)
More personal consumption
Improved health care
Better education
More adequate housing
Equal opportunities for all
The elimination of poverty
Resource conservation
Improved urban transportation
Pollution abatement
City beautification
Encouragement of the arts

the latter ten objectives will experience greater emphasis in the future than they have in the past. The above list is by no means exhaustive; but in a situation where not all objectives can be afforded in the immediate future, it does indicate the range over which priorities have to be determined. It is, of course, essential in a democratic society that the electorate participate fully in the determination of goals and priorities.

USE OF NEW INNOVATIONS

The massive increase in urban population predicted earlier can be catered to only by a tremendous increase in construction activity. Though there have been a number of technological improvements in the construction industry, and a few instances of undoubted increases in efficiency, there is little doubt that this branch of industry has demonstrated an inability to become as productive as others. This is partially due to the instability of the construction industry, which tends to have a cyclical pattern of activity; but it is also due to the nature of the industry, which has to cater to the individual potential home owner as well as to the ambitious downtown redeveloper. However, the future pressure on the construction industry promises to be so great that new innovations in both techniques and production management will have to be incorporated in the future. These innovations range all the way from prefabricated units to the on-the-spot utilization of continuously poured cement for large structures.

A major area of innovation involves the prediction that the general life style of North Americans will change in response to the cybernetic revolution. The cybernetic revolution has been referred to as the second Industrial Revolution, and is just beginning. The basis of the Industrial Revolution was the heat engine that permitted the transformation of energy from one form to another. This resulted in the replacement of natural engines, such as the physical energy provided by human beings and animals, by artificially constructed engines. The second Industrial Revolution comes into being with the appearance of a methodology designed to process not energy but information. This methodology is referred to as *cybernetics,* which is defined as the science of communication and control. The spatial impact of the first Industrial Revolution was such that it necessitated large-scale organization and complex metropolitan growth. The second industrial revolution will most likely have a similar spatial impact, but it will probably permit greater decentralization.

In nonspatial terms, but perhaps of greater significance, is that this second industrial revolution will undoubtedly involve a change in the life style of society that has been as great as that experienced by the first. The need for an ordered and regulated life necessitated by the factory or office schedule of the first will be replaced by a less rigid schedule in the second. This cannot be lightly dismissed as the replacement of the "Protestant work ethic" by a "fun ethic," for it implies a belief that there is, or should be, a great deal more to the human experience than just the mechanistic gaining of a livelihood. If this human experience is interpreted as more recreation, an increased desire for cultural and artistic amenities, improved urban design, greater intellectual and personal freedom, then there will be revolutionary changes in the structure and appearance of future urban communities.

The third type of new innovation necessary for future urban life is a different form of urban transportation. The massive construction and reconstruction of urban areas that is going to be required will make innovation and experimentation feasible. We will assume that the best alternative is the development of some form of personal transit system as suggested previously. This type of system involves the interfacing of cybernetics with individual transport vehicles. Such an interfacing could well be financially feasible in the short term given the colossal overexpenditure on personal transportation incurred today. It is difficult to envisage that an individual really requires a 420 cubic inch internal combustion engine for personal or even family mobility, particularly when the average speed of urban travel is usually less than 25 m.p.h.

PLANNING PATTERNS

The predicted great increase in size and number of urban areas requires planning at the macro or regional scale. Planning of this type must be distinguished from micro or local planning, which involves the layout of units within the urban area. Planning at any level is an attempt at influencing the course of events, and in general involves the application of foresight to achieve certain pre-established goals. We have discussed previously the range of goals pertinent to society in North America and the way in which the priorities and emphasis given to these goals should change in the future. If these changes take place then planning on a continental wide scale for urban areas can occur. Much of the planning literature is concerned with three basic forms of plan—the linear, the circular, and the sector (Reynolds, 1961).

THE LINEAR PLAN

The linear plan is of European origin and became particularly well known when it was proposed as a planning framework for London, England, by the MARS group (Modern Architectural Research Society). The MARS plan featured an arrangement of land uses around a main spine of communication (Foley, 1963, p. 47). Along this main spine are arrayed the major areas of employment and economic activity (Fig. 18.2). The residential areas are located along right-angle offshoots from this main spine and are linked one with the other by the main spine itself or a circumferal belt. Urban growth is facilitated by a simple extension of the spine and the creation of right-angle residential offshoots.

There are several obvious advantages to a plan of this type. In the first place, it does provide a rational procedure for urban growth. Second, it presents a very clear distinction between major land uses, and it does provide a feasible means of interconnection. Third, it emphasizes centrality and the location of

FIG. 18.2. A LINEAR URBAN PLAN. THE MARS GROUP'S PROPOSAL FOR LONDON, ENGLAND. IN THIS PLAN, COMMERCIAL AND INDUSTRIAL AREAS ARE CONCENTRATED IN A CORE PARALLELING THE RIVER THAMES, AND RESIDENTIAL AREAS ARE PLACED IN STRIPS PERPENDICULAR TO THE CORE. (*Source:* Reynolds, 1961, Fig. 17.)

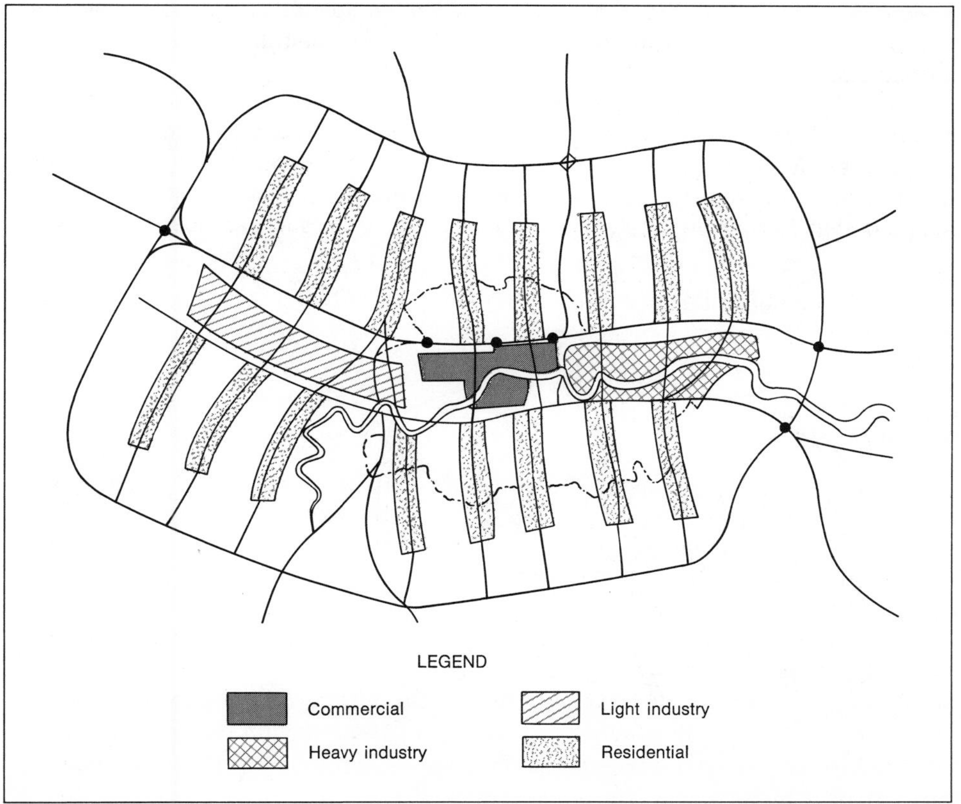

major city-serving activities in an elongated downtown area. Finally it provides for open spaces within an orderly arrangement of land uses that are equally accessible from all residential areas. The major fault in the plan is that it is perhaps too geometric and formal. As applied to London, the major objection was that its implementation would lead to a rather drastic destruction of historical buildings and resorting of land uses on a very large scale. These objections do not of course apply to many North American cities, and certainly not to new urban areas.

THE CIRCULAR PLAN

The circular plan form is developed from a communication system based on ring roads and radials. The radials focus upon a nucleus to a central business area, which is surrounded by a ring and from which the radials spring (see Fig. 18.3). One major advantage of a plan of this type is that it clearly fosters the development of neighborhood units between each radial and ring. Furthermore the plan conforms very closely to the natural evolution of most urban areas, for they have tended to follow this radial–concentric growth. The major drawback becomes apparent, however, when open spaces are being considered, for there are really only two choices—that of a green belt or wedges between the radials.

Green belts have in fact been encouraged as a major device, both for controlling urban sprawl and for providing recreational space for inhabitants of urban areas. In many instances a green belt is considered to be a barrier to urban growth, containing the city and at times providing land for essential services that cannot be located within the urban area, such as hospitals or

FIG. 18.3. A CIRCULAR URBAN PLAN.

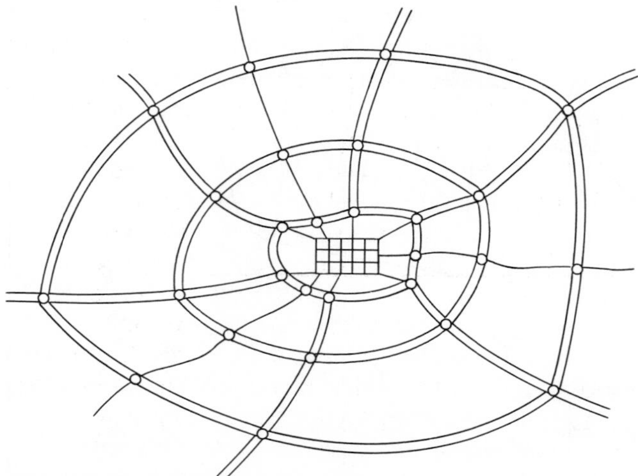

sanatoriums (Coleman, 1969, pp. 45–48). However, the simple introduction of a green belt usually results in the leap-frogging of urban sprawl over the zoned area, so that the green belt becomes a barrier criss-crossed by a variety of modes of communication. As an attempt at planning the development of these urban areas beyond the green belt, authorities in the United Kingdom have developed new towns (Madge, 1962). These new towns in fact form nucleated clusters of residential business and industrial activity beyond the major urban areas, particularly in Greater London, that have been developed especially to contain the emigrating urban population.

Although green belts seem to be an article of faith among many planners, it is doubtful whether they have the great utility attributed to them. Frequently green belts are provided regardless of the type of land involved. It is possible, for example, that potentially good recreational areas may be excluded from a green belt and developed for residential purposes or even commercial activities, simply because they have not been zoned within the green belt. On the other hand, flat, boring, nonrecreational areas may well be included within a green belt because they fall within a planner's geometric conception of design. Thus though one of the philosophical bases of a green belt, that of providing land for recreational purposes, may be quite sound, it is quite feasible to cater to this need without designating an entire ring as a barrier.

One great drawback to green belts is that they are most accessible to people living on the fringe of urban areas and therefore offer an unfair amenity advantage to people living in these peripheral zones. As a means of circumventing this problem, some planners have modified the green-belt concept by proposing wedges that penetrate the urban area to provide open spaces for those people living within the central zone. This modification, however, seems at best a makeshift support to the green-belt concept.

THE SECTOR PLAN

The sector plan concentrates on radials as the dominant framework within which urban development and growth take place. The radials focus upon the urban core, which provides the nucleus for the urban area. The chief lines of communication use avenues along the spine of each radial, and minor nucleations of commercial activities are spaced along each like beads on a string. Probably the best-known plan of this type in Europe is the Copenhagen Finger Plan, and the most discussed similar design in North America is that for Washington, D.C.

In the latter case the plan envisages the development of six radials from central Washington, D.C., one following the Washington-Baltimore corridor and the others connecting the major outlying satellite areas in Maryland and Virginia. Along each of these radials a number of new towns are planned, each of which will offer its own array of services, but they will all be linked to Washington, D.C., as the focus of economic activity for that region (Fig. 18.4). Where the radials connect major urban areas, the radial will in fact become a corridor of movement and will itself become an elongated ribbon of economic

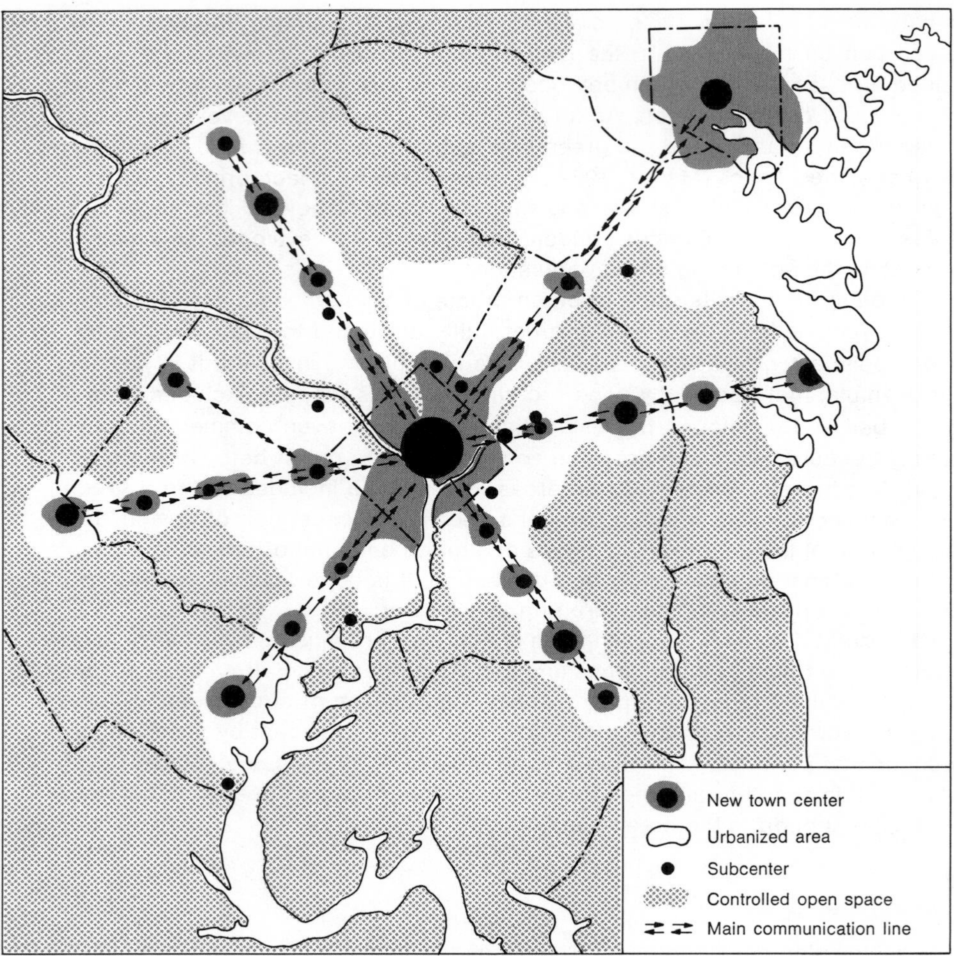

FIG. 18.4. THE SUGGESTED RADIAL CORRIDOR PLAN FOR WASHINGTON, D.C. (*Source:* Maryland-National Capital Park and Planning Commission, 1964, p. 20.)

activity. Between each radial or corridor open land for farming and recreational activities will be preserved.

This plan is basically one that prevents sprawl but channels growth into distinct avenues. Urban growth can take place by extending the radials as well as intensifying the land use, both within the central capital area and along the radial corridors closest to the core. The whole system of course depends on the use of high-speed urban transportation. The spine of each corridor will therefore consist of limited access freeways and rapid transit, as well as railroads for moving bulky goods. It is envisaged, of course, that this mixture of transportation facilities would be designed as a whole rather than as separate units, for they could individually mar the landscape of each corridor. Furthermore, each radial node will have to be planned carefully in terms of optimum size and internal structure.

Thus the sector plan has many advantages over the linear and circular forms. In the first place, it provides a clearly defined framework for urban growth. Secondly it permits the development of urban nuclei in economic modules, so that they do not become too large for the scale of human organization to be overwhelmed. Third, sprawl is avoided, for the areas between each corridor act as buffer zones. Fourthly the hierarchical nodal principle of human organization is kept intact, for not only does each radial settlement focus upon its own central core, but the entire system concentrates on the major focus. Ultimately, of course, all these major foci themselves concentrate on the highest order focus of all. Thus, the system is intuitively appealing to the urban geographer, for it recognizes the spatial interrelatedness of the entire urban system. The feasibility of the plan depends, however, on the efficiency of the transportation system involved.

THE BASIC ELEMENTS OF THE PLAN

The basic elements of the sector plan are fourfold. The first of these is the system of communication which ties the component parts together. The other three are the component parts themselves. The chief component part is the focus of activity, the central city itself. The third element consists of the nodes along the radials, which are the units that cater to overall growth as well as to major residential and minor business commercial and industrial activities. The fourth element consists of the area between the radials, the open land that it is envisaged will be used for farming and recreational purposes. The planning for each of these elements is vital if the whole system is to be viable.

THE COMMUNICATION SYSTEM

Although it can be envisaged that in the future the necessity for personal movement may well decrease, it is nevertheless considered that people will still wish to move around the urban area. The necessity for personal movement, particularly for work purposes, may well decrease as a result of the increasing use of sophisticated communication technology used to control the production or office process. In fact in this sense we may well see a return to the "pedestrian" city, as the work place and the home may be one and the same thing, or at least not very far apart in physical terms, for communication resources may be pooled to form local or neighborhood communication centers. They may be far apart in reality; but the various media of communication available, such as television, telephones, sonic data phones, remote off-and-on line computer terminals, and so forth, will reduce the importance of distance and the daily journey to work in man's life.

However, interpersonal communication, without the use of electronic devices, is very necessary for many business activities, and vital for social, cultural, and recreational purposes. It is envisaged that these latter activities will absorb an increasing share of an individual's life in the future. To facilitate these activities, it is expected that several modes of transportation will be necessary. In the first place the automobile, or some future substitute, will continue to provide the necessary personal or private transportation that most individuals require. Rapid transit will be most efficient for the transportation of people from the smaller nodes along radials to the central city. The mass transportation of people between nodes on different radials would be best undertaken by bus.

For the transportation of goods, it is difficult to envisage any other alternative to rail and truck. The trade-off between truck and rail for the shipment of goods in the future depends on the continuing effort of the railroad industry to compete, and the degree to which trucks are to be permitted to use limited access highways. Obviously the medium- and long-haul advantage of the railroad industry could be restored and emphasized if trucks were banned from all limited access highways. As this event is both doubtful and unwise in a competitive economy, what is really needed is some rationalization of the alternatives available. This can be accomplished in part through design of the facilities to be used for the different modes of transportation.

Transport facilities The transportation system involves, at one level, movement between central cities. Intercity rail lines and limited-access highways can be used for this purpose. They may run in conjunction or parallel with each other and will provide the arteries of heavy traffic. A second level of movement will be that connecting the nodes along the radials with central cities and connecting the nodes on different radials. Here design becomes preeminent, and it is considered that these should be parkways, from which trucks are banned, but buses permitted. Also, rapid transit is to be developed to carry passengers between the radial nodes and the central cities. It is considered that the location of these routes can be designed in conjunction with the parkways, perhaps using the right-of-way along, beneath, or above the median strip. Parkways are also to be used to connect nodes on different radials, and the bus will be the mode of mass transit for this kind of linkage.

The third level of transportation is that involving within-node and within-central city circulation. Here we can envisage the use of parkways, rapid transit, bus, and urban arterials. These latter facilities can accommodate quite heavy volumes of traffic if commercial land use is not allowed to locate continuously on either side of the route. This type of commercial strip, consisting, as it has been observed, of freestanding enterprises, results in congestion due to the multitude of separate entrances and parallel parking. Highway-oriented enterprises of this type should be clustered into planned centers adjacent to the highway with parking and with well-designed entrances and exits from the parking area. Land use clustering of this type will go far toward reducing congestion along urban highways.

THE CENTRAL CITY

The central city poses the biggest problem in the future urban planning. It is the area in which the accumulated fixed investment of capital is the greatest, and it is also the most obsolete area. In most cases it is difficult to envisage anything other than urban renewal on a massive scale, for in most cases a radical resorting of land uses is required. This type of urban renewal is usually undertaken by public agencies, for private redevelopment is usually impossible. Reasons for this have been listed by Bourne (1967, p. 34) as:

1. The units of ownership are too small in most central areas for present redevelopment uses. Thus time has to be spent in accumulating suitable contiguous lots, and this is a complicated procedure.

2. The physical and social environments in many areas are unattractive as both centers of unemployment and residence.

3. The value of land in many areas is excessively high, for it is frequently inflated by overoptimism on the part of the owners, taxation, or inappropriate zoning. Furthermore, land valuations are frequently based on assessments that are not realistic in terms of current conditions.

4. Various legal and financial constraints act as obstacles to renewal, such as zoning, financing, and land titles. For example, the land titles may be in multiple ownership and difficult to trace.

5. Neighborhood and community resistance to change is often sufficiently strong to delay or prevent proposed renewal schemes.

6. The shortage of housing for low-income families and racially segregated groups makes it difficult to remove the existing deteriorated housing which they occupy.

Bourne's (1967, p. 174) study of Toronto indicates that the private redevelopment that does exist takes place primarily in the most favorable areas. These are in the higher income sectors close to subway stations. This is because private redevelopment tends to be middle- and upper-income oriented, and not directed toward families with small children. It is the task of city planning to coordinate private redevelopment opportunities with those designed for the good of the urban area as a whole.

One of the better examples of city planning on a large scale can be seen in Philadelphia (Mitchell, 1960). The relative success of urban renewal and restructuring on a large scale in this case is associated with many factors. In the first place, general comprehensive planning, associated with a desire for government reform, had been pushed by a group of "young Turks" for a number of years. Second, the large number of professional planners available in the area (many of whom were, and are, associated with the University of Pennsylvania) were complemented by the interest of a number of citizens' advisory groups. Third, during the last two decades Philadelphia has been fortunate in having a succession of mayors who have provided the necessary dynamic leadership. Finally the availability of federal funds on quite a large scale during the late fifties and early sixties provided the necessary financial base for the execution of much of the program.

The Philadelphia physical development plan There are two main aspects of the Philadelphia physical development plan that are the bases of the objectives and proposals. The first of these ". . . is concerned with maintaining the eminence of Philadelphia as the central city in a growing metropolitan area," and the second involves ". . . improving the quality of the city's environment as a place in which to live and conduct business" (Row, 1960, p. 177). In order to achieve these aims, two sets of objectives are derived: economic objectives and people objectives. The economic objectives are aimed at improving the competitive position of Philadelphia among the major cities of North America, and the people objectives are concerned with the residential-cultural environment of Philadelphia.

Economic Objectives

The economic objectives of the Philadelphia plan are fourfold. First, the plan aims to maintain the downtown area as the major focus of offices, high-order retail and wholesale activities, cultural amenities, and professional and financial activities. This needs imaginative land use and dramatic architecture. Place de Ville in Montreal is a fine example of an attempt at dramatic but functional renewal on a large scale. Second, there is emphasis on the improvement of major transport facilities that link the primary facilities of the city to each other, to the surrounding residential areas, to the region and the world beyond. Third, the need of industry for space within the city is being met. New industry and the expansion of existing industry are vital for urban growth, and a variety of sites are being made available, close to the city center, in the middle of the city, and at the periphery. Finally, an adequate distribution of tertiary activities is being achieved by the construction of lower-order shopping centers within the city, as well as at the periphery of the urban area. Within many of these centers are to be located smaller cultural and recreational facilities to serve the local community.

People Objectives

A major objective of the Philadelphia plan is to improve the average quality of housing. In some cases this implies demolition of whole blocks; and in others, thinning out to reduce densities. Unfortunately improvements of this type have the effect of removing people from homes, so that alternative residences must be available. In most cities as nearly all areas due for demolition are occupied by the poor, and in the United States these are invariably minority groups, such action is fraught with pitfalls. In fact, it seems that relocation of people in the execution of a plan is the most serious problem and must be approached with the greatest sensitivity and understanding.

With the renewal of large areas of the city and the construction of all or parts of entire sections, it may well be possible to emphasize or create local identity. This is being approached through the organization of the residential area into functional units of three levels: districts, communities, and neighborhoods. Public services of different types are located at each functional level. For example, a major hospital would be located at the district level, and the community-level focus would include facilities such as a library, a satellite health clinic, and a community-level shopping center. Playgrounds and parks are located at every level in the organizational hierarchy.

THE NODES ALONG THE RADIALS

The nodes located along the radials are the areas basically designed to cater to urban growth. In many instances these can be designed as new towns or expanded smaller towns. Their size should be limited to some upper-limit optimum level, perhaps of the order of 200 to 250 thousand people, and they are not meant to be mere satellites of the central city. North America has had some experience with new-town construction, Radburn, Reston, and Columbia (Va.) being the best-known examples. The greatest development of new towns is in Europe, particularly in the United Kingdom, Sweden, and Finland.

The basic feature of British new towns is that they are planned as a whole by a publicly owned development corporation (Edwards, 1964). This corporation oversees and guides the building of the town until it is well settled and then hands the operation over to a locally controlled administration (Lichfield and Wendt, 1969). The land begins and remains in public ownership, though many of the houses and buildings are in private ownership. This public-private ownership relation is an essential feature of new-town construction, as the initial development has to be government funded. The recent new towns of the United States (Reston and Columbia) are private developments, whereas those of an earlier era (Greenhills, Ohio; Greendale, Wis.; and Greenbelt, Md.) were begun under Franklin D. Roosevelt federal government sponsorship (McFarland, 1966). The earliest American new town was Radburn, N.J., designed in 1929 by Clarence Stein and Henry Wright. However, none of these American experiences in the 1930s can really be called new towns, as they are mere suburbanite appendages to their adjacent urban masses. Reston and Columbia are designed as new towns with local employment opportunities, but they seem to be becoming upper- and middle-income suburban Washington exclaves.

The internal structure of new towns The internal structure of these new towns can take many forms. The traditional European design is expressed in Figure 18.5, which is a diagram of the original plan of Crawley in England. The residential parts are divided into several distinct neighborhoods, each with a few thousand inhabitants. Each neighborhood is equipped with schools, churches, a community center, local shopping facilities, and playground areas. The dwellings are of several types: apartments, row houses (town houses), duplex and single-family units; and they are constructed at fairly low densities in order to ensure the

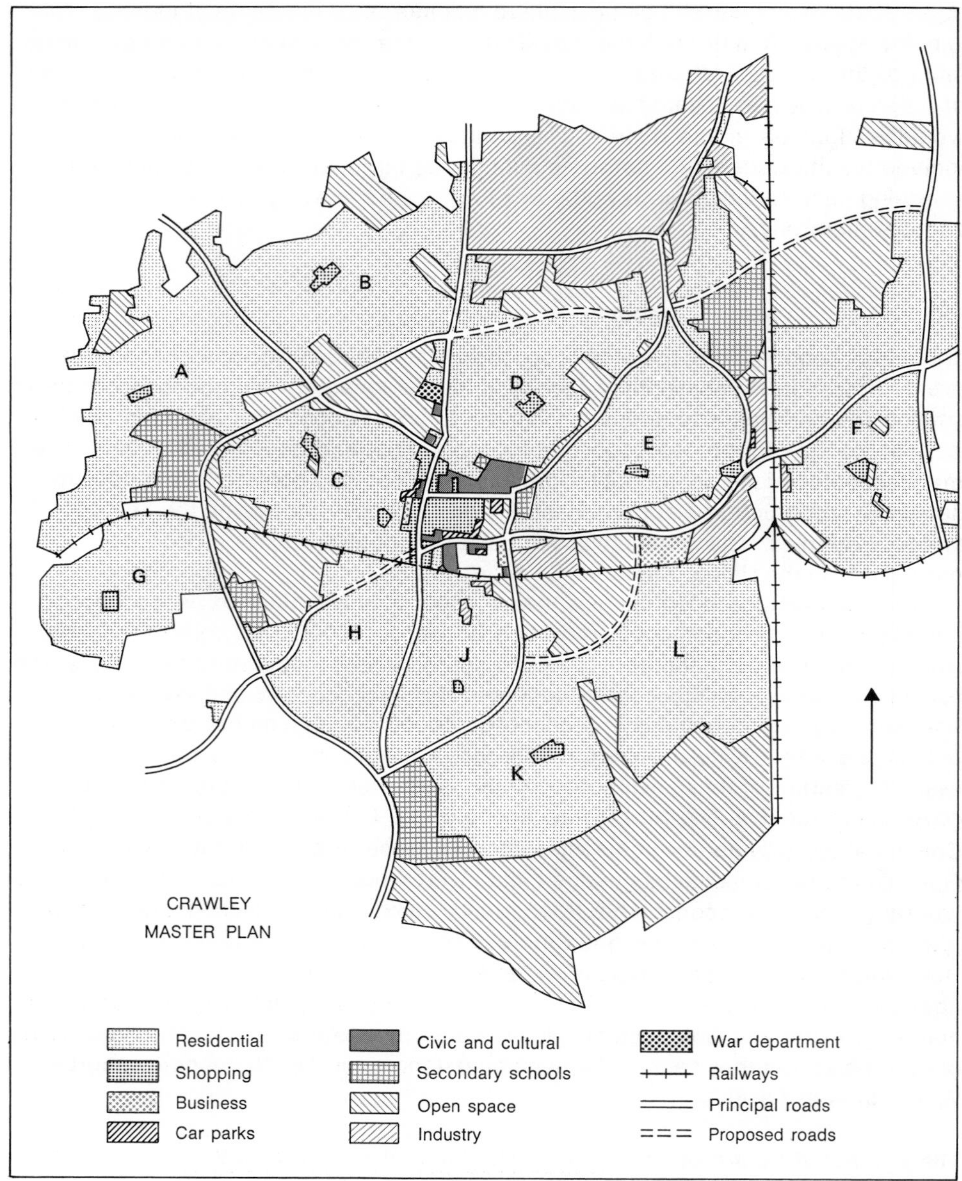

FIG. 18.5. THE MASTER PLAN FOR CRAWLEY NEW TOWN, ENGLAND.

provision of gardens and sufficient areas for children to play. The houses are grouped away from the major roadways, which are used as the dividing lines between neighborhoods.

The manufacturing base of the community is zoned in specific areas either close to the CBD, or in a specific sector close to the principal lines of communication to areas beyond the town. These areas are, in fact, conceived as industrial parks, with their own amenities and integrated design. The CBD is designed to provide the highest-order service facilities for the community. As a consequence, it is the focus of administration, commerce, specialized shopping, and entertainment. It is planned as a distinct element with malls, plazas, and associated parking facilities and is accessible from all the neighborhoods.

The transportation system of the town links these various parts together with a hierarchy of service routes. Footpaths connect the residential areas within the neighborhoods to the schools and neighborhood shopping areas. Residential streets are not designed for heavy traffic, as there are numerous circles and crescents. The major roads within the community connect the residential areas to the factory areas and town center. Finally, these roads connect into major highways which link the community to the national intercity network. Thus there is an internal coherence in traffic design and transport facilities. A major problem with British new towns, however, is that those conceived between 1945 and 1950 are designed to cater to an expected automobile ownership ratio of about 1:15 rather than 1:6, which became the norm during the 1960s.

Megastructures and Platform Cities

Much of the large-scale construction that needs to take place in these radial areas (and in the central cities) may well occur in the form of huge buildings or interlinked complexes. Prototypes of the kind of structure already in construction and operation are Market East in Philadelphia and the John Hancock Center in Chicago. The Marget East structure is, in effect, an elongated (7 block long) miniature platform city, with integrated rapid-transit, bus, truck, and automobile parking facilities arrayed along the lower levels of the structure. The long towers rising from this platform base contain the potential residential, office, industrial, and commercial facilities. The narrowness of the structure and the high density of land use that it implies ensure an abundance of open space in adjacent areas along the entire length. An even greater density of land use is envisaged by the proponents of megastructures. These are envisaged as tall buildings (such as the World Trade Center in Manhattan), occupying a minimal amount of land, serviced at their base by many kinds of public transport media, and within which are located all the facilities desired by the urban dweller.

THE INTERSTITIAL AREAS

The interstices between the radials are clearly defined to prevent sprawl and provide open spaces. The land can be used for a number of purposes: agriculture, recreation, and the location of special facilities. The agricultural activities located within this area should be of the intensive variety, such as truck farming and horticulture, providing fresh commodities for the adjacent urban market. Recreational space would need to be provided in abundance, and a wide variety of uses should be developed. Among the special facilities located in this area would be sanatoria and convalescent homes. It is obvious that great care must be taken to conserve and preserve these interstitial areas. The pressure to use the land for urban construction would be great, and as a consequence it may well be necessary to develop a number of programs concerned with conserving the land. The economic returns should not be viewed in terms of direct economic benefits, but rather in terms of social utility to the urban community as a whole.

Thus, the emphasis of this last chapter has been that an integrated assessment of the goals and direction of North American society is needed if urban North America is to be developed constructively. Although we have but briefly outlined some of the alternatives, it should be apparent that technology is not a drawback to urban devleopment. The technology is available in North America to produce or do almost anything that man desires. What is needed is some assessment of the kind of society that is required, so that the technology and know-how can be used to create the conditions conducive to the development of that society. This is undoubtedly the task of man in North America, for he needs to become as deeply involved in the family of man as he is in his own family.

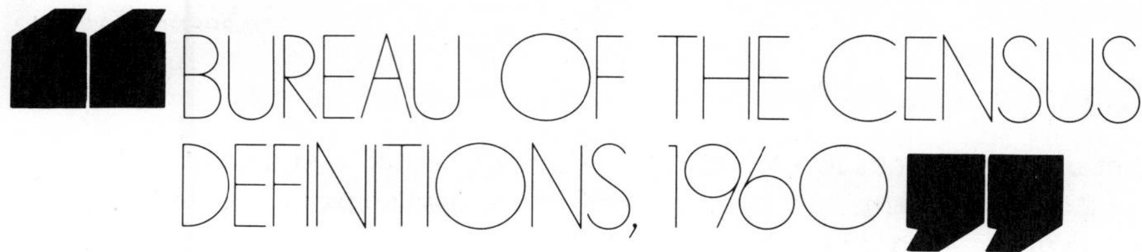

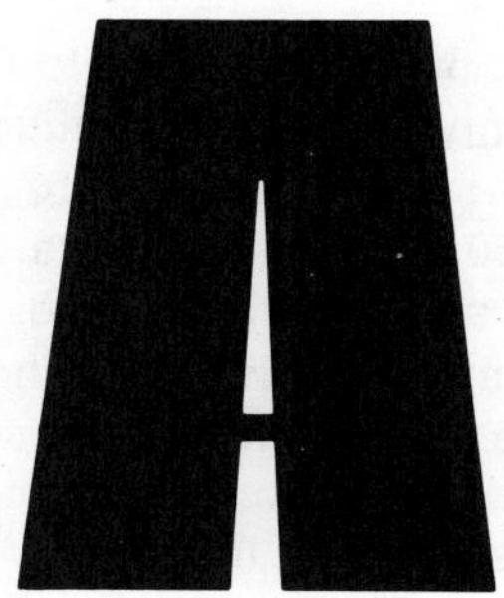

BUREAU OF THE CENSUS DEFINITIONS, 1960

URBAN POPULATION

The *urban population* comprises all persons living in: (1) places of 2,500 inhabitants or more incorporated as cities, boroughs, villages, and towns (except towns in New England, New York, and Wisconsin); (2) the densely settled urban fringe, whether incorporated or unincorporated, of urbanized areas; (3) towns in New England and townships in New Jersey and Pennsylvania, which contain no incorporated municipalities as subdivisions and have either 25,000 inhabitants or more, or a population of 2,500 to 25,000 and a density of 1,500 persons or more per square mile; (4) counties in states other than the New England states, New Jersey, and Pennsylvania that have no incorporated municipalities within their borders and have a density of 1,500 persons per square mile (This applies to only one case—Arlington County, Virginia); (5) unincorporated places of 2,500 inhabitants or more. The population not classified as urban under this definition constitutes the rural population.

This definition of *urban* is substantially the same as that used in 1950. The major difference between 1950 and 1960 is the designation in 1960 of urban towns in New England and of urban townships in New Jersey and Pennsylvania. The effect of the change in definition in 1960 was small, because in 1950 most of the population living in such places was classified as urban by virtue of residence in an urbanized area or in an unincorporated urban place. Thus under the 1960 definition, 125,268,750 persons were classified as urban in the United States; according to the previous definition, 112,548,416 persons would have been classified as urban in 1960.

URBAN PLACES

The count of urban places in 1960 includes all incorporated and unincorporated places of 2,500 inhabitants or more, and the towns, townships, and counties classified as urban according to the above definition.

STANDARD METROPOLITAN STATISTICAL AREAS

Except in New England, the criteria used to delineate an SMSA pertain to county units. An SMSA is a county or group of contiguous counties that contains at least one city of 50,000 inhabitants or more, or twin cities with a combined population of at least 50,000. To qualify as twin cities, two cities must have contiguous boundaries and must constitute, for general social and economic purposes, a single community with a combined population of at least 50,000; the smaller place must have a population of at least 15,000.

In addition to the county or counties containing such a city or cities, contiguous counties are included in an SMSA if they are essentially metropolitan in character and are socially and economically integrated with the central city.

Criteria of metropolitan character (1) At least 75.0 percent of the labor force of the county must be in the nonagricultural labor force. (2) In addition to criteria 1, the county must meet at least one of the following conditions: (*a*) it must have 50.0 percent or more of its population living in contiguous minor civil divisions with a density of at least 150 persons per square mile, in an unbroken chain of minor civil divisions with such density radiating from a central city in an area. (*b*) The number of nonagricultural workers employed in the county must equal at least 10.0 percent of the number of nonagricultural workers employed in the county containing the largest city in the area (the central city); or the outlying county must be the place of employment of at least 10,000 nonagricultural workers. (*c*) The nonagricultural labor force living in the county must equal at least 10.0 percent of the nonagricultural labor force living in the county containing the central city; or the outlying county must be the place of residence of a nonagricultural labor force of at least 10,000.

Criteria of integration A county is regarded as integrated with the county or counties containing the central city or cities if either of the following criteria is met: (1) If 15.0 percent of the workers living in the outlying county work in the county or counties containing the central city or cities of the area. (2) If 25.0 percent of those working in the outlying county live in the county or counties containing the central city or cities of the area.

Only where data for criteria 1 and 2 is not conclusive are other related types of information used, as for example newspaper circulation reports, percent of the population in the county located in the central city telephone exchange area, or delivery service areas of retail stores located in central cities, and so on.

Central cities Although there may be several cities of 50,000 or more inhabitants in an SMSA, not all are necessarily central cities. The central city or cities are determined by the following criteria: (1) The largest city in an SMSA is always the central city. (2) One or two additional cities may be secondary central cities if each has (*a*) at least 250,000 inhabitants, (*b*) a population of one-third of that of the largest city and a minimum population of 25,000. When the criteria for twin cities is met, then both cities are considered to be central cities.

SMSA's in New England In New England, SMSA's are defined on the basis of the administratively more important cities and towns instead of counties. Because cities and towns are used as the basic units, more restricted areas result. To compensate for this, a population density of at least 100 persons per square mile is used as the measure of metropolitan character. In general, the same criteria of integration are applied to New England towns and cities as are applied to counties elsewhere in the United States.

Names and distribution The titles of the SMSA's consist of the names of the central cities followed by the names of the states in which the SMSA is located. The names and distribution of the 212 SMSA's defined on the basis of the above criteria for 1960 are shown in Figure A-1.

STANDARD CONSOLIDATED AREAS

In view of the special importance of the metropolitan complexes around New York City and Chicago, several contiguous SMSA's and additional counties that do not appear to meet the formal criteria for integration, but which do have strong interrelationships with adjacent SMSA's, were combined in 1960 to form the New York-Northeastern New Jersey and the Chicago-Northwestern Indiana Standard Consolidated Areas respectively. The former consists of the New York, N.Y., Newark, N.J., Jersey City, N.J., and Paterson-Clifton-Passaic, N.J., SMSA's, plus the counties of Middlesex and Somerset in New Jersey. The latter area consists of the Chicago, Ill., and Gary-Hammond-East Chicago, Ind., SMSA's.

URBANIZED AREAS

This unit was introduced in 1950 to provide a better separation of urban and rural population in the vicinity of the larger cities. In the 1960 definition, each urbanized area contains at least one city of 50,000 inhabitants together with the following types of contiguous areas which form the urban fringe: (1) Incorporated places within 2,500 inhabitants or more. (2) Incorporated places with less than 2,500 inhabitants, provided each has a closely settled area of 100 dwelling units or more. (3) Towns in the New England states, townships in New Jersey and Pennsylvania, and counties elsewhere classified as urban. (4) Enumeration districts in unincorporated territory with a population density of 1,000 inhabitants or more per square mile. (The areas of large nonresidential tracts devoted to urban land

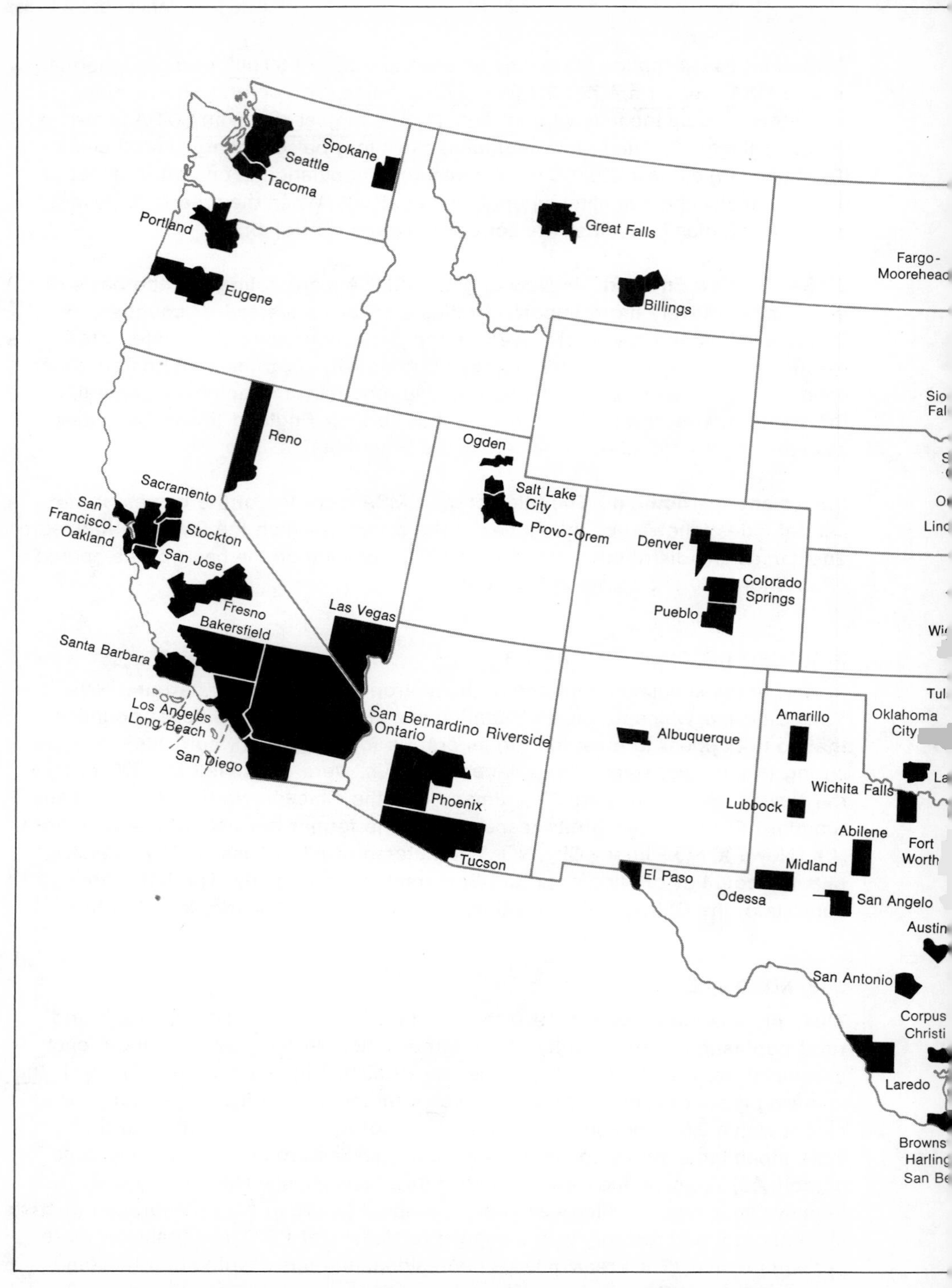

FIG. A.1. STANDARD METROPOLITAN STATISTICAL AREAS IN THE UNITED STATES, 1960.

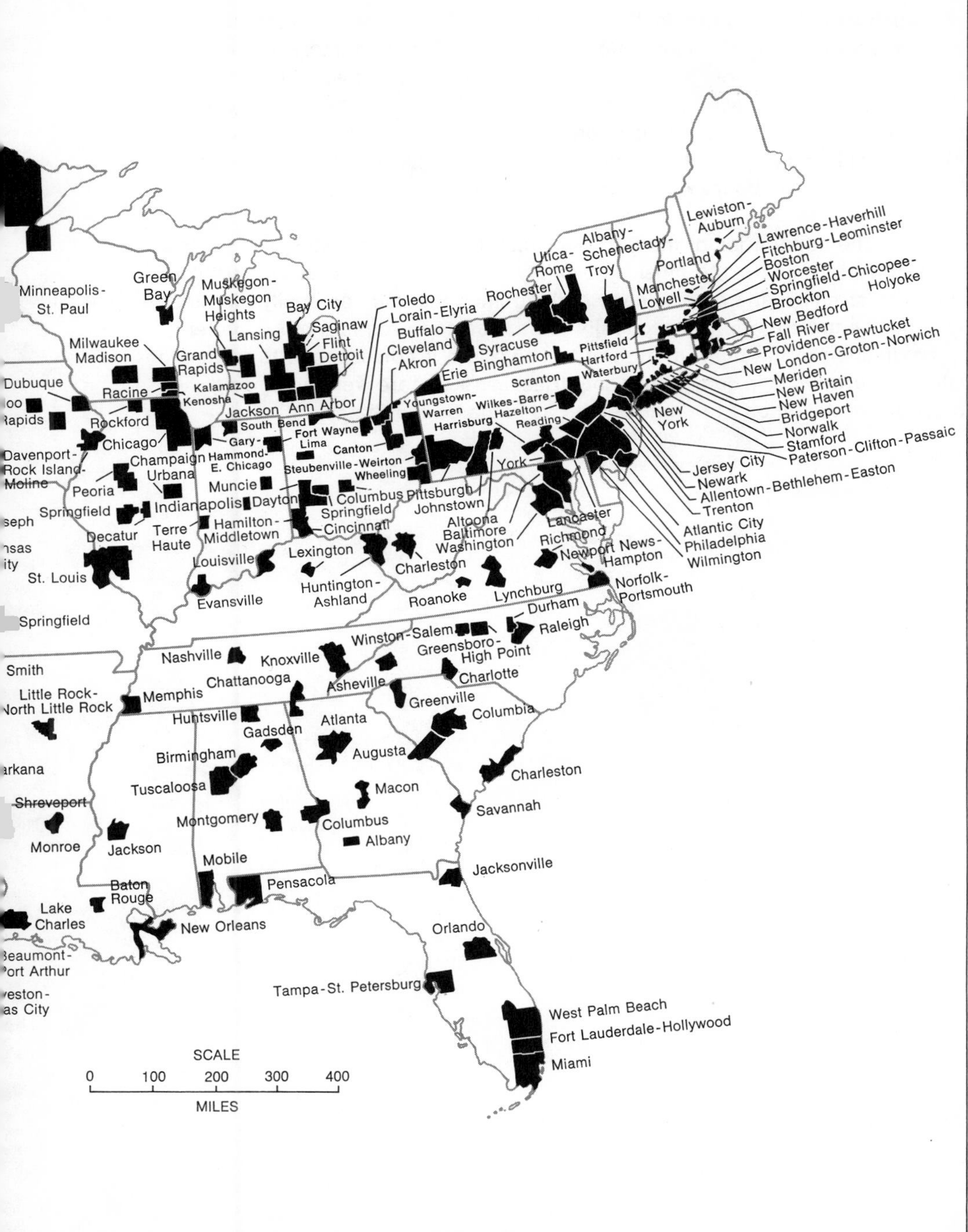

Minneapolis-St. Paul
Green Bay
Milwaukee
Madison
Dubuque
Racine
Kenosha
Rockford
Chicago
Davenport-Rock Island-Moline
Peoria
Champaign Urbana
Springfield
Decatur
St. Louis
Terre Haute
Springfield
Smith
Little Rock-North Little Rock
Shreveport
Monroe
Lake Charles
Muskegon-Muskegon Heights
Grand Rapids
Kalamazoo
Lansing
Bay City
Saginaw
Flint
Detroit
Jackson
Ann Arbor
South Bend
Gary-Hammond-E. Chicago
Fort Wayne
Lima
Muncie
Indianapolis
Dayton
Hamilton-Middletown
Cincinnati
Louisville
Evansville
Toledo
Lorain-Elyria
Buffalo
Cleveland
Akron
Erie
Youngstown-Warren
Canton
Steubenville-Weirton
Wheeling
Columbus
Springfield
Pittsburgh
Johnstown
Altoona
Baltimore
Washington
Lexington
Huntington-Ashland
Charleston
Roanoke
Lynchburg
Rochester
Syracuse
Binghamton
Utica-Rome
Albany-Schenectady-Troy
Scranton
Wilkes-Barre-Hazelton
Harrisburg
Reading
York
Lancaster
Richmond
Newport News-Hampton
Norfolk-Portsmouth
Pittsfield
Hartford
Waterbury
Portland
Lewiston-Auburn
Manchester
Lowell
Lawrence-Haverhill
Fitchburg-Leominster
Boston
Worcester
Springfield-Chicopee-Holyoke
Brockton
New Bedford
Fall River
Providence-Pawtucket
New London-Groton-Norwich
Meriden
New Britain
New Haven
Bridgeport
Norwalk
Stamford
Paterson-Clifton-Passaic
New York
Jersey City
Newark
Allentown-Bethlehem-Easton
Trenton
Atlantic City
Philadelphia
Wilmington
Durham
Raleigh
Winston-Salem
Greensboro-High Point
Nashville
Knoxville
Memphis
Chattanooga
Asheville
Charlotte
Greenville
Columbia
Huntsville
Gadsden
Atlanta
Augusta
Birmingham
Tuscaloosa
Macon
Charleston
Savannah
Montgomery
Columbus
Albany
Jackson
Mobile
Pensacola
Jacksonville
Baton Rouge
New Orleans
Orlando
Tampa-St. Petersburg
West Palm Beach
Fort Lauderdale-Hollywood
Miami
SCALE
0 100 200 300 400
MILES

uses such as railroad yards, factories, and cemeteries were excluded in computing the population density of enumeration districts.) (5) Other enumeration districts in unincorporated territory with lower population density, provided that they served one of the following purposes: (*a*) to eliminate enclaves; (*b*) to close indentations in the urbanized areas of one mile or less across the open end; and (*c*) to link outlying enumeration districts of qualifying density that were no more than 1½ miles from the main body of the urbanized area.

Unlike the boundaries of the SMSA's which follow county lines, the boundaries of urbanized areas for the most part follow features such as roads, streets, railroads, streams, and other clearly defined lines that may be easily identified by census enumerators. Consequently, the urbanized area is a much better approximation to the built-up area of the city; and it corresponds to what are called *conurbations* in some other countries. In 1960 there were according to the above definition 213 urbanized areas in the United States.

LIST OF CITIES BY FUNCTIONAL SPECIALIZATION ON THE HARRIS CLASSIFICATION

States are listed in alphabetic order; the cities, in order of size. Metropolitan districts are marked with a single asterisk and clusters with double asterisks. State capitals in which the political function is clearly dominant are indicated by the letter *P,* those in which the political function is *possibly* dominant are indicated by *P?*

M′ CITIES
(Industrial cities with a marked dominance of manufacturing)

Ala.: Gadsden; *Conn.:* Bridgeport*, Waterbury*, Torrington, Norwich, Danbury, Willimantic; *Ga.:* Rome, La Grange, Griffin; *Ill.:* Rockford*, Elgin, Kewanee, Mount Vernon, Sterling; *Ind.:* South Bend*, Muncie, Anderson, Kokomo, Michigan City, Marion, New Castle, Connersville, Elwood, Goshen; *Iowa:* Newton; *Maine:* Lewiston-Auburn**, Biddeford; *Mass.:* Lowell-Lawrence-Haverhill*, Worcester*, Fall River-New Bedford*, Fitchburg, Taunton, Leominster, North Adams, Gardner, Milfordtown, Southbridgetown, Webstertown, Adamstown, Atholtown; *Mich.:* Detroit*, Flint*, Muskegon-Muskegon Heights**, Monroe, Alpena, Ypsilanti; *Minn.:* Austin; *Miss.:* Laurel; *Mo.:* Hannibal; *Mont.:* Anaconda; *N.H.:* Manchester*, Nashua, Berlin, Dover, Claremont, Rochester; *N.J.:* Bridgeton, Millville; *N.Y.:* Binghampton*, Jamestown, Auburn, Amsterdam, Gloversville-Johnstown**, Lockport, Dunkirk, Corning, Cortland, Fulton, Little Falls; *N.C.:* Winston-Salem*, Durham*, High Point, Gastonia, Salisbury, Concord, Shelby, Statesville, Thomasville; *Ohio:* Youngstown*, Akron*, Canton*, Hamilton-Middletown*,

Springfield*, Lorain, Portsmouth, Steubenville, Elyria, Lancaster, Salem; *Pa.:* Allentown-Bethlehem-Easton*, Reading*, Johnstown*, Lancaster*, York*, Lebanon, Pottstown, Meadville, Coatesville, Berwick, Carlisle, Ellwood City, Hanover, Vandergrift, Waynesboro; *R.I.:* Providence*, Westerly town; *S.C.:* Rock Hill, Greenwood; *Tenn.:* Bristol, Kingsport; *Va.:* Hopewell; *Wash.:* Aberdeen-Hoquiam**, Longview; *W. Va.:* Martinsburg; *Wis.:* Racine-Kenosha*, Beloit, Janesville.

M CITIES
(Industrial cities)

Ala.: Anniston, Decatur, Huntsville; *Calif.:* San Jose*, Eureka; *Colo.:* Pueblo*; *Conn.:* Hartford-New Britain*, New Haven*; *Del.:* Wilmington*; *Ga.:* Columbus*; *Ill.:* Peoria*, Aurora, Joliet, Freeport, Kankakee, Ottawa, Streator, La Salle, Canton; *Ind.:* Evansville*, Fort Wayne*, Richmond, La Porte, Huntington, Bedford, Shelbyville; *Iowa:* Davenport-Rock Island-Moline*, Waterloo*, Muscatine, Fort Madison; *Ky.:* Louisville*, Paducah, Frankfort (P); *La.:* Bogalusa; *Maine:* Augusta (P?), Waterville; *Md.:* Hagerstown; *Mass.:* Springfield*, Pittsfield, Greenfield, Plymouth; *Mich.:* Grand Rapids*, Saginaw-Bay City*, Lansing* (P), Kalamazoo*, Jackson, Battle Creek, Benton Harbor, Marquette, Escanaba, Holland, Sault Ste. Marie, Adrian, Iron Mountain, Niles; *Miss.:* Columbus; *Mo.:* Cape Girardeau; *N.H.:* Concord (P?), Portsmouth, Keene, Laconia; *N.J.:* Trenton* (P?), Dover; *N.Y.:* Buffalo-Niagara Falls*, Albany-Schenectady-Troy* (P?), Rochester*, Syracuse*, Utica-Rome*, Poughkeepsie, Newburgh, Kingston, Oswego, Olean, Batavia, Ogdensburg, Hornell, Geneva, Beacon, Massena, Oneida, Port Jervis; *N.C.:* Greensboro*, Fayetteville, Elizabeth City; *Ohio:* Cleveland*, Cincinnati*, Toledo*, Dayton*, Lima, Zanesville, Mansfield, Newark, Sandusky, Chillicothe, Tiffin, Cambridge, Piqua, Fremont, Fostoria, New Philadelphia, Ashland, Coshocton; *Oreg.:* Klamath Falls, Astoria; *Pa.:* Philadelphia*, Pittsburgh*, Erie*, Williamsport, Beaver Falls, Sunbury, Warren, Chambersburg, Lewistown, Franklin; *S.C.:* Spartanburg, Anderson; *Tenn.:* Chattanooga*, Knoxville*; *Tex.:* Beaumont-Port Arthur*; *Va.:* Lynchburg, Petersburg, Danville, Winchester; *Wash.:* Tacoma*, Everett, Port Angeles; *W. Va.:* Wheeling*, Huntington-Ashland*, Parkersburg, Clarksburg; *Wis.:* Milwaukee*, Oshkosh, La Crosse, Sheboygan, Manitowoc-Two Rivers**, Eau Claire, Appleton, Marinette-Menominee**, Wausau, Watertown.

R CITIES
(Retail centers)

Ala.: Dothan; *Ark.:* Jonesboro, Blytheville; *Calif.:* Fresno*, Stockton*, Bakersfield, Ventura, Santa Rosa, Brawley; *Colo.:* Greeley, Grand Junction; *Fla.:* Orlando, Lakeland, Tallahassee (P); *Idaho:* Boise (P?); *Ill.:* Lincoln; *Iowa.:* Fort Dodge–Boone, Oskaloosa; *Kans.:* Wichita*, Pittsburg, Parsons, Emporia, Newton, Fort Scott, Chanute, Dodge City; *Ky.:* Lexington, Bowling Green; *La.:* Shreveport*, Lake Charles, Lafayette; *Maine:* Bangor; *Minn.:* St. Cloud, Mankato;

Miss.: Jackson* (P?), Clarksdale; *Mont.:* Helena (P?); *Nebr.:* Lincoln* (P?), Grand Island, Hastings, North Platte, Fremont, Norfolk, Beatrice; *Nev.:* Reno; *N. Mex.:* Roswell; *N.C.:* Raleigh (P), Kinston; *N. Dak.:* Grand Forks, Minot, Bismarck (P); *Ohio:* Marietta, Painesville; *Okla.:* Tulsa*, Muskogee, Enid, Shawnee, Ardmore, Chickasha, Lawton, McAlester, Seminole, Ada, Wewoka; *Oreg.:* Medford; *Pa.:* West Chester; *S.C.:* Florence; *S. Dak.:* Aberdeen, Huron, Mitchell, Rapid City, Watertown; *Tex.:* El Paso*, Austin* (P), Corpus Christi*, Amarillo*, Wichita Falls, Laredo, San Angelo, Abilene, Brownsville, Lubbock, Tyler, Paris, Temple, Corsicana, Big Spring, Brownwood, Greenville, Harlingen, Del Rio, Cleburne, Palestine, San Benito, Sweetwater, Pampa; *Utah:* Provo; *Va.:* Charlottesville, Staunton; *Wash.:* Walla Walla; *Wis.:* Madison* (P?), Ashland.

D CITIES
(Diversified cities)

Ala.: Birmingham*, Montgomery* (P?), Tuscaloosa, Selma, Florence; *Ark.:* Little Rock* (P?), Texarkana**, Fort Smith, Pine Bluff, El Dorado; *Calif.:* Los Angeles*, Sacramento* (P), Modesto; *Fla.:* Tampa-St. Petersburg*; *Ga.:* Atlanta*, Augusta*, Athens, Waycross, Brunswick; *Idaho:* Pocatello; *Ill.:* Chicago*, Springfield* (P), Decatur*, Quincy, Bloomington, Jacksonville, Mattoon, Cairo, Centralia; *Ind.:* Indianapolis*, Terre Haute*, Logansport, Vincennes, Peru, Frankfort, Crawfordsville; *Iowa:* Des Moines* (P?), Cedar Rapids*, Dubuque, Burlington, Mason City, Marshalltown, Keokuk; *Kans.:* Topeka* (P?), Hutchinson, Coffeyville, Arkansas City, Atchison, Independence, El Dorado; *Ky.:* Owensboro, Middlesboro; *La.:* Alexandria; *Md.:* Baltimore*, Frederick, Salisbury; *Mass.:* Boston*; *Mich.:* Owosso, Traverse City; *Minn.:* Minneapolis-St. Paul*, Winona, Faribault, Albert Lea, Brainerd; *Miss.:* Vicksburg, Hattiesburg, Greenville, Natchez, McComb; *Mo.:* St. Louis*, Kansas City*, St. Joseph*, Springfield*, Joplin, Jefferson City (P), Sedalia, Moberly; *Mont.:* Great Falls, Missoula; *N.Y.:* New York*, Middletown, Glens Falls, Plattsburgh, Oneonta, Hudson; *N.C.:* Charlotte*, Rocky Mount, Goldsboro, New Bern; *Ohio:* Columbus* (P?), East Liverpool, Ashtabula, Findlay, Wooster, Xenia, Bucyrus; *Okla.:* Okmulgee, Ponca City, Bartlesville; *Oreg.:* Portland*, Salem (P?), Eugene; *Pa.:* Butler, Oil City, Bradford, Du Bois; *S.C.:* Columbia* (P?), Greenville, Sumter; *Tenn.:* Nashville* (P?), Johnson City, Jackson; *Tex.:* Houston*, Fort Worth*, Marshall, Sherman, Denison; *Vt.:* Burlington, Rutland, Barre; *Va.:* Richmond* (P?); *Wash.:* Spokane*, Bellingham, Olympia (P), Bremerton; *W. Va.:* Charleston* (P?); *Wis.:* Fond Du Lac, Stevens Point; *Wyo.:* Cheyenne, Casper.

W CITIES
(Wholesale centers)

Calif.: San Francisco*, Riverside, Redlands, Salinas; *Colo.:* Denver*; *Fla.:* Sanford; *Ga.:* Albany, Valdosta; *Iowa:* Sioux City*; *Kans.:* Salina; *Ky.:* Hopkinsville; *Miss.:* Greenwood; *Mont.:* Billings; *Nebr.:* Omaha*; *N.C.:* Wilson; *N. Dak.:* Fargo; *Okla.:* Oklahoma City*; *S. Dak.:* Sioux Falls; *Tenn.:* Memphis*; *Tex.:* Dallas*, San Antonio*, Waco*; *Utah:* Salt Lake City*; *Va.:* Suffolk; *Wash.:* Seattle*, Yakima, Wenatchee.

S CITIES
(Mining towns)

Colo.: Trinidad; *Ill.:* West Frankfort, Harrisburg; *Mich.:* Ironwood; *Minn.:* Hibbing, Virginia; *Mont.:* Butte; *Pa.:* Scranton–Wilkes-Barre*, Pottsville**, Hazleton, Connellsville; *W. Va.:* Fairmont, Bluefield, Morgantown.

T CITIES
(Transportation centers)

Ala.: Mobile*; *Calif.:* San Bernardino; *Conn.:* New London; *Fla.:* Jacksonville*, Pensacola; *Ga.:* Savannah*, Macon*; *Ill.:* Danville, Galesburg; *Ind.:* Elkhart*; *Iowa:* Ottumwa, Clinton; *La.:* New Orleans*, Monroe; *Maine:* Portland*; *Md.:* Cumberland; *Mich.:* Port Huron; *Minn.:* Duluth-Superior*; *Miss.:* Meridian; *N.Y.:* Elmira, Watertown; *N.C.:* Wilmington; *Ohio:* Marion; *Pa.:* Harrisburg* (P), Altoona*, New Castle; *S.C.:* Charleston*; *Tex.:* Galveston*; *Utah:* Ogden; *Va.:* Norfolk-Portsmouth-Newport News*, Roanoke*; *Wis.:* Green Bay.

E CITIES
(University towns)

Colo.: Boulder; *Fla.:* Gainesville; *Ill.:* Champaign-Urbana**; *Ind.:* Lafayette, Bloomington; *Iowa:* Iowa City, Ames; *Kans.:* Lawrence, Manhattan; *La.:* Baton Rouge (P); *Mich.:* Ann Arbor; *Mo.:* Columbia; *N.Y.:* Ithaca; *Okla.:* Norman, Stillwater; *Tex.:* Denton; *Utah:* Logan.

In the following towns college instruction is an important but secondary function: *Ala.:* Tuscaloosa; *Ariz.:* Tucson; *Colo.:* Greeley, Fort Collins; *Fla.:* Tallahassee; *Ga.:* Athens; *Kans.:* Pittsburg, Emporia; *Ky.:* Lexington, Bowling Green; *La.:* Lafayette; *Mich.:* Ypsilanti; *Miss.:* Columbus; *Mo.:* Cape Girardeau; *Mont.:* Missoula; *Nebr.:* Lincoln*; *Nev.:* Reno; *N. Mex.:* Albuquerque; *N.C.:* Durham*, Raleigh; *N. Dak.:* Fargo, Grand Forks; *Okla.:* Chickasha; *Oreg.:* Eugene; *S.C.:* Rock Hill; *Tex.:* Austin*, Lubbock; *Utah:* Provo; *Vt.:* Burlington; *Va.:* Charlottesville; *W. Va.:* Morgantown; *Wis.:* Madison.

X CITIES
(Resort and retirement towns)

Ariz.: Phoenix*, Tucson; *Ark.:* Hot Springs; *Calif.:* San Diego*, Santa Barbara, Santa Cruz; *Colo.:* Colorado Springs, Fort Collins; *Fla.:* Miami*, West Palm Beach, Daytona Beach, Key West, St. Augustine; *Ga.:* Thomasville; *Minn.:*

Rochester; *Miss.:* Biloxi, Gulfport; *N.J.:* Atlantic City*; *N. Mex.:* Albuquerque, Santa Fe (P?); *N.Y.:* Saratoga Springs; *N.C.:* Asheville*.

P CITIES
(Political capitals)

Washington*, D.C.

Source: Harris (1943), full mimeographed list of cities.

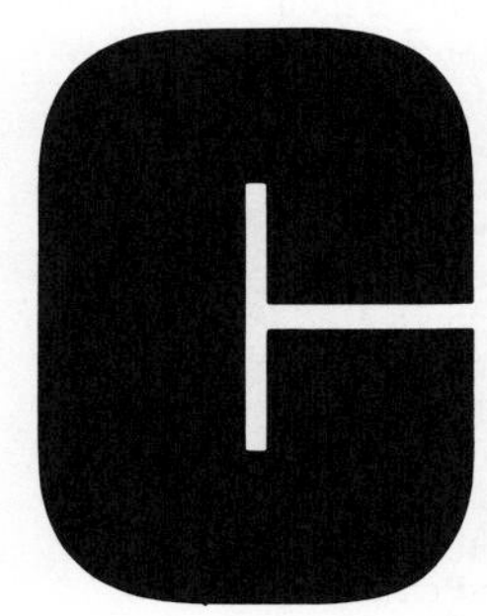

LIST OF CITIES BY FUNCTIONAL SPECIALIZATION IN THE NELSON CLASSIFICATION

Key

	Plus 1 SD	**Plus 2 SD**	**Plus 3 SD**
Manufacturing	Mf	Mf2	Mf3
Retail trade	R	R2	R3
Professional service	Pf	Pf2	Pf3
Transportation and communication	T	T2	T3
Personal service	Ps	Ps2	Ps3
Public administration	Pb	Pb2	Pb3
Wholesale trade	W	W2	W3
Finance, insurance, and real estate	F	F2	F3
Mining	Mi	Mi2	Mi3
Diversified	D		

Alabama

Anniston	Pb
Auburn	Pf3Ps2
Birmingham	D
Decatur	D
Dothan	RW
Florence	D
Gadsden	Mf
Huntsville	RPbF
Mobile	Pb
Montgomery	PbF
Opelika	D
Phenix City	D
Selma	D
Sheffield	T
Talladega	D
Tuscaloosa	Pf

Arizona

Amphitheater	R
Phoenix	PsWF
Tucson	Ps2PfF

Arkansas

Blytheville	R2Ps
Camden	D
El Dorado	D
Fayetteville	Pf2Ps
Fort Smith	RW
Helena	D
Hot Springs	Ps3R
Jonesboro	RTW
Little Rock–North Little Rock	TWF
Pine Bluff	TW
Texarkana	Pb

California

Alisal	W3
Anaheim	W
Antioch	Mf
Bakersfield	Ps
Brawley	W3
Chico	RWF
Corona	W3Ps

Costa Mesa	Mf
El Centro	R3W3PsPbF
Eureka	D
Fresno	PsWF
Fullerton	W
Hanford	R3
Lodi	D
Los Angeles	F
Madera	R2
Merced	R2Pb
Modesto	RWF
Monterey	Ps2R
Napa	D
Newport Beach	F3R
Oceanside	R2PsW
Oildale	Mi2R
Ontario	D
Orange	Pf
Oxnard	Pb3W2
Petaluma	W2R
Pittsburg	Mf
Pomona	W
Redding	R
Riverside	PbWF
Sacramento	Pb3
Salinas	W2RF
San Bernardino	Pb
San Buenaventura	MiPb
San Diego	Pb2PsF
San Francisco–Oakland	F2
San Jose	D
San Luis Obispo	RPfT
Santa Ana	RPbF
Santa Barbara	Ps2F
Santa Cruz	Ps2RF
Santa Maria	RPsW
Santa Paula	W3Pb
Santa Rosa	R2WF
Seaside	Ps2RPb
Stockton	Pb
Tulare	R3W
Visalia	R
Watsonville	W3R

Colorado

Boulder	Pf3Ps2
Colorado Springs	Ps2F
Denver	WF
Fort Collins	Pf2F
Grand Junction	TW
Greeley	RPfWF
Pueblo	Pb
Trinidad	RMi

Connecticut

Ansonia	Mf2
Bridgeport	Mf
Danbury	Mf
Derby	Mf2
Hartford	F3
Meriden	Mf
Middletown	D
New Britain–Bristol	Mf2
New Haven	D
New London	Pb
Norwich	D
Shelton	Mf
Stamford-Norwalk	D
Torrington	Mf
Wallingford	Mf2
Waterbury	Mf
Willimantic	Mf

District of Columbia

Washington	Pb3F

Delaware

Wilmington	D

Florida

Bradenton	RPsF
Brownville–B.–G.	Pb3
Clearwater	Ps2F
Daytona Beach	Ps3F2R
Fort Lauderdale	F3Ps2R
Fort Myers	R2Ps
Fort Pierce	W3RF
Gainesville	Pf3Ps
Hollywood	Ps3F3
Jacksonville	TPsPbFW
Key West	Pb3Ps
Lakeland	F
Lake Worth	R2F2Ps
Miami	Ps3RF
Ocala	R2Ps
Orlando	Ps2F2W
Panama City	Pb
Pensacola	Pb2
St. Augustine	Ps2T
St. Petersburg	Ps2F2R
Sanford	W3
Sarasota	Ps3RF
Tallahassee	Pb2Pf
Tampa	PsW
Warrington	Pb3
West Palm Beach	Ps3RF

Georgia

Augusta	D
Albany	W
Americus	D
Athens	Pf
Atlanta	F2
Brunswick	Ps2
Columbus	D
Dalton	Mf
Decatur	F3W
Dublin	D
Gainesville	W
Griffin	D
La Grange	Mf
Macon	Pb
Marietta	F
Moultrie	D
Rome	D
Savannah	D
Thomasville	D
Valdosta	D
Waycross	T3

Idaho

Boise	F2PbW
Caldwell	RW
Coeur d'Alene	D
Idaho Falls	W2R
Lewiston	R
Moscow	Pf3Ps2
Nampa	T2
Pocatello	T3
Twin Falls	R2W2

Illinois

Alton	D
Aurora	D
Bloomington	F3
Cairo	RW
Canton	D
Carbondale	PfT
Centralia	T3
Champaign	Pb3Ps
Chicago	F
Collinsville	D
Danville	D
Decatur	D
De Kalb	D
Dixon	D
Elgin	D
Freeport	F2
Galesburg	T2
Harrisburg	Mi3
Jacksonville	Pf3
Joliet	D
Kankakee	D
Kewanee	Mf
La Salle	Mf
Lincoln	Pf
Macomb	R
Marion	Mi2
Mattoon	T2
Monmouth	F3R
Mount Vernon	D
Ottawa	D
Pekin	D
Peoria	D
Quincy	D
Rockford	Mf
Springfield	PbF
Sterling	Mf

Streator	Mf
Urbana	Pf3
Waukegan	Pb
West Frankfort	Mi3
Wood River	Mf

Indiana

Anderson	Mf
Bedford	D
Bloomington	Pf3
Columbus	Mf
Connersville	Mf
Crawfordsville	D
Elkhart	Mf
Elwood	Mf
Evansville	D
Fort Wayne	D
Frankfort	T3
Goshen	Mf
Huntington	D
Indianapolis	F
Kokomo	Mf
Lafayette	D
La Porte	Mf
Logansport	T2
Marion	D
Michigan City	D
Muncie	Mf
New Castle	Mf
Peru	T3
Richmond	Mf
Shelbyville	D
South Bend	Mf
Terre Haute	D
Valparaiso	D
Vincennes	R
Wabash	Mf
Washington	T3
West Lafayette	Pf3Ps

Iowa

Ames	Pf3Ps
Boone	T3
Burlington	W2
Cedar Rapids	R
Charles City	D
Clinton	D
Davenport, Ia.–Rock Island–Moline, Ill.	D
Des Moines	F3
Dubuque	D
Fort Dodge	R
Fort Madison	T2
Iowa City	Pf3
Keokuk	D
Marshalltown	D
Mason City	D
Muscatine	D
Newton	Mf
Oskaloosa	R
Ottumwa	D
Sioux City	W2
Waterloo	D

Kansas

Arkansas City	T2
Atchison	D
Chanute	T
Coffeyville	D
Dodge City	W2R2T
El Dorado	Mi
Emporia	T2
Fort Scott	F3T
Garden City	R2
Great Bend	Mi2
Hutchinson	WR
Independence	D
Junction City	Pb3R2Ps
Lawrence	Pf2Ps
Leavenworth	Pb3
Manhattan	Pf3PsPbF
Newton	T3
Ottawa	R
Parsons	T3
Pittsburg	T
Salina	RWF
Topeka	TPbF
Wichita	F
Winfield	Pf

Kentucky

Bowling Green	D
Frankfort	Pb3
Henderson	D
Hopkinsville	RPs
Lexington	PfPs
Louisville	D
Madisonville	Mi3
Middlesboro	Mi2R
Owensboro	D
Paducah	T2
Richmond	PfPb

Louisiana

Alexandria	Ps
Bastrop	Mf
Baton Rouge	D
Bogalusa	D
Crowley	D
Houma	Mi3
Lafayette	D
Lake Charles	D
Monroe	PsW
New Iberia	MiW
New Orleans	TWF
Opelousas	R
Ruston	Pf2
Shreveport	D
West Monroe	RW

Maine

Auburn	Mf
Augusta	Pb2
Bangor	W
Bath	D
Biddeford	Mf2
Lewiston	Mf
Portland	WF
Saco	Mf
Sanford	Mf2
Waterville	D

Maryland

Annapolis	Pf3Pb2
Baltimore	D
Cambridge	D
Cumberland	T3
Frederick	Pb
Hagerstown	D
Salisbury	D

Massachusetts

Adams-Renfrew	Mf2
Boston	F
Brockton	Mf
Clinton	Mf
Fall River	Mf
Fitchburg	Mf
Gardner	Mf
Gloucester	W2
Greenfield	Ps
Haverhill	Mf
Lawrence	Mf
Leominster	Mf2
Lowell	Mf
Marlboro	Mf
Milford	Mf2
New Bedford	Mf
Newburyport	Mf
North Adams	Mf
Northampton	D
Plymouth	D
Southbridge	Mf2
Springfield-Holyoke	Mf
Taunton	Mf
Webster	Mf2
Worcester	D

Michigan

Adrian	D
Albion	Mf
Alpena	D
Ann Arbor	Pf3
Battle Creek	D
Bay City	D
Benton Harbor	Mf
Cadillac	D
Detroit	Mf
Escanaba	T2

Flint	Mf
Grand Rapids	D
Holland	D
Ironwood	Mi3
Jackson	D
Kalamazoo	D
Lansing	D
Marquette	T2Pb
Menominee	Mf
Midland	Mf
Monroe	Mf
Mount Pleasant	PfMi
Muskegon	Mf
Niles	MfT
Owosso	D
Pontiac	Mf
Port Huron	D
Saginaw	Mf
St. Joseph	Mf
Sault Ste. Marie	D
Springfield Place	Mf
Traverse City	Pf
Willow Run	Pf2
Ypsilanti	D

Minnesota

Albert Lea	D
Austin	Mf
Bemidji	R
Brainerd	T3
Duluth, Minn.–Superior, Wis.	T2W
Faribault	Pf2
Fergus Falls	RPf
Hibbing	Mi3
Mankato	W2R
Minneapolis–St. Paul	F2W
Moorhead	W3R
Owatonna	F3
Red Wing	D
Rochester	Pf3Ps2
St. Cloud	Pf
Virginia	Mi3
Winona	D

Mississippi

Biloxi	Ps2Pb
Clarksdale	RPs
Columbus	D
Greenville	D
Greenwood	W2R
Gulfport	Ps
Hattiesburg	D
Jackson	PsF
Laurel	Ps3
McComb	T3R
Meridian	D
Natchez	D
Pascagoula	D
Tupelo	W2
Vicksburg	D

Missouri

Cape Girardeau	D
Carthage	D
Columbia	Pf3Ps
Fulton	Pf3
Hannibal	T
Jefferson City	Pb3
Joplin	W2R
Kansas City	F
Kirksville	RPf
Mexico	D
Moberly	T3
Poplar Bluff	RT
St. Charles	Mf
St. Joseph	W
St. Louis	Ps
Sedalia	T2W
Sikeston	RW
Springfield	TW
Webster Groves	F3W

Montana

Anaconda	Mf
Billings	W2RPsF
Bozeman	Pf2RPs
Butte	Mi3
Great Falls	TF
Helena	Pb3F3
Missoula	PfT

Nebraska

Beatrice	D
Fremont	RW
Grand Island	TWF
Hastings	RW
Kearney	R3Pf2Ps2W
Lincoln	F2
Norfolk	R2W2
North Platte	T3
Omaha	F3W
Scottsbluff	R2W

Nevada

Las Vegas	Ps3
Reno	Ps2F

New Hampshire

Berlin	Mf2
Claremont	Mf
Concord	PfPbF
Dover	Mf
Keene	F
Laconia	D
Manchester	Mf
Nashua	Mf
Portsmouth	D
Rochester	Mf

New Jersey

Asbury Park	Ps3RPb
Atlantic City	Ps3R
Bridgeton	Mf
Burlington	Mf
Long Branch	Pb3
Millville	Mf
Phillipsburg	Mf
Princeton	Pf3
Red Bank	Pb2F
Trenton	Pb

New Mexico

Albuquerque	Pb2PsF
Carlsbad	Mi3
Clovis	T2Ps
Hobbs	Mi3
Las Cruces	Pb2R
Roswell	Ps2RPb
Santa Fe	R2Pb2Ps

New York

Albany-Troy	Pb2
Amsterdam	Mf2
Auburn	Mf
Batavia	D
Beacon	Pf2
Binghamton	R3Mf
Buffalo	D
Corning	Mf
Cortland	Mf
Dunkirk	Mf
Elmira	D
Fulton	Mf2
Geneva	D
Glens Falls	F3
Gloversville	Mf
Hornell	T3
Hudson	D
Ithaca	Pf3
Jamestown	Mf
Johnstown	Mf
Kingston	D
Lockport	Mf
Massena	Mf
Middletown	Pf
Newark	RPf
Newburgh	D
New York–Northeastern N.J.	F2
Niagara Falls	Mf
Ogdensburg	Pf
Olean	D
Oneida	Mf
Oneonta	T3
Oswego	D
Peekskill	T
Plattsburgh	Pf
Poughkeepsie	D
Rochester	Mf

Rome	Mf
Saratoga Springs	Ps2
Schenectady	Mf
Syracuse	D
Utica	D
Watertown	F

North Carolina

Albemarle	Mf
Asheville	Ps
Burlington	Mf
Charlotte	WF
Concord	Mf
Durham	D
Elizabeth City	D
Fayetteville	Ps2R
Gastonia	Mf
Goldsboro	D
Greensboro	F
Greenville	Ps
Henderson	D
Hickory	D
High Point	Mf
Kannapolis	Mf2
Kinston	D
Lexington	Mf
Monroe	D
New Bern	Pb2
Raleigh	F2PfPbPs
Reidsville	Mf
Rocky Mount	T
Salisbury	T
Sanford	D
Shelby	D
Statesville	D
Thomasville	Mf2
Wilmington	T
Wilson	D
Winston-Salem	D

North Dakota

Bismarck	Pb2WF
Fargo	W2F2R
Grand Forks	T
Jamestown	RTPf
Minot	RTW

Ohio

Akron	Mf
Alliance	Mf
Ashland	Mf
Ashtabula	T3
Athens	Pf2
Bellefontaine	T3
Bowling Green	Pf2R
Bucyrus	D
Cambridge	D
Canton	Mf
Chillicothe	D
Cincinnati	D
Cleveland	D
Columbus	F
Conneaut	T3
Coshocton	D
Dayton	Pb
Defiance	D
Delaware	Pf
East Liverpool	Mf
Findlay	D
Fostoria	Mf
Fremont	D
Hamilton	Mf
Kent	Pf
Lancaster	Mf
Lima	D
Lorain	Mf
Mansfield	Mf
Marietta	D
Marion	T
Mount Vernon	D
Newark	D
New Philadelphia	D
Painesville	Mf
Piqua	Mf
Portsmouth	T
Salem	Mf
Sandusky	Mf
Sidney	Mf
Springfield	D
Steubenville	Mf
Tiffin	D
Toledo	D
Troy	Mf
Van Wert	DF
Washington	R
Wooster	Pf
Xenia	Pb3
Youngstown	Mf
Zanesville	D

Oklahoma

Ada	RPs
Ardmore	RF
Bartlesville	Mi3
Chickasha	R
Duncan	Mi3
Durant	R2
El Reno	T3Pb
Enid	RW
Guthrie	Ps
Lawton	Ps2RPb
McAlester	Pb3R
Miami	D
Muskogee	D
Norman	Pf3Ps
Oklahoma City	Pb2F2
Okmulgee	D
Ponca City	D
Sapulpa	D
Seminole	Mi3
Shawnee	D
Stillwater	Pf3Ps
Tulsa	F

Oregon

Albany	R
Astoria	D
Bend	D
Corvallis	Pf3Ps2
Eugene	PfPsF
Klamath Falls	RT
Medford	RWF
Pendleton	D
Portland	WF
Salem	PbF
Springfield	D

Pennsylvania

Allentown-Bethlehem	Mf
Altoona	T3
Berwick	Mf
Bloomsburg	D
Bradford	Mi
Bristol	Mf2
Butler	D
Canonsburg	D
Carlisle	Pb2
Chambersburg	Pb3
Coatesville	Mf
Columbia	MfPb
Connellsville	T2
Conshohocken	Mf2
Donora	Mf2
Du Bois	T2
Easton	Mf
Ellwood City	Mf2
Erie	D
Farrell	Mf2
Franklin	D
Greensburg	F
Hanover	Mf
Harrisburg	Pb3T
Hazleton	Mi2
Indiana	Mi2Pf
Jeannette	Mf
Johnstown	D
Lancaster	Mf
Latrobe	Mf
Lebanon	Mf
Lewistown	D
Lock Haven	D
Mahanoy City	Mi3
Meadville	D
Monessen	Mf2
Mount Carmel	Mi3
New Castle	T
Norristown	Mf
Oil City	D
Philadelphia	F

Phoenixville	Mf
Pittsburgh	D
Pottstown	Mf
Pottsville	Mi
Reading	Mf
Scranton	Mi2
Shamokin	Mi2
Sharon	Mf
Shenandoah	Mi3
State College	Pf3Ps
Sunbury	T
Tamaqua	TMi3
Uniontown	R2Mi2
Warren	D
Washington	D
Waynesboro	Mf
West Chester	Pf
Williamsport	D
Wilkes-Barre	Mi3
York	D

Rhode Island

Bristol	Mf2
Central Falls	Mf2
Newport	Pb3
Providence	Mf
Woonsocket	Mf2

South Carolina

Anderson	D
Brandon-Judson	Mf3
Charleston	D
Columbia	F
Florence	T
Greenwood	D
Greenville	F
Orangeburg	D
Rock Hill	Mf
Spartanburg	D
Sumter	F

South Dakota

Aberdeen	R2WF
Huron	RTW
Mitchell	R2W2
Rapid City	Ps2RPb
Sioux Falls	W2F
Watertown	R2W2

Tennessee

Bristol	D
Chattanooga	D
Clarksville	D
Cleveland	D
Columbia	D
Dyersburg	R
Elizabethton	D
Jackson	T
Johnson City	W
Kingsport	Mf
Knoxville	D
Memphis	W
Morristown	D
Murfreesboro	Pf
Nashville	F
Oak Ridge	MfPb

Texas

Abilene	PsWF
Alice	Mi2
Amarillo	W2TPs
Austin	PbF
Baytown	Mf
Beaumont	D
Big Spring	RT
Borger	Mi
Brownsville	D
Brownwood	RW
Bryan	Pf
Cleburne	T3
Corpus Christi	PsPb
Corsicana	D
Dallas	F3W
Del Rio	RTPs
Denison	T3
Denton	Pf2
Edinburg	W3R
El Paso	T
Fort Worth	D
Gainesville	RMi
Galveston	T2F2
Garland	WF
Greenville	R
Harlingen	RWF
Houston	F
Kingsville	T2
Lamesa	MiR
Laredo	R
Longview	D
Lubbock	RWPsF
Lufkin	D
McAllen	RWF
McKinney	Pf
Marshall	T
Mercedes	W3R
Midland	Mi3
Mission	R
Nacogdoches	D
New Braunfels	Ps
Odessa	Mi3
Orange	D
Palestine	T3
Pampa	Mi2
Paris	R
Plainview	R2
Port Arthur	Mf
San Angelo	RPs
San Antonio	Ps3Pb2F
San Benito	W3
Sherman	D
Snyder	Mi3
Sweetwater	R
Temple	Pf
Terrell	Pf
Texarkana	Pb2
Texas City	D
Tyler	RF
Vernon	R2
Victoria	D
Waco	W
Waxahachie	R
Wichita Falls	RMiPs

Utah

Logan	Pf2R
Ogden	Pb3T2
Provo	Pf
Salt Lake City	F

Vermont

Barre	F
Burlington	Pf
Rutland	T

Virginia

Bristol	D
Charlottesville	Pf
Danville	D
Fredericksburg	D
Harrisonburg	RW
Hopewell	Mf
Lynchburg	D
Martinsville	Mf
Newport News	TPb
Newsome Park	D
Norfolk-Portsmouth	Pb2
Petersburg	D
Richmond	F2
Riverview	Pb3Ps
Roanoke	T2
Staunton	D
Suffolk	W3
Waynesboro	Mf
Winchester	R

Washington

Aberdeen	D
Bellingham	D
Bremerton	D
Everett	D
Hoquiam	Mf
Kennewick	D
Longview	Mf
Olympia	Pb3
Pasco	T2
Port Angeles	D
Pullman	Pf3Ps
Puyallup	D
Richland	Mf2

Seattle	F2
Spokane	F2W
Tacoma	PbF
Walla Walla	D
Wenatchee	RWF
Yakima	W2RF
West Virginia	
Beckley	Mi3
Bluefield	T2WF
Charleston	D
Clarksburg	D
Fairmont	Mi2
Huntington, W. Va.–Ashland, Ky.	T
Martinsburg	D
Morgantown	PfMi
Moundsville	Mf
Parkersburg	D
South Parkersburg	Mf
Weirton	Mf2
Wheeling	D
Wisconsin	
Appleton	D
Ashland	T2
Beaver Dam	D
Beloit	Mf
Chippewa Falls	D
Eau Claire	D
Fond du Lac	D
Green Bay	TW
Janesville	D
Kenosha	Mf
La Crosse	D
Madison	Pf2PbF
Manitowoc	Mf
Marinette	D
Marshfield	W
Menasha	Mf2
Milwaukee	D
Neenah	Mf
Oshkosh	D
Racine	Mf
Sheboygan	Mf
Stevens Point	F3
Two Rivers	Mf2
Watertown	D
Waukesha	D
Wausau	F3
Wisconsin Rapids	Mf
Wyoming	
Casper	Mi
Cheyenne	T3Pb2
Laramie	T2Pf2Pb2
Rock Springs	T2
Sheridan	D

Source: Nelson (1955), Appendix.

ACKERMAN, E. A. [1963], "Where Is a Research Frontier?"; *Annals of the Association of American Geographers,* 53, 429–440.

ADAMS, J. S. [1970], "Residential Structure of Midwestern Cities"; *Annals of the Association of American Geographers,* 60, 37–62.

ADRIAN, C. R. [1961], *Governing Urban America.* New York: McGraw-Hill.

ADVISORY COMMITTEE ON INTERGOVERNMENTAL RELATIONS [1968], *Urban and Rural America: Policies for Future Growth.* Washington, D.C.: U.S. Government Printing Office.

——— [1963], *Performance of Urban Functions: Local and Area Wide.* Washington, D.C.: U.S. Government Printing Office.

ALEXANDER, J. W. [1954], "The Basic–Nonbasic Concept of Urban Economic Functions"; *Economic Geography,* 30, 246–261.

ALEXANDERSSON, G. [1956], *The Industrial Structure of American Cities.* Lincoln, Neb.: University of Nebraska Press.

ALONSO, W. [1960], "A Theory of the Urban Land Market"; *Regional Science Association, Papers and Proceedings,* 6, 149–157.

——— [1964], "Location Theory," in J. Friedman and W. Alonso, eds.; *Regional Development and Planning,* 79–81. Cambridge, Mass.: The M.I.T. Press.

ANDERSON, T. A. and J. A. EGELAND [1961], "Spatial Aspects of Social Area Analysis"; *American Sociological Review,* 26, 392–398.

ANDREWS, R. B. [1953], "Historical Development of the Base Concept"; *Land Economics,* 29, 161–171.

AUROUSSEAU, M. [1921], "The Distribution of Population: A Constructive Problem"; *The Geographical Review,* 11, 563–592.

BARTHOLOMEW, H. [1955], *Land Uses in American Cities.* Cambridge, Mass.: Harvard University Press.

BAUMOL, W. J. [1958], "On the Theory of Oligopoly"; *Economica,* 24, 187–198.

BECKMANN, M. [1958], "City Hierarchies and the Distribution of City Size"; *Economic Development and Cultural Change,* 6, 243–248.

BELL, W. and C. C. MOSKOS [1964], "A Comment on Udry's Increasing Scale and Spatial Differentiation"; *Social Forces,* 62, 414–417.

BERGEL, E. E. [1955], *Urban Sociology.* New York: McGraw-Hill.

BERRY, B. J. L. [1959], "Ribbon Developments in the Urban Business Pattern"; *Annals of the Association of American Geographers,* 49, 145–155.

——— [1960], "The Impact of Expanding Metropolitan Communities upon the Central Place Hierarchy"; *Annals of the Association of American Geographers,* 50, 112–116.

——— [1961], "City Size Distributions and Economic Development"; *Economic Development and Cultural Change,* 9, 573–588.

——— [1963], *Commercial Structure and Commercial Blight.* Research Paper 85, Department of Geography. Chicago: University of Chicago Press.

——— [1964], "Approaches to Regional Analysis: A Synthesis"; *Annals of the Association of American Geographers,* 54, 2–11.

——— [1965], "Internal Structure of the City"; *Law and Contemporary Problems,* 30, 111–119.

——— [1967A], *Geography of Market Centers and Retail Distribution.* Englewood Cliffs, N.J.: Prentice-Hall.

——— [1967B], *Strategies, Models and Economic Theories of Development in Rural Regions.* Washington, D.C.: U.S. Department of Agriculture.

——— [1967C], *Functional Economic Areas and Consolidated Urban Regions of the United States,* Washington, D.C.: Bureau of the Census.

——— H. G. BARNUM and R. J. TENNANT [1962], "Retail Location and Consumer Behaviour"; *Regional Science Association, Papers and Proceedings,* 9, 65–106.

——— and W. L. GARRISON [1958A], "Functional Bases of the Central Place Hierarchy"; *Economic Geography,* 34, 145–154.

——— [1958B], "A Note on Central Place Theory and the Range of a Good"; *Economic Geography,* 34, 304–311.

——— [1958C], "Recent Developments of Central Place Theory"; *Regional Science Association, Papers and Proceedings,* 4, 107–120.

——— [1958D], "Alternate Explanations of Urban Rank-Size Relationships"; *Annals of the Association of American Geographers,* 48, 83–91.

——— and F. E. HORTON [1970], *Geographic Perspectives on Urban Systems.* Englewood Cliffs, N.J.: Prentice-Hall.

——— and J. MELTZER, eds. [1967], *Goals for Urban America.* Englewood Cliffs, N.J.: Prentice-Hall.

——— S. J. PARSONS, and R. H. PLATT [1968], *The Impact of Urban Renewal on Small Business.* Chicago: Center for Urban Studies, University of Chicago Press.

——— and A. PRED [1964], *Central Place Studies: A Bibliography of Theory and Applications.* Philadelphia: Regional Science Association.

——— J. R. SIMMONS and R. TENNANT [1963], "Urban Population Densities: Structure and Change"; *The Geographical Review,* 53, 389–405.

——— and R. TENNANT [1963], *Chicago Commercial Reference Handbook.* Research Paper 86, Department of Geography. Chicago: University of Chicago Press.

BLUMENFELD, H. [1954], "The Tidal Wave of Metropolitan Expansion"; *Journal of the American Institute of Planners,* 20, 3–14.

——— [1955], "The Economic Base of the Metropolis"; *Journal of the American Institute of Planners,* 21, 114–132.

——— [1959], "Are Land Use Patterns Predictable?"; *Journal of the American Institute of Planners,* 25, 60–64.

BOGARDUS, E. S. [1926], "Social Distance in the City," in E. W. Burgess, ed., *The Urban Community,* 48–54. Chicago: University of Chicago Press.

BOLLENS, J. C. and H. J. SCHMANDT [1965], *The Metropolis.* New York: Harper & Row.

BOLTON, R. E. [1965], *Defence Purchases and Regional Growth.* Washington, D.C.: The Brookings Institution.

BORCHERT, J. R. [1967], "American Metropolitan Evolution"; *Geographical Review,* 57, 301–323.

——— and R. B. ADAMS [1963], *Trade Centers and Trade Areas of the Upper Midwest.* Urban Report 3, Upper Midwest Economic Study. Minneapolis: University of Minnesota Press.

BOURNE, L. S. [1967], *Private Development of the Central City.* Research Paper 112, Department of Geography. Chicago: University of Chicago Press.

——— [1968], "Market Location, and Site Selection in Apartment Construction"; *Canadian Geographer,* 12, 211–226.

BOYCE, D. E., N. D. DAY and C. McDONALD [1970], *Metropolitan Plan Making,* Philadelphia: Regional Science Research Institute.

BRAGDON, C. R. [1967], "Territoriality: An Ecological Concept for Urban Planning"; *Planning Comment,* 4, 29–42.

BRIDENBAUGH, C. [1950], *Cities in the Wilderness: The First Century of Urban Life in America, 1625–1742.* New York: Knopf.

BROWNING, C. E. [1964], "Selected Aspects of Land Use and Distance from the City Center: The Case of Chicago"; *Southeastern Geographer,* 4, 29–40.

BRUNN, S. [1968], "Changes in the Service Structure of Rural Trade Centers"; *Rural Sociology,* 33, 200–206.

BRUSH, J. E. [1953], "The Hierarchy of Central Places in Southwestern Wisconsin"; *The Geographical Review,* 43, 380–402.

——— and H. E. BRACEY [1955], "Rural Service Centers in Southwestern Wisconsin and Southern England"; *The Geographical Review,* 45, 559–569.

BRYSON, R. A. and J. E. KUTZBACH [1968], *Air Pollution.* Washington, D.C.: Association of American Geographers.

BUCHANAN, C. D. [1963], *Traffic in Towns.* London: Her Majesty's Stationery Office.

BUNGE, W. [1962], *Theoretical Geography,* Lund Studies in Geography, Series C, 1. Lund, Sweden: Gleerup.

BURGESS, E. W. [1923], "The Growth of the City"; *Proceedings of the American Sociological Society,* 18, 85–89.

——— and D. J. BOGUE [1964], "A Short History of Urban Research at the University of Chicago Before 1946," in E. W. Burgess and D. J. Bogue, eds., *Contributions to Urban Sociology.* Chicago: University of Chicago Press.

BURTON, I. [1963], "The Quantitative Revolution and Theoretical Geography"; *The Canadian Geographer,* 7, 151–162.

BURTT, E. J., Jr. [1961], *"Changing Labor Supply Characteristics Along Route 128";* Research Report 14. Boston: Federal Reserve Bank of Boston.

CAMPBELL, A. K. [1958], "Taxes and Industrial Location in the New York Metropolitan Region"; *National Tax Journal,* 11, 195–218.

CANADA, ECONOMIC COUNCIL OF [1964], *First Annual Review: Economic Goals for Canada to 1970.* Ottawa: The Queen's Printer.

——— [1969], *Sixth Annual Review: Perspective 1975.* Ottawa: The Queen's Printer.

CAPLOW, T. [1952], "Urban Structure in France"; *American Sociological Review,* 17, 544–550.

CAREY, G. [1966], "The Regional Interpretation of Manhattan Population and Housing Patterns Through Factor Analysis"; *The Geographical Review,* 56, 551–569.

CARROLL, J. D. and H. W. BEVIS [1957], "Predicting Local Travel in Urban Regions"; *Regional Science Association, Papers and Proceedings,* 3, 183–197.

CARROTHERS, G. A. P. [1956], "An Historical Review of the Gravity and Potential Concepts of Human Interaction"; *Journal of the American Institute of Planners,* 22, 94–102.

CHICAGO Area Transportation Study, Volume 1 [1959].

CHINITZ, B. [1960], *Freight and the Metropolis.* Cambridge: Harvard University Press.

——— [1965], "New York: A Metropolitan Region"; *Scientific American,* 213, 134–148.

CHISHOLM, M. [1962], *Rural Settlement and Land Use.* London: Hutchinson.

CHOMBART DE LAUWE, P. [1959], *Famille et Habitation.* Paris: Editions du Centre National de la Récherche Scientifique.

——— [1965], *Des Hommes et Des Villes.* Paris: Payot.

CHORLEY, R. J. [1964], "Geography and Analogue Theory"; *Annals of the Association of American Geographers,* 54, 127–137.

CHRISTALLER, W. [1966], *Central Places in Southern Germany,* trans. by C. W. Baskin. Englewood Cliffs, N.J.: Prentice-Hall.

CLARK, C. [1951A], *The Conditions of Economic Progress.* London: MacMillan.

——— [1951B], "Urban Population Densities"; *Journal of the Royal Statistical Society, A;* 114, 490–496.

——— [1957–1958], "Transport—Maker and Breaker of Cities"; *Town Planning Review,* 28, 237–250.

CLARKE, W. A. V. [1968], "Consumer Travel Patterns and the Concept of Range"; *Annals of the Association of American Geographers,* 58, 386–396.

COLBY, C. C. [1933], "Centrifugal and Centripetal Forces in Urban Geography"; *Annals of the Association of American Geographers,* 23, 1–20.

COLEMAN, A. [1969], *The Planning Challenge of the Ottawa Area.* Ottawa: The Queen's Printer.

COX, K. R. [1965], "The Application of Linear Programming to Geographic Problems"; *Tijdschrift voor Economische en Sociale Geografie,* 56, 228-236.

——— and R. G. COLLEDGE, eds. [1969], *Behavioral Problems in Geography: A Symposium.* Studies in Geography, 17. Evanston: Northwestern University Press.

DACEY, M. [1962], "Analysis of Central Place and Point Patterns by a Nearest Neighbor Method," in K. Norborg, ed., *Proceedings of the I.G.U. Symposium in Urban Geography, Lund, 1960,* 55–75. Lund, Sweden: Gleerup.

——— [1965], "The Geometry of Central Place Theory"; *Geografiska Annaler,* Series B, 47, 111–124.

DAVIES, D. H. [1960], "The Hard Core of Cape Town's Central Business District"; *Economic Geography,* 34, 53–69.

DAVIS, J. L. [1965], *The Elevated System and the Growth of Northern Chicago.* Studies in Geography 10. Evanston: Northwestern University Press.

DAVIS, KINGSLEY [1965], "The Urbanization of the Human Population"; *Scientific American,* 213, 40–53.

DE VISE, P. [1960], *A Social Geography of Metropolitan Chicago.* Chicago: Northeastern Illinois Area Planning Commission.

DEPARTMENT OF CITY PLANNING [1961], *Industrial Movements and Expansion, 1947–57, City of Chicago and Chicago Metropolitan Area.* Chicago: Department of City Planning.

DETROIT Metropolitan Area Traffic Study, Part I, 1955.

DICKINSON, R. E. [1948], "The Scope and Status of Urban Geography"; *Land Economics*, 24, 221–238.

——— [1964], *City and Region.* London: Routledge & Kegan Paul.

DODD, S. C. [1950], "The Interactance Hypothesis: A Gravity Model Fitting Physical Masses and Human Behaviour"; *American Sociological Review,* 15, 245–256.

DOXIADIS, C. A. [1966], *Urban Renewal and the Future of the American City.* Chicago: Public Administration Service.

DUE, J. F. [1961], "Studies of State-Local Tax Influences on the Location of Industry"; *National Tax Journal,* 14, 163–173.

DUNCAN, B. [1956], "Factors in Work-Residence Separation: Wage and Salary Workers"; *American Sociological Review,* 21, 48–56.

——— and O. D. DUNCAN [1960], "The Measurement of Intracity Locational and Residential Patterns"; *Journal of Regional Science,* 2, 37–54.

DUNCAN, O. D., W. R. SCOTT, S. LIEBERSON, B. D. DUNCAN, and H. H. WINSBOROUGH [1960], *Metropolis and Region.* Baltimore: The Johns Hopkins Press.

DUNN, E. S., Jr. [1954], *The Location of Agricultural Production.* Gainesville: University of Florida Press.

EDWARDS, K. C. [1964], "The New Towns of Britain"; *Geography,* 69, 279–285.

ERIKSON, E. [1968], *Identity, Youth and Crisis.* New York: Norton.

FEDERAL RESERVE BANK OF KANSAS CITY [1952], "The Employment Multiplier in Wichita"; *Monthly Review,* 37.

FELLMAN, J. D. [1950], *Truck Transportation Patterns of Chicago.* Research Paper 12, Department of Geography. Chicago: University of Chicago Press.

FIREY, W. [1945], "Sentiment and Symbolism as Ecological Variables"; *American Sociological Review,* 10, 140–148.

FISHER, E. M. and L. WINNICK [1951], "A Reformulation of the Filtering Concept"; *Journal of Social Issues,* 45–55.

FLORENCE, P. S. [1953], *The Logic of British and American Industry.* London: Routledge & Kegan Paul.

FOLEY, D. [1963], *Controlling London's Growth.* Berkeley: University of California Press.

FOLGER, J. [1953], "Some Aspects of Migration in the Tennessee Valley"; *American Sociological Review,* 18, 253–260.

FORD, R. G. [1950], "Population Succession in Chicago"; *American Journal of Sociology,* 56, 156–160.

FOX, K. A. and T. K. KUMAR [1965], "The Functional Economic Area: Delineation and Implications for Economic Analysis and Policy"; *Regional Science Association, Papers and Proceedings,* 15, 57–85.

FRIEDLANDER, G. D. [1965], "Airborne Asphyxia—an International Problem"; *Spectrum,* 13–14.

FUCHS, V. R. [1962], *Changes in the Location of Manufacturing in the United States Since 1929.* New Haven: Yale University Press.

GARNER, B. J. [1966], *The Internal Structure of Retail Nucleations.* Studies in Geography, 12. Evanston: Northwestern University Press.

——— [1969], "The Analysis of Qualitative Data in Urban Geography: The Example of Shop Quality"; *Techniques in Urban Geography.* London: Institute of British Geographers Urban Studies Group.

GARRISON, W. L., et al. [1959], *Studies of Highway Development and Geographic Change.* Seattle: University of Washington Press.

GETIS, A. [1963], "The Determination of the Location of Retail Activities with the Use of a Map Transformation"; *Economic Geography,* 39, 1–22.

——— and J. GETIS [1968], "Retail Store and Spatial Affinities"; *Urban Studies* 5, 317–332.

GIBBS, J. P. [1963], "The Evolution of Population Concentration"; *Economic Geography,* 39, 119–129.

GILMORE, H. W. [1953], *Transportation and the Growth of Cities.* Glencoe, Ill.: The Free Press.

GOLDBERG, M. A. [1970], "An Economic Model of Intrametropolitan Industrial Location"; *Journal of Regional Science,* 10, 75–79.

GOLDSTEIN, S. and K. B. MAYER [1961], *Metropolitanization and Population Change in Rhode Island.* Providence: Planning Division, Rhode Island Development Council.

GOLLEDGE, R. G. [1967], "Conceptualizing the Market Decision Process"; *Journal of Regional Science,* 7, 239–258.

GOODWIN, W. [1965], "The Management Center in the United States"; *The Geographical Review,* 55, 1–16.

GOTTMANN, J. [1961], *Megalopolis.* New York: The Twentieth Century Fund.

GREBLER, L. [1952], *Housing Market Behavior in a Declining Area.* New York: Columbia University Press.

GREEN, C. M. [1965], *The Rise of Urban America.* London: Hutchinson.

GREEN, F. H. W. [1950], "Urban Hinterlands in England and Wales: An Analysis of Bus Hinterlands"; *The Geographical Journal,* 96, 64–81.

GREEN, H. L. [1955], "Hinterland Boundaries of New York City and Boston in Southern New England"; *Economic Geography,* 31, 283–300.

GRIGG, D. B. [1965], "The Logic of Regional Systems"; *Annals of the Association of American Geographers,* 55, 465–491.

HAAGEN-SMIT, A. J. [1964], "The Control of Air Pollution"; *Scientific American,* 210, 3–9.

HADDEN, J. K. and E. F. BORGATTA [1965], *American Cities: Their Social Characteristics.* Skokie, Ill.: Rand McNally.

HAGGETT, P. [1965], *Locational Analysis in Human Geography.* London: Edward Arnold.

——— and R. J. CHORLEY, eds. [1967], *Models in Geography.* London: Methuen.

HALL, P. [1966], *The World Cities.* New York: McGraw-Hill.

——— ed. [1966], *Von Thünen's Isolated State.* Oxford: Pergamon Press.

HAMILTON, F. E. I. [1967], "Models of Industrial Location" in R. J. Chorley and P. Haggett, eds., *Models in Geography,* 361–424. London: Methuen.

HAMILTON, W. F. and D. K. NANCE [1968], "Systems Analysis of Urban Transportation"; *Scientific American,* 221, 19–27.

HANDLIN, O. [1959], *The Newcomers.* Cambridge: Harvard University Press.

——— and J. BURCHARD [1966], *The Historian and the City.* Cambridge: The M.I.T. Press.

HARRIS, C. D. [1941], *Salt Lake City: A Regional Capital.* Chicago: University of Chicago Press.

——— [1943], "A Functional Classification of Cities in the United States"; *The Geographical Review,* 33, 86–99.

——— [1954], "The Market as a Factor in the Localization of Industry in the United States"; *Annals of the Association of American Geographers,* 44, 315–348.

——— and E. L. ULLMAN [1945], "The Nature of Cities"; *Annals of the American Academy of Political Science,* 242, 7–17.

HARTSHORNE, R. [1939], *The Nature of Geography.* Lancaster, Pa.: Association of American Geographers.

HARVEY, D. W. [1969], *Explanation in Geography.* London: Edward Arnold.

HATT, P. K. and A. J. REISS, Jr. [1957], *Cities and Society.* Glencoe, Ill.: The Free Press.

HAWLEY, A. A. and O. D. DUNCAN [1957], "Social Area Analysis: A Critical Appraisal"; *Land Economics,* 33, 337–345.

HEIMANN, H. [1967], *Air Pollution and Respiratory Disease.* Washington, D.C.: Public Health Service Publication 1257.

HELFGOTT, R. B. [1959], "Women's and Children's Apparel," in M. Hall, ed., *Made in New York,* 19–134. Cambridge: Harvard University Press.

HELVIG, M. [1964], *Chicago's External Truck Movements.* Department of Geography, Research Paper 90. Chicago: University of Chicago Press.

HILTON, G. W. and J. F. DUE [1964], *The Electric Interurban Railways in America.* Stanford: Stanford University Press.

HOCH, I. [1957], "Rising Land Values Found Along Edens"; *Cook County Highways,* 4, 3–5.

HODGE, G. [1965], "The Prediction of Trade Center Viability in the Great Plains"; *Regional Science Association, Papers and Proceedings,* 15, 87–118.

HOOVER, E. M. [1963], *The Location of Economic Activity.* New York: McGraw-Hill.

——— and R. VERNON [1959], *Anatomy of a Metropolis.* Cambridge: Harvard University Press.

HORWOOD, E. M. and R. R. BOYCE [1959], *Studies of the Central Business District and Urban Freeway Development.* Seattle: University of Washington Press.

HOWARD, E. [1945], *Garden Cities of Tomorrow.* London: Faber & Faber.

HOYT, H. [1933], *One Hundred Years of Land Values in Chicago.* Chicago: University of Chicago Press.

——— [1939], *The Structure and Growth of Residential Neighborhoods in American Cities.* Washington D.C.: Federal Housing Administration.

——— [1960], *Dynamic Factors in Land Values.* Washington, D.C.: Urban Land Institute (Technical Bulletin 37).

——— [1961], The Utility of the Economic Base Method in Calculating Urban Growth"; *Land Economics*, 37, 51–58.

HUFF, D. L. [1960], "A Topographic Model of Consumer Space Preferences"; *Regional Science Association, Papers and Proceedings,* 6, 159–173.

——— [1961], "Ecological Characteristics of Consumer Behavior"; *Regional Science Association, Papers and Proceedings,* 7, 19–28.

——— [1963], "A Probability Analysis of Shopping Center Trading Areas"; *Land Economics,* 53, 81–90.

HUND, J. M. [1959], "Electronics," in M. Hall, ed., *Made in New York,* 241–325. Cambridge: Harvard University Press.

HURD, R. M. [1924], *Principles of City Land Values.* New York: The Record and Guide.

IKLE, F. C. [1954], "Sociological Relationship of Traffic to Population and Distance"; *Traffic Quarterly,* 8, 123–136.

INSTITUTE FOR URBAN STUDIES [1956], *Industrial Land and Facilities for Philadelphia.* Philadelphia: University of Pennsylvania.

ISARD, W. [1956], *Location and Space Economy.* New York: Wiley.

——— [1960], *Methods of Regional Analysis.* New York: Wiley.

——— and R. KAVESH [1954], "Economic Structural Interrelations of Metropolitan Regions"; *American Journal of Sociology,* 60, 152–162.

JACOBS, J. [1961], *The Death and Life of Great American Cities.* New York: Random House.

JAMES, P. E. [1931], "Vicksburg: A Study in Urban Geography"; *Geographical Review,* 21, 234–243.

JEFFERSON, M. [1939], "The Law of the Primate City"; *The Geographical Review,* 29, 226–232.

JOHNSON, J. H. [1967], *Urban Geography: An Introductory Analysis.* Oxford, England: Pergamon Press.

JONASSEN, C. T. [1955], *The Shopping Center Versus Downtown.* Columbus: Bureau of Business Research, Ohio State University.

KAIN, J. F. [1962], *A Multiple Equation Model of Household Locational and Tripmaking Behavior.* Santa Monica, Calif.: The Rand Corporation, Memorandum RM-3086-FF.

——— [1968], "Housing Segregation, Negro Employment, and Metropolitan Decentralization"; *Quarterly Journal of Economics,* 82, 175–197.

——— and J. J. PERSKY [1969], "Alternatives to the Gilded Ghetto"; *The Public Interest,* 14, 74–87.

KARASKA, G. J. [1966], "Interindustry Relations in the Philadelphia Economy"; *The East Lakes Geographer,* 2, 80–96.

KENNELLY, R. A. [1954–55], "The Location of the Mexican Steel Industry," *Revista Geografica,* 15, 41, 109–129; 42, 199–213; 43, 60–77.

KENYON, J. B. [1960], *Industrial Localization and Metropolitan Growth: The Patterson-Passaic District.* Research Paper 67, Department of Geography. Chicago: University of Chicago Press.

——— [1964], "The Industrial Structure of the New York Garment Center," in R. S. Thoman and D. J. Patton, eds., *Focus on Geographic Activity,* 159–166. New York: McGraw-Hill.

KERR, D. and J. SPELT [1965], *The Changing Face of Toronto.* Ottawa: The Queen's Printer.

KING, L. J. [1961], "The Functional Role of Small Towns in Canterbury"; *Proceedings.* 3rd New Zealand Geographical Society Conference, 139–149.

——— [1966], "Cross-sectional Analysis of Canadian Urban Dimensions: 1951 and 1961"; *Canadian Geographer,* 10, 205–224.

KITAGAWA, E. M. and D. J. BOGUE [1955], *Suburbanization of Manufacturing Activity within Standard Metropolitan Statistical Areas.* Oxford, Ohio: Scripps Foundation.

KLIMM, L. E. [1959], "Mere Description"; *Economic Geography,* 35, ii.

KNOS, D. S. [1962], *Distribution of Land Values in Topeka, Kansas.* Lawrence: Center for Research in Business, University of Kansas Press.

LAKSHMANAN, T. R. and W. G. HANSEN [1965], "A Retail Market Potential Model," *Journal of the American Institute of Planners,* 31, 134–143.

LAMPARD, E. E. [1968], "The Evolving System of Cities in the United States: Urbanization and Economic Development," in H. S. Perloff and L. Wingo, Jr., eds., *Issues in Urban Economics,* 81–139. Baltimore: The Johns Hopkins Press.

LANDSBERG, H. E. [1962], "City Air—Better or Worse?"; *Air Over Cities Symposium,* 1–22. Cincinnati: Sanitary Engineering Technical Report, A62–5.

LANE, T. [1966], "The Urban Base Multiplier: An Evaluation of the State of the Art"; *Land Economics,* 42, 339–347.

LANSING, J. B. [1966], *Residential Location and Urban Mobility.* Ann Arbor, Mich.: Survey Research Center, Institute for Social Research, University of Michigan Press.

——— and G. HENDRICKS [1967], "How People Perceive the Cost of the Journey to Work"; *Highway Research Record,* 197, 44–55.

——— C. W. CLIFTON and J. N. MOIZAN [1969], *New Homes and Poor People.* Ann Arbor: Institute for Social Research.

LAPIN, H. S. [1964], *Structuring the Journey to Work.* Philadelphia: University of Pennsylvania Press.

LATHAM, R. F. [1967], "Urban Population Densities and Growth, with Special Reference to Toronto." Kingston: Unpublished Master's Thesis, Department of Geography, Queen's University.

LATHAM, R. F. and M. H. YEATES [1970], "Population Density Growth in Metropolitan Toronto"; *Geographical Analysis,* 2, 177–185.

LEONTIEF, W., et al. [1953], *Studies in the Structure of the American Economy: Theoretical and Empirical Explanations in Input-Output Analysis.* London: Oxford University Press.

LEWIS, O. [1966], *La Vida, A Puerto Rican Family in the Culture of Poverty—San Juan and New York.* New York: Random House.

LICHFIELD, N. and P. F. WENDT [1969], "Six English New Towns: A Financial Analysis"; *Town Planning Review,* 40, 283–314.

LIEBERSON, S. [1963], *Ethnic Patterns in American Cities.* Glencoe, Ill.: The Free Press.

LIEPMAN, K. [1944], *The Journey to Work.* London: Routledge & Kegan Paul.

LIPSET, S. M. and R. BENDIX [1959], *Social Mobility in Industrial Society.* Berkeley: University of California Press.

LITHWICK, N. H. and G. PAQUET [1968], *Urban Studies: A Canadian Perspective.* Toronto: Methuen.

LÖSCH, A. [1954], *The Economics of Location,* trans. by W. H. Woglom. New Haven: Yale University Press. Originally published by Gustav Fischer Verlag.

LOWRY, I. S. [1963A], "Location Parameters in the Pittsburgh Model"; *Regional Science Association, Papers and Proceedings,* 11, 145–165.

——— [1963B], *Portrait of a Region.* Pittsburgh: University of Pittsburgh Press.

——— [1965], "A Short Course in Model Design"; *Journal of the American Institute of Planners,* 31, 158–166.

LUKERMANN, F. [1966], "Empirical Expressions of Nodality and Hierarchy in a Circulation Manifold"; *East Lakes Geographer,* 2, 17–44.

LYNCH, K. [1960], *The Image of the City.* Cambridge: The M.I.T. Press.

MACKAY, R. [1958], "The Interactance Hypothesis and Boundaries in Canada: A Preliminary Study"; *The Canadian Geographer,* 11, 1–8.

MADDEN, C. H. [1956A], "Some Spatial Aspects of Urban Growth in the United States"; *Economic Development and Cultural Change,* 4, 371–387.

——— [1956B], "On Some Indications of Stability in the Growth of Cities in the United States"; *Economic Development and Cultural Change,* 4, 236–252.

MADGE, J. [1962], "The New Towns Program in Britain"; *Journal of the American Institute of Planners,* 28, 208–219.

MARBLE, D. F. and S. R. BOWLBY [1968], "Shopping Alternatives and Recurrent Travel Patterns," *Geographic Studies of Urban Transportation and Network Analysis.* Studies in Geography, No. 16. Evanston: Northwestern University Press.

MARCH, J. G. and H. A. SIMON [1958], *Organizations.* New York: John Wiley.

MARTIN, B. V., F. W. MEMMOTT and A. J. BONE [1961], *Principles and Techniques of Predicting Future Demand for Urban Transportation.* Cambridge: The M.I.T. Press.

MARTIN, F. [1969], "La Théorie de la Croissance Urbaine par Etape"; *Développement Urbain et Analyse Economique.* Paris, France: Cujas.

MARYLAND-NATIONAL CAPITAL PARK AND PLANNING COMMISSION [1964], *On Wedges and Corridors: A General Plan for the Maryland-Washington Regional District in Montgomery and Prince George Counties.*

MAXWELL, J. W. [1965], "The Functional Structure of Canadian Cities: A Classification of Cities"; *Geographical Bulletin,* 7, 79–104.

MAYER, H. M. [1954], "Urban Geography," in P. E. James and C. F. Jones, eds., *American Geography—Inventory and Prospect,* 142–166. Syracuse: Syracuse University Press.

——— [1964], "Politics and Land Use: The Indiana Shoreline of Lake Michigan"; *Annals of the Association of American Geographers,* 54, 508–523.

McFARLAND, J. R. [1966], "The Administration of the New Deal Green Belt Towns"; *Journal of the American Institute of Planners,* 32, 217–225.

McGUIRE, J. W. [1964], *Theories of Business Behavior.* Englewood Cliffs, N.J.: Prentice-Hall.

MEYER, J. R., J. F. KAIN and M. WOHL [1965], *The Urban Transportation Problem.* Cambridge: Harvard University Press.

MITCHELL, J. B. [1960], "Planning and Development in Philadelphia"; *Journal of the American Institute of Planners,* 26, 155–261.

MOORE, D. A. [1954], "The Automobile Industry," in W. Adams, ed., *The Structure of American Industry,* 274–325. New York: Macmillan.

MORRILL, R. L. [1965A], *Migration and the Spread and Growth of Urban Settlement.* Lund, Sweden: Gleerup.

——— [1965B], "The Negro Ghetto: Problems and Alternatives"; *The Geographical Review,* 55, 339–361.

MORRISSET, I. [1958], "The Economic Structure of American Cities"; *Regional Science Association, Papers and Proceedings,* 4, 239–256.

MOSER, C. A. and W. SCOTT [1961], *British Towns.* Edinburgh: Oliver and Boyd.

MOSES, L. F. and H. F. WILLIAMSON, Jr. [1967], "The Location of Economic Activity in Cities"; *American Economic Review,* 52, 211–222.

MUMFORD, L. [1961], *The City in History.* New York: Harcourt Brace Jovanovich, Inc.

——— [1963], *The Highway and the City.* New York: Harcourt Brace Jovanovich, Inc.

MURDIE, R. A. [1965], "Cultural Differences in Consumer Travel"; *Economic Geography,* 41, 211–233.

——— [1969], *Factorial Ecology of Metropolitan Toronto, 1951–1961.* Research Paper 116, Department of Geography. Chicago: University of Chicago Press.

MURPHY, R. E. [1966], *The American City.* New York: McGraw-Hill.

——— and J. E. VANCE, Jr. [1954A], "Delimiting the CBD"; *Economic Geography,* 30, 189–222.

——— [1954B], "A Comparative Study of Nine Central Business Districts"; *Economic Geography,* 30, 301–336.

——— VANCE, J. E. and B. J. EPSTEIN [1955], "Internal Structure of the CBD"; *Economic Geography,* 31, 21–46.

MUTH, R. F. [1961], "The Spatial Structure of the Housing Market"; *Papers and Proceedings of the Regional Science Association,* 7, 207–220.

MYRDAL, G. [1957], *Rich Lands and Poor.* New York: Harper and Row.

NELSON, H. J. [1955], "A Service Classification of American Cities"; *Economic Geography,* 31, 189–210.

——— [1957], "Some Characteristics of the Population of Cities of Similar Service Classifications"; *Economic Geography,* 33, 95–108.

NEWLING, B. E. [1964], "Urban Population Densities and Intraurban Growth"; *The Geographical Review,* 54, 440–442.

——— [1966], "Urban Growth and Spatial Structure: Mathematical Models and Empirical Evidence"; *The Geographical Review,* 56, 213–225.

——— [1969], "The Spatial Variation of Urban Population Densities"; *The Geographical Review,* 59, 242–252.

NICHOLSON, T. G. and M. H. YEATES [1969], "The Ecological and Spatial Structure of the Socio-Economic Characteristics of Winnipeg, 1961"; *The Canadian Review of Sociology and Anthropology,* 6, 162–178.

NIEDERCORN, J. H. and E. F. R. HEARLE [1964], "Recent Land Use Trends in 48 Large American Cities"; *Land Economics,* 105–110.

NOURSE, H. O. [1968], *Regional Economics.* New York: McGraw-Hill.

NOVAK, R. T. [1956], "Distribution of Puerto Ricans on Manhattan Island"; *The Geographical Review,* 46, 182–186.

NYSTUEN, J. D. [1963], "Identification of Some Fundamental Concepts"; *Papers of the Michigan Academy of Science, Arts, and Letters,* 48, 373–384.

——— and M. F. DACEY [1961], "A Graph Theory Interpretation of Nodal Regions"; *Regional Science Association, Papers and Proceedings,* 7, 29–42.

OGBURN, W. F. [1933], *Recent Social Trends in the United States.* New York: McGraw-Hill.

OLSSON, G. [1964], *Distance and Human Interaction.* Philadelphia: Regional Science Research Institute.

OWEN, W. [1966], *The Metropolitan Transportation Problem.* Washington, D.C.: The Brookings Institution.

PARK, R. E. [1929], "Urbanization as Measured by Newspaper Circulation"; *The American Journal of Sociology,* 35, 60–79.

——— and E. W. BURGESS and R. D. McKENZIE [1925], *The City.* Chicago: University of Chicago Press. Reprinted in 1967.

——— and C. NEWCOMB [1933], "Newspaper Circulation in Metropolitan Regions," in R. D. McKenzie, ed., *The Metropolitan Community.* New York: McGraw-Hill.

PASMA, T. K. [1955], *Organized Industrial Districts: A Tool for Community Development.* Washington, D.C.: Area Development Division, Office of Technical Services, U.S. Department of Commerce.

PAULLIN, C. O. [1932], *Atlas of the Historical Geography of the United States.* Washington D.C.: The Carnegie Institution of Washington.

PENDLETON, W. C. [1962], "The Value of Accessibility," Unpublished doctoral dissertation. Chicago: University of Chicago.

PERLOFF, H. and L. WINGO [1961], "Natural Resource Endowment and Regional Economic Growth," in J. J. Spengler, ed., *Natural Resources and Economic Growth,* 191–212. Washington, D.C.: Resources for the Future Inc.

PHILBRICK, A. K. [1957], "Principles of Areal Functional Organization in Regional Human Geography"; *Economic Geography,* 33, 299–336.

PICKARD, J. P. [1959], *Metropolitanization of the United States.* Washington, D.C.: The Urban Land Institute.

PINKEPANK, J. A. [1966], "Serving Twelve Masters"; *Trains,* 26, 36–46, and 42–49.

POPENOE, D. [1969], "On the Meaning of 'Urban' in 'Urban Studies'," in P. Meadows and E. H. Mizruchi, eds., *Urbanism, Urbanization, and Change,* 64–75. Toronto: Addison-Wesley.

POWNALL, L. L. [1953], "The Functions of New Zealand Towns"; *Annals of the Association of American Geographers,* 43, 332–350.

PRATT, E. E. [1911], *Industrial Causes of Congestion of Population in New York City.* Studies in History, Economics, and Public Law. New York: Columbia University Press.

PRED, A. [1963], "Business Thoroughfares as Expressions of Urban Negro Culture"; *Economic Geography,* 39, 217–233.

——— [1964], "The Intrametropolitan Location of Manufacturing"; *Annals of the Association of American Geographers,* 54, 165–180.

———[1965], "Industrialization, Initial Advantage, and American Metropolitan Growth"; *The Geographical Review,* 55, 158–185.

——— [1966], *The Spatial Dynamics of U.S. Urban Industrial Growth, 1800–1914: Interpretive and Theoretical Essays.* Cambridge: The M.I.T. Press.

——— [1967], *Behavior and Location: Part I.* Lund, Sweden: Gleerup.

——— [1969], *Behavior and Location: Part II.* Lund, Sweden: Gleerup.

PROUDFOOT, M. J. [1957], "Chicago's Fragmented Political Structure"; *The Geographical Review,* 47, 106–117.

RAINWATER, L. [1966], "Fear and the House-as-a-Haven in the Lower Class"; *Journal of the American Institute of Planners,* 32, 23–31.

RANNELLS, J. [1956], *The Core of the City.* New York: Columbia University Press.

RATCLIFF, R. U. [1949], *Urban Land Economics.* New York: McGraw-Hill.

——— [1955], "Efficiency and the Location of Urban Activities," in R. M. Fisher, ed., *The Metropolis in Modern Life,* 125–148. Garden City, N.Y.: Doubleday.

——— [1957], "On Wendt's Theory of Land Values"; *Land Economics,* 33, 360–363.

RAY, D. M. [1965], *Market Potential and Economic Shadow.* Research Paper 101, Department of Geography. Chicago: University of Chicago Press.

REES, P. H. [1968], "The Factorial Ecology of Metropolitan Chicago, 1960." Unpublished Master's Thesis, Department of Geography. Chicago: University of Chicago.

REILLY, W. J. [1931], *The Law of Retail Gravitation.* New York: The Knickerbocker Press.

REINEMANN, M. [1955], "The Localization and the Relocation of Manufacturing within the Chicago Urban Region." Unpublished Ph.D. Dissertation, Department of Geography. Evanston: Northwestern University.

——— [1960], "The Pattern and Distribution of Manufacturing in the Chicago Area"; *Economic Geography,* 36, 139–144.

REYNOLDS, J. P. [1961], "The Plan"; *Town Planning Review,* 32, 151–184.

ROSE, H. M. [1970], "The Development of an Urban Subsystem: The Case of the Negro Ghetto"; *Annals of the Association of American Geographers,* 60, 1–17.

ROSSI, P. H. [1955], *Why Families Move.* Glencoe, Ill.: The Free Press.

ROTERUS, V. and W. CALEF [1955], "Notes on the Basic-Nonbasic Employment Ratio"; *Economic Geography,* 31, 17–20.

ROW, A. [1960], "The Physical Development Plan"; *Journal of the American Institute of Planners,* 26, 177–185.

ROWLAND, D. T. [1959], *Urban Real Estate Research.* Washington, D.C.: Urban Land Institute.

SAMUELSON, P. A. and A. SCOTT [1966], *Economics—An Introductory Analysis.* New York: McGraw-Hill.

SENATE COMMITTEE ON PUBLIC WORKS [1963], *A Study of Air Pollution.* Washington, D.C.: Senate Committee on Public Works.

SHEVKY, E. and M. WILLIAMS [1949], *The Social Areas of Los Angeles: Analysis and Typology.* Los Angeles: University of California Press.

——— and W. BELL [1955], *Social Area Analysis: Theory, Illustrative Applications, and Computational Procedures.* Menlo Park: Stanford University Press.

SIMMONS, J. [1964], *The Changing Pattern of Retail Location.* Research Paper 92, Department of Geography. Chicago: University of Chicago Press.

——— [1968], "Changing Residence in the City: A Review of Intra-Urban Mobility"; *The Geographical Review,* 58, 622–651.

——— and R. SIMMONS [1969], *Urban Canada.* Toronto: The Copp Clark Publishing Company.

SIMON, H. A. [1955], "On a Class of Skew Distribution Functions"; *Biometrica,* 42, 425–440.

SKILLING, H. [1964], "An Operational View"; *American Scientist,* 52, 388A–396A.

SKOLNICK, J. H. [1969], *The Politics of Protest.* New York: Ballantine Books.

SMAILES, A. E. [1953], *The Geography of Towns.* London: Hutchinson.

SMALLWOOD, F. [1963], *Metro Toronto: A Decade Later.* Toronto: Bureau of Municipal Research.

SMERK, G. M. [1967], "The Streetcar: Shaper of American Cities"; *Traffic Quarterly,* 21, 569–584.

SMITH, P. J. [1962], "Calgary: A Study in Urban Pattern"; *Economic Geography,* 38, 315–329.

SMITH, R. H. T. [1965A], "Method and Purpose in Functional Town Classification"; *Annals of the Association of American Geographers,* 55, 539–548.

——— [1965B], "The Functions of Australian Towns"; *Netherlands Journal of Economic and Social Geography* (*T.E.S.G.*), 56, 81–92.

SMITH, W. [1964], *Filtering and Neighborhood Change.* Research Report 24, Center for Research in Real Estate and Urban Economics. Berkeley: University of California Press.

SOLZMAN, D. M. [1966], *Waterway Industrial Sites: A Chicago Case Study.* Research Paper 107, Department of Geography. Chicago: University of Chicago.

SPILHAUS, A. [1969], "Technology, Living Cities and Human Environment"; *American Scientist,* 57, 24–36.

STAFFORD, H. A., Jr. [1963], "The Functional Bases of Small Towns"; *Economic Geography,* 39, 165–175.

STEIGENGA, W. [1955], "A Comparative Analysis and a Classification of Netherlands Towns"; *Netherlands Journal of Economic and Social Geography* (*T.E.S.G.*), 46, 106–112.

STEVENS, B. H. and C. A. BRACKETT [1967], *Industrial Location: A Review and Annotated Bibliography of Theoretical, Empirical and Case Studies.* Philadelphia: Regional Science Research Institute.

STEWART, C. T. [1958], "The Size and Spacing of Cities"; *The Geographical Review,* 48, 222–245.

STEWART, J. Q. [1941], "An Inverse Distance Variation for Certain Social Influences"; *Science,* 93, 89–90.

——— [1950], "Potential of Population and Its Relationship to Marketing," in R. Cox and W. Alderson, eds., *Theory in Marketing.* Homewood, Ill.: Richard D. Irwin.

STOKES, C. J. [1962], "A Theory of Slums"; *Land Economics,* 38, 187–197.

STONE, L. O. [1967], *Urban Development in Canada.* Ottawa: The Queen's Printer.

STOUFFER, S. A. [1940], "Intervening Opportunities: A Theory Relating Mobility and Distance"; *American Sociological Review,* 5, 845–867.

STUART, A. W. [1968], "The Suburbanization of Manufacturing in Small Metropolitan Areas: A Case Study of Roanoke"; *The Southeastern Geographer,* 8, 30–39.

TAAFFE, E. J. [1956], "Air Transportation and United States Urban Distribution"; *The Geographical Review,* 46, 219–238.

——— [1962], "The Urban Hierarchy: An Air Passenger Definition"; *Economic Geography,* 38, 1–14.

——— ed. [1970], *Geography.* Englewood Cliffs, N.J.: Prentice-Hall.

——— B. J. GARNER and M. H. YEATES [1963], *The Peripheral Journey to Work.* Evanston, Ill.: Northwestern University Press.

TAUEBER, K. E. and A. R. TAUEBER [1965], *Negroes in Cities.* Chicago: Aldine Publishing Company.

TAYLOR, G. [1942], "Environment, Village, and City"; *Annals of the Association of American Geographers,* 32, 1–67.

TAYLOR, G. R. [1951], *The Transportation Revolution; 1815–1860.* New York: Harper and Row.

THOMAS, E. N. [1960], "Some Comments on Functional Bases for Small Towns"; *Iowa Business Digest,* 1, 10–16.

——— [1961], "Toward an Expanded Central Place Model"; *The Geographical* Review, 51, 400–411.

THOMPSON, W. [1965], *Preface to Urban Economics.* Baltimore: The Johns Hopkins Press.

TIEBOUT, C. M. [1956], "The Urban Economic Base Reconsidered"; *Land Economics,* 32, 95–99.

TORONTO [1966], *Metropolitan Toronto and Region Transportation Study.* Toronto: Parliament Building.

UDRY, J. R. [1964], "Increasing Scale and Spatial Differentiation: New Tests of Two Theories from Shevky and Bell"; *Social Forces, 42,* 403–413.

ULLMAN, E. L. [1943], *Mobile: Industrial Seaport and Trade Center.* Department of Geography. Chicago: University of Chicago Press.

——— [1956], "The Role of Transportation and the Bases for Interaction," in W. L. Thomas, ed., *Man's Role in Changing the Face of the Earth,* 862–890. Chicago: University of Chicago Press.

——— and M. F. DACEY [1962], "The Minimum Requirements Approach to the Urban Economic Base," in K. Norborg, ed., *Proceedings of the I.G.U. Symposium on Urban Geography, Lund, 1960,* 121–143. Lund, Sweden: Gleerup.

——— [1969], *The Economic Base of American Cities,* Seattle, Washington: University of Washington Press.

VAN ARDSOL, M. D. [1961], "An Investigation of the Utility of Urban Typology"; *Pacific Sociological Review,* 4, 26–32.

VANCE, J. E., Jr. [1960], "Labor-shed, Employment Field, and Dynamic Analysis in Urban Geography"; *Economic Geography,* 36, 189–220.

——— [1962], "Emerging Patterns of Commercial Structure in American Cities," in K. Norborg, ed., *Proceedings of the I.G.U. Symposium in Urban Geography, Lund, 1960,* 485–518. Lund, Sweden: Gleerup.

——— [1964], *Geography and Urban Evolution in the San Francisco Bay Area.* Berkeley: Institute of Governmental Studies, University of California Press.

VANCE, R. B. and S. SMITH [1954], "Metropolitan Dominance and Integration," in R. B. Vance and N. J. Demerath, eds., *The Urban South.* Chapel Hill: University of North Carolina Press.

VERNON, R. [1960], *Metropolis 1985.* Cambridge: Harvard University Press.

VINING, R. [1955], "A Description of Certain Aspects of an Economic System"; *Economic Development and Cultural Change,* 3, 147–195.

VOORHEES, A. M., B. SHARPE and J. T. STEGMAR [1955], *Shopping Habits and Travel Patterns.* Washington, D.C.: Urban Land Institute.

WARD, D. [1964], "A Comparative Historical Geography of Streetcar Suburbs in Boston, Massachusetts, and Leeds, England: 1850–1920"; *Annals of the Association of American Geographers*, 54, 477–489.

——— [1968], "The Emergence of Central Immigrant Ghettoes in American Cities 1840–1920"; *Annals of the Association of American Geographers*, 58, 343–359.

WARNER, S. B., Jr. [1962], *Streetcar Suburbs: The Process of Growth in Boston.* Cambridge: Harvard University Press.

WARNTZ, W. [1965], *Macrogeography and Income Fronts.* Philadelphia: Regional Science Research Institute.

WATSON, J. W. [1955], "Geography: A Discipline in Distance"; *Scottish Geographical Magazine*, 71, 1–13.

WEBB, J. W. [1959], "Basic Concepts in the Analysis of Small Urban Centers in Minnesota"; *Annals of the Association of American Geographers*, 49, 55–72.

WEBBER, M. M. [1968], "Planning in an Environment of Change"; *The Town Planning Review*, 39, 179–195, and 277–295.

WEBER, A. [1929], *Theory of the Location of Industries.* Chicago: University of Chicago Press (translation of 1909 German edition).

WEBER, A. F. [1963], *The Growth of Cities in the Nineteenth Century.* Ithaca, N.Y.: Cornell University Press (reprint of 1899 volume).

WEBER, D. [1958], *A Comparison of Two Oil City Business Centers: Odessa-Midland, Texas.* Research Paper 60, Department of Geography. Chicago: University of Chicago Press.

WENDT, P. F. [1957], "Theory of Urban Land Values"; *Land Economics*, 33, 228–240.

——— [1961], *The Dynamics of Central City Land Values—San Francisco and Oakland, 1950–1960.* Berkeley: Real Estate Research Program, Institute of Business and Economic Research, University of California Press.

WHITE, G. F. [1960], "Industrial Water Use: A Review"; *The Geographical Review*, 50, 412–430.

WHITE, L. E. [1963], "Outdoor Play of Children Living in Flats," in L. Kuper, ed., *Living Towns.* London: Grosset Press.

WHITTELSY, D. [1954], "The Regional Concept and the Regional Method," in P. E. James and C. F. Jones, eds., *American Geography—Inventory and Prospect*, 19–69. Syracuse: Syracuse University Press.

WILSON, M. G. A. [1962], "Some Population Characteristics of Australian Mining Settlements"; *Tijdschrift voor Economische en Sociale Geografie*, 53, 125–132.

WINGO, L. [1966], "Urban Renewal: A Strategy for Information and Analysis"; *Journal of the American Institute of Planners*, 32, 144–148.

WINSBOROUGH, H. H. [1961], "A Comparative Study of Urban Population Densities." Unpublished Ph.D. Dissertation, Department of Sociology. Chicago: University of Chicago.

WILLIAMS, W. V. [1967], "A Measure of the Impact of State and Local Taxes on Industrial Location"; *Journal of Regional Science*, 7, 49–60.

WIRTH, L. [1938], "Urbanism as a Way of Life"; *American Journal of Sociology*, 44, 1–24.

WOLFORTH, J. R. [1965], *Residential Location and Place of Work*, Series in Geography No. 4. Vancouver: University of British Columbia Press.

WOLMAN, A. [1965], "The Metabolism of Cities"; *Scientific American*, 213, 179–190.

WOOD, R. C. [1961], *1400 Governments.* Cambridge: Harvard University Press.

WRIGLEY, R. L. [1947], "Organized Industrial Districts"; *Journal of Land and Public Utility Economics* (now called *Land Economics*), 23, 180–198.

YEATES, M. H. [1963], "Hinterland Delimitation: A Distance Minimizing Approach"; *Professional Geographer,* 15, 7–10.

——— [1965A], "Some Factors Affecting the Spatial Distribution of Chicago Land Values, 1910–1960"; *Economic Geography,* 41, 55–70.

——— [1965B], "The Effect of Zoning on Land Values in American Cities: A Case Study," in J. B. Whittow and P. D. Wood, eds., *Essays in Geography for Austin Miller,* 317–333. Reading, England: University of Reading Press.

——— and P. E. LLOYD [1970], *Impact of Industrial Incentives: Southern Georgian Bay Region, Ontario.* Ottawa: The Queen's Printer.

ZELDER, R. E. [1970], "Racial Segregation in Urban Housing Markets"; *Journal of Regional Science,* 10, 93–105.

ZIPF, G. K. [1949], *Human Behavior and the Principle of Least Effort.* New York: Addison-Wesley Press.

INDEX

72 73 74 7 6 5 4 3 2